MW01484228

The Upside-Down Constitution

THE UPSIDE-DOWN CONSTITUTION

MICHAEL S. GREVE

HARVARD UNIVERSITY PRESS
Cambridge, Massachusetts
London, England
2012

Copyright © 2012 by Michael S. Greve

All rights reserved

Printed in the United States of America

Library of Congress Cataloging-in-Publication Data

Greve, Michael S.

The upside-down Constitution / Michael S. Greve.

p. cm.

Includes bibliographical references and index.

ISBN 978-0-674-06191-0 (alk. paper)

1. Federal government—United States.   2. Federal government—
United States—History.   3. Constitutional history—United States.
4. United States. Supreme Court.   I. Title.

KF4600.G748 2012

342.73'042—dc23   2011020224

To my parents

Contents

The Upside-Down Constitution

Introduction

Constitutional Inversion

Constitutions aim to establish workable, enduring frameworks of government and to reduce the vagaries of politics. Yet, uncomfortable though the thought may be, constitutional government also implies the certainty of constitutional change, as well as the distinct possibility of constitutional error. The constitutional enterprise may get away from its founders' expectations and intentions because well-constructed constitutions do not try to settle too much. In Chief Justice Marshall's view, they must be sufficiently open-ended to be "adapted to the various crises of human affairs."[1] More disturbingly, a constitutional order may fall victim to the very political passions and interests that it is meant to contain.

Lately, "Constitutional Development" has emerged as a subfield of political science and constitutional law. But of course, the question of constitutional change and stability is older and more familiar than this academic boomlet. For many decades, it has been the stuff of a very public and, at times, polemical debate. One camp exalts a Constitution that "grows" in response to changing social norms and conditions—in a word, a Constitution that "lives." Another camp takes a dim view of constitutional change. After much change (of the wrong kind), they say, the Founding Fathers' Constitution must be "restored," much like one would rehab deceased parents' crumbling home by shoring up its foundations and removing the accumulated clutter. Still others reject the notion of a Constitution that can be said to grow or deteriorate in any meaningful, directional sense. The drafters of the United States Constitution, they observe, papered over deep disagreements that could not be resolved in a single foundational act. Because the unresolved conflicts carried forward, our politics, institutional arrangements, and constitutional understanding have oscillated—sometimes wildly and violently—between poorly marked, infinitely contestable constitutional boundaries. Finally, there is the dramatic picture of discontinuous change and "constitutional revolutions"—the "revolution" of 1800, for example, which by some lights substituted Thomas Jefferson's Constitution for the one that had been enacted; more clearly and familiarly, the New Deal "revolution" of 1937.[2]

The Upside-Down Constitution presents yet a different picture and argument. Its subject is federalism, that "oldest question of American constitutional law." So far as federalism is concerned, the book argues, the constitutional order has not just grown, deteriorated, or swung too far. Rather, it has been revolutionized in the very specific sense of having been stood on its head. The inversion (we shall see) is readily apparent in particular clauses of the Constitution that have come to assume the opposite of their reasonable meaning, however construed. Those clauses, however, are merely the proverbial canaries. They have croaked on account of a profound atmospheric change—an inversion of the principles and premises on which the constitutional order rests.

Those principles and premises cannot be found *in* the Constitution. Rather, they form its bedrock. Assume them away, and the constitutional structure—as a whole and in its particulars—is rendered pointless and incoherent. The federalism of the United States Constitution presupposes and rests on a handful of such principles and premises. It reflects the long-term calculus of citizens of the United States. It aims to discipline government at all levels, and it aims to curb factional politics and, in that fashion, to produce political and institutional stability. "Our Federalism" (as the Supreme Court likes to call it) embodies just the opposite principles and premises. It serves the interests of politicians, not citizens. It empowers government at all levels. And it unleashes interest group politics and produces a mutable government. Because those orientations are antithetical to the constitutional plan and unattractive in their own right, they are rarely stated forthrightly. But they are the quicksand on which our inverted federalism has come to rest.

Federalism Problems

The notion of federalism's "inversion" departs from conventional wisdom about federalism. Federalism's central, perennial problem, on the standard view, is to preserve a federal "balance" between the states and the nation. At one extreme, the equilibrium is endangered by dissolution; at the other, by wholesale centralization. Political dissolution was indeed once a real danger, which ended only after the Civil War. A total collapse into the center—"consolidation," as the Anti-Federalists called it—was never a real prospect. From the outset, however, apprehensions over an overbearing national government have been a constant theme of our politics. Over the past century, periods of ambitious federal law making—the New Deal, the civil rights revolution, the innovations of the Great Society, the regulatory and fiscal initiatives of the Obama administration—have regularly prompted calls to return power to the states and to restore federalism's balance. Paralleling the political debate, the Supreme Court and constitutional scholars have argued over how much the Supreme Court could and should do to protect the "states as states," the better to preserve federalism's perceived advantages and the states' role in the constitutional system.

Difficult though it is to escape the balance catechism, political scientists and economists who study federalism have come to take a broader view.[3] They have come to recognize that stable federal systems that escape the twin threats of disintegration and nationalization may yet experience serious institutional pathologies. Prominently, painful experience suggests that a mix of centralized tax authority and decentralized spending authority—a common arrangement in many federal systems, including the United States—produces chronic overspending and, in some cases, fiscal ruin.[4] Moreover, well short of disintegration, federal systems can suffer excessive decentralization—a proliferation of virtually autonomous power centers that impose multiple compounding or conflicting burdens on a nation's economy. Excessive centralization and decentralization can occur at the same time, as overlaps of public authority produce thickets of intergovernmental bureaucracies that seem impervious to public accountability, let alone political reform.

A second, related point of scholarly consensus is that federalism is a "they," not an "it." As just suggested, federalism (in its broadest sense) is a mixed blessing. It can promote civic engagement or rank exploitation, innovation or financial and political instability. It can promote political transparency and accountability or compromise it, protect against the ravages of factional politics or amplify them. Salutary and baneful effects often come in bundles. Their mix and overall tendency do not depend on some global balance but on complex institutional and legal arrangements. Depending on those arrangements as well as social and economic background conditions, (de)centralization can make matters better or worse. Federalism can be a promise or a pathology, a blessing or a curse. But the central question is not *how much* federalism; it is *what kind* of federalism.[5]

The Upside-Down Constitution pursues just that question. The inquiry, I hope to show, is far superior to the perennial search for an ill-defined "balance" in allowing us to understand American federalism's historical trajectory and present condition—and most important for my purposes, its *constitutional* contours, logic, and development.

The analysis rests on a simple, binary distinction between two ideal types of federalism. I derive it not from any phenomenological classification but rather from a calculus that might inform a choice for or against federalism, or for or against a particular kind of federalism, *before* a constitution is in place. In that preconstitutional context, one can think of federalism as the constitutional choice of individual prospective citizens of a single polity or, what amounts to the same thing, of a single sovereign "We the people." If those individuals opt for federalism (as opposed to a unitary government), they will choose federalism *of a certain form* and for a certain purpose—to discipline government at all levels. That form of federalism I call "constitutional" or "competitive" federalism. Alternatively, one can think of federalism as a bargain among state governments or local elites.[6] That perspective is perfectly plausible (especially in the formative stages of a political union), but it will generate a very different federalism. The junior governments will yield to central authority only if the move promises to enhance their surplus capacity—very roughly, their ability to tax citizens in excess of the cost of providing public services.[7] This form of federalism I call "cartel" federalism or (in its advanced, contemporary state) "consociational" federalism.

Needless to say, the dichotomy just sketched fails to capture many of the rich nuances and facets of federalism in America, not to mention other countries. Federal systems, including ours, typically combine competitive and cartel arrangements. The notion of states as revenue maximizers is a modeling assumption, not an empirical generalization (let alone an observation). And the idea of an authentic constitutional "choice" seems to correspond with no country's actual experience. For all its simplicity and artifice, however, I hope to show that the heuristic yields important insights into the nature and development of American federalism. The citizens' competitive federalism is, or was, that of the Constitution. The states' federalism of cartels and consociation is ours.

I make no bones about my normative priors: A competitive federalism that disciplines government is worth having. A cartel federalism that empowers government at all levels is pathological, and quite probably worse than wholesale nationalization. However, I shall make no serious effort to defend those intuitions. My central point is to demonstrate that our federalism of cartels and consociation is disconnected from, and indeed antithetical to, the Constitution's competitive structure and logic. Yet nothing in our institutional politics constrains it, and periodic efforts to restore federalism's "balance"—bouts of "devolution" and judicial forays into protecting "states as states"—only reinforce a federalism that, by constitutional design, we were never meant to have. The concluding chapters will take a stab at rehabilitating a modern federalism closer to the Constitution's "genius" (as John Marshall used to say). But the first step is to understand what happened and why. To that end, one has to dig deep, all the way to the foundations.

Constitutional Choices

The Founders, nineteenth-century jurists, and classical and contemporary contractarians all started, or start, with a "dualist" constitutional perspective.[8] They set aside the calculations that citizens, interest groups, or politicians make under already-existing rules and instead ask what the world might look like in a "constitutional moment"—from an "ex ante" position in which the parties choose the rules that will govern their future, "in-period," options and actions. Does federalism make sense from that perspective? And if so, what kind of federalism makes sense? The answer depends on who makes the choice—prospective citizens or states.

The Citizens' Federalism. Suppose that preconstitutional individuals hailing from different polities have decided that they are one nation and that the benefits of establishing a single central government outweigh the costs. To what extent and for what purposes should subordinate governments retain any authority to tax and regulate? Less abstractly: in the *United* States, what good are the states? The question turns out to be very close. Although federalism may make sense under some conditions and on some assumptions, equally plausible assumptions may render a centralized, state-less system a superior choice.[9] For better or worse, though, the first-order choice (federalism, yea or nay) is often foreclosed, and it was foreclosed to the American Founders: if there was to be a union at all, some form of federalism was a foregone conclusion. The constitutional problem was, and is, what *kind* of federalism. That question turns out to have a tolerably clear answer.

Individuals' constitutional choice depends on their expectations about government. They could put their trust in a benevolent government, but that is a high-risk assumption; if it proves wrong, the losses will mount very quickly. It is safer, then, to assume that government will be prone to abuse. "The great difficulty" in forming "a government which is to be administered by men over men," James Madison wrote, is that "you must first enable the government to control the governed; and in the next place oblige it to control itself."[10] For the purpose of controlling the governed, a single central government will do. The point of entrusting a second set of junior governments with authority over the same citizens and territory, therefore, is to oblige government to control itself. *For a single "We the People,"* federalism is worth having if and insofar as it helps to alleviate the government monopoly problem.[11]

Federalism can serve that purpose in two ways. First, federalism limits the central government to procuring public goods that can be provided only at that level, such as national defense. Local public goods are to be provided locally. That arrangement helps to reduce central decision costs, which is worthwhile even if politicians at every level are perfectly benevolent.[12] On any set of less charitable assumptions, however, the central provision of local public goods will result in a level of spending and taxing in excess of *any* jurisdiction's preference, or the level of spending that would obtain if jurisdictions had to tax themselves for the benefit.[13] In short, to the extent that the central government's taxing and spending authority can be limited to goods that are national in scale, federalism can serve as a protection against government error and exploitation.

Second, federalism looks attractive if one assumes that citizens and firms are mobile. In that universe, federalism will enable citizens to choose among varying bundles of public services and the taxes that come with them, and it will force the junior governments to compete for productive citizens and firms. Competition in this sense has many potential advantages. It may allow citizens with heterogeneous preferences to sort themselves into different jurisdictions that offer different bundles of public services (and accompanying tax payments). It may help to disclose information both about what policies work and about citizens' preferences, and it may foster policy innovation. Its principal constitutional advantage, however, is to discipline governments. Citizens will be willing to pay for public services at levels that will vary among jurisdictions. In contrast, states' attempts to collect surplus will induce exploited citizens to exit—to "vote with their feet." This "Tiebout competition" will discipline the junior governments in the same way in which market competition disciplines private producers.[14]

The conventional term for this arrangement is "competitive federalism." Of course, the Founders were unfamiliar with the modern-day economic and public choice theories that sail under that banner, and one has to be careful in projecting those theories backwards and especially in mobilizing them for normative constitutional purposes.[15] Even so, contemporary theory illuminates the elementary calculus of the United States Constitution. If there is to be federalism, it should be a means of reducing decision costs and the dangers of government monopoly and exploitation. That is so because the Constitution, including its federalism, must embody the ex ante preferences of prospective citizens, *to the complete exclusion of the preferences of "states as states."* Examine the Constitution from this vantage: for all the wheeling and dealing that went into it, the Founders managed to protect that central premise. For that reason, they got all the pieces of a competitive federalism architecture almost exactly right—perhaps as right as one can get them.

The States' Federalism. Now invert the perspective, and consider federalism as a bargain among states—that is to say, state officials or political elites. What is their ex ante choice? Unlike individuals, states will embrace federalism as a first-order choice. (They will hardly opt for their own demise.) But they will also have a second-order preference with respect to federalism's form. Prospective citizens will embrace competitive federalism because it promises to reduce government abuse and exploitation all levels. States, in diametrical contrast, will embrace union only if, and to the extent that, it promises to improve their position—the "power, emolument and consequence of the[ir] offices," in Hamilton's words; their "surplus," in the parlance of public choice economists.[16] Much like private producers in economic markets, states "as states" seek supracompetitive returns. To that end, they need a central government that stands ready to *prevent* competition among states and to cartelize the political market. At the same time, a central government that is sufficiently strong to protect the states' surplus may also be sufficiently strong to confiscate it, and states will want to guard against that eventuality.[17]

Most federal constitutions enshrine this federalism-as-a-cartel model. For example, they may grant the central government a de facto tax monopoly (thus suppressing tax competition among states) and guarantee the junior governments a share of the proceeds.[18] The United States

Constitution contains no "fiscal constitution" of this sort. This silence is a first illustration of the Constitution's fiercely competitive structure (and, we shall see, a very important feature). As a matter of institutional practice, however, our federalism has come to approximate the states' cartel ideal. For example, hundreds of federal "conditional funding" programs support, from general taxes, services that states could not hope to provide under competitive conditions for fear that taxed citizens or firms might head for the exits. Federal workplace, employment, and safety standards suppress state competition for mobile labor and capital. And so on. By most measures, American federalism is still among the most competitive in the world; for example, it tolerates a comparatively high level of state tax competition. But there is no mistaking the general tendency.

By all appearances, the cartelization of American federalism confronts no serious constitutional obstacle. The Supreme Court has contributed its share to the process by prohibiting state competition on contentious moral questions, from abortion to the death penalty. And far from viewing the cartelization of American federalism as a constitutional problem, the Court asks whether the system is in "balance"—that is, whether the "states as states," meaning their political institutions and officials, are having a sufficiently good time. That question, we shall see, has no correct or even intelligible answer. It is not part of our constitutional calculus.

Constitutional Change

The central point of the constitutional choice heuristic is to drive the federalism analysis back to a genuinely constitutional perspective and to show that the crucial question, normatively as well as analytically, is not *how much* federalism but *what kind* of federalism. But the perspective also helps to explain federalism's migration from competition to cartel. The explanation emerges if one recasts the ex ante heuristic into an analytic narrative that clarifies the institutional actors' "in-period" incentives.

Once states find themselves operating under a competitive federal order, their dominant strategy is to do in-period what they could not achieve ex ante: organize cartels. To prevent defections and chiseling by procompetitive states, states will require the assistance of a central, coercive agency—that is, the national government.[19] This demand for cartelization is a constant in all federal systems. It is reinforced by potent political and functional demands, and it has been the dominant—though not unbroken—tendency of American federalism. Our constitutional history illustrates both the basic dynamic and the forces that have at times impeded it.

Inversion. State demand for central, cartelizing intervention, I just noted, is a constant. Its *intensity*, however, depends on factor mobility and the scale of economic production. In a world of low factor mobility and limited scale, states collect surplus from local producers and consumers. Under conditions of high factor mobility, national scale of production, and global low-cost financial intermediation, in contrast, ready exit will deplete the states' surplus. To forestall that outcome, states will demand central, "harmonizing" intervention. This dynamic began to unfold in the 1870s and accelerated thereafter. Large-scale industrialization entailed a formidable increase in factor mobility, scale of production, and national financial intermediation, with the expected result: states demanded the harmonization of labor conditions, product standards, and much more. The first demands for systematic federal transfer programs date to the same period.

Although both Congress and the Supreme Court sought to accommodate the demand, bargaining problems—such as state rivalries and defections and disagreements over the distribution of the available surplus—often blocked the creation of state cartels and a systemwide move to "cooperative federalism" (as it would come to be called). However, players who get to play the game often enough will eventually figure out cooperative solutions.[20] Under the added pressure of an exogenous shock (the Depression) and conditions of unusually high political consensus (the landslide election of 1936), political institutions found a way to shift from competition to cartel.[21] Constitutional rules proved inadequate to arrest that joint defection. The Supreme Court abandoned the competitive rules and instead embraced a constitutional order that facilitates the formation of state cartels, usually under national auspices. The cartel federalism of the New Deal Constitution has been "our" federalism ever since.

Later chapters will describe the constitutional dimensions of federalism's complicated renegotiation during the industrial era and the New Deal in some detail. Here, I emphasize two crucial implications. One of them concerns the common notion, dating back to the Founding era and alive to this day, that "states as states" will manfully resist federal encroachments; if they don't, that must be because the central government has corrupted or overwhelmed them. That account has it backwards. One can debate the role of states as relatively autonomous actors in federalism's transformation, but there is no doubt about the direction of their demand *in favor of* central intervention. State resistance to that tendency—that is to say, insistence on competitive conditions—has materialized only under unusual conditions, about which more anon.

The second implication concerns the nature of the New Deal and its federalism. Contrary to its reputation, the New Deal was not a centralizing revolution. Rather, it was a revolution to empower government—to enhance its surplus capacity—at *all* levels. Political scientists and constitutional scholars have often described the transformation as a transition from "dual" to "cooperative" federalism. But that too misses the crucial point: the transition from competition to cartel as federalism's organizing principle.

Impediments. Although the cartelization story just sketched is at odds with our conventional understanding of federalism and its historical trajectory, it mirrors the expectation, shared by the great majority of federalism scholars, that competitive federalism cannot preserve itself.[22] However, exceptional conditions may retard, attenuate, or frustrate the constant state demand for cartelization. American federalism, to the extent that it has remained competitive, has been shaped and protected by two such conditions: sectionalism and constitutional structure.

"Sectionalism" is a social or economic cleavage that produces a persistent division among states across a wide range of political issues. For the purpose of stabilizing competitive conditions, the sectional divide need not be fifty-fifty; however, there must be enough minority states, and the rift between them and the majority must be sufficiently deep, to prevent the majority from bribing or forcing minority states into a federalism cartel. Sectionalism's central role in American federalism is suggested by William Riker's famous observation that the defense of federalism in the United States is a defense of slavery.[23] Riker later qualified his indictment, and the story of American sectionalism is considerably more complicated. (Sectional politics retained great force even after the Civil War had abolished slavery and removed the threat of secession.)[24] Still, Riker's insight points to the fact that sectionalism served as a powerful stabilizing mechanism for competitive federalism—until the New Deal found legislative and constitutional means to break its force and to rope the South into federal cartels. Although that project remained notoriously incomplete (foremost, on the question of civil rights), it is impossible to deny its transformative character.

The constitutional structure theme may seem yet more familiar. Constitutional lawyers in particular are well acquainted with the notion that "political safeguards" (such as the states' representation in Congress) will protect federalism.[25] That, though, is not what I have in mind. Political safeguards protect the interests of the states *as states*. If the states' interests run toward surplus-protective cartels, the structural safeguards will cut in that direction. *Competitive* federalism's structural protections lie elsewhere—in a constitutional silence and a constitutional commitment.

I have already alluded to the procompetitive silence: the United States Constitution has no "fiscal constitution"—no assignment of taxes to levels of government and no explicit provision for revenue sharing between the states and the national government or among states. This entails that state cartels have to be constructed in-period and one at a time, in a bargaining process that (in game theorists' parlance) has no focal point. We shall see that this constitutional design feature has consistently operated as a barrier against state efforts to replicate their ex ante choice—the dystopia of a comprehensive, federally sponsored tax cartel.

The procompetitive commitment is the Constitution's strategy with respect to ordering relations among states and between states and the federal government. The Constitution aims to address federalism's inevitable conflicts and coordination problems—to produce integration—*by law* (as opposed to force or, as just seen, fiscal transfers).[26] Legal integration can be supplied on "positive" terms, through affirmative central legislation; or on "negative" terms, through judicially enforced prohibitions against state interferences. Positive integration will almost always be "harmonizing" and cartel reinforcing. (Later chapters will present the evidence and the reasons.) Negative integration, in contrast, will almost inevitably proceed on competitive terms. Federal courts cannot compel transfer payments among states, harmonize their laws, or pay them money to implement a federal standard. Under a suitably designed Constitution, however, federal courts *can* produce integration on competitive terms: they can forbid states from discriminating against outsiders, taxing or regulating sisterstates' citizens, or blocking entry to and exit from their jurisdictions.

If competitive federalism is your cup of tea, then, you'll want to entrust the federal structure principally to the courts, armed with federal jurisdiction and competition-protective constitutional clauses, while cluttering the federal legislature with obstacles. That, in a nutshell, is our Founders' constitutional arrangement, and it was also our approximate institutional practice throughout the nineteenth century. Cartel federalism, by contrast, calls for just the opposite arrangements: lots of harmonizing, positive integration that forestalls state competition and protects the states' surplus, and a minimal role for procompetitive judicial interventions. Lo, just as the New Deal found means of overcoming obstacles to positive integration, the Supreme Court engineered on the negative side constitutional doctrines that cut back on the federal judiciary's procompetitive interventions. Both moves had profoundly state-empowering objectives and effects. Both were essential elements of the New Deal transformation of the constitutional federalism order—from competition to cartel, and from a federalism for citizens to a federalism for states.

Contents and Polemics

The Upside-Down Constitution is a long trek through the territory just surveyed from thirty thousand feet. Part I establishes the constitutional foundations, followed by the judiciary's elaboration of competitive federalism in Part II. Part III explicates the New Deal transformation, followed by the judiciary's construction of cartels and consociation in Part IV. Part V is devoted to more conjectural and normative thoughts on Our Federalism.

The organization of the book, like its title and the preceding exposition, suggests an abrupt break between the Constitution's competitive federalism and the New Deal Constitution's cartel federalism. Moreover, it suggests a sharp discontinuity between decisive constitutional moments (Parts I and III) and the judiciary's interpretation of the Constitution (Parts II and IV). Those impressions are accurate, up to a point. But the book also pursues deeper and more polemical purposes both with respect to the Constitution's moments and its judicial interpretation.

Moments. Bruce Ackerman famously interpreted the New Deal as a "constitutional moment" in which "We the People" effectively, although informally, amended the Constitution. *The Upside-Down Constitution* riffs on and responds to Ackerman's splendid books, to the point of borrowing the titles for Parts I and III.[27] To his enormous credit, Ackerman recovered the Founders' idea of constitutional politics that differs from ordinary politics in kind and in normative force. His emphasis on that crucial point holds the promise of liberating an aridly interpretive, Court-centered constitutional debate from its self-imposed debilities and limitations. Alas, Ackerman's real achievements are clouded by his outlandish interpretation of the New Deal as a free-form constitutional convention and amendment process.

No one seriously doubts that the New Deal worked a constitutional transformation in a taxonomic sense. However, the fact that to all practical purposes we ended up with a new Constitution marks the beginning rather than the end of controversy. One point of contention has to do with political and institutional dynamics. Undoubtedly, the *political* New Deal played a highly salient role. Its unusual degree of political mobilization and consensus enabled political players to switch from one constitutional model (competition) to another (cartel); and in any event, the drama of

1937/1938 made clear who had won and who had lost the constitutional debate. As "revisionist" scholars have shown, however, the *constitutional* New Deal followed a more gradual dynamic, especially with respect to federalism.[28] Federalism's New Deal transformation had deep intellectual and political roots in the Progressive Era, and it had a great deal to do with secular changes in the country's political economy. None of this is easily telescoped into the politics of the 1930s.[29]

Behind this point of disagreement lurks the much deeper question of whether the politics of the New Deal moment were "constitutional" in any honorific, normatively plausible sense. The hallmark of a constitutional moment, Ackerman argues, is an engaged citizenry. Engagement, though, comes in varying forms. The Founders put their hopes in reasoned engagement—"reflection and choice," in the *Federalist*'s famous phrase.[30] The New Deal never even aspired to that sort of constitutional politics (which is why there is no New Deal equivalent of the Declaration of Independence, the *Federalist Papers*, or the Gettysburg Address). Its explicit program was to cobble together a stable coalition of interests and constituencies. That project, to be sure, proved stupendously successful; but it is antithetical to a truly constitutional enterprise, built on reflection and choice.

This high-level distinction bears centrally on the what-kind-of-federalism choice referred to above. In a constitutional moment of reflection and choice, "We the People" will seek to ensure the blessings of liberty to ourselves *and our posterity*. The calculus is long term, and it excludes any consideration for the welfare of "states as states." That calculus, Part I will show, will utilize federalism to reduce the risk of government monopoly and abuse, to curb the violence of faction, and to generate political stability. These orientations all go together, and they define the federalism program of our Constitution. The New Deal Constitution and its federalism, Part III will show, reflect just the opposite premises and objectives. The New Deal Constitution is solicitous of the states as states—that is, the interest of the political class in accumulating surplus. It thereby unleashes factions (now more charitably called "interest groups") to clamor for a share of the surplus. And in pursuit of those objectives, the New Deal Constitution celebrates political instability and a "Living Constitution." No sentient people, or People, would ever deliberate their way to that arrangement.[31] A federalism of "Them the States and Factions" is coherent in its own warped way. But constitutionally plausible, it is not.

Interpretation. My polemics against the New Deal Constitution may seem to suggest a hankering for the "Old," exiled, pre–New Deal Constitution.

I do indeed have issues with the Progressives and the New Dealers—but not in any conventional, "originalist" sense.

"Originalism," as it has come to be understood, holds that the terms and provisions of the Constitution must be understood in the sense of their "public meaning" at the time of their enactment. As a matter of interpretation, that is surely right; but it cannot be the end of the constitutional inquiry. Foremost, "we must never forget that it is a *constitution* we are expounding"—and not just any old constitution, but a deliberately minimalist constitution that makes politics possible but confidently leaves its shapes and outcomes to future generations.[32] The conspicuous parsimony of the United States Constitution presents an originalist conundrum. It explains why we need interpretive originalism as a constraint on a judiciary that is subject to precious few institutional constraints; but it also renders a narrowly textual, clause-bound exegesis problematic and incomplete. On one side, one cannot make sense of our bare-bones Constitution without some antecedent idea, and ideally a theory, of what the instrument is supposed to do. On the other side, the Constitution will not work without judicially supplied, common-law-like rules that translate the Constitution's text and structure into institutional practice.

Originalism (not in all forms, but in its dominant forms) has set its face like flint against both constitutional theory and common law—for respectable reasons, but to its own detriment. When confronted with the need to articulate, or reason from, the Constitution's normative foundations, originalism turns brutally positivist: judges must enforce the text that the sovereign "We the People" formally ordained more than two centuries ago because they did so ordain. Originalism is parasitic on our "dualist," contractarian tradition; but it does not wish to defend or even understand that tradition (much less answer those who attack it), for fear that the enterprise might lead jurists away from a readable and meaningful text and into the unbounded terrain of natural law sophistry. However laudable that impulse, it produces errors of its own.

When confronted with the incontrovertible fact that the text alone cannot make sense of individual clauses and with the additional, equally obvious fact that our understanding of the instrument has changed greatly over time, originalism responds with intransigent textualism or "fainthearted," ad hoc appeals to stare decisis, tradition, or political exigencies.[33] Even so enriched, however, interpretation alone will not do. A deliberately minimalist, open-ended Constitution consciously invites a more fundamental form of argument. Keith E. Whittington has called that form of argument "constitutional construction." Construction, he writes, implicates fundamental political principles, structures future political practice, occurs at moments of unsettled understanding, develops in interstices of discover-able textual meaning, and provides standards for political conduct.[34] The stuff of this constitutional construction—which in its judicial form might also be termed "structural interpretation"—is constitutional common-law doctrine. Although Whittington, himself an originalist, views this mode of reasoning as legitimate, originalism in its dominant forms seeks to choke it off. Again, it does so for fear that judges might "make it up." And again, we shall see, the attempt produces constitutional errors.

This book attempts, among other things, to explore originalism's char-acteristic blind spots and to cover its open flanks. More clearly perhaps than any other question of constitutional law, federalism reveals the inad-equacies of the conventional originalist understanding. Famously, feder-alism is not "in" our Constitution (although it is "in" many others).[35] It is a structural principle that we infer from individual clauses that would otherwise remain senseless; and this necessary and necessarily inferential reasoning requires some prior, normative understanding of how the con-stitutional structure is supposed to work and what it is supposed to do. At the same time, constitutional federalism is dominated by doctrine—an enumerated powers doctrine, which is inferred from the structure of Arti-cle I; a federal preemption doctrine, usually inferred from the Supremacy Clause; a "Spending Clause doctrine," inferred from a clause that governs taxation, not spending; a state sovereign immunity doctrine, inferred from the general structure of the Constitution but against its text (the Eleventh Amendment); and so forth. The dominance of doctrine over text illustrates that our Constitution is—to employ the fighting words—a *common law* constitution.[36] The term does not necessarily imply a reliance on substan-tive common law or a preference for judge-made rather than statutory law or judicial preeminence, let alone a judicial monopoly of interpretation. Rather, it means that the Constitution requires a robust judicial supply of structural (as opposed to textual) abstract-concrete norms. The abstract side is that the doctrines must be elicited from a Constitution that often fails to spell out—not by accident or lack of foresight, but by design—operational rules that can order public and private conduct within reason-able bounds of specificity and predictability. The concrete side is that the stuff of doctrine comes not from a blackboard but from courts' judgments regarding the actual practices of human beings and their institutions. Because those practices change, the doctrines will elaborate themselves over time, even as the Constitution itself remains the same.

Deep down, originalism suspects all this. Its animosity toward norma-tive constitutional argument and constitutional common law has to do, not with any point of principle, but with its historical origin as a bulwark against the Warren-Brennan Court's rights enthusiasms. Concede to a Court like that an inch beyond the constitutional text and its historical meaning, the thinking went, and there's no telling what newfangled rights it might conjure into law. Federalism presents a challenge to that Manichean originalism. But it also presents an opportunity: it is fundamentally about structure, not rights. So long as the constitutional universe beyond the naked text consists solely of rights, originalists' fears are difficult to gainsay and impossible to dispel. Structure, and especially the Constitution's federal structure, is different: both within the text and outside it, there is much more to work with. Taking the federal structure seriously shows that it is both possible and necessary to articulate constitutional understandings that are more normative and common-law-like than plain vanilla interpretation while remaining tightly yoked to the Constitution.

Something similar is also true of the Constitution more generally. The notion that "We the People" could amend the Constitution without an expressly and self-consciously text-centered deliberation—whether on the fly and in a fevered moment or through rolling Supreme Court adjustments to public opinion polls—would have struck the Founders, and the nineteenth-century jurists in their footsteps, as dangerous folly and possibly insane. In that sense, everyone was an "originalist." But those old-time justices, like the Founders, weren't positivists. They were contractarians. Their opinions teem with reflections on the "genius" of republican government. And they weren't pure textualists; while the text was their starting point, those justices understood the need to make the instrument work as a whole and as well as it would.[37] That, to them, was the point of "the judicial power" conferred by the Constitution they were expounding.

Constitutionalism, Ancient and Modern

I recognize the presumptuousness, and perhaps the implausibility, of my intellectual enterprise. *The Upside-Down Constitution* mobilizes public choice theory against the conventional federalism "balance." It brings competitive federalism theory, never explicitly articulated by the Founders, to bear on constitutional interpretation. It acknowledges the Constitution's openness but insists on its foundational premises and its ascertainable structure. In that fashion, the book stakes out constitutional ground in opposition to both conventional originalism and the New Deal Constitution's progressive heirs. It will not win converts very easily.

Nonetheless, I hope that skeptics will engage the argument—not only because it offers fresh and perhaps clarifying answers to old questions and confusions, but also for urgent practical reasons. America's governments—at all levels—increasingly find themselves in dire financial straits. Americans of all political persuasions have become genuinely worried about the fiscal sustainability of their country's social commitments. It has begun to dawn on members of the body politic that the cause of the present fiscal crisis may be structural rather than purely cyclical. Moreover, these concerns and the accompanying, often shrill debate over the role of government play out against a backdrop of record-low public confidence in our political institutions. Of course, federalism and its dysfunctions are only part of the overall fiscal and political picture. However, as at all critical junctures in American history, federalism is a large part of that picture. Our Federalism—the institutions and instruments that the New Deal Constitution has bequeathed to us—is a principal cause of our current institutional dysfunctions, public discontents, and fiscal imbalances; or so I shall argue. At the same time, "federalism" in a very broad sense continues to serve in some (conservative) political circles as a rallying cry for more democratic, more accountable government. For that salutary program to be successful, however, would require something quite different from a recourse to the familiar themes of "balance" and "original intent." The obsession with "balance" is our federalism's fundamental problem; and an "originalism" solution that surrenders all arms except the Constitution's bare-bones text simply cannot work.

In short, this is a splendid time to re-examine federalism's intellectual foundations and present pathologies. The Founders themselves knew that their bold effort to establish constitutional order for themselves *and their posterity* carried a risk, to the point of certainty, of an unintended turn—perhaps even an inversion. For precisely that reason, they wrote a Constitution that, more than any other, invites argument over its import and foundations—in full awareness of the perils of democratic politics and agitation, but also in fulsome hope that future generations might remember what the Founders were getting at and perhaps, in light of experience and improved knowledge, understand the Constitution's genius in ways surpassing the understandings even of the Founders themselves.[38]

The Upside-Down Constitution responds to that invitation. It illuminates some federalism features that the Founders perceived only imperfectly—and points to many others that they perceived more perfectly than anyone else before or since. In fact, the Founders' understanding of the "compound republic" reached far beyond that of modern-day jurists, political scientists, or economists. If this is a very long book, that is because we have forgotten an awful lot—and find ourselves in dire need of remembering it.

PART ONE

FOUNDATIONS

THE PURPOSE OF PART I is to demonstrate that the United States Constitution adumbrates a particular kind of federalism, which we have come to call competitive federalism. The point of departure is a constitutional moment in which individuals choose the rules that will govern their future interactions. If individuals in that position were to choose any federalism at all, they would choose competitive federalism, to the exclusion of alternative arrangements. To be sure, the Founders did not construe a Constitution in a state of nature or from a contrived original position; they were practical statesmen, not speculative philosophers. And they knew no more of competitive federalism theory than they knew of the marginalist revolution, the Coase theorem, or other intellectual breakthroughs that have allowed us to examine ancient truths in a new light. What the Founders did have, however, was a potent theory of constitutional politics. Their central premise was an insistence that the "utility" of constitutional arrangements, especially including federalism, had to be viewed from the perspective of prospective citizens, as opposed to "states as states." On that foundation rests a constitutional structure that conforms in all essential respects, and countless particulars, to a competitive federalism model. The structure is not a straightjacket; it allows for in-period departures and adjustments. But it is best understood against a competitive baseline.

The constitutional fundamentalism embodied in this analysis resonates with classical contractarian theory, with its modern reformulations (especially James M. Buchanan and Gordon Tullock's *Calculus of Consent*), and with Bruce Ackerman's rehabilitation of constitutional moments and "dualist" constitutionalism. However, it stands in contrast to a judicial federalism jurisprudence (and a flood of academic commentary) that teems with technical difficulties and with inspiring rhetoric—yet is almost devoid of any genuinely constitutional argument. The Supreme Court postulates a free-standing federalism "balance" between the states and the nation, which it then proceeds to adjudicate.[1] Although great controversy surrounds the question of what and how much the justices should do by way of preserving the balance, the major premise (federalism as balance) is shared across the judicial spectrum. So is the minor premise (highly doubtful, we shall see) that the states are perennially endangered by an overbearing national government. This understanding is too widely shared and too deeply entrenched to be easily dislodged, but there are several good reasons to make the effort.

First, the Constitution very conspicuously eschews a balance. Although some federal constitutions do mandate a balance, and although many politicians and publicists of the Founding era agitated for some equilibrating rule, the Constitution instead speaks the language of powers.[2] It establishes a national government, in whose formation and operation the states play a role. It guarantees the states' territorial and political existence, allocates specified powers to the national government's branches and denies specified powers to the states, gives the states a role in the amendment process, and provides a choice of law rule (the Supremacy Clause) for conflicts between state and national law. Within those broad parameters, federalism's balance is left up to us and our politics, not to judicial calibration.

Second, excepting bureaucrats and politicians, it is unclear why anyone should *care* about the balance within an intergovernmental organization chart. Occasionally, the Supreme Court responds that the balance is "constitutionally mandated."[3] Recognizing that it isn't, the justices often embellish one metaphor ("balance") with others. Federalism's balance, they say, is "delicate," and we must respect the "etiquette of federalism" and the states' "dignity"—as if the Constitution were a code of ethics; as if more refined government manners would improve our diet; and as if the Founders had not contemplated *and rejected* state "dignity" as utterly destructive to the constitutional project.[4] In a marginally more rigorous frame of mind, the justices turn consequentialist, as in this oft-cited passage:

> Th[e] federalist structure of joint sovereigns preserves to the people numerous advantages. It assures a decentralized government that will be more sensitive to the diverse needs of a heterogeneous society; it increases opportunity for

citizen involvement in democratic processes; it allows for more innovation and experimentation in government; and it makes government more responsive by putting the States in competition for a mobile citizenry.[5]

Inasmuch as virtually all recent justices have at times relied on this incantation, one might characterize it as an "incompletely theorized agreement"; but it is better described as untheorized burble.[6] Originalist jurists should recoil at grounding constitutional interpretation on a string of bare assertions, especially because virtually none of the perceived advantages is demonstrably part of the constitutional design.[7] But the notion should be equally disconcerting to pragmatic jurists. Were they to consult the scholarship (alas, an uncommon move in federalism cases), they would discover a far more complicated and demoralizing federalism picture than a litany of "advantages" would suggest. In any event, pragmatism cannot tell us how to weigh federalism's supposed advantages or resolve conflicts among them. It cannot even explain why we should not start the analysis with federalism's equally numerous, palpable *dis*-advantages—its frictional costs, for example, or its tendency to multiply access points for rent-seeking factions, or its potential to obfuscate political responsibility.

Third, balance federalism, in its metaphorical or its pragmatic variation, does not merely lack a constitutional foundation but in fact militates against a carefully wrought constitutional structure and against the *kind* of federalism contemplated by the Founders. The *Federalist* spoke often of "balance" and "equilibrium"—but almost always with respect to the separation of powers, and only twice and almost in passing in connection with federalism.[8] Madison's canonical definition of the "compound republic" in *Federalist* 39—the "federalism" of the Constitution—strikes a very different note:

> In its foundation [the Constitution] is federal, not national; in the sources from which the ordinary powers of the government are drawn, it is partly federal, and partly national; in the operation of these powers, it is national, not federal; in the extent of them again, it is federal, not national; and finally, in the authoritative mode of introducing amendments, it is neither wholly federal, nor wholly national.[9]

No suggestion that those structural characteristics somehow balance out, or that the erosion of one could be compensated by strengthening another without effecting a fundamental change in the system. Evidently, Madison deemed the individual features of the constitutional structure of critical importance.

The "compound republic" never made it into our political lexicon— perhaps because the simpler catechism of states' rights and national power lends itself more readily to political combat.[10] For constitutional purposes, however, one should allow that Madison may have captured an insight that our contemporary debate—among jurisprudes, though not among political scientists and economists—has forgotten or suppressed: federalism's effects and advantages depend, not on some global balance, but on specific institutional arrangements and conditions. Suppose, for instance, that we entrust the national government with local land-use regulation, and we permit states to conclude treaties with foreign nations; and suppose that the implicit exchange of functions proves neutral on the dimensions on which we measure government power. Would we rejoice because the system is in "balance"? Or suppose that we permit states to finance their operations by exacting payments from the citizens of other states. Such a federalism will be highly sensitive to the "needs" of a heterogeneous society: citizens in each state will demand lots of free lunches, and they will be prone to discovering needs they never knew they had. Civic engagement will flourish; the greater the opportunities to expropriate outsiders for domestic gains, the greater the incentive to participate in politics. And state governments will be innovative and experimental in responding to those demands. Alas, all states have symmetric incentives, so the perceived local gains from exploitation translate into global losses for citizens (and, we shall see, into advantages for state governments). Should we, would we, still celebrate federalism's advantages?

The Supreme Court has not explicitly embraced an outright inversion of federal and state powers or a federalism of mutually assured state aggression. But it has come very, very close, and it routinely bends the constitutional text and structure to federalism's supposed balance and advantages. "Our federalism" contrives protections for "states as states" in the teeth of the constitutional text, reads specific federalism clauses out of the Constitution, and denigrates the Constitution's Supremacy Clause as "extraordinary" and suspect.[11]

This formless wasteland is a relatively recent creation. "Federalism" first appeared in a Supreme Court opinion in 1939. "Balance" debuted soon thereafter, and the discovery of federalism's "advantages" and "happy incidents" date to the same period.[12] Sophisticated legal theorists defend the federalism embodied in those notions as a "translation" of federalism into a modern world that the Founders could not remotely envision.[13] Something important, however, is often lost in translation. To find out what has been lost and why, one has to go back to the constitutional structure. And to understand that structure, one has to start where the Founders started—with a constitutional moment of reflection and choice.

CHAPTER ONE

Constitutionalism

Constitutional Choice

Tyranny is imposed; a constitution is chosen by people who agree to be governed in accordance with its rules. Classical liberal theory captured the distinction in the notion of a social contract that precedes, establishes, and legitimates institutional politics. Contemporary scholars distinguish between "constitutional" and "ordinary" politics; constitutional choice theorists in the tradition of James Buchanan and Gordon Tullock's *Calculus of Consent*, between "precommitments" and "in-period" choices, and between (prospective) citizens' "ex ante" and "opportunistic" preferences.[1]

Constitutional theory of this description confronts the objection that constitutions cannot actually be chosen in any normatively compelling sense. David Hume, an author much read and revered by the Founders, advanced that view against Hobbes and Locke (constitutional theorists with whom the Founders were likewise very familiar).[2] Its most influential modern version may be that of Friedrich A. Hayek, who insisted that humane institutional arrangements must evolve spontaneously, as a result of gradual social learning and adaptation. "Constructivist" attempts to impose order will produce lots of unintended consequences and, eventually, tyranny.[3] Practical reasons and painful experience support this view. Failed constitutional experiments far outnumber success stories, and attempts to export or transpose successful constitutions to other countries have often proven futile. (The American Constitution in particular has not traveled well. It presupposes too much.) But the Hayekian perspective also has a dark side. In many places, social learning has mostly produced more efficient techniques of usurpation and oppression. Before accepting the harsh conclusion that every society will get the tyrant it deserves, it is worth asking whether deliberate constitutional choice might not be possible for at least *some* societies, under *some* conditions.

The framers of the American Constitution insisted on that possibility. "It has been frequently remarked," the *Federalist* begins, "that it seems to have been reserved to the people of this country to decide, by their conduct and example, the important question, whether societies of men are really capable or not, of establishing good government from reflection and choice, or whether they are forever destined to depend, for their political constitutions, on accident and force."[4] The distinction between "reflection and choice" and "accident and force" expresses the dualism that grounds all constitutional choice theory, and it reflects the same democratic orientation. The choice must be made by prospective citizens—"the people of this country"—alive at a constitutional moment, on behalf of themselves and their posterity.

To be sure, no people and no constitutional convention can choose and "design" a constitution the way Toyota designs automobiles. Preexisting political traditions and institutions will constrain the choices. Entrenched interests and the passions of the moment will play a large role, as will sheer ignorance about how any contemplated set of constitutional rules might play out. Thus, any constitution will involve a lot of compromise and guesswork. One can, however, discern two ex ante orientations that will dominate the deliberations. First, the constitutional subjects will seek to establish a government that is capable of controlling the governed *and itself*—to establish effective government while guarding against abuse. Second, they will seek to ensure political stability, both in the sense of reducing the range of likely political outcomes (tyranny on one side, anarchy on the other) and in the sense of creating a government that, by acting in a moderately predictable fashion, allows private citizens to plan their conduct over time.

We all can, or we think we can, recite the Founders' institutional solutions: the extended republic, checks and balances, the separation of powers, federalism, judicial review. Perhaps, though, the institutional mechanisms are *too* familiar, to the point of making us lose sight of their deeper constitutional logic. That logic emerges in contemplation of the boldness and ambition of the Founders' project.

Constitutionalism: Clubs, Consociations, and Competition

Constitutions are not contracts (although they have contractual elements). They are long-term coordination devices. Individuals, parties, tribes, states, ethnic groups, or social classes agree to play by certain rules, in the hope of procuring gains—effective but limited government, political stability—that cannot be attained under looser, less entrenched arrangements.[5] That generic description, though, encompasses very different accounts of constitutionalism and constitutional choice. One can distinguish two polar types: consociational (or end-state) constitutions and competitive constitutions.[6] The differences between these ideal types arise from the preconstitutional individuals' identity perceptions and, relatedly, their time horizon.

Golf, Anyone?. Suppose some individuals decide to form a club that offers various activities—say, squash, golf, and bridge.[7] (The incentive to cooperate may be to reduce the average cost of a shared public good, such as a clubhouse.) Further suppose the individuals informally agree to solve the basic governance questions through discussion and majority vote. How and on what terms will they agree to cooperate? If the prospective members think of themselves as existential golfers (etc.) and, moreover, have a short time horizon, they might be better off establishing separate clubs, just as ethnic groups in contiguous territories might be better off in separate and independent states. But even if the collective benefits are sufficiently large to dominate the calculus, the best the groups can do is to provide for a distribution of dues and benefits that roughly reflects their relative strength.[8]

Suppose, though, that the prospective members have a long-term view. Youngish squash players anticipate that creaky joints may at some point force them off the courts, onto the golf course, and eventually to the bridge tables in the clubhouse. And suppose the individuals decide to bestow the blessings of club membership on themselves *and their posterity*. Knowing zip about posterity's future preferences, the individuals will want to keep the options open. Instead of attempting to agree on a fixed distribution, they will seek to establish governing institutions and decision rules. Within some protective parameters (for instance, against an irreversible decision by a temporary majority of golfers to flatten the squash courts), they will let the various constituencies compete for resources and decide the appropriate dues levels in-period, pursuant to established rules.[9]

It is true that decision rules have distributive consequences, which the bargainers will seek to anticipate. Golfers may insist that representation and future voting be based on acreage rather than membership. Somebody may insist that the groups be represented equally as groups regardless of size (much as states are represented in the United States Senate). As long as the players know who they are and who they will be, the choice of decision rules may prove as elusive as the choice of end-state distributions. But the opportunistic temptations recede as the time horizon expands. If you don't know your place at a future table, there is no point in loading the dice. "The last shall be first, and the first shall be last": if individuals harbor sufficient uncertainty about their future states, and if their expected payoff is sufficiently large and the payoff period eternal, sheer self-interest may prompt people to act like saints. In matters of constitutional choice (let alone country club management), the stakes are much lower, but the basic idea is the same. Men can leave the state of nature, James Madison observed in allusion to Hobbes and Locke, because "even the stronger individuals are prompted, *by the uncertainty of their condition*, to protect the weak, as well as themselves."[10] Uncertainty both allows and compels individuals to turn from opportunism to reasoned choice, from questions of distribution to institutional rules that promise collective gains.

Consociation and Competition. Political constitutions differ from clubs in many ways, beginning with the fact no one can be compelled to golf. Even so, the club hypothetical illustrates the fundamental difference between consociational and competitive constitutions.

Consociational constitutions are collective, distributional bargains that seek to stabilize some distribution of burdens and benefits among groups. The principal means both of constitutional negotiation and in-period entrenchment is an institutionalized elite cartel. As Arend Lijphart, consociationalism's chief theorist, has written, "consociational democracy means government by an elite cartel to turn a democracy with a fragmented political culture into a stable democracy."[11] Tribal chiefs, religious leaders, party bosses, or peak associations with a monopoly on representing "their" constituencies agree to lock in some distribution of collective entitlements and, moreover, to change that distribution only by consensus among the parties.

What would a pure consociational constitution look like? Although consociationalists have been notoriously imprecise in specifying the institutional characteristics of their model, they favor an electoral system of proportional representation and, moreover, proportionalism in all government institutions. To force compromise and to institutionalize a "culture of consensus," consociationalists favor multiple veto opportunities for all political players. Recognizing that the initial conditions may change (due to demographic changes, for example, or because some parties to the bargain prove more successful than others), consociational constitutions typically provide for mechanisms to recalibrate the original distribution. Often, that task is entrusted to an impartial guardian of the constitution, such as a constitutional court. Throughout, the overriding objectives are to protect the member-groups' collective identities and to lock in an end-state distribution of political and economic entitlements.

Competitive constitutions pursue their objectives by different means—not through coalition building, but through constitution writing.[12] Competitive constitutions do not guarantee, and are not meant to guarantee, any end-state distribution at all. Instead, they seek to establish rules for an institutional repeat game. Ideally, the rules should be "self-enforcing," meaning that multiple and rival institutional actors possess or are given incentives to ensure their observance. Institutionalized competition, not consensus, will keep political outcomes within a range that will generally be perceived as tolerably fair and efficient.

While constitutions typically contain some mix of consociational and competitive mechanisms, there is no doubt about the place of the United States Constitution on the spectrum. The most casual perusal shows it to be wholly anticonsociational. Consociational constitutions are bound to be quite long; like the peace pacts they resemble, they cannot leave much to chance. The United States Constitution is very short. Consociationalists insist on proportional representation and coalition government; our electoral system is unequivocally majoritarian. Consociational constitutions proportion entitlements among the parties to the bargain, especially assets that might become objects of zero-sum political games—civil service appointments, school curricula and governance, language regulations, and officially tolerated (or mandated) religious practices. Our Constitution has nothing to say about any of this, and it proportions nothing except seats in the House of Representatives according to the census. Consociational constitutions spell out social purposes and objectives; ours refrains from loading the dice. In short, the United States Constitution is the prototype of a competitive constitution. It sets up a handful of rivalrous institutions with certain powers, and it mandates certain decision rules. It makes politics possible—and lets the outcomes be what they may.

A constitution of this nature requires a very high degree of confidence that competitive politics and institutions will produce acceptable outcomes—not in every case, but on the whole and over time. It is not clear why anyone would agree in advance to play such an open-ended, high-stakes game. In establishing government, as in all human affairs, people will typically insist on entrenching their partial advantages even if one could show that in the long run everyone would be better off under a different design. Consociationalists despair of putting people in a broader frame of mind, and in divided societies, that may indeed by impossible. Religious, ethnic, or linguistic differences and attachments may run too deep, and politics as a competitive repeat game holds little allure if losing a single round may spell death or ruin.[13] Even under more benign circumstances, however, opportunistic calculations are not easily transcended. The competitive constitutional project requires a willingness and ability to set aside considerations of immediate advantage and to consider the payoffs of long-range coordination. On the possibility of that calculus hangs our Constitution.

Constitutional Politics: Reflection and Choice

Constitutional contractarians, ancient and modern, are competitivists and anticonsociationalists at heart. They derive constitutions not from interest group compromise but from *individual* and *unanimous* choice under conditions of uncertainty.[14] Given the radical uncertainty of a preconstitutional "state of nature," *every* individual will opt for effective, limited, stable government. Unanimity distinguishes legitimate government from usurpation. It is possible if, and only if, the constitution enshrines decision rules, as opposed to distributions (on which no unanimity is ever possible); if the constitutional subjects are in the appropriate, long-term frame of mind; and if they can set aside particularistic attachments to "their" religion, state, ethnicity, and so on.[15]

The Founders understood this abstract theory well enough (they had all read Locke). However, they confronted no state of nature but a series of direct, pressing, specific political problems, and no perfect veil of uncertainty clouded the choices. The delegates to the Philadelphia Convention knew which states were big and which were small. They also knew whether they were debtors or creditors (a crucial divide), and although many of them must have expected that their economic fortunes might change, surely none of them expected to be future slaves. And the document would be submitted for ratification to voters and state conventions whose members were very much aware of their particular interests. In short, America confronted an actual rather than a hypothetical constitutional choice. The question, in that predicament, is whether one should give in to the consociational program of elite compromise—in historical context, compromise among *state* elites—or rather hold on to the competitive constitutional alternative and ideal. Very roughly, the consociational program was, and has been ever since, the Anti-Federalists' prescription. Federalists, in contrast, insisted on the competitive option—a genuine constitutional choice by a single, sovereign people, as opposed to a mere bargain among interests, states, or elites. For reasons just mentioned, abstract theory would prove unpersuasive. What the Federalists needed was a theory of constitutional politics—a theory that would show that there was *enough* room for constitutional "reflection and choice," as opposed to "accident and force."

To that end, people must be persuaded that choice is in fact possible. Utility functions or philosophical abstractions will not do the job, and so Publius appealed to honor, respectability, and the lessons of experience more often than to the dictates of cold reason and interest.[16] The *Federalist*'s true genius, however, is the recognition that constitutional preferences are (as economists now say) endogenous and intransitive. "Endogenous" means that whereas the objective conditions of constitutional choice are what they are (and they had better be favorable), people's preferences will depend on who they think they are, on their risk perceptions, and on their time horizon. The *Federalist* shows that the people have a choice in all those respects and urges them to make the right, constitutional choice. "Intransitive" means that constitutional preferences may cycle. If one-third of voters prefers a reform of the Articles of Confederation, one-third likes the proposed Constitution, and another third holds out for a more perfect document, none of those options may garner a majority—and the wretched status quo would prevail. To forestall that result, someone has to shape and control the agenda. The *Federalist* explains why that is necessary and wholly consistent with constitutional choice.

Constitutional Preferences and Moments. In a sense, Hamilton explains in *Federalist* 1, the question of whether a constitution could be "chosen" had already been answered; the plan of the Convention was being recommended, not imposed. Still, citizens might easily fail to recognize that "accident and force" are the general predicament of mankind and reflection and choice, a rare and unprecedented constitutional moment. It is "more ardently to be wished for, than seriously to be expected," that the constitutional choice

> should be directed by a judicious estimate of our true interests, uninfluenced by considerations foreign to the public good. . . . The plan offered to our deliberations, affects too many particular interests, innovates upon too many local institutions, not to involve in its discussion a variety of objects

extraneous to its merits, and of views, passions and prejudices little favorable to the discovery of truth.[17]

Publius does not hold himself out as an impartial philosopher. In a high-stakes debate, claims to neutrality will be suspect, and Publius admits that "ambition, avarice, personal animosity, party opposition, and many other motives" are apt to operate on all sides of the debate. In any event, Publius has made up his mind, after much "attentive consideration": "I affect not reserves, which I do not feel. I will not amuse you with an appearance of deliberation, when I have decided."[18] Throughout, though, Publius insists that one can *tell* "evidence of truth" from narrow interests, an "enlarged" and "comprehensive" view of the subject from partial concerns, and "sedate and candid consideration" from partisan agitation. There would be no point in putting the people "on guard against all attempts" to distract them from that broader view if they were incapable of acting on it.[19]

How can they? As an initial matter, constitutional choice presupposes an antecedent agreement on who is doing the choosing and for whom the choice is being made. In other words, it presupposes an unambiguous set of choosers—a sovereign "we the people." If people's loyalties to some other collective entity—a tribe, an organized religion, a preexisting state—run too deep to permit agreement on a "we," one cannot have a constitution that is more than usurpation or a consociational peace pact or (as in the European Union) a work-in-progress. The sense of collective identity and the possibility of individual constitutional choice are two sides of the same coin.

Moreover, a deliberate choice is not possible for every people at all times; it requires favorable conditions. By good fortune and "Providence," however, Americans find themselves in such conditions at this particular moment. Publius stresses the fortunate circumstances that enabled individual American citizens to choose *as one people:* a favorable geography that provides natural boundaries and a connected country; and within that connected country,

> one united people; a people descended from the same ancestors, speaking the same language, professing the same religion, attached to the same principles of government, very similar in their manners and customs, and who, by their joint counsels, arms and efforts, fighting side by side through a long and bloody war, have nobly established their general liberty and independence. . . .
>
> To all general purposes we have uniformly been one people . . . each individual citizen every where enjoying the same national rights, privileges, and protection. As a nation we have made peace and war: as a nation we have vanquished our common enemies: as a nation we have formed alliances and

made treaties, and entered into various compacts and conventions with foreign states.[20]

As legions of learned readers have noted, Publius here skirts the slavery question, and his account is jarringly dissonant with the accounts of interstate rivalries and factional politics in later essays. Perfection, however, is not to be expected. Jay's larger point is this: just as there must be *enough* room for "reflection and choice," so there must be *enough* of a real-world basis for a sovereign, "we the people" choice. And although one may justly quarrel with Jay's account, one factor is clearly not overstated—the experience of having fought a common war at great cost. The unifying force of that experience is great, and quite probably essential.[21]

However, constitutional moments are short as well as rare. Reflection and choice presuppose a war that is concluded *and recent*. A prolonged peace is almost as bad as war, albeit for a different reason: it induces forgetfulness and opportunism. The people must choose before a transient moment of constitutional politics passes and ordinary politics again holds sway. In Madison's words:

> *It is too early for politicians to presume on our forgetting* that the public good, the real welfare of the great body of the people, is the supreme object to be pursued; and that no form of government whatever, has any other value, than as may be fitted for the attainment of this object.[22]

"The happiness of the people of America," "the real welfare of the great body of the people," encapsulates the citizens' constitutional, ex ante perspective and the basic criterion of normatively compelling constitutional arrangements. We the people will "forget" that perspective. In-period preferences will be parochial and opportunistic and politics, faction ridden and pathological—perhaps not always, but surely most of the time. With or without a constitution, politicians can count on it, and they will see to it. *But not just yet.* The patriots' sacrifices have purchased the actual possibility of a constitutional choice.

A moment of maximum opportunity is also a moment of maximum danger. Failure to choose means foregone opportunities and, quite likely, future calamity. One way of impressing that critical point is to appeal to people's risk aversion or, more precisely, their desire to minimize their expected regret over the worst outcome under any given scenario.[23] This is the function of the *Federalist*'s dire warnings of anarchy, warfare, and general instability, should the plan of the Convention be defeated. Here, as with Jay's appeals to national unity, one can fault the *Federalist* for exaggeration (though the charge applies with equal force to the Anti-Federalists' hysterics about the impending demise of republican government). But the *Federalist*'s appeal is no mere fearmongering. It is tailored to operate on people's perceptions of the *collective* political risks, as distinct from their partial advantages. Far from trying to cobble together a coalition of the frightened, Publius appeals to "the real welfare of the great body of the people."

How, again, does one encourage that perspective? Extend people's time horizon. "We the People of the United States," says the Constitution's preamble, ordain and establish this Constitution to "secure the Blessings of Liberty to ourselves *and our Posterity.*" The point is huge. It is a preemptive response to Thomas Jefferson's proposal some three decades after the Convention that every generation should be free to write itself a new constitution. Part of the framers' answer to Jefferson's contemporaneous suggestions in that direction—specifically, a proposal to submit conflicts among the branches of government to popular conventions—was utilitarian. A time-limited constitution, or a constitution that can readily be revised by popular conventions, can never earn the "veneration which time bestows on every thing."[24] The force of habit is not to be ignored; its advantages to stable, respectable government are too great. But in the end, what is being venerated has to be worthy of veneration, and it is on that account that populist constitutionalism is self-defeating. Although once-a-generation constitution writers may be more experienced than their predecessors (as Jefferson argued), they know too much about themselves and they discount the future too heavily to look to "the real welfare of the great body of the people." Jefferson's modern heirs often ask why we should feel bound by the "dead hand of the past" and attribute any normative force to the constitutional decisions of centuries past, especially in light of all the moral and democratic progress we have made. The usual inference is that we should update the Constitution. From the Founders' perspective, that enterprise is bound to be an exercise in opportunism or demagogy. A Constitution has normative force if, when, and *because* its authors and ratifiers are capable of looking to posterity.

Agenda Control. Reflection and choice, Publius insists, is possible here and now. However, in constitutional politics as in all politics, preferences may cycle such that option (A) beats (B) beats (C) beats (A) in any pairwise vote. Indeed, anything can happen unless someone controls the agenda. The *Federalist* was clear-eyed in recognizing the problem and candid on the need for agenda control. The gist of the argument appears in *Federalist* 40, but Publius telegraphs it as early as *Federalist* 2.[25]

So far, John Jay implores his audience, the American people have done what they could to seize the constitutional moment. Even "when their habitations were in flames, when many of them were bleeding in the field, and when the progress of hostility and desolation left little room for those calm and mature inquiries and reflections, which must ever precede the formation of a wise and well balanced government for a free people," the people united under the Articles of Confederation. The deficiencies of that instrument having been discovered through painful experience, the Constitutional Convention—"composed of men who possessed the confidence of the people, and many of whom had become highly distinguished by their patriotism, virtue, and wisdom"—met "in the mild season of peace, with minds unoccupied by other subjects" and without "any passion, except love for their country."[26] This helps to legitimize the Convention. It also helps that the delegates were sent by the state governments; Philadelphia was not some NGO confab. In strictness, the delegates had been charged with amending the Articles, not with writing a whole new Constitution. But they had also been charged with rendering the government adequate to its exigencies and to the preservation of the union. Having realized that those objects could not be accomplished through a series of amendments, what were the delegates supposed to do? Which was more important—the end, or the means? Ultimately the delegates took the only responsible course of action.

Here again, Publius omits salient facts. For example, the miracle at Philadelphia occurred not only because the Convention featured many delegates of astounding caliber but also because it was stacked with Federalists—by all accounts, out of proportion to the then-prevailing political sentiments.[27] On any fair reading, however, the striking characteristic of *Federalist* 40 is candor, not equivocation. The delegates, Madison writes, must have deliberated in the anticipation that their plan would be submitted to the people themselves and that popular approbation would "blot out all antecedent errors and irregularities."[28] Madison refrains, however, from staking everything on popular approbation. He knows and confronts the defects of that argument.

One obvious difficulty is that ratification by nine states, rather than all, would suffice to carry the Constitution into effect. In that one instance, Madison volunteers, the Convention did exceed its authority and, in particular, the stricture of Article XIII of the Confederation, which permitted amendment only by unanimous consent.[29] Putting aside questions of strict legality, the departure from unanimity raises the difficult question of how free the tenth state would really be in saying "yes" or "no" to the Constitution. Madison's answer, translated into modern parlance, is that the constitutional choice will pose a game-theoretic problem one way or the other. Whereas any rule short of unanimity (or entirely synchronized voting, a technological impossibility at the time) would produce the "tenth state" problem, a unanimity rule would hold the collective gains hostage to the demands of a single small state (Rogue Island, which had failed to send delegates to the Convention). Even the opponents of the Constitution, Madison writes, failed to press the point because they recognized "the absurdity of subjecting the fate of twelve states to the perverseness or corruption of a thirteenth."[30]

A second problem is that the Convention, by virtue of having met and submitted a plan, has restricted and biased the constitutional choice set. On second thought, though, that is a good thing; inchoate and intransitive preferences need some ordering. When great changes are called for, Madison explains, "it is impossible for the people spontaneously and universally to move in concert towards their object," and "it is therefore essential that such changes be instituted by some *informal and unauthorized propositions*, made by some patriotic and respectable citizen, or number of citizens."[31] Those respectable citizens assembled in the Convention, whose propositions are now before the people. The propositions, moreover, come in a bundle. Up or down, yes or no must be perceived as the *only* options, not as choices from a larger menu—lest the preferences cycle. For that reason, Publius emphasized that an imperfect Constitution is still a plan, as opposed to the Anti-Federalists' lack of a coherent alternative. For the same reason, Publius derided the seemingly attractive third option between chaos and the Constitution—a reform of the Articles—as illusory and ill-advised. And for the same reason, the Federalists refused to open the Convention's product to preapproval amendments.[32]

If all this sounds elitist and antidemocratic, as it did to many Anti-Federalists, note the constraint: at the end of the day, agenda control must produce an actual choice. By way of contrast, the respectable citizens of the European Union periodically assemble to confront voters with yet another four-hundred-page proposal for an "ever closer union." That is a program, not a choice—as is illustrated by the fact that the citizens of European nations get to vote on the politicians' initiatives either not at all, or else as often as it takes to make them say "yes." Choice requires a certain degree of formality and finality. The necessary restriction of the choice set implies the *ability* to say "yes or no" to a concise, understandable plan of action—a written Constitution.

Legitimacy. Constitutional choice, Madison insisted, must look to "the real welfare of the great body of the people." The criterion is utilitarian. But what drives the normative analysis is the distinction between ex ante and in-period preferences, between "reflection and choice" and "accident and force." To make reasoned choice possible, its subjects had to be persuaded that they were in fact one people. Their object would necessarily be imperfect. The agenda had to be structured and controlled. And the Founders' real-world aspiration was not unanimity. It was 50 percent plus one votes in a sufficient number of state conventions, which would take a hard-fought, organized political campaign. Some of the more lurid accounts of that campaign—allegations of Federalist bribes to Massachusetts convention delegates, the (Federalist) postal service's failure to forward Anti-Federalist pamphlets—are probably Anti-Federalist urban legends. But the Federalists certainly manhandled the delegates to the first large-state ratifying convention (Pennsylvania's), and they made sure that the people in the states would vote in the "right" order, hastening the conventions in Federalist states and delaying them in states where approval was uncertain.[33]

One can argue that all this and more—the limited franchise, the Founders' suspicions of the democratic mob, the secrecy of the Philadelphia Convention—obviates the notion of a normatively compelling constitutional choice. One common version of this argument marches modern ideals of democracy and equality into battle and, not surprisingly, finds the Founders defenseless. But that argument, as well as the apologetic response that the Founders did the best they could under the circumstances, misses the Founders' problem. Although they knew Locke well enough to see the appeal of constitutional choice and design, they also knew Hume well enough to understand the deeply problematic nature of that project. One ancient lawgiver, Solon, gave his countrymen not "the government best suited to their happiness, but most tolerable to their prejudices." Another, Lycurgus, mixed "a portion of violence with the authority of superstition," and he succeeded only by renouncing first his country and then his life. Those lessons, Madison writes, teach us "to admire the improvement made by America" in designing constitutions, but they also "admonish us of the hazards and difficulties incident to such experiments, and the great imprudence of unnecessarily multiplying them."[34] The Constitution has to suit the people's happiness, not their prejudices; their ex ante and long-term preferences, not their opportunistic demands. Consent, not violence and superstition, must be the means of adopting it. But those irreducible conditions of legitimate constitutionalism are very dicey. The central problem is to show that choice is possible at all. As James Wilson reminded the Pennsylvania convention, it had not been done in six thousand years.[35]

Serious critics of the Founders' project have understood the force and centrality of the framers' insistence on the possibility of reflection and choice. Charles A. Beard's "economic" interpretation is a prominent, influential illustration.[36] Every legal rule, Beard insisted, has consequences. Because the legal authors can look ahead, the consequences must be the *intended* purpose of the law (its *Zweck*, in the terminology of the German legal theorists on whom Beard relied). The United States Constitution is a thoroughly economic document, and its central guarantees of free internal trade, hard money, and the sanctity of contract benefit identifiable constituencies—merchants, investors, creditors, manufacturers. Those interests, Beard claimed, dominated the Philadelphia Convention and the state conventions, and that explains the substance of the Constitution and its adoption. Beard's theory has been widely criticized on empirical grounds.[37] Its central weakness, however, is that it assumes too much foresight on the part of economic actors. Robert Morris was a rich financier in 1787, only to end up in debtor's prison when his speculative schemes collapsed. Should he have opposed the Constitution? Small landholders, whom Beard identifies as the losers in the constitutional scheme, could expect to suffer under a policy of federal import tariffs, which the Constitution facilitates and which the *Federalist* candidly advocates. On the other hand, unity and a federal monopoly over the common defense, financed through those same tariffs, would free the states from having to maintain large armies and free their citizens from crushing tax burdens.[38] Whose side should the yeoman have taken? Opportunism, prejudice, and class interests are bound to play a role in any constitutional moment. But there remains an ineradicable difference between guaranteeing the enforcement of contracts and handing out an ethanol subsidy, between a constitution and a jumble of entitlements. A constitution that deserves its name will be too open-ended and general, and the writers' and ratifiers' time horizon will be too long, to render pure opportunism rational.[39]

Leviathan and Factions

Consociational constitutions, I noted earlier, attempt to pacify divided societies through an elite pact that promises to stabilize a baseline distribution of entitlements. They attempt to deal with the risk of government exploitation, not by limiting government's reach, but by ensuring fair representation of all socially relevant groups in all institutions. Such instruments typically have a very social-democratic feel. They may regulate the distribution of offices, oil revenues, attendance at international conferences, and foreign aid. In principle, all valued assets and entitlements must flow through the system if it is to remain stable. Competitive constitutions cut in the opposite direction. They look to individual choice and rules, not to coalitions or end-state distributions. What then should the rules look like?

Foremost, individuals will want to protect themselves against force and aggression by outsiders or members of the society. The only effective way to accomplish that objective is to monopolize the use of force. "Safety first" is the inescapable Hobbesian part of the constitutional calculus. If individuals understand basic economics, they will also understand that some desirable goods—in addition to safety—cannot be produced efficiently by private effort and agreement. Some forced exchanges will make everyone better off, and preconstitutional individuals will permit the government to bring those transactions about. However, that grant of authority must be subject to two limiting conditions: acceptable decision costs and adequate safeguards against the risk that government will abuse its powers. In short, the constitutional task is to craft rules that will permit Leviathan to force Pareto-efficient exchanges while limiting, so far as possible, forced exchanges beyond that point.[40]

The continuities between these intuitions and the Madisonian universe are close. The government's protective function—"safety"—is where the *Federalist* starts in making the case for the Union. The danger of foreign attack then prompts a boader inquiry into *"the utility of the UNION to your political prosperity."*[41] Foreign aggression is closely connected to trade wars—by the *Federalist*'s account, often a prelude to or occasion for outright war. From those dangers, the *Federalist* moves easily to the menace of domestic insurrection. Then, the argument appears to take a curious turn. The *Federalist* traces insurrection to poorly ordered domestic politics, moves on to the famous theory of faction in *Federalist* 10, and then returns to international trade disputes.

What is the interest group jazz in *Federalist* 10 doing in the midst of a discussion of warfare and aggression? The answer, I believe, is that "safety" had a more copious meaning to the Founders than it carries for us. Time and again, the *Federalist* describes factional politics as "violence" and "aggression." We tend to take a more benign view and to separate aggression neatly from interest group politics, both because of changed sensibilities and because we have the luxury of a Constitution that has domesticated factional strife. The constitutional choice perspective, in contrast, well-nigh compels one to think of the necessity for government, the potential for abuse, and the necessity of constitutional constraints as a single package. In Madison's famous formulation, semicolons barely slow the train of thought:

In framing a government which is to be administered by men over men, the great difficulty lies in this: you must first enable the government to control the governed; and in the next place oblige it to control itself. A dependence on the people is, no doubt, the primary control on the government; but experience has taught mankind the necessity of auxiliary precautions.[42]

"Dependence on the people"—what we call democracy and what Madison called republican government—is the safest form of government and thus the ex ante choice of the risk-averse. We cannot have a monarch or a House of Lords in America; every branch of government must derive its powers, ultimately, from the people. In this sense, Madison was a lifelong, die-hard republican, to the point of regarding the representation of states rather than people in the Senate as offensive to first principles (though acceptable on pragmatic grounds).[43] But a dependence on the people is not only not enough. In a pure, unmodified form, it is dangerous because the in-period demos is bound to be a self-interested rapacious majority. Hence, the need to "oblige government to control itself" by means of additional, "auxiliary" precautions.

What are those precautions? At one point, Madison calls the principle of representation an auxiliary device. Its beauty is to allow for "the total exclusion of the people, in their collective capacity" from governmental processes and decisions.[44] That exclusion has several advantages. First, representation creates distance between the people and their agents, which may help to dampen populist passions and parochial interests. Second, the people's will can be represented in multiple rival and competing institutions. When properly constructed, those arrangements help to curb the government monopoly risk—specifically, the danger of an "elective despotism" under legislative auspices. Third, the representatives' terms in office and their mode of election can be arranged so as to reconcile the need for energy and stability in government with the "genius" of republican government. For the most part, however, the *Federalist* treats representation as a nonnegotiable baseline of republican government, not as a precaution against its excesses. The true "auxiliary precautions" are the theory of the "extended republic" and the institutional structure of the federal government, especially the separation of powers.

Madison famously expounds his theory of the extended republic in *Federalist* 10 and briefly returns to it in *Federalist* 51. Within the states, *Federalist* 10 argues, citizens will be at the mercy of "factions"—that is, "a number of citizens, whether amounting to a majority or minority of the whole, who are united and actuated by some common impulse of passion, or of interest, adverse to the rights of other citizens, or to the permanent and aggregate interests of the community." Small republics will tend to feature a small number of factions, over a narrow range, which will easily "concert and carry into effect schemes of oppression."[45] An extended sphere mitigates the danger in three ways. First, the larger size of electoral districts will tend to produce better, more public-spirited legislators and create much-needed slack—though hopefully not too much slack—between the people and their agents. Second, a bigger playpen increases the range and number of interests, thus making majorities less likely. Third, the greater range of interests will make factional self-dealing more difficult. High transaction costs ruin a good day for legislators and their clientele, while correspondingly protecting "the rights of other citizens" and "the permanent and aggregate interests of the community." Madison calls the third, transaction cost argument "the most palpable advantage" of an extended republic, probably because it is the least contingent on circumstances.[46]

Federalist 10 is devoted almost exclusively to the protection of "the rights of other citizens," with little attention to the production of public goods. *Federalist* 51 contains a more upbeat suggestion and a more explicit recognition that the protection of rights is a necessary but not a sufficient condition of good government. In the extended republic, Madison avers, "a coalition of a majority of the whole society could seldom take place upon any other principles, than those of justice and the general good."[47] The extended republic is expected to do two things, then: to reduce the aggregate supply of legislation and to bias it toward Pareto-superior outcomes.

Madison's ingenious theory has not held up well in every regard. The framers' hopes in the beneficial sorting effects of the extended republic were soon disappointed. Madison may have overestimated the collective rationality of legislative assemblies, and his theory fails to explicitly account for now-familiar pathologies. Whereas Madison's great fear was *majority* faction, we worry about the ability of small, cohesive interests to exploit a large, underinformed and underincentivized majority.[48] Madison's comforting assurance that majority coalitions would usually be formed on principles of "justice and the general good" fails to take account of logrolling, to the point where entire enactments consist of pure rents. Even so, Madison's formulation of the constitutional problem and his basic solution continue to resonate. Factionalism is the principal pathology of democratic politics and the risk against which a constitution must guard. The basic strategy to that end is not to control the people, because a constitution can do only little in that regard. Rather, it is to discipline the people's *agents* under a constitution that makes politics possible and, at the same time, constrains it. One might dispute whether that project has succeeded. But there is no doubt that it *is* the Madisionian project.[49]

Constitutional Stability

Individuals who choose a constitution wish to escape "the uncertainty of their condition." In other words, they want political stability. But stability is a virtue only up to a point. First, stability must not become sclerosis. Well-ordered societies need ways to adapt to changing circumstances and to escape a stable but bad equilibrium. The practical need for collective in-period decisions raises the question of what cost-effective and normatively attractive constitutional decision rules might look like. Second, the Hobbesian solution—stability at the price of unchecked monopoly— is incompatible with republican principles. So the problem is to render *democratic* societies stable yet adaptable—to entrench ex ante preferences in some institutional framework and then to insulate that framework against the social instabilities and opportunistic demands that it is supposed to contain. Constitutional rules and institutions must do double duty. They have to ensure an acceptable output, and they have to stabilize constitutional arrangements over the long term. For many long papers, Publius strives to show that the constitutional arrangements will produce the requisite stability without, at the same time, depriving government of the requisite "energy" or offending republican principles, rightly understood. Time and again, the *Federalist* inveighs against mere "parchment barriers" and insists on what contemporary theorists call "self-enforcing" rules and institutions: if one can connect "the interests of the man" with "the constitutional rights of the place," rival institutions can be made to check one another. The occupants of the various branches of government must be given "the necessary constitutional means, and personal motives, to resist encroachment of the others . . . .Ambition must be made to counteract ambition."[50]

I have already emphasized the sharp differences between this competitive constitutional model and a consociational bargain that looks for stability to elite coalitions, rather than durable institutional rules. But the constitutional model also stands in stark contrast to consociationalism's more familiar cousin, interest group pluralism. Like consociationalists, pluralists deny that institutions per se can produce political stability; unlike consociationalists, they view political stability not as a product of elite cartels but of fluctuating interest group alignments.[51] To the pluralist mind, the genius of *Federalist* 10 is to have figured that out: So long as there are no *permanent* majorities or minorities, and so long as "cross-cutting cleavages" generate different majority constellations on different issues, the system will remain stable. Today's winners have to figure that they might be tomorrow's losers, and that calculation will temper the urge to oppress and exploit. If some interests manage to entrench themselves, the appropriate response is to make government more democratic, more open to participation by a broader range of interests. Constitutional rules per se yield no stability; they "are mainly significant because they help to determine what particular groups are to be given advantages or handicaps in the political struggle."[52]

Pluralist theory had a profound impact on the post–New Deal Supreme Court's jurisprudence, which accorded a virtually irrebuttable presumption of regularity to interest group bargains but afforded special judicial protection to "discrete and insular minorities."[53] All is in good order with the Constitution, the theory goes, provided we open it to the constituencies the Founders ignored. In some ways, pluralism became untenable some decades ago, when public choice theorists showed that competition among rent-seeking factions usually produces pathologies rather than public benefits and political stability. Pluralism's basic presuppositions, however, have since been embraced by progressive constitutionalists who argue that the Court should take its cues from the democratic demands of successful social "movements." For these scholars, as for the pluralists, accommodation to group demands is the central constitutional objective.[54]

That cheerful view, though, presupposes an antecedent political agreement on what constitutes a "fair" demand or a "democratic" political process. Without that baseline, democratic politics will disintegrate into strife, instability, and demagogy.[55] And that fear, not pluralism (let alone movement politics), tracks the framers' intuitions. Far from putting confidence in factional politics, the *Federalist* identified it as a principal source of "that inconstancy and mutability in the laws, which form the greatest blemish in the character and genius of our governments."[56] "Our governments" here means state governments whose escapades, occasioned by the dominance of faction and the lack of effective institutional constraints thereon, furnished powerful evidence of "the mischievous effects of a mutable government."[57] Externally, Publius writes, an unstable government "forfeits the respect and confidence of other nations." But the "internal effects of a mutable policy are still more calamitous. It poisons the blessings of liberty itself." It induces people to lose respect for their government, and it stifles the productive energies of a commercial republic. "What prudent merchant will hazard his fortunes in any new branch of commerce, when he knows not but that his plans may be rendered unlawful before they can be executed?" None. But there is worse yet:

> Another effect of public instability, is the unreasonable advantage it gives to the sagacious, the enterprising, and the monied few, over the industrious and uninformed mass of the people. Every new regulation concerning commerce or revenue, or in any manner affecting the value of the different species of property, presents a new harvest to those who watch the change, and can trace its consequences; a harvest, reared not by themselves, but by the toils and cares of the great body of their fellow citizens.[58]

Instability rewards habitual rent seekers and invites folks who, under a sensible government, would perforce prove their mettle in the marketplace to instead play on K Street. That sort of pluralist festival is no better than a Hobbesian state of nature played out by other means: "In a society, under the forms of which the stronger faction can readily unite and oppress the weaker, anarchy may as truly be said to reign, as in a state of nature."[59] The quest for stability, then, translates into "auxiliary precautions" that break the violence of faction by institutional means—representation, the separation of powers, bicameralism, long terms in office for senators, the presidential veto, and other devices, all of them operating in an extended republic; all of them calculated to combine the requisite stability with the requisite degree of energy in government and with "inviolable attention due to liberty, and to the republican form."[60]

That endeavor raises the question of how one can insulate institutions from the factional instabilities that they are meant to contain. Publius rejects two strategies: abstract constitutional guarantees, which are bound to be ineffective "parchment barriers" and which would look better in a code of ethics than in a constitution; and the Jeffersonian proposal of direct appeals to the people, which are likely to inflame public passions and to undermine constitutional stability. Neither of those mechanisms, it turns out, is entirely dispensable. The Supreme Court must enforce the written guarantees of a "limited Constitution," and the road for constitutional amendments must be kept open (though not so much to ensure constitutional stability but to correct errors in a praiseworthy but inevitably imperfect structure). But the primary means of ensuring institutional stability is a "policy of supplying, by opposite and rival interests, the defect of better motives."

Almost by definition, the auxiliary precautions that institutionalize this principle are imperfect. One constant challenge, plainly anticipated by Madison, is populist passion. In a constitutional moment, the reason of the public will conclude that stability in government is an essential virtue and that institutional precautions to that end are wholly consistent with republican principles, "rightly understood." In-period, however, that understanding will unravel. While an unsteady, feckless government will always be "odious" to the people, the institutions that are necessary to cure those defects perennially seem to offend "the genius of republican liberty."[61] And sure enough, from the Progressives to the New Dealers to the pluralists to today's apostles of "deliberative democracy," the "undemocratic" features of the Constitution have been the principal target in the campaign for a more up-to-date politics and Constitution.[62]

A second challenge, quite probably underestimated by Madison, is the inordinate difficulty of endowing political institutions with *permanent* rivalrous motivations.[63] What happens when supposedly rivalrous institutions figure out a strategy to maximize their joint surplus, to the citizens' detriment? ("Our Federalism," I suggested in the introduction, is a product of just such a joint defection from the constitutional norms.) Publius provides no direct, explicit answer to the problem. What the *Federalist* does provide, however, is a powerful analytical framework for thinking about institutional and constitutional problems, including unforeseen and unprovided-for events. Against the Madisonian backdrop, and *only* against that backdrop, can one distinguish constitutional development from defection, interpretation from inversion. And no constitutional subject is more in need of that perspective than our federalism.

CHAPTER TWO

Federalism

State attachments, and State importance have been the bane of this Country. We cannot annihilate [the States]; but we may perhaps take out the teeth of the serpents. He wished our ideas to be enlarged to the true interests of man, instead of being circumscribed within the narrow compass of a particular Spot. And after all how little can be the motive yielded by selfishness for such a policy. Who can say whether he himself, much less whether his children, will the next year be an inhabitant of this or that State.

Gouverneur Morris

Federalism?

"Reflection and choice," precautions against the violence of faction, self-enforcing rules as a means to ensure political stability: to what extent do those tightly interwoven premises of competitive constitutionalism carry forward into federalism? Analytically, the answer is straightforward: let prospective citizens—*not states*—choose the arrangements. If they choose a federal arrangement, they will choose competitive federalism rules that promise to curb government surplus, and they will search for means of stabilizing that arrangement against both state and federal defection. The calculus of the United States Constitution, I will now show, conforms elegantly to this model.

Of course, the Constitution was not only calculus and choice but also compromise; and among the Convention's compromises, none ranks more prominent than federalism. The crucial question, however, is what *kind* of compromise—a bargain among interest groups or states, or rather an acceptable choice from a menu of constitutional options that can still be defended from the global, long-term vantage of future citizens of the United States. That distinction was well understood at the time, and it is actually reflected in the Constitution. Its atrocious slavery bargain, marked and marred by the three-fifth formula for representation and taxation, the ill-fated Fugitive Slave Clause, and the Jeffersonian single-generation deal to permit the continued importation of slaves until 1808 was just that—a consociational bargain among interests and states. Its viability was well understood to hang on the stability of the underlying economic forces (a point on which the Founders miscalculated) and, moreover, on an elite pact—effectively concluded at the Convention and desperately maintained by various means thereafter—that everyone shut up about it.[1] On the wrenching slavery issue, the Convention could not see its way clear to a genuinely constitutional solution. On federalism, in contrast, it could and it did. That, at any rate, was the *Federalist*'s contention. While maintaining a shame-faced silence about the slavery issue, Publius mounted an extended defense of the Constitution's federalism arrangements—occasionally on pragmatic, "best that can be done" grounds, but always from a constitutional perspective. Consistently and at times vehemently, Publius insisted on a federalism—the "compound republic"—that rests on the global ex ante calculus of prospective United States citizens, *to the complete exclusion of the states' preferences and perspective.*

From that vantage, the question arises whether one should have states at all and to what end. That question becomes more pressing and difficult yet if one assumes that the central government will be better behaved than state government. Madison, of course, articulated just that expectation—not as a vague speculation, but as a central argument for the union and in the form of the worked-out theory of *Federalist* 10. On that theory, it becomes exceedingly difficult to think of an argument for federalism. It is much more natural to think that the states "as states" should be abolished; and sure enough, Madison (as well as Hamilton) took precisely that position early on. However, the "Father of the Constitution" *lost* the debate on that issue at the Convention. States "as states" survived in the Constitution, and the great little man returned to Virginia in despair over the Convention's abject failure to establish adequate remedies for the states' political vices.

How is it, then, that a few short weeks later, Madison, writing as Publius, managed a sophisticated and, over long stretches, confident defense of the Convention's handiwork, including its federalism? The crucial consideration, it seems to me, is that the proposed Constitution, while retaining the states, was still compatible with the constitutional premise that the project had to rest on the real welfare of the people, as opposed to the interests of states. Publius insists on that premise throughout, and emphatically.

Citizens and States

In mid-June 1787, barely a few weeks into the Convention, James Madison and his allies grew increasingly dismayed. Edmund Randolph, who was supposed to shepherd Madison's Virginia Plan through the Convention, became flustered in the face of the smaller states' objections, confused the argument Madison had scripted for him, and promptly reverted to his usual form—trimming. Small-state delegates fretted over the Convention's authority to undertake a wholesale revision of the Articles and over the states' fate under a "consolidated" government. On June 18, Alexander Hamilton took the floor to stem the bleeding. In the course of what may have been the most powerful—and was almost certainly the most counterproductive—speech of his life, Hamilton insisted that states were, or should be reduced to, mere "corporations." Although that speech later gained notoriety chiefly for Hamilton's encomia to the British system, his remarks on state powers appear to have caused immediate consternation. The very next morning, Hamilton backpedaled, in a manner of speaking: "By an abolition of the States, he meant that no boundary could be drawn between the National & State Legislatures; that the former must therefore have indefinite authority. . . . *As States,* he thought they ought to be abolished."[2]

Predictably, Hamilton's apology failed to reassure states' rights defenders. Thus Mr. Madison rose—and dug in his heels on the line that Hamilton had drawn. The defenders of state prerogatives, he argued, had it all wrong. States as such had no greater claim to autonomy, sovereignty, or political representation than did townships or counties. By that same token, though, states had nothing to fear from a national government. That government (under the Virginia Plan, a far more nationalist concoction than the plan that would eventually emerge from the Convention) would no sooner abolish the states than Connecticut would abolish its townships. And even if that event should come to pass, Madison continued, the general government should soon find itself compelled to reinstate the states.[3]

The argument is hard to credit in substance and difficult to understand in terms of strategy. The former colonies had joined the Articles of Confederation as states, and their delegates voted as states at the Convention. Had the states not already existed, there is no way the Founders would have created anything remotely resembling them. But they did exist, with their own boundaries, institutions, and political traditions. As for strategy, there might have been ways to assuage New Jersey's nervous delegates, but the assurance that their government would henceforth enjoy all the dignity of the Hoboken City Council was surely not among them. So what was Madison *thinking?* The most straightforward explanation is that he believed the "states as municipalities" argument. He deemed it sufficiently important to repeat it in *Federalist* 14 and yet again in the

Virginia Convention, where he confronted head-on, in a debate where the votes counted, the state officials who would be most alarmed at the very real threat to their authority.[4] More is at work, then, than a rhetorical posture or a reflex against the "wicked states" and their irresponsible conduct.[5] Rather, Madison's position is intimately connected with the insistence on the possibility of constitutional choice. The states are not merely extraneous to that project; they are its principal obstacle.

Politicians and the Blood of Thousands. The opening salvo against the states as constitutional actors comes in *Federalist* 1. Apprehending that reflection and choice will be impeded by "extraneous" considerations and interests, Hamilton promptly identifies the principal source of those distractions. Among "the most formidable . . . obstacles," he writes, is

> the obvious interest of a certain class of men in every state to resist all changes which may hazard a diminution of the power, emolument and consequence of the offices they hold under the state establishments . . . and the perverted ambition of another class of men, who will either hope to aggrandize themselves by the confusions of their country, or will flatter themselves with fairer prospects of elevation from the subdivision of the empire into several partial confederacies, than from its union under one government.[6]

Much like public choice theorists reject the notion of a reified "state" and instead think of that construct as a set of self-interested actors, Hamilton reduces protestations on behalf of the states to raw personal self-interest. His maneuver contains a brilliant insight. One can envision a constitutional calculus that makes room for states (or other collective entities)— for example, by stipulating that the states behave as benevolent despots who faithfully represent their subjects' preferences.[7] However, Hamilton's observation that the states' advocates are *officeholders* demolishes any such assumption. Present officeholders will want to maximize the emolument and consequence of their offices *over their own lifetimes.* Men of "perverted ambition" have the same constricted time horizon. Neither can internalize the long-term gains that are the objects of the constitutional project.[8] Their short-term perspective is antithetical to a constitutional choice.

The theme reappears in the pivotal *Federalist* 45. Before transitioning from one demonstration ("the necessity of a government at least equally energetic with the one proposed") to another ("the conformity of the proposed constitution to the true principles of republican government"), Madison takes a final stab at repudiating the Anti-Federalists' most deep-seated objections to the constitutional project.[9] "The adversaries to the plan of the Convention," he begins, "have exhausted themselves in a secondary inquiry into the possible consequences of the proposed degree of power [in the federal government] to the governments of the particular states." The dismissive "secondary" begs the crucial question of whether the states' perspective *should* count for constitutional purposes: if it should, it is neither absurd nor even "secondary" to worry about the likely consequences of the constitutional scheme for states, in their political capacity. Madison inveighs against this argument by disputing its premise, and he does so in an uncharacteristically impassioned tone:[10]

> [If] the union be essential to the happiness of the people of America, is it not preposterous, to urge as an objection to a government, without which the objects of the union cannot be attained, that such a government may derogate from the importance of the governments of the individual states? Was then the American revolution effected, was the American confederacy formed, was the precious blood of thousands spilt, and the hard earned substance of millions lavished, not that the people of America should enjoy peace, liberty, and safety; but that the governments of the individual states, that particular municipal establishments, might enjoy a certain extent of power, and be arrayed with certain dignities and attributes of sovereignty?[11]

Madison goes so far as to accuse Patrick Henry and his cohorts of closet royalism:

> We have heard of the impious doctrine in the old world, that the people were made for kings, not kings for the people. Is the same doctrine to be revived in the new, in another shape, that the solid happiness of the people is to be sacrificed to the views of political institutions of a different form?[12]

Madison's answer was no, or more precisely, not yet. Recall his splendid formulation: "It is too early for politicians to presume on our forgetting that the public good, the real welfare of the great body of the people, is the supreme object to be pursued." That object is not to be sacrificed to the views of "political institutions." In the global constitutional calculus, states are purely instrumental. Their interests "as states"—as political institutions or as affective communities—count for nothing; the only question is what (if anything) they can contribute to "the real welfare of the great body of the people." To the extent that the state sovereignty can be "reconciled to the happiness of the people," the states may keep it. To the extent that it cannot, they must give it up.

The Compound Republic and its Enemies. We shall have to see how far Madison's states-as-mere-instruments perspective carries forward into the Constitution. Its import, though, emerges more clearly in comparison and contrast with alternative federalism ideas and ideals. First among them is the notion against which Madison inveighed so passionately—the notion of constitutionalism and of the United States Constitution as a state pact or compact, rather than the constitutive act of a single sovereign. The Constitution is not ipso facto inconsistent with any notion of state sovereignty and autonomy: if it were, it would cease to be a federal constitution. It is, however, inconsistent with any federalism that mobilizes the interests of the "states as states" against, or apart from, the citizens' constitutional precommitments, as citizens of the *United* States.

A second rival, likewise excluded by Madison's perspective, is the notion of federalism as a means of managing conflicting identities or political loyalties. Many modern federalisms serve that purpose (more or less well), and some theorists even insist that true federalism must implicate state attachments sufficiently strong to elicit "the willingness to die and the willingness to kill."[13] It is an atrocious mistake, however, to project that intellectual matrix backward onto the compound republic. We have of course experienced an existential armed conflict—but not, except in the minds of antebellum romanticists, over "identity." Conversely, we have had our share of identity politics, but not along state lines. American federalism is about interests, not identity; about heterogeneous preferences, not a Hegelian struggle for recognition.[14]

Finally, Madison's perspective blocks the idea of federalism as a consociational, covenantal, or cooperative bargain. For consociationalists, federalism is helpful only so long as state boundaries coincide with tribal, religious, or other divisions.[15] Moreover, those theorists favor an "asymmetric" federalism; each jurisdiction may have its own special relation with the central government, depending on what it takes to rope the respective jurisdiction into the common pool and to prevent defections.[16] And, for consociational theorists, the principal mode of federal politics is negotiation, accommodation, and cooperation. The United States Constitution embodies just the opposite principles. The American states are either accidents of British colonial practice or "rectangles in the prairie"; they *must not be* identifiable along religious, ethnic, or linguistic lines. American federalism is ruthlessly symmetric; the original states, and all states admitted subsequently, entered the union on an equal footing.[17] And although states and national institutions may negotiate and cut bargains, they must do so under a Constitution that—unlike virtually any other federal constitution—provides no baseline for the enterprise.

Over the course of history, it has proven very difficult to sustain the Madisonian perspective. It was not a consensus view among "the Founders" but one side of a fierce and difficult argument, and there is enough "states' rights" stuff in our Founding history and (much more arguably) in the Constitution to have infused constitutional construction and under-standing with permanent ambiguities and tensions. It is all the more important, however, to recover the logic and implications of the Madiso-nian perspective.

States! What Are They Good For?

Follow James Madison on the states-as-mere-instruments point: What *are* states good for? Why should prospective citizens retain the states as part of a long-term calculus? Madison's initial answer—"they shouldn't"—was doomed from the start and, after the Convention, water under the bridge. Thus, the question shifts. How and to what extent can the states' sovereignty and dignity be "reconciled to the happiness of the people"?

"Reconciled to" is a telling choice of words. Reconciled *to*, not *with*. There is no happy compromise between the states' interests and the peo-ple's happiness. One is the baseline; the other must give. And *reconciled*, not "promotes" or "conduces to." State sovereignty, it appears, does no good at all. States as states, Publius seems to say, are a hindrance to estab-lishing and maintaining constitutional government; their mere existence is an obstacle and perhaps a nightmare. That view of the matter is neither self-evident nor obviously correct, either as a general proposition or in historical context.[18] Plainly, though, Publius feared that the interests of state politicians and their clamor of "liberty" would thwart the chance of establishing and maintaining a union. The *Federalist* did not so much talk about the states as rant against those "wretched nurseries of unceas-ing discord," in Hamilton's colorful phrase.[19] Small wonder, then, that there is no worked-out federalism theory in the *Federalist* at all. Publius had a serious theory of the general government, which aims to demon-strate that that government must be "at least equally energetic to the one proposed." He had a serious theory of politics—the theory propounded in *Federalist* 10, which makes it difficult to see why states should continue to exist. Publius even had a theory of why institutions that later came to be identified as bastions of constitutional federalism (prominently, the Sen-ate) might be useful. Those defenses, however, rest on grounds that have nothing to do with "states as states" and in fact impugn the legitimacy of that perspective.[20]

The *Federalist* proffers only two arguments for the states: a decision cost or "sorting" argument and the famous "double security" argument in *Federalist* 51. Upon inspection, neither argument applies to what we now think of as federalism—that is, the regular operation of federal and state politics, partially autonomous and side by side. Sorting is an argument not for state autonomy but for decentralization. The double security applies only in the extreme case of armed rebellion. Neither argument explains what partially autonomous states might be good for in ordinary politics.

Sorting. Federalist 14 responds to the Anti-Federalists' objection that the union is too large for republican government. The natural limit of a republic, Madison argues, "is that distance from the centre, which will barely allow the representatives of the people to meet as often as may be necessary for the administration of public affairs."[21] A large size is good, for reasons rehearsed in *Federalist* 10, but the practicably attainable size is inversely proportional to the amount of stuff that has to be administered. Any attempt to run a vast country from a single location will produce diseconomies of scale and issue congestion—in short, excessive decision costs—at the center. It would be best, therefore, if the center were freed from superfluous tasks. The center will recognize that necessity and let the states operate in their proper sphere. The large size of federal electoral districts will facilitate the election of men with "the most diffusive and established characters," "fit to comprehend and pursue great and national objects."[22] War and national commerce, Publius argued, would provide a suitable and, moreover, amply rewarding occupation for these fine men.

Quite obviously, this is not an argument for autonomous states but rather for mere decentralization. Madison and Hamilton plainly understood the difference; it is what they had in mind in championing the abolition of the states "as states," while retaining them in an administrative, "subordinately useful" role.[23] What stabilizes the division of labor, moreover, is the expectation that the states' affairs—the objects that "concern the lives, liberties, and properties of the people; and the internal order, improvement, and prosperity of the state," as Madison grandiosely put it—are in fact too stupid, perhaps not for words but surely for high-minded federal legislators.[24] On Madison's account, Congress will refrain from meddling not because it lacks the time but because its members will find the pursuit unworthy.

The argument failed to persuade Madison's contemporaries; predictably, state politicians reacted with annoyance at the suggestion that they could be safely entrusted with regulating the height of fences but little else.[25] More than two centuries later, the filtration argument looks entirely forgettable—not so much on account of its aristocratic flavor, but because the mechanism has so obviously failed. In 1789, after a single election cycle, Madison already grumbled that somehow, the wrong people were getting themselves elected to Congress.[26] A century later, when dramatically changed economic, political, and technological conditions increased the need to sort and stabilize national and state functions, the enumerated powers doctrine had to serve as a functional substitute for inoperative institutional dynamics. Later chapters will discuss the extent to which the doctrine can bear that weight. Suffice it here to say that Madison identified a potent argument for decentralization, not federalism, and that he failed to find an effective institutional mechanism to stabilize the arrangement.

Security. *Federalist* 51 returns to the argument concerning factions and the extended republic in *Federalist* 10. Madison now strikes a more state-friendly tone and at last identifies a positive role for the states:

> In the compound republic of America, the power surrendered by the people, is first divided between two distinct governments [state and national], and then the portion allotted to each subdivided among distinct and separate departments. Hence a double security arises to the rights of the people. The different governments will control each other; at the same time that each will be controled [*sic*] by itself.[27]

In the Publius-as-antinationalist pantheon, this "double security" passage is rivaled only by Madison's assurance (in *Federalist* 45) that federal powers are "few and defined." It has a long tradition in American political thought, and it resonates to this day in politics as well as constitutional law. "Just as the separation and independence of the coordinate branches of the Federal Government serve to prevent the accumulation of excessive power in any one branch," the Supreme Court has confidently intoned, "a healthy balance of power between the States and the Federal Government will reduce the risk of tyranny and abuse from either front."[28] However, to the extent that this collection of weasel words ("excessive," "healthy," "balance") means anything at all, it is false to the point of absurdity.[29] In the nineteenth century, states resisted federal power in the defense of slavery, which was not a net gain in terms of reducing tyranny and abuse. Jim Crow legislation is equally difficult to paint as liberty enhancing. Throughout American history, states have erected and defended protectionist barriers to commerce, with highly ambiguous results for liberty. And Madison's assertion that the levels of government will invariably "control" each other seems manifestly in error; very often, they cooperate for mutual benefit and aggrandizement.[30]

Wholly apart from its glaring empirical deficiencies, moreover, the cheerful "federalism protects liberty" interpretation can be sustained only at the price of rendering both Madison and the Constitution incoherent. The "double security" passage gently describes state governments as self-controlled and as featuring separation of powers arrangements comparable to the federal arrangement proposed by the Convention. The plain import of the entire rest of the *Federalist,* in contrast, is that the states' governments were completely *out* of control. High on the list of defects was the lack of any genuine separation of powers. In most states, rapacious legislatures ran roughshod over weak executives and routinely "fixed" inconvenient judicial decisions by legislative fiat. The *Federalist's* confidence in state institutions was practically nil. In the deliberations over the federal separation of powers arrangements, the states' practices served as a foil, not as a blueprint.

The dissonance suggests a fundamental problem. Even if one could rely on states to resist federal usurpations, there is no reason to believe that their institutional incentives will automatically, or even for the most part, translate into security "to the rights of the people." Yes, Virginia may provide a platform to oppose the Alien and Sedition Acts. Would it be impolitic to note, though, that Virginia (as well as most other states) actually had stricter seditious libel laws than the odious federal statute, or to recall Samuel Johnson's famous observation that "we hear the loudest yelps for liberty among the drivers of negroes"? Sedition and slavery point to the systematic problem: Madison expected that state governments would continue to serve as playpens for factions. (His idea that large federal districts will tend to produce wise, public-minded legislators plainly implies that state governments would continue to be run, as they had been, by hacks and demagogues.) It follows that state resistance to federal assertions of power will typically materialize in defense of factional schemes and precisely *not* in defense of the rights of the people.[31]

The constitutional structure reflects this skeptical expectation rather than the conventional interpretation of the "double security" passage. *Federalist* 51 is principally devoted to developing the institutional basis of the separation of powers. That close proximity, as well as the language of the "double security" passage, makes it tempting to view federalism and the separation of powers as a single institutional principle—checks and balances—operating in different directions.[32] On closer reading, however, *Federalist* 51 points to a crucial distinction. A stable separation of powers, Madison argues, requires each department to have a "will of its own" and to be constituted independently, so far as possible. The security against a concentration of powers "consists in giving to those who administer each department, the necessary constitutional means, and personal motives, to resist encroachments of the others." (The means and motives must be *given* because not all departments naturally possess them to the requisite degree.)[33] The House of Representatives, the Senate, and the president are given the means, or what one might call institutional trumps. Most obviously, no law can be enacted without the consent of all three. They are also given the motives to resist one another, as they answer to different constituencies. The arrangement is not wholly symmetrical, for "it is not possible to give to each department an equal power of self-defence."[34] One can even ask whether the framers truly believed in coequal branches or merely cluttered the impetuous legislature with as many obstacles as they could think of. But the basic design of conflicting motives and opposing trumps is clear, and it is clearly intended to produce symmetry and stability.

Not so with federalism. Grant states the natural motives to resist federal aggression: what constitutional means are they given? In substance, none. The states can and will be ornery. The direct exercise of federal authority will often be perceived as obnoxious, and when that happens, the people may turn to their state governments and ask what they are going to do about it. One could say, although Publius never did, that the national government and the states "compete" for the affections of the people.[35] But at the end of the day, the federal government can do what it is empowered to do without the states and against their will. Outside the amendment process, the states' sole *constitutional* protection is the enumerated powers doctrine. That, though, is at most a shield, not a sword. Moreover, it is a doctrine inferred from the text, not a self-enforcing rule, and neither Publius nor his opponents put much stock in such parchment barriers. Predictably, the "double security" passage has gained political prominence and force in American politics, time and again, when states' rights advocates insisted on a constitutional trump or right of interposition—call it a "State-right, veto, nullification, or by any other name" as John C. Calhoun put it.[36] The Constitution, however, contains no such trump, for an obvious reason. Far from ensuring "liberty," the Founders believed, a states' rights trump would produce increased factionalism and political instability. Try as one might, one cannot translate the "double security" into a regularized, let alone a stabilizing, form of institutional competition and rivalry to protect the rights of the people.

What, then, does that passage mean? What Madison had in mind, David F. Epstein has argued, is not federal overreach but incontrovertible usurpation—not the niggling micromanagement of the local watershed, but outright (and probably armed) aggression. Epstein regards not only the conventional reading but also Calhounist interpretations as a misuse of the double security passage. Madison's image, he argues, was not secession by an individual state but resistance to federal aggression against all states—a domestic 1776. Either way, though, the states' trump is extraconstitutional. States protect the rights of the people because, in extremis, they are pretty good places to organize armed resistance to an oppressive government.[37]

Epstein's interpretation makes sense both of Madison and of a central dilemma of liberal government. The conventional reading implies a baseline shift; the same Madison who held out the extended republic as a cure for the ills of faction-ridden states is also supposed to have extolled those self-same states as guardians of liberty. No one, to my knowledge, has explained how that transition is supposed to work.[38] Epstein's interpretation, in contrast, turns on a shift in the mode and the stakes of politics—from ordinary politics to revolutionary, constitutional politics. When politics takes that turn, pathological factionalism gives way to more fundamental concerns and dynamics, and the states secure the rights of the people by providing an institutional platform for a Lockean right to rebellion.

On this reading, Madison appears in his best, brilliant light. No constitution can be entirely self-enforcing; and when the people's agents defect, the people must have some way of revisiting the original bargain. In this sense, all constitutional government implies a right to rebellion. Modern constitutions and theorists have gone to almost comical lengths in trying to accommodate that uncomfortable thought. The German Constitution, for example, guarantees a "right to resistance" in the event that someone should subvert the principles of liberal democracy (the "*freiheitlich demokratische Grundordnung*").[39] That well-meant provision only cements a dichotomy between the crank's futile gesture and the fever of a victorious mob, which will have little use for the niceties of constitutions past. On a different note, Bruce A. Ackerman has interpreted Madison's statement that constitutional politics must be legitimate but not necessarily *legal* as an invitation to amend the Constitution outside the formal Article V process, when (Ackerman says) "We the People" turn from obtuse consumerism to engaged citizenship—as in the New Deal, for instance.[40] At one level, Ackerman is right: Madison did envision the possibility of future informal but nonetheless legitimate constitutional moments. Epstein's reading, however, suggests that Madison entertained a decidedly non-Ackermanian vision of future constitutional moments. They would quite probably involve guns. And unlike Ackerman's plebiscitary, presidency-centered New Deal moment, Madison's constitutional politics would have its institutional focus and basis in the states. The identification of that basis for an otherwise homeless, aridly theoretical right to rebellion is a stroke of constitutional genius. It implies, however, that federalism's double security is an extraordinary backstop, not the normal operation of the political process.

Federalism, After All

On the authority of the *Federalist,* a federalism that is more than mere decentralization does no good except in the event of aggression and for purposes of rebellion. And yet, a potent case can be made for the Constitution's federalism. It does not appear in the *Federalist* or in any other, lesser writings of the Founding era, but it emerges with great clarity when one juxtaposes Madison's position at the Convention with the Convention's product. Madison had agitated for a comprehensive national veto over state laws—an institutional scheme that indeed would have reduced the states to mere "municipalities." The delegates rejected that proposal and instead adopted a genuinely federal solution, embodied in the Constitution's Supremacy Clause and its enumerated powers. This arrangement is very arguably the Constitution's central federalism "compromise," and it is every bit as consequential as the more famous compromise on representation. It can be defended on the grounds of "reflection and choice"; it is probably a *better,* more effective response to the problem of faction than Madison's own Convention program; and while not quite "self-enforcing," it is stabilized by reasonably reliable institutional mechanisms. In short, it rests on firm constitutional foundations—and it embodies what we have come to call "competitive federalism." The theory was not within the Founders' specific contemplation, but it helps us to understand their accomplishment.[41]

The Negative Defeated. The centerpiece of Madison's constitutional agenda and of the Virginia Plan that guided the Convention through its first weeks was a national "Negative" on state laws, to apply *"in all cases whatsoever."*[42] What Madison had in mind was not a federal veto over already-enacted state legislation—a kind of ex post federal preemption of state law. Nor did he hedge his proposal with an enumerated powers proviso that would restrict the exercise of the Negative to national matters. He insisted that no state law of any kind should be allowed to take effect without prior federal approval.[43] Accordingly, the Virginia Plan would have endowed Congress with a single, effectively limitless power "to legislate in all cases to which the separate States are incompetent, or in which the harmony of the United States may be interrupted by the exercise of individual legislation; [and] to negative all laws passed by the several States, contravening in the opinion of the National Legislature the articles of Union."[44] In this fashion, Madison sought to arm the national government with the means to arrest the states' proclivity "to invade the national jurisdiction, to violate treaties and the law of nations & to harass each other with rival and spiteful measures dictated by mistaken views of interest."[45] As the broad sweep of his proposal suggests, however, Madison also aimed to protect citizens from depredations by their own state governments. The Convention, he argued, should "seize the occasion of reforming the national government to treat the internal defects of the states."[46] The reason for that vast ambition—seemingly absurd, considering that the Convention had more than its work cut out in establishing a viable Union—was Madison's conviction that the states' outward aggression and their internal defects had a common source: factionalism. He proposed to tackle that problem at the source, rather than to curb its external manifestations.[47]

Due to Madison's persistence, the Convention was compelled to debate his proposal on three separate occasions. The delegates rejected the Negative on each of those occasions. Even Madison's usual allies denounced the proposal as an excessively nationalistic instrument that would "disgust all the States," thus dooming the constitutional venture.[48] Moreover, the delegates objected, the proposed Negative would sweep too broadly, rendering it both impracticable and unnecessary. It would require states to obtain congressional consent for urgent matters, when the national legislature might not be in session. At the same time, the Negative would compel Congress to concern itself on an ongoing basis with the states' internal affairs. Would Congress have to take action, George Mason asked, every time a state wants to build a bridge inside its territory?[49]

In the end, these arguments—excessive nationalism, exorbitant decision costs—carried the day. Instead of a general congressional legislative power, the Convention adopted the enumerated powers scheme that came to be embodied in Article I of the Constitution. And instead of the Negative, the Convention opted for federal supremacy (embodied in the Supremacy Clause of Article VI, § 2), asserted either through the courts, in the ordinary course of deciding cases and controversies, or through congressional legislation. The crucial difference between the Negative and the Supremacy Clause is the default principle. The Negative would have rendered state laws *inoperative*, pending affirmative congressional approval. The Supremacy Clause, in contrast, permits state laws to be enacted and to remain in effect unless and until a court or the Congress sets them aside. The Convention clearly understood these options as alternatives, and the adoption of the Supremacy Clause promptly followed the rejection of the Negative.[50]

Competitive Federalism. James Madison lost his campaign for a Negative. Even so, he deemed the Convention's product good enough to merit a spirited defense. And in truth, it may have been better than he realized—better, certainly, than his own Convention program.

To ease into the startling argument, note that the Convention actually *retained* a congressional Negative, or the even stronger medicine of an absolute prohibition, for certain classes of state laws. Even as the delegates rejected Madison's entreaties to use the Convention as an opportunity to reform internal state politics, they evidently agreed that certain species of state laws—the "rage" for paper money, debtor relief laws, import duties—posed alarming dangers to sister states and, hence, to the Union. For these classes of state laws, the Convention broke with mere supremacy and instead adopted either an absolute prohibition or the "disgusting" Negative. Most of the specific limitations came to be listed in Article I, § 10 of the Constitution. Among other things, the absolute prohibitions cover state treaties, the coinage of money, bills of attainder, ex post facto laws, and laws impairing the obligation of contract. The Negative applies to state duties on imports and exports, duties of tonnage, standing armies, and state compacts. State acts of these descriptions all require the affirmative consent of the Congress.

Enumerated powers, federal supremacy, specific (absolute or qualified) prohibitions against certain state laws: these central elements of the constitutional architecture are the bedrock of a profoundly *competitive* federalism. Chapter 3 examines the constitutional structure in detail; here, it is sufficient to note its fundamental congruence with competitive federalism principles.

Competitive federalism hangs on a distinction between "internal" state matters and external, "national" affairs. That distinction, in turn, has a vertical and a horizontal dimension. Vertically, it implies that the central government must provide "national" public goods, including the maintenance of a competitive federal (market) order, while leaving states in control over their internal affairs. Horizontally, it implies that "internal" state matters must actually be internal; as we now say, states must not exploit one another or inflict (excessive) "externalities" on one another. Moreover, internal state affairs must not be understood to encompass a right to exclude another state's goods or citizens, both because discriminatory trade barriers—"competitions of commerce" in a wholly undesired sense—are conducive to retaliatory trade warfare and because they wipe out the gains of collective national organization.[51]

These minimal conditions of competitive federalism mirror the constitutional architecture. The vertical dimension of the external-internal distinction is captured in the enumerated powers doctrine—prominently, in the notion that Congress may regulate commerce *among* states but not *within* a state. The horizontal dimension is captured in a slew of vehemently procompetitive provisions in Article I, § 10 and elsewhere—foremost, the Privileges and Immunities Clause (Article IV, § 2), providing that "the Citizens of each State shall be entitled to all Privileges and Immunities of Citizens in the several States." These horizontal federalism provisions are central to the system. Section 10 alone, James Wilson remarked with satisfaction, justified the entire constitutional enterprise. And the Privileges and Immunities Clause, Hamilton diagnosed in *Federalist* 80, "may be esteemed the basis of the Union."[52] Few of the provisions were genuine innovations; virtually all had antecedents in the Articles of Confederation. The Constitution, however, rendered them enforceable—not contingently through congressional legislation, but as absolute or qualified constitutional prohibitions by the federal judiciary.

What Madison Missed: Mobility. I will return to the institutional enforcement choice in a moment, and at greater length in chapter 3. But it is worth pausing over the *types* of state laws that are subject to preemptive constitutional treatment. Virtually without exception, they are the kinds of laws that are highly likely to have deleterious effects on sister-states and their citizens: paper money, impairments of contracts, exclusion and discrimination, and so on. Madison had discussed those exploitative measures as *examples* of the true source of rot—factionalism—to which only a comprehensive Negative would answer. Perhaps the Convention delegates declined to follow Madison's proposal because it would have sunk the constitutional project; perhaps they missed his point entirely.[53] Either way, their choice has an impeccable logic: instead of rooting out state factionalism, the Convention undertook to arrest it at the state borders.

In the immediate aftermath of the Convention, Madison despaired of the attempt to defang rather than annihilate the states. He deemed the distinction between "internal" and "national" affairs—the linchpin of the system—conceptually untenable and politically unstable.[54] And the Convention's attempt to curb factionalism's outward manifestations rather than the disease itself, Madison complained in a long post-Convention letter to Jefferson, was woefully insufficient "1. to prevent encroachments on the General authority. 2. to prevent instability and injustice in the legislation of the States."[55] Encroachments, instability, and injustice would continue unabated because faction-ridden state legislatures have any number of ways to evade the Constitution's specific prohibitions:

> The restraints agst. paper emissions, and violations of contracts are not sufficient . . . . Injustice may be effected by such an infinitude of legislative expedients, that where the disposition exists it can only be controuled by some

provision which reaches all cases whatsoever. The partial provision made [in the Constitution], supposes the disposition which will evade it.[56]

Private rights, Madison continued, would be "more secure under the Guardianship of the General Government" armed with an all-encompassing Negative.

In hindsight, this verdict on the Convention's product looks excessively uncharitable. Madison underestimated its attractions because he missed a crucial point: labor and capital mobility. To be sure, Madison and for that matter Hamilton—the former a rare example of an American to have studied at an institution outside his home state and of another confession, the latter an immigrant and sophisticated economist—were keenly aware of factor mobility.[57] That awareness, however, never entered their theory of federalism and faction in any systematic fashion. Let it enter. The constitutional scheme is a far more effective antifaction arrangement than Madison perceived it to be. The constitutional guarantee of free exit and entry curbs factional politics on the margin where, to Madison's mind, the Constitution left American citizens in the lurch—exploitation by their own state governments. At the same time, the constitutional guarantees against externalities and exclusion promise to curb state factional politics on the margin where it is most likely—one state's exploitation of other states' citizens. Both mechanisms are profoundly competitive. Both, to repeat, are embodied in specific constitutional prohibitions.

Neither mechanism is perfect—not by a long shot. For an obvious example, factor mobility does nothing to curb, and may even exacerbate, the state exploitation of production factors that cannot move (or move only at great cost), such as land or businesses with accumulated local goodwill. Constitutional choice, however, is not a mad chase for perfection but a comparison of least-bad options. By that standard, the Constitution's competitive arrangements look far more promising, anti-faction-wise, than Madison's Negative. Apart from its extravagant decision costs, the Negative is self-defeating. It promises collective gains on the theory that the national legislature is less faction-driven and more broad-minded than state legislatures. On Madison's own premises, though, the connection between the objects of legislation and the quality of legislators runs both ways. Congress, on those premises, will attract individuals with a disposition toward the great objects of national commerce and war. (Large electoral districts will help to get those people elected, but they would not run but for the opportunity to pursue those objectives.) The Negative, however, systematically cuts against filtration: a Congress entrusted with the authority to make local decisions will soon be populated by no one but professional earmarkers. The fact that this happened in any event does not undercut the point that the Negative is incoherent *at an institutional design level*. The competitive constitutional devices are not. To borrow a phrase, they are federal remedies for the diseases most incident to federalism.

What Madison May Have Missed: Political Economy. Grant that mobility may render competitive federalism superior to a nationalist program of faction control; one can still argue that the nifty scheme will prove unstable. Madison did in fact argue along those lines. Neither the Congress nor the Supreme Court, he warned in his post-Convention letter to Jefferson, would consistently protect the union's rightful supremacy—the former because legislators' parochial attachments would all too often block an effective response to state encroachments; the latter because aggrieved individuals would often lack the means or incentives to appeal to the judiciary, whose rulings the states would in any event be reluctant to obey.[58] Here again, Madison got the analysis *almost* right. What he missed, and what has kept American federalism competitive for much of our history, is the political economy of constitutional litigation.

Alexander Hamilton—not coincidentally, an accomplished business lawyer—grasped the point. In *Federalist* 7, Hamilton undertakes to demolish the "utopian" notion that the existing commercial relations among the states would produce an ever-closer union without a decisive constitutional act. The opposite, Hamilton says, might well come to pass:

> The habits of intercourse, on the basis of equal privileges, to which we have been accustomed from the earliest settlement of the country, would give a keener edge to those causes of discontent, than they would naturally have, independent of this circumstance. *We should be ready to denominate injuries, those things which were in reality the justifiable acts of independent sovereignties consulting a distinct interest.* The spirit of enterprise, which characterizes the commercial part of America, has left no occasion of displaying itself unimproved. It is not at all probable, that this unbridled spirit would pay much respect to those regulations of trade, by which particular states might endeavour to secure exclusive benefits to their own citizens.[59]

This brilliant passage contains both a profound institutional insight and a vote of confidence in the constituency for a competitive constitutional order—"the commercial part of America." Thinly hidden in the warning of what would happen if the Constitution were to be defeated is a prediction of what would happen if it were accepted. Intercourse "on the basis of equal privileges" would become a constitutional guarantee in the form of the Privileges and Immunities Clause—"the basis of the union," enforceable by the courts under the federal judiciary's diversity jurisdiction.

Hamilton fully expected, and meant to encourage, "the unbridled spirit of enterprise" to seize on those legal, judicial means. He knew, however, that the Constitution's competitive dynamic is not "self-enforcing" in any mechanical sense; it requires properly incentivized constitutional entrepreneurs and a federal judiciary that recognizes its central place and responsibility in the constitutional architecture. Nothing guarantees the durability of those conditions; one can end up with a clueless commercial class and a judiciary that cannot recognize, or chooses to renege on, constitutional commitments. Those, however, are our failures, not the Founders'.

CHAPTER THREE

Constitutional Structure

When the Constitution is ambiguous or silent on a particular issue, this Court has often relied on notions of a constitutional plan—the implicit ordering of relationships within the federal system necessary to make the Constitution a workable governing charter and to give each provision within that document the full effect intended by the Framers. The tacit postulates yielded by that ordering are as much engrained in the fabric of the document as its express provisions, because, without them, the Constitution is denied force, and often meaning.

William H. Rehnquist

Introduction

The preceding chapter has sketched a few of the Constitution's distinctively competitive federalism arrangements—in particular, those that guarantee cross-border mobility. To show that the Constitution establishes an entire competitive order, this chapter stacks up the Constitution's formal structure against the basic precepts of contemporary competitive federalism theory. The analysis is limited but also quite ambitious. As for limits, I put aside federalism's "political safeguards"—that is, the states' agency in federal political institutions. Those safeguards are best discussed, and will be discussed, in their actual operation over the centuries. I also put aside, for consideration in later chapters, several formal-constitutional matters that bear upon federalism, such as state immunities and (more importantly) individual rights. As for ambition, I aim to show that competition is neither a federalism "value" or advantage that we have discovered ex post nor a Dworkinian abstraction that makes the Constitution appear in its "best light." It is rather a constitutional principle and "tacit postulate" that gives the constitutional clauses force and meaning.

To repeat, the economic federalism theory that I bring to bear on the text reflects insights and empirical experiences that were not within the Founders' specific contemplation. However, Publius plainly envisioned that experience and improved knowledge might produce a better understanding of the Constitution's logic and especially of its political economy. Examining the formal constitutional structure in that light does not produce a "Living Constitution" but rather a fresh understanding of the Founders' work. Moreover, the discovery process runs both ways. Although contemporary competitive federalism theorists envision something very much like the U.S. Constitution, none of them have worked through the architecture with the ingenuity and attention to institutional detail that the Founders brought to the enterprise. Upon close inspection, the Constitution reveals ingenious institutional solutions to some of the problems that have most perplexed contemporary theorists.

Table 3.1 provides a schematic overview. The left-most column shows competitive federalism's objectives (a federal structure; vertical and horizontal coordination, on competitive terms; stability) and the institutional strategies associated with these objectives. The second column, "constitutional criteria," displays minimum conditions of competitive federalism. All are widely accepted among federalism scholars, including critics of competitive federalism. None rest on controversial or esoteric theorems, and none imply any assumption or prediction with respect to competitive federalism's efficiency, stability, or normative desirability. The third column shows the Constitution's corresponding structural principles. Those products of constitutional construction are reflected in, but not exhausted by, individual constitutional clauses; occasionally they are inferred from pronounced constitutional silences.

The structural principles are familiar, most to the point of ennui. The déjà vu provides some assurance that my explication is not some idiosyncratic invention. To be sure, fierce battles have raged over the scope and import of the Constitution's structural principles. My proposal to understand them as interlocking pieces of a competitive architecture is simply another contribution to an ongoing debate that our minimalist Constitution deliberately invites. However, the Constitution also *bounds* the range of disagreement. Try to connect the constitutional pieces under some made-up "dignity" or "balance" slogan: very quickly, the text turns into gibberish, the principles look dubious, and the underlying structure looks senseless or in need of "translation." "Competition," in contrast, makes sense of the clauses, the principles, and the structure. An alarming number of cross-references in this chapter will illustrate that the principles shown in table 3.1 all fit and belong together. They can be understood in light of each other, and they organize a text of remarkable coherence and integrity.

Table 3.1. Competitive federalism and constitutional structure

Objectives/Strategies	Constitutional criteria	Structural principles
Structure		
Vertical federalism	Two levels of government rule the same land and people.	"Dual federalism," a.k.a. "compound republic" (limited, enumerated powers; directness)
Entitlements	The junior governments have primary authority over private conduct within their jurisdictions.	Delegated, enumerated powers
	The national government has primary authority (1) to provide national public goods and	States' rights: territoriality, equality, political integrity
Horizontal federalism	(2) to police the common market and ensure the mobility of goods and (production) factors across jurisdictions.	Nondiscrimination; nonexploitation
Coordination		
Bounded equilibrium	Decision rules, not end-states	Powers, not balance
Jurisdiction	Competition	Federal supremacy
		Exclusivity
Stability		
(Self-)enforcement	The allocation of authority is sufficiently durable to resist alteration by the national government, either *sua sponte* or under pressure from junior governments.	Institutional commitments
Bargains	Revenue sharing among governments is limited, and borrowing by governments is constrained so that all governments face hard budget constraints.	Fiscal autonomy; baseline-free bargaining; transparency

Sources: The "constitutional criteria" of "structure" and "stability" are adopted from Barry R. Weingast's widely accepted minimal criteria of competitive or "market-preserving" federalism. See Weingast, "The Economic Role of Political Institutions: Market-Preserving Federalism and Economic Development," *Journal of Law, Economics and Organization* 11:1 (1995). The criteria for "coordination" are complementary and follow from Weingast's "structure" criteria. For a very similar exposition, see Jenna Bednar, *The Robust Federation: Principles of Design* (New York: Cambridge University Press, 2009), 17, 19–20, 43.

Structure

Competitive federalism implies, first, that there must be "junior," subordinate governments (states) underneath a central government, with sufficient institutional integrity to engage in political and economic competition over some range of activities. It requires, second, a rough division of authority between the central and subordinate governments: States should have autonomy over conduct within their jurisdiction, provided (1) they permit free entry and exit, and (2) their activities do not cause excessive externalities.[1] Enforcement of these provisos is entrusted to the central government. The United States Constitution satisfies these conditions in a unique way. I discuss the structure under three headings: dualism, entitlements, and horizontal federalism.

"Vertical" Federalism: Dualism. Under any federal system, two (or more) levels of government rule the same land and people. The United States Constitution structures this relation as a "dual federalism" arrangement. Dualism denotes, first, the *breadth* of the central government's powers: those powers extend only to certain "enumerated" objects; all else is left to the states. The nineteenth century had an almost physical understanding of separate state and federal "spheres," roughly corresponding to a distinction between the states' "internal" affairs and the "external" or "national" matters committed to the central government. That distinction is often viewed as coterminous with dualism as such, but dualism has two additional features. One of these has to do with the *depth* of the central government's powers: the central government acts *directly* upon individual citizens, without the intermediation or assistance of the states. Dualism's third feature is a firm (though not unbroken) baseline of *exclusivity*: presumptively, any given problem or transaction is governed by federal or state law, but not by both. All three principles have profoundly procompetitive effects. Here, I focus on the enumerated powers and "directness" principles; exclusivity is discussed later, under the heading "coordination."

The distinction between the "breadth" and "depth" of the central government's powers departs from a general tendency to collapse federalism into a simple national-state dichotomy (which in turn produces the inference that federalism requires a federal-state "balance"). We have it on good authority, however, that the conventional dichotomy misreads the Constitution. Madison's already-quoted "compound republic" passage in *Federalist* 39 explains that the federal government's powers are "national" in operation but "federal" in extent. The powers are "federal" in extent (or "breadth") because they are enumerated and limited. They are "national" in "operation" (or "depth") because, to repeat, they operate directly on citizens, requiring no state assistance or intermediation.

The enumerated powers doctrine has rarely been questioned as a matter of first principle, but the scope and construction of particular grants of power have been notoriously controversial throughout our constitutional history. The directness principle has been controversial in a somewhat different way. No one doubts that the Constitution authorizes the national government to act directly upon citizens; everyone recognizes that this feature constitutes the central difference between the Constitution and the Articles of Confederation. The question is whether the Constitution, by *empowering* the national government to act directly on citizens, also *prohibits* it from acting indirectly—that is, through the states. Dualism compels an affirmative answer. Within the limits of its enumerated powers, Congress may "preempt" the states—that is, prohibit them from doing this or that thing. That coordination principle is embodied in the Supremacy Clause (Art. VI, § 2). The Constitution also contains a bargaining principle: the national government may ask the states for their cooperation or offer them payments for the performance of services. However, with certain constitutionally specified exceptions, Congress may not *order* or "commandeer" the states to do anything at all.[2]

Later chapters will discuss the trajectory and the nuances of these principles. What matters here is this: *the "dual" features of the Constitution render the compound republic competitive.* To see the logic, contrast Madison's seemingly labored anatomy with the opposite arrangement—a federal government whose powers are national (unlimited) in scope but federal (indirect) in operation. Enumerated powers entail competition. If the federal government cannot regulate minimum wages or abortion or education, states will have to compete in those domains, whether they like it or not. Under a "national" conception of the central government's powers, in contrast, state competition on any margin can be eradicated and federalism becomes mere decentralization.[3] The competitive force of the directness or anticommandeering principle, in turn, stems primarily from its potential to reduce government surplus at all levels. A central government that may not commandeer states must pay the full political and economic price for enforcing its schemes, instead of hiding those costs in the states. "Cooperative" federalism entails just the opposite result—an excess supply of central, competition-reducing interventions, and appropriable rents for the states as states.[4]

Dual/competitive and cooperative federalism imply very different notions of state autonomy. Under dual federalism, state autonomy means "independence autonomy"—that is, the authority to determine political means and ends, over some range. Under cooperative federalism, in contrast, states possess "administrative autonomy," meaning that the execution of federal law requires their active assistance. It is important to note the difference has do with competition and nothing whatever with "states' rights" or federal "balance." In fact, cooperative federalism may very well be more state friendly than dual federalism. Independence autonomy means state competition, which will diminish the states' ability to accumulate surplus. Administrative autonomy translates primarily into political and economic bargaining power vis-à-vis the central government, which states will often wield for the purpose of procuring rents. For these reasons, states will often prefer commandeering to preemption and administrative to independence autonomy.[5] Many federalisms around the world reflect that preference order.[6] Ours does not. Its point is not to empower states but to discipline them.

Entitlements. The United States Constitution embodies the competitive federalism criteria in table 3.1: primary state authority over internal affairs; primary national responsibility for producing public goods that are national in scale (prominently, national defense) and for the protection of free trade and mobility within the common (domestic) market. This book's appendix contains a schematic overview of the Constitution's individual power-conferring and power-denying clauses. Federal powers (and corresponding prohibitions against the states) fall into four broad categories: (1) commerce, (2) common defense and foreign relations, (3) citizenship and interstate relations, and (4) federal property and institutions. All four categories, and all individual clauses contained within them, conform elegantly to competitive federalism theory.

What of the states' entitlements? As already seen, the Constitution grants the states no "power trump" or veto right against the exercise of federal power. When it comes to the states' authority, the enumerated powers doctrine has to do most of the formal-constitutional work—but not quite all the work. The Constitution contains certain "states' rights" guarantees, or what one might call a state "political existence trump." In oft-quoted judicial parlance, "the Constitution, in all its provisions, looks to an indestructible union, composed of indestructible states."[7] Its state-protective elements help to explain why the states have remained the "default setting" in American politics.[8] They also have potent procompetitive attributes.

Article IV, § 4 guarantees the states a republican form of government, protection against invasion, and protection (upon a state's request) against domestic violence. One purpose of this "Guarantee Clause" is to enable the national government to suppress emerging tyranny or usurpation in a state, whence its baneful influence and contagion might spread to other states. However, the Guarantee Clause is not formulated as a power but as a *duty*. Federal assistance can be "demanded, as a right, from the national government."[9] The Constitution looks to the initial assent not as an incomplete contract that states must make good on (or may renege on) but as a conclusive and irrevocable act. Accordingly, it treats the potential emergence of an autocratic government in any state, even if it were to occur with popular approbation, as an act of aggression against sister-states, which the union is both authorized and obligated to redress.[10]

The states' existence trump further encompasses a principle of *territoriality,* which the Constitution takes very seriously. New states may be added to the Union—but not out of existing states. No state may be broken up, nor may states be joined, without the consent of the state legislature (Art. IV, § 3). The principle embodied in this Joinder Clause runs both ways. Under the Compact Clause (Art. I, § 10, Cl. 3), states may not join with one another (or with foreign nations), without the consent of the Congress. Thus, the Constitution sets its face against organized sectionalism and cartelization—and, in that fashion, aids competitive federalism. Although fifty states (let alone thirteen) do not constitute an atomistic political market structure, the United States encompasses enough and sufficiently robust states to render competition feasible and meaningful.[11]

Next, the Constitution rests on a principle of state *equality*. No individual state enjoys special privileges vis-à-vis the national government or against other states. One strong indication of this feature is the Constitution's frequent resort to nondiscrimination rules. Some such rules (for example, the proviso that indirect taxes must be "uniform," Art. I, § 9) cabin the national government's power. Others (prominently, the Privileges and Immunities Clause) structure relations among states, generally on a principle of mutual nonaggression. In all respects, state equality is strictly formal. Any of the United States may enjoy advantages by virtue of factor endowments (such as size or natural resources) or by legislative grace—but never as a constitutional entitlement.

Formal state equality governs to the exclusion of other mechanisms that are contained in many other federal constitutions and might be but aren't in ours—asymmetric state guarantees, for example, or fiscal distribution formulas and other fairness—or solidarity-enhancing provisions. That formalism, I argued in chapter 2, shows that American federalism is about interest, not identity. Extend the Hegelian thought: the Constitution's arrangement—formal state equality, subject to prohibitions against aggression and monopoly—mimics the logic of liberal market orderings. It is wholly indifferent to the states' initial endowments, establishes neutral rules of autonomy and exchange, and lets the outcomes be what they may. One cannot imagine a more procompetitive federalism baseline.[12]

Consistent with this line of thought, competitive markets presuppose self-directed actors. Accordingly, the Constitution grants the states *political integrity*. That principle is reflected both in the already-mentioned Guarantee Clause and in the Constitution's provisions regarding political representation. States, as the places where representatives, senators, and electors come from, "may be regarded as constituent and essential parts of the federal government."[13] The reverse is not true; the Constitution leaves each state free to design and operate a government of its own choosing. It does require each state to have a "republican form of government"—that is, a legislature. But the election, structure, composition, and operation of that body are left entirely to the states' discretion. Likewise, the Constitution presumes the existence of state courts of some description. But it takes those institutions, too, as it finds them. Even such fundamental questions as the right to vote in state *and federal* elections are, under the original Constitution, left to the states. The constitutional decision to leave the states' political institutions and processes alone (provided only they are "republican") enables states to make independent-autonomous political choices, and it entails that institutional politics itself becomes a competitive margin.

The question of whether the states' existence trump implies any constitutional guarantee beyond the bounds just sketched has produced some of the most confusing and technically challenging debates in all of American constitutional law. Throughout our history, controversies over state sovereign immunity, intergovernmental tax immunity, and supposed Tenth Amendment guarantees against the federal impairment of "essential" state functions have provided ammunition for armies of lawyers. Happily, however, the importance of those questions does not rival their difficulty—so long as one refrains from mobilizing "states' rights" in support of an imagined federalism balance and against dual federalism's competitive structure. Unhappily, as we shall see in later chapters, the Supreme Court has not always resisted that temptation.

Horizontal Federalism. Competitive federalism requires a market-like structure of entitlements and exchanges among states: mobility of goods, services, and production factors across state lines; no (excessive) externalities.[14] The logic is elementary. Mobility makes a system of independent-autonomous states competitive, and each equal state's freedom to govern its own affairs implies a prohibition against governing those of others.[15]

The constitutional rules and principles that structure horizontal state-to-state relations are pristinely procompetitive. As for mobility, the protection of open borders and the common market is the key purpose of several congressional powers, prominently including the power to make commerce "regular." But the foundational mobility requirement is not left to congressional whim. It takes the form of constitutional prohibitions against the states, enforceable by private citizens as of right. Those provisions embody a fundamental precept of American federalism: citizens may freely choose their state and transact business across state lines.[16]

With respect to externalities, the Constitution implies a principle of nonaggression. Each state may legislate upon its own citizens but not upon other states' citizens. Although the prohibition does not appear in the text of the Constitution, its logic is so impeccable that no one has ever seriously questioned it. Its contours, however, have proven fiendishly difficult to discern. The traditional understanding, a rule against "extraterritorial" state jurisdiction, suffers from two shortcomings. First, it does not allow for unambiguous jurisdictional assignments when transactions cover several states with a plausible jurisdictional claim. (In other words, the rule tends to break down when it is needed.) Second, "territory" is not really what we are after. What competitive federalism requires, and what our constitutional logic compels, is a rule against mutual state *exploitation*.[17] The principle is embodied in numerous constitutional clauses. The prohibitions against state tariffs and duties of tonnage, for example, protect not simply against outright exclusion but also, and more broadly, against any state's abuse of a monopolistic market position. The enjoined activities are plainly intraterritorial; what makes them suspect is their exploitative *effect* on other states. The same analysis applies to the prohibitions against state bills of credit, compacts, and laws impairing the obligation of contract; they all serve to curb state acts of aggression against other states.[18]

Although the antiexploitation principle is not easily derived from any individual constitutional clause and, moreover, is difficult to apply in individual cases, the nineteenth-century Supreme Court consistently gave it force and effect. The post–New Deal Court, in contrast, has tended to seize on doctrinal difficulties as a reason for well-nigh throwing in the towel on curbing mutual state exploitation. These opposing impulses, as later chapters will show, illuminate a central structural point: a federal judiciary that surrenders at the horizontal federalism front has surrendered the Constitution's competitive architecture.

Coordination

Competitive federalism demands coordination rules. What should they look like? Recall that constitutional choice pushes toward *decision rules* as opposed to specified end states. That strategy further implies a kind of constitutional minimalism: a constitution should not try to do too much by way of restricting the range of in-period outcomes. (The more restrictive the decision rules, the more they will resemble end-state designations, on which no ex ante agreement is possible.) The Constitution's just-reviewed "horizontal" federalism rules conform to that model. Beyond prohibition against discrimination and exploitation—clear at their core, contestable in application, but never distributional or of an affirmative nature—no state owes any other state much of anything.[19] The Constitution adopts the same coordination strategy in its "vertical," federal-state dimension; it couples a wide but bounded equilibrium of powers with an unambiguous decision rule.

Bounded Equilibrium: Powers, Not Balance. The Constitution's entitlements—federal institutions with limited, enumerated powers; guarantees of the political existence of equal, territorial states—imply that the system must remain federal in some minimal sense. But they mark no balance, only the outer boundaries of a vast range of possible outcomes and constructions—some very nationalist, some very state friendly. That arrangement reflects the calculus of preconstitutional individuals. For them (unlike for state officials), the degree of decentralization per se is inconsequential; what matters is to protect competitive federalism against both state defections and central monopoly. It is impossible to know in advance how these twin risks will shake out—in particular, how much central intervention will be required to sustain competitive conditions.[20] The way to deal with the known unknowns is to cabin the range of outcomes (through institutional devices, textual prohibitions, or both) and to leave the federal-state balance to institutional politics. The fundamental difference between this constitutional arrangement and balance federalism has been noted throughout. But the federalism-as-balance view is sufficiently entrenched, and its errors are sufficiently fateful, to warrant a few additional observations.

For starters, the Constitution's eschewal of any balancing provisions or mechanisms is both conspicuous and intentional. The Constitution *could* have specified sorting criteria to help courts, and perhaps legislators in the first instance, to decide what functions belong where. Madison suggests such a criterion in *Federalist* 14. The federal jurisdiction, he writes, "is limited to certain enumerated objects, which concern all the members of the republic, but which are not to be attained by the separate provisions of any." State governments, on the other hand, will retain authority over "all those other objects, which can be separately provided for."[21] The formulation is strikingly similar to a "principle of subsidiarity," defended by many scholars and contained, for example, in the European Union's treaties.[22] Although one can doubt the effectiveness of a subsidiarity principle, it is at least not tautological. Our own sorting principle, in contrast, *is* tautological. The Tenth Amendment, enacted in large measure to allay fears of federal overreach, reserves all powers not delegated to the federal government "to the States respectively, or to the people." In other words, the federal government has the powers that it has. The tautology is intended; the word "*expressly* delegated," which would have circumscribed federal powers and which had been contained in the corresponding Article of Confederation, was deliberately omitted from the proposed text of what became the Tenth Amendment.[23]

As the Constitution's silence cuts against "balance," so does its minimalism with respect to powers questions. Many of the objections against the proposed Constitution's expansive federal powers could have been deflated, and a federal balance might be more easily maintained, by making the delineation of federal and state powers more specific while permitting a readier recourse to amendments in light of changed circumstances. The Constitution, however, rejects that option and instead embodies an arrangement that is open to highly decentralist and highly nationalist constructions. Even a rough sketch of our perennial federalism debate illustrates that the Constitution provides ammunition to "states' rights" apostles and "nationalists" alike—but no knock-down argument for either side.

The decentralist case typically starts with Madison's famous statement of the enumerated powers principle:

> The powers delegated by the proposed constitution to the federal government, are few and defined. Those which are to remain in the state governments, are numerous and indefinite. The former will be exercised principally on external objects, as war, peace, negotiation, and foreign commerce; with which last the power of taxation will, for the most part, be connected. The powers reserved to the several states will extend to all the objects, which, in the ordinary course of affairs, concern the lives, liberties, and properties of the people; and the internal order, improvement, and prosperity of the state.[24]

In Chief Justice John Marshall's almost equally famous words, "the enumeration [of federal powers] presupposes something not enumerated."[25] By dint of that incontrovertible logic, a constitutional construction that transforms enumerated powers into a collection of "whatever" clauses must be wrong. Conversely, the states' retained and reserved powers cannot be a null set.

The same constitutional raw material, though, also yields a potent nationalist construction. Article I, § 8 enumerates the federal government's powers—what the federal government *may* do. Contrary to Madison's averment, national powers are hardly "few." Section 8 alone contains eighteen clauses, and other powers are scattered throughout the Constitution. And although federal powers are "defined," the harsh fact is that they are *more or less* defined. Many are amazingly broad. Notably, Congress may tax anyone and anything, with the sole exception of exports. Congress also has the power to "make all Laws which shall be necessary and proper for carrying into Execution" all powers vested in the federal government (Art. I § 8 Cl. 18). Article I, § 9 spells out what the federal government may *not* do. Important Bill-of-Rights-style guarantees are listed here: the right to habeas corpus, as well as protections against bills of attainder and ex post facto laws. Section 9 also prohibits Congress from imposing direct taxes except in proportion to the census, from taxing state exports, and from granting preferences to particular ports. Article I, § 10 lists what the *states* may not do. They may not pass ex post facto laws, enact laws impairing the obligation of contracts, have treaties with one another or with foreign nations, or coin money. Section 10 also contains a list of things that states may not do without the consent of the Congress. They must not tax imports or exports, keep armed forces, or have compacts with one another or with foreign nations. Note again the want of a state power trump. Our Constitution contains no list of protected state powers or functions. Where it mentions state powers, it abrogates them.

That constitutional feature, replies the decentralist, simply reflects the principle of copious reserved powers. But the response looks doubtful. The "reserved" powers are purely residual, and the list of state prohibitions encompasses just about everything sovereign states do for a living: control the borders, coin currency, protect citizens against foreign attacks, prefer them to outsiders. The Constitution effectively monopolizes these functions in the national government and imposes (typically explicit) corresponding disabilities on the states. Under such conditions, it is hard to see the point of being a state.

There is no way of deciding the dispute by way of constitutional argument. But that is just the point: In *rejecting* a preset balance, the Constitution *invites* sustained argument over its structure—not just arid theoretical argument, but political argument, backed by real (and shifting) constituencies and institutions. That mode of keeping constitutional argument alive in ordinary politics, not some imaginary balance, is at the heart of our open, minimalist constitutional structure.[26]

The *Federalist* buttresses this interpretation, albeit indirectly. Illustrious readers have argued that Publius nearly despaired of prevailing over state sentiments; that he expected (or hoped) that states and the general government would settle into some form of regularized, equilibrium-protective competition for the people's affections; or that he expected (or hoped) the states would wither away.[27] One can mobilize the *Federalist* for all those interpretations, but it is unlikely that any single reading captures Publius's "true" views. The *Federalist*'s tone in discussing formal constitutional arrangements is confident and assertive. It turns diffident and occasionally dissonant on federalism's political economy. Apprehensions about the states' centrifugal tendencies alternate with reassuring noises to the effect that the states have nothing to fear, and again with subtle suggestions that the states could cease to play an important role if "manifest and irresistible proofs of a better administration" of the federal government should overcome "all [the] antecedent propensities" that attach citizens to their state governments.[28] The best interpretation is that Publius viewed all those scenarios as plausible—with no clear sense of the discount rates, but with a very clear sense that much would depend on constitutional construction in real-time politics. Much of the *Federalist* was devoted to the constructive task, as were Hamilton's and Madison's efforts in the New York and Virginia ratifying conventions. Promptly after ratification, both men devoted themselves to constitutional construction at an institutional level, with a clear understanding that the early precedents would carry great future weight. The fact that they soon came to blows illustrates the price, but also the genius, of a Constitution that leaves much of the federal architecture open to politics, argument, and construction.

Jurisdiction: Supremacy and Exclusivity. Constitutional openness with respect to federalism end-states does not mean imprecision or indecision with respect to decision rules—quite the opposite. European federal constitutions and the European Treaties, which uniformly do aim at a federalism balance, speak delicately of federal and state "functions" or "competencies," capable of migrating up and down the intergovernmental chain of command in accordance with felt necessities and demonstrated "competence." Those concepts reflect the administrative, between-law-and-politics nature of European federalisms. The U.S. Constitution, in contrast, speaks unequivocally of *powers*—that is, the legal authority to do this or that thing or an equivalent prohibition. In the nature of things, the scope of those powers is contestable. But the Constitution is very pre-cise, often to the point of redundancy, in specifying who has the power (or, occasionally, the obligation) to do what. Jurisdiction is the constitutional ballgame, and it is played in accordance with decision rules, as opposed to goals, objectives, or distributions. The central rule, the Supremacy Clause of Article VI § 2, is harsh and unequivocal:

> This Constitution, and the Laws of the United States which shall be made in Pursuance thereof; and all Treaties made, or which shall be made, under the Authority of the United States, shall be the supreme Law of the Land; and the Judges in every State shall be bound thereby, any Thing in the Constitution or Laws of any State to the Contrary notwithstanding.

The framers' core meaning is as clear as their capitalization rules are mysterious: The Supremacy Clause encapsulates Madison's compound republic. National sovereignty is not boundless. Laws must be made "in pursuance of" the Constitution—that is, within the scope of the enumer-ated powers, and through the constitutionally mandated procedures of bicameral approval, presentment, and veto. Within that domain, how-ever, any federal law trumps any contravening state law, including state constitutional law. There can be no state enclaves from federal supremacy and no judicial "harmonizing" of federal and state law.[29] *Supreme* federal powers means *plenary* federal powers, so far as they extend. There is nei-ther any implied reservation of state powers nor any constitutional com-mand of federal courtesy or forbearance vis-à-vis the states. Conversely, *enumerated* powers means that the powers end where they end. Wherever that line may fall, federal power does not brood or hover over the states. Thus, the Constitution reflects a deep bias toward *exclusive* federal or state jurisdiction, consistent with the constitutional assignments.[30]

As noted earlier, exclusivity is a close constitutional cousin of the enu-merated powers and directness (or "anticommandeering") principles. And like its relatives, it is intensely disputed—most plausibly, on the grounds that not all federal powers are exclusive. The conventional starting point is Hamilton's discussion in *Federalist* 32. The Constitution, Hamilton writes, makes federal powers exclusive in three cases: where it explicitly qualifies them as such, where the grant of a federal power is mirrored by a corresponding prohibition against the states, and where federal powers are "exclusive" by nature. Hamilton instances the power to establish "uni-form" rules (for bankruptcy or—Hamilton's example—naturalization) "because if each state had power to prescribe a DISTINCT RULE, there could be no UNIFORM RULE." With these exclusive powers, Hamilton contrasts the *non*-exclusive power of taxation. With the stated exceptions and provisos of Article I § 9 and § 10, Hamilton writes, the power to tax is "manifestly a concurrent and co-equal authority in the United States and in the individual states." States, he contends, retain the authority to tax "in the most absolute and unqualified sense"; federal interference "would be a violent assumption of power, unwarranted by any article or clause of its constitution." Hamilton infers this from the structure of the Constitution and the nature of the taxing power. Dual taxes on the same base, he says, can be "inconvenient"; but unlike rules governing primary conduct, they cannot conflict or be "repugnant" to one another.[31]

The exposition is a brilliant piece of misdirection. On Hamilton's account, "state governments would clearly retain all the rights of sovereignty which they before had, and which were not, by that act, *exclusively* delegated to the United States." Concurrent powers, it appears, are the baseline, subject to alienation "only" in the three listed cases.[32] Another peek at the appendix, however, suggests Hamilton's inordinately liberal use of "only": *virtually without exception,* federal powers are accompanied by corresponding prohibitions against the states. Many of the remaining federal powers are either explicitly exclusive or else fall under Hamilton's "uniformity" reasoning. (For example, if states as well as Congress could "fix" weights and measures, they would no longer be "fixed.") And Hamilton's discussion of taxation, his lone example of a nonexclusive power, plainly overstates the case both in constitutional terms and as a matter of political economy.[33] Push hard enough, and the Constitution appears to foreclose any notion of concurrent federal and state powers.

Although some of Hamilton's disciples articulated just that proposition, we shall see shortly that the Supreme Court never followed them, or him. Precisely because the exclusivity principle is not unbroken, however, it is important to not lose sight of its underlying logic. Notwithstanding its close association with Hamilton, exclusivity per se has nothing to do with nationalism: It says nothing about what is exclusive to whom. It has to do, rather, with *competition.* Concurrent powers imply a duty to comply with (at least) two sovereigns, without any ability to migrate from one to the other and with the usual result that the more restrictive set of rules dominates. Exclusivity, in contrast, means "one problem, one sovereign."[34] Horizontally, that principle is firmly embedded in the constitutional rules that enable individuals to migrate from one sovereign to another, thus compelling junior sovereigns to compete. The same principle, operating vertically, subjects private conduct to federal or state rules *but not both.* Of course, federal intervention will often block state competition on some margin. However, the same intervention will—on an exclusivity reading—also block additional state regulation and so arrest what, under a concurrent powers reading, would be a one-dimensional race toward higher levels of intervention.

We have already seen that "dualist" independence-autonomy is actually a much harsher, less state-friendly rule than cooperative federalism's surplus autonomy. The same logic applies to the question of concurrent and exclusive powers: The procompetitive rule is the state-restrictive rule. On both points, libertarians have to be Hamiltonians first.

Stability

Contemporary federalism scholars widely agree that federalism may be harder to sustain than any other constitutional arrangement.[35] By all accounts, it is harder still to stabilize *competitive* federalism. Many federal systems, Australia, Germany, and the United States among them— and the European Union, if it counts as "federal"—have proven stable in the sense of escaping the twin dangers of disintegration or wholesale centralization. All of them, however, have moved from competitive arrangements to intergovernmentalism and cartels. Pervasive interstate externalities, inequalities among states (many of them undeserved), or states' underinvestments or failures to coordinate a viable infrastructure may prompt political responses that eventually overwhelm any initial commitment to decentralized, competitive arrangements.[36] State defections (such as state protectionism or exploitation) may necessitate massive central interventions, with no assurance that those interventions will be procompetitive or remain limited to the problem at hand. At the same time, states will often *demand* central interventions to dampen interstate competition. In short, centrifugal and centripetal forces both cut against competitive arrangements, and competitive federalism confronts, in the intergovernmental setting, the dilemma that confronts all liberal government: a general government that is strong enough to protect competition is also strong enough to wipe it out, *sua sponte* or upon state demand. The problem has no easy solution and perhaps no reliable "self-enforcing" solution at all. However, the Constitution contains two ingenious procompetitive mechanisms: incentive-compatible institutional commitments and baseline-free bargaining against a background rule of fiscal autonomy. In addition, the Constitution, rightly construed, requires a principle of transparency in intergovernmental bargains.[37]

Institutional Commitments. In the introduction and chapter 2, I suggested a partial solution to the competitive stability problem: "negative" integration, led by a federal judiciary armed to the teeth with procompetitive federalism provisions. These mechanisms are part of a broader constitutional principle and strategy: *the Constitution biases the institutional system toward procompetitive outcomes by committing different sets of federalism problems to the political branches and to the federal judiciary, respectively,* in accordance with the underlying federalism risks and the branches' capacity and propensity to provide competitive responses.

Consider again the basic difficulty of constructing a central government that is sufficiently strong to ensure competition, yet not so strong as to destroy it. How does the Constitution guard against those twin risks? The central protection against centripetal federalism risks are the Constitution's supermajoritarian features—the separation of powers, checks and balances, bicameralism. Although the chief purpose of those arrangements is to curb factionalism, they contain an important structural protection for competitive federalism: imperial federal ambitions and state demands for fiscal or regulatory cartelization will have to overcome the built-in supermajoritarian hurdles.[38] However, the obstacles that impede factionalism and cartelization also impede timely, decisive measures against the states' centrifugal tendencies—that is, defections that pose a threat to sister-states or to the Union. There is no way of solving this problem by recalibrating federal legislative incentives or majority rules. Any institutional arrangement that might make it easier for Congress to counteract state defections would simultaneously pave the way for increased factionalism and federal centralization.

The Constitution's solution is to change the default rules that operate on the states *in the absence of any congressional intervention,* such as the Privileges and Immunities Clause and the prohibitions of Article I § 10. Those constraints have two things in common: they are market protective and procompetitive, and *they are redundant* in the sense that the prohibited state activities could be enjoined *by Congress* under its enumerated powers.[39] Their point, then, is not to create federal powers but to switch the first-line enforcement authority from the Congress to the federal courts—plainly in the expectation that in an alarming fraction of cases, Congress would fall down on the job.[40] In short, centripetal risks to competitive federalism—unilateral monopolization, state-induced cartelization—are principally committed to the political institutions, where supermajoritarian obstacles impede the effort. The most potent centrifugal federalism risks—exit-and-entry restrictions, exploitation—are principally committed to the federal courts.[41]

The institutional design does not envision an impartial judicial "guardian of the Constitution"—a kind of benevolent despot on reserve. Rather, it contemplates that the Supreme Court's institutional incentives systematically push toward competitive federalism outcomes. A Supreme Court that vigorously enforces federal constitutional norms will by and large enhance its own authority. To the extent that judges *like* to augment the consequence of their offices, the incentive will operate as a counterpoise to the states' centrifugal incentives. To the considerable extent that the norms principally entrusted to the Court's care are procompetitive, institutional ambition and competition will sail in tandem. These dynamics, moreover, are reinforced by institutional propensities and limitations. Think of federalism as a common-pool problem (like, say, a fishery): states will perennially seek to overfish the commons. Will a central legislator adopt a property rights solution and decide what belongs to whom? Eventually, perhaps—but only after all *regulatory* options have been tried and failed, and only when the common pool faces collapse.[42] Courts, in contrast, naturally gravitate to competitive and property rights solutions. When faced with an instance of state protectionism or exploitation, courts can let it pass or, consistent with empire-building incentives, say "no." What courts *cannot* do—not so much because they are prohibited but because they are institutionally incapable—is to "harmonize" state demands and arrange for side payments to create that harmony. By and large, then, courts cannot supply "positive" integration. They can only supply "negative" integration—that is to say, integration on procompetitive terms. The procompetitive bias is a matter of fairly stable judicial incentives and limitations, not of contingent judicial preferences.[43]

We shall see that the institutional commitments work well under some economic and political conditions but tend to fail under others. Unmistakably, though, they mobilize the comparative advantages and pathologies of governmental institutions for competitive federalism ends. The courts are good at producing integration on competitive terms. The Congress is designed to be good at dithering, which is a splendid reason to entrust it with political demands for cartelization. In a second-best world without a benevolent despot, the commitment strategy may be the best we can do.

Fiscal Autonomy: Bargains without Baselines. Competitive federalism requires state tax competition, which in turn requires tax autonomy for both levels of government. The demand for federal tax autonomy ranked high on the Federalists' agenda, and they unequivocally prevailed on the point at the Convention. Conversely, if the states are to survive as relatively autonomous entities that are capable of competing, the central government must be disabled from occupying their revenue sources. The prospect that the federal government under the Constitution would surely do so was the Anti-Federalists' dire lament. How then does one protect bilateral tax autonomy?

Most modern federal systems attempt to do so by means of tax assignments, typically in accordance with purported efficiency criteria. Local governments tax property, states tax consumption, the national government taxes income. (A principal reason for those assignments is to curb "inefficient" tax competition.) The U.S. tax system has gradually moved toward roughly those assignments, but not on account of any constitutional provision. The Constitution contains virtually no tax assignments; its background rule is federal and state tax autonomy, almost across the board.[44] That deliberate design choice, like the institutional commitment principle, is imperfect, but quite probably a competitive second-best.

Article I, § 8, Clause 1 grants Congress the power "to lay and collect Taxes, Imposts and Excises, to pay the Debts and provide for the common Defence and general Welfare of the United States." This general grant of power is subject to one procedural proviso, two limitations on the objects of taxation, and two nondiscrimination rules. The procedural proviso, not applicable to any other congressional enactment, is that "all Bills for raising Revenue shall originate in the House of Representatives." The substantive limitations are, first, that "no Tax or Duty shall be laid [by Congress] on Articles exported from any State"; and second, a long-expired clause prohibiting the imposition of a tax or duty on slave imports in excess of $10 per head prior to the year 1808. The nondiscrimination rules apply to indirect and direct taxes, respectively. Indirect taxes must be "uniform throughout the United States." With respect to direct taxes, the Constitution mandates state apportionment "in Proportion to the Census."[45]

The Constitution is still more parsimonious with respect to the states' tax powers. Article I, § 10 bars them from laying imposts or duties on imports or exports and duties of tonnage. In conjunction with the limitations that apply to the federal government, those provisions establish the only unequivocal tax assignments of the Constitution: no one may tax exports; only the national government may impose an import tariff. With those exceptions, state and federal tax powers run concurrent over the entire tax base. Conspicuously, the Constitution makes no explicit provision for asymmetries or equalization. It permits concurrent taxation and commands formal state equality—and lets the outcomes be what they may.[46]

The minimalist system holds out the prospect of robust tax competition, both vertically (where states and the federal government compete for the same tax base) and horizontally among states (where factor mobility limits the states' appropriable surplus). That state of affairs, however, is persistently threatened. Tax autonomy and competition may collapse on account of unilateral defections—monopolization by the center or exploitative state taxation, either of which may produce an "overgrazing" of the tax base.[47] Or tax autonomy and competition may erode in a process of intergovernmental bargaining. States may collectively lock themselves into a fiscal cartel, or they may individually run up debt in anticipation of a federal bailout. Table 3.2 shows the possibilities (they are not mutually exclusive).

Note that only one competitive federalism risk, monopoly, emanates from the central government. Historically, moreover, that risk—a target of much Anti-Federalist agitation—has proven the *least* likely scenario, both in the United States and elsewhere (most likely because the states' agency in federal institutions blocks the move). The remaining three risks all flow from the states' unremitting incentive to suppress tax competition. Exploitative taxation, tax-and-spend cartels, and excess borrowing and spending are merely different forms of that constant orientation.[48]

On a closely related note, table 3.2 illustrates an apparent discontinuity between the constitutional scheme and much of the modern federalism literature, which focuses primarily on the bargaining risks—cartels and moral hazard. On those issues, the Constitution is essentially silent. Nothing bars the states from accumulating debt in the hope of, or in reliance on, a national bailout.[49] And nothing in the Constitution seems to bar the states from locking themselves into a federally sponsored tax cartel by surrendering their tax autonomy to the federal government in exchange for a share of the revenue.

It is tempting to conclude that the bargaining risks simply eluded the Framers. Had they thought about collusion and moral hazard, they might well have adopted formal constitutional limitations on state borrowing and federal transfer payments. However, modern federalism theory casts grave doubt on the utility of that approach.[50] It rather suggests that the Founders' silence contains great wisdom. The Constitution's lack of tax assignments and distributive, revenue-sharing formulas deprives

Table 3.2. Competitive federalism risks: taxation

	Centralization	State defection
Coordination	Federal monopoly	State tax exploitation ("extraterritorial taxation")
Bargaining	Cartel ("fiscal federalism")	Moral hazard (excess borrowing/spending)

would-be conspirators of a focal bargaining point. State demand for fiscal cartelization is a constant, and speculative state borrowing gambits are recurring events. No federal constitution can do much about either. A federal constitution can, however, force government actors to *improvise* tax cartels, as opposed to legislating against a preset baseline. Baseline-free bargaining will tend to render any agreement haphazard and piecemeal, and disagreements over distribution will often thwart even a unanimous consensus on a "cooperative," surplus-maximizing solution.[51]

Transparency. The baseline-free bargaining arrangement can be defeated. If government actors can figure out distributions that make all governments better off (and repeat players *will* eventually hit upon that cooperative solution), the competitive federalism game is up. States will surrender their independence autonomy in exchange for federal cash transfers; Congress will "spend its way around" enumerated powers limitations. Are those bargains around the constitutional entitlements subject to any constraints—and if so, of what sort?

The answer is best derived by process of elimination. At one extreme, a constitution could prohibit any and all intergovernmental bargains. However, although cooperation is prone to abuse, it may also produce gains all around (for example in the production of public goods, such as a national system of roads or telecommunications). It would therefore be foolish and futile to foreclose all bargains ex ante. At the other extreme, a constitution could permit governments to bargain for any purpose, on any terms. That arrangement, though, would leave nothing of the Constitution. Thus, bargaining must be subject to constraints. For an obvious example, two levels of government cannot by bargain create a power that neither possesses. (Congress may not pay states to close down newspapers.) Nor can one government transfer a nondelegable power to another.[52]

The question of whether federal-state bargains are subject to any additional constraints has a long and storied constitutional past. On one, "Madisonian" account the spending power is cabined by the enumerated powers and by the constitutional requirement that all taxation, and therefore (presumably) all spending, must be for the "general Welfare" (Article I, § 8, Cl. 1). Over time, however, the opposite, "Hamiltonian" position has prevailed: Congress may spend regardless of enumerated powers constraints, and there is no judicially enforceable "general welfare" limitation. For reasons discussed in chapter 7, I take this to be the correct position. It tends to prompt the immediate objection that governments' ability to bargain around constitutional entitlements eviscerates the entire carefully calibrated federal structure. However, that is not so.

First, the federal government cannot spend money that it has not raised. (It may *borrow* money but will have to pay it back—unless, of course, it is allowed to debase the currency, an arrangement the Founders viewed as a form of organized theft.)[53] There is, then, a fiscal constraint; but it operates on the tax rather than the spending side. Second, state-federal bargains are just that—*bargains,* "in the nature of a contract."[54] The deals will typically be enshrined in a federal statute that can be looked up in the United States Code. Unlike (regulatory) enumerated powers statutes, however, spending statutes do not come with the state-law-displacing force of the Supremacy Clause. Their legal consequences flow not from their nature as federal law but rather from the states' acceptance of the bargain: no acceptance, no legal consequence. Congress cannot "spend its way around" constitutional limitations *without the states' consent*—which it may invite but never compel. Third, the contractual nature of spending legislation has important consequences with respect to the *terms* of intergovernmental bargains. The terms must be clearly stated and, in doubtful cases, must be construed against the party that wrote the bargain—to wit, the Congress.

In contemporary doctrine, that constitutional canon is called the "clear statement rule." Unfortunately, the Supreme Court has not always been precise about the scope and the rationale of that doctrine, and it has at times proffered it as a state-protective "balance" rule. In its correct application, the doctrine governs *spending* legislation exclusively; and it has to do, not with protecting "states as states" but with what the Court, in more lucid moments, has called "accountability"—that is, with keeping intergovernmental bargains transparent *for citizens.*[55] This transparency principle is intimately linked to the already-expounded constitutional principles of "directness" and "exclusivity."

We have seen that Congress, within the ambit of its enumerated powers, may entirely displace—"preempt"—state authority, no questions asked. But we have also seen that Congress may *not* "commandeer" state officials into its service. Why? The answer is not that commandeering is more obnoxious to states than a mere prohibition. Rather, it is that state defiance of a federal prohibition is more easily monitored *for citizens* than is the shirking of an affirmative command. Put differently, "cooperative" federal-state arrangements pose a risk of strategic behavior, including intergovernmental collusion against citizens, in a way in which the direct and preemptive exercise of federal authority does not.[56]

These basic principles and considerations carry forward into government bargains. For reasons mentioned, the central government may bargain with subordinate governments to provide services, just as it may bargain with Catholic Charities or Boeing. The bargains may be good or bad, pro- or anticompetitive. Any and all bargains, however, will drive up citizens' monitoring costs. An enforceable transparency requirement, to the effect that each bargain must clearly state its terms and conditions, helps to counteract that effect.

At first impression, the notion of transparency as a federalism principle may seem paradoxical. The most transparent political system—in terms of the traceability of public decisions—is a pure autocracy, where all commands issue from a single sovereign. Federalism confounds that simple picture, and observers from Tocqueville on forward have noted American federalism's messiness and the great difficulty of telling who governs what.[57] Government bargains may further obscure the picture; but surely, that is a matter of degree—no? No. The confusion that attends a system of multiple governments is comparable to what East Germans encountered after the fall of the Berlin Wall. East Berlin's shops were highly transparent; no advertisement or merchandise obstructed the view, and once you had seen one store, you had seen them all. West Berlin's shopping malls presented a very different, utterly confounding picture. But although consumers in competitive markets—for goods or for public policy—often feel at sea, the system as a whole brings to light information that would remain suppressed in a monopolistic setting. By serving as a means of individual preference revelation, federalism enhances transparency after all. That benefit, however, accrues *only in a competitive setting*.[58] It evaporates when everything on offer turns out to be a joint product and when consumers can no longer tell who is responsible for the defects. The rule that the conditions of intergovernmental agreements must be clearly stated is imperfect. But it is entirely continuous with competitive federalism's constitutional structure.

Conclusion

My attempt to read the Constitution as a coherent structure and through a competitive federalism prism runs counter to two pervasive tendencies in contemporary federalism theory and constitutional thought. One tendency is the temptation to collapse the structure into a "balance" among "coequal sovereigns." I have explained why I believe that approach to be mistaken. The other tendency is to lose the forest for the trees, and the structure over the specific clauses. Any plausible constitutional construction must give each individual clause force and meaning. At the end of the day, though, the clauses are part of a larger formal architecture, whose understanding requires both some antecedent theory of how the instrument is supposed to work and a report to doctrines—enumerated powers, anticommandeering, and for that matter, federalism—that are not "in" the document in any direct, literal sense.

That mode of structural or "intratextual" analysis is not beyond reproach. Constitutional silences may be oversights or punts, rather than design decisions; specific clauses may be historical quirks or redundancies, rather than pregnant illustrations of an ingenious design. And the premise of internal coherence is something we bring to the Constitution as an article of faith.[59]

It is, however, a very old and honorable article of faith. For at least the first century of our constitutional history, no jurist thought that one could understand the Constitution without some political theory of its antecedent commitments; and none thought that the Constitution could work, or was ever intended to work, without an inferential, common-law-like mode of judicial power and reasoning. The nineteenth-century construction of our competitive Constitution, Part II will show, depended on just these forms on constitutional argument.

PART TWO

COMPETITIVE FEDERALISM

N o FEDERAL CONSTITUTIONAL ORDER implements itself. Its elaboration—the translation of general constitutional commands into abstract-concrete norms that are capable of governing private and official conduct, its adaptation to changing economic and political circumstances—is a sustained work of construction, partly political and partly legal. That elaboration during the nineteenth century is the subject of Part II. No statesman or judge of that formative period consciously thought about "competition" as a constitutional or federalism principle. If the country nonetheless ended up with a fiercely competitive constitutional order, the explanation is not some ruse of competitive reason. Rather, the competitive federal order rose principally on the foundation of what I have called the Constitution's "institutional commitment" principles. The working out of the constitutional rules was largely left to the Supreme Court, which ensured that it would proceed on procompetitive terms. At the same time, sectional forces sharply circumscribed the states' and the political branches' ability to bargain around the constitutional norms.

Much of my emphasis is on constitutional doctrine and its intrinsic logic. However, I do not mean to suggest that constitutional construction is a purely theoretical exercise (or for that matter a judicial monopoly). It is also and always about the projection of power—specifically, in the present context, about the projection of federal *judicial* power on recalcitrant states. The point bears emphasis because even some of the most learned scholars have tended to underestimate it. Writing at the end of the century, for example, Sir Henry Maine saw the secret of America's stupendous economic growth in "the [constitutional] prohibition against levying duties on commodities passing from State to State." That prohibition, Maine said, "secures to the producer the command of a free market over an enormous territory of vast natural wealth, and thus it secondarily reconciles the American people to a tariff on foreign importations as oppressive as ever a nation has submitted to."[1] The Founders, it appears, had hit upon a winning formula: vast scale, free trade, and competition at home; mercantilism and protectionism abroad. Alfred D. Chandler, Jr., writing many decades later, linked the explosive growth of industrial capitalism to the same factor. The emergence of a wide national market, he argued in his magisterial works, was the principal prerequisite for the rise of large, vertically integrated manufacturing corporations and for the operation of the "visible hand" of a managerial class that, over time, learned how to organize and run such firms.[2] These observations capture much of federalism's dynamic of the nineteenth century, but they tend to slight the judiciary's crucial role. Contrary to the whiff of Smithian liberalism that hangs over Maine's oft-quoted statement, the domestic market required not simply a rule against state duties on commodities but also rules against state barriers to the free flow of capital and labor, rules against state disruptions of network industries (such as railroads and telegraphs), and rules against state-imposed barriers to firm integration (that is, corporations). By that same token, Chandler's national market was not simply a function of geography (westward expansion) and reduced costs of transportation and communication. It was primarily a product of dramatically reduced state barriers to trade and industrial organization, especially organization in a corporate form.

All those procompetitive rules and arrangements were supplied almost exclusively by the federal judiciary. They did not enforce themselves but rather had to be imposed day in, day out on recalcitrant states. And none of them had a plausible, politically supplied substitute. At the time of John Marshall's death in 1835, there was no national bank. There was no national system of bankruptcy (despite the explicit grant of congressional power), no navigation act extending the federal admiralty power, no federal law of negotiable instruments in interstate commerce, and no federal statute governing extraterritorial state taxation.[3] (Congressional activity increased with and after the Civil War, but it remained sporadic even then.) What did exist throughout was a United States Supreme Court willing and able to use its ample Article III powers, so far as political circumstances would permit. Part II explores, in this context, the doctrines deployed by the Court over the nineteenth century: the Commerce Clause, especially in its "dormant" state; (chapter 4); the treatment of business corporations (chapter 5); and the "federal general common law" of *Swift v. Tyson* notoriety (chapter 6). Those interconnected doctrines do not exhaust the federalism universe, but they were critically important in the creation of a working federal order, and they cover enough ground to illuminate the central, common themes.

The judiciary's dominance over so wide a swath of American political and economic life, and in particular over questions of what the states were and were not permitted to do, raises the question of why the institutional arrangement should have proven so durable. States, I insisted earlier, detest competition and procompetitive constitutional rules; yet that was what the Supreme Court consistently served up. Why did the states not resist? The short answer is that they did resist, often by simply ignoring the Court and its pronouncements. What failed to materialize was a sustained, successful effort to trump the Court's rules through anticompetitive fiscal or regulatory arrangements, procured in and through the institution that is in the business of supplying that demand: the United States Congress.

As chapter 7 will show, that was not for lack of trying. However, the deep sectional divisions that produced the Civil War perforce made it impossible for the states to bargain around the constitutional norms and the Supreme Court's competitive federalism rules. And although the Civil War ended the exit threat that had hung over the Union, sectional dynamics retained much of their force. Under the peculiar conditions of the late nineteenth century, the then-dominant political coalition, based in the industrial states, used fiscal side payments (principally, the proceeds of the tariff) to purchase the acquiescence of states and state-based interests to the Supreme Court's construction of a competitive federal order. This constellation accommodated the country to the purest form of competitive federalism that the United States, and perhaps any democratic country, has ever known.

Competitive-federalism theorists are perennially torn between the normative attractions of their models and the recognition that competitive federalism is possible only under very unusual political conditions. The following chapters partake of that ambivalence. The American federalism of the late nineteenth century is not a model. It is a historical outlier, and the political conditions that stabilized it could not and did not last. Even so, there is merit in explaining why competitive federalism is the Founders' constitutional child and its cooperative replacement, a bastard. These chapters attend to the first part of the task.

CHAPTER FOUR

Commerce and Competition

Introduction: The Two-Sided Commerce Clause

Competitive federalism confronts two dangers: central interventions that destroy competition among states, and anticompetitive practices by junior governments (protectionism, exploitation, and balkanization). The constitutional design problem is to identify and stabilize a competitive equilibrium—put differently, to figure out a set of rules and arrangements that promises to minimize the joint costs of error on either side.

Although the problem can be traced throughout the constitutional architecture, one of its focal points is the Commerce Clause. On one side, the clause grants Congress the power to "regulate Commerce . . .among the several States." On the other side, the "negative" or "dormant" Commerce Clause is generally thought to forbid certain state interferences with interstate commerce, even in the absence of a congressional prohibition or regulation. On the affirmative side, the problem has been to cabin a power that—especially in conjunction with the Necessary and Proper Clause—appears to permit Congress to centralize or harmonize a vast range of economic activities. On the negative side, the problem has been to identify a firm constitutional basis and a workable conceptual framework for a judicially enforced dormant Commerce Clause.

In the modern understanding, the affirmative Commerce Clause extends to any and all economic conduct that affects interstate commerce, whereas the dormant Commerce Clause prohibits state taxes and regulations that discriminate against interstate commerce. That formulation, though, is a product of a long process of trial, error, and adaptation. This chapter traces roughly the first century of that process, beginning with the Supreme Court's antebellum interpretation of the Commerce Clause in a relative handful of notoriously inconclusive cases from *Gibbons v. Ogden* (1824) to *Cooley v. Board of Wardens* (1851). Still, the nineteenth century ended with a Commerce Clause that was strikingly well suited to the demands of a competitive economy and an equally competitive federalism. The trajectory, I hope to show, can be understood as a gradual approximation, under rapidly shifting economic and institutional conditions, of a competitive constitutional baseline.

Virtually all of the nineteenth-century action took place on the negative, "dormant" side of the Commerce Clause. In that context, the Supreme Court embraced a remarkably expansive conception of interstate commerce. It is widely thought that competitive federalism requires a small, strictly limited central government that provides ample room for decentralized decision making, but this is actually wrong. The states' room to compete is also a room to defect from the competitive ground rules. Competitive federalism is more likely to be the product of *broad* federal power over the economy, coupled with institutional norms and real-world conditions that bias the central government's output toward competition. One such set of conditions is legislative restraint and judicial dominance over the terms of interstate commerce. The conjunction of just these conditions—the Supreme Court's discovery of an expansive (dormant) Commerce Clause, coupled with legislative quiescence and judicial dominance over interstate commerce—explains the rise of a competitive federal Constitution over the course of the nineteenth century.

Whence the Dormant Commerce Clause?

The "dormant" Commerce Clause metaphor is a misnomer in two respects. First, "its intended point is that the *Commerce Clause* is always awake, even when *Congress* is asleep."[1] Second, the doctrine has for much of American constitutional history led a very vibrant existence and appeared, in various permutations, in hundreds of Supreme Court cases.[2] It was, however, off to a slow start. John Marshall's canonical Commerce Clause pronouncements in *Gibbons v. Ogden* date to 1824, more than three decades into the nation's existence. Prior to the Civil War, the Court decided no more than a dozen or so cases implicating the clause, over a very narrow range of interstate transactions and state laws. And not until 1872 would the Supreme Court unambiguously enjoin the operation of a state statute pursuant to the dormant Commerce Clause.[3] The picture, however, changed dramatically thereafter. By 1932, the dormant Commerce Clause had felled some 180 state laws, and it would retain much of its vitality throughout and after the New Deal.[4]

The dormant Commerce Clause is a *federalism* doctrine, and it is an unambiguously *competitive* doctrine. The affirmative commerce power lends itself to pro- or anticompetitive purposes: Congress may break monopolies or make them, liberate interstate commerce or restrict it, regulate commerce or balkanize it. The judicially enforced dormant Commerce Clause, in contrast, cuts in only one direction; regardless of its precise formulation, it mows down state-imposed obstacles to interstate commerce. The demise of those obstacles exposes producers in each state to interstate competition, bars states from procuring local advantages by means of exploiting outsiders, and compels states to compete for productive citizens and industries. The purpose of the dormant Commerce Clause is commonly couched in terms of "economic union" or "interstate harmony" rather than "competition." But the competitive effect is unmistakable and, if not exactly the object of the dormant Commerce Clause, then certainly its acknowledged result. The dormant Commerce Clause, the Supreme Court has said, encapsulates the proposition that no state may attempt to "suppress or mitigate the consequences of competition between the states."[5]

Notoriously, though, the dormant Commerce Clause is not literally *in* the Constitution. By its terms, the constitutional language—"Congress shall have Power . . . to regulate Commerce . . . among the several states"—does not prohibit the states from doing anything at all, and there are reasons against inferring such a prohibition. Article I, § 10 explicitly prohibits certain state interferences with interstate commerce—prominently, import and export duties, as well as duties of tonnage. In addition, the Privileges and Immunities Clause (Art. IV, § 2) compels each state to grant the citizens of all other states the same privileges and immunities that it grants its own citizens. In other words, state commercial discrimination against out-of-state citizens is verboten. Those specific prohibitions suggest that anything that is *not* prohibited remains permitted to the states until and unless Congress affirmatively exercises its power to regulate interstate commerce. On that theory, the negative Commerce Clause should be dead, not dormant.

In the late nineteenth century, this thinking found a powerful advocate in Harvard's James B. Thayer, and prominent modern-day scholars and justices have echoed his position. There is no exclusive commerce power, they say. The dormant Commerce Clause is pure politics—a free-trade equivalent of *Lochner* and its fanciful notions of substantive due process and liberty of contract.[6] However, the critics' position has never prevailed. Every Court in American history—nationalist and states' rights, activist and deferential, laissez-faire and decidedly not—has enforced some version of the doctrine. Why?

A first-cut answer is that one cannot make the Constitution work without the dormant Commerce Clause or something very much like it. Justice Robert H. Jackson captured that thought in calling the construct one of the Constitution's "great silences."[7] Oliver Wendell Holmes, no great fan of judicial creativity in constitutional matters, put the point directly. The nation, he famously remarked, could survive without judicial review (which, for what it's worth, is also not "in" the Constitution). It could *not* survive without the dormant Commerce Clause.[8] Felix Frankfurter, another apostle of judicial deference and sworn enemy of laissez-faire ideology, was the Woody Allen of the dormant Commerce Clause: although *Professor* Frankfurter may not have been afraid of its death, *Justice* Frankfurter did not want to be around for the event.[9] In short, even *Lochner*'s implacable enemies perceived a crucial difference between substantive due process and the dormant Commerce Clause: the Constitution works just fine without one but not without the other.

At a second, deeper level, one can understand the dormant Commerce Clause as a Marshallian mode of argument, operating on the Madisonian fear that the specified prohibitions of Article I, § 10 would be insufficient to police the states. Experience would soon bear Madison out. Some academic dispute surrounds the extent of commercial warfare among the states under the Articles of Confederation, as well as the question of how formative that experience was in the framing and ratification of the Constitution.[10] There is little disagreement, however, about the states' record *under* the Constitution. During the early nineteenth century, states acted as "masters in their own houses, imposing schemes of mercantile licensing and taxation, forbidding or conditioning the entry of unfavored articles of commerce, prescribing marketing practices and procedures, devising inspection laws to better their competitive position relative to sister states, in brief, acting freely on all matters respecting trade and traffic, whatever the interstate ramifications."[11] Nor did states behave any more cooperatively in later decades, when the constitutional rules had become much clearer. Throughout the nineteenth century, the supposedly uninhibited domestic market was in fact a system of "rivalistic state mercantilism."[12] The only meaningful political check on that conduct was the United States Supreme Court.

The Marshallian mode of argument is the presumption that the Founders were too wise and patriotic to give us an imperfect Constitution.[13] The Constitution fails to prohibit directly many things that would destroy the Union if left unchecked, such as state taxes on the Bank of the United States. It also fails to provide explicitly for a great many "necessary and proper" instruments, such as certain forms of federal jurisdiction or, for that matter, a federal authority to establish a Bank of the United States. However, Marshall and his contemporaries refrained from mobilizing the Constitution's deliberate minimalism against the Constitution itself. Rather, so long as the document would bear the construction, they inferred the prohibitions and powers that make the Constitution work, and work well, from its structure, general spirit, and "the genius of republican government"—*our* republican government, but also the general principles on which all republican government rests.[14]

Marshall did not conclusively embrace the dormant Commerce Clause on these (or any other) grounds. But he came very close, and the train of thought is reasonably straightforward. The specific prohibitions of Article I, § 10 and Article IV, § II, I suggested earlier, appear to cut against a "dormant Commerce Clause." On second thought, however, they *support* that construct. This is certainly so in a directional sense; parallel to the operation of the dormant Commerce Clause, the textual provisions entrust the judiciary, not the Congress, with policing state interferences that would prove detrimental to free internal commerce and interstate harmony. One could object, of course, that the textually prohibited forms of conduct—import and export duties, tonnage duties, state compacts, deprivations of privileges and immunities—are so distinctly and uniquely bad as to warrant special constitutional safeguards, whereas redress for more humdrum, inconsequential, and arguable state interferences with national purposes can—and given the structure of the Constitution, must—be left to Congress exclusively. Only an idiot, however, would write a Constitution of that import. A specific prohibition, Madison warned, already "supposes the disposition which will evade it."[15] That disposition is easily acted upon because all the directly prohibited state laws have close substitutes: any lawyer knows how to impose an import tax or a tonnage duty, or how to deprive out-of-state citizens of equal privileges and immunities, without actually saying so. Therefore, faithful judicial interpretation cannot rest on literalism or an implied premise of state-side brain death. It demands a constitutional safeguard against circumvention. That safeguard, we have come to call the "dormant Commerce Clause."

Four closely connected themes run through the Commerce Clause cases of the nineteenth century: a distinction between national and local affairs, a second distinction between interstate commerce and the states' police powers, the question of concurrent versus exclusive state and federal powers, and the question of federal supremacy. All four themes illustrate the functional, can't-do-without-it reasons for the dormant Commerce Clause, its procompetitive thrust, and its operation as a constitutional principle against circumvention. All four go back to the Supreme Court's first serious engagement with the Commerce Clause in *Gibbons v. Ogden* (1824).

Commerce and Competition

The famous *Gibbons* case presented the question of whether a monopoly charter issued by the State of New York to a steamboat ferry service on the Hudson River barred a potential rival from operating a competing ferry service between New Jersey and New York. The Supreme Court's clear answer was "no." Less clear was the basis of the decision. A concurring opinion by Justice Johnson contained the first unambiguous statement of the dormant Commerce Clause: states have no power to interfere with the commerce of the United States, regardless of whether or not Congress has chosen to prohibit the particular activity. John Marshall's majority opinion granted the "great force" of that argument but eventually backed off and instead held that the New York monopoly conflicted with the unencumbered exercise of a coastal trading license that the would-be competitors had obtained under a federal statute.

An important clue to the case and to the origin of the dormant Commerce Clause lies in asking why *Gibbons* was a Commerce Clause case. Why did Daniel Webster, counsel for plaintiffs, take that then-untested vehicle for a spin when other constitutional candidates seemed at hand? The short answer is that none of the alternatives held much promise. One candidate was the maritime jurisdiction of the United States. At the time of *Gibbons*, that jurisdiction was clearly established, and indeed, the 1789 Judiciary Act had given the federal courts near-exclusive maritime jurisdiction. But the Supreme Court's authority to administer federal common law in this domain was extremely sensitive, and the Court sought to avoid giving offense to the states—for example, by extending maritime jurisdiction only to the high seas and tidal waters rather than all navigable waters (which would have included inland waterways).[16] *Gibbons*, which did involve waters of the United States but also presented a direct confrontation with the state's control over its harbors, partakes of that caution.

Nor did the Constitution's explicit nondiscrimination provisions offer much help. Obviously, the Import-Export Clause did not cover the case.

More interesting, the Privileges and Immunities Clause did not cover it, either. The monopoly charter was originally held by New Yorkers. But they had apparently won it in a competition open to all comers, and by the time of *Gibbons*, both parties to the litigation were New Jersey citizens.[17] What is more, it was not at all clear that *any* state monopoly grant would be vulnerable to the clause, inasmuch as such grants excluded even the state's own citizens from operating a competing business. The only way to defeat that logic was to move the issue beyond the state's legislative jurisdiction. Hence, Webster's insistence that navigation constitutes interstate commerce. He won on that point, as he had to.

What else, though, constitutes "commerce among the states"? Later generations of scholars and justices would confidently aver that Marshall defined the commerce power "with a breadth never yet exceeded."[18] But although *Gibbons* contains some expansive passages (including Marshall's notorious definition of commerce as "intercourse"), closer examination suggests a different reading. Webster took care to confine his argument to commercial navigation among different states, as distinct both from other forms of interstate transport and from in-state navigation.[19] Marshall followed that lead. The only incontrovertible holding of *Gibbons* was that the commercial transport of persons between states and across the majestic Hudson constitutes "commerce among the states," and subsequent cases suggest that *Gibbons* was not meant to reach much further. For example, in *Willson v. Black-Bird Creek Marsh Co.* (1829), the Marshall Court sustained a state law authorizing the construction of a dam obstructing a navigable but small and in-state creek.[20] Even the constitutional status of railroads remained doubtful for quite some time.[21]

Marshall's expansive dicta, moreover, were accompanied by an insistence on the commerce power as an *enumerated* power. The enumeration implies a limitation—some line where the power ends and the residual (nondelegated, reserved) powers of the states begin. Because the Constitution has no name for and contains no systematic account of the reserved powers, the language for the federal-state demarcation must be borrowed from elsewhere. In *Gibbons*, Marshall takes two stabs at the problem. His first effort is the time-honored distinction—familiar from the debates over the Stamp Act and from the *Federalist*, and common currency at the time—between internal (state) affairs and the states' external conduct, or the sorts of things that "concern more states than one." "Interstate commerce" (as the Supreme Court would later say in shorthand, though Marshall did not) must be *commerce*, and it must be *among* states. That field, wide though it may be, does not encompass "that commerce, which is completely internal, which is carried on between man and man in a

State, or between different parts of the same State, and which does not extend to or affect other States." That formulation was hardly reassuring to states' rights apostles: it is hard to think of transactions that are "completely" internal or do not "affect" other states in some way. On a more conciliatory note, though, Marshall described the area of reserved powers as "that immense mass of legislation, which embraces every thing within the territory of a State, not surrendered to the general government."[22]

Marshall provides examples of that mass: "inspection laws, quarantine laws, health laws of every description, as well as laws for regulating the internal commerce of a State, and those which respect turnpike roads, ferries, &c."[23] Despite the suggestion of continuity ("the internal commerce of a State"), though, Marshall is no longer talking about an internal-external distinction. He is rather talking about a different distinction between the regulation of interstate commerce as such and what came to be known as the states' "police power," a copious category that encompasses just about any state law regarding the health, safety, and welfare of citizens and the general administration of a state's affairs, except perhaps a tax. The police power is not coterminous with "internal" state regulation because many exercises of the police power, such as inspection laws or laws respecting turnpikes etc., are anything but "completely internal."

Both the internal-external distinction and the distinction between interstate commerce and the police power would live a long and tortured life. After the Civil War, the territorial approach developed into a set of formal distinctions between commerce on the one hand and manufacture, production, mining, and agriculture on the other. The police-power approach gave rise to distinctions between "direct" and therefore prohibited state regulations of interstate commerce and permissible state laws that regulate interstate commerce only "indirectly" or incidentally. Both distinctions suffer from the same basic difficulty: they are indispensable at a conceptual level but all too often fail at an empirical, descriptive level. *Some* external-internal distinction is required by the constitutional text and structure. Likewise, there must be *some* meaningful distinction between a legitimate state policy objective and protectionism in disguise, lest interstate commerce and competition founder on what Justice Holmes called "the convenient apologetics of the police power."[24] Yet in the cases that become the stuff of political conflict and of litigation, the categories typically do not refer to physically separate sets of activities. Usually, they refer to the *same* activities under different descriptions. There is no way of drawing the distinctions without reference to their purpose—in other words, without some antecedent, normative idea of how the constitutional system as a whole is supposed to work. The nineteenth-century development of the Commerce Clause can be understood in light of one such conception: competition.

Internal-External. If the commerce power extends no farther than to activities that occur physically outside a state, it covers little beyond commerce on the navigable waters of the United States. That observation had occurred to Marshall in *Gibbons*, and he took care to spell it out more fully in the very next Commerce Clause case, *Brown v. Maryland* (1827). At issue was a Maryland license tax on wholesalers dealing in imported goods. The Court deemed the statute to violate both the Import-Export Clause and a federal Commerce Clause statute. The fact that the tax applied to the in-state sale of goods rather than imports (or the act of importing) per se was of no consequence. The power of Congress, Marshall said, "is coextensive with the subject on which it acts, and cannot be stopped at the external boundary of a State, but must enter its interior."[25] Similarly, shortly after Marshall's death, the Court held that the Commerce Clause authorized Congress to criminalize the theft of goods from shipwrecked vessels even above the waterline and within state boundaries. And in an opinion by Chief Justice Taney, the Court determined that Congress could regulate, pursuant to the Commerce Clause, service vessels that never left the safe harbor of Mobile, Alabama.[26]

Cases of this latter sort—and note that they precede the New Deal by many decades—are best understood and analyzed not as Commerce Clause cases simpliciter but as applications of the Necessary and Proper Clause.[27] The theft of stranded goods, for example, is neither commerce nor interstate, but the federal criminalization is necessary and proper to protect commerce among the states. Among other advantages, that analysis points to the central or, at any rate, the initial rationale for an expansive Commerce Clause. That rationale was the recognition that *the first and last leg of any interstate commercial transaction*—the departure and docking of a ferry, the formation and execution of a contract, the sale of interstate goods at auction—*must of needs be local events.* More often than not, though, the power to block the local event is the power to block the entire transaction. Thus, the commerce power "must enter the interior" of each state: "The grant [of power] should be as extensive as the mischief."[28]

Should Mr. Gibbons's ferry be permitted to steam into the "local" New York dock—or be forced to row the last mile? Is an insurance contract between parties from different states tied to the place of execution or performance—or an instrument of interstate commerce? Is a state law requiring a transcontinental express train to stop at every hamlet a "local" regulation—or an imposition on interstate commerce? Is a license tax on the privilege to trade in foreign goods a local event—or an obstruction of interstate commerce?[29] As cases of the sort multiplied, the Supreme Court very nearly jettisoned the internal-external distinction and, by the 1880s, "came close to announcing that the nation's economy was a seamless web stretching from sea to shining sea—a legal vision that is usually credited to the New Deal."[30]

Not until the New Deal did the Court pursue that vision to its conclusion. For more than a half-century, the justices continued to mobilize the internal-external distinction and its close cousins (such as the distinction between manufacture and commerce)—not, however, out of fondness for empty formalisms, but rather on account of an institutional and profoundly competitive calculus. The commerce power expanded in the context of the *dormant* Commerce Clause. In that context, more federal judicial power is unambiguously procompetitive, while a residual domain of reserved state power threatens to operate as a license to expropriate interstate commerce and those who engage in it. Full *judicial* control over interstate commerce, however, drags in its wake full *congressional* authority over the same range of conduct. When Congress utilizes that authority, the results are bound to be anything but procompetitive. In fact, federalism and the states might quickly go out of business altogether. That recognition, we shall see later, prompted the Supreme Court in those decades to hang on to the internal-external categories, reluctantly and in full awareness of the costs of pulling back at the dormant Commerce Clause front.

Police Powers. Marshall's internal-external distinction in *Gibbons* focused on the situs of any given transaction; his second distinction between interstate commerce and the states' police powers, on the nature or purpose of the state's regulation. In later decades, "the police power" was at times used as a subject-matter distinction and as a categorical limit to the commerce power.[31] That has to be wrong: there is no implied limitation, police power or otherwise, to the Supremacy Clause. The police-power analysis makes perfect sense, however, when it serves to distinguish in the first instance not between inviolable state and federal spheres but *between different types of state law.* A "police power" regulation is a state law that serves a legitimate public purpose. The opposite is what the nineteenth century called "partial" regulation, meaning naked interest group transfers.[32] In the Commerce Clause arena, that vital distinction plays out as a means of arresting factionalism at the state borders while protecting legitimate exercises of state autonomy against federal overreach. Table 4.1 illustrates the train of thought.

Table 4.1. Commerce Clause trade-offs

	Police-power justifications	
Interstate effects	Weak	Strong
Weak	Null set (I)	"Indirect effect" (III)
Strong	"Direct effect"/"discrimination" (II)	Hard cases (IV)

The left-hand column contains "partial" legislation. States are free to stage rent-seeking festivals, provided there is little or no cost to interstate commerce (quadrant I). Commerce Clause challenges to those sorts of laws are bound to be rare because few plaintiffs will come forward. Tolerance, however, must end where factionalism spills across states borders. The pre–New Deal Court captured laws of this description under the headings of a "direct regulation" of interstate commerce; the post–New Deal Court invalidates them under the heading of "discrimination" (quadrant II). In the right-hand column, a state law with a powerful police-power rationale but a modest effect on interstate commerce (quadrant III) qualifies as a permissible "indirect effect." Quadrant IV contains the hard cases, wherein potent public-regarding state purposes conflict with equally potent Commerce Clause effects. The police-power/Commerce Clause analysis attempts to reduce this set to a minimum. Close scrutiny of the state's proffered police-power justifications kicks the outcome either upward or leftward. The scheme captures what the Court is actually doing in dormant Commerce Clause cases (as distinct from what it says it is doing): it stacks up the states' police power justifications against the costs to interstate commerce.

To some minds, that inquiry seems far removed from a genuinely constitutional test.[33] But the analysis is in fact closely analogous to the Import-Export Clause (Art. I, § 10), which reads as follows:

> No State shall, without the Consent of the Congress, lay any Imposts or Duties on Imports or Exports, except what may be absolutely necessary for executing its inspection Laws: and the net Produce of all Duties and Imposts, laid by any State on Imports or Exports, shall be for the Use of the Treasury of the United States; and all such Laws shall be subject to the Revision and Controul of the Congress.

State duties are an imposition on external, interstate commerce, which Congress could mow down under even the most restrictive interpretation of the Commerce Clause. Evidently, however, the Founders considered such duties sufficiently destructive to erect special safeguards: a requirement of congressional preapproval and a requirement that excess funds be paid over to the United States Treasury. The clause exempts state inspection laws—on the *Gibbons* intuition, which would maintain its hold throughout the nineteenth century, that such laws are the embodiment of health and safety (read: police-power) legislation.[34] Reflecting a fear that states will abuse the exemption as a subterfuge for protectionism, the clause ordains that duties imposed for purposes of administering inspection laws must be *absolutely* necessary. It then confiscates the states' excess duties, which is a good reason for states not to bother to collect them at all.

The Import-Export Clause allows only one police-power purpose (inspection); demands an extremely tight nexus between that purpose and the imposition ("absolutely necessary"); and confiscates the states' surplus (that is, the difference between the proceeds of inspection duties and the cost of administering the system). The dormant Commerce Clause of needs covers a far wider range of impositions and justifications. Moreover, the Supreme Court cannot order the states' surplus to be deposited in the U.S. Treasury; hence, the applicable tests must block surplus accumulation at the front end. The structure of the constitutional test, however, remains parallel to the Import-Export Clause.

The analysis surfaces most clearly in cases dealing with state quarantine laws.[35] *City of New York v. Miln* (1837) upheld a state law that required all incoming boats into New York to first provide a passenger roster and then to post bond against their becoming charges against the City of New York—a good way to make the operators more selective in choosing whom to transport. Most crucial, this provision did not generate excess funds that could be diverted for unrelated purposes. In the *Passenger Cases* (1849), in contrast, one of the defendant states (New York) dedicated the proceeds it received from a de facto head tax on immigration to maintaining a marine hospital, with the surplus to be paid "to the treasurer of the Society for the Reformation of Juvenile Delinquents in the city of New York, for the use of the society."[36] The state defended this arrangement as a police-power exercise to protect public health, safety, and morals. By all appearances, however, the state had imposed a protective tariff in order to fund its own local operations, wholly apart from any health or safety risk arising from the movement of persons across state lines. Justice McLean, in one of many inchoate opinions rendered in the case, was probably right to invalidate the tax on the ground that no state should be allowed to finance its entire operations through impositions on interstate commerce.[37] But the devil is often in the details. The size of the exaction and the direction of the payment count for a great deal in the analysis.

Cooley v. Board of Wardens of Port of Philadelphia (1851), one of the last antebellum Commerce Clause cases, confirms the point. At issue was a Pennsylvania ordinance that required incoming vessels from out of state to employ a local pilot—unless they chose to use their own pilot and to contribute a sum equal to one-half the required fee to a pension fund for "the relief of distressed and decayed pilots, their widows and children."[38] Once again the generation and distribution of surplus funds escaped the Import-Export clause; once again, the protectionist elements that loomed in the *Passenger Cases* were at work. The Court sustained the regulation as relating to matters of peculiar local importance, which sounds persuasive so long as one follows the Court in defining the subject-matter as "pilotage." But although there is a potent case for requiring local pilots for the Philadelphia harbor, a statutory obligation to contribute to the local pension fund bears a less compelling relation to port safety. And when (as in *Cooley*) the local regulation is limited to ships from foreign nations and other states, and when the pilot requirement is waivable but the pension payments are not, the suspicion hardens that the *Cooley* Court should have probed more deeply.[39]

In *Cooley*, as in the earlier decisions in *Miln* and the *Passenger Cases* and as in countless later cases, the dormant Commerce Clause functions as a backstop means of controlling state impositions that operate as close equivalents of unequivocally and directly prohibited state laws—prominently, import tariffs and duties of tonnage. Unlike the internal-external distinction, the police power inquiry treats interstate commerce as a seamless web; in the fashion of the Import-Export Clause, it seeks to square the constitutional mandate to protect interstate commerce with the state's police power justifications. The explicit pronouncement of this test (effectively, the analysis captured in table 4.1) would come only in 1938.[40] In later decades, the test hardened into an antidiscrimination principle, which uses a state's willingness to treat its own citizens no better than outsiders as a proxy for a legitimate police power rationale. In that formulation, the dormant Commerce Clause looks less like an Import-Export analogue and more like an extension of another procompetitive and antifactional constitutional provision, the Privileges and Immunities Clause. That close proximity, though, is as old as *Brown v. Maryland*, which could and perhaps should have been decided as a discrimination case.[41] It reflects, not a desperate judicial contrivance to find a home for a vagrant doctrine, but rather the continuity of that doctrine with the constitutional structure.

Exclusivity. The dormant Commerce Clause doctrine is closely associated with the notion of an *exclusive* commerce power. (In fact, so long as one insists that that doctrine must derive from that specific clause alone, it is hard to see where else it could come from.) Although widely doubted nowadays, the exclusive commerce power was the orthodox position in Federalist circles for well over a generation after the founding. Daniel Webster's argument in *Gibbons v. Ogden* denounced the very idea of a general concurrent power in the States as "insidious and dangerous." Admit it, Webster warned, and "no one can say where it will stop."[42] Even Anti-Federalists implicitly conceded the force of the exclusivity position and instead fought their nationalist foes over the scope of that exclusive power. To some extent, the initial appeal of an exclusive commerce power has to do with the fact that its inherent logic—"one problem, one regulator"—struck the Founders and their immediate successors as more compelling than it seems to us modern sophisticates, wedded as we are to the idea that economic complexity requires regulators and tax collectors to descend in swarms. Two additional factors, however, help to explain why an initially compelling exclusive commerce power became less so over time: the scope of the commerce power and judicial expectations with respect to the congressional response.

"On the whole," a close student of the Founding era concluded more than six decades ago, "the evidence supports the view that, *as to the restricted field which was deemed at the time to constitute regulation of commerce*, the grant of power to the federal government presupposed the withdrawal of authority pari passu from the states."[43] The italicized phrase is crucial. It makes perfect sense to treat the Commerce Clause as exclusive in venues that no state can claim as its own—the lower Hudson River, for example: full speed ahead for steamboat traffic, and damn the local monopolies. However, as the scope of "commerce among the states" expands, the states' power to govern their own affairs diminishes. And yet, the Supreme Court needed an expansive commerce power to give bite to the dormant Commerce Clause. Therein lies a dilemma. Exclusivity and an expansive commerce power both serve the same purpose—to block state interferences with a free, competitive internal market. Paradoxically, however, the constructs work against each other: as one becomes more plausible, the other becomes less so.

The second factor affecting the exclusivity doctrine, judicial expectations vis-à-vis Congress, is best explained by recalling Hamilton's argument that a federal power to enact "uniform" laws implies exclusivity.[44] Several years before *Gibbons*, the Marshall Court had considered that argument—and rejected it. In *Sturges v. Crowninshield* (1819), it held that there was no exclusive or dormant Bankruptcy Clause, notwithstanding the congressional power to make "uniform" laws of bankruptcy.[45] In the absence of affirmative congressional legislation, the Court said, states were free to enact bankruptcy and insolvency laws (although the state laws at issue in *Sturges* were found unconstitutional on other grounds). What, then, emboldened Webster in *Gibbons* to argue for an exclusive Commerce Clause, and why did Marshall find "great force" in that contention?[46] The most plausible answer has to do with institutional considerations and, in particular, with the outcomes attendant to the expected congressional response, or rather the lack thereof. If a dormant, exclusive Bankruptcy Clause bars states from enacting bankruptcy laws, then *no* bankruptcy law will exist unless Congress acts—which for most of the nineteenth century, it didn't.[47] In contrast, congressional inaction in the wake of a dormant Commerce Clause ruling brings about the desired state of affairs—commerce and competition. Nothing irregular happens if Congress fails to act because the judicial injunction against state impositions *is* the regulation. The exclusive national commerce power flows naturally toward the competitive baseline and parallel to the terms of the grant of power.

The difficulty is that the exclusivity construction depends on the certainty that Congress will fail to respond; for what happens when it does? Suppose (by way of real-world example) the Court declares that certain state liquor regulations violate the dormant Commerce Clause, and Congress responds by authorizing those regulations: is that federal statute constitutional? The tempting answer is yes. The dormant Commerce Clause is not a hard constitutional rule but rather a rule of constitutional common law, which governs only until and unless Congress says otherwise. Constitutional law abounds with such rules—for a famous example, the rule that states may not tax the instruments of the United States government.[48] That answer, however, is highly suspect if the commerce power is truly exclusive: a power of that nature cannot be delegated to the states.

Both problems—the scope of exclusivity and the delegation problem—powerfully affected the development of the Commerce Clause in the late nineteenth century, but their origins already appear in the antebellum cases. *Brown* illustrates the problem of scope. Exclusive federal control over import duties is not some constitutional inference; it is right there in the text. How far, though, does the prohibition against the states extend? Marshall responded by yoking the state's license tax to the plainly prohibited end, the imposition of a duty or impost on imports. The two taxes differ in their incidence in that a license tax on importers is not sensitive to the volume of goods sold, while the direct tax on imports is. But the need to prevent the circumvention of the constitutional prohibition against taxes on imports led Marshall to strike down the tax on importers as a noxious variation of a tax on imports. Justice Thompson's dissent questioned the coherence of that principle because it barred state duties only on the first in-state wholesale transaction, by wholesalers. By its logic, Thompson argued, the purported principle should forbid state-imposed duties on imported goods at *any* stage of sale and distribution—in Thompson's mind, an obviously untenable proposition.[49]

Marshall attempted to cut off this difficulty by suggesting, without any great confidence, that the constitutional injunction applied so long as imported goods remained in their "original package." That doctrine would gain notoriety in the late nineteenth century, when it was read to prohibit the state regulation or taxation of liquor in its "original form or package" (while permitting regulation once the package had been broken, deliberately or by accident). In that deployment, the doctrine produced much litigation, legislation, jokes of the "Professor, your package of books is leaking" variety, and an unending stream of sneering law review articles. The legal-realist snorts, however, miss the question of why the justices thought they needed the obviously ludicrous original package doctrine, and they tend to miss its crucial flaw.[50] The need arises from the exclusivity premise: interstate commerce has to stop someplace, lest the states go out of business. The flaw is that any stopping point will produce sharp discontinuities. Although that difficulty arises under any doctrine that seeks to identify a point at which interstate commerce ends and internal commerce begins, exclusivity heightens the contradiction, for it suggests that federal and state jurisdictions are *mutually* exclusive. Thus, interstate commerce is either immune from any state imposition, including impositions that apply to in-state actors and transactions. That sort of unwarranted advantage looks more like forced entry than like competition. Or else, interstate commerce is subject to expropriation. A dormant Commerce Clause of that description is both implausible and unstable. Regardless of where one draws the line, it will crumble under the weight of incessant litigation and clever attempts at evasion.[51]

Cooley illustrates both a related aspect of the scope problem and, in blazing light, the delegation problem. Justice Curtis's opinion deemed the commerce power exclusive with respect to subjects that "are in their nature national, or admit only of one uniform system, or plan of regulation."[52] Though widely criticized as arbitrary and incoherent, the *Cooley* formulation at least tackled the scope problem head-on.[53] Moreover, what the *Cooley* Court was angling for—but lacked the constitutional and economic language to express—was a solution to one of federalism's central coordination problems: the state-sponsored disruption of network industries, or what the Supreme Court later came to call "balkanization." The problem with the test is that it is grossly underinclusive. While capturing cases of balkanization, it fails to cover equally common cases of protectionism and exploitation. To illustrate, *Cooley* appears to bar prohibitive taxes and regulations on railroad property but not on the property of supermarket chains, which can always renounce the local business in a state without suffering a mortal blow to their operations elsewhere. On account of that incongruity, the Supreme Court soon recognized that *Cooley* could be *a* test but not *the* test for an exclusive Commerce Clause.

Cooley fared no better with respect to its second prong—the delegation problem. If the commerce power is truly exclusive, Justice Curtis pronounced, "certainly Congress cannot re-grant, or in any manner reconvey to the states that power."[54] At some level, over some range, that has to be right. If *Cooley* nonetheless proved "the zenith of the no-delegation school of constitutional thought,"[55] that is because the proposition cannot be *generally* right. Suppose the Court in an ambiguous case sets aside state law on the grounds that the subject admits only of one plan of regulation (think passenger service requirements for delayed aircraft).[56] Suppose further that Congress disagrees: in that event, it is difficult to fathom a congressional response that would *not* regrant or reconvey to the states the power they just lost at the hands of the Supreme Court. It is equally difficult to see why the negative Commerce Clause should then be understood to constrain the full and free congressional exercise of the affirmative Commerce Clause.

The delegation problem was a prominent theme of Commerce Clause jurisprudence between the Civil War and the New Deal, and the Supreme Court experimented with varying solutions. In one line of cases, it declared that the dormant Commerce Clause barred state interferences with interstate commerce not on account of exclusivity but because congressional silence was tantamount to a congressional "will" that commerce shall be free. That formulation certainly avoids the delegation problem—but only at the considerable price of resting the dormant Commerce Clause on a nonexistent congressional will. In other cases, the Court held that Congress could constitutionally "divest" an article of commerce (prominently, liquor in its original package) of its interstate nature; or that Congress could, without running afoul of the nondelegation rule, retroactively adopt varying state laws as its own, as opposed to a prospective surrender of federal authority to the dictates of future state laws.[57] Predictably, those attempts to save the nondelegation village by burning it down proved unavailing. In the end, the Court concluded that the commerce power is concurrent over virtually its entire range.[58]

The de facto demise of the nondelegation doctrine had, and has, undeniable advantages. It clears the way for a broad dormant Commerce Clause, based on the realization that an interstate commerce that must "struggle for Congressional action to make it free" is already dead.[59] Moreover, it avoids the awkward suggestion that the judiciary's authority under the Commerce Clause power is broader than that of Congress. It does, however, have two serious drawbacks—a doctrinal problem and a competition problem. The doctrinal problem, which the Old Court clearly perceived, is that the demise of exclusivity might leave the dormant Commerce Clause—so long as it is viewed as a clause-bound *Commerce Clause* doctrine—without a solid foundation. The competition problem is that a Commerce Clause sans exclusivity can address state laws that look like infractions on interstate commerce or on the rights and interests of other states—protectionism, exploitation, and balkanization. What, though, if states *agree* on such policies and demand and obtain them from Congress?

Against that anticompetitive threat, a nonexclusive Commerce Clause is helpless. Its very premise is that the dormant Commerce Clause truly goes to sleep when Congress has spoken. In the twentieth century, when Congress began to speak with regularity, the difficult theoretical question of congressional "reconveyances" caused a learned, long-running, but eventually inconsequential dispute between the Harvard and Columbia law faculties. The objections to a redelegation of federal commerce powers, a prominent participant summarized in 1954, remained "formidable."[60] They had not, however, prevented "a flexible and resourceful cooperative-federalism"—that is, a federalism that offers the states a ready congressional escape from the competitive demands of the dormant Commerce Clause.

Supremacy's Domain. The faithful judicial construction of constitutional norms, we have seen, requires an interpretive rule or principle against state circumvention. The same anticircumvention rule operates at the level of statutory (rather than constitutional) construction. It is elementary that federal law trumps any contravening state law, and by the time of *Gibbons*, even Anti-Federalists conceded that the Supremacy Clause to that extent meant what it said. It is not easy to say, however, what constitutes a contradiction or conflict between federal and state law. If federal law tells a private citizen to do *A* and state law tells him to do *B* instead, the conflict is manifest. What, though, if state law says "more than *A*"—for example, by requiring a state permit on top of a federal coastal trading license? The principle against circumvention says that federal statutes must be read to block such state laws along with direct violations, lest political compromises arduously hammered out in Congress founder on a barrage of hostile state legislation. In the modern era, this intuition is captured in a doctrine of "implied preemption." That term was unknown in the nineteenth century, but the doctrine itself plainly existed. The Supreme Court applied it under a variety of constitutional clauses, from the Militia Clauses to the Fugitive Slave Clause.[61] The principal field of action, though, was the Commerce Clause. Here, the statutory construction principle against circumvention is continuous with the dormant Commerce Clause, which forbids certain state laws when Congress has remained silent; surely, a like prohibition ought to attach when Congress has spoken, albeit not very clearly or exhaustively. Webster's *Gibbons* argument captured the affinity between the dormant Commerce Clause and statutory preemption:

> The States may legislate, it is said, wherever Congress has not made a *plenary* exercise of its power. But who is to judge whether Congress has made this *plenary* exercise of power? Congress has acted on this power; it has done all that it deemed wise; and are the States now to do whatever Congress has left undone? Congress makes such rules as, in its judgment, the case requires; and those rules, whatever they are, constitute the *system*.
>
> All useful regulation does not consist in restraint; and that which Congress sees fit to leave free, is a part of its regulation, as much as the rest.[62]

It may seem odd to infer a prohibition against the states from statutory silence. But then, what is the alternative? A concurrent state power that reaches right up to a literal constitutional or statutory prohibition invites states to do by evasion and subterfuge what they may no longer do directly, thus defeating the purpose of those prohibitions.

Gibbons itself illustrates a related point—the potential of broad statutory constructions to serve as a close substitute for an (exclusive) dormant Commerce Clause. There was no need to decide whether the Commerce Clause was exclusive, Marshall wrote in reply to Webster's argument and Justice Johnson's concurrence, because the federal statute at issue had affirmatively foreclosed New York's monopoly grant. That, though, seems doubtful, if not downright "esoteric."[63] The federal statute designated certain U.S. vessels as "entitled to the privileges of ships or vessels employed in the coasting trade" and established a procedure for granting licenses to that effect, whence Marshall inferred that a federal license conferred a "right to trade." Chancellor Kent, in the New York decisions in *Gibbons*, had read the statute as simply freeing American vessels from the duties and inconveniences that were routinely encountered by foreign vessels operating in American waters, and Justice Johnson's concurrence in *Gibbons* took the same position.[64] One could say, perhaps, that state monopoly grants would deprive American ships of their trading advantages and, to that extent, "conflict" with the federal coasting license. Even that latitudinarian construction, though, effectively substitutes a regulatory statute that Congress could have enacted for the mercantilist statute that it did enact.[65]

Marshall pressed a similarly forced construction of a federal statute in *Brown*. In the Commerce Clause portion of his opinion, he invoked a federal tariff statute "which authorize[d] importation" on payment of certain duties by merchants and thereby, according to Marshall, established a federal "right to sell," which states could not then encumber by levying taxes on its exercise.[66] The point of the tariff law, though, was to distinguish foreign from domestic goods, not to allow importers to ply their trade without hindrance by the states. And because merchants had a "right to trade" with or without special leave from Congress, it is hard to see what the tariff law could add to their constitutional position.[67]

It is not altogether clear how dispositive the federal statutes really were in *Gibbons* or *Brown*. Marshall's reliance on an act of Congress in *Gibbons* may have been an effort to avoid a decision on the exclusivity question in the very first Commerce Clause case to reach the Court. The statutory riff in *Brown* may be dicta as the Court had already found the Maryland tax to violate the Import-Export Clause. And Marshall sidestepped statutory niceties when he found it convenient to do so.[68] Statutory preemption may only be as potent as the surrounding context makes it.

Behind the apparent confusion lurks the same difficult institutional, competitive calculus that appears in the dormant Commerce Clause cases of the late nineteenth century. A statutory preemption doctrine that unequivocally displaces concurrent state power is profoundly procompetitive. Even if the federal statute is itself anticompetitive in substance, wholesale preemption will bar states from piling additional or differing demands on top of the federal floor. In nineteenth-century parlance, the system will remain "dual": private parties confront a single (federal or state) requirement and regulator, not a cascade of impositions. Accordingly, the Supreme Court in the late nineteenth century administered a doctrine of "latent exclusivity," which left states free to regulate unless and until Congress had spoken—at which point any and all state regulation in that field had to give way, regardless of whether or not they "conflicted" with federal law and regardless of whether Congress had intended that result. The plausibility and the effects of that arrangement, however, hang on the assumption that the Commerce Clause has limits and, moreover, on judicial expectations concerning the disposition of Congress: combine latent exclusivity with a busybody Congress and a limitless Commerce Clause, and the system threatens to collapse into the center. Reasons of this sort eventually prompted the Supreme Court to jettison latent exclusivity and to adopt a far more state-friendly preemption doctrine.[69]

Conclusion

The Supreme Court's Commerce Clause watchword throughout the nineteenth century was "union"—political and economic integration, not state competition. Under the conditions of the nineteenth century, however, those turned out to be the same things. The Constitution, both in its specific provisions and its general structure, provided the raw materials for a competitive federalism, and it established a federal judiciary with the legal authority and the institutional incentives to give force and meaning to those provisions and that structure. Congress, meanwhile and for the duration of a century, made few meaningful contributions to the crucial integrative task of regulating interstate commerce. The field was dominated by the Supreme Court, and that meant integration had to proceed on competitive terms or not at all.

The dormant Commerce Clause is one manifestation of that dynamic. Its purpose, I have argued, was to prevent states from accomplishing through subterfuge and evasion ends that are prohibited by the Constitution. The logic is not altogether inescapable. One could contend, for example, that it rests on an exaggerated fear of the states' centrifugal tendencies. States, like all commercial republics (except perhaps more so), "will never be disposed to waste themselves in ruinous contentions with each other. They will be governed by mutual interest, and will cultivate a spirit of mutual amity and concord."[70] That cheerful expectation was widely held at the time of the Founding, and it reverberates today in neoliberal trade and federalism theories. The Constitution, in contrast, rests on the contention that theories of this sort are too unreliable to serve "as a practical maxim for the direction of our political conduct."[71] In a world without politics, federalism is an assignment or coordination problem. In the real world, it is first and foremost a control problem. The dormant Commerce Clause was a judicial answer to that problem. We shall see in the next chapter that it was an *indispensable* answer: no other doctrine could do the job.

CHAPTER FIVE

Corporations

Introduction

The subject of this chapter is an oft-told but endlessly fascinating story: the rise of corporate capitalism in nineteenth-century America. In the early years of the Republic, a relative handful of corporations operated under special, single-issue state charters. Often, the charters conferred monopolistic privileges, and corporations' operations were restricted to the chartering state. Corporate charters had the advantage of allowing the pooling of large sums of money (often for large infrastructure projects), and states competed with each other for capital in the national and international markets. But there was no state competition for corporate charters. A century later, corporations had become the dominant form of American business, and they operated under general incorporation laws rather than special legislative charters. Chartered in a single state of their own choosing, they competed freely (though by no means unmolested) in all states. Conversely, states competed vigorously for the opportunity to issue charters.

Both of these arrangements—the national operation of corporations (with its attendant tendency to erode local monopolies) and state competition for corporate charters—are central to the transformation of the United States from economic backwater into global powerhouse, from a fragmented, agrarian economy into large-scale, dynamic corporate capitalism.

Both are profoundly competitive. Both are products of law and legal institutions. In those respects, this chapter covers now-familiar ground. But the subject provides occasion to introduce two additional themes.

First, the controversy over the legal status of business corporations that raged over the nineteenth century illustrates the interdependence of legal doctrines. Chapter 4 alluded to the Supreme Court's aggressive deployment of the dormant Commerce Clause—after a handful of mostly inconclusive antebellum cases—in scores of cases beginning in the 1870s. This chapter will reveal the reason for that development: one cannot protect interstate commerce without protecting actors *in* interstate commerce. The dormant Commerce Clause provided a means of protecting corporations *at a time when other clauses and doctrines did not*. Its meteoric rise can only be understood in that context.

Second, the chapter illustrates both the force of the Constitution's institutional commitments and the demand-driven dynamics of constitutional construction. Judicial doctrine is not wholly self-directed; much of it depends on the ebb and flow of cases and on the litigants' choices. Alexander Hamilton, as noted in chapter 2, put confidence in "the unbridled spirit" of "the commercial part of America," which would deploy its entrepreneurial spirit on constitutional as well as commercial margins. So it came to pass, on the constitutional ground Hamilton had anticipated: the Privileges and Immunities Clause and the federal courts' diversity jurisdiction.

Of Privileges, Immunities, and Jurisdiction

The nineteenth century witnessed a protracted struggle over the "citizenship" status of corporations. It implicated two constitutional provisions: the Privileges and Immunities Clause (Art. IV, § 2, Cl.1) and the grant of federal diversity jurisdiction in Article III—that is, the extension of the judicial power of the United States to controversies "between a State and Citizens of another State" and "between Citizens of different States."

The Privileges and Immunities Clause declares that "the Citizens of each State shall be entitled to all Privileges and Immunities of Citizens in the several States." That formulation encapsulates Article IV of the Articles of Confederation:

> The better to secure and perpetuate mutual friendship and intercourse among the people of the different States in this union, the free inhabitants of each of these States, paupers, vagabonds and fugitives from justice excepted, shall be entitled to all privileges and immunities of free citizens in the several

States; and the people of each State shall have free ingress and regress to and from any other State, and shall enjoy therein all the privileges of trade and commerce, subject to the same duties, impositions and restrictions as the inhabitants thereof respectively.[1]

In a confusion of words that Madison described as "remarkable," Article IV speaks variously of "free inhabitants," "free citizens," "people," and again "inhabitants."[2] In keeping with the Constitution's overall economy of language, the Convention adopted the single term "citizens," deleted the "paupers" exception, and dropped the language following the semicolon—evidently on the theory that the "privileges of trade and commerce" were already encompassed by "Privileges and Immunities" of citizens. In substantially that form, the clause emerged from the Convention's Committee on Detail. It engendered very little discussion and so entered the Constitution as a brief, confidently stated nondiscrimination rule.[3]

The principal change between the Articles and the Constitution is the enforcement mechanism. The constitutional enforcement agency is the United States Supreme Court; and on account of the interstate constellation of cases that are likely to arise under the Privileges and Immunities Clause, the principal enforcement path is diversity jurisdiction. Few clauses in the Constitution are yoked together so intimately. The substantive and the jurisdictional grant go together, and both refer to "citizens."[4]

The Privileges and Immunities Clause embodies a fiercely procompetitive principle: citizens choose their state, not the other way around. Whatever exactly may be embraced under "privileges and immunities," moreover, the commercial core is unmistakable. Citizens may freely enter and exit each state for commercial purposes and, while on the premises, may conduct business in the same way, on the same terms, as the host state's own citizens. All this is pretty much beyond serious argument. However, the question of whether *corporations* enjoy protection under the clause was intensely controversial and, moreover, of enormous practical consequence for much of the nineteenth century. Treat corporations as "citizens" under the Privileges and Immunities Clause, and state (as well as private) economic competition will be unleashed with full force. Deny them that status, and state protectionism will thrive: each state has a right to exclude corporations, which implies a right to admit them on any condition a state may see fit to impose. Treat corporations as legal entities whose citizenship status in the chartering state holds good in all states, and they gain access to federal courts and their diversity jurisdiction; declare them legal constructs that "cannot be found" outside the incorporating state's territory, and corporations are at risk of forfeiting the federal courts' protection.

The Supreme Court's answer to the problem was ambivalent throughout the nineteenth century and in some ways has remained so. Corporations have *never* counted as citizens for purposes of the Privileges and Immunities Clause (or after the enactment of the Fourteenth Amendment, as citizens for purposes of the Privileges *or* Immunities Clause of that amendment).[5] In contrast, the general rule for diversity jurisdiction, from the 1850s forward, was that corporations were to be "deemed" citizens of their state of incorporation (and of no other state), regardless of their inability to attain that status under the Privileges and Immunities Clause. It is difficult to think of a constitutional justification for that dual regime and to believe that "citizen" should mean one thing in Article III and another in Article IV, especially in light of the close connection between the clauses at issue.

Throughout the contentious debate, that connection remained present to combatants on all sides. The opponents of diversity jurisdiction—at various times, debtor interests and their political patrons, Populists, Progressives, and New Dealers—often insisted that the Privileges and Immunities Clause, read in context, can apply only to natural persons. Ergo, their argument runs, neither the Court nor for that matter Congress can constitutionally extend the protection of the clause, *or of diversity jurisdiction*, to corporations.[6] Hamiltonian apostles of nationalism and commercialism tended to run the argument in the opposite direction, from jurisdiction to citizenship: surely, individual citizens within one state cannot be deprived of access to federal court just because they chose to organize as a corporation rather than a partnership.[7] Defining the range of the Privileges and Immunities Clause on the grounds of "naturalness" is bad essentialism. What one needs is a coherent theory of the purpose of the clause. About that purpose, there is no shred of doubt; see *Federalist* 80. And if corporations, as the dominant form of interstate commerce, are excluded from the reach of that bedrock clause, the constitutional purpose—"the basis of the union"—is defeated.

What, then, accounts for the appeal and stability of a constitutional formula—corporate citizenship for diversity but not for Privileges and Immunities purposes—that looked untenable to so many? Sheer fortuity, we shall see, had something to do with it. So did slavery: over the debate regarding corporate citizenship hung the question about the privileges and immunities of blacks who were free in some states and slaves in others. (If they could freely enter and exit states, who knows what other privileges they might claim.) But the initial prompt, and the constant throughout the century-long debate, was the Supreme Court's determination to vindicate the Constitution's competitive purposes without producing an epic political blowback and a mortal threat to the Court's jurisdiction.

Beginnings

The Supreme Court's earliest serious engagement with the citizenship status of corporations is a group of cases known as *Bank of the United States v. Deveaux* (1809), suits in diversity that turned on the citizenship of the corporate plaintiffs and their members. In declining jurisdiction, Chief Justice John Marshall held that a "mere legal entity, a corporation aggregate, is certainly not a citizen; and, consequently, cannot sue or be sued in the courts of the United States, *unless the rights of the members, in this respect, can be exercised in their corporate name.*"[8] To translate the italics into plaintext: so long as all members of a corporation are citizens of the incorporating state, the corporation may sue and be sued in diversity, in federal courts. The emphasis is on "all." In an earlier case, *Strawbridge v. Curtiss* (1806), the Court (again per Marshall) had held that diversity—under the diversity provision of the 1789 Judiciary Act—meant "complete" diversity: so long as any shareholder of a defendant-corporation resides in the plaintiff's state (or vice versa), federal courts lack jurisdiction.[9]

The oddity of *Deveaux* was widely noted at the time, and soon-developing difficulties in applying the rule of the case did nothing to improve its reputation. When the U.S. government subscribes to the stock of a state-chartered corporation (as it often did), does the corporation cease to be a citizen of its home state? When a corporation raises capital across the country and in foreign markets (as many did), does it become a citizen of all states where some incorporators reside? None? Should one look only to the original incorporators or to all present owners? To the corporation's directors, perhaps? And what of corporations chartered in multiple states (again, a common practice at the time)? Difficulties of this sort, which would soon occupy the Court to no end, were entirely foreseeable. Why, then, the curious *Deveaux* ruling?

On one account, the case fits the "John Marshall, capitalist and nationalist" story line. What Marshall should have said, the argument runs, is that corporations, as artificial legal entities, cannot be "citizens"—period. His insistence on looking to the individual incorporators was simply a means of keeping the federal courts open to at least *some* corporations.[10] That reading (we shall see shortly) is right in a fashion—but not because the notion that corporations cannot be citizens is either self-evident or obviously correct. At least, it was not thought to be so at the time of *Deveaux*. Joseph Story thought that corporations *were* citizens, as did Justice Bushrod Washington, Daniel Webster, and (if Story is to be believed) John Marshall.[11] British common law cases, as well as the law of nations, had long treated corporations as "inhabitants" of particular countries or places, and American students of Coke and of the British common law would have known that.[12] (Marshall knew it; he discussed some of those cases in *Deveaux* but brushed them aside.) The word "citizen," although open to some dispute, provides no conclusive reason to reject the common-law view. Article IV of the Confederation (quoted earlier) had spoken of "inhabitants," and the substitution of "citizens" in the Privileges and Immunities Clause was intended not to restrict its range of application but solely to prevent the absurd consequence of enabling one state to confer citizenship on persons in other states—in other words, to make privileges and immunities *within* the United States dovetail with the national government's monopoly over uniform rules of naturalization.[13] There is ample room, then, to look beyond the specific word to the Constitution's logic.

Counsel in the insurance cases decided alongside *Deveaux* forcefully pressed arguments along these lines. The right to sue *and be sued* in diversity, one lawyer (John Adams) reminded the Court, runs both ways. The point of diversity jurisdiction is to curb local bias; and that risk is multiplied when the out-of-state plaintiff encounters not an individual but a powerful, well-connected corporation on its home turf. Declare corporations to be noncitizens, and state protectionism will run rampant; make their status hang on the citizenship of its incorporators, and any state corporation can escape federal jurisdiction through the simple device of having a single nominal shareholder in the plaintiff's state. Another counsel explained, on a strikingly modern-sounding note, that in his industry (insurance) diversity jurisdiction was practically nothing *but* corporate litigation. Banish corporations, and the Court's diversity docket will be reduced to high-stakes divorce cases while insurance markets and commercial law sink into a morass of state litigation.[14] Those arguments—perhaps not the common law jazz, for the Chief was never much of a common lawyer, but surely the structural and consequentialist arguments—were plainly calculated to appeal to Marshall's instincts and his style of reasoning. Why did they fail?

Contingency and politics. At the time of *Deveaux*, corporations were deeply suspect, especially in the South, where they were widely associated with aristocratic, Federalist machinations. Marshall feared that corporate citizenship, and hence access to federal court and possibly free entry, would have caused profound political repercussions.[15] That interpretation is buttressed by the little-known facts of *Deveaux*: it was a suit against Georgia officials who had waltzed into the bank's branch office and left with $2,004 in silver, in payment of a state tax on the bank's branch and its business. Sound familiar? *Deveaux* presented the question that would arrive on John Marshall's doorstep a decade later under the Court's "arising under" (as we now say, "federal question") jurisdiction. Arguably, Marshall could have saved himself and the country a heap of trouble on the Bank issue (and on the status of corporations) had he decided the question of *M'Culloch* right then and there in *Deveaux*.[16] But given the explosive issue, and what with the still-more incendiary *Fletcher v. Peck* on the docket, likewise involving the State of Georgia and federal jurisdiction, one can see why Marshall chose to punt.[17] The pronouncement that corporations were "certainly" not citizens blunted the expected hostile response. It had the unfortunate side effect of placing a large segment of interstate commerce beyond the federal courts' protection. Hence, the proviso that the *members* of a corporation might still invoke diversity jurisdiction. The awkward *Deveaux* construction was Marshall's way of preserving a role for the federal judiciary without subjecting states immediately and across the board to the discipline of a constitutional free-trade regime for corporations.

After Marshall's death in 1835, the Taney Court skinned the corporate cat in a somewhat different fashion. In *Bank of Augusta v. Earle* (1839), the question was whether banks chartered in one state (Georgia) may do business in another (Alabama).[18] Unlike *Deveaux*, *Bank of Augusta* addressed the citizenship status of corporations under the Privileges and Immunities Clause, rather than Article III. As in *Deveaux*, however, the Bank of the United States was again a party to the litigation, though now organized as a state institution under the laws of Pennsylvania. Arguing for the bank, Daniel Webster insisted that the Privileges and Immunities Clause, contra Marshall and the language of *Deveaux*, did cover corporations. The Court squarely rejected that contention. A corporation, Chief Justice Taney wrote, can have no existence outside its charter state; it "must dwell in the place of its creation, and cannot migrate to another sovereignty."[19] However, Taney proceeded to embrace an implied consent theory: a corporation's right to operate in another state should be presumed as a matter of interstate comity unless a state has explicitly (typically, by affirmative legislation) repudiated that presumption. This free-trade-with-an-opt-out construction departed from Marshall's *Deveaux* strategy of looking behind the legal form to the corporators' citizenship, but it pursued the same ends: protect the Supreme Court's jurisdiction; strike a blow for free interstate commerce without forcing the states tout de suite under its discipline.[20]

The Supreme Court had some difficulty in adhering to the formula. It actually jettisoned *Deveaux* altogether in *Louisville Rail Co. v. Letson*

(1844), which boldly declared any corporation to be "a citizen of the state which created it."[21] If that is right, then the Privileges and Immunities Clause applies with full force and diversity jurisdiction is available to corporations to the same extent, on the same terms, as it is available to individuals or partnerships. But the Court soon backpedaled. In *Marshall v. Baltimore & Ohio Railroad Co.* (1853), it reverted to the formula of *Deveaux*: a corporation cannot be a "citizen"; the right to sue and defend must be based on citizenship of its members.[22] To the obvious difficulty of ascertaining the incorporators' citizenship, the Court responded with a strong and eventually conclusive presumption that a corporation is composed entirely of citizens of the state of incorporation. The resort to that increasingly "violent fiction" to sustain jurisdiction "indicates two things: A strong conviction that the spirit and purpose of the Constitution required [the justices] to give corporations the rights of citizens in the federal courts; and a profound aversion to reaching such a result by the simple and direct method of calling a corporation a citizen."[23]

The source of that aversion is no mystery: state courts, especially in the South and West, had gone ballistic over *Letson*—unmistakably, *on account of its competitive potential and implications.*[24] The trouble with the Court's mid-century formula—no corporate citizenship under the Privileges and Immunities Clause, a conclusive presumption of citizenship for purposes of diversity jurisdiction—wasn't that it rested on legal fictions. The trouble was that it rested on fictions that could not withstand the force of relentless litigation and creative state legislation. Put aside awkward questions of what to do with entities incorporated in several states, which repeatedly occupied the Court: the far nastier problem was that *Bank of Augusta* explicitly recognized the states' authority to revoke the implied consent to the operation of foreign corporations. (Alabama, the losing defendant-state in *Bank of Augusta*, exercised that option faster than you can say "interstate comity.") Grant the premise, and the promise of comity becomes an empty shell. A state that may exclude corporations altogether may condition their operation in the state on their consent to surrendering privileges—*including the privilege of invoking the federal courts' diversity jurisdiction.* With dreary regularity, states utilized that option, either by demanding a surrender of diversity jurisdiction up front or by expelling corporations that had the audacity of removing a case to federal court. Now what?

Throughout the nineteenth century, and as late as 1906, the Supreme Court formally held to the position that states may exclude corporations entirely and that the power to exclude implies the power to discriminate or expel for good reasons, bad reasons, or no reason at all. Despite that insistent formalism, however, or perhaps on account of it, the Supreme Court found ways around the vexing power to exclude. One path was the Commerce Clause and the other, the doctrine of unconstitutional conditions. The unlikely starting point of both strategies was Justice Stephen Field's decision and opinion in *Paul v. Virginia* (1869).

The Law of the Gilded Age

Paul v. Virginia was a test case to challenge a Virginia statute that required foreign insurance companies—but not Virginia-chartered corporations— to purchase and deposit with the State Treasurer upwards of $30,000 worth of Virginia-issued bonds. A companion statute barred anyone from serving as an agent for any insurance company that had failed to meet the licensing requirement. The named plaintiff had set himself up as an agent for out-of-state insurance companies, meticulously complied with every licensing condition except the deposit requirement, executed a contract with a Virginia citizen, was duly fined, sued and naturally lost in the Virginia courts, and filed a writ of error with the Supreme Court. The plaintiff, or rather his New York-based employers, raised two claims. First, they charged up the Hamburger Hill on which Webster and Co. had fought in vain and argued, yet again, that corporations were citizens under the Privileges and Immunities Clause. Second, they argued that the Commerce Clause rendered the Virginia statute unconstitutional.

Justice Field, writing for a unanimous Court, roundly rejected both contentions. He reaffirmed the no-corporate-citizenship holding of *Bank of Augusta* and rejected the contrary notion as utterly inconsistent with both the Privileges and Immunities Clause and the states' sacred police powers. Citizenship for *limited liability* corporations, he wrote, would allow those entities to exercise the privilege of doing business in another state without assuming the attendant liabilities.[25] That advantage, he added, would be "utterly destructive of the independence and the harmony of the States," especially in light of modern conditions:

> There is scarcely a business pursued requiring the expenditure of large capital, or the union of large numbers, that is not carried on by corporations. It is not too much to say that the wealth and business of the country are to a great extent controlled by them. And if . . . corporate powers and franchises could be exercised in other States without restriction, . . . the most important business of those States would soon pass into their hands.[26]

Field seems to have understood the insurers to demand a right to exercise special privileges conferred by their home state charters in a foreign state—obviously, an untenable position.[27] However, even a presumed right to do business on no better than nondiscriminatory terms, Field continued, would eviscerate the states' autonomy. "They could not charter a company for any purpose, however restricted, without at once opening the door to a flood of corporations from other States to engage in the same pursuits."[28] And that result would be intolerable. In Field's understanding, the states' police powers included the right to shield domestic corporations from extra-territorial competition.

Field dismissed the Commerce Clause claim with equal firmness. He admitted that the Commerce Clause, unlike the Privileges and Immunities Clause, protects corporations as well as partnerships and individuals. Insurance contracts, however, "are not articles of commerce in any proper meaning of the word." Though the contracts may be made among parties from different states, they do not become effective until they are executed in a particular place. "They are, then, local transactions, and are governed by the local law."[29] They are therefore beyond the protection of the Commerce Clause.

Paul was a clever test case that backfired on the client but inadvertently produced huge gains for other industries. The holding that "insurance is not interstate commerce" survived repeated attacks until 1944, when it was overturned by the Court but, wartime distractions notwithstanding, promptly reinstated by that inveterate guardian of interstate commerce, the United States Congress.[30] All other pieces of Justice Field's architecture, in contrast, were soon demolished under an invigorated Commerce Clause and a novel doctrine of unconstitutional conditions.

The Commerce Clause Revisited. The rise of the dormant Commerce Clause after the Civil War was prompted, ironically enough, by Justice Field's language in *Paul*—plainly dictum, not a holding—that the Commerce Clause, unlike the Privileges and Immunities Clause, protects corporations along with all other participants in interstate commerce. It follows that the negative Commerce Clause trumps the states' right to exclude; and "if the right to exclude is denied, the right to admit on condition necessarily falls with it."[31] Corporations soon availed themselves of this opening. The pioneers, predictably, were firms that unlike insurers were undoubtedly engaged in interstate commerce, such as railroad and telegraph companies. *Pensacola Telegraph Company v. Western Union Telegraph Company* (1877) provides an early example. An 1866 act of Congress had authorized telegraph companies (under certain conditions) to operate lines along military or post roads of the United States. A Florida statute, enacted barely six months later, granted the Pensacola Telegraph

Company a monopoly over telegraph lines in two counties, including incoming and outgoing lines across state borders. Seven years later, the state repudiated that exclusive grant and issued to a railroad company a franchise, eventually transferred to Western Union, to build telegraph lines along its right of way. Pensacola Telegraph sued on the Contract Clause. The Supreme Court held that the first grant was preempted under federal law and, moreover, violated the Commerce Clause. In a vehement dissent, Justice Field (the author of *Paul*) argued that the local transportation monopoly was beyond the scope of the Commerce Clause. But even if the corporation had engaged in bona fide interstate commerce, Field continued, he would defend the state's right to exclude it. He described as "novel and startling" the majority's notion that "if a corporation be in any way engaged in interstate commerce, it can enter and do business in another state without the latter's consent."[32]

Precisely that novel and startling notion, though, was well on its way to becoming official doctrine. Between the 1870s and the New Deal era, the Commerce Clause was the stuff of hundreds of Supreme Court decisions and one of the Court's principal means of curbing state protectionism. That heavy reliance, though, brought back to life and exposed to glaring light a conceptual problem from *Gibbons* to *Cooley*: what exactly *is* "commerce among the states"? As just noted, the Court started with the stuff that fits a dictionary definition, as well as *Cooley*'s formula of "inherently national" matters—interstate transportation and communication, and the sale of goods across state lines. What, though, of industries that do not fit that account? And what of the in-state transactions of interstate corporations? To cover this ground, the Supreme Court created a doctrine of unconstitutional conditions.

Unconstitutional Conditions. *Paul*, as noted, held that the right to exclude includes the right to impose any and all conditions. If a corporation *consents* to conditions that might otherwise violate the Constitution, then there is no violation—unless the corporation had an unqualified right to be admitted in the first place. Still, in the teeth of *Paul*, the Supreme Court soon developed a doctrine to the effect that state-imposed conditions must not be "repugnant" to the Constitution or laws of the United States. This "unconstitutional conditions" doctrine was pressed by the industry that, under the plain holding of *Paul*, could not avail itself of its emerging Commerce Clause exception: insurers.

State laws imposing requirements on foreign insurers dated back to the 1820s. Many of those statutes reeked of protectionism, but others responded to genuine differences in regulating domestic and foreign firms—notably, the difficulty of obtaining legal process when the person of the defendant could not be found in the jurisdiction.[33] For example, states enacted statutes that enabled them to sue foreign corporations by serving process on their in-state agents. Statutes of that description *have* to be constitutional: they merely put foreign firms on a par with local firms (which can always be "found" within the jurisdiction). Similarly, it seems good sense to require a corporation, as a condition of doing local business, to designate an agent on whom process may be served.[34]

Where, though, are the limits? The rationale on which the state may impose conditions in the first place is that the foreign corporation, by exercising the privilege of conducting business in the state, has given its implied consent to the state's requirements—which seems to suggest that it "must take the legal premises as it finds them."[35] Over time, however, the Court came to reject that absolutist position, for the same reason that accounts for its heavy resort to the Commerce Clause: a desire to block states from defeating the Court's authority by conditioning insurers' operations on a surrender of the right to invoke federal jurisdiction. In 1874, the justices took a baby step by holding that a foreign corporation's agreement not to invoke federal jurisdiction could not bar removal to federal court if a corporation chose to exercise that option.[36] Two years later, however, in *Doyle v. Continental Insurance Co.*, the Court held that a state could in that event expel the corporation. Justice Bradley's dissent contains perhaps the first clear statement of the unconstitutional conditions doctrine:

> Though a State may have the power, if it sees fit to subject its citizens to the inconvenience, of prohibiting all foreign corporations from transacting business within its jurisdiction, it has no power to impose unconstitutional conditions upon their doing so. Total prohibition may produce suffering, and may manifest a spirit of unfriendliness to sister States; but prohibition, *except on conditions derogatory to the jurisdiction and sovereignty of the United States,* is mischievous, and productive of hostility and disloyalty to the general government. If a state is unwise enough to legislate the one, it has no constitutional power to legislate the other.[37]

The right to exclude remained nominally intact for another three decades. Increasingly, however, the Court's decisions charted byways, and the emergent unconstitutional conditions doctrine gradually lost its nexus to the protection of federal court jurisdiction. For example, the Court held that state court jurisdiction requires service of process on a sufficiently representative agent, as opposed to any clerk in the foreign company's employ. Similarly, it held that the state's undoubted right to require designation of an agent who can be served confers state jurisdiction only with respect to business within the enacting state, not to the corporation's conduct elsewhere in the nation.[38] Quite often, the Court arrived at such holdings in reliance on constitutional provisions that, unlike the Privileges and Immunities Clause, offered protection for corporations and their operations. A milestone in that development was *Allgeyer v. Louisiana* (1897), wherein the Court construed a state law prohibiting insurance contracts with nonlicensed out-of-state firms as an interference with the insurance *customers'* constitutional liberty.[39]

In 1910, the unconstitutional conditions doctrine sprung the confines of insurance litigation and met up with the Commerce Clause. The reason for that convergence was the Court's subject-matter distinction between in-state and interstate commerce, or rather, the unworkability of that distinction. Time and again, the Court had declared that the in-state leg of an interstate transaction, or the in-state business of an interstate corporation, could be taxed and regulated separately, even in a patently discriminatory manner. After all (the theory went), the interstate corporation could always "renounce" the local business.[40] But that formulation does not cover all-too-common state attempts to hold an interstate corporation's local business hostage. Thus, Kansas required all foreign corporations to pay a certain percent of their total capital stock as a condition of doing business within the state. In a pair of cases, *Western Union Telegraph Co. v. Kansas* and *Pullman Co. v. Kansas* (1910), both decided 5–4, the Supreme Court enjoined the state officials. One can read the cases either as unconstitutional conditions cases or as extensions of the Commerce Clause (or perhaps the Due Process Clause) to cover the extraterritorial taxation of interstate commerce.[41] Either way, and unequivocally, they stand for a de facto repeal of the right to exclude.

Justice Holmes's dissents stated the traditional syllogism: the power to exclude encompasses the power to discriminate. The Supreme Court, however, never looked back. *Doyle* and its progeny were soon overruled, and Justice Bradley's dissent in *Doyle* (quoted earlier) was declared the Court's official doctrine.[42] In *Frost & Frost Trucking Co v. Railroad Commission* (1926), the Court expounded the unconstitutional conditions doctrine as a general principle, transcending its origins in concerns over federalism, corporations, interstate commerce, and federal jurisdiction. The doctrine, Justice Sutherland declared, applies even to a state's imposition of licensing conditions on *in-state* users of the state's own highways.[43] In that formulation, the doctrine lives to this day, even as its original purpose—to protect diversity jurisdiction and interstate commerce—has fallen into desuetude.

Constitutional Entrepreneurship

Robust Commerce Clause protection for interstate enterprises, an unconstitutional conditions doctrine for enterprises and operations beyond
the purview of the Commerce Clause, firm judicial insistence on diversity jurisdiction: those three key features of the law of the Gilded Age
contributed greatly to an intensely competitive federalism that helped to
integrate the national economy and to break down local monopolies. But
there is both more and less to the picture painted so far. There is more
to it because the Supreme Court's doctrines unleashed state competition
for corporate charters—a pristine embodiment of competitive federalism
or the first clear example of a state "race to the bottom," depending on
who gets to tell the story. There is less to the picture because the Supreme
Court's Commerce Clause doctrine ("no state regulation of interstate
commerce") soon proved incoherent and weirdly *anti*-competitive, a recognition that prompted another doctrinal adjustment.

The Law of the Traitor State. The central advantage of the corporate
form, at least initially, was the ability to pool large amounts of capital. For
the most part, states cherished that arrangement: it allowed the tax-free
funding of large-scale projects such as canals and, later, railroads.[44] Each
state had to compete with all the rest for perfidious Albion's capital. That
constraint, however, is as nothing to the competition at the end of the century—competition for corporate charters. "Competition" anno 1810 or so
was what every (state) legislature wants it to be: a low-volume, high-rent
business wherein corporate charters were auctioned off to the highest bid-
der. Corporate chartering a century later was the opposite: high volume,
low transaction costs, with next to no legislative intermediation. Why did
legislatures go along with that transformation? The answer, Henry Butler
has powerfully argued, is that few of them ever did. The transformation
from competing state industrial policies to competitive federalism was
forced upon the states.[45]

The development of corporate charters during the nineteenth century
comprises three periods. During the first period, corporate charters were
a special, usually monopolistic privilege doled out by state legislatures,
chiefly for industrial policy purposes. That period came to an end in the
late 1840s, after a panic had thrown eight states into default on their
bonds and most others into severe financial distress. Within a decade,
provisions for general incorporation were written into the constitutions
of most states by way of constitutional amendment. (New states typically

adopted those provisions as part of their constitutions.) However, the constitutional reforms did not in fact end special corporate charters. Rather, they established a "dual" chartering regime: general chartering for some, special charters for others. Butler persuasively interprets this shift as the state monopolists' strategy of price discrimination. General charters provided a means of reaping some revenue from a rapidly increasing number of firms that might otherwise eschew the corporate form altogether. At the same time, the continued availability of special charters allowed states to capture rents from producers who, for one reason or another, were willing to pay for privileges that were unavailable under general charters.

The third phase of corporate chartering was the arrival of general corporate chartering laws *to the exclusion* of special charters. In 1875, New Jersey—a state with a long, lucrative tradition of granting corporate charters, including charters that allowed the corporations to operate outside the state—enacted the first truly general corporation statute, a prototype of modern American corporate law. A key provision of the statute made New Jersey charters available to corporations domiciled in other states, so long as they had an office and an agent in New Jersey. The law imposed filing fees and franchise taxes, but the rates were low and imposed on a tax base (capital stock) that left nothing to the discretion of tax administrators. Evidently, the New Jersey legislature hoped that incorporation volume and attendant revenues would more than offset proceeds from continued price discrimination. The move paid off handsomely: New Jersey dominated the market for incorporation for almost four decades.[46]

The emergence of general incorporation and state competition for corporate charters is largely attributable to now-familiar legal developments. The Supreme Court's sustained interventions against protectionist trade barriers facilitated the emergence of large, nationally operating firms—first in transportation and communications, then in manufacturing—with a need to pool large sums of capital, ideally under the laws of a single state. That option, though, was of doubtful value so long as states had a right to exclude foreign corporations. It was the demise of that doctrine, beginning with *Paul*, that prompted the adoption of New Jersey's incorporation law and the ensuing competition for corporate charters.

That competition did not begin in earnest until 1888, when the early adopter (New Jersey) made a second move to maintain its dominant position. At the time, many industries confronted barriers to integration (and, ahem, cartelization). Voluntary coordination, often through trade associations, tended to founder on the difficulty of making the agreements stick.[47] One response to this problem was the legal form of a trust, evidently invented by the Standard Oil Company's legal counsel: companies turn stock over to board of trustees, authorized to make binding decisions for all members, in exchange for certificates of equal value.[48] Predictably, those beasts quickly came under attack in the courts, state legislatures, and soon enough the Congress. Another, more flexible and elegant means of integration, corporate cross-ownership under the umbrella of a holding company, was generally unavailable because state constitutions required special legislative acts for the formation of a company authorized to hold stock in other companies. In its 1888/1889 session, however, the New Jersey legislature, responding to the entreaties of a former governor and a creative New York corporation lawyer, repealed that constitutional requirement. The "New Jersey Holding Company" quickly became the dominant form of large-scale corporate organization. By 1894, incorporation fees and taxes, largely paid by corporations doing business in New York, constituted New Jersey's entire budget. The Garden State maintained its dominance until 1913, when Governor Woodrow Wilson's Progressive leadership prompted a substantial restriction on permissible corporate activities in New Jersey and a unilateral surrender of its advantages to Delaware.[49]

The corporate story at this point is intertwined with the emergence of antitrust law and, in particular, the Sherman Act of 1890—at the time of its enactment and for some time thereafter, not so much a "consumer welfare" manifesto but a quasi-constitutional response to the problem of state-chartered trusts with monopolistic tendencies and price effects across the country.[50] Although it took time and effort to work out the respective domains of corporate law and antitrust law, the law eventually settled on the formula that corporate (state) law governs corporations' "internal affairs," whereas antitrust law (and later securities law) governs their market position and conduct. That arrangement implies state competition for charters, while subjecting the anticompetitive extraterritorial *effects* of corporate conduct to federal control and redress. In principle, that is the true and correct competitive federalism arrangement.

Commerce: Subject-Matter Versus Discrimination. In its modern version, the negative Commerce Clause operates as an anti-discrimination rule, parallel or analogous to the Privileges and Immunities Clause. As noted repeatedly, though, the Supreme Court started in the 1870s with the notion of "interstate commerce" as a cabined and exclusive sphere of federal activity, distinct from the equally inviolable sphere of state police powers. The move from the subject-matter conception to the modern antidiscrimination rule was not some convulsive constitutional "revolution" anno 1937 or thereabouts but a gradual transformation, which set in almost as soon as the categorical approach had been formulated.[51] One can understand that migration as a competitive federalism move. The supposedly commerce-protective subject-matter approach produced undesired anticompetitive results, for which the antidiscrimination rule promised redress.

The conventional modern perception is that the Court's categorical distinction between interstate commerce and the states' police powers— and between "commerce" and "manufacture," between the verboten "direct" regulation and a permissible "indirect" effect of police power regulations on interstate commerce, between a product in its "original package" (which is immune from state regulation and taxation) and the same product commingled with the "great mass of property" in the state—had laissez-faire purposes and effects: by placing certain matters beyond the reach of Congress, it compelled states in those domains to tax and regulate under competitive conditions. In fact, however, neither an anti-Congress orientation nor laissez-faire ideology had anything to do with the matter. The Court formulated its subject-matter distinctions long before it occurred to anyone that Congress might actively regulate anything except navigation, railroads, and telegraphs—industries that undoubtedly fell within the Commerce Clause. Moreover, post-*Paul* Commerce Clause doctrine was respectful and even solicitous, both in intention and in fact, of congressional authority. In the absence of a federal statute, the Court proceeded on the assumption that Congress had "willed" commerce to be free. When a federal statute was at hand, however, the justices construed it as preempting any and all state regulation, conflicting or not, in that field. On many occasions (for example, railroad employers' liability), the Court practically begged Congress to speak; and when it did speak, the Court consistently acceded, albeit rarely without reminding Congress to observe the distinction between interstate and in-state transactions.[52] Similarly, the notion of categorical Commerce Clause distinctions as laissez faire would have struck combatants at the time as very odd. The distinctions protected firms that run railroads— but not firms that build the cars (that was manufacture, not commerce) or provided the capital (that was banking or insurance, and therefore not commerce).[53] Understandably, large segments of American business took a dim view of the Court's doctrine. Populists, on the other hand, rather liked it. The distinction between "commerce" and "manufacture" notoriety, for example, operated as a limit on Congress only rarely and secondarily. In the context of the dormant Commerce Clause, where the distinctions first developed and cases came in bundles, the doctrines had a distinctly *pro*-regulatory effect.[54]

Why, then, did the Court initially construe the negative Commerce Clause in analogy to the categorical Import-Export Clause, rather than the antidiscriminatory Privileges and Immunities Clause?[55] The first, already-suggested attraction of the Commerce Clause was to escape the Privileges and Immunities Clause and to conceptualize (corporate) interstate commerce, not as a bargain in which a state may exact concessions, but as a jurisdictional category—put differently, to move interstate commerce beyond the states' legislative jurisdiction. To do that work, the power to regulate interstate commerce *had* to be exclusive. That, in turn, means that interstate commerce must end someplace. Regardless of where one might want to draw the line, there has to be *a* line—a subject-matter distinction.

Second, the exclusive Commerce Clause was a necessary means of breaking down sectional barriers to trade and competition. The genius of a nondiscrimination rule is to hold local interests hostage to interstate commerce and competition: if a state wants to exploit out-of-state interests, it must inflict like misery on the same domestic interests, which it will be loath to do. But what if there *are* no comparable in-state interests? What if all corporations that employ "peddlers" (that is, sales agents) are based in New York or Ohio—and Nebraska or Kansas taxes peddlers in a "nondiscriminatory" fashion? A fine illustration of the problem is *Woodruff v. Parham* (1868), decided near-contemporaneously with *Paul*. At issue was a Louisiana tax on sales at auction. Justice Miller, writing for the Court, held that the Import-Export Clause applies only to foreign commerce, not to interstate commerce. Having so held (probably erroneously), Miller fumbled his way to a Commerce Clause theory. If the Louisiana scheme were shown to be *discriminatory*, he said, the Court might well strike it down.[56] The telling rejoinder appears in Justice Nelson's dissent. Louisiana knew (Nelson said), and everybody else knew, and everybody knew that Louisiana knew, that the tax affected only out-of-state interests. The neutral form of the tax was a lousy disguise for its patently discriminatory purpose and effect. No flabby neutrality rule would forestall such maneuvers; only a categorical prohibition would do.[57] To this day, no-local-hostages cases present a nasty Commerce Clause problem, albeit one that remains at bay in a context of highly diversified state economies.[58] At the time, though, the problem was common, and it implicated profound sectional and economic divisions—northeastern producer states versus southern and western market states, Wall Street versus Main Street. In that context, subject-matter distinctions that protected interstate commerce from any hostile state action held real appeal.

Alas, a legal rule that blocks one bad result often produces unintended results in another dimension and application. The Court's categorical distinctions introduced sharp discontinuities—between industries that are wholly immune from state regulation and industries that must accept whatever bargain a state may offer, between the interstate leg of a railway transport and its last in-state mile, between the free interstate shipment of liquor and its total prohibition in dry states. Each of those problems produced its own difficulties and, eventually, accommodations between the Court and the Congress. The overarching problem, however, was that the Court's categorical distinctions were ill-suited to a central issue of late nineteenth-century capitalism—vertical firm integration. On the one hand, a categorical "no tax on interstate commerce" rule hands interstate corporations an unwarranted advantage over local actors, whose operations are subject to state taxation and regulation. On the other hand, the same rule exposes interstate firms to ruthless exploitation: there is no point to vertical integration if state trolls can expropriate the gains by taxing the final "in-state" transaction. Corporations soon figured this out and pushed for a move from categorical distinctions to non-discrimination.

We owe to I. M. Singer and Company both the sewing machine and significant advances in Commerce Clause doctrine.[59] By 1860 or so, Singer had found that existing local wholesalers were incapable of supplying consumer credit or demonstration and repair services. Over the next two decades, therefore, the company created its own distribution network, consisting of more than five hundred stores that also served as a base for a large force of door-to-door salesmen. States responded in the usual fashion—through stepped-up enforcement of licensing laws against peddlers and through tax laws that put the sellers of out-of-state products at a profound disadvantage. While the Privileges and Immunities Clause forbade states from discriminating against out-of-state sellers, *Brown v. Maryland* permitted them to discriminate against out-of-state *products*, once they had been removed from their "original package." States routinely availed themselves of that option.[60]

Singer had a powerful incentive to break those barriers, and it had the muscle. Like the insurers in *Paul*, Singer urged its local agents to ignore state laws so as to invite prosecution and conviction and then hired high-powered law firms to contest the state laws. In 1876, the strategy bore fruit. In *Welton v. Missouri*, the Supreme Court invalidated a state law that required peddlers—defined as persons selling commodities "not the growth, produce, or manufacture of this State"—to pay a license fee for the privilege of doing local business. Frankly admitting that the law was consistent with *Brown*, the Court nonetheless declared it unconstitutional. The prohibitory force of the Commerce Clause, it held, "continues until the commodity has ceased to be the subject of discriminating legislation by reason of its foreign character"—that is to say, up to and including final retails.[61]

For Singer, this extension of the original package doctrine was a mere beachhead, exposed to a barrage of hostile fire. Virginia, in one variation on a common theme, enacted a license fee scheme that effectively forced Singer and similar companies to disband their state sales force. The Supreme Court invalidated that scheme too. On this occasion, it departed from *Brown*'s subject-matter distinctions and at last focused on the incidence and discriminatory effect of the state's law.[62]

A similar pattern unfolded in the meat industry. The invention of the refrigerated railroad car sharply reduced transportation costs, relative to on-the-hoof transport; secondarily, it generated increased economies of scale in production (that is, slaughter and processing). In short order, the "Big Four" Chicago meatpackers, led by the Swift Company, proved able to ship dressed beef over long distances. But Swift did not become dominant simply because of the refrigerated railroad car. Rather, "he was the first to appreciate the need for a distribution network to store meat and deliver it to the retailers."[63] That effort met with vehement opposition by entrenched interests all along the distribution chain. Railroads refused to buy refrigerated cars; when Swift built his own, the rails refused to carry them. Local wholesalers, organized in 1886 as the National Butchers' Protective Association (BPA), organized boycotts and mobilized local prejudice—a losing cause, in light of the national firms' low prices and the high quality of their products.[64]

The local monopolists' best bet was "federalism"—specifically, the states' unquestioned right to ensure their citizens' health and safety. That claim was more than colorable, given the real risk of sales of spoiled goods to consumers who cannot readily ascertain the quality of the product. Even so, the Chicago producers prevailed in *Minnesota v. Barber* (1890), substantially on the grounds that the states' proffered health rationales were pretextual and without empirical foundation.[65] Legitimate health and safety concerns, the Court insisted, would have to be met in a fashion less fraught with protectionist risks. And just as the sewing-machine cases exposed one irrational consequence of the Marshall Court's doctrine (to wit, the interruption of an integrated chain of production and distribution), the meat-packing cases exposed the dichotomy between interstate commerce and state health and safety legislation—by the lights of *Gibbons*, the heart and soul of internal state affairs—as untenable. *Barber* produced another round of evasive state maneuvers (such as discriminatory inspection fees), enacted at the BPA's behest but promptly struck down by the Court.[66] Cases of this sort would soon proliferate. The Court continued to employ the language of "interstate commerce" and "police powers," but it did so for purposes of analysis rather than segregation. It treated interstate commerce as an integrated system and then stacked up the interest in protecting that system against the states' police power rationales. Prohibited "discrimination" is when the state loses.

The transition was far from painless. For decades, the Court agonized over bottlenecks in a "stream of commerce" and puzzled over whether logs, wheat, and livestock had "come to rest" somewhere in that stream.[67] The systemic source of the agony was the difficulty of locating the competitive balance. An antidiscrimination rule extends to the final in-state transaction and, moreover, protects interstate commerce not only against flagrant discrimination but also against state "balkanization"—that is, disruptions of integrated industries and transactions. However, the same broad understanding of interstate commerce on the "affirmative" side of the Commerce Clause has the price of allowing the *Congress* to reach further into the states' theretofore "internal" commerce—in other words, to mow down state competition. Hence, the justices' reluctance to surrender the subject-matter categories altogether.

In the end, subject-matter categories proved unstable. Perhaps (one can speculate) the commerce/police-power distinction might have produced a rough balance between the states' unwarranted exactions on interstate commerce and interstate corporations' excess profits. Two could play the game: for every state that exploited the discontinuities to reap rents by taxing vertical integration, there was a corporation that arbitraged the same distinctions to the states' detriment.[68] A rough average reciprocity of exploitation, however, could not last. State-side, it was unacceptable to market states, where the ratio of foreign corporations' in-state operations to their overall size was too small to allow the state to reap a "fair" share of the corporations' national profits and proceeds; recall the *Kansas* cases in 1910. Corporate-side, the old distinctions were a nightmare for firms whose business model depended on seamless vertical integration; recall the archetypal sewing and meat-packing cases. Litigation dynamics, coupled with the Court's recognition of the economic realities, produced an intensely procompetitive dormant Commerce Clause—an encompassing antidiscrimination rule with bite.

CHAPTER SIX

Federal Common Law

Introduction

Among the doctrines and cases covered in these chapters, none is more discredited than the "federal common law" of *Swift v. Tyson* (1842). Reduced to its essentials, the question in *Swift* was this: in "diversity" cases among parties from different states, what law are federal courts to apply when no federal statute or constitutional provision governs the dispute? *Swift* held that in certain "commercial" cases of this nature, federal courts should apply a federal general common law, largely independent of the common law decisions of individual state courts.

Swift and its progeny of hundreds of Supreme Court decisions were overruled in *Erie Railroad Co. v. Tompkins* (1938). "There is no federal general common law," *Erie* famously declared, and the federal courts have no authority to invoke that "brooding omnipresence in the sky" on their own steam.[1] A federal general common law that displaces otherwise applicable state law, in areas where Congress has ordained no such result and where it may even lack the authority to impose it, seems at war with basic principles of federalism and the separation of powers. In *Swift*-style cases, *Erie* declared, federal courts must follow the rules of the state in which they sit, including that state's common-law rules.

It has become well-nigh impossible to approach *Swift* except through the prism of *Erie*. But there are reasons to make the effort. Among those reasons is this striking fact: the notion that a federal general common law offends federalism was unarticulated and, so far as one can tell, never even occurred to any jurist of the antebellum era. To be sure, *Swift* was written by Joseph Story, an apostle of national power. The case, however, was a *unanimous* decision by the Taney Court, which was stacked with Southerners. Nor was *Swift* a rallying point of states' rights resistance. Long and many times before the case hit the law books, its reasoning had been endorsed by rabid states' rights advocates.[2] The eventual decision went almost unnoticed except by the financial press and by Harvard law students, to whom the author of the opinion assigned the case as a moot court exam. In that light, one ought to step outside *Erie*'s shadow and contemplate the possibility that *Swift* actually got some things right, federalismwise and otherwise. Those things appear in sharp relief when one understands the decision against a competitive constitutional baseline.

Competition and Contracts

Conflicts of law are preprogrammed in a federal system. In the vertical, federal-state dimension, the Supremacy Clause provides an unambiguous choice-of-law rule. Horizontal, state-to-state conflicts are more difficult, both because more than two legal systems can conflict and because the constitutional premise of state equality prohibits a systemic preference for any individual state's rules. Left to proliferate without some ordering principle, though, conflicts of law will diminish the gains from organizing under a federal system—prominently, the gains of unimpeded commerce, conducted on the basis of equal privileges and immunities. That danger will appear particularly grave if one believes that such conflicts will typically arise from state protectionism and bias against outsiders, rather than sheer fortuity. On that analysis, the coordination problem poses two systemic risks: the risk that state *law* will be biased against outsiders and the risk that the state *forum* will be biased. The Constitution adumbrates both risks. It seeks to guard against state law bias both through direct prohibitions against the states, such as the Contract Clause, and by granting Congress authority to trump state law within the bounds of its enumerated powers. It guards against the forum risk primarily by committing disputes among parties from different states to the federal courts, at the initiative of either party and regardless of whether the dispute involves any federal law.[3]

Like much else in the Constitution, this grant of "diversity jurisdiction" implies an inordinate reliance on the federal courts. A more direct and obvious solution would be to simply supplant state law with federal law. There is nothing odd about a federal statutory law of contract or torts, and many federal systems have adopted that solution. (We have instead opted for a Uniform Commercial Code that is neither uniform nor a code. That *is* odd.) But federal uniformity is not really a *federalism* solution. To the extent that one believes that decentralized systems of lawmaking may under some circumstances improve the legal product, it is also not a *competitive* solution. And for good or ill, Congress in the nineteenth century was thought to lack the power to reach matters of this sort under its enumerated powers.

What, then, is the competitive federalism solution to the problem of divergent and probably biased state law? The first-cut answer is contractual: let the parties to any given interstate transaction *choose* their law, and give them access to an impartial forum. (Choice of law alone will not do the job because a sufficiently biased state forum will abrogate, ex post and at the request of the in-state plaintiff, an explicit law choice provision among the parties.) That solution is straightforward where the parties have explicitly chosen the state law that will govern their transaction in the event of a dispute. But what if they have not?

One option is to let the dispute be governed by the law of the state where a lawsuit is first filed. That, in a nutshell, is the *Erie* regime. It is the anticompetitive solution par excellence because it maximizes two things: post-contractual opportunism by parties to commercial transactions and the homeward bias of state courts, who know that the federal courts to whom a case may be removed will in any event have to follow the forum state's law.

A second option is to let any dispute be governed by the laws of the place where a contract was formed (or the physical res of a dispute is located or a tort among strangers occurred). This "territorial" or lex loci rule already had a long tradition in the common law and the law of nations at the time of the American Founding. It was followed by American courts for much of the nation's history. In the late nineteenth century, scholars generated an imposing system of territorial jurisdiction and choice of law.[4]

A third solution goes back to the contractual baseline: adopt as a default rule the legal rules that the parties likely *would* have chosen, had they thought about the matter and made an explicit ex ante choice. In some contexts, that might well be lex loci. Real estate disputes, for example, may be best handled in situ. Because the asset cannot move, lex loci provides an unambiguous basis for the parties' bargains and, moreover, offers the prospect of winding up multistate disputes in a single place. Too, the rule comes with implicit competitive federalism protections.

Many investors have a wide range of choices among properties and the state laws that attach to them, and state law that is known to discriminate against outsiders will deter foreign investment. The choice of lex loci in this context is territorial in substance, but for contractual reasons. Its advantages are so obvious that the rule should be imputed to the parties, barring some explicit agreement to the contrary.

By parity of reasoning, lex loci looks unattractive in contracts over moving goods or intangibles. It is hard to believe that parties would want to have their relations governed by the sheer happenstance of when some document landed in another's mailbox or by where exactly a good happened to be on its journey. The difficulties are compounded when the items pass through many hands in many jurisdictions. In those settings, an independent assessment of the parties' intentions—independent, that is, of the state law of whoever happens to sue first—is more likely to provide a fair and efficient legal solution. An independent federal rule of decision guards against the risks of opportunistic party behavior and state bias, both in its legal and its forum dimension. At the same time, it preserves the benefits of competitive federalism for parties and states alike. If the independent law is no good, parties can opt into superior state law. And if states wish to maximize economic transactions within their jurisdiction, they will be inclined to offer such law.

Swift did not speak the language of competition or federalism. But it very clearly recognized the underlying problem, and it provided an ingenious contractual and constitutional solution.

Swift . . .

Swift arose over a highly speculative, legally dubious scheme involving tracts of land in Maine, financed through promissory notes and bills of exchange.[5] Like countless other such enterprises, the scheme collapsed in the panic of 1837. Swift, the cashier of a bank in Portland, Maine, had been paid with a bill of exchange that had been drawn by one of the scheme's perpetrators and had been signed and accepted by Tyson, a New York investor. With the endorsement of that bill to Swift, Tyson became indebted to Swift. The central question was whether Tyson would have to make good on the debt even if he could show that the original transaction had been tainted by fraud. Put more generally, *Swift* involved the central question of negotiable instruments: Can the holder of such an instrument enforce his claims regardless of the equities among the original parties?

Or do those equities travel with the instrument through *n* number of hands, until it is either satisfied or else becomes the stuff of litigation?

The question was vital to the commercial world of the antebellum era, when America suffered from a chronic lack of specie and negotiable instruments served as a source of liquidity and as the chief medium of exchange in long-distance transfers of capital and credit. The question of whether the instruments were in fact negotiable divided state courts. New York law at the time was unsettled, and Swift's attorney filed his case in the *Federal* Court for the Southern District of New York—quite probably to escape the local bias he would surely encounter in a state forum. What he could not escape was the local jury, which (pursuant to the judge's instructions) ruled for Tyson.

The appeal to the Federal Circuit Court principally revolved around the disputed facts of the case. But it also gave rise to the question of whether § 34 of the Judiciary Act was relevant to the case. That section read as follows:

> The laws of the several states, except where the constitution, treaties or statutes of the United States shall otherwise require or provide, shall be regarded as rules of decision in trials at common law in the courts of the United States in cases where they apply.[6]

The appellate judges could not agree on the application of that provision. One judge—under the odd rules of those times, the same judge who had presided over the case at trial—insisted that New York law, as declared by the New York courts, should govern. The other judge would not accept that view, and under then-existing rules, the case was appealed to the Supreme Court on a certificate of division.

The Supreme Court, in an opinion authored by Justice Joseph Story, determined that § 34 was inapplicable. By the New York courts' own lights, there was no statutory or plainly established New York law on the question at issue—only the courts' own latest pronouncements. "In the ordinary use of language," Story declared in a famous passage, "it will hardly be contended that the decisions of courts constitute laws. They are, at most, only evidence of what the laws are, and are not, of themselves, laws."[7] He explained that § 34 is "limited in its application to state laws strictly local; that is to say,

[1] to the positive statutes of the state, and the construction thereof adopted by the local tribunals, and

[2] to . . . rights and titles to real estates, and other matters immovable and intraterritorial in their nature and character.[8]

Without "the slightest difficulty," the Court determined that § 34 did *not* "extend to contracts and other instruments of a commercial nature, the true interpretation and effect whereof are to be sought, not in the decisions of the local tribunals, but in the general principles and doctrines of commercial jurisprudence." To determine those principles and their correct application to the question at hand, Story first surveyed a sizable number of English and American state court decisions, which (on Story's reading) supported the notion of negotiability. Second, he determined that the practice of receiving negotiable instruments in payment of preexisting debts was "according to the known usual course of trade and business" and "for the benefit and convenience of the commercial world." The contrary doctrine of the New York courts "would strike a fatal blow at all discounts of negotiable securities for preexisting debts." Thus, whatever the equities among the original parties may have been, third parties who accepted a bill of exchange in the ordinary course of business were bound by its obligations.[9]

To understand the reach and the limits of *Swift*, one has to understand its basic assumptions and its context. *Swift*'s central point was to vindicate party autonomy—more precisely, the ex ante expectations among merchants dealing across state or international borders. *Swift* enforces that principle in a limited context: "contracts and other instruments *of a commercial nature.*" "Commercial" did not mean "anything having to do with economic exchange," such as a retail sale to consumers, a real estate transaction, or the execution of a will. And "common law," in this context, did not mean "whatever judges do." Rather, it meant contractual relations *among businessmen.* We can assume three things about these sets of transactions. First, the participants act on conditions of rough equality, thus obviating concerns over asymmetric information and unequal bargaining power among the parties and setting to naught any state's proffered interest in protecting citizens-consumers against foreign depredation.[10] Second, commercial actors operate in a world of generally accepted rules and expectations, generated sometimes by positive legal norms but more often by common practices that are enforced primarily by bonding, reputation, and a shared sense of their general utility. In adjudicating those informal rules, courts do not really make law; they merely give force to well-understood implied terms of contract—"the known usual course of trade and business," in Story's terrific formulation. Third, regular market participants can be expected to know those rules. In that context and for those reasons, it makes sense to let the parties choose their own law. For the same reasons, it make sense to impute to the parties an ex ante commitment to abide by the rules and to hold them to their bargains. It does *not* make sense to let parties escape into their own local law after the fact.

The logic, as just noted, has limits. In wholly in-state transactions among parties from the same state, it seems strained to impute any intent other than recourse to local law and the local courts. Accordingly, *Swift* applies only in diversity cases. Whatever exactly the "federal general common law" may be, it is not a basis for invoking the federal courts' federal question jurisdiction. Two further limitations appear in the block quote above. (1) Arguably, businessmen should be charged with a duty of acquainting themselves with the local positive law and its judicial interpretation when conducting their business in other states. (The question, we shall see, is difficult, and *Swift* gives an ambiguous answer.) (2) With respect to in rem disputes over immovable, intraterritorial objects such as real estate, the autonomy premise implies knowledge of and consent to the local law. Hence, the doctrine of *Swift* does not extend to those matters.

What merchants *cannot* be charged with is advance knowledge of another state's common law. Why? In the absence of any statutory law, local courts will adjudicate any dispute under the very same principles of commercial law on which an independent (federal) forum would rely. As Story emphasized, the confused New York precedents relied on by the lower courts ruling in *Swift* had been decided on exactly those grounds. The only thing that contracting parties can be presumed to "know" about each other's forum is that it will likely have a homeward bias. Thus, to hold a party to the common law of the plaintiff's home state is to impute a mutual intent to settle any disputes under the law of whoever sues first. That imputation, and any jurisdictional regime based on it, is nuts. Even if lawyers and businessmen can bargain around bad rules, a "follow-the-home-state-law" rule is a de facto tax on interstate transactions. We do not have a Constitution and federal courts to tax interstate commerce. We established those institutions to facilitate and protect it.

. . . and the Constitution

Swift is not a constitutional case, and it was not viewed by any justice as "a federalism case." However, *Swift*'s understanding of law is continuous with the Constitution in three related respects: the Constitution's territoriality principle; its grant of diversity jurisdiction under Article III; and its substantive provisions, especially the Contract Clause and the Commerce Clause. The *Swift* Court was aware of the continuities. They would soon serve as means of "constitutionalizing" *Swift*, which in turn prompted much of the criticism of its progeny. Where the Constitution and its explicit grants of powers end, rings the objection, politics begins, and that is not the judiciary's business. *Swift's* answer is that the commercial law is provisional and revisable at will by Congress or by any individual state. It is a default rule, not a primary and preemptive constitutional rule. Precisely that quality accounts for *Swift's* initial attraction and the unanimity of the decision, for its stupendous rise, and for its eventual downfall.

Territoriality. The precept that equal states may legislate for themselves but not for or on each other is a bedrock proposition of constitutional federalism. No one seriously doubts the proposition; the question is how to identify workable, federalism-conforming standards of territoriality. *Swift* identifies such a standard or baseline for commercial transactions: contract.

Although *Swift* itself does not mention "territoriality," its author had a very clear grasp of the point. Long before *Swift*, Story articulated it forcefully in *Van Reimsdyk v. Kane* (1812). Like many cases of the era but unlike *Swift*, *Van Reimsdyk* involved a state statute governing—with the usual purpose of abrogating—a foreign debt contracted through a bill of exchange. Story would have none of it. A contract made in one state or foreign country, he insisted, "cannot be discharged by a mere positive regulation of another country." Although federal courts must generally follow § 34, a "limitation must arise *whenever the subject-matter . . . is extra-territorial*." Any other arrangement, Story continued,

> would enable the state legislatures by local regulations, to dry up the sources
> of the federal jurisdiction, and annihilate public as well as private credit; it
> would set the citizens of the different states in array against each other, and
> enable a fraudulent debtor to retreat into another state, and there by a formal
> surrender of his property and a settled residence, to set at defiance the claims
> of all his absent and honest creditors.[11]

The case for a federal general common law that displaces not just state courts' common law but also statutory law is extremely difficult. For reasons discussed later, Story's position is not completely beyond the pale, but it clearly strains the language of § 34 and, more broadly, the federal courts' authority.[12] On balance, it seems straightforward that state statutes of the kind described by Story are directly prohibited by the Constitution, in particular by the Contract Clause. What matters in the present context, however, is the underlying logic. In a contractual context, we have a way of identifying "extraterritorial" state law: it involves citizens from different states and, ipso facto, at least two sets of state law. There is no prima facie reason to credit a pro-debtor state's law over the less forgiving law of another state (presumably, the creditor's). Indeed, there is a powerful reason not to do so: presumably, the debtor chose the forum precisely because it promised the abrogation of a validly entered agreement. The idea that federal courts must follow the forum state's law by virtue of the bare fact that the plaintiff has chosen it is a "territorial" rule all right. But it is the worst imaginable rule, productive of all the mischief described by Story. The right rule honors the parties' ex ante commitments, not their opportunistic litigation choices.

Swift entails the possibility of two sets of laws within one and the same state—one for "diverse" parties, another for purely domestic disputes (unless the local courts choose to follow the Supreme Court's understanding of general common law). That seeming oddity would in the Progressive Era become a prominent theme of anti-*Swift* agitation, but it is spurious in the context of a contractual understanding.[13] By way of a close contemporary analogy, American companies routinely subject their international agreements to international arbitration. No one believes that those agreements constitute an assault on the sovereignty or territorial integrity of the United States; no one seriously argues that arbitration agreements create two sets of laws within our territory. (If those fears were real, we would not render international arbitration agreements enforceable in U.S. courts.) The difference is that arbitration agreements require an affirmative exercise of party autonomy, whereas *Swift* presumes it. We shall see shortly, however, that the presumption is just that—a presumption, not an ironclad rule.

Diversity. By its terms, *Swift* is grounded in and limited to the federal courts' diversity jurisdiction. The commercial law is not a *source* of federal jurisdiction; that would indeed be inconsistent with a constitutional system of delegated powers. Rather, it is a means of exercising jurisdiction that has been granted—in this case, diversity jurisdiction.[14]

To positivist, post-*Erie* minds, the distinction between the common law as a body of law and a mode of judicial reasoning—fundamental to *Swift* and its era—misses the mark on two points: the underlying notion that judges can independently "find" law (as opposed to making it up), and the notion that diversity jurisdiction authorizes federal courts to engage in that mode of inquiry. The easiest way to explain the latter, crucial point lays in the fact, curious at first sight, that the federal common law of admiralty and maritime jurisdiction—the field where the battle over federal common law was first waged—has survived to this day. The common explanation (or at any rate rationalization) is that Article III of the Constitution explicitly confers subject-matter jurisdiction over "all Cases of admiralty and maritime Jurisdiction." The grant of diversity jurisdiction, in contrast, goes to the constellation among parties, not to subject-matter. Its purpose, the positivist argument runs, is to give citizens access to an impartial *forum*, not to a separate body of *law*, declared independently of the will of either Congress or the states. With respect to the apprehended bias of substantive state law, the Constitution provides for two sets of complementary remedies: direct prohibitions against the states, such as the Contract Clause; and federal legislation pursuant to some enumerated power. Those are the arrangements the states accepted, and all they accepted. Their presence in the Constitution proves that a federal common law, supplied by the federal judiciary, is an affront to federalism.

Strange as it may sound, *Swift* did not reject this line of reasoning, implicitly or explicitly. *Swift* does not entitle diversity litigants to a different, made-up body of law. To the contrary, in deciding commercial law cases, the Supreme Court looked to the same principles and doctrines under which the state courts decided cases. (*Swift*'s examination of New York law and the decisions of "the several states" was not merely a polite nod; it was a look for instruction and illumination.) Still, the heart and soul of diversity jurisdiction is the protection of parties against local bias, and that purpose would be defeated if federal courts had to slavishly follow the forum state's common law. Why? Principally, because the local courts and their law are bound be biased in a way in which federal courts are not. However, "the litigant in the federal court is entitled to the law as it is, not simply to the local judicial reflection of the law."[15] To reject the Supreme Court's right to an independent determination is to destroy the purpose of diversity jurisdiction.

Contracts and Commerce. Swift is continuous with substantive (rather than jurisdictional) constitutional provisions that protect interstate commerce and those engaged in it against. The Commerce Clause, the Privileges and Immunities Clause, and the Contract Clause are the most prominent examples. All embody *Swift*'s central objective: protect the gains from interstate commerce and, to that end, protect the commercial class from bias and unfair surprise in foreign state jurisdictions. The continuity is not a matter of ephemeral constitutional "values" or atmospherics. If anything, the nineteenth-century affinity between common law and constitutional law is too close for modern comfort: in case after case (though not in *Swift* itself), general common-law arguments ran together with constitutional claims—most frequently, the Contract Clause and the Commerce Clause.[16]

There were breakpoints and differences. Prominently, *Swift* principally aimed to discipline state courts. Those institutions were arguably beyond the scope of the Contract Clause, which is explicitly directed at state legislatures. (It says that no state may "pass any bill" impairing the obligation of contract.) *Swift*'s ability to cover the common but constitutionally under-provided-for cases of state judicial expropriation may have been one of its attractions. Further, the general common law predictably provided a more nuanced framework for contractual relations than the bare language of the Constitution—even if read against a common-law background—could readily provide. The best illustration of this difference and its implications is the famous *Dartmouth College* case, which arose over the question of whether changes to the college's colonial charter violated the Contract Clause.[17] It is unambiguously "a Contract Clause case" because the plaintiffs' lawyers (though aided by Justice Story, whose ex parte contacts in the matter caused much bitterness) could not find a way to manufacture a diversity case.[18] It was brought instead as a federal question case, which technically cut off the entire body of general law bearing on the questions at hand, including the central question of whether the charter was a "contract" in the first place. John Marshall solved the plaintiffs' problem by reading much of the general law into the Constitution, thus producing what looks even by Marshall's standards like a remarkably aggressive take on the document.[19]

Although the Contract Clause is no longer with us, Marshall's mode of constitutional argument is far more familiar to us now than the common-law discourse of the nineteenth century. Story's mercantile law may no longer brood or hover over the states; but the enlightened opinions of mankind and the Constitution of Zimbabwe do, usually under the copious umbrella of the Fourteenth Amendment.[20] Whether that is a better way of making sense of the constitutional architecture is a different question.

Constitutional Problems? Erie declared *Swift* unconstitutional. To see why the *Swift* Court did not perceive any such problem, it is best to set aside three anti-*Swift* arguments that played major roles in *Swift*'s eventual demise but, in the end, obscure rather than advance a sensible understanding of the decision, its place in the constitutional architecture, and its difficulties.

The first, narrow argument is that Story misread § 34. In the 1920s, the eminent Charles Warren claimed to have found historical evidence showing that the authors of the Judiciary Act had in fact meant to include state common law under the heading of "laws of the several states." We can safely put that objection aside as Warren's purported evidence has been discredited. Although not demonstrably correct, Story's interpretation is entirely plausible.[21] Two broader objections to *Swift* derive from hostility to the federal courts' diversity jurisdiction per se and from Justice Holmes's legal positivism. Both ideas would figure prominently in *Swift*'s demise. Neither, however, contributes to a constitutional understanding of *Swift* and its progeny. (Chapter 10 will expound on these cursory remarks.)

Stripped of those latter-day concerns, the constitutional difficulty with *Swift* is this: The national government is a government of delegated and limited powers. That goes for the federal courts as well as for the other branches. No federal statute authorizes the Supreme Court's general common law. (It would then no longer be "common law" but instead be captured by the "except" clause of § 34). And there is no constitutional delegation of power, either. Diversity jurisdiction determines only what court is to hear what sorts of cases, not what law that court is to apply in those disputes.

This line of argument ought to have traction in a system of limited government; and so indeed it did. The advocates of common law had a three-part response. We have already encountered the first two parts: One, the common law could never be a *basis* of federal jurisdiction, only a means of exercising jurisdiction that had been conveyed by the Constitution and the Judiciary Act or some equivalent statute. Two, "federal general common law" was not a separate body of law but an independent assessment of what that law was (and technically, the federal determinations remained *state* law). The third part of the answer was that the commercial law was provisional, both vis-à-vis Congress and vis-à-vis the states. Congress may grant or withhold diversity jurisdiction, and it may independently and sua sponte supplant federal common law. At the same time, federal general common law lacked *preemptive* effect. It could be "localized" both by private parties (for example, through a contractual clause specifying a particular state's law) or by states, through statutory legislation.[22]

The *Swift* formula is of one piece with judicial constructions encountered in earlier chapters—prominently, the corporation law of *Deveaux*: free commerce as a constitutional baseline, state legislation as an opt-out. On the post-Marshall Court, that formula held great appeal. For nationalists like Story, it offered an avenue to advance integration without dramatic, backlash-inducing constitutional declarations. Conversely, for the Taney Court's Jacksonian justices, it offered a way to hold on to state sovereignty without endangering the union. This helps to explain why none of the justices, including the most vehement states' rights defenders ever to occupy the Bench, perceived a federalism problem in *Swift*. And it explains why the supposedly Anti-Federalist Taney Court was more assertive on federal common law matters, both in admiralty cases and in diversity cases, than the nationalist Marshall Court.[23] In historical context, then, the general common law was anything but brooding abstraction. It was a pragmatic response to federalism's coordination problems. Nor was it a manifestation of judicial imperialism. It was a constitutional avoidance canon.

The problem was not *Swift*'s basis or construction; the problem was containment. Beginning in the 1850s, the Supreme Court extended the principle of *Swift* to an ever-widening range of state common law. Moreover, it applied federal common law even when state legislatures had enacted, and state courts had conclusively interpreted, a "localizing" state statute. Arguably, those extensions were not warranted by the original *Swift* formula. They would provide much fodder for relentless attacks on *Swift*, and they eventually contributed greatly to its demise.[24] It is important, however, to understand the fundamental reasons for those extensions: the pro-competitive thrust of the *Swift* principle and the states' protectionist and exploitative impulses pushed in opposite directions.[25] The conflicts multiplied and intensified in tandem with progressive economic integration, industrialization, and sectional divisions among states. Eventually, those forces proved more than the Supreme Court could handle. *Swift* was eminently plausible so long as federalism looked like a coordination problem. When it proved to be a control problem, *Swift*'s elegant formula disintegrated.

Swift Extensions

Swift contained two fundamental ambiguities. The first ambiguity was the "breadth" of general common law. Obviously, the construct encompasses the law of negotiable instruments. But what else was included? Soon after *Swift*, the Court unanimously extended the ruling to cover insurance contracts.[26] But would the rule extend to bills of lading, as a means of contracting away liability for acts of negligence? To carriage contracts or municipal bonds? The second ambiguity concerned the "depth" of the *Swift* principle. Story's formulation in *Swift*, as noted, extended only to state common law, as distinct from state constitutions, statutes, and authoritative state judicial interpretations of those instruments. That formulation rendered federal common law consistent with § 34 and with broader principles of federalism and the separation of powers. In theory, it also permitted the development of a coherent, uniform commercial law, available to all merchants in interstate commerce—and to the extent that state courts or legislatures chose to adopt the general common law, also to in-state actors and transactions.

The general law can do its work safely within the bounds of federalism and § 34 so long as states see the genius and the wisdom of the construction. At an abstract level, one might expect the states to resist the option of "localizing" the law. That strategy, one should think, would be harmful to party expectations and to the state's interest in retaining a reputation as a reliable place for business. From a global perspective, excessive localization of the law governing interstate transactions would retard commerce and comity among states. With a bit of gentle judicial guidance, the justices of the post-Marshall era hoped, states would surely see the point.[27]

They did not. *Swift* encountered the same force that doomed the corporate law formula of *Deveaux*—factional forces that drove the states' mercantilist rivalry and their protectionist and exploitative tendencies. States stubbornly resisted the *Swift* doctrine.[28] The courts of New York, having been repudiated in *Swift*, consistently refused to be governed by its doctrine, apparently for the remainder of the nineteenth century.[29] Similarly, state legislatures routinely localized their law in response to cases decided on the principle of *Swift*. Quite often, they did so to reverse the outcome in an individual controversy.

Confronted with that resistance, what were the federal courts to do? Surely, the general law, diversity jurisdiction, and the authority of the federal judiciary could not be ousted quite so easily. If the principle of *Swift* was to have any force, it needed an anticircumvention doctrine. Cases articulating this rationale began to crop up in the 1840s. A famous example is *Rowan v. Runnels* (1847). A Virginia creditor had sued a Mississippi debtor on a contract involving a sale of slaves imported into Mississippi, entered into after the enactment of the Mississippi Constitution and its prohibition on the importation, for sale, of slaves after May 1, 1833. (The prohibition was intended to protect the value of the local slave population against large-scale importation from Virginia's Tidewater region.) A Mississippi judge and jury ruled for the in-state defendant, relying on a Mississippi Supreme Court decision that had held the constitutional provision to be self-executing, meaning legally effective without implementing legislation. In *Rowan*, the Supreme Court reversed, notwithstanding the Mississippi Supreme Court's conclusive interpretation of the state constitution. The explanation for this ruling, seemingly outside *Swift*'s four corners, is that a virtually identical case, involving the same state constitutional provision and a very similar, near-contemporaneous contract, had reached the justices earlier. In *Groves v. Slaughter* (1841), the Court had held the constitutional provision to *lack* self-executing force. It had felt free to do so—a year before *Swift*, but entirely consistent with its holding—because no conclusive state court interpretation existed at that time. The Mississippi Supreme Court's subsequent ruling to the contrary effectively "overruled" the Supreme Court and enabled the state courts to abrogate contracts of the sort in question on a retroactive basis.[30]

Chief Justice Taney rejected that obstinate maneuver. His opinion in *Rowan* conceded that federal courts must generally defer to state courts on interpretation of state constitutions "from the time they are made." No such comity, however, could extend to the retroactive invalidation of contracts with citizens in other states, lest diversity jurisdiction "become utterly useless and nugatory."[31] The basis of this decision is not altogether clear. Taney mentions the Contract Clause, but almost in passing. Ultimately, the assertion of the Court's authority seems to rest on an implied grant within the compass of "the judicial power" and on a broad understanding of scope and purposes of diversity jurisdiction.[32] The power to exercise diversity jurisdiction, one could say, must include the power to protect that jurisdiction against manifest state evasion. The same conjunction of constitutional concerns reappears in *Watson v. Tarpley* (1856), where a Tennessee resident had sued a Mississippi resident on a bill of exchange. Mississippi law favored the in-state debtor-defendant in the circumstances at issue. A unanimous Supreme Court decided for the plaintiff, in derogation of the Mississippi statute. Any state law that impairs the contractual rights of nonresidents or divests federal courts of cognizance of such cases, the Court declared, would constitute "a violation of the general commercial law, which a State would have no power to impose, and which the courts of the United States would be bound to disregard."[33]

One can read *Rowan* and *Watson* as consistent with *Swift*, but that interpretation seems forced in light of *Watson*'s broad language. In substance, it is clear what is going on here: the Taney Court was determined to police the principle of *Swift* and unwilling to let the states eviscerate the federal courts' authority. It is not easy, however, to formulate a *Swift*-protective principle that does not compromise, more or less overtly, the implicit federalism restrictions of *Swift* itself. The federal courts' authority to police state court interpretations of state constitutions and laws must rest on some basis other than the general common law as formulated in *Swift*. That basis must of needs be constitutional, as *Rowan* and *Watson* recognized. One can therefore say that *Swift* became "constitutionalized." Conversely, and perhaps better, one can say that in cases like *Rowan* and *Watson*, the general common law operated as a kind of Contract Clause in disguise. For the Taney Court, federal general common law provided a means of protecting interstate commerce without superintending, on a constitutional basis, the states' domestic affairs (such as debtor relief laws). It allowed the Court to throttle back on Marshall's and Story's Contract Clause without throwing the door wide open to state protectionism and exploitation.[34]

The difficulties were twofold. One, a *Swift* doctrine that covers state statutes and noncommercial matters really does demand a constitutional foundation. Two, the Supreme Court in the end lacked the institutional clout to force procompetitive norms on unwilling states. Cases involving railroad finance and railroad employer liability, two particularly fertile fields of federal common law litigation, illustrate the dynamics.

Railroad Bonds. The operation of general law as de facto Interstate Contract Clause is illustrated powerfully by railroad bond cases. Midwestern local governments often sought to attract developers and especially railroads with offers of aid, usually financed by floating local bond issues. State constitutions and statutes (many enacted in the wake of the panic of 1837) often restricted those issues in various respects. Equally often, those restrictions were ignored, either inadvertently or with a willful intent to dishonor the bonds once they had been sold or resold to investors, predominantly out-of-state. More often than not, state courts sanctioned those maneuvers.

In one view, bond issues look "purely local" in *Swift*'s sense. They could not issue from anywhere except a local sovereign, whose acts (unlike negotiable instruments framed by private parties) are matters of public record. That view, though, seems artificial and oblivious both to the brutal political abuses on the frontier and to the practical considerations that drove *Swift*—the liquidity of financial markets and the marketability of commercial paper in the far-away secondary markets in the East and in Europe.[35] The force of these considerations appears in *Gelpcke v. Dubuque* (1864), an early and notorious bond case. The Iowa legislature had authorized localities to float railroad bonds, and the Iowa Supreme Court had repeatedly declared those authorizations constitutional—until the schemes went belly up and the Iowa Court, in a sharp reversal and at variance with the law in the great majority of states, determined that the authorization violated the Iowa Constitution after all. With that ruling, both the in-state and out-of-state bondholders were out of luck. The U.S. Supreme Court reversed on principles of general law. The justices were scandalized by the political shenanigans that had induced the Iowa Supreme Court's about-face. "We shall never immolate truth, justice, and the law," the Court intoned, "because a State tribunal has erected the altar and decreed the sacrifice." Only Justice Miller (who hailed from the Iowa town of Keokuk) dissented, as he would in many municipal bond cases. State courts, he predicted, would not yield to the Supreme Court's general law pronouncements, with the result that to all practical intents, two sets of laws would govern in the states—the state courts' law, applicable to in-state creditors; and the general common law, for the benefit of "stockbroker[s] of Wall Street."[36]

Over time, municipal bond defaults reached some $100 million to $150 million. In a pattern familiar from chapter 5, states barred railroad and other companies from doing business in the state unless they surrendered their right to invoke the federal courts' diversity jurisdiction. Counties reorganized themselves to escape payment, and state judges consistently sided with the debtors.[37] Three decades after *Gelpcke*, the Supreme Court had decided some three hundred bond cases. Those cases were a counterpart to the railroad tax cases under the dormant Commerce Clause. As Justice Miller's invective against Wall Street illustrates, the underlying question was whether the proceeds of rail development would end up in the Eastern states or in the rural West and South. The bond cases dealt with the investment end of that question, the tax cases with the operating profits. And in neither set of cases was the Court able to discipline local governments in any consequential way. The Supreme Court is, or can be, very good at setting default rules. It cannot realistically function as a regulatory agency, least of all in a context that involved intense sectional and economic divisions.

Railroads: Employer Liability. Harms among strangers had traditionally been thought to be covered by lex loci delicti, rather than general common law. *Swift*'s conceptual apparatus rested on presumptions of party autonomy and mutual consent, as reflected in accepted business practices. That construction makes neither practical nor conceptual sense in the context of torts among strangers. On the other hand, lex loci made little sense on railroads, where the costs of configuring work practices and technical equipment to the demands of each state along a transcontinental trip can be very high. What to do?

Baltimore & Ohio Railroad Co. v. Baugh (1893) was a diversity suit by a fireman injured by a train accident, allegedly caused by an engineer's negligence, that occurred in Ohio in the course of an interstate trip. The central question in *Baugh*, as in numerous cases before and after, was whether the railroad employer was liable for an employee's negligence that caused injury to a fellow-servant employee. Justice Brewer, writing for the Court, acknowledged the need for "the exercise of mutual respect and deference" between federal and state courts. The state courts' rules on property and action, especially the law of real estate and the interpretation of state statutes and constitutions, would always be binding in federal courts. Even so, federal courts would exercise "independent judgment in cases not foreclosed by previous adjudication"; indeed, it would be a "dereliction of their duty" not to do so.[38] Brewer seemed impressed by two considerations: the fact that the Ohio Supreme Court had apparently considered the question as one of general law, and the need for a uniform fellow-servant rule for interstate carriers. Congress, Brewer observed, had legislated upon railroads (though not fellow-servant rules) in the Interstate Commerce Act and subsequent enactments. The Baltimore and Ohio Railroad was plainly an interstate carrier. As trains pass from state to state, Brewer asked rhetorically, "must the rights, obligations, and duties subsisting between [the railroad] and its employees change at every state line?"[39] Having answered in the negative, Brewer decided the case under general common law rather than Ohio's more plaintiff-friendly liability law. Baugh lost.

Justice Stephen Field submitted a vehement dissent—not inappropriately characterized as a rant—that contains the first full-scale attack on *Swift* by any justice. "There is no unwritten general or common law of the United States on the subject" of fellow-servant liability, Field insisted. "Indeed, there is no unwritten general or common law of the United States on any subject." Field conceded that he himself had in many cases confidently followed the doctrine of *Swift*, but he now considered those opinions in error.[40] And in a passage that would come to figure prominently in *Erie*, he argued that the imposition of general law in these types of cases violated first principles of dual federalism and the states' "autonomy and independence" in their proper sphere.[41]

It is not altogether clear what prompted Field's departure. Plainly, the Court's employer-friendly disposition of the case—quite arguably, a deviation from more plaintiff-friendly precedents, including an important opinion by Field himself—had something to do with it.[42] Field's hostility to large corporations, already on display in the constitutional cases reviewed in chapter 5, was another probable factor. In the end, though, it is hard to deny that the *Swift* doctrine had in fact reached, and perhaps exceeded, the outer limits of its plausibility. Brewer's ruminations about the Interstate Commerce Act and the needs of interstate commerce suggested that *Baugh* had a constitutional backdrop. It was natural for Field to respond at that level.

It is also possible, though, to understand the Court's sustained application of federal common law and Brewer's discussion of interstate commerce in a different light—as a call for, or perhaps an implicit bet on, federal legislation. Field's doctrinaire dualism, with its concomitant suggestion that state courts and juries might gobble up and dissipate the proceeds of interstate railroad operations, held very little appeal. On the other hand, the justices had struggled with railroad liability matters without much success in finding a viable formula. The sensible solution might be a federal *legislative* rule, and by the time of *Baugh* (1893), that was no longer an elusive proposition. After all, Congress had already established the Interstate Commerce Commission to regulate railroad rates in interstate traffic, and it was not far-fetched to think that judicial insistence on the inherently federal nature of that traffic might prompt congressional regulation of liability standards.[43] Congress eventually enacted that statute, the Federal Employers' Liability Act, in 1906, declaring employer liability for fellow-servant injuries the general rule. Although the Court declared that act unconstitutional on the grounds that it covered purely in-state as well as interstate commerce, it left little doubt that a more narrowly crafted statute would be sustained. Armed with what amounted to a set of drafting instruction, Congress reenacted substantially the same statute while restricting its scope to interstate commerce. So revised, the act easily passed judicial muster.[44]

There was more than one irony here. The coextensive reach for federal common law and federal legislative authority had played a major role in the early years of the republic, especially in the area of maritime law, where the issue first arose. The fear that federal judicial authority would drag congressional authority after it had then been a Jeffersonian refrain, which induced Story and his nationalist brethren to tread lightly.[45] Some eight decades later, the fact that federal common law had paved the way for congressional intervention proved of benefit to Progressive forces. Conversely, the railroad corporations that had for decades defended federal courts and federal law as a bulwark against state exploitation argued in the *Second Employers' Liability Cases* that Congress had no business interfering with the states' traditional prerogatives over tort law. (In a real sense, they no longer knew what side they were on.) The Supreme Court brusquely rejected that argument.[46] The long-running argument over federal general common law would henceforth be fought on statutory terms.

Conclusion

Legislative-judicial accommodations of the sort just sketched were a prominent feature of the law of the Gilded Age. They played out in different arenas and in different forms. The congressional "reconveyance" of state authority was one such form; the compartmentalization of anti-trust and corporate law was another; the partial substitution of legislative or administrative standards (for example, under the Interstate Commerce Act) for common-law adjudication was a third. In each case, Congress intervened against the backdrop of a judicially developed, procompetitive baseline. In each case, the interventions were prompted at least in part by the Court's inability to function as a de facto regulatory agency. In each case, the Supreme Court continued to police the legislative interventions with an eye toward reminding legislators to remain respectful of the constitutional parameters; and more often than not, the congressional schemes provided for a continued judicial role. In no case did the Court bar the door to congressional action.

I do not mean to paint a picture of political and institutional harmony. The issues over which the judicial doctrines reviewed in these chapters held sway were areas of intense sectional conflict and of social, political, and economic turmoil, and it typically took decades to work out the institutional solutions. In retrospect, the jurisprudence of the time looks to many like a reactionary judiciary's hold-out campaign against the pain-fully obvious necessities of the modern state.[47] It looks that way, how-ever, mostly because we know who eventually won. All things considered, the dominant pattern—legislative intervention against a background of procompetitive default rules—was not a bad means of constitutional adaptation. It left room and time for the constructive development of pro-competitive adaptations and coordination rules—corporate law, the dor-mant Commerce Clause (for all its seeming confusions), federal liability rules for common carriers in interstate commerce. The residual force of the constitutional background rules dampened the political hyperactivity and feverish innovation that would characterize later periods of constitu-tional adjustment.

That force, however, depended on sectional divisions among states—the same sectional divisions that made the doctrine of *Swift* first attractive and in the end unworkable. I will return to this constant theme one last time at the end of the next and final chapter on competitive federalism, dealing with its nineteenth-century fiscal aspects.

CHAPTER SEVEN

The Fiscal Constitution

Within a constitutionally designed federal structure, we would predict that there would be constant pressures by competitive lower-level governments to secure institutional rearrangements that would moderate competitive pressures. One obvious such arrangement would be one that established a uniform tax system across all jurisdictions. . . . And the logical body to administer any such agreement is the higher level of government.

Geoffrey Brennan and James M. Buchanan

The representatives of the States and of the people . . . will naturally incline to obtain means from the Federal Government for State purposes. . . . We should then not only 'lay and collect taxes, duties, imposts, and excises' for Federal purposes, but for every State purpose which Congress might deem expedient or useful. This would . . . constitute a sort of partnership between the two in the Treasury of the United States, equally ruinous to both.

President James Buchanan

Introduction

Recall the fiscal federalism principles from chapter 3. Competitive federalism demands substantial fiscal and in particular tax autonomy for all levels of government, as well as a low level of intergovernmental fiscal transfers. Such an arrangement confronts a risk of unilateral defection, either by the central government (through the imposition of a tax monopoly) or by states (through taxes that exploit other states' citizens); and bargaining risks, either in the form of federal tax-and-spend cartels, instituted in response to state demand, or of excessive state borrowing in expectation of a federal bailout. All four risks played a role in nineteenth century politics and constitutional debate; all four were held at bay. The first section of this chapter sketches the Constitution's parsimonious tax assignments and explains why a federal tax monopoly, though dreaded by many Anti-Federalists at the time of the Founding, has not been a real threat to American federalism. In contrast, exploitative state taxation has been a constant temptation and peril. It was addressed in the nineteenth

century in the constitutionally envisioned fashion—by judicial intervention. That is the subject of the fourth section. The intervening sections
deal with federalism's bargaining risks: fiscal cartelization and excessive
state borrowing. While both dangers proved very real over the course of
the nineteenth century, the constitutional structure and practice remained
vehemently competitive. Fiscal transfers to state and local governments
remained limited throughout, and the national government spectacularly
declined to bail out debt-ridden state governments.

This resilience with respect to bargaining risks contrasts sharply with
the contemporary picture. The New Deal and, on a grander scale, the
Great Society blanketed vast areas of government with "cooperative"
fiscal transfer programs. In more recent experience, the long-standing
precommitment against federal bailouts of state and local governments
appears to have collapsed. The question, then, is why fiscal federalism
remained competitive for such an extended period, only to surrender so
completely later on. The natural temptation is to attribute the dramatic
shift to constitutional causes and culprits. The modern Congress, the story
goes, routinely "spends its way around" enumerated powers limitations. It
offers federal funds that the states cannot afford to refuse and, in the same
breath, establishes federal bureaucracies to micromanage state and local
affairs. The perverse fiscal incentives practically force states to create and
expand programs that erode their fiscal autonomy; when the programs
prove unsustainable (as in the wake of a financial crisis), the states have
no choice but to beg for a bailout. All around, states seem at the mercy
of Congress, and nothing seems to be left of federalism. If that unhappy
fate befell us only in the twentieth century, surely the explanation must
be sought in the demise of constitutional norms that had theretofore
stiffened the states' collective spine to resist federal entreaties—perhaps
the enactment of the Sixteenth Amendment in 1913, which provided the
national government with ample income-tax revenues to bribe states into
compliance; or the Seventeenth Amendment, also ratified in 1913, which
deprived state governments of their representation as states in the federal
councils; or the New Deal Court's demolition of constitutional limitations
on the congressional spending power.[1]

This story has currency among many constitutional scholars, but we
shall see that it is untenable. Its central error is the notion that federal
conditional funding is a centralizing imposition on the states. It is not.
Rather, it is a response to state demand. And although the demand has
varied in intensity, it has been a constant throughout the history of the
Union. Some 130 years before James Buchanan, *President* James Buchanan
apprehended the danger without the aid of public choice theorems, based

on experience. State and local demands for federal transfer payments had trickled into the very first Congress and soon become a mighty stream. The real question, then, is why those demands, which our modern federalism seems to accommodate with such ease and generosity, went largely unmet in the nineteenth century.

Neither fiscal constraints nor state representation had anything to do with the matter. No meaningful fiscal constraints existed, and the representation of states as states cannot possibly reduce state demand for federal transfers and bailouts.[2] Nor are affirmative constitutional limitations a likely explanation, for the excellent reason that the Constitution contains no such limitations. Rather, competitive federalism's nineteenth-century resilience has to do with what the Constitution does *not* do and say. Federally sponsored tax-and-spend cartels—that is, "cooperative federalism"—require a coordination point or baseline on which subordinate governments can negotiate a bargain. So do bailouts. As explained in chapter 3, however, the Constitution abjures any predetermined distributional baseline. Consequently, states must coordinate tax-and-spend cartels or bailouts on an open field; and under nineteenth-century conditions, sectional divisions among states blocked any such bargain. For reasons discussed in later chapters, the states managed to overcome those obstacles in the twentieth century, which goes to show that our bare-bones, minimalist Constitution provides no *insurmountable* barrier to federalism's built-in tendency toward cartelization. Quite arguably, however, it impedes that tendency as effectively as one can reasonably hope.

Federal Taxation

The Constitution prohibits states from taxing imports and exports, and it prohibits federal taxes on exports from any state. In that fashion, it protected Southern "staple" states from a federal assault on their economic basis (the export-oriented plantation economy) while giving the national government a monopoly over import tariffs. With those exceptions, the Constitution contains no tax assignments. States and the federal government may concurrently tax the same people, assets, and transactions at any rate they may see fit.[3]

The ratification debates resounded with Anti-Federalist alarms to the effect that the Constitution's open-ended tax structure would in short order produce a federal tax monopoly and impoverish the states. Publius dismissed those apprehensions as baseless. Considerations of political economy and administrative convenience, Hamilton argued, would naturally produce a segregation of revenue sources. For the most part, his analysis proved correct. Constitutionally barred from imposing tariffs, states came to rely on internal property and poll taxes (as Hamilton anticipated), as well as benefit taxes and fees and royalties from incorporation.[4] The federal government, for its part, relied almost entirely on the tariff, the one revenue source that the Constitution explicitly monopolizes in the federal government. Thus, throughout the nineteenth century (except in wartime), mercantilism abroad went hand-in-hand with minimal federal taxation at home and with fiscal competition among states.

The paucity of tax assignments in the Constitution is a deliberate and foundational design decision—and a somewhat ironic one, since the road to Philadelphia started with a debate, and initially a broad consensus, over tax assignments. The embarrassing experience with the requisition system of the Articles had persuaded political leaders that the Union had to be endowed with an independent source of revenue. Just about everyone's federal tax of choice was a tariff on foreign imports. An impost had been proposed twice as an amendment to the Articles of Confederation and, on both occasions, foundered on the opposition of a single state (Rhode Island in 1781, New York in 1783). Still, the impost seemed to offer an attractive remedy for the Union's ills. It could be enforced easily and with minimal intrusion in the states' affairs, and it would not have to be apportioned among states—thus obviating, or so it seemed, any need for a difficult debate over representation and slavery. And even a very modest impost would suffice to pay off the war debts and to restore public credit.

On account of these attractions, a federal impost was a core position of constituencies who advocated a reform of the Articles, as opposed to a brand-new Constitution. Against this tempting position, Federalists mobilized two mutually reinforcing arguments. The first, institutional argument was that an impost could not in fact be added quite so easily to the Articles. It would require a surrender of the unanimity principle, lest it founder on the hold-out problem that had thwarted the proposal twice before. Moreover, a Union with the power to impose a tariff would require enforcement authorities and a judicial apparatus to protect against private evasion (for example, by smugglers) and against state infringement. The existing powers of the Union, however, already looked troublesome to adherents of republican government. Its central principle, representation of states in a collective body, was bearable only on account of the congressional unanimity requirement and state enforcement of Union law—precisely the features that had blocked the impost and caused political "imbecility" in the first place. Heaping additional central powers on the rickety Articles would be intolerable. Think hard enough about the tax question, and you have to rethink the institutional structure.

The Federalists' second, economic argument was that the impost would perhaps fund the debt of the last war and restore public credit—but fail in the event of the next calamity. War tends to bring trade and hence tariff revenue to a halt. And because few people lend on a diminishing stream of profits, credit too would dry up when it would be most needed. In the ordinary course of events, the Union would have neither a need nor any inclination to resort to nontariff revenues. In extremis, however, it would probably have to do so, and it would be dangerous folly to block that option ex ante. That argument implied a Union with its own internal revenue agents and authority, which further strengthened the case for fundamental constitutional reform.

The Federalists prevailed. The tax arguments that had provided such a powerful impulse *for* the Constitution survived *in* the Constitution, and the national government obtained full and direct tax authority over any conceivable tax base, save only for exports. Federalists and Anti-Federalists alike often described that authority as "unlimited" or "unqualified." What they meant was that federal taxation was unlimited with respect to the tax rate and to the tax base (save only for the prohibition against taxing exports and, prior to 1808, the importation of slaves). But the shorthand characterization is not entirely accurate. The Constitution imposes formal constraints on the taxing power, depending on the mode of taxation: an unfortunate apportionment rule for direct taxes and an eminently sensible uniformity rule for indirect taxes. Both constraints would have potent effects on the tax structure, though not always the intended effects.

Apportionment. The choice of an apportionment rule for direct taxes was part and parcel of the sordid compromise over slavery and representation. To break the Convention deadlock over how to count slaves for purposes of representation, Gouverneur Morris proposed "that taxation shall be in proportion to Representation."[5] Morris subsequently amended his proposal to apply only to "direct" taxes—probably to meet the objection that the impost, which was plainly an indirect tax and which had the huge advantage of not having to be apportioned, would have to apportioned after all. To distill the bargain to its essence, the South obtained the political protection of "extra" representation inherent in the three-fifths clause. For the North, the conjunction of taxation and representation implied that the South might be taxed—via apportionment—for its dubious privilege.

To this compromise, we owe one of the most alien, ill-understood, and unworkable provisions of the Constitution. "Alien" because the compromise effectively breaks with the constitutional principle that the federal government acts on individuals, not states. (Apportioned taxes look an awful lot like requisitions in drag and, in the antebellum era, were even raised in that fashion.)[6] "Ill-understood" because not a single member of the Convention appears to have had the foggiest notion of what might qualify as a "direct" tax, let alone how it might in practice be apportioned, assessed, and enforced.[7] "Unworkable" because the apportionment requirement effectively eviscerates the grant of power. Because an apportioned tax is sensitive to the distribution of tax burdens *among* states, it is insensitive to the differential burdens on constituencies *within* or *across* states. To illustrate the absurd consequence: If today's federal income tax were apportioned, the average tax rates would range from 9.2 percent in the richest state (Connecticut) to 17.9 percent in the poorest state (Mississippi).[8] Obviously, a tax with such attributes is extremely unlikely to be enacted. Short of a federal head tax (which is apportioned by definition), apportionment very nearly means that no direct tax can be laid at all.

The point, which completely eluded the Convention, was brought home soon enough in *Hylton v. United States* (1796), dealing with a federal luxury tax on carriages. One of only three constitutional proceedings prior to 1801 to be decided by (seriatim) written Supreme Court opinions, *Hylton* was an Alexander Hamilton production, which assumed the trappings of a legal case only through a series of collusive maneuvers among the parties. However, neither the obvious collusion, nor the lack of a final lower court judgment from which appeal to the Supreme Court could be had, nor even the lack of the statutory quorum of four justices, prevented three justices (Iredell, Paterson, Chase) from rendering a decision.[9] Alas, their opinions shed little light on the constitutional distinction between direct and indirect taxes. They can be read to stand for the Hamiltonian position that the apportionment requirement can apply only to taxes that can by their nature be apportioned; and in the justices' view, the carriage tax was not of that kind. The opinions identified the paradigmatic cases on either side: poll taxes or taxes on land are plainly "direct," whereas excise taxes are plainly "indirect." But the justices did not offer any coherent constitutional or economic matrix or rationale for determining the constitutional status of other forms of federal taxation.

The need for a coherent answer was less than pressing for most of the nineteenth century. Administrative and enforcement costs made direct taxes unattractive for the federal government; ample tariff revenues made them unnecessary. (Wartime experiments with direct taxes were typically ended upon the cessation of hostilities; only the Civil War would change this pattern.) However, the apportionment question reemerged when the Supreme Court's decision in *Pollock v. Farmers' Loan & Trust Co.* (1895) declared an unapportioned federal income tax unconstitutional.[10] *Pollock* is widely viewed as a plain example of judicial excess. As Owen Fiss has observed in his splendid book on the Fuller Court, however, the Court's reasoning was respectable, if not exactly compelling. To simplify, *Pollock* held that a tax on income derived from land had to be treated like a tax on land itself; in other words, it had to be apportioned. The Court then treated the remaining portions of the income tax statute as nonseverable, meaning that they had to fall along with the tax on income derived from land. Against the holding stood a few precedents, based on loose language in *Hylton*, to the effect that only poll and land taxes were subject to apportionment. In favor of the holding (at least with respect to income derived from land) stood the argument that a tax on the proceeds of a good or asset is a tax on the good or asset itself. That holding, while not free from doubt, rested on the well-accepted anticircumvention principle of *Brown v. Maryland*.

Whence, then, the modern discomfort with *Pollock*? Fiss attributes it to the air of disingenuousness that hangs over the Court's insistence on mobilizing a federalism rule for antiredistribution purposes.[11] Consistent with this view, one can interpret the Sixteenth Amendment, which overturned *Pollock* and authorized Congress to tax incomes "from whatever source derived, without apportionment among the several States, and without regard to any census or enumeration," as a triumph of modern social-democratic orientations over antediluvian federalism notions. The true problem, however, is not the abuse of the apportionment rule; it is the rule itself. As noted, the rule had an antiredistribution purpose all along—to wit, the protection of agrarian and slave-holding interests against the mercantile Northeast. Conversely, the redistributive income tax at issue in *Pollock* had a federalism dimension. As Fiss notes, it captured practically nothing except dividend income, thus hitting prosperous taxpayers who lived primarily in the industrial Northeast and effectively exempting agrarian states and interests. This dimension was vivid to the *Pollock* Court, both because it figured prominently in the political debate (the tax was popular in the West and the South and vehemently resisted in the Northeast) and because it was urged by counsel, who argued that the predictable geographic incidence of the tax violated the uniformity requirement. The Court rejected the argument (rightly so, to my mind), was thus brought back to the apportionment question, and blew it. Federalism-wise, there *is* something troublesome about tailoring a federal tax to hit taxpayers in particular states. And yet, apportionment is the wrong response for the reason mentioned: to the extent that apportioned taxes can be imposed at all, they will almost invariably impose higher tax rates on individuals in poor states. That is a federalism rule alright, but one without any procompetitive rationale to commend it. Nor did the Founders perceive any such rationale: apportionment made it into the Constitution as part of the slavery bargain. The Sixteenth Amendment excised a remnant of that bargain and corrected a structural error.

Uniformity. The constitutional uniformity requirement applies both to the tariff and to "indirect" internal taxes, such as excise taxes. Like the apportionment rule, the uniformity requirement depends in its operation on the state-to-state heterogeneity of the tax base. Unlike that ill-fated rule, uniformity has both a potent procompetitive rationale and salutary rather than perverse effects. Given a geographically heterogeneous tax base, a "uniform" tax base and rate for every state in the Union will imply a very different tax load or incidence for different states and constituencies. The expected differences may make it hard to pick up a sufficiently broad political consensus to sustain a revenue-maximizing tariff or excise tax. Thus, uniformity may operate as a de facto budget constraint, akin to a supermajority requirement. Like any other budget constraint, though, the uniformity constraint can be overrun: by manipulating the base, legislators can eviscerate the budget constraint and tailor the tax structure to political or revenue needs.[12]

At times, this danger materialized. Massive manipulation of the tariff for protectionist and parochial ends after 1824 prompted South Carolina's vehement opposition to the "tariff of abominations." It also prompted arguments to the effect that the uniformity requirement, properly understood, prohibited such maneuvers. The Constitution authorizes Congress to "lay and collect Taxes, Duties, Imposts, and Excises, to pay the Debts and provide for the common Defence and general Welfare of the United States." "To pay," John C. Calhoun argued, means something like "in order to pay." Hence, the Constitution authorized only revenue tariffs but not protective tariffs for the benefit of particular industries or regions.[13] The argument is better than its reputation (a lot better, we shall see shortly, than the more popular notion that the just-quoted General Welfare Clause imposes a *spending* restriction on Congress). It is too refined, however, to serve as a meaningful restraint. Even the purest revenue tariff will affect domestic consumers, producers, and states in different ways and to varying degrees, with the result that the distinction between revenue tariffs and protectionism is quickly lost. And in truth, South Carolina's real bone of contention was not Henry Clay's manipulation of the tariff but its underlying structure. Even a "clean" revenue impost would protect, and did protect, Northern manufacturers at great cost to the Southern export economies. Put differently, the tariff did indirectly what the constitutionally prohibited export tariff might have done directly.

It is on account of this sectional division that the uniformity rule operated as a de facto budget constraint throughout the antebellum era. The threat of secession by Southern states limited manipulation of the tariff and, moreover, imposed an upper bound of political acceptability on tariff rates. Most important, the budget constraint had potent effects on the spending side. It played a central role in the contentious antebellum debate over "internal improvements," to which I now turn.

Spending Constraints: Internal Improvements

In a once-influential book on *The American Partnership*, the late Daniel J. Elazar argued that American federalism was cooperative ab ovo.[14] His book provides an informative account, still of great interest to students of public administration, of nineteenth-century federal-state cooperation. At a theoretical level, however, Elazar's book is to fiscal federalism what Felix Frankfurter's Commerce Clause is to constitutional law—an ingenious but ultimately unpersuasive attempt to show that the Founders, and all who followed in their footsteps, had been New Dealers all along. It is true that nineteenth-century federal and state fiscal affairs were never hermetically sealed. For example, the federal government shared plentiful tariff revenues and western lands with the states. Occasionally, Congress initiated and supported infrastructure projects of national significance such as the Cumberland Road; more commonly, it authorized transfer payments for local purposes, such as lighthouses or the dredging of harbors. Overwhelmingly, however, the virgin continent was despoiled by states, which competed vigorously for infrastructure investments. Federal transfers remained modest and sporadic, and they had more to do with party machines than with institutionalized intergovernmentalism.[15] Federalism remained profoundly "dual"—that is to say, competitive.

Historians and political economists have puzzled over this pattern, both because it so markedly differs from twentieth-century practice and because antebellum conditions were highly favorable for federal infrastructure investments. Except in wartime, the tariff threw off more revenue than the national government knew what to do with, and the logical place to dissipate the proceeds was internal development. For the immediate post-Founding generation, that strategy had a profound constitutional dimension: Washington, Madison, and even Jefferson, along with Hamiltonians and Whigs, hoped that roads and canals would knit the far-flung nation together and enhance people's confidence in their government. The available supply of funds, moreover, met with a real and forcefully articulated state demand. Beginning with the First Congress, states sent petitions to Congress—initially, for federal funds for post and military roads; soon thereafter, for money to support projects of all descriptions. State governors, accompanied then as now by well-connected lobbyists, trooped to Washington to argue the overwhelming justice of their demands, and nary a ditch, swamp, or dirt path in the country failed to assume national significance. As near as we can tell, those demands reflected the voters' authentic preferences. There was no protolibertarian resistance to "big government" at the time. The political debate was over whether the *national* government should fund internal improvements.[16]

The question proved "one of the most persistent and contentious issues of antebellum American politics."[17] From the outset, the debate had strong constitutional overtones. Madisonian and Jeffersonian defenders of a "strict construction" insisted that Congress lacked constitutional authority to spend on internal improvements, except perhaps projects that were truly national in nature. Averments of this sort, often contained in presidential messages accompanying vetoes of particular spending bills, seem to suggest that the Constitution contains a limitation on the spending power—now forgotten, but well recognized and effective way back when. That view, however, is mistaken. The Constitution does in fact erect powerful (but not insurmountable) obstacles to federal spending, but that is not on account of some textual parchment barrier. Its procompetitive effects had to do with two different factors operating in conjunction: constitutional silence on the spending question, and the sectional and ideological divisions of the antebellum era.

Constitutional Silence. The Constitution contains no "Spending Clause" at all. Rather, Congress's power to spend is commonly (though not without interpretive difficulty) inferred from its power, granted in Article I, § 8, Clause 1 of the Constitution, "to lay and collect Taxes, Duties, Imposts and Excises, to pay the Debts and provide for the common Defence and general Welfare of the United States." The question is how to read the last, "general Welfare" clause of this provision. Hamilton, in an over-the-top moment, suggested that the power to "provide for the . . . general Welfare" was an *independent* power, implying that it empowered Congress to tax, spend, and do all other things (such as regulate or establish a bank).[18] But if that reading were correct, the enumeration of powers elsewhere in the Constitution would be unnecessary and perhaps counterproductive. Thus, the General Welfare Clause must operate as a limitation on the power to tax, not as an independent grant of power. On an alternative, "Madisonian" interpretation, the spending power is cabined by the enumerated powers. But that cannot be right, either: the enumerated powers, in conjunction with the Necessary and Proper Clause, *already* authorize taxation and spending. Lest the General Welfare Clause be rendered empty, it must be read to embrace some objects outside the confines of the enumerated powers. What, then, are they?

Perhaps the most natural reading is that the objects of federal spending must be genuinely national, as opposed to purely local. This was the declared ground of the antebellum opposition to internal improvement funding. However, the historical record casts grave doubt on plausibility of that position. For one thing, Congress can always fund roads and canals under some enumerated power, such as the power to establish post roads—regardless, it would appear, of whether the expenditures satisfy some independent "general welfare" criterion. Thus, even a strict Madisonian understanding of the General Welfare Clause cannot do as a constitutional matter, and did not do as a practical matter, what it is supposed to be doing—to check a free-spending, earmarking, parochial Congress.[19] For another thing, the opponents of internal improvements were less than fully consistent in their position. The first comprehensive plan for a system of national improvements, which would serve as a gold standard for many decades, was drawn up in 1808 by Albert Gallatin, Secretary of the Treasury under (of all presidents) Thomas Jefferson. Under the same administration, Congress authorized and began to fund the construction of the National (Cumberland) Road, the single largest improvement project of the antebellum era. Those undertakings may well have satisfied a "national" or "general welfare" test. Throughout that era, however, Congress routinely authorized funding for lighthouses, harbors, and sundry other local projects, with nary a peep of opposition from presidents—such as Andrew Jackson—who loudly advertised their "strict construction" bona fides. Some of the spending was devoted to the territories and seaboards and could arguably qualify as "general" because those areas did not belong to any individual state. But Jackson also agreed to fund the National Road. He vetoed spending on the Maysville Road, on the well-rehearsed grounds that federal spending had to be "general, not local, national, not State." The Maysville Road was part of an embryonic interstate highway system, just like the National Road. But whereas the National Road facilitated settlement of the old Northwest by "Butternuts" who voted Democratic, the Maysville Road ran through Henry Clay's backyard. No one at the time took Jackson's constitutional bluster very seriously.[20]

The oddity here is not the opportunistic deployment of a constitutional theory. Rather, it is the routine deployment of a perceived constitutional distinction that is incoherent and unsustainable even in theory, let alone in the rough-and-tumble of politics. Every econ freshman can invent "externalities" that render local projects of general importance; as noted, so could antebellum politicians. Conversely, every "general" or "national" good—say, an army base or a lighthouse—has local aspects in production or consumption. A road or canal of national significance has to be built *somewhere*, with the natural result that legislators from other places, whose constituencies are taxed for the project but do not reap its rewards, will oppose the measure.[21] The internal improvements debate thus illustrates a result that political economists can derive on a blackboard: unguided spending from a common pool will tend to occur either not at all or else, on "universalist" terms—that is, in accordance with some scheme that benefits *all* legislators. Any rational, national plan of internal improvements will be systematically underfunded.[22]

One can think of two mechanisms that would obviate the dilemma. The United States Constitution, however, forecloses one of them and fails to provide for the other. Option 1 is benefit taxation: the legislature could build individual projects of national significance with taxes imposed on the more-or-less immediate beneficiaries in the particular location. That is how states typically financed large-scale projects, such as the Erie Canal. The federal government, however, did not and does not have that option; by providing that direct taxes must be apportioned and indirect taxes must be uniform, the Constitution takes benefit taxation off the table. Option 2 is a predetermined fiscal distribution formula. As noted, however, the Constitution conspicuously fails to provide for such a spending baseline.

The constraining effects of the Constitution's silence on this point, as well as the pro-spending attractions of a distribution formula, were clearly felt by the participants in the internal improvements debate. The natural move was to borrow a spending formula that the Constitution enshrined for direct taxation—state apportionment according to the census. Apportionment was a common element of proposals for a constitutional amendment to authorize federal spending on internal improvements, starting with Jefferson's. Members of Congress who felt shortchanged by some proposed spending scheme sometimes suggested that the Constitution already required apportionment on the spending as well as the tax side.[23] And apportionment occasionally found its way into spending legislation as a means of saving internal improvements from oblivion, and Congress from itself. An 1836 Deposit-Distribution Act, for example, ordered state banks to "deposit" some $37 million of federal funds with the states according to electoral votes (thus including three-fifth of slaves).[24] But although the apportionment solution was no more contrived and certainly more coherent than the notion of a general welfare limitation, it had too many problems to gain sustained acceptance. There was no reason to expect that proportionate federal spending within states would in any way correspond to national interests. The surface appeal of apportioning federal revenues dissolved upon the recognition that those revenues were raised through the tariff—not an apportioned tax but a uniform tax, with known and highly controversial distributive effects. Given the mismatch, spending apportionment was highly unlikely to be perceived as "fair." Finally, and perhaps most fateful, apportionment inevitably implicated the slavery question. For all these reasons, the internal improvements debate perennially reverted to the illusory, incoherent distinction between "national" and "local" improvements.

Sectionalism. The account so far leaves two features of the internal improvements debate unexplained: the durability of a constitutional doctrine that could not and did not do what its advocates wanted it to do, and the persistence of federal spending restraint despite high state demand and ample revenue supply. Both features had to do with the ideological and sectional divisions of the antebellum era.

The internal improvements debate ran together with two other, equally contentious questions: the Bank of the United States and the tariff. In conjunction, those issues defined a profound divide: Hamiltonian supporters of the Bank and tariff-financed improvements on one side, Jeffersonian opponents of all those positions on the other. Neither Jefferson nor his followers and successors, I noted earlier, opposed federal infrastructure spending per se. What they hated was the "corruption" that to their minds accompanied federal internal improvements—the "boundless patronage to the executive, jobbing to members of Congress & their friends, and a bottomless abyss of public money."[25] That style of politics, Jeffersonians associated with Hamilton and his Bank (and later, with Henry Clay and his "American system"). They entertained a loftier vision of a truly republican politics, more in keeping with the principles of 1776 and unpolluted by party and corruption. The constitutional faith in republican government explains Jefferson's seeming inconsistency—his harangues against internal improvements, and his support for the National Road and especially for Gallatin's national plan.[26] The "general versus local" riff on the spending power has to be seen in this light: for all its incoherence and constitutional implausibility, it was the only formula that allowed Jeffersonians to escape the dilemma between chronic underinvestment and pork barreling and to support public-regarding federal investments while opposing Hamiltonian politics.

For better or worse, though, the formula proved no more plausible in practice than it did as a matter of constitutional exegesis. Only Congress, Gallatin intoned in submitting his plan, "embracing every local interest, and superior to every local consideration," was "competent to the selection of such national objects" of internal improvement. In a nod to reality, Gallatin hedged his national system with a proposal to "do substantial justice" and produce "general satisfaction" by making "compensatory grants" to "a number of local improvements" in New England and the South, whose voters and representatives might insist on such side payments to recognize the good sense of the system.[27] But that concession limped behind the reality that Congress, far from being "superior to every local consideration," had already proven incapable of considering anything else. In an ironic but predictable twist, Gallatin's report, with its prospect of large-scale federal funding, turned a theretofore manageable trickle of local requests into a veritable torrent.[28] In an equally predictable irony, presidential vetoes that were intended, sometimes sincerely, as a means of policing improvement spending against pork barreling and corruption tended to make the system *less* general. Universalist bills containing small-scale, local projects routinely sailed through Congress and hardly ever encountered a veto, for the splendid reason that every member of Congress had been fed. Vetoes almost invariably hit large-scale projects that arguably *were* of general, national significance, such as the Maysville Road.

The Jeffersonian ideal celebrated a near-final hurrah in 1816, when President James Madison, on his last day in office, vetoed a comprehensive internal improvements bill. After the War of 1812, Madison himself had advocated greatly enhanced federal funds for internal improvements. His veto—on all accounts, one of the most surprising in American history—was prompted by republican hang-ups: he could not stomach the pork that it had taken Henry Clay to produce the bill.[29] Republican commitments still echo in the internal improvement veto messages of James Monroe, the last of the Founder-presidents. Below the surface, however, the recognition that the game was up had already settled in.[30] That recognition coincided with a transformation of the party system. Under Jackson and then Van Buren, Democrats migrated from the position that executive patronage and congressional pork-barreling were inherently corrupt to the position that those institutional practices were "corrupt" in the hands of Federalists and Whigs but rather less problematic, potentially democratic, and in any event highly useful to the heirs of republican principles. Pork-barrel spending became bipartisan and more universalist. Andrew Jackson managed to build a reputation as a fierce opponent of federal improvements—while spending twice as much on such projects as all his predecessors combined.[31]

If internal-improvements spending remained nonetheless both limited and controversial, that is because everyone knew where the money would come from—the tariff.[32] The tariff was beloved in the North because it cemented a political coalition that included just about every interest except the Southern plantation economies: a growing manufacturing sector that liked tariff walls, Western states that hoped to benefit from an investment of tariff revenues in internal improvements, abolitionists determined to drive the Southern slave economies to the wall. The Southern aristocracy had a very different view, but its members saw the connections with equal clarity. "Destroy the tariff and you will leave no means of carrying on internal improvement," South Carolina Senator William Smith intoned in 1830. "Destroy internal improvement and you leave no motive for the tariff."[33] It is thus incorrect to suggest that the "states as states" nobly resisted federal entreaties; as seen, federal spending measures that did not implicate the basic sectional division encountered no organized opposition. What did exist was vehement opposition by *some* states, notably Virginia, to any spending scheme that appeared to threaten the peculiar institution in the South.

Given the profound sectional division, there was no way of rolling over the South or of bribing individual Southern states into a minimum winning spending coalition. The stakes were too high and the divisions in Congress too close. Northern defections from the pro-improvements coalition were common. Once New York had built the Erie Canal on its own nickel, it naturally opposed federal funding for competing canals elsewhere.[34] And over the entire debate hung the threat that Southern states, when pushed to the brink, might exit the union. Slavery and sectionalism, not some constitutional spending constraint, stabilized competitive fiscal federalism in the antebellum era.

Moral Hazard: The Debt Crisis

State borrowing on the (implicit) credit of the central government bears strong similarities to cooperative fiscal transfer programs. Both state stratagems serve to escape federalism's competitive pressures. But whereas grants or transfer programs are preapproved by the central government and thus allow the federal government to limit its exposure, state borrowing in the expectation of a federal bailout offers no such safeguard. Alas, when states expect that the center will cave and that disproportionate rewards may go to the most brazen, all will be tempted to borrow recklessly. The only meaningful defense against this malignant form of fiscal decentralization is the center's credible commitment against bailouts.

As with respect to fiscal transfers in general, the Constitution at first sight seems deficient in stemming the peril of bailout expectations. Nothing in the Constitution bars states from borrowing money (although they are compelled to pay their debts in real money). And nothing bars the federal government from paying the states' debts, sua sponte or upon the states' request. Thus, the stage seems set for irresponsible state bets on federal assistance. The scenario seems particularly likely because constitutional government in the United States *started* with a bailout—to wit, the assumption of the states' war debts. The federal government also repaid states for expenditures they had incurred in the War of 1812, and a few other federal measures (such as federal subscriptions to the stock of state improvement corporations) arguably created further precedents for federal debt relief.

A serious test of the federal government's commitment occurred in the years between 1837 and 1843.[35] At the time, as noted, states competed aggressively in providing infrastructure. While some funded projects through benefit taxation, others used a system of tax-free finance; state-chartered banks and internal improvement corporations sold debt instruments, very often to European investors. Those schemes sailed into trouble in the wake of a sharp deflation (a "panic," as it was then called) in 1837. Some states, especially in the West, responded with yet more aggressive borrowing. The game was up in 1840, when banks collapsed and the bottom dropped out of the speculative land market that had supported the borrowing spree. (This was the same chain of events that gave us *Swift v. Tyson* and the early reform of state corporation law.) In 1841/1842, several states defaulted on their obligations.

Plans for a federal bailout surfaced in 1839, well before the crisis had hit with full force. In 1843, after years of debate, a congressional committee submitted a proposal for federal assumption. The committee rehearsed predictable arguments: historical precedents for assumption; the dearth of state funds and available revenue sources; and the danger that state defaults would halt the construction of projects that, though state-initiated, were of national, interstate importance. To those arguments, one could have added others. Prominently, British and Dutch investors pressured the United States government for intervention, arguing (probably with some justice) that the funds had been extended in reliance on the credit of the United States. In 1842, the United States was entirely cut off from international credit.

Even so, no bailout materialized; the committee's report and proposal never even received a vote in Congress. A number of factors, including the individual states' widely differing practices and debt levels, help to explain the striking result. Clearly, though, the structural features of the Constitution are among those factors. In the absence of a constitutional baseline or established practice, interstate variegation made it impossible to generate political consensus. The congressional committee proposed to distribute federal funds not in proportion to actual state debt but rather in proportion to state population (apparently including the three-fifths formula).[36] Debt relievers, like internal improvers, went to the only formula they knew. Predictably, though, the prospective·apportioned payments bore no systematic relation to individual state debt levels, let alone the level of national interest (such as the severity of interstate spillovers) or the degree of political culpability and corruption that had produced individual states' fiscal crisis. Like the internal improvements debate, the assumption debate revolved not around a distribution that would be "fair" relative to a known baseline; it was about what the appropriate distribution baseline ought to be. Especially for an institutional system that demands considerably more than $n/2 + 1$ votes in a single political body, that is often too much to handle.

As in the improvements debate, the decisive factor was not what the Constitution says but what it does not say. It contains no mandate for redistribution, no distributive baseline, and no general supervisory authority over the states' taxing, spending, and borrowing decisions. In the years between 1837 and 1843, Jonathan Rodden has written, "those limitations clearly bolstered the credibility of the center's commitment to stay out of the states' budget difficulties."[37] Scholars generally credit two subsequent developments to that resolve: constitutional prohibitions against tax-free finance, enacted by many states in the aftermath of the crisis; and a remarkably firm expectation among investors and politicians that the federal government will hold firm against bailout demands. Sometimes, the Constitution's silences speak audibly.

State Taxation: Competitive Federalism
in the Gilded Age

Fiscal federalism's political economy after the Civil War and the end of Reconstruction differed in salient ways from that of the antebellum era.

The Civil War had solved the secession question; state exit was no longer a realistic option or threat. The exigencies of war had produced a national government with theretofore barely imaginable powers, as well as a bureaucratic apparatus to administer them. (Some emergency measures and powers, such as the income tax, were discontinued, and others remained in place or were reconfigured for postwar needs.) And rapid industrialization changed the face of the nation. Two of its consequences are of special significance in the context of state taxation: increased factor mobility and increased integration both at the firm and a macroeconomic level.

Competitive federalism models have states competing for productive citizens and firms. In the real world, in contrast, states compete for each other's tax dollars. The Constitution plainly adumbrates the danger of "extraterritorial," exploitative state taxation. The Founders' dire fears on this score are reflected in the decision to commit the protection of competitive conditions in the first instance to the judiciary, rather than Congress. The Import-Export Clause, the Tonnage Clause, the Legal Tender Clause, and the Contract Clause foreclose the most obvious and attractive exploitative stratagems. In addition, the Constitution contains a broader, structural principle against state evasion of the textual norms; recall the discussion of *Brown v. Maryland* and the dormant Commerce Clause.

Although evasive state maneuvering is a constant, the enormous increase in factor mobility in the late nineteenth century intensified competition among states and threatened to erode their surplus. The temptation to exploit outsiders rose in proportion, and cross-border economic integration multiplied the opportunities to do so. These dynamics, as well as increased public demands on government, prompted an ever-more intense state scramble for exploitable revenue sources. Chapters 4 through 6 described the states' determined effort to expropriate the profits of national corporations operating within their borders. The Supreme Court intervened often and energetically to curb those tendencies, principally under the dormant Commerce Clause and, occasionally, the Due Process Clause.

Tax cases, not regulatory cases, were the primary focus of the dormant Commerce Clause at the time. But there is little mileage in tracing the Court's twists and turns on the taxation of railroad cars or intangibles (such as stocks), or on the distinction between a state tax *on* interstate commerce and on income derived *from* such commerce. An air of randomness and futility hangs over the long-forgotten tax cases. Its cause is not difficult to discern: the Court's formal and, in particular, its territorial categories were mismatched to the underlying problem. Tax exploitation has to do primarily with the incidence of a given tax and with a state's abuse of a monopolistic position—not with territory per se, and not with the form or name of a tax. Thus, a state tax on the "last mile" of railroad does not become unproblematic by virtue of the bare fact that the track is located within the state, and a state severance tax on coal is not automatically unproblematic because it is imposed at the point of production rather than export. Conversely, a nondiscriminatory state tax does not become suspect when it is imposed on interstate as well as in-state businesses. This mismatch between form and substance produced errors in both directions. Occasionally, a legitimate state tax fell by the wayside. More commonly, states reconfigured an exploitative tax in conformity with the Supreme Court's categories.

Scholars at the time suggested that the Court's Commerce Clause meant that states may tax just about anything so long as they call the tax by the right name.[38] Only legal-realist silliness, however, would dismiss the Court's entire jurisprudence as a joke or a laissez-faire crusade. Even an inadequate constitutional deterrent with a high error rate in close, litigated cases may well be preferable to no deterrent at all. And the alternative to judicial constraints on exploitative state taxation was (and is) just that: *no* constraint. In a few regulatory arenas, the Congress of the Gilded Age effectively displaced the Supreme Court's dormant Commerce Clause regime with federal administrative schemes, beginning with the establishment of the Interstate Commerce Commission in 1887 and with increasing frequency thereafter. However, whereas federal legislative intervention was becoming available for the purpose of regulating individual industries, it was not an option with respect to tax schemes that cut across numerous industries and all states. Congress lacked (and still lacks) any capacity to establish jurisdictional boundaries to prescribe which state may tax what and whom. Confronted with the certain prospect of a state tax free-for-all, what was the Supreme Court supposed to do? What it did do was to try and make the Commerce Clause categories work as well as they could.

In an institutional and political context, that *was* what the Court was supposed to do, or rather what the dominant political coalition at the time, assembled under the umbrella of the Republican Party, expected it to do.[39] That coalition rested on three interlocking positions: the tariff; the gold standard; and an open internal market or, more to the point, the opening of the southern plantation economies to the industrial corporations based in the Northeast and around the Great Lakes. *That* was the central Commerce Clause issue at the time; and the state tax question was whether the gains from industrial innovation and economic integration would get stuck in the southern "market states" or be repatriated to the industrial capital and working class in the North. When trade barriers and state-protected monopolies fell in the South and West, northern producer states benefited.

Regime politics does not translate seamlessly into constitutional categories. A constitutional prohibition that operates against one state operates against all.[40] In an immediate political sense, then, the Court's doctrines were overbroad. The governing coalition, however, was well aware that it could not possibly replicate the Supreme Court's procompetitive regime by means of legislation. It thus had a reason to discount the overbreadth problem—and it had a way of dealing with it: the tariff (along with revenues from excise taxes on alcohol and tobacco that had remained in place after the Civil War) provided a resource with which to compensate Republican constituencies for occasional competition-induced losses. The revenues found their way into the party's constituencies by way of Civil War pensions (which overwhelmingly wound up, both by program design and through sheer corruption, in northern Republican states) and through programs that in the antebellum era had sailed under the "internal improvements" umbrella, such as the annual pork fest of the Rivers and Harbors Bill.[41]

In some ways, these Gilded Age federalism arrangements look transitional. The dissipation of tariff revenues to local interests resembles antebellum practice, and even the sectional divide of the Gilded Age looks like antebellum America—though now clearly dominated by the North and operating without a state exit threat. At the same time, the age spawned spending programs that, in retrospect, look like the beginning of cooperative federalism or perhaps American "state building."[42] However, the political economy of the Gilded Age had a distinctive fiscal federalism logic. On the tax side, the tariff had lost any real connection to mercantilist ends. It was purely a means of generating political rents with which to cement an inchoate GOP coalition and to purchase its acquiescence to the Supreme Court's constitutional program. On the spending side, programs that would later come to be viewed as forerunners of a new federalism were not conceived as national, programmatic policy but rather as ad hoc responses to a cacophony of state and local demands.[43] And their purpose and effect was not "cooperative" but profoundly procompetitive: fiscal side payments served as the Republican majority's means of protecting procompetitive constitutional norms. By way of close analogy, the sensible way of maximizing the benefits of an international free-trade pact among unequal partners is to compensate losers on the side, as opposed to larding up the agreement with "harmonizing" workplace or environmental protections. The political economy of the Gilded Age accomplished an analogous result, on a systemwide basis, by means of institutional separation: the Supreme Court policed internal free-trade rules while the Republican majority in Congress made the side payments. That arms-length arrangement is the most extreme manifestation of the Constitution's institutional commitment principle and the most competitive federalism we have ever known.

Coda: Competition and Constitutional Construction

It is tempting to think that constitutional regimes with a high degree of intellectual coherence, institutional plausibility, and normative attractiveness should be stable, at least unless and until they are hit by some exogenous, malignant force. To many contemporary political economists, the competitive federalism of the Gilded Age has come to look like a model. And modern-day admirers of the Old Court and its federalism often suggest that we had a perfectly coherent Constitution, until the Progressives destroyed it.[44] Their position is not mere romanticism; it captures something of the spirit of the Gilded Age. Lord Bryce's best-selling *American Commonwealth*, which in many ways canonized the then-dominant understanding, has an end-of-history feel: the vexing citizenship and secession questions having been settled by the Civil War, American federalism had reached its apotheosis. The preceding chapters sketched, at the level of constitutional doctrine, the federalism arrangements before Lord Bryce's eyes—"two governments, covering the same ground, commanding, with equally direct authority, the obedience of the same citizens," "distinct and separate in their action," "each set doing its own work without touching or hampering the other."[45]

I owned up to my affection for that order at the outset, and I have explicated its distinctly competitive features. At the same time, however, the chapters in this part have emphasized that the working-out of a competitive federal order depended on the Supreme Court's dominance in superintending competitive arrangements against the perennial threat of state defection. That dominance, in turn, hung on the peculiar political economy and alignments of the period, which could not and did not last. In short, one should not overestimate the stability of the institutional arrangements of the Gilded Age or reify an "Old" (or "true" and "original") Constitution.

That note of caution invites a further and final reflection on constitutional construction at competitive federalism's end. As suggested earlier, the justices of the Gilded Age did not set out to create a specifically competitive federalism. Their jurisprudence rather reflected the formalism of Thomas Cooley's *Constitutional Limitations*, and on account of the justices' emphasis on categorical, conceptual distinctions, their federalism would come to be called "dual" rather than "competitive."[46] Constitutional formalism, however, is continuous and congruent with competitive federalism—not entirely so (more in a moment), but to a large extent. Stack up the doctrines reviewed in this and the preceding chapters against the competitive federalism criteria in Table 3.1: the congruence is near-perfect. Moreover, it has deep roots. Howard Gillman, among other "revisionist" scholars, has emphasized the Old Court's constitutionally rooted hostility to factional politics and "partial" laws.[47] We have come to associate that disposition chiefly with *Lochner*—that is, a *rights*-oriented jurisprudence. But it is also at work in the *structural* decisions of the period. Uniformly, the federalism doctrines reviewed in these chapters had the purpose and effect to break the institutionalized force of factions at the state level.

Similarly, Owen Fiss has emphasized that the justices of the Old Court were constitutional contractarians at heart.[48] I argued in chapter 1 that there is a close connection between contractarianism and competition as a constitutional principle, and that connection was very much at work in federalism's formulation in the late nineteenth century. Contractarian constitutionalism was by no means averse to empirical argument or demands for doctrinal innovation. Constitutional entrepreneurs such as I.M. Singer and the "Big Four" meatpackers consistently presented briefs that were heavy on the economics of large-scale industrial production and marketing, and they sketched for the justices constitutional rules that would accommodate those demands. More often than not, those arguments found a receptive judicial audience. However, the justices would have recoiled at any suggestion that their embrace of novel doctrines amounted to a change in the Constitution itself. Precisely *because* they were mindful and confident of the Constitution's precommitments, they felt free to elaborate doctrines that would make it work in a rapidly changing, increasingly complex and interdependent society. Under then-prevailing conditions, their constitutionally grounded and disciplined common law formalism was singularly suited to the elaboration of competitive federalism rules.

As already hinted, however, the congruence was incomplete. Justice Stephen Field's hostility to corporations marks one discontinuity. (The escape of those entities from the control of an individual state struck Field and his fellow formalists as a dangerous form of private lawmaking.) In addition, "dual" federalism partook of a rigid territorialism, which misapprehended *Swift*'s contractual logic and produced jurisdictional doctrines that in the end were mismatched to the demands of a competitive economy and federalism.[49] Perhaps the most significant discontinuity, however, concerns the very point at issue: "dual" federalism's competitive dynamic.

That dynamic was no secret at the time—certainly not to the corporate lawyers who invented trusts and the modern corporate charter, and not to the Progressives. Much of that ascendant political movement's agenda was to forestall the states' "race to the bottom." The Progressives' uncharitable view of state competition will play a large role in Part III; my observations here concern the Old Court's inadequate response. The best illustration is *Hammer v. Dagenhart* (1918), the famous "child labor" case. In defense of the federal statute barring the interstate shipment of goods produced in factories that employed child labor, the federal government's brief invoked the specter of a "race to the bottom": in the absence of a federal standard, pro-regulatory states would find themselves at a disadvantage, and no socially beneficial legislation would be forthcoming. The Supreme Court majority responded that

> [t]here is no power vested in Congress to require the states to exercise their police power so as to prevent possible unfair competition. Many causes may cooperate to give one State, by reason of local laws or conditions, an economic advantage over others. The Commerce Clause was not intended to give Congress a general authority to equalize such conditions.[50]

The passage hints at an important insight: grant the national government the authority to equalize conditions on *this* margin, and the equalization of other and eventually all disadvantages would be sure to follow. At the end, nothing would be left of federalism. However, the majority missed a larger point. Dissenting in *Hammer*, Justice Holmes (joined by Justices Brandeis, McKenna, and Clarke) noted that the shipment across state borders of goods produced with child labor is undoubtedly interstate commerce. The notion that Congress may only facilitate but not restrict such commerce, he continued, was untenable: the Court had crossed *that* bridge earlier, when it permitted the federal regulation, for prohibitory purposes, of interstate trade in noxious goods, such as lottery tickets and prostitutes.[51] It did not matter, Holmes wrote, whether "the supposed evil precedes or follows the transportation. It is enough that, in the opinion of Congress, the transportation encourages the evil."[52]

Is it? Against a competitive baseline, "precede or follow" makes *all* the difference. The import of harmful goods into a state that does not want them is a harm in a way in which the import of goods produced under objectionable conditions is not—precisely *because* the evil follows rather than precedes the transportation. (On this principle, international free trade agreements, including the World Trade Organization, generally allow member-countries to block the import of goods on account of their harmful properties or effects but not on account of their production under inferior social or environmental standards.) Holmes's point was that the Constitution contains no competitive baseline. If that is right, though, Congress may do just what the majority said it could not: equalize conditions among states.

In *Hammer*, the Old Court failed to articulate a direct response not only to Holmes's rank positivism ("the opinion of Congress is enough") but also to his egregious political economy. Instead, it retreated to the formal distinction between "manufacture" and "commerce." This would become a pattern. Time and again, we shall see in Part III, the Old Court declined to engage the dubious economic theories that Holmes and especially Brandeis would bring to the Court, the Constitution, and its federalism. Eventually, of course, the Progressives' jurisprudence triumphed.

For reasons already stated, it is unlikely that a more confident and direct response to the Progressives—a defense of competitive rather than "dual" federalism—could have changed the course of events. But the implicit "what if" question also suggests a wrong picture of how judicial doctrine and ideology evolve. Chief Justice Taft and Justice Sutherland were smart enough to recognize that the Progressive justices' economic arguments were as wrong as they were ostentatious. (They were sufficiently inane to make even Justice McReynolds look like Milton Friedman.)[53] However, jurists and especially justices do not reconfigure their mental maps so easily. Formalism had brought the Old Court to a coherent view of the Constitution, and to an exalted institutional role. Thus, when confronted with the Progressives' challenge, the Old Court's justices failed to realize that the formalism that had once been their strength was rapidly turning into a liability. Throughout their illustrious tenures, Taft and Sutherland fought with one hand tied behind their backs. In that intellectual respect, they left the field to the architects of a new, vehemently anti-competitive federalism. That edifice is the subject of Part III.

PART THREE

TRANSFORMATION

When, in the course of human events, it becomes necessary for a nation to repair the fabric which unites its many agencies of government, and to restore the solidarity which is vital to orderly growth, it is the duty of responsible officials to define the need and to find a way to meet it. . . .

Through established agencies of cooperation, through uniform and reciprocal laws and regulations, through compacts under the Constitution, through informal collaboration, and through all other means possible, our nation, our states, and our localities must fuse their activities with a new fervor of national unity.

"Declaration of Interdependence," drafted and signed by state and local
government representatives at a national conference in 1937.

T O REPEAT: THE CONDITIONS THAT SUSTAINED competitive federalism could not and did not last. Profound political, economic, and social changes—including the shift from a tariff to an income tax economy, the emergence of populist and Progressive social movements, and the expanded franchise—had potent effects on American federalism's practice and constitutional understanding. Progressive theorists denounced the traditional constitutional understanding as hopelessly inadequate to the complexities of industrial capitalism and agitated for a "Living" Constitution more in keeping with the times and with popular demand.[1] Some three decades later, they got their wish. The Old Constitution disappeared, and a very different Constitution—the "New Deal Constitution"—took its place.

I understand the logic and genesis of the New Deal Constitution and its federalism from the same constitutional choice perspective that I have brought to bear on the Founding. On Madisonian premises, constitutional choice must be the ex ante choice of prospective citizens. That premise translates into a competitive federalism that curbs factionalism, disciplines government at all levels, and seeks to ensure stability through self-enforcing norms. Invert the perspective, and suppose that the constitutional choice were made not by citizens but by states. What constitutional federalism rules would *they* choose? They would choose the rules that the New Deal has bequeathed us. The organizing principle of that Constitution is the systematic suppression of political and economic competition among states. Its objective is not to check factionalism but to promote it, not to discipline Leviathan but to empower government at all levels, not to ensure constitutional stability but to make the Constitution itself more responsive to democratic demands. The inversion of the constitutional choice perspective, from citizens to states as the subjects of constitutional choice, produces an inverted Constitution. After the New Deal, that Constitution is ours. Its organizing principle is the opposite of competition: cartels at every level.[2]

The forms and dynamics of that federalism are the subject of this part. Chapter 8 explains why states, under conditions of an integrated and highly mobile economy, would opt for the New Deal Constitution's federalism. The gist of it is that states loathe competition and will seek to suppress it. That anticompetitive impulse is captured in the New Deal's metaphors: the "race to the bottom," states as "laboratories of democracy," and federalism as "balance." Chapters 9 through 11 discuss the New Deal Constitution's federalism doctrines and innovations—perhaps in greater detail than even patient readers will want to bear. I hope to demonstrate, though, that the constitutional choice story illuminates not only the New Deal's Broadway productions (the Commerce Clause!) but also its abandoned alleyways (the Full Faith and Credit Clause, anyone?) and its subterranean infrastructure of federal jurisdiction, choice of law, preemption, and other nauseating tunnels. Chapter 9 shows that the New Deal's Commerce Clause—seemingly a profoundly nationalist construct—is better understood as an accommodation to the demands of states and their interest group clientele. Chapter 10 returns to an earlier theme: jurisdiction is half the constitutional ballgame. The cornerstone of the New Deal edifice is *Erie Railroad Co. v. Tompkins* (1938), which greatly expanded the powers of states and especially state courts. Chapter 11 describes the New Deal Constitution's fiscal federalism.

Before journeying into this fiercely contested territory, I reiterate several notes of caution, first flagged in the introduction, about the nature of the expedition. Its purpose is not to present the true and correct history of American federalism. Rather, the point of the constitutional choice story is to present an "analytic narrative" that serves to clarify the incentives and interests of (some of) the principal institutional actors and especially the states, meaning their political officials and elites.[3] I cheerfully concede, and will emphasize at times, that federalism's renegotiation during the Progressive Era and the New Deal was a complicated, discontinuous, messy affair; that state demand for cartelization is by no means the only force to destabilize competitive federalism; and that path dependencies, political forces and external shocks, and sheer contingency played a powerful role and produced a far more multi-faceted and fascinating federalism picture than my just-so story suggests.[4] For all that, I hope to show, the story provides an antidote and corrective to deeply entrenched misconceptions about American federalism. Among them are the notions of the New Deal as a nationalist imposition on the states, the notion that federalism consists in a "balance" of power between Washington and the states, the notion that the New Deal Constitution somehow "translated" federalism into a new context, and above all Bruce A. Ackerman's notion of the New Deal as a "constitutional moment."

What I call the "New Deal Constitution" is not coterminous with the *political* (First or Second) New Deal of the Roosevelt Administration, let alone any particular set of policies. Nor can its creation be telescoped into a few months following the 1936 election or the announcement of Roosevelt's Court packing plan and the Supreme Court's famous "switch in time." Those events were *institutionally* significant because the unusual degree of political consensus allowed political actors to renegotiate the constitutional bargain for good; they were *politically* significant because they made clear who had won, and who had lost, the constitutional debate. For all their drama, however, they were part of a prolonged constitutional reconstruction. At one end, the momentous economic and social changes that drove the transition from competitive to cartel federalism developed over time, and the institutional and judicial responses—the states' increased demand for federal intervention, the invention of "cooperative" federal funding programs, the revision of the Commerce Clause and of federal preemption, the brawl over the federal courts' diversity jurisdiction—long predate the New Deal.[5] At the other end, the New Deal's federalism was not fully worked out until the 1950s. The New Deal Constitution, as I understand it, is the constitutional construction and the set of entrenched institutional norms and practices that we inherited at the end. That Constitution has an internal logic and coherence, even if the notoriously improvisational political New Deal did not.

Precisely its logic and coherence, however, dispel the notion of the New Deal Constitution as an authentically *constitutional* product. To his great credit, Ackerman insists that constitutionalism rests on a credible choice of prospective citizens—"We the People." His insistence on that irreducible Madisonian premise pushed Ackerman into positions that have drawn ready criticism: his invention of a New Deal that never was, his exaltation of an engaged citizenry that has more in common with a third-world mob than with the Founders' idea of democratic deliberation, and his disturbing notion of informal constitutional amendments.[6] The deeper, more radical point of the following chapters is to examine the result—that is, the New Deal Constitution's forms and substance. From the vantage of a Madisonian constitutional moment, that Constitution looks senseless. Understand it instead as an inverted, anti-constitutional choice by "states as states," and lo: the doctrines are altogether functional and coherent. The constitutional pudding contains no proof of anything. It does, however, provide food for a debate over constitutionalism, and the Constitution, that is worth having.

The New Deal Constitution's genius is to obviate that debate. Its heirs and defenders, left and right, have lowered their sights; unlike Ackerman, they feel no urgency to defend the Madisonian baseline. But they also lack the nerve to repudiate that baseline outright. Their federalism encomia are invariably accompanied by assurances to the effect that federalism's "balance" and states' rights are a means to something else—pragmatic "advantages," "active liberty," or something of the sort. And yet, the federalism inquiry perennially reverts to the question of whether the "states as states" are having a good time. The headnoted "Declaration of Interdependence" sums up the convictions that underlie the New Deal's federalism: the urgent need for a new constitutional beginning, aggressive antiformalism, and the commitment to "solidarity" and to intergovernmentalism as a method and an objective. Citizens disappear from the constitutional calculus; the envisioned constitutional project is an enterprise by, of, for, and among government agencies and "responsible officials." In that fashion, the "Declaration" seeks to erase the gulf that separates the people's earnest, wrenching decision to make a new and violent beginning from the politicians' cabal to augment the power, emolument and consequence of their offices.

There is nothing inherently absurd or impractical about an intergovernmental federalism cartel. One can even call it "constitutional," in the sense that many federal constitutions embody it. But it is not the project of the United States Constitution. It is an inversion.

CHAPTER EIGHT

Constitutional Inversion

Introduction

The Constitution, I argued in chapters 1 and 2, embodies three precommitments: the citizens' ex ante perspective ("reflection and choice") as the constitutional baseline, safeguards against the violence of faction, and self-enforcing norms as a means of ensuring stability. These principles in turn translate into a competitive constitutional structure and federalism. The New Deal Constitution embodies just the opposite commitments. Its federalism reflects the interests of "states as states," not of citizens. It seeks to unleash interest group politics, not to discipline them. And it eviscerates the Constitution's self-enforcing, stabilizing mechanisms to make room for a more "democratic" Constitution. These precepts translate into a vehemently anticompetitive federalism—"New Deal federalism," or "cartel federalism."

This chapter explicates the interrelated constitutional inversions and their political economy. It concludes with a schematic overview of the structure of the New Deal Constitution, explored at greater length in subsequent chapters. It begins, though, with a brief discussion of two more familiar accounts of the New Deal's federalism: the story of the New Deal as centralization and the notion of a transition from "dual" to "cooperative" federalism. Although both stories have come under considerable scholarly fire, they retain sufficient life to warrant a direct discussion and repudiation. That exercise prepares the ground for the true story—the migration from competition to cartel as federalism's central organizing principle.

Familiar Stories

Few constitutional stories are more familiar than the notion of the New Deal Constitution as a response to increasing social and economic complexity. The problems of a mass society, industrialization, and corporate capitalism, all extending over an entire continent, commanded changes in a Constitution written over a century earlier for an agrarian society of some four million people. So said the Progressives and the New Dealers; and because history is written by the winners, their story has currency today. One of its versions interprets the New Deal as (belated) centralization.[1] Another version describes it as a transition from "dual" to "cooperative" federalism. Neither version is plausible, however. The centralization story fails to account for the distinctively state-protective features of the New Deal Constitution. The cooperative federalism story distorts their nature. The New Deal Constitution's target wasn't dualism per se; it was competition.

Centralization? On Weberian accounts of the New Deal as a centralizing revolution, federalism in America looks like religion in America—a hang-up or neurosis, which modernizing tendencies have not fully overcome. This, however, is at odds both with what the New Dealers thought they were doing and with the institutions and the Constitution they produced. Certainly, the New Dealers greatly expanded the functions of the national government and made way for that expansion through a dramatic reinterpretation of the Constitution. But they never made the mistake of thinking that federalism must be a zero-sum game, such that the national government can gain power only at the states' expense. Rather, they recognized that federalism can serve to empower both the federal government and the states, instead of disciplining either. The New Deal, then, was not a revolution in favor of central government but a revolution in favor of government at *all* levels. Its state-friendly orientation is reflected in standard measures of government centralization, in regulatory arrangements, and in constitutional doctrine.

Revenue figures tell a familiar story of government growth over the course of the New Deal—and a less-familiar story about centralization. Although federal revenues rose considerably with the onset of the New

Deal, an increasingly large share found its way into state and local budgets. Between 1932 and 1940, federal outlays for cooperative fiscal programs exploded from $250 million to almost $4 billion, accounting for fully 75 percent of the growth in the federal government's non-military expenditures. Newly enacted grants programs involved the national government in many activities theretofore beyond its purview, but they also enabled the states to procure federal funds for activities that previously had to be financed from own-source revenues.[2]

Regulatory and social policies reflect the same state-protective pattern. Not a single New Deal regulatory regime unambiguously trumped or displaced the states. For example, the Securities Act of 1933 and the Securities Exchange Act of 1934, which established a federal regime to govern corporate disclosure and the stock exchanges, explicitly declined to preempt state regulators and instead layered the newly created Securities Exchange Commission (SEC) on top of the states' "blue sky" laws (so called because they aimed to prevent scam artists from swindling credulous investors into buying "the blue sky"). The regulation of telecommunications has a very similar structure, as does labor law, agriculture policy, and the regulation of power generation and transmission, transportation industries, and deceptive business conduct. Similarly, virtually all New Deal social legislation, from unemployment insurance to welfare benefits, afforded the states an important administrative and political role, and the expansion of federal tax credits and transfer payments enhanced state capacity.[3]

Finally, *constitutional doctrine* assumed a distinctly state-friendly trajectory. Conventional wisdom has it that in 1937 or thereabouts, the Supreme Court surrendered a judicially enforceable federalism principle of limited, enumerated powers, leaving the states to fend for themselves in the political process. That account, however, is woefully incomplete. Just as the political New Deal expanded government at all levels, so the constitutional New Deal coupled the demise of restraints on the national government with doctrines that unshackled *the states* from constitutional constraints. In a pathbreaking article, Stephen Gardbaum has inventoried the New Deal's state-liberating doctrines: the demise of "substantive due process," a state-protective reformulation of the dormant Commerce Clause and of federal preemption, the death of *Swift v. Tyson* and its substitution with the doctrine of *Erie Railroad Co. v. Tompkins*, and other doctrines that greatly expanded the jurisdiction of state courts both vis-à-vis federal courts and territorially.[4] We will encounter all these doctrines in later chapters. They partake of a constitutional transformation that remade federalism in accordance with the states' interests and demands.

Coordination, Cooperation, and Cartels. The conventional sobriquet for the New Deal's federalism is "cooperative."[5] That term of convenience, coined by leading Progressives and New Dealers, glosses over a divide, usually traced to Theodore Roosevelt's "New Nationalism" and a competing tradition of Woodrow Wilson's "New Freedom," between bureaucratic centralizers and adherents of a more decentralized, Jacksonian politics. What united those camps, though, was the conviction that the old "dual" federalism impeded an effective response to a stupendous increase in social and economic complexity. That reality, the Progressives and New Dealers insisted, demanded cooperation among governments.[6]

Institutional proposals to that end took varying forms. Early on, the "uniform law" movement sought to harmonize state law without federal intervention or changes in the constitutional architecture. Another popular proposal, the extensive use of interstate compacts, bore some fruit in areas such as natural resource management and criminal law enforcement. Traces of that era are still with us. The Uniform Commercial Code is one; the American Bar Association, originally founded for the promotion of uniform state laws, is another. On the whole, though, the accomplishments remained modest, in turn prompting demands for more structured intergovernmentalism *under federal auspices.* The logic of this transition is elementary. State "cooperation" and cartels will often founder on state disagreements or, subsequently, on defection or cheating by individual states. Blocking such maneuvers requires central intervention by the federal government. "Cooperative federalism" is an umbrella term for federal programs of that description.

Federalism poses coordination problems at the best of times, and the Progressives and New Dealers were obviously correct that the greatly increased economic scale and integration of the industrial age posed them with increased frequency and severity. However, the central question was, and is, not "coordination, yea or nay," but rather coordination *on what terms*—competition or cartel?[7] On one side, "dual" federalism rarely impeded genuine coordination efforts. What it blocked, not always but too often to suit Progressive tastes, was cartelization. On the other side, the Progressives' and New Dealers' initiatives rarely coordinated anything, while consistently establishing intergovernmental or industrial cartels.

"Dualism impedes coordination" was a prominent Progressive and New Deal theme. Edward S. Corwin, among other leading legal lights, complained that the Supreme Court's rigid distinction between interstate commerce and the states' police powers had created a jurisdictional no-man's-land in which *no* government was competent to act.[8] Before the turn of the century, that contention had some plausibility in a few settings. Corwin's principal example was antitrust law and, in particular, the Supreme Court's overwrought decision in *E. C. Knight* (1895), which did seem to immunize corporate perpetrators of nationwide conspiracies against any government's reach.[9] Another example was alcohol regulation, where the Supreme Court's "original package" doctrine effectively thwarted dry states' unilateral efforts to remain dry. Both problems, however, were soon remedied: the antitrust problem, through an adjustment by the Supreme Court; the booze problem, through federal legislation (the 1890 Wilson Act and the 1913 Webb-Kenyon Act, both of which the Supreme Court sustained).[10] Corwin held to his "no man's-land" theory long after those successful adjustments, and President Roosevelt still peddled it to the public in 1937.[11] By that time, though, the idea that the old federalism created insoluble coordination problems or barred energetic national action was demonstrably wrong. Nothing precluded the national management of interstate network industries (such as railroads), the federal regulation of bottleneck industries in interstate commerce, or federal safety laws and their enforcement by state and local officials; constitutional impediments to those schemes had been removed long before the New Deal.[12] Nor did the old Constitution pose insurmountable obstacles to the New Deal's national social and economic objectives. Nothing barred the hiring of unemployed artists to adorn post offices with Soviet Realist murals or the establishment of the Civilian Conservation Corps. And nothing prevented the New Deal from establishing the pristinely national Social Security system.[13] What the Old Constitution did often impede, not always but often for federalism-related reasons, was coordination in the form and for the purpose of establishing state or industrial cartels. That description fits any and all of the federal enactments that met with judicial disfavor over the years: federal child-labor standards in *Hammer v. Dagenhart* (1918); the Agricultural Adjustment Act in *Butler* (1936); the National Industrial Recovery Act in *Panama Refining* (1935) and in the unanimous *Schechter Poultry* decision (1935); and the Guffey Act in *Carter v. Carter Coal* (1936).[14]

The New Deal's own "cooperative" programs and doctrines further belie the notion that coordination per se had much to do with its agenda. Federal minimum standards for labor practices coordinated nothing because states remained free to legislate on top of those standards. The New Deal's strategy of granting states a concurrent role in industry regulation—a consistent practice even where wholly national regulation would have made a lot more sense—did not solve coordination problems but rather created them.[15] So too with fiscal programs. Coordinationwise, it would make eminent sense to monopolize redistributive programs at the federal level. (The federal government has a comparative advantage at redistribution because it can tax on a nationwide basis and it knows how to move gobs of money.) Running the programs through state bureaucracies involves high administrative costs, fiscal distortions, policy slippage, political gamesmanship, and outright theft. The New Dealers were well aware of those problems but, evidently, not terribly impressed by them.[16] And so, we shall see, with constitutional doctrine. The New Deal's state-friendly innovations, though touted as solutions to federalism's coordination problems, instead created such problems in abundance.

If the New Deal was about solving coordination problems, it did a rotten job of it. In truth, though, the Progressives and New Dealers were never interested in "coordination." For all their handwringing over the complexities of the industrial age, only one of federalism's perceived coordination problems truly concerned them: competition among states. Their colorful name for that problem was the "race to the bottom."

The Race to the Bottom. Competitive federalism embodies a harm principle, analogous to the harm principle that obtains in private markets.[17] Among states, as among individuals, the legal order must protect against the risks of force, fraud, and monopoly. In contrast, injuries from competition—the private firm's loss of customers, a state's loss of productive citizens—*must not* count as redressable harms. Roughly, that was the old constitutional arrangement. The New Deal Constitution, in diametrical contrast, defines interstate competition *itself* as a collective action problem—as a "race to the bottom."

The evidence of that "race," the Progressives and New Dealers believed, was all around. One notorious example was corporate law, where state charters allowed corporations to escape into (allegedly) irresponsibly lax jurisdictions, notably Delaware. A second "race" frustrated state efforts to tax wealthy and, as it turned out, highly mobile individuals. (Florida's emergence as a tax-free retirement haven dates to this period.) A third instance was workplace regulation such as child labor laws, minimum wage laws, maximum work hours laws, laws regarding unionization and, later, the provision of social services to the indigent, disabled, and elderly. Time and again, it appeared, fear of competition prevented enlightened states from responding to urgent social problems and demands.

Most modern economists doubt that jurisdictional competition systematically produces collective action problems and socially undesirable outcomes. For a prominent example, the state "race" for corporate charters that troubled the Progressives is now widely viewed as a potent vehicle for maximizing shareholder value.[18] More broadly, scholars have come to doubt, both for theoretical reasons and for lack of empirical evidence, that competition for mobile production factors will systematically induce jurisdictions to undersupply public goods, such as environmental amenities. Under most reasonable assumptions, the level of such goods will reflect the local demand, which may be quite high even when the tax price is substantial.[19]

It may seem hard to be equally sanguine about the effects of competition on redistributive programs. With respect to public goods (the basic intuition runs), taxpayers get what they pay for. Some will want a small and inexpensive bundle of goods; others, a more comprehensive and expensive package. At any point in time, lots of people may be on the move. That, though, is no "race to the bottom." It is a sorting process that produces a rough equilibrium, at least in principle. Redistribution, in contrast, is an uncompensated loss to the payer and a pure windfall to the payee. Each state must apprehend that redistribution will induce immediate exit by mobile taxpayers, as well as an unwanted "welfare magnet" effect. The equilibrium point, it appears, is zero redistribution. It is surprisingly hard, however, to find contemporaneous evidence of a "race to the bottom."

Among the issues that agitated the Progressives and New Dealers, none was more salient and emotional than child labor. Federal legislation on the subject was declared unconstitutional in the race-to-the-bottom case par excellence—*Hammer v. Dagenhart* (1918), where a narrow 5–4 majority of the Supreme Court invalidated, as exceeding Congress's powers under the Commerce Clause, a federal statute prohibiting the interstate shipment of goods from any factory employing children under the age of fourteen. Four years later, the Court invalidated, now by a 6–3 vote, a federal tax designed to accomplish the end already found unconstitutional in *Hammer*.[20] Efforts to prohibit child labor by means of constitutional amendment remained unavailing, and child labor remained unregulated at the federal level until 1938.

What happened in the real world? Figure 8.1 shows the percentage of the labor force comprised of children (ages 10–15) between 1880 and 1930.

All states had already adopted child labor laws by the time of *Hammer*, albeit of varying stringency. Those differences reflected a deep sectional difference between the poor South and the wealthier states especially in the Northeast, which held throughout the period. (Demand for federal intervention predictably came from high-wage industries in those states, such as the Massachusetts textile industry.) Even so, state-level prohibitions toughened over time, and one observes a sustained improvement in economic and social conditions. State laws probably did little to reduce child labor.[21] Rising prosperity, perhaps facilitated by a lightly regulated economy, appears to have been a much bigger factor. Either way, child

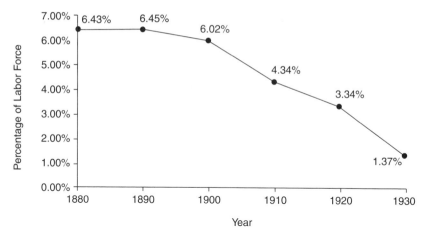

8.1. Percentage of workforce comprised of children. Source: Bicentennial Edition: Historical Statistics of the United States, Colonial Times to 1970: Chapter D, Series 75 and 80. Available online at http://www.census.gov/prod/www/abs/statab.html.

labor had already been cut almost in half at the time of *Hammer* and effectively disappeared by 1930. Prior to the onset of the Great Depression, virtually all other social indicators show a similar improvement. It hardly mattered, though; the "race to the bottom" easily survived the evidence and flourished as an all-purpose rationale for federal intervention.

However, the New Deal was not content to merely compromise competitive federalism's harm principle; it inverted it. Even as competition turned into an "externality," actual externalities *ceased* to count as harms. Both at a legislative and a constitutional level, the New Dealers affirmatively encouraged states to tax and regulate their neighbors and interstate commerce, several times over. Unlike competition, the state exercise of such "extraterritorial" state authority does present an acute danger, not just of inefficiency but of exploitation, mutual aggression, and tit-for-tat retaliation—a "race to the bottom," if you will. The New Dealers, however, viewed extraterritorial legislation as a virtue of their federalism. They called it "experimentation," about which more anon.

From a constitutional and a commonsense vantage, a federalism that blocks the states' ability to compete while encouraging aggression among them looks decidedly weird. Weirder still is its designation as "cooperative." The oddness, however, disappears when one looks at federalism from the states' vantage: the New Deal's inverted Constitution is the federalism they want.

Constitutional Inversion, Part 1:
A Federalism for States

The New Deal Constitution's federalism, I have insisted, inverts the foundational principles of the Madisonian, competitive Constitution. It moves from the citizens' "reflection and choice" to the states' interests as federalism's baseline; from safeguards against the violence of faction to an embrace of interest group politics; from constitutional stability, ensured through self-enforcing norms, to a more democratic, "Living" Constitution. The remainder of this chapter tackles this constitutional transformation one inversion at a time. The explanation moves from a simple, bare-bones model to a richer account that more fully captures the logic and the political economy of the New Deal transformation.

I begin in this section with a hypothetical constitutional choice story: if states (uncertain, like individuals, about their in-period position) could choose their federalism rules ex ante, they would choose the New Deal Constitution. A second step examines the states' constitutional choice perspective "in-period," under conditions roughly resembling those of the early twentieth century. At a third stage, I show that the seemingly abstract constitutional choice analysis has a great deal of real-world traction in explaining the New Deal Constitution's genesis, political economy, and contours.

Federalism: The States' Choice. The constitutional baseline is the global ex ante calculus of prospective citizens, to the exclusion of the states' perspective. Invert the scenario, and imagine that states got to choose federalism rules ex ante. What would the rules look like? To a large extent, the answer depends on what one means by "state." As a first approximation, one can think of states as autocratic revenue-maximizers—"Leviathans," or in a yet-more inflammatory metaphor, "stationary bandits."[22] The stylized assumption is not strictly necessary, and I shall relax it in a moment. However, it helps to guard against the tendency to think of states in a reified, romanticized way, and it is continuous with the Founders' intellectual universe. States, Hamilton and Madison warned, are run by politicians with interests and incentives—by men who seek to augment the "power, emolument, and consequence of the offices they hold under the state establishments." The Leviathan hypothesis imagines that these men could make an unconstrained federalism choice.[23]

Are Leviathans capable of consenting to *any* federal union? Why, yes. For example, small states may band together so as to economize on collective defense expenditures, in the hope that some portion of the savings will accrue to each member-state in the form of appropriable surplus.[24] Calculations of this sort may run over a range of issues, so that union (rather than a mere defense pact) becomes an attractive option. Beyond this point, though, and with respect to the Union's internal organization, the states' calculus becomes very complicated. One might think that states will cede authority to the center only so far as is absolutely necessary to perform the purposes of federal organization and, in all other respects, insist on what I have called their "independence autonomy"—that is, a right to govern their own affairs to the exclusion of the central government. But this assumption—a close twin of the common misinterpretation of federalism as a "double security"—hangs on the Leviathans' assumptions about the constitutional world to come.

The crucial complication is that political union will likely mean a common citizenship and free movement of citizens across state borders. Free domestic trade may enhance citizens' productive capacity and, presumably, each Leviathan's tax capacity. However, free movement also entails increased competition among states. At the limit, in a "pure Tiebout" world, free and costless exit for all production factors may wipe out all available state surplus. That calculation may not matter much, and states may insist on independence autonomy, so long as exit remains very costly and state economies remain localized. In contrast, under conditions of an open economy, states will trade their independence autonomy for surplus. Like private producers in economic markets, they will demand the central organization of interstate cartels, even at a considerable risk of interference with their independence autonomy.

The Leviathans may have a reservation price—that is, some point at which they will refuse to accept a federally sponsored cartel. But they will seek to exact that price on the *distribution* side, not by means of protecting independence autonomy. In political as in economic markets, prohibiting competition on one margin prompts competition on another (less efficient) margin.[25] The recognition of this displacement effect pushes states to what I will call their Hobbesian demand—an omnipotent central government, capable of reaching any private conduct and suppressing competition among states in any dimension. That surrender of independence autonomy, however, must be paid in the coinage that Leviathans value and recognize—surplus. I will call this the states' "Lockean proviso."[26] The most natural answer to the states' demands under open-economy conditions is a comprehensive tax cartel—that is, a federal tax monopoly (the Hobbesian demand) coupled with guaranteed federal-to-state transfers in accordance with a constitutional distribution formula (the Lockean proviso). Some federal constitutions conform to this solution both as a matter of history and design. The United States Constitution is antithetical to it. The New Deal Constitution, we shall see, approximates it.[27]

In-Period State Choice. The ex ante analysis of state constitutional choice, like its individual-choice counterpart, is merely a thought experiment. However, it yields useful predictions about how states will behave in-period, and it helps to understand the New Deal transformation and its political economy. To that end, I abandon the autocracy assumption and substitute a more conventional assumption about state politics: democracy, or interest group politics. This move implies a change in the dissipation of state surplus: autocrats will want to spend on concubines and castles; elected officials, on constituencies. (We can be confident of this generalization because officials who fail to do so won't be officials for very long.) However, state politicians will still seek to produce surplus, for the reasons that worried Hamilton and Madison: a lack of any encompassing interest (they are supposed to look to their own constituents' interests, not those of other states or the nation), and a short time horizon extending to the protection of their tenure.

The general expectation is that states, at the constitutional stage, will have to accept *some* competitive arrangements as the price of union. The American states, we have seen, had to swallow a brutally competitive Constitution. However, given the dispositions and incentives just sketched, states will seek to take back the constitutional concessions in-period. Thus, state demand for cartelization is a given. Its intensity, however, will vary with the cost of exit and other factors that affect the degree of interstate competition.[28]

For most of the nineteenth century, the economic conditions of a largely agrarian society, dominated by small scale producers with high exit costs (such as farmers and artisans), gave states few occasions to demand federal protection against having to compete with other states. Even then, though, states fought the Supreme Court at every turn; and with the rise of industrial capitalism, the competitive rules began to bite. Vertically integrated national corporations mowed down local, state-protected monopolies and incorporated in "friendly" state jurisdictions. Wealthy retirees migrated to states without an inheritance tax. Black labor began to migrate northward. Investment capital at last operated in a truly national financial market. For state governments, increased factor mobility and economic integration entailed more intense competition and a decreased ability to collect surplus.[29]

Can one reverse the competitive tide and return the economy to localism? Something like that agenda impelled the Populist movement of the late nineteenth century. It may have spurred the antitrust movement in the 1880s and 1890s, and it sustained the campaign against national chain stores in the 1930s.[30] That crusade, an early anti-Walmart movement, was supported by state and local governments and by an odd coalition of local merchants, Huey Long and his populist rabble, the Ku Klux Klan (which apprehended that chain stores would sell to and even employ Negroes), and Progressive adherents of democratic localism—prominently, Louis Brandeis. The movement's objective was to neutralize national chains' "unfair" advantages (such as economies of scale) vis-à-vis local stores, primarily by means of differential state taxation. The campaign succeeded in many states. It produced confusing Supreme Court decisions on the taxation of interstate commerce and some of Justice Brandeis's most effusive encomia to local self-determination.[31] It also produced the federal Robinson-Patman Act (1936), which sought to counteract the national chains' cost advantages in purchasing. Still, the anti-chain store movement collapsed by the end of the decade, when it had become obvious that consumers demanded the chains' lower prices and competent service and when the stores came up with yet another capitalist contrivance, the shopping cart.[32] To generalize the demoralizing experience: although a few local industries may succeed in entrenching themselves in some protectionist pocket (given sufficiently dumb federal laws and constitutional doctrines), conditions of high mobility and large economic scale frustrate any systemwide return to localism. Thus, the states' best move is a federalism that enlists the central government in creating and protecting state cartels.

States pursued that strategy through the institutional mechanism that the Constitution provides—their agency within the national government. Time and again, we shall see (especially in chapters 9 and 11), states demanded an expansion of national authority coupled with a surplus-protective state proviso. The states' litigation positions reveal a very similar pattern. No state ever defended the "old," competitive Constitution against the perceived or real impositions of an overbearing Congress. It was left to corporations, Justice Robert Jackson wrote in 1941, to carry "the states' rights plea against the states themselves."[33]

Patterns of Accommodation. Following a great many federalism scholars, I have so far treated states as players in a federalism "game." Models of this sort have their problems.[34] For starters, states are not unitary actors with well-defined preferences. Additional complications arise when the model is used to explain, not the formation of a federal union, but a renegotiation of federalism under an existing union with preexisting federal institutions, social divisions, national parties, and interest groups (a complication to which I will attend in a moment). All those actors and factors are interdependent, and a plausible historical account would have to look a whole lot more complicated than a stylized $n + 1$ (n states, one central government) federalism model. Still, the narrative helps to make sense not only of the timing and dynamic of the New Deal transformation but also its contours.

For "states as states," federalism is an enforcement problem; pro-competitive free-riders and chiselers persistently undermine the desired cartels. In the first instance, though, it is a bargaining problem. Even unanimous intergovernmental agreement to maximize surplus—a "Declaration of Interdependence," passed with devout intentions on all sides—may founder on disagreements over the distribution of the proceeds.[35] The United States Constitution presents this problem in a particularly acute form. As seen in earlier chapters, it contains no distributional baseline of any kind. And without a focal point, state bargaining will prove costly and complicated.

Against these impediments to in-period cartelization stands the intuition that actors who play a game often enough will eventually find a cooperative solution. The states did find that solution—"cooperative federalism"—but they did so in fits and starts, one bargain at a time, over the pre–New Deal decades. A *systemwide* move to cartel federalism and its constitutional entrenchment had to await the crisis conditions and the extraordinary degree of partisan-political consensus of the New Deal.[36] Even then, however, the fact that cartel federalism, lacking a constitutional baseline, had to be improvised in-period had potent effects both on its scope and its forms.

As for scope, cartelization became the dominant but not the exclusive mode of federal organization. In some venues, cartel federalism encountered formidable obstacles—foremost, sectionalism. Pre–New Deal, sectionalism frustrated child labor legislation; post–New Deal, it blocked, for the better part of three decades, "cooperative" federal programs that directly threatened the racial caste system in the South.[37] Other impediments arose from path dependencies and "preempted policy space."[38] For example, our federalism appears to have problems in eliminating competitive advantages possessed and cultivated by a few states or even a single state. The durability of Delaware's corporate law regime, as well as the successful resistance of a few small states without a sales tax to a federal sales tax cartel, illustrates the point.[39] Similarly, entrenched regulatory regimes may resist cartelization; the resilience of the "dual" banking system, created in the 1860s on dual federalism premises, is an example.[40]

As for cartel federalism's forms, in-period construction produced a singularly haphazard and incoherent form of "cooperative" federalism. Its contours vary widely across policy sectors, without regard to considerations of distributional equity or economic rationality. Within each intergovernmental policy silo (as well as overall), the distribution of power and surplus—federalism's "balance"—often lurches from a pro-state distribution to centralization, and back again. Even so, the system is extremely resilient. The New Deal Constitution, we shall see, has found ways of preventing defection by even the worst-off institutional actor.

Constitutional Inversion, Part 2: From Factions to Interests

For James Madison, state politics was particularly the domain of faction. The constitutional architecture is calculated to suppress its poisonous effects. The New Deal Constitution rests on the same premise but inverts its valence. Instead of lamenting the states' factional tendencies, Progressives and New Dealers celebrated them under the heading of "pluralism" or interest group politics. This inversion is closely linked to the New Deal Constitution's federalism for "states as states." The New Dealers did not care for states on account of some antebellum romanticism but because states are terrific places to both mobilize and satisfy interest group claimants. Put differently, states that are empowered to collect surplus are in a position to dissipate it to political constituencies. This calculus connects the New Deal Constitution's federalism to its politics. It can be summarized under three headings: experimentation, dynamic federalism, and exploitation.[41]

Experimentation. The classic exposition of New Deal federalism "experimentation" is Justice Brandeis's famous dissent in *New State Ice Co. v. Liebmann* (1932):

> There must be power in the states and the nation to remould, through experimentation, our economic practices and institutions to meet changing social and economic needs. . . . It is one of the happy incidents of the federal system that a single courageous state may, if its citizens choose, serve as a laboratory; and try novel social and economic experiments without risk to the rest of the country.[42]

Brandeis's metaphor has appealed not only to proponents of democratic localism but also to some modern conservatives and to economists who stress the virtues of local learning and "adaptive efficiency."[43] Political institutions, they say, should be capable of adapting to changing economic circumstances and divergent social preferences. Much can be said for the piecemeal diffusion of new policies; when we do not know what we are doing, it is best not to do it everywhere, all at once. A state-based process may facilitate gradualism and, therefore, feedback and institutional learning. All those advantages, however, depend on institutional and legal preconditions about which the "laboratory" metaphor itself is silent. Foremost, a great deal depends on whether states experiment under competitive or noncompetitive conditions.

As noted, it is not at all frivolous to describe the pre–New Deal trajectory of child labor legislation as a process of successful state experimentation. That experiment, though, was conducted under competitive conditions and persistent exit threats. For precisely that reason, it was *not* the "experimentation" that Brandeis and the rest had in mind; it was a "race to the bottom" that required power in "*the nation* to remould" and experiment on the world. The Progressives' and New Dealers' enthusiasm for state "laboratories" was limited to arenas where states could experiment without fear of competition.[44]

New State Ice, the paradigmatic case, arose over an Oklahoma statute prohibiting the manufacture, distribution, and sale of ice without a certificate of public convenience and necessity. Contra Brandeis, Oklahoma was not a "single courageous state" whose "citizens chose" to stage a "novel experiment." Rather, well-connected producers found themselves threatened by competition and by an invention called the refrigerator, and so helped themselves to market entry and output restrictions, in conspiracy against consumers and potential competitors.[45] Against this idiocy, competitive federalism provides little effective protection. The monopoly overcharge would have to be very large to induce exit, and due to the economics of the ice business, the erosion of monopoly profits through out-of-state competition was a remote prospect at the time. For that reason, the Old Court employed the Due Process Clause as a coarse screen that permitted states to experiment with public health, safety, and morals legislation while blocking faction-driven, "partial" legislation. For the same reason, the New Deal Constitution scuttled the doctrine.[46]

Dynamic Federalism. The central dynamic of competitive federalism is— well, competition. The New Deal Constitution's federalism is dynamic in two different senses. The first has to do with the migration of interest group demand: a federalism that liberates the concurrent state and national "remoulding" of economic conditions entails that some agency, some level of government, is always open for business. As one near-canonical text put it:

[A] system of many power centers is well suited to meet the infinite variety of expressed needs. . . . Because there are many points for decision, citizens and citizen groups have multiple opportunities to influence decisionmaking. If a group does not get satisfaction at one place, it can try another. And if the second is unresponsive, there may exist a third or fourth.⁴⁷

Contra Mick Jagger, you *can* always get what you want. Alas, someone has to pay for "the infinite variety of expressed needs." Those people now have to guard, not against one potentially bad actor, but against many, including the worst among them. In a Madisonian universe, that is a state of nature. It is the apotheosis of the New Deal Constitution.

The second dynamic has to do with the spatial distribution of interests. Redistributive interests that cannot win on a national level might yet win in a few states—because they are concentrated in a "single state," and/ or because that state is in a position or sufficiently "courageous" to defy competitive pressures.⁴⁸ Having prevailed, the interests may well be able to enlist state officials and even their erstwhile in-state opponents—for example, taxpayers or producers who pay the costs of the experiment— in a campaign to ramp the experiment up to national scale, with an eye toward spreading the costs across the nation or toward "leveling the play- ing field" by regulatory means. (Many of the political New Deal's policy innovations followed just this pattern.) "Experimentation's" federalism strategy isn't policy diversification; it is island hopping. Less flippantly, the New Deal Constitution's federalism is a response to the *national*-scale weakness of distributional coalitions in American politics.

Exploitation. James Madison, we have seen, despaired of arresting fac- tionalism at the states' borders. The Convention disagreed with him; to that rejection, we owe our competitive federal, rather than national, Constitution. But the constitutional solution makes sense only against the background agreement that factionalism is actually bad. If it is good, the logical move is to *promote* interest group exploitation of other state's citi- zens: they are less likely than in-state constituencies to notice the imposi- tion because the costs are spread more widely, they cannot fight back at the ballot box, and they have no exit. Oklahoma's fabulous scheme was unlikely to have any price effects outside the state. In that sense, Brandeis was right to describe the experiment as "without risk to the rest of the country." In short order, however, the Supreme Court liberated the states to experiment on each other's citizens. The encouragement of exploitative state action, we shall see, is a cornerstone of the New Deal Constitution in its mature, developed state.

Constitutional Inversion, Part 3:
Stability and Structure

Competitive federalism reflects, or reflected, a precommitment to constitutional stability in a dual sense. Self-enforcing constitutional rules are designed to limit the range of equilibrium outcomes (to guard against the perils of a "mutable government") and, at the same time, to ensure the durability of the constitutional arrangements as such. Both orientations are anathema to a political movement that celebrates interest group politics. Such a movement will want *in*-stability, both in terms of output and of constitutional structure. Because that sounds unappealing, more honorific terms will soon come to mind. The New Deal's terms, and soon the Supreme Court's watchwords, were "democracy" and a "Living Constitution." Rivers of ink have flown over this change in constitutional understanding; what matters here are the dramatic shifts in the Supreme Court's institutional role and its federalism.

The Court. The point of a competitive constitutional structure, to repeat, is to ensure stability understood both as limiting the output of factional legislation and as ensuring the durability of self-enforcing rules. Although the Supreme Court is not the only or even the most vital check on the system, it is *a* vital check: its raison d'être is to prevent institutional agents' defections from the agreed-upon, competitive rules of the game. In the competitive constitutional setting, the Supreme Court is a "Structure Court" that acts as a constitutional antitrust enforcer: when institutional actors unilaterally break the rules, or when intergovernmental conspiracies are clearly afoot, the Court must step in—not, mind you, to protect the competitors, but to protect citizen-consumers.

The New Deal Court surrendered the structure function not only on separation of powers questions, where it had never played a serious role, but also on federalism questions, where it had. The demise of the enumerated powers doctrine is widely viewed as the most obvious illustration of the Court's newfound deference or abdication to democratic demands. As suggested, however, the New Deal Court also assumed a highly deferential role vis-à-vis the states. Thus, unilateral defections became more viable not only for the Congress but for all levels of government. Opportunities for intergovernmental "cooperation" waxed correspondingly (or rather exponentially), while the Court's interest in distinguishing cooperation from intergovernmental collusion and conspiracies waned.

The judicial abandonment of a competitive structure raises two questions. First, having procured a Constitution that is less structure and more "democracy," what is the Court still good for? Second, *whose* democratic demands are now supposed to prevail? At the end of the day, a Court that has made room for a more democratic politics and Constitution will want to make it safe for the constituencies on whose behalf it made the move in the first place. To that end, it will have to decide who deserves advantages and disadvantages in the political struggle.[49] That cannot be done by the uncertain means of rejiggering the constitutional structure and process. It requires a direct allocation of rights. Thus, having surrendered its function as a "Structure Court," the Supreme Court will have to become a "Rights Court." Having liberated the people's agents from constraints, the Court must now constrain the people themselves.[50] The Supreme Court recognized and advertised this intimate connection between structural abandonment and rights enthusiasm as early as 1938. *Carolene Products*, emblematic of the New Deal Court's policy of letting unvarnished interest group swinishness pass without judicial scrutiny, famously footnoted the Court's intention of protecting rights (of a certain description).[51]

Even so, the immediately following chapters postpone the rights question for consideration in Parts IV and V. The first, chronological reason for doing so is that the "rights revolution," although embedded in the New Deal transformation, had to await those later decades and intervening events. The second reason is our tendency to let judicial style cloud constitutional substance. The rights revolution was a decidedly "activist" judicial intervention and an affirmative act of constitutional construction. The antecedent demise of structure, in contrast, sounds in judicial deference and humility. In substance, however, the demise of the Constitution's competitive structure and its replacement with cartel federalism was no less an audacious act of constitutional construction than the rights revolution. Far from surrendering federalism, the New Deal Court radically reconceived it.

Conclusion

The constitutional choice story oulined in this chapter highlights, and leads back to, the initial point of departure: *what* federalism, not how much, is the central question of political organization and development. Political economists are well aware of the difference. Decentralization, they have found, can discipline government and retard its growth. That effect, however, crucially depends on competitive (constitutional) background conditions. Allow governments to collude vertically or horizontally: decentralization will cease to have the expected disciplining results and may in fact enhance the growth of government.[52]

That anticipated effect is the point of the Declaration of Interdependence of the New Deal's federalism. This chapter has provided an account of the political economy of the shift, or inversion, from competition to cartel. The following chapters deal with the corollary shifts in central principles of constitutional structure and construction. Table 8.1 juxtaposes the principles of the competitive federal Constitution, originally shown and discussed in chapter 3, with the inverted principles of the New Deal Constitution.

Table 8.1. Competitive federalism versus cartel federalism: constitutional structure

Strategies	Competitive federalism	Cartel federalism
Structure		
Federalism	"Dual federalism," a.k.a. "compound republic" (limited, enumerated powers; directness)	Intergovernmental cartels
Entitlements	Delegated, enumerated powers	Congressional omnicompetence
	States' rights: territoriality, equality, political integrity	(Tenth Amendment enclaves)
	Nondiscrimination; nonexploitation	Exploitation
Coordination		
Bounded equilibrium	Powers, not balance	Vertical balance
Jurisdiction	Federal supremacy	Supremacy-minus
	Exclusivity	Concurrent powers
Stability		
(Self-)enforcement	Institutional commitments	Judicial deference/ abstention canons
Bargains	Fiscal autonomy; baseline-free bargaining; transparency	Fiscal transfers; "cooperation"

Contemporary constitutional scholars understand these doctrinal shifts as a federalism "translation." After the inevitable demise of the enumerated powers doctrine, their theory goes, the Supreme Court adjusted other pieces of the constitutional architecture to restore, or at least approximate, the original federalism balance.[53] But although that understanding is in keeping with the New Dealers' own pronouncement, the fact is that one cannot mix and match the elements of Madison's "compound republic" without affecting institutional outcomes and dynamics. The supposed "translation" masks a profound shift from competition to cartel, from government discipline to empowerment, from a federalism for citizens to a federalism for states. Perhaps the New Deal "translation" illustrates that courts are not particularly good at identifying the best moves in a second-best world.[54] But I am more inclined to think that the New Dealers knew what they were doing.

CHAPTER NINE

Commerce, Cartels, and Concurrent Powers

Commerce: The States' Choices

The Commerce Clause territory, like Gaul, is divided into three parts: the scope of congressional power under the clause; the question of coordinating concurrent state and federal regulation, or federal preemption; and the dormant Commerce Clause. In all three areas, the New Deal Constitution accommodated the state demand for surplus-protective doctrines, with one important qualification.

The states' preferred rule under competitive conditions, I have argued, is an all-encompassing federal commerce power. That construct is a central accomplishment of the New Deal revolution, marked by the transformation of the Commerce Clause from *Hammer v. Dagenhart* (1918) to *Wickard v. Filburn* (1942). I emphasize the underappreciated *institutional* aspects of that familiar story. Far from trampling on the states, the expansion of federal commerce powers enhanced their capacity to collect surplus. Even the Commerce Clause, exhibit A in every account of a supposedly nationalist New Deal, was a state-friendly doctrine and a response to state demand.

The states' demand for a Hobbesian federal commerce power, I have further argued, will be hedged with a Lockean proviso to prevent the federal government from expropriating local surplus. That proviso requires a continued state power to regulate even after the federal government has entered the field. Federal legislation, therefore, should not be exclusive but should rather leave room for concurrent, more stringent or expansive state legislation. Post–New Deal preemption doctrines serve precisely this function.

Finally, I have suggested that a Constitution for "states as states" will contain a states' right to exploit each other's citizens, subject to certain limitations. One constitutional distillation of this arrangement is the dormant Commerce Clause, covered in the third part of this chapter. The pre–New Deal version of the doctrine often operated as a categorical restraint on the states. In its post–New Deal version, it bars only a certain subset of state activities—those that "discriminate" against interstate commerce. Moreover, the doctrine effectively lost its "extraterritoriality" prong—that is, the prohibition against state laws that do not discriminate against but nonetheless exploit interstate commerce. I will explain why a doctrine with those contours *may* be consistent with the New Deal's cartel federalism. However, even in its post–New Deal formulation, the dormant Commerce Clause is a procompetitive rule. It cuts against every other New Deal doctrine—the demise of the Due Process clause, modern preemption doctrine, and *Erie*. Thus, its survival is a bit of a mystery. Perhaps the best explanation is that the Constitution requires something like the dormant Commerce Clause as a pure functional necessity.

The Hobbesian Commerce Clause

The transformation of the enumerated powers doctrine and the Commerce Clause is, or is thought to be, thoroughly familiar. The pre-New Deal Constitution embodied a categorical distinction between separate, mutually exclusive federal and states spheres. In the late nineteenth century, when cases testing the boundaries became the daily diet of the law, the categorical distinctions came under enormous pressure, which increased with the growth of an industrialized corporate economy and rapid economic integration. Judicial attempts to shore up the internal-external distinction with further epicycles—such as the distinction between "commerce" and "production" and the distinction between "direct" and "indirect" effects on interstate commerce—proved equally contestable. Soon enough, the Supreme Court's conceptual edifice invited legal-realist ridicule.[1] Eventually, the enumerated powers doctrine collapsed. It was at last discarded in *Wickard v. Filburn* (1942), which held that the Commerce Clause authorizes Congress to regulate not only interstate commerce but also transactions that are neither "interstate" nor even "commercial"—in that case, farmer Filburn's consumption of his own wheat on his own farm. Legal scholars continue to debate the logic and timing of the transformation. Perhaps the Supreme Court collapsed under raw political pressure when it held, in *NLRB v. Jones & Laughlin* (1937), that the federal government could regulate labor relations, at least in factories that were directly connected to interstate commerce. Or perhaps that decision was a laudable attempt to adjust the old distinctions to novel economic circumstances, an effort that was unnecessarily discarded in *Wickard*. But there seems to be a general agreement that the New Deal's Commerce Clause is an unambiguously nationalist, centralizing doctrine. That view, I believe, mistakes the political economy of the Commerce Clause, and therefore the reasons for its transformation.

Commerce and Complexity: Two Views. Progressives and New Dealers propagated an expansive Commerce Clause with two somewhat different lines of argument. At times, they described it as a restoration of an original Commerce Clause that had been recklessly trashed by the *Lochner* Court's laissez-faire reactionaries. This understanding, developed in a torrent of tendentious books and articles, is encapsulated in *Wickard*'s oft-cited observation that Chief Justice Marshall's opinion in *Gibbons v. Ogden* described the Commerce Clause "with a breadth never yet exceeded."[2] That, though, was at best a mildly charming self-deception at the time, and modern scholarship demonstrates it to be baseless.[3] At other times, the New Dealers insisted that the conceptual distinctions of the "horse and buggy" era were no longer workable in a complex modern economy. That argument, too, surfaced in *Wickard*. The effective exercise of the unquestioned congressional power to regulate interstate commerce, the Court explained, often requires the regulation of local activities that, in the aggregate, *affect* commerce.[4]

There are reasons to doubt that the New Dealers actually believed their own "complexity" burble. Foremost, we shall see, the supposedly untenable categorical distinctions survived on the dormant Commerce Clause side, despite the complexity of it all. Moreover, the New Deal systematically "stabilized" industries under separate regulatory umbrellas—banks here, insurance companies there, securities markets elsewhere. That strategy makes sense, if at all, only on the assumption that one can stabilize one segment of the economy without creating dislocations elsewhere—in other words, on the basis of indifference to or ignorance of economic complexity. Far from attempting to govern the world as a global commons, the New Deal attempted to manage it as a collection of cartels; and it was *that* purpose that drove the New Deal's take on the Commerce Clause. As noted earlier, all the schemes that had been invalidated by the pre–New Deal Court, from *Hammer* to *Schechter*, fit the cartel description. Perhaps the finest illustration, though, is *Wickard* itself.

The case is often taught as a reductio ad absurdum: why is a family farmer's home-baked bread the feds' business? But the folklore misses the context. After the destruction of U.S. export markets in the wake of the Smoot-Hawley tariffs, the country confronted persistent overcapacity in many agricultural commodities, including wheat. The New Deal vowed to curb "overproduction" and "destructive competition" through federal production quotas, and that objective required national control over local events. Filburn did not bake bread in worrisome quantities; rather, he fed the wheat to his cattle. That made him part of a very real threat—a mass migration of local producers from a controlled commodity (wheat) into an uncontrolled one (livestock). To avert that scenario, the New Deal had to block the exits. A distinction between national and in-state events would only prompt evasions and, in the end, bring the entire program to a fall. Concede the cartel premise, and *Wickard* is an easy case: the local *must* be national.[5]

The argument that the transformation of the Commerce Clause had to do, not with complexity, but with the New Deal's dreadful economic policies and objectives is a standard refrain among modern-day libertarian critics of the New Deal and its Constitution.[6] As just seen, I share that view. However, the libertarian position—"stick with the old distinctions"—has its own difficulties. One such difficulty is that those distinctions were developed on the dormant side of the Commerce Clause, as a shield against *judicial* intervention.[7] There are reasons to doubt that the same distinctions will work when deployed against *Congress*. This is particularly so because the commerce power, as all enumerated powers, operates in conjunction with the Necessary and Proper Clause. That clause disappeared from the pre–New Deal Commerce Clause cases for the splendid reason that it would have rendered the Court's categorical distinctions impotent. It resurfaced soon enough, however, and cast a large shadow over the enterprise of limiting congressional powers.[8]

The second, more fundamental difficulty has to do not with doctrine but with institutions. Enumerated powers limitations, wherever one might wish to locate them, are parchment barriers. They will retain force and stability only so long as they are sustained by some extralegal, political and institutional dynamic. What sustained dual, competitive arrangements throughout the nineteenth century was sectionalism. Large-scale, rapid industrialization, however, and especially the great increase in capital and labor mobility, drastically changed the landscape and the states' calculus. States experienced intensified competition as a loss of autonomy, and they clamored for federal intervention to block "destructive" competition. The political economy that had sustained the Commerce Clause collapsed, and the demise of the old understanding was a foregone conclusion well before the New Deal.

Commerce Powers: The Demand Side. In its modern usage, "cooperative federalism" refers primarily to federal grants programs. Its original focus, however, was not the spending power but the Commerce Clause. Well into the 1930s, "national-state cooperation [was] almost always conceived of in terms of federal consent to state action," and a steady stream of learned books and articles addressed that thorny problem.[9] Modern constitutional sensibilities make it hard to perceive what the problem might have been. Presumably, federalism means that the states may do as they wish, so long as no federal law or constitutional provision stands in the way. Why and for what might they need federal *consent*? The answer has to do with the traditional distinction between mutually exclusive categories of interstate commerce and state police powers. Even in dualism's heyday, the justices acknowledged a gray area where the characterization of private conduct and its regulation was less than clear-cut. The classic case was the liquor trade. What is one to make of a federal statute, enacted in response to a genuine coordination problem, that authorizes the states to regulate booze arriving from out of state in its "original package" on the same terms and conditions that apply to the state's domestic sales, up to and including prohibition? If the subject matter falls under the police power, Congress exercised a power that it does not possess. (The fact that the states demanded the federal intervention cannot make a constitutional difference.) If the subject matter constitutes interstate commerce, the legislation is likewise dubious. Congress cannot delegate to the states a power that the Constitution confers *exclusively* on Congress.

The Supreme Court tackled this conundrum with a series of legal fictions, such as the notion that Congress could constitutionally "divest" a product (liquor in its original package) of its interstate character, whereupon it would be commingled with the great mass of property in the state and, accordingly, subject to police-power regulation.[10] Superficially, such fictions permitted the Court to sustain the jurisdictional understanding. But if one examined what the Court actually did (as opposed to what it said), a very different principle had emerged by 1937. Supposed congressional "intrusions" into the states' police powers and their Tenth Amendment domain were permissible, *so long as and because a significant majority of states consented.* In a powerful, oft-cited 1938 article, Frank

Strong observed "on the whole a striking correlation between [Supreme Court] judicial behavior and the climate of state policy as expressed in statute and common law."[11] In an impressive display of empiricism, the author compiled the instances in which many, most, and sometimes all states had already enacted regulatory statutes by the time Congress regulated the same subject-matter and the Supreme Court ruled on—and consistently sustained—the constitutionality of the federal enactments. The long list includes antitrust law, food and drug regulation, and interstate traffic in harmful products such as lottery tickets, liquor, and loose women. It includes the regulation of criminal activities, such as the Anti-Narcotic Act (1914), the National Motor Vehicle Theft Act (1919), the National Firearms Act (1934), and antikidnapping statutes. It includes bona fide regulatory enactments, such as the Federal Bills of Lading Act (1916), the Packers and Stockyards Act (1921), and the Grain Futures Act (1922), along with such interest group rackets as a 1902 federal tax on colored oleomargarine. At the tail end is the National Labor Relations Act of 1935, sustained in *NLRB v. Jones & Laughlin* and its companion cases.[12]

Only two Commerce Clause cases of the period appear inconsistent with this pattern. One is the invalidation of federal child-labor legislation in *Hammer v. Dagenhart* (1918), despite the earlier enactment of prohibitions against child labor in all states. The other is *Schechter Poultry* (1935), which invalidated, on Commerce Clause and other grounds, the National Industrial Recovery Act and its administrative machinery to impose "fair" industry codes. Strong makes a persuasive case, however, that those two cases also fit the overall picture. At the time of *Hammer*, only some sixteen states had standards that were substantially equivalent to the federal standard. The consensus against child labor in general masked a substantial *sectional* disagreement among states, which was sufficiently deep-seated to last another two decades.[13] The federal enactment struck down in *Hammer* did not look like a collective state demand for "cooperative federalism" but rather like an attempt by some states to put others at a disadvantage. Ditto, Strong argues, with *Schechter*. All states at the time sported "little FTC Acts" that, like the Federal Trade Commission Act itself, prohibited unfair and deceptive business practices. However, only sixteen states had "little NRAs," and those were very different beasts. The federal government argued in *Schechter* that the NRA's "fair" labor codes were merely the equivalent of the FTC Act's prohibition against "unfair" business practices. But the Supreme Court unanimously rejected that transparent maneuver on the grounds that the detailed, *pre*-scriptive NRA code provisions were light years removed from the common-law-like, *pro*-scriptive provisions of the FTC Act.[14] In fact, the NRA marked a sharp break with earlier industrial and antitrust policy, federal and state alike.

Strong's account fails to distinguish between procompetitive federal laws and outright cartels. The point of the Webb-Kenyon Act, for example, was to allow dry states to remain dry and wet states, wet—in other words, to compartmentalize liquor regulation along state lines. That sort of coordination rule is one thing; a federal tax on oleomargarine, on top of (and in response to) dairy states' efforts to stamp out unwanted competition, is an entirely different proposition. But then, the distinction also gradually disappeared in the Supreme Court's decisions. Against the background expectation that states will surely resist federal encroachments, state consent to once-suspect exercises of federal powers suggests that Congress probably possessed those powers all along. Perhaps the last echo of the old understanding is *Ashton v. Cameron County* (1936), arising over a 1934 amendment to the federal Bankruptcy Act that permitted local governments, with the permission of the state, to file for bankruptcy in federal court, in the hope of escaping their bond obligations. Justice McReynolds, writing for a majority of five justices, declared the scheme an encroachment upon state powers and in excess of federal authority— plainly, on account of the apprehension that the levels of government had conspired to abrogate the Contract Clause.[15] Justice Cardozo's dissent, however, articulated the ascendant understanding that state "consent will preserve a [federalism] balance threatened with derangement." To insist on state dignity even where "the state disclaims the affront and is doing all it can to keep the law alive," Cardozo wrote, "is to make dignity a doubtful blessing."[16] That understanding soon prevailed. While the principle that "neither consent nor submission by the states can enlarge the powers of Congress" technically remained intact (as it has to this day), state consent became the implicit measure of congressional power.[17] The question of what exactly the states were consenting to effectively dropped from sight.

Is there some magic threshold number to signify a sufficient state consensus? Unlike the modern Supreme Court, which on controversial state laws (such as the death penalty) undertakes periodic head counts of states, and sometimes of foreign countries, to determine whether it is confronted with a legitimate policy disagreement among states or another noxious display of Southern exceptionalism, the Old Court never addressed the point directly.[18] Strong's evidence, however, suggests that the magic number was close to thirty-six—three-fourths of forty-eight, which then happened to be the threshold for constitutional amendments pursuant to Article V. Cooperative federalism's progress, Strong writes, "might not inaptly be denominated a de facto amending process under which the registered will of a preponderant majority becomes, without operation of the formal amendment mechanism, the national will."[19]

There are some parallels here to Bruce Ackerman's world of informal constitutional amendment. For example, much as Ackerman labors to distinguish constitutional moments from politics as usual, Strong muses over the indicia of sufficient state consent.[20] (Should one insist on formal state legislation, or will something less do—perhaps, the litigation position of three dozen states in a Supreme Court amicus brief?) More telling, though, are two salient differences. Ackerman envisions a constitutional *moment*, which hangs on a general election that in the author's telling looks a lot like a national plebiscite. Strong's process, though equally informal, is more gradual, and it remains tied to the Constitution's distinctively federal features. His account is consistent, not with a "We the People" story, but with a state cartel story. In fact, it *is* that story.

The Lockean Proviso: Preemption

States as states, we have seen, will insist and did insist on an all-encompassing federal commerce power. But they will also insist on "Lockean provisos" to protect state surplus accumulation under a federal regime. The most important proviso, and the one here at issue, is concurrent state regulation as opposed to exclusive federal regulation. The New Deal Constitution accommodates that demand. I first describe the trajectory of preemption law and then discuss two of its central features: its state-protective aspects and its emphasis on an improvisational federalism "balance."[21]

From Exclusive to Concurrent Powers. In the nineteenth-century universe of separate, mutually exclusive state and federal spheres, there could be no truly concurrent state and federal powers. Hence, there was no federal "preemption" doctrine to determine when and to what extent federal law trumped state laws governing the same subject matter. There was of course a doctrine, interpreting the Supremacy Clause, on conflicts between federal and state law, covering what we now call "implied preemption." But under the strict "dual" understanding of the time, the question was jurisdiction, not preemption. In its now-common legal usage, "preemption" made its first appearance in 1917.[22] It surfaced, naturally enough, in the gray areas of overlapping state and federal authority where the Court also developed its consent-based Commerce Clause.

The Court's initial move was to supplement the exclusive Commerce Clause, in the limited area left for concurrent state power, with a preemption doctrine of "latent exclusivity." Once Congress had exercised its enumerated powers, its intervention displaced state regulation in the entire field—regardless of whether state law conflicts with federal law, and regardless of whether Congress had intended wholesale preemption.[23] That nationalist doctrine made sense so long as congressional interventions remained more or less sporadic and, moreover, cabined by the enumerated powers doctrine. As federal legislation increased in scope and frequency, however, and as the Commerce Clause assumed far broader contours, adherence to latent exclusivity threatened a wholesale collapse into the center. Thus the Supreme Court gradually moved toward a more attenuated, state-protective doctrine of federal preemption. That doctrine has two basic elements.

First, the touchstone of whether and to what extent state regulation is preempted in the sea of concurrent powers is a matter of congressional intent. In outright conflicts between federal and state law, of course, the Supremacy Clause dictates that federal law must prevail and state law must give way. Also, Congress may expressly trump nonconflicting state laws; that, too, follows straightforwardly from the Supremacy Clause. But there is no warrant to set aside state laws that do *not* conflict with federal law and that may even promote congressional objectives. Thus, unless Congress has plainly intended to preempt, federal statutes should be understood to leave state law intact. One can understand this doctrine as the mirror image of the states' consent to federal law—as a form of congressional consent to continued state activity in a potentially exclusive federal domain. Second, the New Deal Constitution supplements the congressional intent baseline with a "presumption against preemption." Its classic formulation is *Rice v. Santa Fe Elevator Corp* (1947): in preemption cases, the judicial inquiry "start[s] with the assumption that the historic police powers of the States were not to be superseded by the Federal Act unless that was the clear and manifest purpose of Congress."[24] Countless preemption cases recite this language, without paying attention to the facts of *Rice*. Those facts, however, prove highly instructive.

The statute at issue, the 1931 Warehouse Act, entrusted the United States Secretary of Agriculture with regulatory authority over warehouse operators that chose to operate under a federal license. Rice, a grain dealer and customer of the Santa Fe warehousing operation, brought suit under the Illinois Public Utility Act, claiming that Santa Fe had discriminated against it in setting and maintaining storage rates by opting for a federal operating license, which (unlike extant state requirements) entailed no rate regulation. Among other remedies, the case sought to have Illinois regulators set appropriate rates for Santa Fe's operation. The demand, volubly echoed by state regulators, shows some nerve. The operative language of the federal statute provided that "the power, jurisdiction, and authority conferred upon the Secretary of Agriculture under this Act *shall be exclusive with respect to all persons securing a license hereunder.*"[25] This language was express, unequivocal, and unadulterated by any savings clause in favor of state law. Moreover, the exclusive federal regulation kicked in only *at the operators' own choice.* For warehouses that continued to operate under a state license, the statute established neither a floor nor a ceiling: states remained free to regulate to their hearts' content. The blow to state authority, if any, had nothing to do with the Supremacy Clause. It had to do with the federal government's decision to offer a regulatory option at variance and in competition with the states'.

Undeterred, the *Rice* Court performed a maneuver that it would soon execute in more important regulatory arenas, such as antitrust law: it transformed a crystal-clear statute, informed by pre–New Deal exclusivity presumptions, into a concurrent powers construct.[26] Rice had claimed, for example, that no conflict existed with respect to setting rates. While Illinois had that power, the secretary of agriculture was authorized only to disallow rates that were adjudged exorbitant. Instead of rejecting that claim out of hand—a conclusion that should follow from the "exclusive" language and structure of the act—Justice Douglas (writing for the majority) looked closely at the legislative history to determine whether Congress had desired a single system of regulation, so that the state would have to yield. Examining the statutory provisions on a retail-only basis, he concluded that the state scheme survived in areas where no conflict was evident (for example, in obtaining prior approvals for such matters as construction and insurance, which were regulated under Illinois law but not under the federal statute). The bias in favor of concurrent regulation was sufficient to sustain the state's authority over these matters.

Justice Frankfurter's dissent lurched even more sharply in favor of concurrent jurisdiction. In Frankfurter's view, preemption turned on the demonstration of an actual conflict between state regulation and the actions of the secretary. No such conflicts, Frankfurter thought, could be shown. For one thing, the statute imposed on the secretary a duty to cooperate with state officials. Further, it had failed to "establish a compulsory, uniform, nation-wide system for the regulation of grain warehouses." Notably, the secretary of agriculture—unlike state regulators—lacked the authority to fix rates. Finally, Frankfurter argued, congressional appropriations under the statute failed to increase after the 1931 enactment, again belying the notion that the statute was intended as a serious regulatory scheme. Plainly, Frankfurter's concern was not a diminution of the states' police powers per se. Had there been a federal price-fixing scheme, he would have found preemption. What concerned Frankfurter was the competition left in the system. "As a result of today's decision," Frankfurter lamented, "the gates of escape from deeply rooted State requirements will be open."[27] There you have the New Deal Constitution's baseline: cartels at every level.

Empowering States. The post–New Deal Court consciously deployed its preemption canon as a federalism "translation" and as a balance-preserving corrective to the expansion of congressional power. Harlan Fiske Stone's dissent in *Hines v. Davidowitz* (1941) spelled out the link and articulated the position that *Rice* would make black-letter law:

> At a time when the exercise of the federal power is being rapidly expanded through Congressional action, it is difficult to overstate the importance of safeguarding against such diminution of state power by vague inferences as to what Congress might have intended if it had considered the matter or by reference to our own conceptions of a policy which Congress has not expressed and which is not plainly to be inferred from the legislation which it has enacted.[28]

Something usually gets lost in translation, however. In Madison's universe, the national government's powers were "federal"—meaning limited—in their extent but "national"—meaning direct and, as a rule, exclusive of contravening state law—in their operation. The New Deal Constitution inverts the arrangement. On the Commerce Clause side, it renders federal powers effectively unlimited. On the preemption side, the Supremacy Clause becomes suspect: legal supremacy no longer attaches automatically but must be expressly stated or clearly implied, subject to a contravening presumption against preemption. In this maneuver to preserve a federalism "balance," the constitutional logic is inverted. The states "swap" autonomy for surplus, and the formerly competitive system assumes a vehemently pro-state, proregulatory bias.

The Old Court's latent exclusivity doctrine protected a rough competitive equilibrium by presenting the states with a stark choice. "No federal intervention" meant state autonomy but also competition under the Court's grim, commerce-protective rules. Federal intervention would end (or at any rate displace) competition but, on account of latent exclusivity, curb state autonomy *without producing any surplus*. After all, why would anyone lobby a state legislature, agency, or court on an issue on which those bodies, by dint of federal legislation and its judicial construction, may no longer act at all?[29]

The New Deal understanding of preemption, in contrast, liberates the states to lock themselves into federal regulatory cartels. It achieves this result by precluding federal surplus monopolization. The focus on congressional intent ensures that the states will be protected through the ordinary operation of the political process. Theoretically, Congress could mimic the old world by making latent exclusivity explicit; it could speak "with drastic clarity" and preempt states entirely.[30] Ironclad preemption provisions, however, are exceedingly rare, for the obvious reason that our political institutions do not operate that way. The judicial presumption against preemption, moreover, reinforces the state-protective force of a preemption regime that rests on congressional intent.

What is being protected here is not state independence autonomy but surplus. Federal regulatory statutes establish a floor that will govern regardless of what any state may wish to do or ordain. The preemption question is whether those same statutes also establish a *ceiling* on state action. Latent exclusivity means both a floor and a ceiling, in the same breath and enactment. Preemption under New Deal auspices, in contrast, is all floor and no ceiling (unless Congress has said otherwise). Now consider, first, the effects of a federal statute that responds to a genuine coordination problem, such as interstate externalities and exploitation: here, the anti-preemptive presumptions imply a sustained ability on the part of states to inflict costs on each other, which can no more yield a net gain in state autonomy than my right to stick a fist in your face yields a net gain in individual rights. Anti-preemptive presumptions protect "federalism" and the states only on the assumption that the relevant measure is the authority of "states as states"—that is, the authority of *regulators* and their clientele.

Consider, next, a federal preemption statute that regulates primarily in-state conduct and effects (rather than externalities); again, it is odd to view the preemptive ceiling in isolation from the regulatory floor. The regulatory floor liberates proregulatory states from having to compete on some regulatory margin, at some cost to procompetition states. (If no such defectors existed, there would be no point to the statute.) The procompetition states lost and, postenactment, cannot shirk or defect.[31] Proregulation states, in contrast, may under permissive preemption rules defect from the federal standard—upwards. For them, the federal minimum standard is a double victory: it eliminates competition, and it liberates them to play the same game again. Latent exclusivity precluded that result because federal intervention blocked state defections in either direction. The New Deal Court's preemption doctrine, in contrast, couples an ironclad federal floor with a permeable ceiling and so institutionalizes Louis Brandeis's one-way experimentation.

Balance and Improvisation. The preemption baseline is that of the entire New Deal Constitution: the will of the Congress shall prevail. But the formula does not answer how one is to understand and construe that will, and the judicial posture of deference conceals important institutional dynamics. Congress's intent to preempt, *Rice* said, must be "clear and manifest," which suggests that overcoming that presumption will be an uphill battle. Yet, the next sentences announce and organize the rules of "implied" preemption—that is, a preemptive intent that is *not* explicitly stated:

> The scheme of federal regulation may be so pervasive as to make reasonable the inference that Congress left no room for the States to supplement it. Or the Act of Congress may touch a field in which the federal interest is so dominant that the federal system will be assumed to preclude enforcement of state laws on the same subject. Likewise, the object sought to be obtained by the federal law and the character of obligations imposed by it may reveal the same purpose. Or the state policy may produce a result inconsistent with the objective of the federal statute.[32]

Justice Frankfurter suggested in his dissent in *Rice* that the notion of an implied but nonetheless "clear and manifest" intent is inherently contradictory. Although that may go too far, the canons do pull in opposite directions: the presumption against preemption, toward the states; implied preemption, toward federal power. The *Rice* majority itself recognized the difficulty:

> It is often a perplexing question whether Congress has precluded state action or by the choice of selective regulatory measures has left the police power of the States undisturbed except as the state and federal regulations collide.[33]

Perplexing, indeed. The ambivalent *Rice* formula commands impressionistic, statute-by-statute interpretation, and it is the source of a universally lamented "muddle" in preemption law.[34] If it has nonetheless withstood the test of time, that is because it embodies two basic orientations of the New Deal Constitution, cartelization and improvisation.

Very often, states are well-situated to construct cartels. In those situations, they deserve protection against federal interference: Katie, bar the "gates to escape from deeply rooted State requirements." *Rice* captures this state-protective side in its presumption against preemption. Just as often, however, cartelization requires national management of industry sectors by expert administrative agencies. The New Deal was still informed by production values. It aimed to stabilize industries, not to destroy them.[35] That model requires protection against collateral attack and state interference. *Rice* captures this nationalist side in a judicial willingness to imply federal preemption where Congress has failed to express it.[36]

The second function of *Rice*'s ambiguity is to serve as a cooperation-facilitating device. The Constitution, we have seen, precludes cooperative federalism in the form of a grand, once-and-for-all bargain; institutions and interest groups must cut their deals one statute at a time. Attempts to forge a deal are often blocked by high bargaining costs, uncertainty over the magnitude of the expected gains, and disagreement over the distribution of the expected gains both among states and between them and the national government. Preemption provisions determine the surplus distribution. If that question had to be settled conclusively at the time of enactment, few agreements would come about.[37] Thus, the best strategy for surplus-maximizing governments is to agree on rules that promise aggregate gains and to haggle over the distribution of the proceeds somewhere down the road. The best background rule to that end is the ambivalence of *Rice*. It lops off the tail ends of the distribution—federal surplus monopolization through the presumption against preemption, deal-breaking state evasions and defections through implied preemption. Ambiguity within this range allows institutional actors to regulate first and sort out the details later, in administrative agencies and, eventually and with dreary regularity, in the courts.

Dormant Commerce

The third part of the Commerce Clause territory is the reach of the clause in its "dormant" or "negative" state. It too underwent a transformation in the New Deal. After a brief description of the doctrinal change, I present some constitutional choice analytics and empirics to suggest that the transformed dormant Commerce Clause, appearances notwithstanding, may fit the New Deal Constitution. As already suggested, however, the doctrine remains far more continuous with the pre-New Deal Constitution than any other piece of the New Deal architecture.

Doctrine. The pre–New Deal Court employed the dormant Commerce Clause as a jurisdictional limitation on state regulation and taxation: states must not (directly) regulate or tax interstate commerce. The New Deal Court abandoned this framework and substituted a neutrality rule: henceforth, only *discriminatory* state regulations would be found unconstitutional. The analysis turns on three specified federalism risks: state discrimination in the form of local protectionism, balkanization, and cost exportation. The canonical exposition appears in *South Carolina State Highway Department v. Barnwell Brothers* (1938):

The commerce clause, by its own force, prohibits discrimination against interstate commerce, whatever its form or method, and the decisions of this Court have recognized that there is scope for its like operation when state legislation nominally of local concern is in point of fact aimed at interstate commerce, or by its necessary operation is a means of gaining a local benefit by throwing the attendant burdens on those without the state.[38]

An equally seminal decision that same year, *Western Live Stock v. Bureau of Revenue*, developed a very similar test for taxation. Interstate commerce, the Court held, cannot claim immunity from state taxation; it "must pay its way" on a par with intrastate commerce.[39] De facto tariffs are barred, however, and taxes must be fairly apportioned among states to avoid multiple burdens on interstate commerce. The timing of these decisions may suggest that they were part of an opportunistic Supreme Court "switch in time." As discussed in earlier chapters, however, the old categorical distinctions had begun to erode long before 1937. Moreover, neither the empirics nor the tenor of the 1938 decisions confirm the suspicion of a sudden about-face.

In the years between 1922 and 1929 inclusive (roughly covering the Taft Court), the justices decided fifty-two dormant Commerce Clause cases by written opinion.[40] The states prevailed in 55 percent of those cases. In the next eight-year period, covering the Hughes Court prior to President Roosevelt's appointments, the states prevailed in almost 80 percent of fifty-five cases. All but six cases were decided without dissent, an extraordinary level of unanimity especially for a Court that was supposedly deeply divided on matters of state and federal powers. Although states fared better still in the immediate post–New Deal period, from 1938 to 1945 (they did not lose a regulatory case until 1945 and won twenty-four of thirty tax cases), their good fortune continued a trend that well predates the New Deal Court.

Likewise, dormant Commerce Clause decisions long before the New Deal began to mirror the Court's state-friendly determinations under the "affirmative" Commerce Clause, where state consent sanctified federal interventions. But although the "consent" determination involved some implicit guesswork, the states' dormant Commerce Clause preferences were transparent and unequivocal. In case after case, the states pushed up against the Old Court's doctrine. The justices were confronted with a bewildering array of state taxes and regulations, typically configured to steer clear of the latest Supreme Court pronouncements. The most confident defender of the old jurisdictional boundaries must have been tempted to mumble "complexity" and to throw in the towel. Instead, however, *Barnwell* and *Western Live Stock* looked for a workable constitutional formula without throwing the door open to utter mischief. In the fashion of a federal common lawyer, Justice Harlan F. Stone, the author of both opinions and of many other leading dormant Commerce Clause decisions of that era, attempted to synthesize the rules of prior decisions.[41] By citing rafts of cases for each leg of the inquiry, Stone showed that the risks of protectionism, balkanization, and cost exportation were what the old conceptual distinctions had been aimed at all along. What Stone added is that the antidiscrimination regime—"interstate commerce must pay its way, without suffering discrimination or exploitation"—was not a series of syllogisms but rather a framework for pragmatic analysis.

Stone's synthesis is an impressive judicial accomplishment—far superior in many respects to the well-intentioned but ultimately incoherent formula of *Cooley*. At some level, though, his framework remained wedded to the old subject-matter distinctions. An insistence that *all* state discriminatory burdens on interstate commerce must end is to say that the states should go out of business. Since that cannot be the purpose of the dormant Commerce Clause, the Court must weigh the magnitude and directness of the effects on interstate commerce against the state's police power justification. The first part of that inquiry looks suspiciously like the old categories (internal affairs versus interstate commerce, direct versus indirect effects). The second part of the test, the judicial probing of the state's proffered police-power justifications, looks suspiciously like an interstate version of *Lochner*.

In modern dormant Commerce Clause cases, *Lochner*'s ghost is usually invoked by justices who profess adherence to originalism rather than New Deal precepts. But the post- and pro–New Deal justices also perceived the affinity.[42] They knew that wholesale abandonment of the dormant Commerce Clause was the logical conclusion of the New Deal Constitution—and, moreover, a rare conclusion for which its advocates could marshal impressive support. J. B. Thayer, Felix Frankfurter's teacher at Harvard, had argued that there was no such thing as a judicially enforceable dormant Commerce Clause, and Professor Frankfurter probably held the same view.[43] And yet, no justice of the post–New Deal era believed that states should be allowed to defeat the dormant Commerce Clause "by simply invoking the convenient apologetics of the police power" (among them, the "convenience" of segregating passengers on interstate motor carriers).[44] Stone eloquently articulated that position before he became a member of the Court, and he held to it throughout his illustrious tenure.[45] Even the most diffident enforcers of the dormant Commerce Clause never jettisoned it. In an "amusing irony," Justice Frankfurter's very first Supreme Court opinion, *Hale v. Bimco Trading, Inc.* (1939), declared a discriminatory state tax in violation of the dormant Commerce Clause (on a claim, mind you, that the plaintiff-appellant had apparently failed to plead).[46]

The political environment helps to explain why the post–New Deal Court's fondness for the dormant Commerce Clause reached a zenith in the immediate postwar period.[47] Brandeisian values of local self-determination, in defense against corporate capitalism, took on very different connotations when the task at hand was to rebuild the national economy and, in the global arena, to reintegrate the vanquished Axis powers into a world economy. And the breathtaking parochialism displayed by the Congress of the time may have given pause even to staunch defenders of legislative supremacy and judicial deference.[48] However, the dormant Commerce Clause survived even as those transient considerations abated. In part, that adherence to a nonconforming doctrine reflects the New Deal Constitution's ambivalence, already noted in the preemption context, between state empowerment and production values. In other part, the dormant Commerce Clause may have lasted because the New Deal Court stripped it from the element that states most loathe—the injunction against exploitative, extraterritorial state regulation.

Exploitation. *Barnwell*, quoted earlier, identified three Commerce Clause risks: protectionist exclusion of interstate commerce; the "balkanization" of interstate networks (as in *Barnwell* itself); and exploitation, or the deliberate infliction of interstate externalities. What are the constitutional choice analytics for citizens and states respectively? Citizens, ex ante, would desire constitutional rules that guard against all three risks.[49] The states' preferences are more uncertain, but one can harmonize them with the New Deal's dormant Commerce Clause.

With respect to protectionism, the states' ex ante preferences hang on assumptions about gains from trade, the domestic political process, factor mobility, and other variables. Their best choice, though, *may* be the rule that we have—a general, poorly policed prohibition, coupled with the option of a federal override.[50] With respect to balkanization, it is hard to see what states could gain ex ante from a rule that allows each to defect from an interstate (Nash) equilibrium that has no obvious distributional consequences.[51] Thus, the antibalkanization rule of *Barnwell* may make sense. Assume these conjectures to be right: what is the states' ex ante position on *Barnwell*'s exploitation leg?

Arguably, the surplus-maximizing rule will permit universal cost exports. For citizens, that rule creates a negative-sum game. For surplus-maximizing states, in contrast, full extraterritorial authority serves the

same purpose as a universal federal commerce power: it potentially eliminates Tiebout competition. It does so without the need for, and the risks
of, federal intervention, and it has the added advantage of accommodating the domestic demand for taxing and regulating outsiders.[52]

The states' proviso is that the exploitation must remain undetected by
each state's citizens, lest it invite retaliation. Thus, for example, the dormant Commerce Clause should freely permit the exploitation of another
state's consumers *but not* of its public utilities.[53] Arguably, the New Deal's
dormant Commerce Clause developed over time to accommodate this
position. In cases dealing with the balkanization of networks, such as
Barnwell, as well as in protectionism cases of the *Bimco Trading* variety,
a close judicial monitoring of the states' police-power justifications kept
them from spinning out of control. The exploitation analysis, in contrast,
has followed a more erratic course.

The Commerce Clause, *Barnwell* had declared, forbids any state scheme
that "by its necessary operation is a means of gaining a local benefit by
throwing the attendant burdens on those without the state." Only five
years later, however, in *Parker v. Brown* (1943), the Court unanimously
sustained the very prototype of such a scheme. California, which at the
time supplied some 95 percent of the nation's raisin production, had organized an output cartel to limit the national supply of California raisins
(more precisely, the supply from Raisin Proration Zone No. 1). *Parker*
sustained that arrangement against three challenges. The Court ruled that
state-sponsored cartels, as opposed to wholly private ones, are immune
against antitrust challenges. It found that California's scheme was not
preempted by federal agriculture laws and regulations, inasmuch as both
promoted the same general objective of "stabilizing" commodity markets. And it held that massive cost exportation—the manifest purpose
and effect of California's output limitations—did not violate the dormant
Commerce Clause.[54]

Parker owes its fame to its eponymous antitrust exemption for state
cartels, which (with some wrinkles) governs American law to this day.
That rule is explicitly anticompetitive and state-protective. The *Parker*
Court effectively admitted as much in rejecting the plaintiff's dormant
Commerce Clause claim on the remarkable theory that California had
regulated only the in-state *production* of raisins, not their *sale* in interstate commerce.[55] Precisely that distinction, of course, had been supposedly abolished in *Wickard v. Filburn*. It is conceivable that the justices
missed the connection between the cases, but not bloody likely: *Wickard*
and *Parker* were argued on the same day in October 1942 and decided,

both unanimously, with a few weeks of each other. What harmonizes the decisions is the cartel principle. The national government's control over local events and the states' license to exploit monopolistic advantages are two sides of that same coin.

Another six years later, in *H. P. Hood & Sons, Inc. v. Du Mond* (1949), a divided Court seemingly shifted course again. It found a dormant Commerce Clause violation when New York denied Hood a license to build a new receiving facility in New York State in order to ship its raw milk for processing in the Boston, Massachusetts, market. The ground on which New York's commissioner denied the license was chiefly his statutory authority to prevent "destructive competition in a market already adequately served." In invalidating the license denial, Justice Jackson's majority opinion relied principally on the distinction, "deeply rooted in both our history and our law," between economic protectionism and legitimate police-power regulations.[56] The dissenters (Justice Black, joined by Justice Murphy; and Justice Frankfurter, joined by Justice Rutledge) argued primarily that the states' power to enact "local" laws against destructive competition followed easily from *Cooley* and, of course, *Parker v. Brown*. They had a point; there was no evidence that the out-of-state destination of the dairy-applicant's products played any role in New York's license denial. The license denial in *H. P. Hood* was far less troublesome than the raisin cartel that survived in *Parker*.

Parker and *Hood* have since continued their uneasy coexistence, but with a pronounced shift toward the pro-cartel position. *Hood* is a bit of a period piece; it continues to be cited for its economic unity encomia but not for its holding. The antitrust immunities of *Parker*, in contrast, have expanded, and periodic pleas to reform that odious doctrine so as to curb its exploitative potential have fallen on deaf ears.[57] Something similar has also happened under the Privileges and Immunities Clause and under the dormant Commerce Clause, where a doctrine of state proprietary functions or "market participant" exemption broadly protects discriminatory and especially cost-externalizing state activities.[58] With respect to regulation, the only form of cost exportation that is prohibited under the dormant Commerce Clause is the direct state regulation of transactions in other states.[59] With respect to taxation, the last remaining barrier is a prohibition against the state taxation, or the imposition of state tax collection obligations, on sellers who have no physical nexus to the taxing jurisdiction, such as catalogue or Internet sellers. The post–New Deal Court first parked the underlying extraterritoriality concern in its crowded due process garage and then moved it to the dormant Commerce Clause shed, where it is gravely exposed and probably slated for removal.[60] I will examine the wreck in chapter 13.

THE proposition that the dormant Commerce Clause, despite its residual competitive thrust, is consistent with the New Deal Constitution rests on the claim that the states' preferred arrangement is a mutual aggression pact: I exploit your citizens and you are free to exploit mine, provided no citizen catches on to us. As noted at the outset, I proffer this explanation with less than complete conviction. Some empirical evidence supports the contention. One piece of evidence is *Parker*: not one of the states whose citizens presumably paid the price of California's raisin cartel objected even as an amicus.[61] Another piece of evidence is the Supreme Court's tendency to invalidate state laws on dormant Commerce Clause grounds far more often in cases brought by states than in cases brought by private parties.[62] However, one can also think of alternative and perhaps more plausible explanations. Dormant Commerce Clause claims brought by corporate plaintiffs are bound to be strategic; thus, the judiciary's focus on the presence of states as parties may serve as a rough screen to separate opportunistic from bona fide claims.[63] Moreover, exploitation does not easily lend itself to a manageable judicial test. Once one gets beyond brazen schemes à la *Parker*, the question becomes how much is too much, and it is difficult to think of a principled answer.[64] Finally, exploitation is not readily subsumed under the political values that are thought to sustain the dormant Commerce Clause. Outright exclusion and balkanization invite tit-for-tat retaliation; exploitation, within the bounds stated, will not. It may be a concern from an "economic unity" perspective of the dormant Commerce Clause, but not from a political perspective that emphasizes interstate comity.

Perhaps, then, the dormant Commerce Clause has survived the New Deal for the reason suggested by Oliver Wendell Holmes: at the end of the day, the Constitution cannot live without it.[65] To rock-ribbed advocates of judicial restraint and clause-bound originalism, the idea of staying the judges' hands and to "let Commerce struggle for Congressional action to make it free" may hold some appeal. But as Justice Robert Jackson observed, Congress cannot be relied on to do its part to protect economic union; if anything, it can be relied on *not* to do that part.[66] If that is so, the constitutional architecture presupposes a dormant Commerce Clause, or something very much like it.

CHAPTER TEN

Erie's Federalism

Were we bereft of the common law, our federal system would be impotent. This follows from the recognized futility of attempting all-complete statutory codes, and is apparent from the terms of the Constitution itself.

Robert H. Jackson

Erie Matters

Erie Railroad Co. v. Tompkins (1938) is one of the most central decisions, not just in the New Deal's Constitution but in the entire history and architecture of American constitutional law. Justice Brandeis's opinion, joined in toto by four other justices, declared that *Swift v. Tyson* and its progeny of hundreds of cases were not simply wrong but unconstitutional. *Erie* captured that holding in a famous dramatic formulation: "There is no federal general common law."[1] Henceforth federal courts would in diversity cases cease to divine such a law and instead follow the rules, common law as well as statutory, of the state in which they sit.[2] To the New Deal's opponents, the decision represented the "triumph of the Harvard Law School, acting through the not undistinguished quartet of Gray, Holmes, Brandeis and Frankfurter, over the prostrate body of the Constitution."[3] To the New Dealers, in contrast, *Erie* encapsulated "our federalism" more than any other single decision. *Erie*, John Hart Ely has characterized—disapprovingly, but accurately—the "general sense" of an entire generation of judges and legal scholars, "implicates, indeed perhaps it is, the very essence of our federalism."[4] *Erie* greatly augmented the states' powers, and especially state courts' power, over interstate commerce. In so doing, it greatly enhanced state autonomy *in the sense of surplus accumulation* and, correspondingly, weakened the power of national institutions to curb that tendency. That, indeed, is "the very essence" of the New Deal's federalism.

Justice Brandeis's opinion deliberately obscures that essence. It combines statutory, pragmatic, and constitutional arguments, all calculated to demonstrate *Swift*'s irredeemable flaws. The arguments do not mesh easily, and *Erie*'s federalism content depends on which strand one chooses to emphasize. The most persuasive interpretation, the first part of this chapter argues, is to read *Erie* in the way just suggested, as a means of augmenting state surplus. Under *Swift*, corporations' access to the federal courts and their general common law perennially eroded that surplus. *Erie*, in contrast, vindicates the *plaintiff*'s choice of state law and, by tying federal courts to state law, leaves corporate defendants no exit. In a strategic sense, *Erie*'s federalism has a constitutional pedigree; as noted in earlier chapters, the Constitution itself relies on the litigation incentives of private (mercantile) interests for the federal courts' enforcement of procompetitive, open-economy rules. *Erie* mimics the strategy but inverts its addressee and its purpose. It mobilizes plaintiffs' opportunistic state forum choices to enhance state power over interstate commerce.

That enterprise proved problematic in two different respects. On the one hand, *Erie*'s precise holding could not fully accomplish its broader social purpose without further plaintiff- and state-empowering revisions of closely related doctrines, especially those governing choice of law questions and personal jurisdiction. Those arcane but vitally important doctrines are discussed in the second part of this chapter. On the other hand, *Erie*'s diffidence with respect to the common-law powers of federal courts proved unsustainable. In short order, the Supreme Court recognized certain enclaves of federal common law. Moreover, it developed an imposing body of "new" or "specialized" federal common law supposedly derived, unlike the general law of *Swift*, from congressional statutes or constitutional provisions. These doctrines are best understood as a tacit acknowledgment of Justice Robert Jackson's insight: a federal system bereft of the Court's common law is impotent. As shown in the third part of this chapter, however, *Erie*'s enclaves and especially the breadth of the new federal common law suggest a striking conclusion: *Erie*'s injunction governs, almost exclusively and of all things, the state regulation of *the interstate commerce of the United States*. Put differently, *Erie* protects state "autonomy" in the domain where the potential for surplus production is greatest, and most destructive of competitive federalism. Precisely on that account, *Erie* is the heart and soul of our federalism.

Erie's Federalism

Erie was decided on April 25, 1938, during a Supreme Court term full of surprises. The decision struck the legal profession like a thunderbolt. Since around 1930, the Supreme Court had gradually retreated from some of *Swift*'s more far-fetched applications, often with the support of conservative justices and to general acclaim.[5] It was widely expected that the trend would continue. Instead, *Erie* made a radical break.

From Swift *to* Erie. Attacks on *Swift* and its extensions had been building for a good half-century. Perhaps the most forceful attack, certainly at the level of legal theory, was legal positivism. In a series of famous dissents in federal common-law cases, Justice Oliver Wendell Holmes insisted that law had to be traceable to some sovereign's command. The notion of a "general common law," a "brooding omnipresence in the sky" that could be "discovered" by judicial oracles, was a fallacy. He would not overrule *Swift*, Holmes wrote, but it should not be allowed to spread into new fields.[6]

A second attack focused on *Swift*'s potential to produce in a single state two sets of law (federal and state) for in-state and out-of-state parties, depending on the constellation of the parties and, in some cases, corporations' manipulation of their legal status. These attacks reached a fever pitch after *Black & White Taxicab & Transfer Co. v. Brown & Yellow Taxicab & Transfer Co.* (1928). The parties to the case were two competing cab companies at a railroad station in Bowling Green, Kentucky. Brown & Yellow contracted with the railroad company to grant it a monopoly. Because Kentucky law prohibited such contracts, Brown & Yellow reincorporated under the law of Tennessee, which allowed them, and the contract was executed in that state. The company admittedly took those steps to create diversity jurisdiction and, once in federal court, argued that under federal common law, the case should be decided not under the local Kentucky law but under the law of its (Brown & Yellow's) state of incorporation. Without probing the grounds or the good sense of the alleged jurisdiction, the Supreme Court upheld the contract on principles of general law. The decision created enormous controversy and proposals in Congress to abolish federal diversity jurisdiction and to overrule *Swift*.[7]

A third attack on *Swift* was constitutional. The judicial creation of substantive rules of decision, it was said, was incompatible both with the separation of powers—inasmuch as it implied a judicial power even beyond the scope of congressional authority—and also with federalism. Federal courts, the argument went, had no business interfering with state court authority, which was every bit as much a part of the states' sovereignty as state legislation. The origin of this criticism—somewhat unlikely, we shall see—was Justice Stephen Field's dissent in *Balt. & Ohio R.R. Co. v. Baugh*, the 1893 fellow-servant decision discussed in chapter 6.

A fourth line of attack focused on *Swift*'s historical foundations and, in particular, on Story's understanding of § 34 of the Judiciary Act and its "laws of the several states" language. In a celebrated study, Charles Warren purported to demonstrate that the authors of the Judiciary Act had in fact intended to include state courts' common-law decisions under that description. If that was right, then *Swift* had been wrong (although not necessarily unconstitutional) all along.[8]

All four lines of attack appeared in *Erie*, a case arising over humdrum facts. Late one night, plaintiff-respondent Tompkins was walking on a path running parallel to a railroad track. He was struck by a protruding object from a passing train, which severed his arm. His suit turned on the duty of care owed by the railroad to strangers. Under the law of Pennsylvania, where the accident occurred, the railroad would have escaped liability. Tompkins, however, sued in federal district court in New York (where the Erie Railroad was domiciled) and insisted on having the case litigated under federal common law—which, like the law of most states at the time, held the railroad liable for occurrences of this sort. A federal jury returned a verdict of $30,000. The judgment was affirmed by the Court of Appeals, explicitly on the grounds that the question was governed by general common law. The Supreme Court granted certiorari.

Throughout the litigation and the Supreme Court proceedings, the parties assumed the validity of the *Swift* doctrine and its applicability to the case. Over the voluble dissent of Justices Butler and McReynolds, however, the Court sua sponte declared *Swift* overruled. And over a concurring opinion by Justice Reed, who argued that the case should be decided on statutory grounds, the majority rested its decision on the Constitution. After perfunctory account of the facts and history of the case, Justice Brandeis presented his argument in sections numbered "First" to "Fourth."

First, the opinion observes, criticism of *Swift* had been mounting. "The recent research of a competent scholar" (Charles Warren) established that Story's interpretation of § 34 of the Judiciary Act, since codified as the Rules of Decision Act, had been erroneous. (A footnote to this passage presents Warren's evidence.) Brandeis adds that criticism of the doctrine of *Swift* "became widespread" after *Black & White*, which he then summarizes.

Second, Brandeis turns to *Swift*'s "defects, political and social." The decision, he writes, had produced legal uncertainty rather than uniformity. At the same time, Brandeis continues, *Swift*

> introduced grave discrimination by noncitizens against citizens. It made rights enjoyed under the unwritten 'general law' vary according to whether enforcement was sought in the state or federal court; and the privilege of selecting the court in which the right should be determined was conferred upon the noncitizen. Thus, the doctrine rendered impossible equal protection of the law.[9]

The discrimination, Brandeis claims, had become "far-reaching," both because of the doctrine's expansive reach and on account of the "wide range of persons held entitled to avail themselves of the federal rule" by creating diversity. Corporations, he adds, could accomplish that objective even without a change in residence, through simple reincorporation, "as was done in the Taxicab Case." If this were merely a matter of statutory construction, this section of the opinion concludes, the Court should not overrule the century-old *Swift* doctrine. "But the unconstitutionality of the course pursued has now been made clear, and compels us to do so."[10]

The placement of that pronouncement notwithstanding, *Swift*'s unconstitutionality is *not* the just-mentioned "equal protection of the laws" problem. Justice Brandeis did not believe that the Equal Protection Clause protected imbeciles from forced sterilization; surely, he did not want it to protect classes of litigants.[11] The real constitutional concern appears in the next section of the opinion, labeled "Third":

> Except in matters governed by the Federal Constitution or by acts of Congress, the law to be applied in any case is the law of the state. . . . There is no federal general common law. *Congress has no power to declare substantive rules of common law applicable in a state* whether they be local in their nature or 'general,' be they commercial law or a part of the law of torts. And no clause in the Constitution purports to confer such a power upon the federal courts.[12]

The italicized phrase, widely viewed as *Erie*'s constitutional holding, does not mean (Brandeis stresses) that § 34 was itself unconstitutional: "We merely declare that in applying the doctrine this Court and the lower courts have invaded rights which in our opinion are reserved by the Constitution to the several states."[13] Brandeis concludes, "Fourth," that the Court of Appeals' decision under general law was in error. Its decision was reversed and the case was remanded for further proceedings consistent with the opinion.

It is quite difficult to forge this collection of arguments into a single coherent whole. Many of the complications, however, arise from taking Justice Brandeis's statutory and constitutional arguments at face value. They are better understood as strategic and instrumental—instrumental, that is, to Brandeis's overriding objective of fixing *Swift*'s "defects, political and social." That reading renders *Erie* continuous with the New Deal Constitution.

Statutory Law and the Constitution. On the narrowest interpretation, *Erie* was a statutory decision: *Swift* had simply misread § 34. However, this reading not only flies in the face of the opinion but also renders the decision baseless. Charles Warren's purported evidence has been proven wrong to the point of certainty.[14] The New Dealers extolled Warren's "discovery," and Brandeis probably led off with the statutory argument because it had the great attraction of connecting *Swift* and especially its later extensions to the New Deal's narrative of a Constitution that had been hijacked by laissez-faire ideologues. (*Black & White* was to diversity jurisdiction what *Hammer* was to the Commerce Clause.) But although the political utility of Warren's claims was obvious, their juridical purchase was doubted from the outset. Even Frankfurter privately suspected that the "competent scholar" had probably found what he had wanted to find. Brandeis himself seems to have been reluctant to place much weight on Warren's claims, which explains why his opinion moves on to constitutional arguments.[15]

Those arguments caused considerable consternation at the time. Renowned scholars, not at all hostile to the New Deal, echoed Justice Reed's concurrence and wondered why Brandeis did not simply rely on the statutory argument and *Swift*'s practical defects. A quarter-century later, Henry Friendly—once Brandeis's law clerk and then a justly revered federal judge—suggested that Brandeis had no other option: his task was to bury *Swift* six feet deep, and the statutory argument would not do.[16] That sounds plausible as a matter of judicial strategy. But what exactly *was* unconstitutional about *Swift*? It was, Brandeis writes, the presumed judicial "power to declare rules of decision which Congress *was confessedly without power* to enact as statutes."[17] That cryptic sentence is open to several federalism interpretations: an enumerated powers federalism, an enclave theory, and process federalism. None of these readings is persuasive, but their implausibility sheds light on the federalism that *Erie* does adumbrate.

"Confessedly" may mean something like, "rules of decision that the courts at the time considered beyond congressional power." One can think of examples that would have buttressed Brandeis's point. For example, despite the Court's holding (still good law at the time) that insurance was not interstate commerce and thus, presumably, beyond congressional reach at least under the Commerce Clause, the Court routinely decided diversity cases in that area under general law. But Brandeis did not provide any examples or authority. Instead, he stated (without citing a precedent in an opinion otherwise bursting with case citations) that "Congress has no power to declare substantive rules of common law applicable in a state."

Now *there* is a sentiment to warm libertarian hearts: "Congress has no power." But one cannot plausibly read the sentence as an endorsement of enumerated powers federalism. First, *Erie* was decided after *Jones & Laughlin*, when that federalism had lost purchase. Second, this is Brandeis writing, not Brewer or Butler. Third, it seems clear that Congress could reenact, and could have reenacted even in 1938, the entire corpus juris of general common law that was declared unconstitutional in *Erie*.[18] Thus, if *Swift* was unconstitutional because it supplied substantive rules of decision that Congress cannot enact (as opposed to the rules that it has failed to enact), *Erie*'s constitutional holding would lack any bite.

On a second interpretation, *Erie* stands for an enclave federalism. Although congressional powers are effectively unlimited, the Tenth Amendment or some equivalent constitutional principle may still cordon off certain areas of state policy (the common law of tort and contract, perhaps?) from federal intervention. Some *Erie* passages suggest an enclave interpretation, and John Hart Ely, writing in 1974, worried that some post-*Erie* cases came close to endorsing it.[19] But the enclave view has never been a dominant strand of *Erie*'s interpretation—to my mind, not so much on account of its inherent implausibility but because it might have hampered the development of the new federal common law, where the Supreme Court was eager to wipe out state enclaves even in areas where Congress had most likely left them.[20]

On a third interpretation, *Erie*'s federalism operates in conjunction with separation of powers concerns. *Erie*'s holding is that federal courts must not supply substantive rules of decision *without a constitutional or congressional warrant*, which neither the general vestment of "the Judicial Power" in Article III nor the grant of diversity jurisdiction per se supplies. In creating substantive federal common law, the federal courts must take their bearings from the Congress. The arrangement protects federalism, the argument concludes, because the states are represented in Congress but not, of course, in the federal judiciary; and because the supermajoritarian features of the legislative process provide an implicit federalism protection.[21]

This structural or process federalism interpretation captures the New Deal's commitment to legislative supremacy and its faith in the political process. Moreover, by throttling back on the more extravagant constitutional averments in *Erie*, the argument connects the constitutional piece of the puzzle to *Erie*'s pragmatic concerns over the absurdity of having two sets of laws govern a single state. *Erie*'s binary regime—no federal common law, or else a constitutional norm or a congressional enactment that sweeps the boards (unless Congress says otherwise)—remedies that problem, at least conceptually. However, putting aside that the reading is hard to square with Brandeis's opinion, it cannot easily contain the legal materials that it is meant to organize—*Erie*'s domain, as defined by its enclaves and the "new" federal common law in its statutory and constitutional derivations. For example, in a potent and nearly persuasive 1975 article, Henry Paul Monaghan argued that constitutional common law is compatible with *Erie* and its federalism because it can be *overruled* by Congress.[22] That is technically true of the dormant Commerce Clause; at the time of Monaghan's writing, it was also true of the *Miranda* rules and other constitutionally inferred criminal protections. It is *not* true, however, of many other doctrines that are generally viewed as constitutional common law—for example, the "one man, one vote" principle of the reapportionment decisions.[23] Monaghan avoided the problem by reserving the "constitutional common law" term for reversible doctrines. (The nonreversible doctrines that look like common law will have to be called something else—constitutional "interpretation," for example.) That strategy, though, saves not much besides the dormant Commerce Clause and federal immunities. Moreover, the reversibility criterion is depressingly thin. In the absence of a judicial rule, congressional fumbling allows the states to go their merry ways. In contrast, when a (state-restrictive) federal common-law rule is in place, the states must overcome all the obstacles that impede congressional legislation. For this reason, it is hard to connect a process federalism reading of *Erie*—one that would accommodate the "new" constitutional common law—to a muscular notion of *federalism*. Comparable difficulties, we shall see, afflict any attempt to reconcile *Erie* with its enclaves and with the new federal common law in its statutory variety.

"Defects, Political and Social". Looking to statutory and constitutional arguments for an explanation of *Erie*, Edward A. Purcell has argued in a masterful book, is to look in all the wrong places.[24] Brandeis's central, intensely political concern, according to Purcell, was to remedy the *Swift*-induced lack of effective state control over interstate commerce and

corporations. Purcell's insistence on reading *Erie* through the prism of Progressive ideology departs from some of the orthodoxies of civil procedure and federal courts scholarship.[25] Perhaps for that reason, however, it yields a coherent view of *Erie*'s federalism.

At the time of *Erie*, diversity jurisdiction according to *Swift* was not a question of arid jurisprudential speculation. For a half-century it had been arguably *the* central battleground between the states and their clientele on one hand and the Supreme Court, its Constitution, and national corporations on the other. Progressive theorists and partisans explored any number of ways to curtail corporate America's access to the federal courts and their common law. The cleanest way was an outright abolition of diversity jurisdiction. But that was obviously not within the Supreme Court's authority, and although *Black & White* prompted renewed efforts by Congress to curb diversity jurisdiction, corporate interests blocked virtually all those attempts. Another option was to attack the legal fiction that made corporations citizens, for diversity (but not some other) purposes, of their domicile state but no other state. If corporations could be made "citizens" in every state where they do business, diversity jurisdiction could be defeated by competent plaintiffs in any of the host jurisdictions. That strategy also proved futile. *Erie* was the culmination of a third strategy—the abolition of federal general common law. Diversity jurisdiction would continue to exist, but it would be rendered impotent.

Although *Erie* artfully disguises its ideological purposes, they break to the surface in Brandeis's account of *Swift*'s "defects, political and social." *Swift*, Brandeis writes, had produced disharmony rather than legal uniformity and, by creating two sets of laws within states, had encouraged forum shopping and unfairness among classes of litigants. That characterization has an appearance of common-sense neutrality (all those in favor of unfairness or forum shopping, say "aye"), but it is highly misleading. Forum shopping had indeed become a sport for what Brandeis antiseptically called a "wide range of persons" in the decades prior to *Erie*. For the most part, however, plaintiffs sought to avail themselves of a favorable *state* court jurisdiction. Then as now, the shopping spree was largely driven by plaintiffs' firms that specialized in procuring large damage awards by dragging corporate defendants into hostile jurisdictions.[26] Manipulation of diversity jurisdiction was a small part of the overall picture. Major corporations shunned particularly hostile states, but they rarely changed their legal domicile for the purpose of creating diversity jurisdiction. *That* game was mainly the domain of occasional third-tier players, and by all appearances, it was very small domain. The *Black & White* case was indeed absurd. But it was also singular, and hardly warranted the overruling of a century's worth of precedents.[27] In short, Brandeis's professed dismay over forum shopping is a distraction.

The real issue surfaces in an easily missed mistake in the opinion, in a passage quoted earlier. "The privilege of selecting the court in which the right should be determined," Brandeis writes, was under *Swift* "conferred upon the non-citizen." This statement anchors the charge that diversity jurisdiction "discriminates" against citizens—and it is manifestly wrong.[28] Under *Swift*, a party to a diversity case could sue in his own court or in his opponent's court or in federal court under federal common law (the *Erie* constellation). That holds true regardless of which party to the underlying transaction sues first. Where, then, is the "unfairness"? Nowhere.[29] Brandeis's problem, it turns out, is not the initial venue and its law. His problem is the diverse defendant's right to *remove* a state court case to federal court and federal law. In that situation, the noncitizen indeed has an advantage that the in-state defendant, whose rights (unless they are federal) will in all events be adjudicated by the local courts and under local law, does not possess. And although *Erie* speaks aridly of "citizens" and "non-citizens" and of a "wide range of persons" who availed themselves unfairly of diversity jurisdiction and federal common law, Brandeis knew full well who those "non-citizens" were: corporations, which dominated upwards of 80 percent of the Supreme Court's diversity docket.[30]

Fairness and Federalism. Does "unfairness" between citizen and noncitizen defendants matter? The question, it turns out, has nothing to do with "equal protection" (even in a metaphorical sense). It is foremost a *federalism* question. The answer depends on whether one takes the citizens' federalism perspective or the states'—*Swift*'s perspective or *Erie*'s.

Swift, we saw in chapter 6, sought to protect the parties' ex ante expectations. Its regime gibed with the federalism distinction between local and national, interstate affairs. With respect to immovable objects (such as land), *Swift* reasonably presumed that contracting parties would subject their disputes to the law of the local jurisdiction. With respect to general commercial contracts among parties from different states, the presumption ran the other way: barring some evidence to the contrary, one assumes that each party would ex ante want the option of escaping local bias in the other party's home state. In this conceptual universe, the "unfairness" complaint is very nearly incomprehensible. When a plaintiff in a diversity case chooses a federal court and its law to adjudicate a commercial dispute, the defendant can hardly complain of unfairness; both sides knew of that symmetrically available opportunity when they struck their bargain. When either side sues in its own state court and the defendant removes to federal court and federal law, there is no unfairness, either. The defendant's opportunistic move occurs only after the plaintiff has already made *his* opportunistic move. Against *Swift*'s baseline, a rule that checks opportunistic litigation choices by either party is the embodiment of fairness.[31]

Erie circumvents this logic through a subtle but fateful shift of the perspective. It focuses not on expectations among parties but on unfairness among *classes of litigants, at the time of litigation.* It is this two-front shift, from ex ante bargaining expectations to ex post litigation opportunities and from individual parties to classes of litigants, that produces Brandeis's "unfairness." In-state business litigants are trapped in state law while diversity defendants get to choose between state and federal common law: unfair! The wildly differing initial positions and expectations have disappeared from sight; what grates is that out-of-state defendants have an exit. Allow that maneuver, and "the gates of escape from deeply rooted State requirements will be open."

That sentence does not appear in *Erie*. It appears, attentive readers may recall, in Justice Frankfurter's dissent in *Rice*, the foundational preemption case discussed in chapter 9. The misdirection is my clumsy way of highlighting *Erie*'s continuity with the New Deal's preemption regime. Although the two cases deal with different classes of fugitives—*Rice* with in-state enterprises, *Erie* with out-of-state corporations—they are congruent in all other material respects. Just as Frankfurter's *Rice* opinion elides the difference between federal preemption and the warehouse operators' *choice* of a federal license and instead obsesses over their advantages over the left-behind, state-licensed competitors, so *Erie* views federal general common law as an illicit escape. Neither *Swift* nor the Warehouse Act of *Rice* interfered with state autonomy; they merely offered a competitive alternative to entrenched state regimes. By Brandeis's and Frankfurter's lights, however, the bare existence of that alternative is an assault on the states' autonomy. Competition itself is a harm.

Also, the two opinions embody the same starry-eyed assumptions about state autonomy and interest group politics. *Swift* afforded protection not simply against the risk of biased local juries and judges but also against the real force behind that risk: state factionalism, which may at any point frustrate the legitimate undertakings of American citizens in interstate commerce. Federal general common law cannot always provide relief inasmuch as states can always opt out of it through legislation. However, *Swift* forced the factions to obtain state legislation—a more arduous but also a more responsible process than the rush to the friendliest county court. *Erie*, in contrast, treats the operation of state politics not as a factionalist menace to political stability but as a salutary expression of democratic state experimentation, which should in fairness reach national as well as local enterprises. Perhaps diversity jurisdiction and federal general common law were necessary in the olden days as a safeguard against state prejudice against foreigners as such. But that danger, so dreaded by the Founders, no longer exists.[32] In a more enlightened modern age, diversity jurisdiction operates simply as a subsidy for national corporations. Its abolition being outside the federal judiciary's reach, the rule that federal courts must follow state courts' rules of decision is the constitutional choice. Or so *Erie* asks us to believe.

Can *nothing* be said for *Erie*'s unfairness argument? Au contraire. The contention that local businesses may be subject to discrimination—relative to more mobile economic actors or (what amounts to roughly the same thing) to actors who have access to federal common law—has real bite, although not for a reason that Louis Brandeis would have endorsed. Factional exploitation is the coin of the political realm; the question is how one deals with it. The Old Court attempted to curtail the states' rents, as in *Lochner* and *New State Ice* (the majority opinion, not Brandeis's let's-hear-it-for-monopoly dissent); to expose local monopolies to foreign competition, as under the dormant Commerce Clause; and to open an exit and an impartial forum, as in *Swift*. In its original formulation, *Swift* was far more state-friendly than *Lochner*; any state could erase "unfairness" any day of the week by adopting the general common law, judicially or legislatively. Indeed, *Swift* actually invited states to serve as laboratories and to provide *better* law than the federal common law.[33] In so doing, a courageous state might hand its local businesses an advantage, and noncitizens might choose its law by contract. As noted, though, neither Brandeis nor the New Deal cared for *that* sort of experimentation. "Experimentation" cuts only one way, and "fairness" means to maximize the states' surplus by choking off the exits. *Erie* was the centerpiece of that agenda.

Erie Extensions

As noted earlier, *Erie* is a bit of a halfway house. Instead of abolishing diversity jurisdiction, it emasculates it by tying federal courts to state court determinations. That effect, moreover, depends on two related doctrines that are not encompassed by *Erie*'s precise holding. First, *Erie*'s core holding—federal courts will in diversity cases follow the rules of the state courts where they sit—does not decide *which* state law governs in cases where typically more than one state's law may apply. If defendants could routinely avail themselves of their home-state law, much of *Erie*'s proplaintiff thrust would be eviscerated. Second, *Erie* does not determine the reach of state courts' jurisdiction over noncitizen litigants. The more limited the reach of jurisdiction, the more limited *Erie*'s impact. Over time, the Supreme Court resolved both the first, "choice of law" question and the second, "personal jurisdiction" question consistent with *Erie*'s social-political purpose: reduce the power of federal courts over the states' regulatory choices; allow states to extend their extraterritorial powers; throttle back on constitutional limitations and their enforcement by federal courts; enhance state authority by empowering plaintiffs and by closing off the exits for defendants. State courts make the calls; the federal courts follow.

Choice of Law and Jurisdiction. At the time of *Erie*, choice of law and personal jurisdiction questions were still governed by traditional territorial doctrines. As for choice of law, the American Law Institute's *First Restatement of Conflicts*, which embodied the lex loci understanding, was published just before *Erie*, and the *Erie* Court seems to have assumed that on remand, the case would be decided under the laws of Pennsylvania (the place of the accident), not those of the plaintiff's chosen New York venue.[34] Moreover, the Supreme Court, notably including *Erie*'s author, assumed that state courts' doctrines with respect to both the choice of law and personal jurisdiction were constitutionally constrained by the Full Faith and Credit Clause and by the Due Process Clause. In a series of *Erie*-era cases arising primarily over insurance contracts and workmen's compensation statutes, the Supreme Court held that both clauses forbade wholly extraterritorial applications of state law and, moreover, required a constitutional balancing of competing state jurisdictional claims.[35] Within a decade, however, both the traditional understanding and the constitutional constraints disintegrated. A mere three years after *Erie*, in a unanimous and extremely cursory opinion in *Klaxon Co. v. Stentor Electric Manufacturing Co.* (1941), the Supreme Court held that federal courts must follow state court determinations even on the choice of state law.[36] This doctrine, one of the most important applications of *Erie*, reinforces *Erie*'s proplaintiff orientation. *Erie* guaranteed plaintiffs their choice of *a* state law, to the exclusion of federal general common law. *Klaxon* effectively guaranteed them the state law of their chosen forum. The demise of constitutional constraints on choice of law ran roughly parallel. By the 1950s, the Supreme Court declared state courts' choice of law determinations constitutionally permissible unless the choice is so unreasonable, and so completely unconnected to the dispute at hand, as to offend "traditional notions of fair play and substantial justice."[37]

The law of personal jurisdiction moved on a similar trajectory. Traditional territorial rules of jurisdiction turned on a party's (typically the defendant's) physical "presence" in a given state. While those rules had become very messy in the pre-*Erie* decades, the general trend was toward a relaxation of rigid presence requirements. The breakthrough came in the Supreme Court's *International Shoe* decision (1945), which held that any "minimum contact" suffices to expose a defendant to the jurisdiction of the local courts. Here as in the choice of law area, the constitutional (due process) requirements eroded: virtually any passing contact with the forum jurisdiction subjects an out-of-state party to suit.[38]

A Federalism for Plaintiffs and States. The rules of *Klaxon* and *International Shoe*, operating in tandem, expose parties in interstate commerce to suit virtually anywhere, in a forum and under a state law of the plaintiff's choosing. A diverse defendant may still be able to escape the *personal* bias of the local courts by removing the case to a federal court, but the *doctrinal* bias of the local law will follow him into that forum. Among other consequences, this regime encourages relentless forum shopping for hospitable state venues. Post-*Erie*, moreover, that temptation runs not over two sets of laws (federal and state) but over fifty. To the extent that one takes *Erie*'s lamentations about opportunistic litigation and "unfairness" at face value, the decision looks like a miserable failure.

In that light, should one view *Klaxon*, *International Shoe*, and the demise of constitutional limitations on the choice of law and jurisdiction as part and parcel of an "*Erie* regime"? In terms of contemporaneous judicial expectations, the answer may well be no. *Erie*, as noted, was decided against a backdrop of territorial assumptions about choice of law and jurisdiction, and in a world where the Full Faith and Credit Clause and the Due Process Clause had real purchase. Significantly, Brandeis as well as Holmes insisted that the choice of state law had to be cabined by federal law and federal courts. Holmes, with customary insouciance, routinely decided conflicts cases under "what seems to us [the justices] the proper rule," regardless of whether that was the rule of any actual state.[39] Brandeis likewise insisted that the Full Faith and Credit Clause and the Due Process Clause limited plaintiffs' and state courts' choice of law.[40]

Respectable arguments support this view. Presumably, *Erie* did not mean to block vertical forum shopping only to replace it with plaintiffs' bargain hunting among favorable state laws. *Especially* if a substantive federal common law is unavailable, one might think, the choice of law question must be governed by federal common law. The same considerations of fairness that should prevent classes of citizens from invoking the convenient escape of federal common law should likewise bar identifiable classes of citizens—plaintiffs—from *their* opportunistic forum choices. (As William Baxter has put it, unconstrained choice of law is like having baseball calls made not by umpires but by the first player who manages to rule on a disputed event.)[41] Over the years, many New Dealers sharply criticized *Klaxon* on these grounds.

And yet, the justices who decided *Klaxon*, unanimously and only three years after *Erie*, evidently viewed it as a natural extension; and on balance, that is the better view. First, *Erie*'s target was not "forum shopping" in the abstract. Its aim was to promote the states' autonomy to apply their own rules to out-of-state defendants. Defendants' escape into federal law defeats that objective; but then, so does a diverse defendant's escape into his own home-state law. On that reasoning, federalism demands that the venue and law choice must be the plaintiff's, and the plaintiff's alone. Second, if one takes Holmes's positivism and its regurgitation in *Erie* seriously, it is hard to escape the *Klaxon* consequence. Positivists have nothing coherent to say about conflicts of law; their premise that law must come from some sovereign blocks any *legal* answer to the question of which sovereign gets to rule in cases of conflict.[42] Third, an independent federal judicial inquiry into state courts' choice of law and jurisdictional rulings looks a lot like the federal common law that *Erie* sought to demolish.[43] Henry Hart and other *Klaxon* critics sought to escape that logic by insisting that choice-of-law questions had traditionally been viewed as "procedural," in contradistinction to the "substantive" rules of decisions to which *Erie*'s constitutional holding was addressed. But apart from the fact that Brandeis (for one) thought little of that distinction, it is too subtle to survive the recognition that the choice of law is not a warm-up pitch but often the entire ballgame.[44] An independent federal common law on choice of law would undo the gains of *Erie* by again permitting defendants to evade the plaintiffs' choices. Over *Erie*, and indeed over the New Deal's entire Constitution, hangs a giant No Exit sign. Why let defendants escape through the air ducts?

The "no exit" observation points to a fourth continuity between *Erie*, its *Klaxon-International Shoe* progeny, and the New Deal Constitution. Perhaps one can envision a post-*Erie* world in which federal courts monitor plaintiffs' forum choices and state courts' jurisdictional reach—a world where each individual state exercises regulatory autonomy over interstate commerce within its boundaries and "without risk to the rest to the country," as Justice Brandeis wrote in his seemingly unrelated *New State Ice* dissent. But the post–New Deal Court never seriously entertained that option. Instead, it followed *Erie*'s gravitational force, for the same reason that prompted the *Parker* Court to ignore the "without risk" proviso. The loadstar of *Erie*'s federalism is interest group politics and state surplus. If those are good things, why should they should stop at the borders? The New Deal quest for state autonomy *always* spills across borders because that is where the surplus is. Justice Brandeis's courageous little state may don the cloak of democratic localism, but it is an imperialist at heart.

The New Federal Common Law

Erie's contours and understanding have fluctuated over the decades— partly as a result of reinterpretations by its great expositors, partly as a result of *Erie*'s interplay with other doctrines, partly as a result of broader political and legal changes. On one side, *Klaxon* and *International Shoe* extended *Erie*'s logic. One the other side, *Erie*'s expansion was bounded by the judicial creation, beginning in the 1940s, of a "new" federal common law. It differs from the law of *Swift* in two respects.

First, unlike *Swift*, the new federal common law binds state courts and other authorities under the Supremacy Clause. State courts were never compelled to follow the federal common law of negotiable instruments; they are of course compelled to follow the federal common law of libel announced in *New York Times Co. v. Sullivan* (1964) and the federal courts' interpretations of the Sherman Act.[45] In short, the new federal common law is much deeper and more "nationalist" than the old. Second, the new federal common law is much broader than the old. In particular, it is not tied to diversity jurisdiction.

How much broader depends on what exactly one means by "federal common law." No commonly accepted definition exists. In one widely cited formulation, the Supreme Court identified two categories of federal common law: federal rules of decision that are "necessary to protect uniquely federal interests," and areas where Congress has authorized federal courts to develop substantive federal law.[46] The first part of this formula circumscribes a set of "enclaves" of federal common law in the strictest sense. *Erie*'s injunction notwithstanding, federal courts will supply substantive rules of decision without an explicit, substantive grant of authority from the Constitution or the Congress. The rules of maritime law are an example; rules governing interstate compacts, another. The universe of supposedly "authorized" exercises of federal common-law making is far more uncertain and controversial. The Supreme Court has inferred such authority, not only from explicit statutory language, but also from broadly worded statutes (such as the Sherman Act) and, as mentioned, from constitutional as well as statutory provisions. Although one can call the elaborate edifice of modern antitrust law or search-and-seizure rules "interpretation," the enterprise looks a lot like judge-made common law.[47]

As the definition of "federal common law" expands, *Erie*'s domain contracts and begins to look exceptional. In the world imagined in *Erie*, one might paraphrase Grant Gilmore, there would be no federal common law. In the actual post-*Erie* world, there is nothing but federal common law, and due process is meticulously observed.[48] But one need not push the definition of "federal common law" very hard or much beyond its widely accepted parameters to discern the basic thrust and import of *Erie*'s regime: the *only* form of federal common law that is deemed to offend the Constitution, federalism, and the separation of powers is the general common law of *Swift* and the web of commercial interstate relations that it protected prior to *Erie*.[49] That pattern may appear discordant with *Erie*'s spirit of judicial deference. It is, however, perfectly in keeping with its ideological purpose, and its federalism.

Enclaves. The "federal interest" segment of post-*Erie* federal common law contains a somewhat disjointed set of doctrines. It originated on the very day of *Erie*, in an opinion likewise authored by Justice Brandeis, in a case involving the interpretation of an interstate compact. Such cases, the Court declared, had to be decided under federal common law because adjudication under either state's law would obviously be prejudicial to the other.[50] In later decades, "uniquely federal interests" came to encompass the unhampered operation of the federal government's own instruments, such as its financial paper. It expanded further when the Court held that the Constitution, of its own force, protects not only the federal government but also its contractors from liability lawsuits, based on state law, that seek redress for injuries suffered from manufacturing defects (in the leading case, a soldier's death in a helicopter crash). In the general understanding, cases in maritime law are also to be decided under federal common law. And there is a doctrine (once robust, although now of uncertain scope) that bars state law-based actions that would compromise the foreign policy objectives and prerogatives of the United States.[51] Two common features of these enclaves merit attention: their progovernmental orientation and their stark contrast with the *Erie* regime.

The progovernment bias is best illustrated by *Clearfield Trust* (1943), involving the question of whether the United States' delay in asking for reimbursement of its payment on a fraudulently endorsed check barred recovery of the sum (a princely $24.20) from the Clearfield Trust Company. The company had accepted the bad check and submitted and received payment on it from the U.S. government. Applicable state law would have barred recovery by the United States, but the Supreme Court declared that rule "singularly inappropriate":

> The issuance of commercial paper by the United States is on a vast scale and transactions in that paper from issuance to payment will commonly occur in several states. The application of state law, even without the conflict of laws rules of the forum, would subject the rights and duties of the United States to exceptional uncertainty. It would lead to great diversity in results by making identical transactions subject to the vagaries of the laws of the several states.[52]

What bothered the justices was what bothers the Chamber of Commerce—the sheer inconsistency of state laws. Note the irony behind the *M'Culloch*-on-steroids decision in *Clearfield Trust*: *Erie* had promised legal certainty for confused businessmen—and a fortiori, one would think, for more resourceful actors, let alone an actor with the power to declare binding rules for all states. Displaying little confidence in *Erie*'s promise, the *Clearfield Trust* Court considered the need for a judicially created uniform rule "plain." And on second thought, the general common law is not as bad as all that:

> While the federal law merchant developed for about a century under the regime of [*Swift*] represented general commercial law rather than a choice of a federal rule designed to protect a federal right, it nevertheless stands as a convenient source of reference for fashioning federal rules applicable to these federal questions.[53]

The Court did not explain why concerns over the "vagaries" of state law do not apply with equal force to any financial institution (say, a federally chartered bank) in interstate commerce. A few years after *Clearfield Trust*, it held that the law of that case does *not* protect private bank transactions in U.S. paper.[54] *Clearfield Trust* sprouted two diverging branches—one, protecting federal governmental interests; the other, denying protections against hostile state legislation for private parties, even those with comparable economic functions and dealing in the same instruments.

The dramatic difference between *Erie* and its enclaves is best illustrated by the federal common maritime and admiralty law that was "grandfathered" into *Erie*. Carnival Cruise Lines' contracts—long, small-font documents that were sent to prospective passengers only *after* they had booked and paid for a voyage—specified that any disputes arising out of the transaction (including accidents at sea) would be litigated in the courts of Florida, the company's domicile. In *Carnival Cruise Lines v. Shute* (1991), the Supreme Court sustained those clauses, despite the obvious inconvenience to a Washington plaintiff who had suffered a slip-and-fall injury at sea and wished to litigate in her own state's courts. Presumably, the Court reasoned, purchasers are compensated implicitly for the choice-of-forum clause in the price of their tickets, and that advantage merits protection against opportunistic litigants. That proposition is widely accepted among economists—but not in American law: forum selection clauses in consumer contracts are generally unenforceable under any state law.[55] And under *Erie*'s iron logic, state law will govern.[56]

The boundaries of the federal common law, as drawn in *Clearfield Trust*, *Carnival Cruise Lines*, and similar cases strongly suggest that the protection of interstate commerce per se is *not* a "uniquely federal interest" of the sort that would warrant a federal common law. This is so even where the risk of state interference is sufficiently severe to warrant federal rules of decision for federal institutions, for their private contractors, and for private enterprises whose instruments of commerce happen to float. The cut points are all-decisive: defendants will either operate under federal protection or else, in the *Erie-Klaxon* world of institutionalized state aggression. At the outer margins, where protectionist state legislation poses a political risk of retaliation by other states, the dormant Commerce Clause provides a modest guardrail. In virtually all other respects, interstate commerce must rely on Congress for protection.

"Authorized" Federal Common Law. Having delegitimized the general common law of *Swift*, the New Deal Court had to rest the new federal common law on a different foundation. Unlike *Swift*'s law, the theory runs, the new federal common law is rooted in substantive constitutional or congressional grants of authority. Those roots, however, have often proved shallow. One is hard pressed, for example, to find the *Miranda* warnings "in" the Constitution. Similarly, some congressional statutes that have been read to invite or authorize the creation of federal common law provide an exceedingly slight basis for doing so. The universe contains, for example (though somewhat uneasily), the Rules Enabling Act and, under it, the Federal Rules of Civil Procedure.[57] More broadly, the new federal common law encompasses the judicial construction of broad statutes that if taken literally would shut down the country. A classic example is the Sherman Act, which by its terms prohibits any agreement "in restraint of trade or commerce." That language prohibits any kind of contract. Because that cannot be the purpose of the act, federal courts

apply a "rule of reason" to distinguish permissible from impermissible agreements, along with some categorical prohibitions against obviously anticompetitive practices. Virtually the entire apparatus of American competition law is a judicial creation, and the Supreme Court has described the Sherman Act as an invitation for that creation.[58] It has said the same of other statutes (for example, those that create common-law-like employment and liability obligations for railroads and other firms). Eventually, the intuition set in that, come to think of it, *every* federal statute invites federal courts to vindicate the purposes of the Congress. If Congress dislikes securities fraud, for example, that warrants the judicial creation of a private cause of action for that offense, regardless of Congress's failure to provide for it. And if Congress dislikes race discrimination, that warrants a judicial rule of tolerance vis-à-vis race-conscious schemes that the text of the pertinent statute affirmatively forbids.[59]

The vast scope and often tenuous foundations of the new federal common law raise the question of how much is left at the end of the day of *Erie*'s domain. It also raises the questions of how and why a foundational decision that was initially understood and intended as a monument to both federalism and judicial restraint could instead become an engine for a vast expansion of both federal (preemptive) law and judicial assertiveness. Part of the answer, surely, has to do with shifting political alliances and institutional allegiances. *Erie* presumed, in good New Deal spirit, that Progressive politics demands judicial deference. When that configuration began to crumble in the 1950s, *Erie*'s institutional commitment had to give way to Progressive substance—on civil rights, the First Amendment, reapportionment, the rights of criminal defendants, and much else besides. It was one thing to subject national corporations to the tender mercies of Alabama courts and their common law of torts. It was a very different thing to subject the *New York Times* to Alabama's common law of libel, in the midst of the civil rights struggle. Thing one called for federal judicial deference to state law. Thing two called for a federal common law of libel, a novelty with little resemblance to the common law of any state or nation.[60] Especially in its constitutional variety, the new federal common law ties the *Erie* regime to the formula of *Carolene Products* and *West Coast Hotel*: a muscular role for federal courts in enforcing the guarantees of the Bill of Rights, a very deferential role with respect to the great mass of "economic" regulation, federal as well as state. As the "Rights Revolution" took hold, the new federal common law triumphed while *Erie* disappeared in the federal courts and civil procedure corners.

There is much to this story. But it is a bit too tidy, and it sleights important features of the post-*Erie* regime. For one thing, the post–New Deal

Court remained committed to the notion of "judicial federalism"—that is, the notion that federal courts should treat state courts as equal partners in a cooperative venture, the better to protect federalism's balance. That general disposition is reflected, for example, in the broad doctrines of federal court abstention that renounce federal jurisdiction, in deference to state courts.[61] Second, and more important, not all new federal common law reflects a liberal agenda. Practically from the get-go, the new federal common law was shaped not only by Progressive ideology but also by institutional demands—the same institutional demands that prompted sensible New Dealers to hang on to the dormant Commerce Clause and implied preemption.

Erie's suggestion, or perhaps its myth, is that we can run a complicated federal system with a minimalist federal common law because political bodies—"the sovereign," in Holmes's oddly un-American parlance—can always supply the requisite rules. America, however, has no sovereign in that simple sense; and the new federal common law implicitly recognizes that the New Dealers' ersatz "sovereign," the United States Congress, needs a ton of judicial help. Some of *Erie's* more thoughtful apologists have acknowledged the point, although not always directly. In a famous 1964 address and essay "In Praise of *Erie*—and of the New Federal Common Law," Judge Henry Friendly defended *Erie's* solution—leave federal questions to the feds and state questions to the states—as "so beautifully simple, and so simply beautiful, that we must wonder why a century and a half was needed to discover [it]."[62] Even at the time, though, that defense required heroic effort, and on closer reading, Friendly's essay actually runs counter to its cheerful conclusion. Acknowledging the dire need for a coherent ordering of interstate relations, it celebrated "new" federal common law extensions, on the barest of congressional hints, to matters that would have struck Justice Story as beyond the reach of any federal institution. Perhaps Judge Friendly's position reflects a genuine belief in a "synthesis" between the functional demands of a federal Constitution and the precepts of *Erie* (as Friendly insisted); perhaps, the judge's adulation of "his" justice.[63] Either way, Friendly's confidence in *Erie's* beauty, simplicity, and symmetry of form grossly understates the centrifugal force of *Erie's* core holding and grossly overestimates the ordering capacity of federal political institutions.

Two things, however, must be said in Friendly's defense. First, the great judge very clearly perceived the institutional problem of legislative pusillanimity.(He embraced highly creative federal common-law constructions for precisely that reason.)[64] Second, Friendly wrote before *Erie's* centrifugal force had become fully evident—before the invention of sprawling class actions, migrating asbestos claims, and a roving plaintiffs' bar. More than four decades later, those exploitative tendencies are painfully manifest, as is the inability of Congress to respond. In that context, continued insistence on *Erie*'s indelible rightness suggests a very different, uncharitable but perfectly plausible interpretation. On a widely held theory (reviewed earlier), *Erie* protects federalism by committing substantive federal rules of decision to Congress, where the states are represented. However, the true protection for the "states as states" is not their representation in Congress. Rather, it is the certainty that *Congress will consistently fail to enact, and federal courts will under* Erie *refuse to supply, federal rules of decision in a specified domain*—the state exploitation of interstate commerce. So viewed, *Erie*'s legacy dovetails with the New Deal's ambivalent preemption doctrine. It instrumentalizes Madison's auxiliary precautions against factionalism at the federal level to protect and promote factionalism in the states—unless the justices, in their own discretion, decide that things have gotten out of hand. Later chapters will trace the contours and the effects of this arrangement.

CHAPTER ELEVEN

Fiscal Federalism

Introduction

The New Deal's fiscal instruments—federal tax credits, grants-in-aid, and conditional funding programs—embody the New Deal's "cooperative federalism," and they form the warp and woof of the American welfare state. Building on Progressive initiatives, the New Deal greatly expanded fiscal intergovernmentalism and entrenched it in the institutional architecture of American federalism. A federal inheritance tax, coupled with an offset of up to 80 percent for tax payments to states—was introduced in 1926. It served as a model for, among other things, the unemployment insurance title of the 1935 Social Security Act, which coupled a tax credit for employers in participating states with certain program requirements for those states. An early, very modest federal grants-in-aid program, the Federal-Aid Road Act of 1916, became a template for numerous, far more ambitious federal transfer programs. The 1921 Maternity Act, which extended partial federal funding to states that agreed to participate in a federal maternal health program, was precursor to the New Deal's Aid to Families with Dependent Children (AFDC). In contrast to their Progressive forerunners, the great majority of New Deal programs proved effectively permanent.

Even upon casual inspection, the New Deal's fiscal programs illustrate that the New Deal was not a "nationalist" revolution but rather created a new form of federalism. While the federal initiatives of the 1930s of course involved the national government in domains theretofore beyond its purview, they also built state capacity and enabled states to run programs that, to all practical intents, had been beyond their abilities.[1] And we shall see that the New Deal's fiscal federalism conforms to the model of a state cartel not only in its state-friendly disposition but also in all other salient respects: the states' demand for federal intervention, the obfuscation of any distinction between coordination and cartel, and the institutional bias in favor of interest group politics and government enlargement at all levels.

The formal constitutional questions in the fiscal domain are few and limited. There was no Commerce Clause to reconstruct, no Contract Clause to demolish, no *Swift v. Tyson* to contend with. In the handful of decisions in this area, the Old Court's justices arguably missed the competitive logic of dual federalism and the anticompetitive thrust of the New Deal project. Even a clear-eyed recognition of the direction, however, would have made little difference. The harsh fact is that the Constitution offers no robust, judicially enforceable defense against federally sponsored fiscal cartels among states.

If fiscal cartelization in the United States nonetheless confronts limits, that is not on account of some explicit constitutional provision but for reasons of political economy (sectionalism) and on account of the Constitution's structural features, particularly its lack of a distributional baseline or focal point. Both factors, we saw in chapter 7, played a large role in blocking the emergence of cooperative fiscal federalism. The genius of the New Deal was to find institutional ways and means to overcome sectionalism without splitting the political coalition inside the Democratic Party.[2] Limits remained; cooperative programs that directly threatened the racial caste system in the South, especially education, would have to wait until the 1960s. Moreover, due to the Constitution's deafening silence on federal-state fiscal relations, a full-scale, systematic fiscal cartel was never within reach or seriously contemplated. Within those bounds, however, the New Dealers found ways to improvise an endless array of fiscal cartels, one policy arena at a time.

The Taxing Power, My Dear

In the turbulent days of 1935, when the Roosevelt administration's lawyers scrambled to draft the Social Security Act in a way that would pass Supreme Court muster, Labor Secretary Francis Perkins related her woes to

Justice Harlan Fiske Stone at a Washington tea party. "The taxing power, my dear," the justice is said to have stage-whispered in the secretary's ear, "you can do anything under the taxing power."[3] That advice—and accurate prediction, it soon turned out—encapsulated not only an accurate assessment of the votes on the Court but also the broader recognition that the Constitution, as written and as interpreted by the Court, imposed very few limitations on the national government's powers to tax and spend. Any looming constitutional issues could be avoided, and eventually were avoided, by careful legislative drafting and competent legal advocacy.[4]

The central event, well preceding the New Deal, was the transition from a tariff economy to an income tax economy following the enactment of the Sixteenth Amendment in 1913. Beginning in the 1920s, the expansion of the national government's fiscal reach prompted the taxed parties, and occasionally a state, to search for constitutional restraints. All those attempts, however, proved essentially futile. In 1926, for example, Congress provided that any estate subject to state taxation could offset that liability against up to 80 percent of a federal inheritance and estate tax that had been created a few years earlier. The measure was calculated to curb rampant state tax competition for wealthy retirees.[5] Private plaintiffs attacked the federal inheritance tax on the theory that the Tenth Amendment, or something like it, bars the federal taxation of objects that are tied to a particular situs. The Supreme Court roundly rejected that claim. In a later case, it likewise rejected Florida's claim that the federal inheritance tax credit infringed on the state's constitutionally guaranteed fiscal autonomy. The federal demolition of Florida's competitive position, Justice Sutherland declared in a perfunctory (and unanimous) opinion, was not a judicially redressable harm.[6]

The more respectable argument that Congress may not tax for *regulatory* purposes had a bit more traction, though only for awhile. The Court occasionally relied on the doctrine—most prominently, when it held that a federal tax on the interstate shipment of products from factories that employed child labor was an illicit means of accomplishing a regulatory purpose that had already been declared unconstitutional in *Hammer v. Dagenhart*.[7] But the doctrine was never rigidly followed. For example, it is hard to envision a tax that is more nakedly calculated to serve a regulatory purpose than a targeted federal tax on interstate shipments of oleomargarine, with an expected revenue yield of zero; yet the Supreme Court early on sustained that obnoxious tax.[8] The notion of an impermissible regulatory tax celebrated a final hurrah in *United States v. Butler* (1935), which invalidated the Agricultural Adjustment Act (AAA).[9] Soon thereafter, the Court effectively discarded the doctrine on the grounds that *every* tax has some regulatory purpose. Henceforth, the Court would refrain from scrutinizing congressional policy choices in this area.[10]

Latitudinarianism also prevailed on the spending side. At the time, it was still plausible to argue that Congress's taxing and spending powers are cabined by the scope of enumerated powers. In 1935, however, in the otherwise mangled opinion and decision in *Butler*, the Supreme Court unanimously rejected this "Madisonian" understanding and instead adopted the rival "Hamiltonian" understanding, which holds that Congress may tax and spend for objects outside the range of enumerated powers. That understanding, the Court correctly observed, had been accepted and followed all along.[11] Along the same lines, the Supreme Court held in a later case that Congress's power to tax for the "general Welfare of the United States" did not imply a judicially enforceable prohibition against federal spending on purely local problems and events, at least so long as those local problems were apparent all across the country.[12]

The conjunction of broad federal taxing and spending powers raised additional questions with potent federalism implications. *Butler* suggested that two constitutional rights—a permissible tax and a permissible spending measure—may yet make a constitutional wrong.[13] The AAA provided price supports for farmers who agreed to take acreage for certain commodities out of production, and it financed those payments through a tax on the processors of those commodities. A narrow majority of the Court described this arrangement as a regulatory interference with a subject-matter—agriculture—that was reserved to the states by the Tenth Amendment. The insistence on the states' prerogatives, though, looks like makeweight. What irked the Court's conservatives was the transfer from one set of identifiable actors to another specified group. What the decision seemed to say, though, is that so long as the tax and spending sides of any legislative bargain *look* sufficiently separate, the arrangement is constitutionally permissible. On that reading, payment of the taxes into the government's general revenues rather than an earmarked fund, or payment from general revenues rather than a dedicated tax, will break the impermissible linkage. The drafters of the Social Security Act, in a bow to *Butler*'s commands, stuck the benefit provisions into Title I through Title VI of the act, put the corresponding tax provisions into Title VIII and Title IX, and separated the two sides of the transactions through Title VII, establishing the Social Security Board. In addition, Congress and the administration took pains to emphasize that for constitutional purposes, old-age contributions went into and out of general revenues, thus rendering inapplicable *Butler*'s objections to the AAA.[14] In substance, *Butler* proved little more than a set of drafting instructions for lawmakers.

Ironically perhaps, *Butler* got the underlying problem very nearly backwards. Typically, it is not the linkage but the *decoupling* of taxing and spending decisions that induces fiscal distortions and exploitation. The AAA's cross-subsidies were plain for all to see. Remove the linkage: taxes become common pool contributions and spending demands, claims on that common pool. Within the pool, between money in and money out, anything can happen. It usually does; when cross-subsidies become more opaque, they also become more common.

The Supreme Court missed this point not only in *Butler* but also in its earlier decision in *Massachusetts v. Mellon* (1923). In that case, the Commonwealth challenged the federal Maternity Act, which provided federal funds for maternal health programs to states that agreed to abide by certain grant conditions. Massachusetts argued that the nominally voluntary act left it no choice but to cooperate, thereby violating constitutional principles of federalism. Individual Massachusetts citizens brought a companion case, styled *Frothingham v. Mellon*, claiming that the Maternity Act violated their rights as taxpayers. The orchestrated litigation shows an acute awareness of cooperative federalism's central problem. The "coercion" whereof Massachusetts complained was *not* a feared imposition of onerous grant conditions but the fiscal asymmetry of the Maternity Act. Massachusetts taxpayers would be taxed for the costs of the program regardless of whether or not Massachusetts itself chose to participate. A nonparticipating state would leave its taxpayers' money on the table and available for distribution to other, participating states. The only way to escape the de facto exaction would be to participate.

The force of the argument depends on keeping both sides of the transaction in view. The Supreme Court, however, separated them and determined that neither the Commonwealth nor the individual taxpayers could invoke the Court's jurisdiction. For purposes of federal taxation, the Court held, the obligation runs directly between the citizens and the national government. States may not interpose their parens patriae authority in the relation; they lack standing to assert the taxpayers' rights. Taxpayers qua taxpayers, in turn, lack standing to complain of federal spending decisions.[15] Once both sides of the transaction had been found beyond judicial purview, the perceived federalism problem vanished. If Congress enacted the Maternity Act with the purpose of tempting states to yield their authority, Justice Sutherland wrote for the unanimous Court, "that purpose may be effectively frustrated by the simple expedient of not yielding."[16] The laconic observation seems to miss the nasty incentives and fiscal asymmetries at the heart of the plaintiffs' case. For better or worse, though, the Constitution provides no ready handle to force taxing and spending decisions into a single, unified judicial inquiry that might constrain "cooperative" schemes.[17]

If such a lever existed, states would rarely use it. In *Massachusetts v. Mellon*, the state argued alongside its citizens, against a federal cooperative scheme. That constellation has rarely recurred; with respect to cooperative spending programs as with respect to cooperative regulatory programs, the defense of the old federalism was left to private litigants.[18] In 1937, the Supreme Court entertained a corporation's constitutional challenge to certain sections of the Social Security Act on the grounds that the tax and conditional funding regime of the Act effectively deprived states of their autonomy, thereby violating the Tenth Amendment. The relevant provisions established a national—but primarily state-administered—system of unemployment insurance by crediting 90 percent of any employers' payments to a qualified state unemployment insurance plan against its federal payments. The states joined the federal defendants, and Justice Cardozo's opinion for the Court made much of the fact. Rejecting the plaintiff's Tenth Amendment claims, Cardozo effused over congressional efforts to "find a method" by which "public agencies may work together to a common end."[19] The notion that such arrangements might imperil states' rights, he maintained, was untenable. Indeed, national intervention empowered states to undertake initiatives that they would otherwise have to abandon on account of competitive pressures. In any event, Cardozo continued, no federal influence would be felt without the states' consent. And consent, he wrote (echoing the Commerce Clause decisions of the period), "will preserve a balance threatened with derangement."[20]

The power to tax indeed proved all that the New Deal needed, or at least most of what it needed. Constitutional revolutionaries are wont to attack the reactionaries' weakest front, and after several false starts (and with a little help from Justice Stone), the New Dealers discovered that the taxing power was that front.

The Demand Side

Cooperative fiscal federalism was an invention of the Progressives, which the New Deal institutionalized on a massive scale.[21] I focus on three prominent aspects of the transition, closely paralleling the discussion of regulatory cartels in chapter 9: the difference between cartel and coordination, the solicitude of states and interests, and the institutional system's tendency to expand government at all levels.

Cartels, Not Coordination. The distinctive, innovative feature of Progressive and New Deal fiscal programs was the conscious design and deployment of intergovernmental schemes as a means of reducing fiscal competition among the states. No nineteenth-century program had this feature; all instruments of the New Deal's fiscal Constitution share it. Federal tax credits for state tax payments, for example, serve no purpose *except* to curb state tax competition.[22] Likewise, federal conditional grants programs institutionalize vertical-horizontal conspiracies—that is, collusive arrangements under which a vertical agreement (federal taxes and transfer payments to states coupled with funding conditions that prohibit defection or product modifications) serves to suppress horizontal competition among market participants (the states).

Cooperative fiscal instruments have rarely been used to remedy bona fide coordination problems among states, such as interstate externalities or an undersupply of public goods that are national in scale. Even programs that nominally purport to address coordination problems have rarely served that purpose. Highway construction, perhaps the most urgent infrastructure issue of the pre–New Deal decades, provides an instructive example.

The Federal Aid Road Act of 1916, one of the earliest federal grants-in-aid programs and a model for the New Deal and for many subsequent federal enactments, provided $75 million in federal highway aid, which states had to match on a fifty-fifty basis. Those grants, though decidedly modest by modern standards, constituted about half of all federal aid to the states at the time. Offhand, one can think of two coordination problems that might warrant federal intervention in this area: the need to make roads connect at the state borders, and the risk that state jurisdictions might undersupply a national public good (either by not building interstate roads at all or by building them to inferior standards). Neither problem, however, had much to do with the 1916 act or subsequent appropriations. The border problem usually solved itself on account of a path dependency of the most literal sort; highways were built or paved where the cart paths ran. Likewise, there was no undersupply problem.

Although many states initially funded road construction through bond issues, a consensus quickly emerged that the costs should be borne by users. The gasoline tax proved a reasonably good proxy for highway use, and it quickly became a mainstay of state finances. Besides being fair and easily collectible, its user fee features made it popular both among private and commercial users and with the general public. State politicians protected the political consensus by enacting gasoline tax exemptions for off-road vehicles (airplanes as well as tractors); by taxing interstate commerce in proportion to its in-state highway use; and by monitoring, to the point of fastidiousness, the diversion of gasoline taxes to other uses. To the extent one can reasonably expect, competitive federalism conformed to the economists' models. State taxes financed the construction of a very respectable road system that roughly balanced supply and demand on a local and a national basis. Federal funds amounted to no more than 2 percent of all spending on roads during the period and had no demonstrable supply effect. To be sure, not all was bliss. Road construction and vehicle standards exemplify the sort of network issues where uniformity is at a high premium, and the commendable aspiration of making interstate commerce pay a fair share of in-state road use still poses a risk that that commerce will pay more than its share (as a result of state exploitation) or less (as a result of clever evasion). However, federal enactments did virtually nothing to address those genuine problems. It was left to the Supreme Court to rectify them, as best it could, under the dormant Commerce Clause.[23]

If the Road Act and its successors "solved" imagined coordination problems while leaving the real ones unattended, what *was* its point? The principal and intended effect, it appears, was to centralize and professionalize the administration of road construction in the several states.[24] In all states, federal funds and funding conditions helped central administrators to beat down local governments in disputes over rights-of-way and road design. This was not some federal scheme; it was the states' agenda. The most potent lobby for federal road legislation was the American Association of State Highway Officials which, having been founded in 1914, wasted little time in turning to its calling of lobbying Congress.[25]

At the time, the professionalization and centralization of state highway administration may well have been worth the modest federal investment. Over time, however, it becomes hard to tell those virtues from bureaucratic empire building, interest group favoritism, and fund substitution. The Eisenhower administration's legendary interstate highway program in the 1950s was financed with a $25 billion federal gas tax. Although a program of that scale is bound to have *some* supply effect, much of the federal money simply displaced state spending. Certainly, the federal program greatly increased construction costs: among its central provision was a mandate that all federal and state contractors must pay Davis-Bacon (that is, union) wages. A federal funding statute of this sort solves a problem for the states, especially those with powerful unions and concrete lobbies. What it fails to solve is a federalism or coordination problem.

Redistribution: States and Interests. Redistribution, as opposed to the federal coordination of public goods or scale problems, soon emerged as fiscal federalism's central arena. No surprise here: to the Progressives' and New Dealers' minds, the fear that state-level redistribution might induce factor migration was a "race to the bottom."[26] The puzzle lies in the states' prominent role in the architecture of the American welfare state. If federalism's central flaw is its inherent limit on redistributive policies, why have a federal rather than national solution?

There is no obvious reason to enlist states in the enterprise; there are good reasons to by-pass them. Wholly national redistribution policies (such as Social Security and, in recent decades, the Earned Income Tax Credit) work with comparatively high accuracy and low administrative overhead. In contrast, intergovernmental fiscal arrangements entail high transaction and monitoring costs, as well as principal-agent problems that have no clean solution. A federal attempt to ensure through stringent grant conditions and close monitoring that federal funds reach the intended beneficiaries will effectively turn state administrators into federal deputies and, to the extent that states must match federal funds, will commandeer substantial state resources. Conversely, independent state administration will entail a loss of efficiency and accuracy. (State "flexibility," a supposed advantage of cooperative federalism, is a different name for a federal "implementation deficit.") Too, a disproportionate number of poor people usually live in poor states with a low level of public expenditures and little tax capacity, with the result that a federal matching grant will tend to exacerbate disparities among the states and, moreover, fail to reach many intended beneficiaries.[27]

The New Dealers understood these difficulties very well. Field agents charged with implementing cooperative programs perennially complained to Washington headquarters that state officials were politically unreliable, corrupt, and incompetent.[28] And it was quite clear that cooperative programs had undesired distributive consequences. The American South, identified by President Roosevelt as the "Nation's Number One Economic Problem," received less funding under federal programs than any other region.[29] Why then did the New Dealers embrace cooperative arrangements with such striking regularity, while conspicuously eschewing—with the exception of Social Security—wholly national solutions? The best answer is that they had identified a positive role for the states— to compensate for the weakness of redistributive coalitions in American national politics.

In explaining the uniquely prominent role of states in the formation and the architecture of the American welfare state, political scientists have emphasized path dependencies and, in particular, the crucial influence of preexisting state institutions. At one extreme, path dependencies help to explain why neither the 1935 Social Security Act nor any other piece of New Deal legislation addressed the pressing issue of workmen's compensation: all states had such policies in place at the time, and although many worked poorly, they were protected by bureaucratic and commercial interests.[30] At the other extreme, Social Security became a wholly national program in large part because virtually no state had adopted anything of the kind. "Cooperative" New Deal programs (such as work relief, unemployment insurance, and AFDC) lie between those poles. Importantly, however, they were not simply designed "around" preexisting state efforts; they also built on and leveraged those efforts. Put differently, path dependencies presented not simply a constraint but also an opportunity point, in the form of an articulated state *demand* for federal intervention. Jane Perry Clark, a prominent scholar close to the New Deal in time and disposition, emphasized that

> a realistic view of the situation may indicate that it is frequently a mistake to regard grants-in-aid as devices for raising standards of state administration, but that grants should be thought of as means for raising funds for state services without resort to the politically embarrassing expedient of state taxation.[31]

The New Deal's ready accommodation of that demand, and its conspicuous fondness for cooperative fiscal federalism, hardly means that state lobbies ran roughshod over the Roosevelt administration, nor even that state demand was the most important determinant of federal policy. Rather, New Deal redistributive policies turned cooperative because the demand of states *as states* was required to redistribute much of anything at all.[32]

To see the point, start with the Madisonian insight that the range of interest groups is usually narrower within states than in the country at large. This implies significant differences *among* states. It also implies that an interest group coalition that cannot prevail at the national level may yet win in *some* states—in LaFollette's Wisconsin, for a nonrandom example. Having won once, the coalition will continue its campaign in other states and in Washington, where it will propose to encourage and extend the lead states' experiments by means of federal funding. Those experiments are of vital importance to a national redistributive initiative because the demand for federal intervention will now enjoy the support of the enacting states *as states*. That includes the states' lawmakers, its bureaucracies, and the interests that will have coalesced around the program. It may even include state constituencies that originally opposed the program; inasmuch as they are now among the payors, they will support an effort to transfer a portion of the cost to the federal government.

The federal intervention will likely take the form of a conditional federal grant rather than wholesale nationalization. Federal legislators who would vote against the policy if its full costs appeared in the federal budget may well vote *for* it if those costs can be partially hidden in state and local budgets. Legislators who believe that redistributive objectives would be better served under a wholly national policy will likewise converge on a cooperative program, for fear of losing the support of vital state-based constituencies (for example, public-sector unions). Moreover, and perhaps most important, the division of expenditures between levels of governments produces a fiscal illusion on the part of taxpayers. Preenactment, taxpayers who would oppose a tax-and-expenditure program if it were proposed to them as a single state-level bundle may nonetheless support a relatively cheap federal program to "assist the states." Postenactment, an even wider group of taxpayers can be relied on to favor matching state expenditures because the federal grants will reduce the price of the funded service at the state level. (State citizens who are unwilling to tax themselves for a $10 program may be willing to pay $5 once the federal government offers to match the effort.) Moreover, each state's citizens will pay for the federal program expenditures one way or the other; the only question is whether or not to collect federal payments. The response, as noted, is a foregone conclusion.

Due to its fiscal illusions and asymmetries, fiscal federalism inflates the local demand for services and pushes redistributive programs beyond the authentic preferences of local jurisdictions, and beyond the level that would obtain under an exclusive assignment of taxing and spending authority to either level of government. In the fiscal arena as elsewhere, cooperative federalism serves to enhance the growth of government at all levels.

Bias and Entrenchment. Chapters 9 and 10 showed that the New Deal's preemption doctrine and the *Erie-Klaxon* regime embody an option, not for states per se, but for the most interventionist state—the one that is most willing and able to serve as an opportunity point for proregulatory interests. The New Deal's fiscal programs illustrate the same strategy of mobilizing Madisonian insights—the diversity of an extended republic, the states' propensity toward factionalism—for anti-Madisonian, anti-competitive ends. Distributional coalitions will naturally migrate to the most accommodating state. That lead state will then be eager to transfer a portion of its costs to the federal government and to draw all states into a tax-and-spend cartel.

This process is the central to the Progressives' and New Dealers' embrace of federalism's virtues. "We ought to get the full benefit of experiments in individual states before attempting anything in the way of other Federal action," Louis Brandeis wrote in 1912.[33] As noted, Brandeis did not have in mind Delaware's experiment with corporate charters or North Carolina's experiment with child labor laws; that sort of thing was a race to the bottom. Experimentation, Brandeis thought, was worth having only under noncompetitive conditions and, moreover, when it serves as a prelude to, and as a political support-building exercise for, a push for federal assistance. The point of state experiments is not to let laggard states lag but to go national, by means of inducing the lead states to push for federal offers that the laggards cannot refuse. Federalism is when the dominoes tip in only one direction.

The cascade is not a foregone conclusion. Harmonizing federal legislation may fail to materialize; in that sense, the lead states have to be "courageous," as Brandeis put it. That difficulty, however, is compensated by fiscal federalism's entrenchment effect. Once a "cooperative" scheme has been adopted, the asymmetric financial structure of the arrangement— that is, the fact that local taxpayers will pay for the federal program one way or the other—ensures a quasi-preemptive effect and, moreover, a tendency to further expansion. In flush times, state and local governments will expand federally funded programs to maximize federal transfers; in times of fiscal constraint, they will be loathe to cut those programs for fear of "losing" federal dollars.[34] The near-ineluctable tendency of cooperative fiscal programs is onward and upward.

Constitutional Structure and Fiscal Cooperation

Cooperative fiscal federalism is a way of bargaining around constitutional entitlements. Given the breadth and scale of such arrangements, it seems tempting to conclude that our political institutions have successfully declared their interdependence and seceded from the competitive constitutional order; and in many ways, this is true. However, the constitutional structure has left deep marks on the New Deal's fiscal federalism. The Constitution's lack of a distributional baseline, we saw in chapter 7, helped in the nineteenth century to forestall a lurch into cooperative fiscal federalism. In the twentieth century, it produced a singularly haphazard fiscal federalism. The in-period construction of American fiscal federalism "on the fly" and under an open-ended Constitution had two consequences: a disconnect between taxing and spending decisions, coupled with a level of tax competition that no truly "cooperative" federal system tolerates; and a pattern of continuous improvisation and intergovernmental conflict.

Full-scale fiscal cartelization requires a recognition of federal taxing and spending linkages and, moreover, the suppression of state tax competition. Many modern federal constitutions—for example, Canada's and Germany's—contain explicit provisions on these questions; and invariably, they link taxing and spending provisions.[35] Virtually alone among all federal systems, however, the United States has never come anywhere near this scenario.[36] Tax autonomy has prevailed even when a federal tax monopoly, coupled with the redistribution of the proceeds to the states, would have improved the position of *all* states and when, moreover, it was the only way of preventing an erosion of the state tax base and the attendant revenues.[37] The most likely explanation is that tax autonomy is the states' "reservation position" or Lockean proviso—their safeguard against a wholesale expropriation of the surplus that accrues to cooperative fiscal arrangements. A surrender of that entitlement, in return for a "fair" and stable return, would have to be ex ante. It cannot be procured ex post at a subconstitutional level, due to inordinate bargaining costs, rampant opportunism, and the central government's inability to precommit to the protection of a "fair" state share.

Any attempt to bring rhyme and reason to cooperative fiscal federalism, then, will have to be made on the distribution or spending side. Even here, however, the obstacles are insurmountable. For want of a distributional baseline and because of the sequential consideration of individual programs, any distributional inequities will have to be resolved on a program-by-program basis. Thus, in comparison to other federal systems, our cooperative federalism is singularly improvisational. All federal systems experience continuous disputes over the vertical and horizontal distribution of fiscal resources, but no other country sports a fiscal system that does not even attempt to approximate any kind of baseline. The U.S. tax and transfer system generates massive inequities and imbalances both among states and vis-à-vis the supposedly intended social service beneficiaries.[38] That was true of the historical New Deal programs. It has been true ever since, and seven decades after the fact, it is safe to describe the system's dysfunctions as intractable. If the system has nonetheless proven extraordinarily resilient, that is because the features that may seem to render it vulnerable also help to stabilize it.[39]

The disconnect between taxing and spending decisions ensures that the states' contributions to the system—more precisely, the state taxpayers' contributions—rarely become an object of political attention even in donor states. For every dollar that some New York cherry grower, welfare client, teacher, or concrete contractor receives under some federal grant program, New York taxpayers will have paid a disproportionate amount.

New York's representatives often complain about the "unfairness" of being a permanent donor state. They are far less vocal, however, about the underlying dynamic. Federal transfers are largely paid from income tax revenues, which are paid largely by wealthy households, a large number of which are domiciled in New York. Short of importing millions of welfare recipients, there is no way of ensuring a roughly fair bargain for New York State *on the distribution side alone.* The only way to ensure an equitable bargain for the Empire State is a relinkage of taxing and spending decisions—in plain English, a tax cut for hedge-fund managers. If New York's representatives rarely push the point, that is because they need not stand behind their state's excessive but imperceptible common pool contributions. They do, however, get to and usually do stand next to the federally funded cherry trees. The fact that New Yorkers, including quite possibly the tree owner himself, may have been played for suckers is of no practical consequence. What guarantees the system's stability is the lack of transparency and the state politicians' interest in the "emolument and consequence" of their offices.

Similarly, the need for incremental, program-by-program decision making prevents individual programs from foundering on broader, intractable disagreements over distributional inequities that characterize the system as a whole. Narrower, program-specific objections can then be met by making side payments to recalcitrant states and constituencies within each particular program, through the same implicit agreement that makes federal preemption statutes possible: agree to create intergovernmental surplus, and leave potentially deal-breaking distributional questions for another day. (A federal grants-in-aid statute can no more settle distributional questions than a federal preemption statute can settle jurisdictional lines and fix a "federalism balance"; were it to try, it would never be enacted.) Hence, federal grant and transfer programs—like federal preemption statutes—are characterized by a constant wrangling over the proceeds. Payments to state and local governments go up and down (mostly up); funding conditions are tightened, relaxed, and tightened again; statutes go from categorical, highly prescriptive programs to "devolutionary" waivers and block grants and back again. These periodic shifts can entail important policy consequences, and they are obviously salient for governmental actors at all levels and for their constituencies. Thus, the administration of federally funded programs is accompanied by voluble state protests about "unfunded mandates" and federal complaints about state and local governments' "waste" and shirking. However, one must not mistake the squabbling for instability. The permanent renegotiation of federal-state bargains affects only the distribution of power and resources *among* government actors, not the institutional stability of the intergovernmental machinery as such.[40] The default response to intergovernmental conflicts is to pump more money into the system. But even when federal-state bargains deteriorate to the states' detriment, state officials' response is not a demand for independence; it is "give us more money and leave us alone." Federal legislators, for their part, are equally unlikely to advocate "disentanglement"—that is, either a wholesale program cancellation or a federal take-over—as an alternative to malfunctioning cooperative programs. Legislators who oppose a given program will want to minimize federal outlays; those who support it will accept partial funding as the price of sustaining its political base. Unlike competitive federalism, then, cooperative federalism is self-enforcing: nobody can defect.

Conclusion

Cooperative fiscal federalism raises a challenge to the image of a seamless competitive Constitution: Why would its architects leave the fiscal front so unprotected? In particular, what is the point of enumerated powers if Congress can always tax and spend around them? Earlier chapters suggested two answers. First, the original Constitution was hardly oblivious to the prospect of fiscal end-runs. The Founders thought, however, that the prohibitions against paper money and unapportioned direct taxes would constrain the national government's taxing powers. The demise of those constitutional limitations long before the New Deal produced a stream of more (and cheaper) dollars with which to bargain around dual federalism's constraints and to create intergovernmental fiscal cartels. Once that logic kicked in, the game was up; and as we have seen, the Supreme Court accepted the result well before the New Deal.

Second, at least so long as there is a hard budget constraint on the central government, it is quite plausible—even for constitutional designers less nationalist than Hamilton or Madison—to live with federal fiscal powers that wheel freely beyond enumerated powers. The federal power to tax can never compromise state authority in the same way that federal regulation can block state ambitions. A federal tax on some set of assets or transactions may impinge upon the states' revenue-raising capacity; but then, a state tax may compromise the federal government's tax effort. The constitutional background norm is mutual accommodation, not federal supremacy. On the expenditure side, meanwhile, the binding force of federal spending statutes flows from the state's acceptance of the bargain, not from the federal government's authority to trump state law. Without the states' acceptance, federal spending statutes—Medicaid, education, homeland security—would turn into congressional press releases. In that important sense, Justice Sutherland was right: the lure of a federal grant is not "coercion."[41]

This line of argument may seem unduly formalistic. State acceptance of federal bargains—even on very onerous conditions—is typically a foregone conclusion. Fiscal federalism's asymmetry leaves states no other options; hence, the federal power to spend has proven the power to destroy. That predicament, however, is not a result of constitutional imperfections or judicial fecklessness. Neither is it a federal imposition on defenseless states. It is rather a function of state demand and its political mobilization, and thus part and parcel of the New Deal Constitution's federalism for "states as states." Later chapters explore whether that federalism is subject to meaningful constitutional or fiscal constraints.

PART FOUR

OUR FEDERALISM

PART III DESCRIBED THE NEW DEAL CONSTITUTION as an inversion of the constitutional order—from competition to cartel, from "the true welfare of the great body of the people" to the interests of "states as states", from checks against factionalism to interest group mobilization, from constitutional commitments to democratic demands. In some areas, the baseline shift was almost instantaneous. Judicial scrutiny of federal "economic" legislation was officially abandoned in *Carolene Products* (1938). *Hammer v. Dagenhart* was overruled in *United States v. Darby* (1941). The enumerated powers doctrine was effectively declared dead in *Wickard v. Filburn* (1942). *Lochner* was so thoroughly discredited after *West Coast Hotel v. Parrish* (1938) that it did not have to be formally overruled.[1] To these prompt, decisive shifts, the New Deal owes a great deal of its reputation as a revolution or a constitutional moment.

The preceding chapters have already intimated, though, that the working-out of a new federalism was far more protracted and complex, institutionally as well as doctrinally, than a "revolution" or "inversion" metaphor suggests. The New Deal Constitution, as we have inherited it, took shape in encounters with and adaptation to profound political forces and events: World War II, the creation of an administrative state, the civil rights movement, the Great Society, the collapse of the New Deal coalition, and the "culture wars" and the rise of conservative politics. In each of these encounters, the New Deal's anticompetitive commitments remained foundational, but they were extended, sharpened, and radicalized.

Part IV traces this dynamic in four federalism dimensions: rights, fiscal federalism, regulation, and horizontal federalism. Table IV.1 provides a schematic overview. For each federalism dimension, the middle column shows the anticompetitive themes of the New Deal Constitution. The right-hand column shows the organizing principles of what the Supreme Court often calls "Our Federalism." Paradigmatic cases appear in italics.

The New Deal's *rights* agenda was devoted, nominally at least, to the perfection of pluralist and, in that sense, competitive New Deal politics. Our Federalism has abandoned that position and instead mobilizes rights for the purpose of imposing an enlightened consensus in areas where state competition is still robust and, moreover, not easily suppressed by Congress. I call this orientation "consociational" because it approximates the role of courts and constitutional review in consociational democracies, identified in chapter 1 as the polar opposite of our competitive Constitution. The

Table IV.1. Federalism dimensions

	New Deal Constitution	Our Federalism
Rights	Pluralism	Consociation
	United States v. Carolene Products Co. (1938), n. 4	*Lawrence v. Texas* (2003)
Fiscal federalism	Cooperation	Entitlement
	Charles C. Steward Machine Co. v. Davis (1937)	*Maine v. Thiboutot* (1980)
Regulation	Cartel	Empowerment
	Rice v. Santa Fe Elevator Corp. (1947)	*Wyeth v. Levine* (2009)
Horizontal federalism	State experimentation	Exploitation
	S.C. State Highway Dept. v. Barnwell Bros. (1938)	*United Haulers Ass'n v. Oneida-Herkimer SWMA* (2007)
	Erie Railroad Co. v. Tompkins (1938)	*Klaxon Co. v. Stentor Electric Manufacturing. Co., Inc.* (1941)
		International Shoe Co. v. Washington (1945)

New Deal Constitution's *fiscal federalism* formula was "cooperation"—that is, bargains between states and the federal government. A point of that arrangement was to institutionalize redistribution on a grander scale than either level of government could achieve on its own. Our Federalism augments that anticompetitive capacity by empowering its supposed beneficiaries to enforce the bargains in court by means of entitlements and private rights of action. The New Deal Constitution's *regulatory* commitment was cartelization. It required (among other things) a preemption law that reconciled, however uneasily, the federal government's ability to impose market order with the states' ability to collect surplus. Our Federalism has a more centrifugal orientation: it further empowers the states, on the theory that more regulation—on top of a federal regulatory "floor"—is ipso facto better regulation. In federalism's *horizontal* dimension, the New Deal Constitution's enthusiasm for "laboratories of democracy" was still hedged with the proviso that states should experiment on their own citizens "without risk to the rest of the country." Our Federalism affirmatively encourages state exploitation of other states' firms and citizens because that is where most of the surplus is.

Chapter 12 describes the first three shifts; chapter 13, the fourth. Both adopt a broad, institutional perspective. The more Court-centered chapter 14 traces judicial federalism's doctrinal developments under the Rehnquist-Roberts Court. The individual pieces of the picture are thoroughly familiar to constitutional scholars and to political scientists. Integrating them into a unified conceptual framework helps to transcend the preoccupation of our federalism debate with the question of "balance" and, more narrow still, the question of whether the Supreme Court has any business in protecting the "states as states" vis-à-vis the Congress. That question has agitated constitutional scholars to no end, but it misses most of what is interesting and important about post–New Deal federalism.

The common reference point of the balance debate is an enormously influential 1954 article by Herbert Wechsler, arguing that the states' constitutional protection lay in the political process and especially the states' federal representation in Congress, to the exclusion of any judicially enforceable rules.[2] The debate between advocates of Wechsler's "process federalism" and proponents of a more assertive judicial role in protecting federalism's balance has raged ever since; it reached a crescendo when the Rehnquist Court's conservative majority jettisoned process federalism and aggressively protected states' rights vis-à-vis the Congress. However, the debate teaches next to nothing about constitutional federalism. Neither side has a *federalism* theory at all, only a theory about judicial review of federal legislation that might affect states.[3] Neither side has much to say about the Court's own effect on federalism's vaunted balance, especially including the effect of judicial rights proliferation on state autonomy; nor do the combatants consider the judiciary's state-empowering doctrines, from *Erie* to preemption. The entire debate narrows to a handful of "vertical" federalism doctrines. Even in that constricted domain, moreover, Wechslerians and their opponents alike unquestioningly accept the New Deal premise that federalism is what the "states as states" want it to be. The notion that there might be a difference between constitutional federalism and state demands—just as there is a difference between market orderings and the opportunistic demands of the Fortune 500—never enters the picture.

What states want is to accumulate surplus, which requires protection against competition. The New Deal Constitution accommodated that demand to a very considerable extent. The Wechsler question does not suggest a reversal of that move; it merely asks whether the interests of states as states warrant any *additional*, judicially supplied surplus protection. In a partial and wholly unintended sense, Wechsler's answer—they do not—may have been right: it is hard to see why the Supreme Court should systematically augment the states' surplus, both because the Constitution provides no obvious warrant for that enterprise and because the political process pushes in the desired direction all on its own. Either way, though, the answer is of little constitutional moment because the question is, in Madison's fine word, "secondary."[4] The primary federalism question is not *how much* federalism but *what* federalism—competition or cartel, a federalism for states or for citizens. Unlike the balance question, that question has a constitutional answer. The process federalism debate can never get to that answer because it has blocked the question.

I intend to resurrect the suppressed constitutional question, not only to awaken the legal profession from its dogmatic slumber, but also, and primarily, on account of its real-world significance. The political federalism debate, no less than the lawyers', has been preoccupied with federalism's vertical balance. Periodically, it has taken the form of popular discontent with excessive centralization and governmental "New Federalism" initiatives. It is hard to gainsay the good sense behind those discontents. No one seriously believes that we need a federal "czar" for domestic violence; or a federal security force that trolls, in the middle of a war against terror, after gravely ill pot-smokers; or a U.S. Corps of Engineers that regulates mud puddles. What the debate misses is that nationalist legislative excess is not our only federalism problem. The Supreme Court's rights production also is, or can be, a federalism problem. Cooperative federalism's metamorphosis into an unsustainable entitlement state is a federalism problem. The proliferation of uncoordinated, semiautonomous power centers, and in particular the judicial empowerment of state legislatures, courts, and juries to regulate the commerce of the United States fifty times over, is a federalism problem.

All these pathologies have reached unprecedented proportions; all flow from the New Deal Constitution. But the most fateful effect of that Constitution, and the true measure of its resounding success, is the constriction of our constitutional memory and imagination to a "balance" question that the Constitution itself conspicuously eschews. The first step to recovery is to acknowledge the loss of memory; the second step, to examine its consequences. That is the program of these chapters.

CHAPTER TWELVE

Federalism after the New Deal: Rights, Revenues, and Regulation

Introduction

This chapter examines federalism's post–New Deal trajectory in the rights arena, where the Supreme Court aggressively expanded constitutional entitlements; the fiscal arena, which is characterized by a sustained expansion of cooperative federalism programs; and the regulatory arena, where we have witnessed a dramatic expansion of both federal and state authority. In terms of our conventional federalism debate, these developments seem discordant. Federalism's balance swings now this way, now that; the Supreme Court's stance vis-à-vis the states, from confident, centralizing activism (as with rights) to deference and decentralization (as with respect to states' regulatory powers). However, the seemingly disparate tendencies gain coherence if one understands federalism's trajectory as an extension and radicalization of the New Deal Constitution's anticompetitive precepts—from rights pluralism to consociation, from fiscal cooperation to entitlements, and from regulatory cartels to empowerment.

Rights: From Pluralism to Consociation

The signal and in many ways defining moment of constitutional law after the New Deal is the "rights revolution" of the Warren-Brennan era. Its federalism aspects are best understood as a sequence of two connected shifts: an institutional shift from structure to rights as the Supreme Court's principal business, and a subsequent shift from pluralism to consociation and social consensus as the judiciary's rights polestar.

I introduced "consociation" in the introduction and in chapter 1 as the polar opposite of our competitive Constitution. Consociationalism thinks of a constitution not as a self-enforcing order that organizes competitive politics but as a cartel among elites. Competitive and consociational constitutions may both rely on constitutional courts to help superintend the initial bargain, but the judiciary conforms to very different roles and expectations. To oversimplify a bit, competitive constitutions need structure courts; consociational constitutions need rights courts.[1]

Structure courts principally serve to curb democratic *agency* risks— that is, the danger that the people's representatives (agents) may defect from a competitive constitutional structure that is supposed to keep them in check. The constitution may entrust the enforcement of its structure to private litigants and, to that extent, couch structural guarantees (free internal trade) in the form of rights (privileges and immunities). As we have seen, the United States Constitution adopts that strategy. Structure, however, remains the lodestar. If a competitive constitution is "in every rational sense, and to every useful purpose, A BILL OF RIGHTS," its Bill of Rights will, conversely, conform to and aid the constitutional structure and its purposes.[2] A structure court will remember that intimate two-way connection.

Rights courts guard against the very different risk that the people themselves, rather than their agents, may defect from the constitutional bargain and violate minority rights. That orientation coheres with consociational systems that attempt to stabilize an initial social bargain and elite consensus and to adjust both to changing circumstances. Competitive politics and structure are ill suited to that end because the link between institutional rules and distributional outcomes is too tenuous and unpredictable. Accordingly, consociational courts operate principally by means of egalitarian or identity-based rights. The principal objective of judicial review is not, or at least not primarily, to guard against the persecution of a lone individual; it is to block the oppression of a socially relevant group.[3]

Many modern constitutional courts were established under rights-laden consociational constitutions, for consociational purposes, and have therefore been rights courts ab ovo. The United States Supreme Court, in contrast, turned from structure to rights in the wake of the New Deal. Initially, its rights jurisprudence remained nominally committed to a pluralist and, in that sense, competitive politics. That orientation, however, could not and did not last. In recent decades, the Supreme Court's jurisprudence has come to approximate the consociational model.

From Structure to Rights. The Supreme Court signaled its transition from structure to rights as early as 1938, in *Carolene Products'* famous footnote 4. While declaring a horrendous interest-group racket beyond judicial purview, the Court also declared itself open for other sorts of business—the enforcement of "specific" Bill of Rights guarantees and the protection of "discrete and insular minorities."[4] The surrender of structure was a fait accompli by 1940. The arrival of the rights Court was delayed by World War II. Beginning with the Warren-Brennan Court, however, Bill of Rights guarantees came to loom very large. *Brown v. Board* (1954) was the beginning. Subsequently, the Court extended the Equal Protection Clause to a widening array of contexts (such as reapportionment) and constituencies (most consequentially, to women). At the same time, the justices "incorporated" most Bill of Rights provisions into the Fourteenth Amendment, thereby making them applicable to the states. In the 1960s, the Court hit upon a formula that permitted the justices to embrace substantive due process again without, at the same time, inviting a second coming of *Lochner.*[5] The result of that jurisprudence was *Roe v. Wade* (1973) and its progeny.

In addition to this constitutional dimension, the rights revolution had a statutory and an equity component. Concurrent with expansion of constitutional rights, the Supreme Court began in the 1960s to read federal statutes, especially statutes that condition federal funds on the states' observance of statutory requirements, in a rights-granting way. Congress fostered that development by legislating a flood of federal entitlement statutes. The expansion of the federal courts' equitable and remedial powers moved on a parallel and roughly contemporaneous track. Encouraged by the Supreme Court, federal district courts embarked on ambitious, long-lasting ventures to reform school districts, prisons, mental institutions, and other state and local agencies by means of consent decrees and broad, "structural" injunctions.

The question of whether and to what extent this rights proliferation is continuous with the New Deal Constitution has been a matter of considerable contention, much of it among the New Deal's heirs.[6] The answer depends on whether one looks to institutional or to political and ideological commitments. At an institutional level, judicial rights entrepreneurship appears to run counter the Progressives' and the New Dealers' professed commitments in favor of democratic politics and against an "activist" federal judiciary. Leading New Dealers, most prominently Felix Frankfurter, articulated this view as the Warren-Brennan Court hit its stride; conservative scholars and justices continued to echo the theme as the Court's rights production accelerated. By any measure, however, substance has triumphed over professed institutional commitments. Arguably, the New Deal's commitment to judicial deference and democratic politics effectively ended in 1938, just as soon as the Court had been stacked with reliable New Deal partisans. In any event, the institutional commitment did not hold because it *could* not hold against the political logic of the New Deal Constitution.

From Pluralism to Consociation. Carolene Products suggests a commensurability between structural abandonment and rights proliferation. Like the New Deal Constitution writ large, the decision unfettered political institutions from structural constraints for the explicit purpose of making politics and the Constitution more "democratic"—that is to say, more open to unconstrained politics. The obvious risk is that politics will allow the powerful to triumph yet again over the New Deal's demos. Therefore, the Court must be vigilant about rights so as to guard against the heightened risk to disempowered minorities and individuals. From this vantage, less structure and more rights both serve the same democratic ends: rights (of a certain description) help to ensure that everyone has access to an open-ended politics. Far from trumping democracy, they serve as a corrective or backstop to democratic process failures or pathologies.

This effort to square the post–New Deal Court's increasingly aggressive rights tack with the New Deal's ostensible institutional commitments to democratic politics, pluralism, and judicial deference has spanned decades, from Robert Dahl to John Hart Ely to contemporary defenders of a judicially reinforced "deliberative" democracy.[7] Ultimately, however, neither Footnote 4 nor pluralist, process-oriented elaborations of the *Carolene Products* agenda describes the Court's post–New Deal jurisprudence very well.[8] *Brown v. Board of Education* seems to fit the account, as do many of the Court's energetic First Amendment interventions. Eventually, though, not *all* specific constitutional guarantees merited judicial solicitude, whereas some unspecified or highly unspecific "interests" and "values" (education, privacy, nonestablishment of religion) did.[9] Only a very convoluted argument, if any, would lead one to describe women—who became a judicially favored class in the 1970s—as a minority, let alone a "discrete and insular" one. And a First Amendment jurisprudence that affords greater protection to internet pornography than to political campaign speech is quite probably driven by something other than an overriding regard for an open political process.[10]

A moment's thought suggests that the notion of a poststructural but nonetheless procompetitive rights jurisprudence is very nearly incoherent. A Court that surrenders the constitutional structure to an overwhelming political coalition will in all likelihood configure its rights jurisprudence to the demands of that same coalition. Lo, just as the post–New Deal Court's abandonment of structure signaled a judicial capitulation to the winning political coalition, so its rights agenda played out the coalition's program.[11] This commitment to constituency politics is the real-world basis of the "Living Constitution" from the New Deal to William Brennan to contemporary "democratic constitutionalists." It also ties that jurisprudence to the Court's federalism, and ours.

The New Deal Constitution's strategy of unleashing pluralist politics and, in particular, politics on behalf of redistributive constituencies calls for judicial deference vis-à-vis Congress, vis-à-vis experimenting state legislatures, and vis-à-vis state courts. All those doctrines sound in structural surrender.[12] Judicial deference must end, however, where state politics threatens to undermine the New Deal consensus and coalition, where state competition rears its head, and *where Congress has no ready means of providing a remedy*. Here, the commitment against competition must sound in judicially supplied rights. Accordingly, the Court's constitutional rights agenda has come to be dominated by issues that do not readily lend themselves to a federal legislative solution on account of their intrinsic characteristics: high salience and high levels of state heterogeneity of a kind that is not readily reduced by means of fiscal side payments.

Almost by definition, this judicial program often prompts state resistance in a way in which federal legislation rarely does. The Court's first, paradigmatic, nominally minority-protective but substantively majoritarian rights foray, beginning with *Brown*, produced massive resistance. Of course, the civil rights struggle is sui generis in many ways. For one thing, race is different from anything else in American politics. For another thing, the fundamental shift in federalism relations wrought by the civil rights revolution rests on the firm basis of the Civil War amendments. (The constitutional problem is the delayed arrival of that Second Founding, not its eventual implementation.) Finally, the Court's civil rights course did not sustain the New Deal coalition but rather broke the bipolar coalition inside the Democratic Party and, in so doing, contributed to a fundamental realignment in American politics. For all that, the Court's civil rights jurisprudence also suggests, or rather became formative for, a deeper and lasting federal pattern—the harmonization of state politics and policies under a consociational rights umbrella.[13]

Through the civil rights debate runs a perennial dispute over whether those rights are of an individual-rights-against-the-state nature (say, the right not to be excluded on the basis of race from a neighborhood school) or of a more egalitarian, distributional kind (the right to attend a racially integrated school). That same ambivalence and dispute runs through the Court's entire rights jurisprudence. At the individual rights end lie the constitutional guarantees, especially in criminal proceedings, that the Supreme Court "incorporated" and thus made applicable to the states. At the opposite end of the spectrum lie later-adopted and incorporated rights, foremost the right to abortion; although they make take the form of an individual right, their essence is constituency politics. The rights are ascriptive, identitarian, and/or distributional. Everyone knows whose they are.

These differences have consequences. First, constituency rights have tended to prompt lasting controversy, in a way in which individual rights have not. (For example, the 1960s agitation over criminal rights has long subsided. The debate over the public display of religion has not and will not.) Second, constituency rights partake not of the New Deal's nominal, let-the-chips-fall pluralism but rather of Progressivism's deeper commitment to the in-period demos, as opposed to the dead letter of the Constitution, as the lodestar of constitutional review. The rights question that drives the Court is not whether a lone individual needs protection against the mob, it is whether intense controversies over private conduct and social mores should be governed by competitive politics or by the Court. More often than not, the answer is "the Court." And more often than not, the Court's answer is pristinely, self-consciously consociational: the constitutional aspiration is an enlightened social consensus.

That orientation, in turn, has federalism consequences. Where policy rifts run nationwide (as with affirmative action), the Court tends to take its bearings from elite institutions, such as Harvard University and the U.S. military.[14] However, some social policy disagreements continue to have a strong sectional dimension, and it is here that the rights rubber hits the federalism road. Figure 12.1 shows the distribution of states on controversial social issues—gay rights, the Equal Rights Amendment, and abortion. It also includes the death penalty (a true individual rights issue, but one that has served as a marker for broader political and ideological concerns). For a reason to be revealed momentarily, the map also shows the distribution of "right to work" laws, which are a tolerably good proxy for states' general regulatory climate.[15] The parameters are explained in the legend. States in a minority position on four or five issues are shown in different shades of gray.

12.1. Distribution of controversial social issues by state. Sources: For data on sodomy laws, see *Lawrence v. Texas*, 539 U.S. 558 (2203); and Human Rights Campaign, "State Laws," online at http://www.hrc.org/laws_and_elections/state.asp. For ERA data, see National Council of Women's Organizations, "Ratifications," online at http://www.equalrightsamendment.org/ratified.htm. For death penalty data, see Death Penalty Information Center, "Facts About the Death Penalty," online at http://www.deathpenaltyinfo.org/documents/FactSheet.pdf. For state's classification as "high-risk Roe," see Center for Reproductive Rights, "What if Roe Fell?" 2007, online at http://www.reproductiverights.org/pdf/Roe_PublicationPF4a.pdf. For data on "Right to Work" laws, see National Right to Work Legal Defense Foundation, "Right to Work States," online at http://www.nrtw.org/rtws.ht.

The picture (need I say?) maps the division of the Jim Crow era and the divisions of the industrial era. The forces that drove Southern exceptionalism for so much of American history—race and economic backwardness—no longer dominate. Race, though still divisive, has ceased to be a dividing *federalism* issue.[16] In the economic domain, most states of the

Old South are probably more competitive than the once-dominant industrial and financial states around the Great Lakes and along the Northern seaboard. (I included right-to-work laws for that reason.) Sectionalism lives on, however, in the social domain.[17] The Supreme Court is doing what it has done throughout American history—drum the South into compliance with national norms.

The continuity, however, hides a crucial difference. The Supreme Court's aggressive posture on federal jurisdiction (in the antebellum era) and on open-market doctrines (for the decades spanning the turn of the twentieth century) had vehemently procompetitive federalism effects, even if the Court did not always clearly articulate or rely on that structural rationale. Even *Lochner* and its progeny arguably had a competitive rationale, as did the decisions and laws that broke the back of state-enforced segregation.[18] In contrast, the modern Court's exertions to drag the South into postmodernity lack any such rationale. In the social domain, federalism problems—spillovers, exploitation, "races to the bottom"—are highly attenuated, if not altogether nonexistent.[19] Yet it is precisely in this domain that the Supreme Court has been at its most centralist. To be sure, Justice Brennan's Constitution, just as Justice Brandeis's, encourages state "experimentation"—provided, however, that it can cut in only one direction.[20] Genuine, open-ended state policy competition is the enemy of the Court's consociational consensus.

Fiscal Federalism:
From Cooperation to Entitlement

Chapter 11 described the New Deal's fiscal federalism as a tax-and-spend cartel. The post–New Deal era wrought two extensions of the New Deal Constitution: an enormous, sustained fiscal and programmatic expansion, and a shift from intergovernmental bargaining to judicially enforced entitlements as the operative principle of fiscal transfer programs. The system has proven exceptionally resilient. Over some seven decades, cooperative fiscal federalism has met with only two serious challenges. The first coincided with the first Reagan administration; cooperative federalism emerged bloodied but, in the end, with renewed vigor. The 2008/2009 financial crisis has produced a second, more profound challenge with uncertain outcome.

Growth and Entrenchment. The postwar era provides impressive evidence of fiscal federalism's tendency toward expansion. In 1950, the count

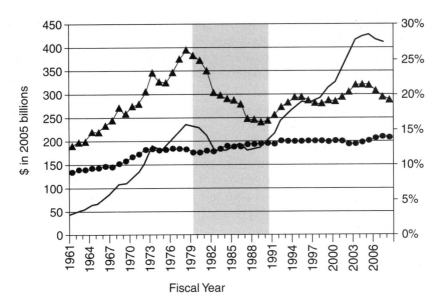

12.2. Fiscal federalism trends, 1961–2008. Sources: GDP: U.S. Department of Commerce, Bureau of Economic Analysis (available online at http://www.bea .gov/national/nipaweb/SelectTable.asp?Selected=N); federal spending: U.S. Federal Budget (http://www.gpoaccess.gov/usbudget/fy11/hist.html); state and local data: U.S. Census Bureau (http://www.census.gov/govs/estimate/). The Rockefeller Institute of Government graciously provided a compilation of this data.

of federal aid programs stood at 68; in 1960, prior to the Great Society, at 132. At the end of that period in 1970, scholars counted 530 programs; by 2006, the number had grown to over 800.[21] Fiscal measures show the same tendency. After modest, steady growth in the 1950s, federal transfer payments to state and local governments grew dramatically in the 1960s and 1970s, declined in the 1980s, and resumed their explosive growth soon thereafter. Figure 12.2 displays the trend lines beginning in 1961.

The federalism debate of the past half-century has resounded with complaints to the effect that an overbearing central government has dragged or bribed unwilling states into destructive and centralizing bargains. As noted earlier, though, this account is not altogether plausible; and figure 12.2 illustrates that by some measures, fiscal federalism has had a long-run tendency *in favor of the states*. First, state and local own-source revenues (excluding federal transfers) increased from under 9 percent of GDP in 1961 to almost 14 percent by 2007.[22] This marks a continuation of a longer-term trend (state and local revenues were roughly 6 percent of GDP after the Korean War), and it contrasts with a remarkably constant level (18 percent to 20 percent) of federal revenues to GDP over the entire time frame. It prevailed over forces that by all rights should depress state and local tax capacity, such as increased capital, labor, and consumer mobility, and the transition from an industrial to an information and service economy that is much less tied to local factor endowments. The most plausible explanation, as noted in chapter 11, is that federal transfer programs expand the states' tax capacity and surplus, at least up to a point.

Second, federal transfer payments over the half-century between 1960 and 2010 have taken the shape of a continuous, sharply upward curve, with a break in the 1980s (shaded in figure 12.2). The principal driver of this trend is not the political New Deal but the Great Society and its "cooperative" programs for public services and redistribution (as distinct from the infrastructure investments, such as the highway program, that had previously dominated fiscal federalism). Two Great Society initiatives, both enacted in 1965, loom especially large: the Elementary and Secondary Education Act (ESEA) and Medicaid. Both programs surmounted the sectional divisions that had perennially frustrated social reformers before, under, and after the New Deal. Both brought innovations that would prove formative for American federalism.

The ESEA for the first time provided general funding to school districts with a certain number of poor children. Although earlier efforts had produced some federal education funding for K–12 education (such as "impact aid" and funding under the National Defense Education Act), more ambitious and systematic proposals had always foundered on Southern opposition, amplified by disputes over the inclusion of parochial schools and their students and by generalized resistance to federal interference with what were then perceived to be pristinely local affairs. In the heady days of 1965, after a resounding electoral victory for the Democratic Party, the ESEA's architects overcame that opposition.[23]

The ESEA's principal effect was and is regulatory. In addition to programmatic requirements in the statute itself, federal funds drag in their wake an array of compliance requirements with federal civil rights statutes, especially the antidiscrimination provisions of Title VI of the Civil Rights Act and of Title IX of the 1972 Education Amendments, which prohibit sex discrimination in federally funded programs. Medicaid's innovation, in contrast, was primarily fiscal. Under the statute, the federal government reimburses states for health-care expenditures incurred for federally approved services and constituencies (initially, those covered by what was then Aid to Families with Dependent Children, or AFDC, a New Deal program that was radically reformed in 1996). The reimbursement formula is exceedingly generous. It has traditionally ranged from 50 percent for the wealthiest states to over 75 percent for the poorest. Moreover, Medicaid is an *uncapped* matching grant. Federal transfers depend on the states' expenditure decisions, without any federal fiscal constraint.

Education policy and Medicaid developed in continuity with their initial design features. In education, regulatory and programmatic debates have continued to dominate. The federal share of primary education funding doubled from 4.4 percent to 8.8 percent after the ESEA's enactment but has grown only modestly since, even as programmatic requirements expanded considerably (especially under the 2001 No Child Left Behind law). Under Medicaid, the general long-term tendency has been federal *de*-regulation, coupled with an astounding expansion of federal transfer payments. Initially enacted as a modest addition to the much larger (but wholly federal) Medicare program, Medicaid has since grown to include many nonpoor groups and an ever-growing array of services. For the most part, the coverage expansion was driven by states; Democratic and Republican administrations alike liberally granted federal waivers to accommodate the demand. Medicaid and closely related health programs account for an ever-growing share of federal transfers and for most of fiscal federalism's expansion over the past two decades.[24]

What education programs and Medicaid have in common—with each other and with virtually all other grant programs—is their progressive entrenchment. Though intensely controversial at the time of its enactment, the ESEA became virtually immune to any serious political challenge soon thereafter.[25] The innocent little Medicaid program, too, quickly became sacrosanct, notwithstanding its escalating costs.

From Cooperation to Entitlements. In the course of the Great Society, fiscal federalism's expansionary dynamics were reinforced by judicially enforced entitlements. The New Deal thought of "entitlement statutes" as entitlements *for the states*, meaning that transfer payments were allocated in accordance with a predetermined formula.[26] Conditions attached to the funds were just that—funding conditions, which were (and still are) enforceable by federal agencies through administrative means or the threat of withholding future funds in the event of continued failure to perform. Modern statutes, in contrast, are principally entitlement statutes *for individuals*, meaning the third-party beneficiaries of federal-state bargains. With that shift, the regulatory terms and conditions of federal-state bargains are put under the superintendence of federal courts, prompted by individual litigants who claim to have been harmed by a state's failure to pay benefits or to provide a statutorily specified service.

The federal judiciary played an instrumental role in this development. In the 1960s, concurrent with the constitutional rights revolution, the Supreme Court substantially expanded private rights of action and, moreover, transported them into federal funding statutes, with stupendous effects. Most major federal entitlement statutes—both conditional funding statutes and federal statutes that regulate private and public parties, such as Title VII of the Civil Rights Act—have been shaped and implemented largely through private litigation. For example, the federal judiciary played a prominent role in determining AFDC entitlements and eligibility rules. The development of affirmative action programs under federal civil rights statutes was in large measure the courts' accomplishment, as was the Byzantine edifice of sexual harassment law.[27]

A particularly potent vehicle for private programmatic litigation was § 1983 of Title 42 of the United States Code. Originally enacted in 1871 to provide federal court jurisdiction to enforce federal rights against the states, § 1983 played only a very small role until the 1960s, when the Supreme Court began to expand its scope.[28] For some time, that expansion ran parallel to the judiciary's coinage of statutory rights of action. After a handful of Supreme Court decisions had throttled back on statutory rights creation, § 1983 came to serve as a yet more potent substitute: *Maine v. Thiboutot* (1980) effectively authorized the private enforcement of federal law—including funding conditions—even and especially where Congress had failed to provide for that mechanism.[29] In that fashion, the Court converted a vast array of theretofore discretionary federal programs into entitlement statutes. Education programs and Medicaid proved particularly fertile fields of litigation.

This is not to say that the Supreme Court's course was a slow-motion coup d'état against the political branches of government. Occasionally, Congress overruled a judicial proentitlement decision—typically, when that decision threatened to unravel a tenuous congressional coalition in support of the program.[30] But the general pattern of the 1960s, 1970s, and to some extent the 1980s was collusive entitlement production.[31] At times, the Court took the initiative in creating entitlements, and Congress ratified the step. At other times, Congress put expansive private entitlements on the books, for which the Supreme Court provided yet more expansive interpretations. Now and then, the Court clipped entitlements; on those occasions, Congress often "restored" supposedly lost rights to what they had never been before.[32] But although the terms of collusion between Congress and the Supreme Court differed across issues, statutes, and time, the basic expansionist dynamics worked across the board.

In light of the judiciary's ambitious role, the state and local defendants' weakened position, and the confrontational style of policy making, the switch from state to private entitlements appears to depart from New Deal presumptions. As explained earlier, however, cooperative fiscal programs are best understood as a response to the weakness of redistributive coalitions in American national politics. Entitlement statutes and litigation extend that logic by putting statutory enforcement at the command of those coalitions. The rights at issue do not entitle anyone to any particular benefit; rather, they give advocacy groups a kind of property right in the administrative process. In turn, they tend to create insulated policy silos, populated by advocates, federal and local bureaucrats, and congressional subcommittees with a common interest to expand "their" programs.[33] Regardless of the distribution of resources within the silos at any given point, the arrangements are institutionally stable and fiscally expansionary so long as the money lasts.

Nor is this institutional pattern necessarily at odds with the New Deal strategy of empowering state and local governments. Although officials with general responsibility (such as governors) often chafe under entitlement litigation over schools, prisons, health programs, welfare agencies, and other institutions, state agencies often welcome it. Federal court orders or consent decrees provide leverage for an agency's claim on the state budget. Sustained federal court supervision over a school district or a state's Medicaid program or prison system (a common result of entitlement litigation) looks like the antithesis of federalism and states' rights—until one recognizes that state agencies quite probably invited the litigation and, in any event, vehemently resist any restoration of political controls.[34] It is thus very hard, but also beside the point, to speculate over the aggregate effects of entitlement litigation on the federal-state balance. The crucial effect is entitlement-driven entrenchment and expansion.

Challenges. Fiscal federalism's entitlement engine began to sputter under Chief Justice Rehnquist's tenure, when the Supreme Court shifted toward more restrictive doctrines. To some extent, a parallel trend occurred in Congress. Its principal manifestation is the 1996 welfare reform, which repealed the panoply of judicially created entitlements under the former AFDC and categorically forbade judicial enforcement of any entitlements under the reform package.[35] These adjustments of the terms of intergovernmental programs, however, were quite modest and in any event swamped by sustained fiscal and programmatic expansion.

A central reason for that resilience, we saw in chapter 11, is that cooperative fiscal federalism responds to state demands. To be sure, funding conditions constrain state governments' discretion, and the clamor over "unfunded mandates" has been a constant of the federalism debate over many decades. Funded programs—especially *generously* funded programs—crowd out unfunded programs, exacerbate boom-and-bust budget cycles, and over time may ruin state finances. State politicians' limited time horizon, however, implies a very steep discount rate for destructive long-term effects. Although conditional funding may look unattractive relative to a hypothetical baseline of pure money-for-nothing fiscal transfers, state politicians find it vastly preferable to a disentangled, condition-free but *competitive* fiscal system. The most onerous transfer program still liberates them from having to serve domestic constituencies with wholly state-generated surplus, dampens interstate competition, and acts as a driver for local tax effort. These incentives are far too powerful to be broken by earnest policy reformers or incremental adjustments; only a severe exogenous shock can rattle the system. One such shock occurred in the early 1980s; another, with the financial crisis beginning in 2008.

The challenge of the early 1980s had two sources: the Federal Reserve Board's decision to wring inflation out of the economy, which ended the political strategy of redeeming promises to state and local governments in cheaper dollars; and the collapse of a formerly stable consensus on cooperative federalism, which prompted an ambitious "New Federalism" initiative by the newly elected Reagan administration. The economic shock subsided with the fall of the Soviet Union and the dissipation of the "peace dividend" to worthy recipients, including state and local governments. The political shock subsided even earlier. Soon after its inception, the New Federalism foundered on the resolute opposition of its supposed beneficiaries—the states.

Reagan's New Federalism reflected a broad, growing sense among the electorate, policy makers, and experts that cooperative programs had failed to work. In 1981, the congressionally funded, nonpartisan Advisory Commission on Intergovernmental Relations (ACIR) summarized its comprehensive review of cooperative federalism programs as follows:

> Regarding national purpose, the record indicates that federal grant-in-aid programs have never reflected any consistent or coherent interpretation of national needs. . . . Regarding fiscal equity, the record indicates that federal aid programs have never consistently transferred income to the poorest

jurisdictions or individuals. Neither do most existing grants accord with the prescription of "externality" theory. . . . Regarding economic efficiency and administrative effectiveness, the record indicates . . . serious obstacles to the successful implementation of intergovernmental programs.[36]

The growth of federal programs, the ACIR continued, had produced "rising levels of political alienation, the increasing atomization of national political processes, and the growing overload of major decisionmaking institutions."[37] Let "cooperation" metastasize and drag enough interest groups and governments into its orbit: in the end, no one is responsible for anything.[38]

The core of Reagan's "New Federalism" initiative was a proposal, based on expert recommendations (mostly from the Brookings Institution), to disentangle cooperative federalism by means of a welfare "swap": the federal government would assume full funding responsibility for Medicaid and food stamps in exchange for the states' assumption of full responsibility—including revenue responsibility—for AFDC and other welfare programs. The swap was carefully calculated to improve the fiscal condition of all states, both on a current and prospective basis (as Medicaid payments were growing much faster than welfare obligations). Its central assumption was that perennial state complaints over "unfunded mandates," onerous grant conditions, and deteriorating state finances would translate into state support for disentanglement on fiscally advantageous conditions.

That assumption proved gravely mistaken. Neither state officials nor the welfare lobby were remotely prepared to entertain the swap proposal, and it was never even introduced in Congress.[39] Confronted with the states' and their clientele's vehement protests, the Reagan administration abandoned its disentanglement objective and instead endeavored to stem the flow of federal money to state and local governments—as shown in figure 12.2, with notable but transitory success. Statutory mandates soon again proliferated, and transfer payments (especially for Medicaid) resumed their growth.

In retrospect, the failure of the Reagan administration's structural, distinctly competitive federalism initiative looms very large as a missed opportunity to reform a fiscal federalism that, in the aftermath of the 2008/2009 financial crisis, looks not simply inefficient and demoralizing but positively ruinous. Among scholars, somewhat academic worries that large-scale transfer programs are inconsistent with competitive federalism and, moreover, rarely achieve their stated objectives have given way to outright alarm. The principal concern, buttressed by the experience of federal countries around the world, is that a toxic combination of central taxing authority and local spending authority consistently induces moral hazard—that is, local overspending and implicit bets on a federal bailout. A common first-order response has been a series of undercover bailouts, often in the form of nominally programmatic, policy-oriented measures that aim to plug holes in local budgets. As those measures prove inadequate and productive of additional moral hazard, restoring the center's precommitment against bailouts proves well-nigh impossible. No federal system can prevail over a coalition of local politicians, statutory beneficiaries, and bondholders.

American federalism has reached this crossroads. The flattening of the state/local revenue line in figure 12.2 suggests that ever-increasing federal transfers have for some time now failed to spur local tax effort. Instead, funded programs have crowded out unfunded programs at the state and local level, exacerbated state and local governments' budget difficulties in economic downturns, and induced them to maintain spending levels by underfunding pension and other retirement obligations. For well over a decade and especially in the course of the 2008/2009 financial crisis, the federal government has staged a series of de facto bailouts, and it seems safe to say that the national government's commitment against such measures has collapsed.[40]

Among the forces that erode competitive federalism, fiscal transfers are the least susceptible to constitutional constraints and judicial control. However, fiscal federalism confronts an upper bound of affordability. It is this constraint, not any constitutional rule, that may compel a fundamental renegotiation of American federalism and federal-state relations. This book's conclusion contains additional remarks on that subject.

Regulation: From Cartel to Empowerment

In the regulatory as in the fiscal arena, the conventional account of federalism's post–New Deal fate is a march toward centralization. An oft-cited 1992 ACIR study pictured a tsunami of federal preemptive statutes and an attendant emasculation of federalism and state autonomy. "Of approximately 439 significant preemption statutes enacted by the Congress since 1789," the ACIR found, "more than 53 percent (233) have been enacted only since 1969."[41] The burst of federal regulation prompted widespread concern over excessive centralization, which informed the "New Federalism" initiatives of the Nixon and Reagan administrations and, in the 1990s, calls for "devolution" of federal authority. Here again, however, the conventional view is wrong. The true story is the radicalization of the

New Deal Constitution—that is, a shift from cartel to state empowerment as federalism's baseline.

Transcending Rice. After the demise of the enumerated powers doctrine, federalism questions in the regulatory arena revolved principally around subconstitutional questions—foremost, the federal preemption of state law. Under the New Deal Constitution's formula of *Rice v. Santa Fe Elevator Corp.*, the congressional intent baseline and judicial anti-preemption presumptions protected state regulators' surplus. However, by allowing for judicially implied preemption, the formula left room for the New Deal's nationalist side and its administrative model, the management of sectorally defined industries under the auspices of expert agencies. Precisely because preemption jurisprudence never attempted to resolve these conflicting impulses, it could be tailored to the demands and dynamics of individual industry or policy sectors. At the same time, the New Deal model dampened both interest group and state-federal frictions. Once a firm or industry had locked itself into a federal regulatory regime and paid off the officially recognized interest groups, it enjoyed protection from collateral attacks from private as well as public parties, including states.[42] Serious preemption disputes were comparatively rare, and the interest group alignments were quite fluid.[43]

Beginning in the 1960s, however, the political and institutional compromises embodied in the New Deal model collapsed. Far from expertly regulating industries in the public interest, it appeared, agencies actually cartelized industries to the detriment of consumers and other broad constituencies that could not easily be organized to provide a counterweight to concentrated producer interests. In the 1960s and 1970s, the critique of "captured" agencies produced a "Reformation of American Administrative Law" and a style of business regulation quite at odds with the New Deal model.[44] A raft of environmental, consumer protection, and health and safety statutes enacted in response to intense public demand were defined by subject-matter (air, water, product safety, workplace safety) rather than industry. Heightened skepticism of neutral expertise prompted the enactment of provisions that invite judicial review of agency action at the behest of broad classes of "concerned citizens." And whereas the New Deal cartel model was inspired by *production* values, the "new" or "social" regulation was driven by *consumption* values. Less risk or damage to health, safety, and the environment is always better, "regardless of the cost."[45]

At first impression, the federal regulatory statutes of the 1960s and 1970s (such as the Clean Air Act, the Clean Water Act, and the Occupational

Safety and Health Act) do look like nationalist occupations of previously state-owned ground. However, the statutes adhere to the New Deal's pro-state precepts in three respects: they establish a federal regulatory floor, thus liberating states from having to compete on those margins; they usually provide for joint, federal-state administration; and they leave ample room for ambiguity, negotiation, and judicial interpretation.[46] Moreover, the increased emphasis on consumption values has gradually eroded the New Deal's residual nationalist impulses. Against a background expectation of agency capture, implied preemption looks like an excuse for recalcitrant federal agencies to serve as a refuge for beleaguered industries against bolder, more entrepreneurial state regulators. The better strategy is to unleash states to regulate on top of the federal floor, freed from any recrudescent threat of preemption. More regulation is ipso facto better regulation; and because that is so, preemption should rarely be legislated and never be judicially implied. Advocates of this position have appropriately dubbed it "empowerment federalism" because it empowers governments and proregulatory interests at all levels.[47] Contemporary doctrine has come to approximate it by way of a detour and a confrontation with a profound challenge to the regulatory state. Here as in the fiscal arena, the challenge materialized under the first Reagan administration, for closely related reasons.

Challenge. Roughly a decade after the capture critique of the administrative state had gained hold and produced the "new" social regulation, it prompted a very different reform strategy—a sharp curtailment of regulatory processes and institutions, with an eye toward creating room for market mechanisms. The deregulation of airlines, trucking, railroads, and antitrust all followed this train of thought.[48] It hearkened back, not to the cooperative New Deal, but rather, though for the most part unwittingly, to "dual" federalism's exclusivity logic. Deregulatory statutes invariably impose a regulatory ceiling or uniform standard from which states may not deviate one way or the other. They *have* to do so: one cannot deregulate airlines, truckers, railroads, or financial institutions without affirmatively prohibiting state and local governments from reregulating them. Unlike either New Deal statutes or the new social regulation, then, deregulatory statutes compromised the autonomy that states care about—the ability to collect and dissipate surplus. It was thus the supposedly federalist Reagan revolution, *not* the supposedly nationalist regulatory enthusiasm of the 1960s and 1970s, that had the most profound and controversial effects on federalism law and relations in the regulatory state.

The inherent contradiction between decentralization and deregulatory objectives was not obvious to an administration that inclined to the mistaken belief that decentralization equals less government. Perhaps the mistake was encouraged by regulatory initiatives of the 1970s that had in fact produced state resistance to more expansive and stringent federal regulation of private and public transactions. One example, which loomed large at the time, is natural resource management, where the enforcement of new or strengthened federal statutes produced bitter brawls that confronted federal agencies and nationally organized environmental constituencies with producer interests, often supported by the affected states, in such sectors as forestry, ranching, farming, mining, and fisheries. Similarly, the new social regulation brought a few legal innovations that seemed to revamp federalism relations to the states' detriment. For example, the Clean Water Act (among other statutes) permits state agencies to administer the regulatory regime on their own unless they cede enforcement authority to the EPA. Such "conditional preemption" statutes initially prompted much state concern and litigation.

Conflicts between proregulatory federal moves and state authority, however, have been uncommon and, moreover, transitory. The effort to remake resource-based state economies (especially in Western and Mountain states) in accordance with an emerging national environmental conscience initially produced the "Sagebrush Rebellion" of the 1980s. Due to a variety of factors—the de facto U.S. policy of exporting extractive industries to foreign countries, the changing demographics of Western and Mountain states, and the reorientation of their economies from resource extraction to tourism—the rebellion soon burned out, and the federalism dimension of natural resource policy has become much less prominent. State opposition to conditional preemption has likewise subsided—in part because the Supreme Court narrowly sustained those provisions; in larger part because state administrators have discovered that conditional preemption may in fact enhance state authority.[49] None of these conflicts have left a lasting mark on American federalism law and relations. In sharp contrast, federal deregulatory statutes, as well as regulatory "ceilings" and uniform standards, have become a focal point of intense political and ideological conflict and a fertile field of federal initiative, state evasion, and incessant litigation over the scope of federal preemption. It is no exaggeration to characterize this once-placid backwater as federalism's central battlefield.[50]

Conflict and Empowerment. The waning of regulatory enthusiasms in the 1980s and the transition of national institutions to deregulation in some areas and more cost-conscious and incremental regulation in others produced a conflictual federalism environment that differs markedly from the consensual style of the post–New Deal era. Proregulatory constituencies did not simply call it a day. Rather, they migrated to the states, whose incentives to retain a regulatory role parallel the constituencies' interventionist interests. Conversely, business constituencies have gravitated to the federal government, whose preemptive legislation has proven the only viable defense against aggressive state regulation. The pattern holds across the entire spectrum of regulation. Even in the environmental arena, where one might expect state resistance to national proregulatory moves, state demand for *more* federal regulation, coupled with a dispensation from federal preemption, has become the norm, as have coalitions between state regulators and environmental advocacy groups.[51] As those political alignments have become more entrenched, the fronts have hardened. Regulatory federalism is still "cooperative" in the sense that few regulatory schemes separate exclusive federal and state responsibilities. But the terms of concurrent authority are subject to fierce political and legal conflict over the distribution of the available private and public rents.

Several closely related institutional consequences bear mention. Prominent among them is a migration from legislative and administrative standard setting to litigation as the dominant form of state regulation. Federal preemptive statutes are typically aimed at state legislatures and regulatory authorities. Provisions of this sort threaten a wholesale confiscation of the states' regulatory rents, and states routinely attempt to evade that outcome. They may call their laws and regulations by a different name, so that a clearly preempted waste management standard becomes a purportedly non-preempted "workplace safety" rule; or they may pursue the prohibited end by supposedly non-preempted means, as when a federal prohibition against the state regulation of airline fares prompts state controls over the advertising of those fares.[52] A much more common, successful, and consequential state move is a migration from statutory and administrative requirements to common law liability. That strategy is attractive because common-law standards are arguably not the kind of "standards" that Congress intended to preempt. Moreover, many federal preemption statutes contain "savings clauses" that exempt common law from their reach.[53] Hence, the federal preemption of state *tort* law has become a central and intensely controversial question of federalism law.[54] At the same time, the states' dominant avoidance strategy has produced a dramatic shift of power from state legislatures to state attorneys general and courts; a parallel migration of interest groups; and symbiotic alliances between proregulatory constituencies, attorneys general, and an all-purpose enforcement contingent, the plaintiffs' bar. Increasingly, business "regulation" has taken the form of indictment, prosecution, and settlement.

Public and private litigation, threatened or actually commenced, has prompted the reorganization of entire industries (such as tobacco and, prior to their collapse, investment banks) and generated more or less formalized regulatory frameworks.[55] Such regimes often escape federal preemption because they are instituted with the regulated industries' consent. Finally, increased conflict between states and the national government has prompted increased cooperation among states. When federal preemption blocks any state from regulating, all states stand to gain from a successful reassertion of state authority. Hence, the modern regulatory landscape features an unprecedented level of horizontal cooperation among states, typically along functional lines. The deregulation of airlines and antitrust law prompted the National Association of Attorneys General (NAAG) to form task forces on those matters, with an eye toward reestablishing state regulatory controls over airlines and to protecting state enforcement authority over state and federal antitrust law. Regulation-by-litigation initiatives, though typically initiated by individual states, usually result in multistate settlements encompassing substantially all states, often because the regulated firms or industries insist on universal consent as a condition of settlement. State amicus cooperation in regulatory cases, as well as cooperation in direct litigation to compel more stringent federal regulation, has been professionalized and routinized. State coordinating bodies and task forces have come to assume a role of de facto regulatory agencies, somewhere between states and the nation.

Later chapters will discuss these features of our regulatory federalism and especially their legal and constitutional aspects in detail. Suffice it here to note their ambivalent relation to the New Deal Constitution. Contemporary regulatory federalism differs from the New Deal model in its confrontational style; its single-minded orientation toward consumption values and more regulation, as opposed to efficient management; and its confidence in generalist judges, juries, and trial lawyers, as opposed to experts. All the while, however, the underlying premise has remained constant. Competition is the enemy in all its forms but one—"empowerment," or "competition," both between the states and the federal government and among states, for escalating regulatory and liability standards.

Conclusion

Although my emphasis has been broadly institutional rather than court centered, it is appropriate to end with a brief remark on the Supreme Court's role in the federal scheme of things—more precisely, with a note of caution against the common and understandable, but nonetheless misleading, temptation to identify constitutional construction with judicial activism and, in turn, with centralization. Those tendencies do in fact coincide in the Supreme Court's consociational, constitutional rights jurisprudence. Other federalism domains, however, show different patterns. In the fiscal arena, the Court's "activism" ran largely in tandem with the legislature's; and as noted, it is far from clear that the shift from bargains to entitlements had unequivocally centralizing effects. The conventional metrics in this context fail to capture the crucial dynamic—the Court's eager cooperation in an expansive, vehemently anticompetitive institutional system. The Court's role is yet more ambivalent in the regulatory arena. Although much ink has been spilled over the Supreme Court's unwillingness to rein in the national regulatory state and the judiciary's supposed solicitude of federal preemptive purposes, the historical and institutional context suggests a very different interpretation. The Court's jurisprudence has played out against the background of the New Deal demise of the enumerated powers doctrine and of exclusivity-based preemption rules; and those, recall, were judicial-deference and state-protective moves. Post–New Deal preemption doctrine is a remnant of the old, competitive Constitution, not a New Deal–inspired instrument of centralization. That doctrine, moreover, has manifestly failed to contain the contemporary state flight into litigation in lieu of legislation.

That unambiguously centrifugal, state-empowering force has in turn been unleashed by the most state-empowering New Deal decision of all—*Erie*, without which state courts could never have become suppliers of state-sponsored, national-scale regulation. The close connection between the regulatory state and horizontal federalism, between the move from cartel to empowerment and from experimentation to exploitation, is the subject of the next chapter. It illustrates that judicial deference and state-empowering moves, no less than aggressive and centralizing moves, are deliberate acts of constitutional construction.

CHAPTER THIRTEEN

From Experiments to Exploitation

The extraterritoriality principle is not to be located in any particular clause. It is one of those foundational principles of our federalism which we infer from the structure of the Constitution as a whole.

Donald H. Regan

We decline to embark on the constitutional course.

Franchise Tax Board v. Hyatt

Introduction

The Constitution sought to contain the states' factional propensities at the state borders. The New Deal Constitution pursues the opposite orientation of liberating factions, now called "interest groups," to launch their schemes in the several states, as well as in Congress. In its original Brandeisian formulation, "experimentation" still came with the caveat that states should experiment "without risk to the rest of the country." As suggested earlier, though, the qualification is not altogether coherent. If interest group politics is a good thing, federalism should allow states to experiment on other states' citizens. The post–New Deal Court has accommodated that strategy by eviscerating the Constitution's horizontal federalism rules—that is, its prohibitions against "extraterritorial" state action. By moving from state-by-state experimentation to mutual exploitation among states as the operative federalism baseline, Our Federalism radicalizes the New Deal Constitution's anticompetitive thrust.

The first part of this chapter sketches this trajectory in the context of state taxation. Recall that the Constitution thwarts the states' preferred anticompetitive solution—a comprehensive, federally sponsored tax cartel. Thus, the states' next-best means of suppressing tax competition is (in-period) tax "harmonization." We shall see, however, that this strategy has also proved largely unavailing. Voluntary state tax harmonization has consistently foundered on the problems of cheating and defection that bedevil all cartels. More surprisingly, attempts to block defections by means of federal legislation and under a federally superintended state tax cartel have likewise proved futile. To this institutional dynamic, rather than any constitutional injunctions, American federalism owes its unusually high level of state tax competition.

However, this is not quite the end of the analysis. *Perfect* extraterritoriality—that is, universal state jurisdiction to tax individuals and firms to the ends of the earth—will wipe out all tax competition: no taxpayer will have an exit, and no state can provide a tax haven. From the vantage of individual-citizen taxpayers (and of perfectly benevolent state officials with a long-term view), such a regime of universalized mutual aggression is a dystopia. For surplus-maximizing (and imperfectly monitored) state officials, in contrast, a collusive agreement to tax each others' citizens regime is—under perfectly plausible assumptions—a highly attractive arrangement. Because a perfect extraterritoriality rule prevents unilateral defections, it may allow states to establish and maintain tax cartels even without central intervention, provided they can agree on some distribution formula. The second part of this chapter presents an example of such a spontaneous state tax cartel, the 1998 Master Settlement Agreement (MSA) on tobacco litigation. The MSA never received the congressional consent that, under the Compact Clause of Article I, § 10, is required for any agreement among states. However, the Supreme Court has roundly rejected legal challenges to the MSA on these and closely related grounds. So far as the justices are concerned, the plain text of the Constitution has ceased to limit the states' extraterritorial ambitions.

The third section returns to the centerpiece of the New Deal Constitution's federalism, *Erie Railroad Co. v. Tompkins*. By substituting state courts' and juries' parochial determinations in lieu of the federal general common law, *Erie* laid the groundwork for a further extension of its inherent anticompetitive and proplaintiff logic. Subsequent expansions of state courts' extraterritorial powers invited plaintiffs to shop for hospitable jurisdictions and so enshrined a systemic federalism preference, not simply for state courts and their law over federal law, but over a wide range of private conduct, for the law of the most exploitative state. That dynamic, in turn, is closely related to the extensive use of civil liability, rather than legislative or administrative standard setting, as the states' principal regulatory strategy under Our Federalism.

Through the entire discussion runs an underappreciated theme—the near-total incapacity of *Congress* to order horizontal state relations. Congress is institutionally incapable of ordaining rules that determine which state may own or govern what; at most, it can substitute a uniform federal rule for divergent state rules. The Founders understood this, which is why they committed horizontal federalism's protection principally to the federal courts. Pragmatic New Dealers—Harlan F. Stone, Robert Jackson—likewise understood it. More theoretically minded New Dealers—Felix Frankfurter, Hugo Black—may have believed that Congress, under inspired presidential leadership and aided by a cadre of expert agencies, might be able to provide horizontal rules of the road. No such uncertainty, however, afflicts modern-day purveyors of Our Federalism. They *know*, based on ample experience, that Congress cannot and will not provide. Far from reasserting judicial federalism norms in light of that recognition, however, they have stayed their hand and deliberately amplified federalism's exploitative tendencies. Save for the small territory covered by the dormant Commerce Clause, horizontal federalism has collapsed into preemption doctrine; and even in that small habitat, it is an endangered species. When asked to enforce horizontal federalism's ground rules, the justices demur: "We decline to embark on the constitutional course."

State Taxation

Throughout American history, it has fallen to the Supreme Court to create "virtually the entire body of federal constraints upon state [tax] power," chiefly under the dormant Commerce Clause.[1] Over the post–New Deal decades, those constraints have weakened greatly. Although restrictions against *discriminatory* state taxation are still enforced, the Court has tolerated an enormous expansion of *extraterritorial* taxation. The institutional consequences of this move require a brief review of the changed legal landscape.

Taxing Commerce. The pre–New Deal Court approached state tax cases with the same doctrines that it applied in regulatory cases: discriminatory state taxes were prohibited; nondiscriminatory taxes on interstate commerce were forbidden if they were deemed "direct" rather than incidental. However, that latter test, closely tied to dual federalism's exclusivity principle and categorical distinctions, was fraught with difficulties. First, it tended to exclude interstate commerce from the reach of any state, thus handing it an unwarranted advantage over in-state commerce.[2] Recognizing the difficulty, the Court gradually poured more palatable wine into the old doctrines while officially denying that anything had changed. Increasingly, the justices found local taxable events, thus putting interstate commerce on a par with in-state commerce.[3] Second, exclusivity rules make much less sense in tax cases than in a regulatory context. Even under a strict dualist understanding, the federal government may tax what (arguendo) it may not regulate. By parity of reasoning, the Supreme Court held that states may tax at least *some* things that they may not regulate.[4]

Predictably, these moves often produced multiple, compounding state tax burdens on interstate commerce. Hence, the Supreme Court strove to assign tax authority, not simply to "the states" but to particular states and, ideally, to a single state. It sought to capture the constitutional considerations under the heading of a prohibition against "extraterritorial" taxation, derived from the Commerce Clause and the Due Process Clause. Time and again, the Court proclaimed that "no state may tax anything not within her jurisdiction without violating the Fourteenth Amendment."[5]

Alas, a constitutionally grounded, workable concept of (state) jurisdiction is hard to come by.[6] Territorial notions work well enough for real property, whose immobility allows unambiguous jurisdictional assignments—but less well for tangibles, and not at all for intangibles (such as stocks). Over time, therefore, the Court moved from physical extraterritoriality to the more realistic objective of ensuring that assets and transactions would be subject to taxation in *some* place, but *only* in one place. In tax as in regulatory cases, the formula on which the Court settled was Harlan F. Stone's. In *Western Live Stock v. Bureau of Revenue* (1938), the Supreme Court (per Justice Stone) held that state taxes on interstate commerce are constitutional so long as they are nondiscriminatory, fairly apportioned, and consistent, meaning that they can be imposed by all states without exposing the taxed entity to double taxation. The objective was to make interstate commerce pay its way without being subject to discriminatory burdens.[7]

With some modifications, the *Western Live Stock* formula has remained the lodestar for constitutional state tax cases.[8] Over time, however, the tests that serve to capture extraterritoriality concerns receded into the background, in tax as in regulatory cases. Although wholly extraterritorial and "direct" taxation and regulation are still prohibited, any slight physical "nexus" to a jurisdiction now suffices to expose out-of-state entities to tax payment and collection obligations. The leading Supreme Court decision, *Quill v. North Dakota* (1992), abolished due process limitations on the state taxation of interstate sales and, moreover, suggested that the Commerce Clause might require a "nexus" only so long as state and local tax efforts pose an "undue burden" on interstate commerce.[9] The determination of whether a sufficient nexus exists is effectively left to state courts, courtesy of the Tax Injunction Act.[10]

Collective Action Problems. In one sense, the near demise of territorial limitations is in the states' interest. Each state need only find *some* locally taxable event, massage its apportionment formula, and (theoretically) come out a winner.[11] However, a tax system that allows the same base to be taxed two, three, or four times will also allow many transactions to go entirely untaxed. So long as taxpayers have an escape, rampant arbitrage will erode the states' tax base and revenues. For a full century, therefore, states have sought to organize tax cartels, with and without congressional help. Two types of taxes illustrate the futility of these efforts: sales and use taxes and business activity taxes.

Constitutional questions over state sales taxation took on great urgency in the pre–New Deal era. Broad-based sales taxes had become a major state revenue source, and they suffered most from the "immunity" of interstate commerce against state taxation. With respect to interstate sales, the tax posed two interrelated problems. The first question was whether the taxable sale should be attributed—"sourced," in tax law lingo—to the seller's home or "origin" state or to the purchaser's "destination state." The second question was enforcement: given the insurmountable difficulties of collecting the tax from consumers, may a state impose tax collection obligations on out-of-state sellers?

Initially, it was unclear whether states could impose *any* consumption or "use" tax on imported goods, inasmuch as a tax exclusively on out-of-state goods might be said to discriminate against interstate commerce. However, the Supreme Court eventually sustained use taxes—equivalent to the applicable in-state sales tax—as a nondiscriminatory compensating tax.[12] That left the collection problem, and the states actively pursued coordinated responses. In the early 1930s, North Carolina officials circulated a proposed federal law authorizing nondiscriminatory consumption taxes in destination states, and the Oklahoma Tax Commission prompted the state's federal representative to introduce a more comprehensive bill. In contrast to comparable federal statutes that had facilitated the state *regulation* of interstate commerce, however, state demand for federal *tax* harmonization went unheeded then and has gone unheeded ever since. The principal reason is that any apportionment rule has profound distributive consequences. If all sales are taxable in the destination state, sellers will be indifferent to the tax rate in their home jurisdiction. In contrast, when interstate sales are sourced and taxed in the origin state, interstate sellers domiciled in low-tax jurisdictions will enjoy cost and pricing advantages over their competitors in high-tax jurisdictions, which will prompt fierce tax competition among states. (That result will also obtain under a destination rule unless states have an effective way of compelling out-of-state sellers to collect and remit the tax.) At the time, the seemingly technical sourcing question had a profound sectional dimension: "consumer states" such as Oklahoma and North Carolina insisted on destination rules, whereas "producer states" such as New York resisted that proposal. On account of that divide, the states' proposal went nowhere.[13]

Anticipating as much, states explored voluntary means of tax coordination. In 1935, state tax commissioners met in Cincinnati to discuss, inter alia, sourcing rules for the taxation of interstate sales. Origin taxation, the commissioners agreed, would hand an unfair advantage to producer states, to the detriment of the consumer states that were perceived to be most desperately in need of revenue. With unerring instinct, the commissioners settled for the anticompetitive rule: tax interstate sales at the consumer's point of purchase.[14] To this day, however, states have found no effective means of collecting use taxes from either their own citizens or "remote" sellers without a nexus to the consumer state. Catalogue sales and, more recently, Internet sales have prompted sustained state efforts to expand the definition of a nexus that permits the imposition of sales tax obligations on remote sellers, to "harmonize" state taxation, and to prompt Congress to beat states without a sales tax into submission. Those initiatives have foundered, and tax competition has survived, for the same reasons that foiled state efforts in the 1930s—state divisions, expectations of cheating, and congressional paralysis in the face of those forces. In fact, the plea for congressional intervention has produced wholly unintended results: Congress has repeatedly codified the *Quill* regime and shielded "remote" sellers from direct state tax collection.[15]

The history of business activity taxes sheds additional light on the states' inability to organize seamless tax cartels. In *Northwestern States Portland Cement Co. v. Minnesota* (1959), the Supreme Court greatly expanded the states' authority to tax business income in interstate commerce.[16] Congress quickly slapped a moratorium on the state taxation of interstate business income of firms whose foreign-state operations did not exceed minimal activities (such as solicitation and delivery). That "safe harbor" moratorium satisfied neither the states nor corporate America, and for several years, Congress earnestly pursued a solution to the vexing problem of interstate taxation. Again, those efforts came to naught. The temporary "moratorium," in effect to this day, was enacted only because the status quo ante *Portland Cement*, however unsatisfactory, provided a judicially improvised baseline. The far harder task of producing a coherent solution proved beyond Congress's capability.

In response to these difficulties, a 1967 Multistate Tax Compact (MTC) established a standing Multistate Tax Commission, composed of member states' tax administrators. The member-states endowed the Commission with regulatory authority to determine rules for the allocation and apportionment of business income among member-states and other multistate tax issues, subject to the member-states' participation and subsequent approval of the regulations. The MTC's ostensible objectives are to facilitate the proper determination of multistate taxpayers' state and local tax obligations, to promote uniformity, to facilitate taxpayer convenience and compliance, and to avoid duplicative taxation. But the compact has never achieved those coordination objectives; and in truth, it was never meant to. The MTC was formed not because Congress had failed to solve tax coordination problems but for fear that it might.[17] And the MTC's purpose was not tax coordination but rather tax harmonization—that is, the suppression of (locational) tax competition.

One way of coordinating the state taxation of interstate business income is to allocate all income, for taxation purposes, to the company's domicile state. Such an "origin rule" is unambiguous and easily administered. But it is also fiercely procompetitive, as firms will sort themselves into low-tax jurisdictions. It is therefore the rule that states love to hate, and it was precisely the traditional allocation of business income to domicile states that prompted the MTC's creation by consumer states. The rule favored by those states is the "full apportionment" of interstate business income to all states where a firm conducts operations or its products happen to wind up. Unlike an origin rule, full apportionment produces nightmarish coordination problems. Its principal advantage—from the states' perspective—is to suppress interstate tax competition for firms. A corollary principle of unitary taxation, which treats corporations and their subsidiaries as a single entity for purposes of taxation, prevents corporations from escaping taxation through clever restructuring. Moreover, it enables a state to capture a foreign corporation's income even if the corporation's subsidiary in the state earned no income or even incurred losses.

From the outset, the MTC was widely viewed as a tax cartel and as a cabal "of a group of small states trying to increase their revenues by 'feeding off' 'eastern' businesses."[18] And from the outset, the MTC pushed apportionment and unitary taxation principles to the outer constitutional limits, and occasionally beyond.[19] Again, however, these efforts have foundered on holdout problems and defection. The Commission can cajole, and it can advance its "recommendations" in cooperation with state officials by exploiting agency and monitoring problems at the state level. But it cannot truly enforce any particular market order, even on its members. Efforts to overcome those obstacles by means of congressional intervention have foundered, here as in the sales tax arena, on the states' own insistence on maintaining their tax autonomy.[20]

Implications. As suggested earlier, the modern Court has been highly deferential in policing state taxation. At one level, this is understandable. An integrated national economy puts territorial notions of jurisdiction under enormous pressure, and the distance between constitutionally derived doctrines and a viable framework for interstate taxation in all its bewildering complexity becomes ever wider.[21] Add New Deal-ish, pro-state enthusiasms to the mix, and judicial abdication becomes a well-nigh foregone conclusion. And yet, judicial surrender at this front has real costs. In the 1980s, for example, the Court took up a series of cases involving state efforts to tax corporate subsidiaries—including the subsidiaries of non-U.S. firms—under expansive notions of unitary taxation. The attempt to develop manageable constitutional rules proved futile, and the Court soon abandoned the field.[22] Unleashed state aggression produced a diplomatic crisis with America's trading partners over the states' application of unitary taxation and worldwide combined income principles to foreign corporations doing business in the United States. Those corporations and their governments complained bitterly, through diplomatic and legal channels, about the states' tactics, which they and, for the most part, the United States government believed to contravene international tax treaties. The long-running dispute was settled only well over a decade later, after much litigation and diplomatic exertions.[23]

The perennial call in hundreds of law review articles and trade publications is for congressional guidance. But although the good sense of that demand is hard to gainsay, Congress has intervened, and will intervene, only under extremely rare and limited conditions. Congress can codify a preexisting judicial baseline, as it did in the business tax "moratorium" and in repeatedly codifying the *Quill* rule. And occasionally, Congress has provided uniform tax rules in response to the demands of discrete groups of taxpayers, such as railroads, pensioners, and naturally, members of Congress.[24] Outside these confines, however, "the empirical evidence and the public choice theory cast doubt on the likelihood of Congress ever enacting legislation mandating uniformity."[25] State tax coordination will either come from the federal courts, or else not at all. Under Our Federalism, the prevailing answer is "not at all."

Tax Cartels and Compacts

No one is very fond of uncoordinated state taxation. Even so, the present regime has one redeeming feature: the last remaining barriers to extraterritorial taxation, especially including *Quill*'s nexus requirement, are in fact a vital protection for state tax competition. So long as constitutional doctrines leave taxpayers *some* escape, state tax cartels will founder on state defections and private tax arbitrage. In contrast, universal state tax authority may facilitate a near-seamless state tax cartel. The so-called Master Settlement Agreement on tobacco litigation (MSA) exemplifies that nasty logic.[26]

The Master Settlement Agreement. The MSA, signed in November 1998 by the attorneys general of forty-six states and the major U.S. tobacco manufacturers, provides for the companies' payment of over $200 billion to the states over a period of twenty-five years. (Thereafter, payments are to run in perpetuity.) In addition, the agreement established a nationwide regulatory regime for the sale and marketing of tobacco products. The MSA had its origins in liability lawsuits that many (not all) states had brought against tobacco producers, ostensibly to recoup Medicaid expenses attributable to smoking-related illnesses. The first such lawsuit was filed in 1994, at the suggestion of an antitobacco trial lawyer (and subsequently with his cooperation) by Mississippi's attorney general. By mid-1997, thirty-one states had filed similar lawsuits. Mississippi's lawsuit settled for $3.6 billion in July 1997; Florida's case settled a month later for $11.3 billion. At that stage, adverse developments—including the legislative abrogation of common-law liability defenses in some states—had already induced the tobacco companies to sue for peace. In June 1997, tobacco lawyers, plaintiffs' attorneys, and attorneys general hammered out a comprehensive agreement known as the "Resolution." A precursor to the MSA, the Resolution provided for a comprehensive financial settlement of all pending state lawsuits, projected at $368.5 billion over twenty-five years, in return for expansive protections against civil liability for the settling manufacturers. The Resolution also would have conferred authority on the federal Food and Drug Administration (FDA) to regulate nicotine as an addictive drug. The parties submitted the proposed legislation to Congress. In June 1998, however, the bill died, largely because antitobacco and public-health advocacy groups had loaded it with provisions that proved unacceptable to the tobacco industry.[27] The parties then met in secret to negotiate an agreement along the lines of the Resolution, though more moderate in scope. Total industry payments to the settling states were reduced to roughly $206 billion by 2025. (Four nonparticipating states had reached earlier agreements with the industry, totaling $40 billion, which were preserved under the MSA.) Provisions for the FDA regulation of tobacco products, which obviously would have required federal approval and legislation, were stripped, and the expansive civil liability limitations contained in the Resolution were replaced with narrower protections from state-initiated lawsuits against the industry. The MSA was released in November 1998, and all state attorneys general promptly approved it. Unlike the Resolution, the MSA was not presented to the Congress for approval.

The obvious question is why the states on their own were able to bring about a result that the United States Congress was evidently unable to achieve. Part of the answer is that the Resolution collapsed in Congress under the weight of interest group conflicts. In other words, it failed for the constitutionally envisioned reason. And so the MSA's architects moved to closed-door negotiations, where the range of interests could be restricted to state officials, tobacco interests, and trial lawyers.[28] In executing this move, the MSA parties did not merely respond to congressional indecision and interest group conflict. They also counted on those forces. Congress, they calculated, had failed to approve a grand bargain; but it would not affirmatively prohibit it, either. In much larger part, though, the answer has to do with the MSA's extraterritorial, exploitative dynamics.

Extraterritorial effects are endemic to products liability proceedings. The defendant-firms in the tobacco cases had no way of internalizing the cost of settlement (none of the state cases reached a verdict) to any plaintiff-state. At the same time, they had every incentive to pursue a settlement that would impose the cost on consumers, rather than shareholders and workers. The firms proffered just such a settlement to the states and the plaintiffs bar, in exchange for a substantial chunk of the profits. (More on the mechanics anon.) When the contours of that lucrative bargain became clear and state support had reached critical mass, extraterritoriality dynamics trumped the holdout and defection problems that ordinarily thwart state cartels. Consumers in each state would pay the tobacco tort tax regardless of whether or not their state joined the MSA. At the same time, the MSA put money on the table and, much like a federal grant-in-aid program, promised to distribute it to participating states in accordance with an agreed-upon formula. A nonparticipating state would simply leave "its" share of the MSA proceeds available for distribution to participating states. Renegade states protested, but they had no effective way of resisting the settlement dynamics.[29]

A Near-Perfect Cartel. The MSA is not a metaphorical cartel in the sense that all government regulation "cartelizes" markets by eliminating the supply of the prohibited conduct. It is an actual, naked cartel—a collusive agreement to limit output and raise prices and to share the monopoly profits among the producers, states, and the trial bar.[30]

The MSA accomplishes this result through a set of fiendishly clever provisions. For the four "Majors" who at the time supplied close to 99 percent of the U.S. cigarette market, the MSA payment obligations implied a cost of some 35 cents per pack. Continued price competition would have meant that the payments would come substantially off the producers' hide—the intended result of liability litigation, one would think, but not one that was likely to procure the industry's consent or, for that matter, to ensure its ability to pay. The MSA forestalled that result by ensuring that *consumers* would pay virtually all of the costs, and more, associated with the MSA (short of a tipping point at which price elasticities reduce tobacco consumption).[31] First, the MSA allocated the manufacturers' share of the payments in proportion to current and future market share—not, as one would expect in a liability lawsuit, in proportion to the producers' contributions to the alleged harms. A higher market share means higher payments, rendering price competition pointless. Second, the MSA provided the majors with protection against competition by smaller producers and new market entrants. Smaller manufacturers were permitted to join the MSA without incurring proportionate payment obligations, provided that they agreed to stabilize their sales at pre-MSA levels. To induce acceptance of that bargain and to suppress new market entrants (who, by definition, have caused none of the damages that the MSA is supposed to redress), an MSA "model statute," to be enacted by all member-states, requires nonparticipating manufacturers to make payments, equivalent to roughly 150 percent of the "damage" payments they would incur under the MSA, into an escrow account, supposedly in anticipation of future costs and liabilities.

The MSA enforces this order through a regime of interstate transfer payments. If the MSA causes the participating manufacturers to suffer sales losses exceeding 2 percent of their aggregate market share, they may reduce their base payments to the states by 3 percent for each percent market share loss above that level. In other words, a 10 percent decline in aggregate market share entitles the participating manufacturers to a 24 percent reduction in (adjusted) base payments to the states. The entire reduction is imposed on states that have failed to enact a model statute that "fully and effectively neutralizes" the participating manufacturers' cost disadvantages attributable to the MSA. Such states may lose their entire allocable share. These incentives guaranteed prompt and universal state enactment of the MSA model statute. Over the years, most states have also enacted various laws, urged by the National Association of Attorneys General (which administers the MSA), to protect the MSA's intricate design against evasion by renegade manufacturers and cost-conscious consumers.[32]

The MSA has not quite lived up to signatories' hopes. Despite all precautions, the Majors have lost over 10 percent of market share, in turn prompting reductions of the originally envisioned payments. Even so, the MSA closely approximates the ideal of a self-enforcing, surplus-maximizing state cartel. Perfect extraterritoriality produced state unanimity: ex ante, no state could hold out; ex post, none can defect. And the MSA's proceeds are pure surplus. No consumer has seen a nickel of the supposed "damages" or obtained any other relief, yet all must pay a steep excise tax that no legislator, federal or state, has ever voted on. The proceeds of the bargain have accrued to an unholy alliance of trial lawyers, "Big Tobacco," and the states.

Constitutional Limitations?. The Constitution's Compact Clause (Art. I, § 10, Cl. 3) provides that "no state shall, without the Consent of the Congress . . . enter into any Agreement or Compact with another State, or with a foreign Power." Plainly, the MSA is a compact among the states; and plainly, Congress did not consent to the MSA. A more direct constitutional violation is difficult to envision. The violation, moreover, is conjoined with an appalling policy innovation—that of a publicly protected monopoly, enjoyed by the nastiest of industries, that operates without any restriction on or supervision of its pricing or profits. On these accounts, the MSA has been called "the constitutional crime of the century."[33] Federal courts, however, have uniformly rejected Compact Clause, antitrust, and other challenges to the MSA; and the Supreme Court has repeatedly and, it is fair to say, conclusively rejected petitions for certiorari.[34] However dismaying, the judiciary's record of indifference makes sense in the context of the New Deal Constitution's anticompetitive, exploitative logic. The historical trajectory of the Compact Clause illustrates the point.[35]

The Compact Clause is among the qualified prohibitions of Article 1, § 10, identified in chapter 2 as applications of the Madisonian "Negative" over state laws. Unlike ordinary state laws, which go into effect and remain in effect until and unless Congress preempts or the courts enjoin them, state laws that are subject to the "Negative" require affirmative congressional consent to become operative. The Constitution reserves this adverse treatment for laws that are highly likely to imperil sister-states and, hence, the harmony of the Union, such as import duties, tonnage duties, and for good measure, acts of war.

At first impression, it may seem curious that the Constitution should treat state *compacts* on a par with overtly hostile state acts. Unlike those acts, compacts promise gains that might fail to materialize under alternative modes of resolving interstate disputes (litigation or federal regulation). Against that cheerful prospect, however, stand two considerations. First, compacts may serve as a means of coordination *or cartelization*. States may collude to exploit other states, and any such aggression would ipso facto threaten the harmony of the union.[36] Second, Coasean enthusiasm should be tempered in this setting by a recognition that states are not principals but agents. The agents are hard to monitor even when acting alone, within the sphere of their respective jurisdictions. When their responsibilities are commingled or transferred to a third party, the monitoring costs increase exponentially.[37] Thus, the Constitution strikes a balance between the expected risks and benefits of state compacts. The congressional consent requirement imposes the burden of procuring legislative majorities in both houses on the proponents of a compact, thereby reducing the costs that states incur in monitoring and countermanding bargains that might adversely affect them and their citizens while still allowing unobjectionable bargains to go forward.

Throughout the nineteenth century, the Supreme Court understood the constitutional arrangement and its purpose. Foremost, it understood the Compact Clause, not as an act of nationalist unkindness, but as a horizontal protection *for the states*. Its point, Chief Justice Taney wrote in 1854, is "to prevent any compact or agreement between any two States, which might affect injuriously the interest of the others."[38] On account of that danger, Taney had written earlier in *Holmes v. Jennison* (1840), the constitutional injunction "prohibit[s] every agreement, written or verbal, formal or informal, positive or implied, by the mutual understanding of the parties."[39] The Court continued to adhere to this uncompromising position with respect to state agreements involving foreign powers (as in *Holmes*).[40] However, an understandable desire to facilitate useful cooperative state ventures gradually prompted a more limited reading of the "domestic" Compact Clause.

A milestone in that development was *Virginia v. Tennessee* (1893), involving a border dispute between the two states. "Looking at the object of the constitutional provision" rather than its text, Justice Field's opinion pronounced that the clause requires congressional consent only for state agreements "directed to the formation of any combination tending to the increase of political power in the states, which may encroach upon or interfere with the just supremacy of the United States," as distinct from agreements "to which the United States can have no possible objection or have any interest in interfering with."[41] Field's interpretation was committed to dual federalism: to discourage a Compact Clause interpretation that might prompt needless federal-state entanglement, Field effectively imported the basic distinction between enumerated (commerce) powers and police powers into the Compact Clause. The approach is fraught with problems—not least, because *joint* state exercises of the police power are unlikely to be purely internal to each state.[42] Even so, *Virginia v. Tennessee* need not have wrought much damage; its misleading passages on the scope of the Compact Clause were plainly dicta. (A later part of the opinion held that Congress had in fact approved the state agreement at issue.) Progressive scholars, however, soon mobilized Field's ill-advised musings for cooperative ends. An influential 1925 law review article by Felix Frankfurter and James M. Landis celebrated "the imaginative adaptation of the compact idea" to increased regionalism and "the overwhelming difficulties confronting modern society."[43] Although Frankfurter and Landis did not argue for dispensing with the congressional consent requirement, they furnished the intellectual apparatus—and the soothing rhetoric of cooperation, flexibility, and localism—that later generations of scholars and judges would put to that purpose. The Supreme Court increasingly encouraged states to utilize compacts as a means of resolving boundary disputes, water rights questions, and pollution problems. By 1959, the justices celebrated compacts as a manifestation of "imagination and resourcefulness in devising fruitful interstate relationships," "extraconstitutional forms of legal invention," and the "interplay of living forces of government to meet the evolving needs of a complex society."[44]

Two decades later, cooperative federalism effusions gave way to complete incomprehension. In *U.S. Steel Corp. v. Multistate Tax Commission* (1978), the Court sustained the multistate tax compact described earlier. Writing for a majority of seven justices, Justice Powell roundly rejected the contention that the MTC violated the Compact Clause because Congress had failed to consent to the agreement.[45] The clause, the Court said, covers only state agreements that may affect federal supremacy, and the MTC supposedly posed no such danger.

The *MTC* majority placed great weight on *Virginia v. Tennessee* and its suggestion that the clause covers only compacts that "may encroach upon or interfere with the just supremacy of the United States." The Court then deployed that supposed "rule" to cast aside the concerns over state collusion that had played such a prominent role in the nineteenth-century cases. It acknowledged that the MTC—unlike the once-and-done border demarcation between contiguous states in *Virginia v. Tennessee*—established an ongoing regulatory regime of manifest interest to sister-states. However, the majority continued, states are similarly affected by any number of policies enacted by individual sister states. That is so. Individual state policies, however, are not constitutionally disfavored. State compacts are. As Justice White's dissent pointed out, "The [Compact] Clause must mean that some actions which would be permissible for individual States to undertake are not permissible for a group of States to *agree* to undertake."[46]

The *MTC* majority did not bother to respond. Instead, having effectively excluded horizontal federalism concerns from constitutional consideration, it proceeded to minimize the MTC's effects on federal supremacy. "The pertinent inquiry," it observed in professed agreement with *Virginia v. Tennessee*, is one of "potential, rather than actual, impact upon federal supremacy."[47] That test would allow play for the Compact Clause by requiring congressional consent even if no *affirmative* violation can be shown. It is not at all clear, however, that the *MTC* Court actually applied that test. Elsewhere, it declared that "*on its face the Multistate Tax Compact contains no provisions* that would enhance the political power of the member States in a way that encroaches upon the supremacy of the United States." In that formulation, the test is not a "potential impact" rule but an *actual* conflict between compact language and a federal rule.[48] *No* state compact requires congressional approval unless it violates ordinary principles of conflict preemption or else, declares an invasion of federal supremacy in haec verba. The Compact Clause, it appears, is empty.

On a charitable reading, the *MTC* Court's loose language may have been prompted by a desire to uphold what, in the end, seemed a harmless state agreement. Any state could freely enter and exit the compact; and as noted earlier, the MTC lacked the authority and the means to impose its rules even on member-states. In contrast, a binding agreement that establishes a state cartel in effect as well as aspiration might, on this reading, be distinguishable from the MTC and require congressional consent.[49] However, the judiciary's cavalier treatment of the MSA renders that interpretation untenable.

Unlike the MTC, the MSA satisfies all the "classic" attributes of a state compact. By its terms, it is a binding agreement among states, and it establishes a permanent administrative body for its ongoing interpretation and enforcement.[50] Recall, moreover, that the MSA imposed a national tax and regulatory regime without the vote of a single legislator, state or federal. Even many of the state attorneys general who signed the agreement had no choice; opting out would have meant a loss of MSA revenues, while the state's citizens would still pay the MSA tax. State legislatures faced the same unappealing choice in enacting an MSA-commandeered "model statute." In short, ex ante no state could freely withhold its consent once the contours of the bargain had taken shape. Ex post, no state can exit the agreement without severe detriment to itself.[51] And in its substantive provisions, the MSA runs up hard against important, well-recognized federal statutes and concerns, starting with antitrust law. An agreement of that description should require congressional consent even under the crabbed "encroachment" theory of *MTC* unless that theory means what it seems to suggest: *no* state agreement will violate the Compact Clause unless it is already preempted or otherwise unlawful.[52]

By the same token, the MSA practically screams for a recognition of the horizontal federalism purposes of the Compact Clause. Even under the modern Court's latitudinarian jurisprudence, one has to assume that a national excise tax would be unconstitutional if a single state sought to impose it. (Minnesota may not tax the sale of a Virginia-produced cigarette in Maryland.)[53] The fact that the states *conspired* to impose that tax renders the measure more suspect, not less so—if the Compact Clause still counts for something, that is. Moreover, the MSA is a textbook example of a "naked" cartel to restrict output and raise prices, in flagrant violation of the federal Sherman Act. Its legality thus hangs on its alleged antitrust immunity under *Parker*'s state action doctrine. *Parker*, however, dealt with the unilateral state exploitation of market power by a single state.[54] That federalism-based exemption, whatever its warrant and appropriate scope, cannot possibly immunize multistate agreements to *create* market power. The Compact Clause is not necessary to arrive at this conclusion. But it supports the federalism reasoning at a constitutional level, and it supplies the constitutionally mandated remedy: congressional consent.[55]

The MSA prompted a number of legal scholars to call for a rehabilitation of the Compact Clause.[56] If the Supreme Court has proven deaf to their suggestions and to expertly litigated, well-supported Compact Clause challenges, that may be because the MSA so perfectly embodies Our Federalism's logic: "cooperative" in form, maximally exploitative in substance. For the most part, the logic can be accommodated at the level of doctrine and constitutional interpretation—for example, a constricted dormant Commerce Clause. In contrast, when the logic runs up against an unequivocal constitutional provision, the judiciary confronts an awkward choice. It can enforce the clause at issue, but only at the price of a sharp discontinuity with the remainder of its federalism doctrine. Or it can read the clause out of the Constitution. That has been the modern Court's preferred strategy. Among its victims is the Compact Clause.

Horizontal Empowerment Federalism:
The Litigation Explosion

A half-century ago, American liability rules still bore a firm resemblance to those of other common-law countries. That is no longer so. American civil liability rules are notoriously more expansive and litigation (as opposed to ex ante regulation) plays a much larger role than in any other country. Scholars have advanced any number of explanations—among them, a peculiarly American culture of "adversarial legalism," ideological confusions, efficient adaptation to industrialization and economic integration, and idiosyncrasies of American legal practice, such as contingency fees and class action rules.[57] A good case can be made, however, that the "tort crisis" or "liability explosion" is in large measure a *public law* phenomenon and a horizontal federalism problem.[58] That case rests on *Erie* and its extensions.

Erie *Extended. Erie* choked off defendants' escape into federal general common law. At some level, it reflected a Brandeisian commitment to state experimentation "without risk to the rest of the country." It entitled a plaintiff only to *a* state law—but not necessarily to his own state's law, in cases where another state might have an equally plausible claim to governing the transaction, and certainly not to the most favorable state law. As noted in chapter 10, however, those inhibitions soon gave way to a more thorough-going adaptation of *Erie*'s logic. One critical move was a revision of choice of law doctrines; the other, an expansion of personal jurisdiction.

The central choice of law case is *Klaxon Co. v. Stentor Electric Manufacturing Co.* (1941), which extended *Erie*'s holding—federal courts will in diversity cases follow state law—to state courts' choice of law determinations, no matter how biased. At some variance with *Erie*'s ostensible concerns over forum shopping but consistent with its general tenor, federal courts soon focused, not on curbing that tendency, but rather on maximizing its potential. To that end, two constitutional constraints had to give way: territorial doctrines, embodied primarily in the Due Process Clause, that restricted plaintiffs' ability to reach out-of-state defendants; and the constitutional rule that states must give "Full Faith and Credit" to sister-states' law.

The central case on jurisdiction is *International Shoe* (1945)—not a liability case but a tax case, where the Supreme Court held that state personal jurisdiction attaches to any defendant with "minimum contacts" to that state unless the suit offends "traditional notions of fair play and substantial justice."⁵⁹ The question was whether the International Shoe Company, a Missouri corporation operating in Washington (among other states), could be compelled to contribute to Washington's unemployment insurance fund for its employees in that state. The obvious answer was yes, and that result would have obtained even under the old territorial rules. *International Shoe* owes its landmark status to the "minimum contacts" language, which soon became the operative judicial test for both Due Process and Full Faith and Credit purposes.

A minimum-contacts rule may be a sensible response to the realities of an integrated economy. It will hardly do to let economic actors roam in each state's jurisdiction while remaining immune from all but their respective home-state rules on account of some anachronistic legalism. However, a legal regime that exposes private actors to suit and liability in any number of jurisdictions—with no ready way of avoiding hostile jurisdictions, and with no recourse to federal general common law—should by all rights be especially attuned to the heightened risks of opportunistic plaintiff behavior and judicial home-state bias. The Constitution, by instructing each state to give "Full Faith and Credit" to sister-states' "public Acts, Records, and judicial Proceedings," provides a ready handle, and very arguably a mandate, to curb what Justice Robert H. Jackson called "the disintegrating influence of provincialism."⁶⁰ The post-New Deal judiciary, however, took just the opposite tack and, with respect to public Acts, effectively read the Full Faith and Credit Clause out of the Constitution. Constitutionally unshackled, state choice-of-law doctrines soon assumed a pronounced homebound bias.⁶¹

That bias received a potent justification in the conflicts-of-law scholarship of the post-*Erie* decades, which thoroughly repudiated the traditional, territorial learning. Brainerd Currie, the Robespierre of that "Conflicts Revolution," criticized the old learning as utterly incoherent—among other reasons, because it often compelled state courts to prefer another state's law to their own. His approach, called "interest analysis," makes the choice of law hang on the intensity of the interests that competing *states*—not parties—have in seeing their own law applied in any given case. From that vantage, conflicts cases typically require a balancing of competing state interests; and that, Currie insisted in good positivistic fashion, is an inherently legislative task, not a judicial or jurisprudential one. In all but the most extreme cases, the forum state should simply apply its own law. This, Currie sought to demonstrate, is what courts had actually done all along under the cloak of lex loci rules (and to the extent that they had failed to do so, the cases had been wrongly decided).⁶² Post-*Erie*, virtually all state courts abandoned lex loci rules and adopted Currie's approach or some equally convoluted way of saying that the will and the law of the local forum shall prevail. The beatification of that view occurred in 1971, in the ALI's *Restatement (Second) of Conflict of Laws.*[63]

Currie conceded that the Full Faith and Credit Clause should still bar particularly far-fetched applications of home-state law—those where the forum's "interests" are wholly elusive. That category, though, comprises a small fraction of cases, and in 1981, in *Allstate Insurance Co. v. Hague*, the Supreme Court effectively reduced it to a null set. The case arose over a deadly automobile accident in Wisconsin, among Wisconsin citizens. The victim had obtained insurance policies for three vehicles, issued in Wisconsin, each covering him for loss incurred from accidents with uninsured motorists but limiting recovery to $15,000. Because Wisconsin law prohibited the "stacking" of such policies (for a total recovery of $45,000), the decedent's widow, having moved to Minnesota, sued under that state's law, which permitted stacking. The Minnesota Supreme Court sustained that choice of law, and the Supreme Court affirmed. Minnesota's choice of law, Justice Brennan's plurality opinion declared, was constitutional because Mr. Hague, though a resident of Wisconsin, had been "a member of Minnesota's work force" and regularly commuted there (though not in connection with the accident); because "Allstate was at all times present and doing business in Minnesota" and should therefore not be surprised to have occurrences in some other corner of the planet adjudicated in Minnesota and under Minnesota law; and because the claimant had moved to Minnesota for reasons unrelated to the suit and the advantages of Minnesota law.[64] None of these factors had anything to do with the dispute, but no matter.

Another two decades later, in *Franchise Tax Board v. Hyatt* (2003), a unanimous Supreme Court explicitly embraced *Allstate*'s implied "whatever" holding and declared the Full Faith and Credit Clause a nullity with respect to public acts. In a case brought by a Nevada citizen, in Nevada courts and under Nevada law, against California government officials—a context where the federalism implications of choice-of-law questions are particularly vivid—the Court determined that Nevada courts need not respect the defendant-officials' immunity under California law. Consummating a long-established trend, the *Hyatt* Court conclusively rejected California's position that the Full Faith and Credit Clause had to retain some independent meaning. "We decline," Justice O'Connor wrote, "to embark on the constitutional course of balancing coordinate States' competing sovereign interests to resolve conflicts of laws under the Full Faith and Credit Clause."[65]

Technically speaking, the Full Faith and Credit Clause still bars the application of state law to parties with no relation to the jurisdiction. And the Due Process Clause bars punitive damages—but not other types of relief—that are based on an intent to punish a defendant's conduct in other jurisdictions (where that conduct may have been lawful).[66] Shadowboxing at the absolute outer margins, however, barely disguises the general pattern. Prominent scholars—William Baxter, John Hart Ely, and Douglas Laycock among them—have argued that a systematic bias for home-state law sits poorly with a constitutional clause that demands *full* faith and credit to sister states' public acts.[67] But the Supreme Court has declined to follow that path. *Erie*'s and *Klaxon*'s irreducible baseline, the Court has said, is that forum shopping privileges are "reserved for plaintiffs."[68] That teaching is nowhere to be found in the Constitution, but it is as firmly entrenched as anything in the document.

No Dealing With Erie. If *Erie* entrenches a preference of state over federal general common law, its extensions entrench the preferences of the most proregulatory, protax state. *Klaxon, International Shoe,* and closely related rules governing diversity and removal jurisdiction encourage plaintiffs to sort themselves into the plaintiff-friendliest jurisdiction. Unless defendants have some means of avoiding that jurisdiction or price their products in accordance with the local litigation risk, its rules will dominate. Due to the logic of concentrated benefits and dispersed costs, no other state will resist the imposition. Rather, states will "compete" by becoming yet more hospitable to plaintiffs.[69] Ample evidence illustrates this dynamic. *International Shoe*, for example, prompted the enactment of general purpose "long-arm" statutes that extend state jurisdiction to the outer limits of the Constitution, which within two decades spread to virtually all states.[70] Similarly, the conflicts revolution and the demise of constitutional doctrines that restrained free-form choice of law facilitated the evisceration of "inefficient," defendant-protective doctrines and the tort-ification of contract law.[71]

Erie's exploitative tendencies have hardly gone unnoticed. Celebrated scholars have advanced proposals for the federal coordination of choice of law while leaving substantive tort and contract to the states and *Erie* itself unchallenged.[72] What unites this Lost Cause Hall of Fame is the hope in an institutional capacity that Congress simply does not possess. Congress has never heeded the call for horizontal ordering rules, and it never will. At most, Congress can manipulate vertical, federal-state forum rules; legislate targeted prohibitions; or substitute uniform, substantive federal law for state law by means of preemption. The first two strategies are exceedingly rare.[73] The third is a losing game of chicken. The *Erie* regime affirmatively invites state "experimentation" and then dares Congress to catch up with the inventions of the most entrepreneurial, exploitative state. The notion that Congress possesses that capacity, and that the federal system was ever supposed to work in that fashion, is wishful thinking—or else, a cynical manipulation of "federalism" nostrums for factional ends.[74]

Any federal system has to live with tax and regulatory spillovers. A federal system can, however, control *excessive* spillovers, especially including deliberate exploitation—provided it has the appropriate legal framework. The Constitution's horizontal federalism rules, coupled with its grants of federal jurisdiction, supply that framework. That solution, however, presupposes an appreciation of the constitutional structure and of the need for its common-law elaboration, as well as a judiciary cognizant of its institutional responsibilities within the federal system. Our Federalism embodies the opposite regime: a legal framework that entrenches exploitation, and a judiciary that mistakes its complicity in that scheme for deference.[75] The entire structure of horizontal federalism has been driven into preemption law and, more narrowly still, the doctrine of implied preemption. Superficially, appeals to "the intent of Congress" allow the justices to harmonize the actual Constitution's structural imperatives with the New Deal Constitution's state-friendly precepts and its posture of judicial deference. But the attempt to tackle the centrifugal tendencies of American federalism with the repertoire of the New Deal Constitution would be problematic even if the justices understood the nature of the enterprise. The following chapter shows that they do not.

CHAPTER FOURTEEN

The Supreme Court's Federalism

Introduction

Over the past generation, judicial federalism has taken some seemingly curious turns. Beginning in the late 1980s and with increasing determination thereafter, the Rehnquist Court embarked on a "federalism revolution" that was widely viewed as a fundamental challenge to the New Deal Constitution. Liberal scholars and advocates vehemently denounced the Court's supposed resurrection of a pre–New Deal "Constitution in Exile" or even of an "antebellum" jurisprudence, while some conservatives placed high, perhaps equally fanciful hopes in the Court's agenda.[1] The debate reached a crescendo circa 2000, when the Court's conservative "Federalist Five" prevailed in a string of cases over enumerated powers, state sovereign immunity, and statutory federalism questions.

The Rehnquist Court's federalism fizzled soon thereafter, even before the end of the Natural Court. Obituaries, however, proved premature as federalism reemerged as a major theme of judicial, scholarly, and public debate in a different doctrinal arena, with an inverted political valence. The new judicial federalism's focus is not vertical but horizontal federalism; not statutory entitlement litigation but business regulation, and federal preemption in particular. In that arena, the pro-state ramparts have come to be occupied, not by conservatives (who are said to trim their pro-state sails in deference to probusiness commitments), but by progressives.

Journalists as well as scholars (especially those of an "attitudinal" persuasion) have a ready explanation: nobody is a "principled" federalist, and the justices simply vote their political preferences.[2] But that notion is too crude to be right; and for the most part, it is actually wrong. The dominant theme of judicial federalism's revolution, denouement, and political inversion is continuity with the New Deal Constitution. Conservatives have failed to escape its gravitational pull; liberals have sought to extend it.

The hallmark of the Rehnquist Court's federalism was the repudiation of Wechsler's "process federalism"—that is, the notion that the states' protection should be left to the political process, not the judiciary. In rejecting that tenet of the New Deal Constitution, however, conservative justices *embraced* the New Deal's formulation of the federalism question as vertical balance. Failing to grasp that the New Deal's point was not to oppress states but to suppress competition among them, they contrived to help the "states as states." That agenda could never be more than a curlicue on a New Deal Constitution that already protects state surplus by numerous means. A meaningful, procompetitive challenge to the New Deal Constitution was never within the Rehnquist Court's contemplation. Indeed, when a more competitive constitutional federalism appeared on the horizon, the Court balked and steered in the opposite direction.

The most conspicuous manifestation of this tendency is the Court's consistent failure to connect its balance federalism to broader questions of constitutional rights and constitutional structure. A federalist *rights* jurisprudence would give states greater latitude in regulating their own citizens' mores. A federalist *structure* jurisprudence would block state attempts to exploit interstate commerce and each others' citizens. The rights move would primarily cover "moral" or "social" questions; it would have the justices do *less* by way of superintending state policy choices in those domains. The structure move would extend over regulatory and economic matters; it would have the justices to do *more* by way of controlling exploitative state conduct. Both these complementary moves are, or would be, profoundly procompetitive—and both have been rejected by the Supreme Court. Although the rights move had three votes on the Rehnquist-Roberts Court, it has foundered on the majority's adherence to an expansive consociational rights jurisprudence. The structure move may never have had a single vote. In federalism's regulatory and horizontal domains, the prevailing trend has been toward a federalism of state empowerment and exploitation. Conservative justices have resisted this trend only intermittently and half-heartedly. Unable to escape the New Deal Constitution, they can no longer explain, even to themselves, why the progressives' program should *not* carry the day.

This chapter begins with a brief summary of the Rehnquist Court's federalism and then turns to its limitations. In the rights and fiscal federalism domains, the Court's self-imposed limitations flow from an unwillingness to surrender consociational rights. In the regulatory and horizontal domains, they reflect the justices' inability to conceive of a federalism beyond balance, closely coupled with judicial "deference" nostrums that likewise spring from the New Deal Constitution.

The Rehnquist Court's Federalism

The Rehnquist Court's federalism, as understood by scholars and by the Court itself, consists principally of "vertical" cases and doctrines. It encompasses a handful of enumerated powers cases and a long stream of cases dealing with the powers of Congress vis-à-vis "states as states."

Enumerated Powers. The Rehnquist Court's enumerated powers foray began with the 1995 decision in *United States v. Lopez*, where the Court held—for the first time since 1936—that a federal statute (the Gun Free School Zones Act, which criminalized the possession of guns on school grounds) exceeded the powers of Congress under the Commerce Clause. Although Chief Justice Rehnquist's opinion for the majority professed to start with "first principles," the opinion actually proceeded more modestly by reordering extant precedents in a common-lawyerly fashion, without overruling any of those cases. The crux of the matter is the "aggregation" principle of *Wickard v. Filburn*—that is, the notion that congressional power extends not only to interstate commerce but also to local activities and events that in the aggregate "affect" that commerce. *Lopez* explicitly affirmed that principle.[3] However, the Court added that the aggregated activity must itself be of an "economic" nature and, moreover, linked to interstate commerce in some more-than-speculative way. The federal criminalization of gun possession on school grounds, the *Lopez* majority declared, exceeded those bounds.

The true holding of *Lopez* may be more limited, but also more direct, than its somewhat contrived conceptual framework suggests. The Constitution, the majority said, supposes *some* distinction between national and local affairs. On the theories proffered in defense of the Gun Free School Zones Act, though, it would be impossible to discern any limit to the commerce power. Hence, the statute had to fall. That line of reasoning also supported the Court's decision and opinion in *United States v. Morrison* (2000), which invalidated a provision contained in the federal Violence

Against Women Act that created a federal cause of action for victims of violence "motivated by gender."[4]

After those twin decisions the Court temporized and eventually, in *Gonzales v. Raich* (2003), took back much of what it seemed to have promised. *Raich* dealt with a California statute that permitted the cultivation and use of marijuana for noncommercial medicinal purposes under certain limiting conditions. The Federal Controlled Substances Act (CSA) classifies marijuana as a Schedule I substance, criminalizing its possession and use under all circumstances. The Supreme Court sustained those provisions as part of a comprehensive statutory scheme that regulates interstate commerce.[5]

The cases just summarized principally address the Article I powers of Congress. Fourteenth Amendment legislation—that is, the power of Congress to enforce the provisions of the Amendment, under its § 5, "by appropriate legislation"—is subject to two different enumerated powers constraints. One is the so-called "state action doctrine": federal law must be directed toward public rather than purely private conduct. The second limitation is a means-ends test: § 5 legislation must be "congruent and proportionate" to a demonstrable constitutional violation.[6]

Over time, the congruence and proportionality test attracted growing criticism. Some critics have argued that the standard is mismatched with the constitutional rule (that is, the distinction between rights enforcement and rights creation). Others have noted that the standard is highly manipulable; necessitates a judicial parsing of the legislative record and evidence more appropriate to an "arbitrary and capricious" review of administrative action; and opens up the awkward prospect that the constitutionally permissible scope of federal legislation, including long-existing legislation, may wax and wane over time—perhaps with objective conditions and changing state law but more likely with shifting Supreme Court majorities.[7] On the most explosive question, the continued constitutionality of the "preclearance" provision of § 5 of the Voting Rights Act, the justices punted and, instead of examining the provision under the congruence test, adopted a strained statutory construction that allows covered local jurisdictions readier means of "bailing out" of § 5.[8]

Scholars agree that the Supreme Court's enumerated powers decisions have not amounted to any serious challenge to the powers of Congress. Even so, the enumerated powers question refuses to go away, and legislative innovations—for a prominent example, an individual mandate to purchase health insurance, contained in the 2010 health-care reforms—continue to prompt agitation and litigation over the scope of congressional authority. Chapter 15 will revisit the question.

Federal-State Relations. Cases dealing with the relation between the political branches of the national government and the "states as states" were the principal venue of the Rehnquist Court's federalism, both in sheer number and in terms of practical impact. They have also been the central arena for the sustained debate over "process federalism." Wechsler's position celebrated a final hurrah in *Garcia v. San Antonio Metropolitan Transit Authority* (1985), which sustained—in a departure from then-recent precedent—the application of the Federal Labor Relations Act to state and local employees. *Garcia* explicitly reaffirmed process federalism and, moreover, renounced the notion of "traditional" state authority as a judicially protected Tenth Amendment enclave as "unsound in principle and unworkable in practice."[9] However, the close, 5–4 *Garcia* decision was in tension with a general pro-state jurisprudence even at the time. Soon, the conservative majority found pathways around *Garcia* without ever formally overruling it.[10]

The broadest, most potent of the Rehnquist Court's vertical federalism doctrines is the so-called "clear statement" rule. It holds that Congress must not be presumed to alter the federal-state balance lightly; hence, the Court will require a clear statement that Congress in fact intended that result. In its most aggressive formulation, the clear statement requirement is not simply a canon of statutory interpretation but a *constitutional* rule. The statement must appear in the text of the statute; it cannot be inferred from the statute or lifted from legislative history. Moreover, it must be "unmistakably clear."[11]

The clear statement rule originated in cases dealing with federal spending statutes and, in particular, statutes that condition the receipt of federal funds on a surrender of state sovereign immunity. Soon, however, it came to cover any statute that, to the justices' minds, threatened the "usual" federal balance. Thus, federal courts will not enforce *any* funding condition at the behest of a private litigant unless both the condition and the private litigant's entitlement are made unmistakably clear in the language of the statute. The clear statement rule also governs federal entitlement statutes that apply to state and local governments as well as private actors, such as the Fair Labor Standards Act and the Age Discrimination in Employment Act.[12]

Three additional lines of decisions dovetail (and partially overlap) with the clear statement rule. In one increasingly restrictive line of cases, the Rehnquist Court cut back on the rights of private litigants to enforce statutory requirements, regardless of whether those entitlement claims are raised under a federal spending statute, a regulation pursuant to such a statute, or § 1983.[13] A second, very controversial line of cases expanded the states' sovereign immunity, both against direct federal impositions and under federal conditional spending programs. Beginning with a pathbreaking decision in *Seminole Tribe of Florida v. Florida* (1996), the Supreme Court held (very roughly) that Congress may not abrogate sovereign immunity—that is, expose states to lawsuits for damage remedies—under statutes enacted pursuant to its Article I powers.[14] Congress *may* still abrogate sovereign immunity under the Fourteenth Amendment, but only so long as that remedy is congruent and proportionate to an underlying constitutional offense and, moreover (and again), unmistakably stated in the statutory language.[15]

The third line of cases, consisting of a mere two decisions, holds that the federal government may not "commandeer" state officials to administer federal law. Commandeering, in the Court's parlance, means the unilateral federal imposition of affirmative obligations, as opposed to both a federal prohibition (that is called "preemption") and a state's voluntary assumption of affirmative obligations in exchange for some benefit (typically, federal funding). *New York v. United States* (1992) forbade Congress from commandeering state legislators; *Printz v. United States* (1997) extended that prohibition to the commandeering of state executive officers.[16] *Printz* met with controversy and hostility out of all proportion to its near-inconsequential holding, the invalidation of a federal statute requiring state enforcement officers to administer temporary federal gun registration requirements. The reason, chapter 15 will show, is that *Printz* rediscovered important pieces of a competitive federal architecture, albeit in a truncated form. The salient fact for present purposes is that no Supreme Court case to date has followed the holding or the reasoning of *Printz*.

Federalism's Limits: Balance and Rights

As the Rehnquist Court drew to a close, its judicial federalism doctrines frayed. The enumerated powers holding in *Raich* and the once-and-done-with fate of *Printz* are emblematic of an across-the-board failure to extend, and often an outright retreat on, the reach of sovereign immunity, § 1983, and "congruence and proportionality."[17] Why did the Rehnquist Court's signature project and hoped-for legacy end on a whimper?

The prevailing answer is that the Court encountered insurmountable obstacles—the enumerated powers doctrine according to *Wickard*; the spending power; and the expectation that a Congress bit too often would eventually bite back. Confronted with those obstacles, one or another member of the conservative majority blinked. The Rehnquist Court took on the federalism front what it thought Congress would give it—which, at the end of the day, wasn't all that much.[18] The account is plausible. Foremost, virtually all of the Court's judicial federalism doctrines are "second look" doctrines: Congress can always legislate around them. Commerce Clause limitations can be overcome by inserting a jurisdictional predicate in a statute, or by enacting a "local" rule as part of a larger statutory scheme that regulate commerce among the states.[19] More obviously still, vertical federalism doctrines do not cabin the enumerated powers of the Congress, only the ways in which Congress may exercise those powers. The clear statement rule has considerable bite, but Congress remains free to overrule the Court's restrictive decisions. And even with respect to seemingly categorical federalism rules (such as the anticommandeering rule and the injunction against unilateral federal abrogations of sovereign immunity pursuant to Article I), Congress can remedy constitutional disabilities by means of spending legislation.

The difficulty with the "take what they give us" story is that it renders the Rehnquist Court's federalism perplexing ab ovo.[20] Surely, the enumerated powers and spending power obstacles should have occurred to the justices at the outset. And occur they did: *Lopez*, the first enumerated powers case, went out of its way to reaffirm *Wickard*. Or consider the spending power: in *South Dakota v. Dole* (1987), while sustaining the imposition of a federal minimum drinking age as a condition of receiving federal highway funds, the justices hinted that federal grant conditions might be unconstitutional if they lacked any nexus "to the federal interest in particular national projects or programs," suggesting that a particularly egregious mismatch between miniscule funding and substantial impositions might render a statute constitutionally suspect.[21] However, the Court never pursued this line of thought, leaving Congress free to spend its way around any judicial federalism barriers. What, then, is the point of imposing them in the first place? Beyond spooking the New Deal Constitution's partisans, it is hard to see what the "Federalist Five" could or did hope to accomplish.

A better explanation of judicial federalism's rise and expiation is that the justices connected very different ideas and objectives with the notion of federalism.[22] They agreed that federalism had to mean "balance" and "power to the states," and they agreed on renouncing the Wechslerian position. That surface consensus, however, fails to connect "vertical" federalism to the larger constitutional structure. Moreover, it suppresses all the crucial "what federalism" questions: state power on what margin and to what end? When those questions broke to the surface, the federalism consensus crumbled. In the end, the Rehnquist Court's federalism foundered not over how hard to push but over what to push *for*. The Court's decisions on constitutional rights and entitlements illustrate that the point.

Rights and Competition. Even as the Rehnquist Court pursued its federalism agenda, it continued to insist on its authority to adjudicate questions of abortion, gay rights, sex discrimination, the death penalty, and other intensely contested matters.[23] This dual agenda is manifestly incoherent. By the Court's own lights, federalism's point is to enable citizens to govern themselves closer to home. But if they are not permitted to diverge from the judiciary's postmodern orientations, it is difficult to see what they *are* allowed to decide, and why. Social policy was and is the one area where the justices might give federalism bite without, at the same time, dragging the Court into a suicidal campaign against the regulatory state. And yet, the Rehnquist Court never pursued that option. Its central theme was a consociational rights jurisprudence, informed by a morbid fear of a more competitive, decentralized politics.[24]

That orientation not only limited but also washed back into the Court's enumerated powers jurisprudence. *Lopez* and *Morrison* pointed in a "moral federalism" direction; both suggested that the commerce power does not extend to transactions that are *neither* interstate *nor* "economic" (meaning something like the voluntary exchange of goods and services).[25] That line, roughly, would allow citizens in the several states to govern themselves on matters of social policy while leaving the economy to Congress.[26] However, the Court eventually failed to pursue this logic under the Commerce Clause (or for that matter the Fourteenth Amendment), and it is difficult to separate that failure from its rights enthusiasms. For instance, the Court's decisions often cite family relations as a Commerce Clause ad absurdum: if Congress can regulate *this*, the argument runs, it could also regulate divorce, and that cannot be right.[27] At the same time, however, the Court has reserved to itself the right to regulate questions of family law—parental notification requirements for abortions by minors, for example, and probably gay marriage. Surely, though, the power of Congress vis-à-vis the states must reach as far as the Court's. Lo, there goes the enumerated powers line.

Perhaps one could harmonize these lines of thought. A responsible judicial federalism must guard against particularly severe state deprivations of civil rights. But a Court that pulls the civil rights trigger to dispel mere *stereotypes* about *men* will have a hard time explaining what policy choices it will ultimately tolerate.[28] And in truth, the Court's animosity to policy competition has reached well beyond core constitutional rights. It was hardly a coincidence, Richard A. Epstein noted in the wake of *Lopez*, that the Supreme Court had tagged (noneconomic) crime prevention as a distinctly unsuitable Commerce Clause objective. When it comes to ordinary crime, one need not apprehend a state "race" to a low-regulation "bottom." If anything, federalism dynamics might prompt states to *over*-regulate.[29] Sure enough, the federalism majority's fragile consensus collapsed over "lifestyle crimes" (such as marijuana use), where states might compete by going either way.[30]

Entitlements: Missing the Point. The preeminent theme of the Rehnquist Court's federalism, as noted, was "vertical" federalism. Although cases in that venue come under varying legal rubrics (Eleventh Amendment immunities, Tenth Amendment protections, clear statement canons, etc.), almost all boil down to the question of private entitlements vis-à-vis state and local governments, under federal statutes. On that account, the Court's vertical doctrines had the potential of reversing one of the extensions of the New Deal Constitution—the move from the New Deal to the Great Society, from cooperation to entitlements as the organizing principle of fiscal federalism. Again, however, the Court failed to execute.

The Warren-Brennan Court's entitlement jurisprudence, we saw in chapter 12, played out the logic of New Deal federalism: if the point of cooperative federalism programs is to compensate for the weakness of distributional coalitions at the national level, then the Court should lend a hand and put the intended beneficiaries of those programs in charge of their enforcement and expansion. The Rehnquist Court renounced the partnership with the Congress and switched to a posture of noncooperation: if Congress wishes to create or expand entitlements, it will have to do so on its own.[31] That line of thinking, exemplified by the clear statement rule and restrictive § 1983 decisions, has potent procompetitive rationales. For starters, it revokes the Court's own participation in an intergovernmental cartel for the production of entitlements. Moreover, and as a result, the terms and dynamics of cooperative federalism shift from litigation-driven entitlement politics to intergovernmental bargaining. The power of third-party claimants weakens both in the implementation process and at the antecedent legislative stage: the more resistant federal judges are to entitlement fabrication, the harder distributional coalitions will have to insist on explicit entitlements at the front end.

It is telling, however, that the Rehnquist Court never quite articulated this or any other systematic, nonbalance rationale for its entitlement jurisprudence.[32] Instead, it rested its decisions on a state-protective rationale that, as noted in chapter 12, is empirically doubtful and often at odds with the states' own preferences. As a result, the Court never realized the potential of its noncooperation stance, even though doing so would not have taken very much. *Maine v. Thibotout* (1980), for example, which produced an explosion of third-party claims under § 1983, is by all accounts a gravely wounded duck. Suggestions to put the bird out of its misery appeared in Supreme Court opinions and (consequently) petitions for certiorari, and on one occasion, the justices came close to overruling *Thibotout*, albeit sub silentio. In the end, however, the Court—well, ducked the question and instead continued to decide cases on a retail, one-entitlement-at-a-time basis.[33]

Unsurprisingly, that strategy soon suffered the backwash of rights enthusiasms that also afflicted enumerated powers decisions. In estimating the effect of entitlements on federalism's "delicate balance," the Court's true sorting criterion is not the federalism cost of the entitlement but its perceived value to the claimant—not the "dignity" of the state but the sanctity of the plaintiff class. Doctrines on sovereign immunity and clear statements took shape in cases over the entitlements of not-so-suspect classes, such as religious organizations, commercial interests, Native American tribes, and the elderly (a "minority" to which all of us belong or hope to belong one day). When the interests of racial minorities, women, or the disabled were at issue, the Court's federalism usually faded.[34]

This calculus has the paradoxical but predictable effect of making judicial federalism appear purely opportunistic, as a smokescreen to be thrown up when the Court thinks it can get away with stripping entitlements. The larger truth, though, is that rights enthusiasms will eventually trump federalism scruples, all the more so when the scruples are unsupported by any credible evidence or constitutional theory. The Federalist Five assumed that state and local governments need judicial protection, but they never deemed it necessary to supply a scintilla of evidence in support of that premise. Nor did they bother to explain why anyone other than bureaucrats should care about balance or protecting states. The purported federalism revolution was a strange first in American constitutional history—a display of judicial aggressiveness in response to no obvious problem, on behalf of no discernible constituency, and to no plausible end. Small wonder that it faded.

Structure: Derangement

With the transition from the Rehnquist Court to the Roberts Court, the federalism debate assumed a very different coloration. As "states' rights" cases fizzled, "business cases" took center stage. Those cases range from antitrust to patents, from private rights of action to statutory interpretation, from the Federal Rules of Civil Procedure to preemption and the dormant Commerce Clause. Probusiness, antistate outcomes in a large number of cases soon prompted harangues to the effect that conservative justices were surrendering their states' rights orientation to corporate interests.[35] That allegation, however, does not survive a first encounter with the empirics, let alone any serious examination.

It is true that the Court's business docket, though seemingly removed from federalism, is in fact its fulcrum. For reasons rehearsed in chapter 12, the New Deal's federalism pits states and their clientele—prominently, the plaintiffs' bar—against productive enterprises in interstate commerce. It is also true that under the Roberts Court, business litigants have often prevailed. What is emphatically *not* true is that the pattern is distinctly conservative. Few "probusiness" decisions have featured the 5–4 blocs that so reliably oppose one another in cases over God, guns, and gays. Conversely, "antibusiness" cases have been produced by very heterogeneous coalitions of justices, often including the most conservative and ostentatiously originalist justices.[36] The pattern defies any superficial political or attitudinal explanation. Its true explanation is this: just as the Rehnquist Court's federalism was constrained and ultimately defeated by its post–New Deal rights agenda, the Roberts Court has been unable to escape the New Deal Constitution's structure.

Perhaps because the justices read the newspapers, they have come to recognize that the commerce of the United States requires protection against cascading state impositions. To curb some of the more exotic legal flora that has sprouted in the several states, large majorities of justices have followed good sense and contained state law claims under narrow statutory interpretations of federal law, by means of tightening pleading standards, and by means of federal preemption.[37] However, the justices will not allow themselves to have a judicial or constitutional theory of the landscape. Two tenets of the New Deal Constitution block the perspective: *Erie*, and the notion of federalism as balance.

Erie naturally dovetails with empowerment federalism because its holding commands solicitude of the state courts that have, precisely on account of that solicitude, emerged as principal engines of interstate exploitation. *Erie*'s holding, though, is fatefully entangled with its "myth"; its injunction against the federal *general* common law of *Swift*, with broader propositions about the common-law powers of federal courts. And no one is more eager to unchain *Erie*'s ghost than the Court's originalists—foremost, Justice Scalia and Justice Thomas. In their minds, *Erie* encapsulates juridical commitments far beyond its holding—judicial restraint and deference to Congress, textualism, resolute opposition to judicial common-law reasoning between text and raw politics. For Justice Thomas (though perhaps not Justice Scalia), those precepts operate in tandem with a firm commitment to a state-protective federalism.[38] When these orientations prevail, conservative originalists unite with progressives to push the Constitution from cartel to empowerment, from experiment to exploitation.

These conclusory and perhaps somewhat esoteric averments are readily illustrated. The Supreme Court's treatment of federal common law provides ample evidence of its unwillingness to reconsider horizontal federalism questions. Its decisions on the dormant Commerce Clause and federal preemption illustrate the trajectory of originalist thought and its perplexing congruence with a radicalized New Deal Constitution.

Federal Common Law. Decades ago, Henry Friendly and other sober New Dealers recognized that *Erie* had to be contained by means of a "new" federal common law and, ideally, by federal statutes that would either preempt the states or order relations among them.[39] Alas, that recognition never congealed into a notion that there might be something wrong with *Erie* itself. And alas, four decades later—after an *Erie-Klaxon*-spawned "litigation explosion," after the emergence of a potent and well-organized litigation industry, and in the teeth of overwhelming evidence of congressional imbecility—the same ambivalence pervades the Supreme Court's jurisprudence under Judge Friendly's one-time law clerk and best-known disciple, Chief Justice John Roberts. The justices recognize that a workable federalism cannot live with *Erie*—that Congress and administrative agencies, unaided by constructive judicial doctrines, are incapable of arresting centrifugal state tendencies. They have responded to *Erie*'s defects, social and political, by protecting enclaves of federal common law and by experimenting with *Erie*-cabining statutory or quasi-constitutional interventions, only to abandon them in the teeth of unshakeable New Deal presumptions.

In some venues, especially maritime law and antitrust law, the justices have pushed federal common-law constructions, often based on economic theories emanating from the vicinity of Hyde Park, without giving much thought to the question of how or why the Court's confident judicial orderings might fit together with its diffidence with respect to federal common law in general.[40] Similarly, supposedly procedural statutes have come to serve as safe havens against state abuse. One example is the Rules Enabling Act, which entrusts the federal judiciary with creating and administering its own procedural rules, provided that substantive rights remain unaffected. The Federal Rules of Civil Procedure have brooded over *Erie's* tovu vabohu a principio, and they continue to hover as a kind of ersatz Constitution for defendants who would otherwise find themselves at the mercy of state courts.[41] Another example is the Federal Arbitration Act (FAA), a pre–New Deal statute that facilitates binding arbitration in lieu of litigation. Beginning in the 1980s, the Supreme Court discovered—without much credible legal evidence, and plainly in response to an increasingly aggressive litigation industry—that the statute applies in state as well as federal courts and, moreover, preempts state laws that interfere with arbitration agreements. Over the years, FAA preemption has come to assume an amazing breadth and depth.[42]

In other venues, the pattern has been one of judicial intervention, confusion, and eventual surrender. When the justices encounter defendants in extremis—state law class-actions over wholly foreign events and transactions, punitive damage verdicts over actions that are legal in most states, and the like—they sense that something is not quite right with the New Deal Constitution. Typically, they park their concerns and reasoning under the Due Process Clause, which they can no longer understand as a structural guarantee against exploitative, "extraterritorial" state action but only as a fundamental fairness garage.[43] On the second or third go-around on the same issue (and, occasionally, the same case), it transpires that the exploitation problem is sufficiently systemic to require a theory, not just a gut check. Once that recognition sets in, the justices equivocate and then retreat. Cases dealing punitive damages imposed under state law illustrate this trajectory; the Court's treatment of multistate class actions and extraterritoriality has followed a similar pattern.[44] The case law gains a coherence of sorts—though not intellectual or constitutional coherence—against the foundational *Erie* baseline. The justices protect *Erie's* traditional enclaves and, as with the FAA, occasionally carve a new preemptive or common-law enclave for the unarticulated purpose of allowing good sense and judicial orderings to reign. In *Erie's* core domain, the justices remain at sea.

Strikingly, the *Erie-Klaxon* promontory overshadows even vertical federalism canons. In the *Hyatt* case, briefly discussed in chapter 13, the plaintiff, a former California resident, sued California tax officials in Nevada courts, under Nevada law, over conduct for which California law would have provided immunity. Here, the Supreme Court's latitudinarian approach to the Full Faith and Credit Clause ran up against state sovereign (as well as statutory) immunity against lawsuits for monetary damages—the sanctissimum of the Rehnquist Court's vertical federalism. Yet the Court disposed of the case unanimously and without a hint at or a cite to its sovereign immunity cases. Under *Seminole Tribe* and its progeny, a federal statute abrogating state immunity would be flat-out unconstitutional; on the authority of *Hyatt*, a sister-state common-law doctrine with the same effect is constitutional.[45] In vertical federalism cases, state "dignity" and sovereign immunity attenuate the force of the Supremacy Clause; in horizontal cases, those notions count for nothing. States may do to each other what federalism forbids the national government to do to the least of them.

Commerce and Preemption. With respect to the dormant Commerce Clause, the Court has continued to operate within the basic New Deal framework. Facially discriminatory state statutes are almost per se illegal. Statutes that discriminate de facto are subject to probing police-power scrutiny, although that scrutiny subsides when statutes discriminate among rather than within industries.[46] Nondiscriminatory statutes that impose an "undue burden" on interstate commerce *may* be unconstitutional, but the judiciary's balancing test is extremely lenient.[47] Extraterritorial regulation and taxation is permitted, save only for a very narrowly defined category of "wholly extraterritorial" impositions.[48] The Court has left this framework largely intact, even if the pattern of decisions and articulated rationales (or rationalizations) has appeared inconsistent and incoherent to many legal scholars and some justices.

Preemption law defies any easy summary. One can, however, discern two key trends. First, the federal preemption of state tort law has gained ever-growing prominence and sparked increased controversy on and off the bench, for reasons explained earlier. Second, the case law reflects an increased (though not unbroken) trend toward a precise parsing of the statutory text as the touchstone of preemption analysis. On one side, text-only analysis has cast doubt on the New Deal "presumption against preemption," at least in express preemption cases. On the other side, it has produced increased judicial reluctance to imply preemption from the structure and purpose of federal statutes, while placing great emphasis on statutory magic words that express a congressional intent to preempt.[49]

Underneath the slow-moving, meandering decisional current, dormant Commerce Clause doctrine and implied preemption law have prompted much turbulence. The most significant source of commotion has been an energetic initiative by Justice Scalia and Justice Thomas to rethink and perhaps abandon both doctrines. Both justices have denounced the dormant Commerce Clause doctrine as a warrantless judicial invention—as "a sort of intellectual adverse possession" and as "unsound and illegitimate."[50] Paralleling this trend, the conservative originalists have increasingly come to resist preemption claims, especially implied preemption. Justice Thomas has stated his categorical position against implied ("obstacle") preemption with great clarity and rigor. Justice Scalia, who would cabin rather than abolish the dormant Commerce Clause, has taken an analogous position on preemption: while not categorically opposed to implied preemption, he has been profoundly skeptical of (to his mind) latitudinarian agency interpretation of statutory preemption provisions.[51]

To date, the originalists' positions have affected outcomes only in a handful of cases, albeit important ones. As noted, however, the dormant Commerce Clause and the implied preemption doctrine of *Rice v. Santa Fe* are the pale New Deal shadows of the old, competitive Constitution. Let the New Deal Constitution, Peter Pan-style, lose that shadow; it can *really* fly. The drift of preemption law points to that liberation, and the originalist justices' propensities propel it. (Parallel developments under the dormant Commerce Clause are lamented in chapter 16.)

The central preemption battle has been the question of whether federal health and safety statutes or agency regulations impliedly preempt state law (especially state tort law) when the federal standards establish not a minimum "floor" but rather an *optimum* standard. The principal case for the proposition that federal health and safety standards—even in the absence of an express provision—should be so understood is, or was, *Geier v. Honda Motor Co.* (2000). Justice Breyer's opinion for the 5–4 *Geier* majority explained that excessively strict standards can increase risk just as unduly lax ones can (for example, by discouraging innovation). For that reason, jury-imposed liability standards beyond the federally determined optimum conflict with federal law and should be deemed preempted.[52] *Wyeth v. Levine* (2009) points in the opposite direction. The case arose over a tragic injury to a patient whose doctor and nurse, in an act of flagrant malpractice, had administered a drug in direct contravention of the federally approved warning label. The wording of that label conformed with—in fact, was practically dictated by—Federal Drug Administration (FDA) requirements. Like *Geier*, *Wyeth* posed the question of whether the federal standards constitute a preemptive optimum or rather a mere federal floor. By a 6–3 majority (including Justice Breyer), the Court decided against preemption.

It is too much to say that *Wyeth* overrules *Geier*, but the shift in the underlying premises is unmistakable.[53] *Geier* said not a word about "federalism"; indeed, it pointedly failed to respond to the dissenters' vehement states' rights protestations. *Wyeth*, in contrast, celebrates federalism, and it subjects the implied preemption of "traditional" state authority (including, evidently but absurdly, the labeling of pharmaceutical products in interstate commerce) to a strong "presumption against preemption"—the functional analogue of a clear statement rule that loads the dice against the Congress. The FDA's claims of expertise are given the judicial back of the hand; state juries, *Wyeth* strongly implies, are better positioned to interpret the agency's regulatory regime than is the agency itself.[54]

In a no-holds-barred concurrence, Justice Thomas sharply rejected the majority's "presumption against preemption" and instead advocated something close to a *conclusive* presumption against implied ("obstacle") preemption. To protect federalism's "delicate balance," Justice Thomas insists, "pre-emptive effect [must] be given only those to [sic] federal standards and policies that are set forth in, *or necessarily follow from*, the statutory text . . . Pre-emption must turn on whether state law conflicts with the text of the relevant federal statute or with the federal regulations authorized by that text."[55] It must not turn, as in Justice Thomas's estimation it has in far too many cases, on judicial constructions of congressional "purposes" or on "tensions" with supposed but unlegislated federal "objectives." The "Court's entire body of 'purposes and objectives' pre-emption jurisprudence," his *Wyeth* opinion declares, "is inherently flawed."[56]

As goes implied obstacle preemption, so goes the background rule of federal exclusivity still recognized, albeit reluctantly, in *Rice*. No federal statute embodies exclusivity more pristinely that the National Bank Act (NBA) of 1864, which shields the banking operations of federally chartered institutions against investigation and prosecution by the states (while leaving state banks almost exclusively to state supervision and regulation). *Cuomo v. Clearing House Association*, decided a few weeks after *Wyeth*, effectively ended that system. Justice Scalia's majority opinion, joined by the Court's liberal bloc, held that the NBA's express prohibition against the exercise of state visitorial powers—roughly, ongoing oversight over corporate affairs—over national banks does not preempt state authority to sue such banks for alleged violations of state laws of general applicability, including, of all things, discriminatory lending laws. The Office of the Comptroller of the Currency (OCC), which administers the NBA, had interpreted the relevant statutory provision to preempt state lawsuits targeted at the banks' federally authorized operations (such as lending) but not general matters of zoning or contract law. The Court rejected that interpretation as so unreasonable as to merit zero judicial deference. Henceforth, banking regulation will be a "cooperative" federal-state enterprise. The majority opinion's lodestar is *Rice*—not its ambivalent majority opinion, mind you, but Justice Frankfurter's states' rights dissent.[57]

Ideological Convergence. *Wyeth* and *Clearing House* illustrate an increasingly common convergence of liberal justices and one or more conservatives on empowerment federalism. It is no great mystery why progressives would push in this direction. The preemption doctrine of *Rice* accommodated the New Deal in its centralist, confident, cartelizing posture: agency expertise, policy coherence, the regularity of the Administrative Procedures Act. Now that that model has lost normative force, progressive preemption doctrine conforms to a more state-friendly, Brandeisian New Deal tradition: multiply access points for factions and ensure that the most aggressive regulator dominates the universe. More regulation is better regulation, always and ipso facto. A preemption doctrine of that description is congenial to a progressivism that no longer believes in politically managed progress, only in interest group deals; whose political aspirations rest on trial lawyers, not experts.

The conservatives' more perplexing affinity for this program correlates not with *political* ideology, which would obviously dictate just the opposite position. It rather correlates with *judicial* ideology—i.e., originalism. Conspicuously, though unsuccessfully, originalism has sought to mobilize the New Deal's hostility to *Lochner* against modern-day rights enthusiasms. But originalism has also inherited the New Deal's animosity against federal common law, both in the specific sense of *Erie* and in a broader, more generic sense: anything beyond the bare constitutional or statutory text is politics, with which judges must have nothing to do. Implied (obstacle) preemption is "fundamentally flawed" when, and because, it strays from text into statutory purposes and structure. The dormant Commerce Clause is "illegitimate"—pure federal common law, and *Lochner* in drag.[58] In this frame of mind, conservative originalists unite with the New Deal's heirs to wipe out the remnants of a competitive constitutional order. The defense of those remnants has increasingly fallen to centrist justices with less-than-complete confidence in the enterprise. Empowerment federalism is carrying the day because in a real sense, it no longer has an enemy.

Conclusion

For a few brief years, the Rehnquist Court's federalism captured the imagination of political and legal elites. Almost in spite of itself, it contained the seeds of doctrines that would facilitate a more decentralized, competitive politics—a federalism not for "states as states" but for citizens; a federalism that would discipline government at all levels, as opposed to divvying up the intergovernmental surplus in accordance with a made-up "balance." It was not to be. Whenever embryonic competitive constitutional doctrines bumped into more foundational prejudices and presumptions, they were promptly aborted. The Court's rights umbrella leaves no daylight for a federalism beyond lace curtain sentiments of state dignity and "etiquette";[59] and in *Erie*'s shadow, no constitutional thought can sprout. And so the Rehnquist-Roberts Court remained wedded to the New Deal Constitution and, in some fateful ways, extended it.

In emphasizing these continuities, I may have made too much of doctrine and too little of judicial politics and raw votes. But for a few unfortunate Supreme Court appointments, moral federalism would have triumphed, say conservatives. The defeat of such appointments and the centrist drift of Republican appointees reflect the Supreme Court's tendency to articulate a rough national consensus, respond progressive proponents of "democratic constitutionalism." Regardless of their comparative plausibility, however, both those narratives capture only the rights side, not the structure side and empowerment federalism's slouch toward dominance. And neither side can articulate or even imagine, any more than the justices, a federalism beyond balance. This constriction of our constitutional memory and imagination marks the true triumph of the New Deal Constitution.

PART FIVE

THE STATE OF OUR FEDERALISM

COMPETITIVE FEDERALISM, I have argued, is the only federalism to which prospective citizens would precommit. The United States Constitution is best understood as embodying that precommitment. For all its compromises and imperfections, Part I showed, the Constitution's central organizing principles reflect the ex ante calculations of individuals as distinct both from the calculations of "states as states" and from opportunistic interest group bargains. That singular, exceptional feature explains the Constitution's option for competitive politics and political institutions, prominently including competitive federalism.

Constitutional government is not only design but also development and construction. Parts II through IV described the working out of a competitive order during the nineteenth century, the Constitution's inversion under the New Deal Constitution, and the radicalization of that program under Our Federalism. My principal purpose has been to show that the "competition-cartel-consociation" matrix makes sense of American federalism's constitutional development. Unmistakably, though, the heuristic suggests that the constitutional project seems to have disintegrated in a rather fundamental sense. The forces that stabilized competitive arrangements for over a century—sectionalism, and the organizing force and gravitational pull of a procompetitive constitutional framework—greatly weakened, to the point of allowing a wholesale defection from the competitive bargain.

Contrary to widely held beliefs, the dominant form of that defection is not progressive centralization. Rather, the federal system has centralized and disintegrated in different dimensions, at the same time. Persistent demand for anticompetitive arrangements has produced centralization in domains that by all rights ought to remain local, while pushing toward decentralization where a national monopoly is the sensible solution. Both propensities have reached unprecedented proportions. Under Our Federalism, the central government regulates local storm drains, our children's grade-school curricula, and conflicts between your plan to build a home on your property and a toad's desire to procreate in the same location. (As a rule, the toad wins.) Domestic violence—spousal abuse, not armed insurrection—has become a care of the general jurisdiction on account of its supposed connection to interstate commerce. Your parking spot at the mall, your office jokes, your children's playground conduct—these and countless other matters close to home have become of federal concern.[1] Conversely, the failed state of California has contrived to regulate transaction between European citizens and companies conducted on European soil some eight decades ago. And California has vigorously asserted a right to its own global warming policy, said to be virtuous and valuable precisely because its costs and benefits do *not* accrue primarily, let alone exclusively, to California citizens. Such legislative initiatives, moreover, pale against state judicial interventions. Products and profits disappear in hellhole jurisdictions; entire industries are reorganized in multistate settlements. Those practices are more often enabled than checked by central institutions.[2]

The unprecedented reach of the federal government (including the Supreme Court) and the equally unprecedented reach of state and local governments do not somehow cancel each other out or produce a happy equilibrium. Rather, they produce a two-sided problem. On one side, in a vast and diverse country, local matters rarely managed easily or well from a single center. On the other side, it is hard to believe that California will govern the ecosystem any better than it has governed itself, or that in a federalism game of mutually guaranteed exploitation, every state comes out a winner.

Bilateral overreach produces a further problem. Its usual consequence is not the substitution of a federal monopoly for local control or vice versa. Rather, it is concurrent government powers over the full range of human affairs. In the regulatory domain, private conduct becomes subject to multiple, often conflicting impositions, with the strictest regulator typically dominating private choices. In the fiscal domain, government sinks into a morass of intergovernmental collusion, moral hazard, and eventually financial crisis. In both domains, federalism erodes political accountability and transparency.

What can be done about it? Perhaps, nothing. Throughout, I have emphasized Our Federalism's self-reinforcing tendencies and its extraordinary political and institutional resilience. Once ordinary, in-period, democratic politics has triumphed over competitive arrangements, one cannot look to the same kind of politics as a means of reviving those arrangements. Hopes in the Supreme Court as the guardian of an "original" Constitution seem equally illusory; the justices cannot resurrect a lost "Constitution in Exile." Moreover, it is not obvious that anything *should* be done about federalism's fate. The constitutive, anticompetitive features of Our Federalism—rights proliferation, entitlement politics, empowerment, exploitation—have made the Constitution more open to the demands of distributional coalitions and progressive social movements and more conducive to "active liberty." To many minds, that is all to the good.

Obviously, that view is not mine. However, any high-level normative debate would be somewhat beside the point. In ordinary political times, would-be reformers are howling at the moon: Our Federalism will lurch, as it has lurched, from one level of dysfunction to the next, higher level. The question is how federalism responds to acute crises and external shocks.

By any measure, the 2008/2009 financial crisis and its aftermath constitute such a shock. In a word, our government is broke. Many municipalities and some states are effectively insolvent. In the heyday of the crisis, political institutions resorted to the usual "remedy" of pumping more money into the intergovernmental system. Temporary bailouts, however, only steepened the states' financial cliff. Increased transfer payments cannot provide a lasting solution to our federalism problems—most obviously because the federal government also lacks the money.

Encrusted federalism cartels may survive even the most severe external shocks. Argentina's federalism is an example; the fate of Germany's federalism after reunification is another.[3] It is also possible, however, that some federal systems, in response to crisis conditions, are capable of revisiting and renegotiating the basic federalism bargain. Chapter 12 described the Reagan administration's "New Federalism" initiative; chapter 14, the Rehnquist Court's federalism agenda. The political reforms proved transitory; the Court's agenda, confused and misguided. Even so, the experience suggests that American federalism possessed, and may still possess, a latent reform capacity.

That capacity, in my estimation, has to do with the fact that America still sports the most competitive politics and federalism of virtually any country—most likely because America is still somewhat exceptional.[4] And the central exceptionalism dimension, here as so often, is constitutionalism. The United States has the single most procompetitive constitution in the world—uncluttered by any commitment to distribution or solidarity; abundant in explicit procompetitive federalism provisions; hardwired with procompetitive institutional arrangements that are much less easily dislodged or cast aside than a few obnoxious textual provisions. Also, the United States has a political culture that is uniquely willing to go back to first constitutional principles, even if its institutions have made it very hard to act on that impulse.

In that light, it is worth exploring what a competitive federalism jurisprudence in this day and age, with a lot of water over the dam, might actually look like. Regardless of how much the federal judiciary could ultimately achieve by way of curbing institutional dysfunctions, surely, it should not makes matters worse. A bit more ambitiously, a plausible federalism jurisprudence should be responsive to the federalism problems that we actually have—not an imaginary "balance" problem; not the problems of the nineteenth century; not the day-to-day, partisan-political issues that prompt politicians and agitators on all sides to chant "federalism" slogans; but rather the systemic problems and pathologies the Constitution is supposed to contain.

The contours of such a jurisprudence are the subject of the following chapters. The central theme, predictably, is a federalism beyond "balance." A competitive federalism jurisprudence would repudiate all of the four anticompetitive commitments of Our Federalism identified in Part IV: consociational rights, entitlement proliferation, empowerment federalism, and exploitation. Chapter 15 discusses rights and federal-state relations (roughly, federalism's vertical dimension); chapter 16, federalism's empowerment and exploitation strands (roughly, its horizontal dimension). In all four arenas, a federalism jurisprudence beyond balance would start with the constitutional commitments that I have sought to capture under the umbrella of "competition." It would rest on and reinforce the constitutional principles and strategies elucidated in chapter 3.

Two themes of the discussion bear a brief mention up front. First, some of the usual federalism suspects prove much less vexing and important than is widely believed. The question of state sovereign immunity is an example; another, more controversial example is the enumerated powers doctrine. Conversely, some foundational cases of the New Deal Constitution that we have come to take for granted prove central and deeply problematic; *Erie* is the starkest example. Even readers who disagree with my take on particular cases and doctrines may find some merit in federalism's reorientation to those questions and away from balance-inspired marginalia. Second, and perhaps a bit surprising, the contemporary Supreme Court has at times rediscovered important pieces of federalism's constitutional architecture—most likely because it is very hard to eradicate altogether the formal Constitution's competitive features.[5] Those nuggets of constitutional reasoning, strewn amid the rubble of the New Deal Constitution, suggest that a competitive federalism jurisprudence need not be a root-and-branch operation. It does, however, presuppose a coherent understanding of the constitutional structure, which the justices lack.

The concluding essay (chapter 17) returns from constitutional doctrine to institutional questions. Normative constitutional argument tends to bring out the worst in constitutional theorists; their view of what the world ought to look like often overwhelms their analytical understanding. The distillation of that tendency, in the context of the contemporary constitutional debate, is the notion that a sufficient number of justices with the right disposition will surely restore the "original" Constitution to its full glory. That court-centered perspective is not mine. Rather, my emphasis is on the larger political and institutional context—more precisely, the prospect that grave financial distress and pervasive institutional failures may prompt a renegotiation of America's basic federalism arrangements. I am agnostic on the likelihood and the likely direction of that process; there is simply too much contingency in the system to hazard any confident prediction. However, it is *conceivable* that our Constitution has sufficient resonance to prompt a rediscovery of its competitive logic. Chapter 17 provides some thoughts on what that rediscovery might look like, and what it would take.

CHAPTER FIFTEEN

The Court, the Nation, and the States

Our federalism is not Europe's.

Antonin Scalia

Introduction

This chapter, as just advertised, addresses federalism's vertical, federal-state dimension. I begin with the Supreme Court's own role in this theater—that is, with the question of constitutional rights. The basic proposition is straightforward: competitive federalism would require the Supreme Court to repudiate its consociational rights agenda. Importantly, that program differs from an anti-"activist," William-Brennan-in-reverse agenda in substance and in its general orientation. Its central objective is not to stop making up rights but to reconnect rights jurisprudence to the constitutional structure. A full elaboration of that agenda is beyond my scope and ambition; I shall simply suggest the possibility of the enterprise and its general direction.

I then turn to the doctrines that govern relations between federal political institutions and the states. Here again, the basic proposition is straightforward: banish "balance" from respectable federalism discourse and, instead, reconstruct the logic of Madison's compound republic. The crucial move is to distinguish between—instead of collapsing into a murky balance—the "breadth" and the "depth" (in Madison's terms, the "federal extent" and the "national operation") of the federal government's powers. Make that move, and the constitutional principles expounded in chapter 3 fall into place: limited, enumerated powers; exclusivity and directness; and transparency.

Rights: Competition and Consociation

Rights and structure are calculated to protect constitutional precommitments by different means, against different threats. Structural norms guard against defection by the people's agents; rights, against defection by temporary democratic majorities. One can envision a rights-less, purely structural constitution, coupled with a constitutional court that is a pure structure court.[1] Our own Constitution, however, combines structure and rights—not as a foul compromise, but within an architecture that makes the two fit together. The problems of modern-day jurisprudence have to do, not with rights per se, but with rights that do not fit, and indeed undermine, the competitive architecture.

The starting point is the primacy of structure over rights in the *Federalist*'s theory. The Founders took it for granted that no constitution can prevent the demos from going bad, least of all by means of a list of rights. What a constitution *can* do is to prevent the people's agents from defecting from a competitive institutional order. Checks and balances—self-enforcing rules and competitive politics—are the principal means to that end. This is what Hamilton had in mind in calling the Constitution "to every useful purpose, a BILL OF RIGHTS."[2]

Even so, structure is not quite everything. The Constitution itself, Hamilton awkwardly observed, contains individual rights guarantees, such as habeas corpus. And of course, the soon-ratified Bill of Rights added many important individual rights protections. The question is whether one should understand rights—in relation to structure—as a rival or a complementary constitutional strategy. The most plausible approach, prominently championed by professor Akhil Amar, is to read the Bill of Rights as a Constitution and in continuity with the structure.[3] Compellingly, Amar understands constitutional rights guarantees as part of a structural framework that is principally designed to check agency problems. Less compellingly, he invests his interpretation with thoroughly populist and nationalist presumptions. Constitutional rights guarantees are better understood in continuity with a *competitive* structure and, more particularly, a competitive *federal* structure.

Even at a purely formal level, the constitutional text strongly suggests the continuity of rights and structure. A competitive constitution, we saw in chapter 1, will be minimalist, and it will specify powers and decision rules rather than end states. The Constitution's rights guarantees have the same formal structure. The list is notoriously short, at least in comparison with modern, rights-rich constitutions.[4] Moreover, there are no distributional rights guarantees in the Constitution, just as there are no structural distribution formulas. With rights as with the institution's apparatus, the architecture reflects a bold confidence that we can leave an awful lot to politics—so long as we get the ground rules right.

Further, the Constitution contains no abstract rights trumps against "the State" in toto. Rather, rights guarantees in the Constitution and in the Bill of Rights typically run against particular institutions. The arrangement is profoundly *federal* in that the most common and conspicuous line of distinction and differentiation runs between the states and national institutions.[5] It is profoundly *competitive* in that both the inventory of rights and their pairings with institutions are consistent with competitive federalism's constitutional calculus and, in crucial respects, supportive of its institutional operation. One set of rights, which I call *enforcement rights*, give force to competitive federalism's structure; they are intimately joined to what I have called the Constitution's "institutional commitment" principle. Two additional sets of rights address situations in which competitive federalism dynamics must be expected to fail. *Externality rights* run against the national government, which by definition cannot be subject to competitive federalism discipline. *Compensating rights* cover situations in which federalism competition among states will likely fail to operate.

All of the Constitution's textual rights fit at least one of those three categories (although I shall refrain from demonstrating the point and instead make do with illustrations). But the continuities between structure and rights run deeper than a clause-by-clause analysis would suggest. Constitutional law features some rights and constructions (such as the incorporation of certain rights against the states) that lack an unambiguous textual anchor. If those constructs have nonetheless become generally accepted, that is because they cohere with, and even reinforce, the competitive structure. Conversely, many other modern-day rights coinages remain intensely controversial because they flunk the structure test.[6] On these *consociational rights*, competitive judicial federalism would have to retreat.

Enforcement Rights. In important domains, the Constitution mobilizes rights as a structural, competition-protective enforcement mechanism. The chief domain, as it happens, is federalism. The most instructive example is the Privileges and Immunities Clause of Article IV, § 2, entitling the "the Citizens of each State . . . to all Privileges and Immunities of Citizens in the several States." Although the clause sounds to modern ears like a high-toned universal rights guarantee, its text actually suggests a very different, structural purpose. The protection belongs only to *citizens*, to the exclusion of foreigners; and it runs only against the states, not the federal government. The clause is not a natural law abstraction, but rather an institutional commitment device. If one could entrust the enforcement of a competitive structure that disciplines the people's agents *to* those agents, the protection of privileges and immunities should by all rights be an Article I grant of power.[7] That strategy, however, is self-defeating, and the constitutional answer to the difficulty is a grant of right and corresponding jurisdiction. The Privileges and Immunities Clause is "the cornerstone of the union" because it supplies the "soft arm of the magistracy" with a torso of properly incentivized plaintiffs.[8]

Beyond the Privileges and Immunities Clause and similar textual guarantees, the structure-conforming logic explains several enforcement rights that are nowhere in the literal text but have not, on that account, caused any great consternation or controversy. The most prominent example is the judicially recognized "right to travel" from state to state. No one knows where precisely the right comes from; it has no more clause-specific support than the controversial "right to privacy." Still, despite its oblique derivation and debate over its precise scope, no one seriously doubts its existence. The best answer to that perplexity is structural conformity. The bedrock—competitive—principle of American federalism is that citizens choose their state, and the "right to travel" is a term of convenience for a set of private claims to enforce that principle.[9] Similarly, the *Ex Parte Young* doctrine, which permits private plaintiffs to sue a state's officers for violations of federal rights even when the state itself may not be so sued, is universally acknowledged to be a "fiction." Historically, it was the product of the laissez-faire Court that brought us *Lochner*. If neither its fictional character not its embarrassing affinity to *Lochner* has dented the unquestioned acceptance of *Ex Parte Young*, that is again because the federal structure requires it.[10] On a closely related note, no one seems to know precisely why and pursuant to what private plaintiffs may directly enforce the dormant Commerce Clause or for that matter any of the constitutionally specified antidiscrimination rules, from the Port Preference Clause to the Tonnage Clause; or why private parties may litigate federal preemption claims in the absence of statutory authority.[11] In each case, we infer the private right from the general structure because that is the only way to make the structure work.

Externality Rights. Some constitutionally specified rights spring from a straightforward Lockean calculus. When expected externality costs (that is, the costs of the bad things government can do to you) are very high, the sensible ex ante strategy is to drive up decision-making costs—that is, to enlarge the majorities that will be required to bring the feared outcomes about. That calculus applies most urgently to the loss of very highly valued goods, such as life or liberty (in the elementary sense of imprisonment); and to situations where competitive mechanisms are unavailing because the individual has already been tagged for special, adverse treatment. Ex ante, *everyone* will want protection against those events.[12]

Up to a point, this calculus coheres with a competitive federalism calculus and with our constitutional structure. Foremost, it coheres with the initial understanding that Bill of Rights guarantees run only against the national government, not against the states.[13] Oppressive state governments face an exit threat. That structural protection against monopoly is unavailable against the central government; rights provide a remedy. The objection remains, though, that the rights aren't really structural. Far from curbing agency problems, they protect against the prospect that the people's representatives might do bad things that the demos *wants* them to do. Precisely because this is so, it is important to recognize the system-conforming limitations of externality rights: formalism and individualism.

By "formalism," I mean a categorical abstraction from any in-period social calculus. Overwhelmingly, (externality) rights are formulated, not as private claims to be stacked up against public purposes, but as prohibitions against specified forms of government conduct.[14] The prohibitions are categorical both vis-à-vis the government and private actors. On one side, the government may not escape the constitutional injunctions if it finds a sufficiently nifty reason for doing so.[15] On the other side, the prohibitions do not carve out sacrosanct realms of private autonomy, any more than the Constitution carves out realms of state autonomy. *No* contract term is immune against legislative interference, provided the obligation of contract is left unimpaired. *Any* private property and perhaps even all of it may be taken for public use, provided just compensation is paid.[16] Life, liberty, and property *may* be taken, so long as due process is observed. In short, no primary private conduct seems immune against public regulation.[17]

By "individualism," I mean that constitutional rights are "minority-protective" not in the sense of providing a quasi-consociational safeguard against politically induced losses for minorities, including permanent, "discrete and insular" political (or racial, ethnic, or religious) minorities. *That* sort of protection the Constitution leaves to competitive politics, within constitutional constraints (most importantly, the Equal Protection Clause). Rather, externality rights cover situations in which a lone individual finds himself confronted with the combined might of the community. Criminal process protections are prototypical.

With externality rights as with enforcement rights, the constitutional logic helps to explain why some rights have become well accepted despite their lack of an unequivocal textual basis. Both the exclusionary rule and the *Miranda* rule are extratextual constitutional common-law constructions; both were intensely controversial at the time of their creation and application to the states. If both have nonetheless become firm fixtures in the constitutional landscape, that is probably because they work in the formalistic and rigidly individualistic fashion of textually specified rights. We find it hard to imagine that anyone would harbor a contrary ex ante preference or that state competition might fruitfully operate in this domain.[18]

Compensating Rights. Competitive federalism helps to make sense of rights that hold, or have at times been deemed to hold, good against the states. In many areas, for many actors, in the ordinary course of events, state competition provides adequate antimonopoly protection. That is not so, however, when exit costs become prohibitive—for example, for small producers with accumulated local goodwill or (more often yet) for consumers in markets that, for one reason or another, are shielded from interstate competition. Calculations of this sort plainly informed *Allgeyer v. Louisiana*, perhaps the first "substantive due process" case. It is not implausible to understand *Lochner* and its progeny and, in more recent decades, *Griswold* and the incorporation of Bill of Rights guarantees against the states in this light, as protections against local monopoly.[19]

How much confidence should one have in competitive dynamics in this setting? It seems incontrovertible that some local depredations are too awful and stubborn to be left to competitive dynamics. From this vantage, the Civil War amendments can be viewed as a structure-compatible adjustment. Of course, the amendments worked a major change in federalism's architecture; and of course, it seems obtuse to view the wrenching struggle of the Civil War and its aftermath through a competition lens. And yet, it remains important to recognize that the amendments rendered the constitutional structure *more* competitive, not less so.

First, the amendments belatedly undid the Convention's slavery bargain—as explained, the one part of the Constitution that departed from a constitutional perspective and instead enshrined a consociational interest group compromise. Second, and conversely, the amendments made the blessings of a competitive Constitution, voice and exit, available to people theretofore held in bondage. Third, the amendments did this not by force of creating new rights but rather by defining, as a matter of federal law, *who counts* as a person and a citizen. At the end of the day, no federal system can leave that determination to its constituent units. The monopoly follows directly from the nature of the federal constitution as the constitutive act of a single, sovereign people. And the logic of the amendments, as of American citizenship in general, is inclusion, not the extension of new and more expansive rights.[20]

The post-Reconstruction Supreme Court read the Civil War amendments in continuity with the constitutional logic and structure. One essential element of the synthesis is the state action doctrine of the *Civil Rights Cases* (1883): federal legislation must actually be addressed to curbing government abuse, as opposed to rearranging local market conditions. A second limitation arises from the *Slaughter-House Cases* (1872), which held that the Privileges or Immunities Clause of the Fourteenth Amendment protects only the rights held by individuals *as United States citizens*. On this reading, the amendment expands citizenship and, in so doing, breaks down protectionist barriers that had been impervious to competitive dynamics. But the Court rejected the broader, rights-creative interpretation urged by the plaintiffs, largely on the grounds that it would leave far too little of federalism.[21]

Although the late nineteenth-century Court has been widely, and rightly, criticized for throwing in the towel on Reconstruction, a great deal can be said for its attempt to stick with the structure and to resist the rights sirens. When given a chance to work, the structure did work: the local monopolies of the *Slaughter-House Cases* soon eroded—courtesy not of a rights-proliferating Court but of the Chicago meatpackers, operating under the Supreme Court's robust protection of interstate commerce. The true scandal was not the Court's adherence to the Constitution's competitive logic but its repeated failure to pursue it in direct confrontations with the Southern social structure—for notorious examples, the failure to protect *interstate carriers* against segregationist state laws and to make a rival, federal judicial forum available to black citizens where the local ones could not possibly be trusted.[22]

The tension between compensating rights and competition is still with us; it lurks just underneath the surface of highly salient constitutional debates. Economists are bound to observe that exit is always costly and, moreover, that states (and for that matter local governments) provide "bundled" products. No single policy stick in the bundle causes sufficient pain to induce exit, but what's the objection to having a federal court end the exploitation? On the left, advocates are apt to mobilize this sort of argument in defense of *Griswold* and its progeny. On the right, libertarians urge courts to drop "David's Rights Hammer" on the purveyors of local grassroots tyranny. The camps converge on the same prescription: overrule the *Slaughter-House Cases*.[23]

The conventional objection to this orientation is that it would grant too much power to the Court and leave too little to democratic politics. The argument has undeniable force; but then, it is also hard to say anything nice about the "democratic" politics and federalist "experimentation" on display in *Lochner, Nebbia, New State Ice,* or *West Coast Hotel* (or, for that matter, the silliness of prohibiting the sale of contraceptives to unmarried individuals). Juristocracy or interest group rackets: pick your institutional poison. I cannot think of a compelling global answer to the dilemma, but I can think of potent arguments that cut in favor of reliance on competition.

To the extent that the attempt to compensate for failures in the federalism "market" relies on substantive rights that protect private primary conduct, it is in tension with a formal constitutional structure that provides no sanctuaries for private actors but instead tries to get the rules of the game right. And whatever confidence one may have in the rights strategy, it seems strangely out of date. Universal rights are an appropriate strategy for an immobile, localized society, provided it can institutionalize a trustworthy guardian. A modern, highly mobile and dynamic society is better off with jurisdictional competition and parochial rights.[24] Greater mobility lowers exit costs while correspondingly raising the error costs of central intervention and entrenchment. Government still comes in bundles and exit is still costly, but attempts to make competitive federalism more "efficient" (by unbundling government services or by neutralizing locational advantages) will produce enormous error costs and threaten the system's adaptive efficiency, regardless of whether those efforts are undertaken by federal legislators or judges.

We naturally resist that intuition when it comes to civil rights. With respect to truly universal guarantees of American citizenship, that instinct is surely right and, for reasons mentioned, consistent with the constitutional calculus. Beyond that range, however, civil rights quickly become a matter of conflicting preferences and difficult trade-offs. With several leaps of logic, one can categorize rape and domestic violence as "gender based" and "discriminatory" and, in that fashion, conjure up an equal protection rationale for a federal remedy for private acts of aggression that are already subject to criminal and civil penalties under state law. (The state action predicate for the remedy is the supposed failure of many states to prosecute and punish offenders with sufficient vigor and consistency.) It is exceedingly unlikely, however, that the failure has much to do with official hostility to women as a class. It *is* likely that state laws and practices reflect imperfect compromises between competing objectives. Rape is a horrible fate; but then, so is a baseless allegation of rape.

The task of minimizing the joint costs of error on either side is terribly difficult, and the federal government and courts are no more likely to get it right than any state. The better part of wisdom is to let people in the various states govern themselves.[25]

What Doesn't Fit: Consociational Rights. Enforcement rights are an essential means of sustaining a competitive federal structure. Externality rights and compensating rights are consistent with a competitive structure, even if there is considerable room for disagreement over the extent to which one should rely on rights or on competitive dynamics. None of this, in contrast, holds for modern-day rights that are shorthand for, or shortcuts around, collective decisions about distributive fairness or intensely contested moral questions that may agitate a community of free and equal citizens. Conservative jurists have inveighed against some of those rights because they are "group rights" rather than "individual rights" (as with affirmative action); against other rights (such as abortion) because they flow from a "substantive due process" construct that allows judges to enact their own moral code freed from any meaningful constitutional constraint. Both objections partly capture the deeper problem—the disconnect of modern-day rights from the constitutional logic, and their close affinity to the consociational notion of constitutionalism as interest group bargaining and consensus. The modern-day rights that have caused sustained controversy obviously reflect, not any ex ante calculation, but the demands of in-period politics and constituencies. They govern the outcome of political questions on which individual citizens may often find themselves in a minority, but never alone, and on which preferences run now this way, now that. The judicial entrenchment of those rights is akin, not to the Seventh or Fourteenth Amendment but to the Eighteenth Amendment, establishing Prohibition—a supposedly enlightened policy choice, constitutionalized in response to vocal constituency demands but later repealed.[26]

The Supreme Court's consociational rights jurisprudence can and has been criticized on many grounds—its tendency to generate rather than to dampen social conflict; its tendency to promote constitutional instability (the Court's rolling constitutional amendments must be adjusted periodically to an ever-shifting enlightened consensus); its elitist orientation; its antidemocratic, juristocratic implications. All those critiques converge on the point here at issue—the systematic suppression of a competitive politics. That tendency is the natural effect and the intended point of the Supreme Court's self-consciously consociational ventures into "culture war" rights. It is at war with a competitive federal structure and Constitution.

Whither Rights?. The preceding discussion could easily be extended to show that competition is the genius of the Establishment Clause; or that the perennial brawl over the Equal Protection Clause—as an individual guarantee against being singled out for adverse treatment or, alternatively, as a consociational assurance of concern and respect—is, at bottom, a fight over whether the Constitution is a *constitution* or an interest group bargain; and that a judicial truce at this front would yield big gains in terms of a more competitive, democratic politics. Cultural politics is highly entrepreneurial, and one side is as good as the other in mobilizing public opinion and mass support. It revolves around issues that require difficult, often vexing moral judgments but very little technical or other expertise, let alone questions on which judges could claim any special competence. Moreover, the crucial issues come with a kind of built-in structure theme. Culture war issues are conflictual rather than allocative, states remain heterogeneous, and interstate externalities are negligible. On those issues, there is every reason in the world to trust the democratic process, and a *federal* democratic process in particular.[27]

All those arguments push in the same direction: read rights in a structural context and they begin to make sense. Alas, they also converge on the same difficulty. *Conceptually*, a system-conforming rights jurisprudence isn't all that hard (and enough is left in our constitutional memory to make it possible). *Institutionally*, it is inordinately hard. It would require a rights court that has staked its power and prestige on political constituencies to revert to a competitive structure. There are reasons to doubt that it could ever be done; chapter 17 contains some thoughts on that question. The minimum condition, though, is this: no Court will, or should, recommit rights-based constituencies to an unconstrained political "process" that simply regularizes civil warfare. Any plausible effort to deconstitutionalize consociational rights will have to reconstitutionalize a structure that inspires confidence in competitive politics.

Enumerated Powers: Breadth

A competitive Constitution presupposes limited federal powers. A sensible take on that question must steer a middle course between opposing positions, both untenable. On one side, the New Deal's intellectual heirs hold that enumerated powers have no judicially enforceable limits and that the Commerce Clause in particular authorizes Congress to do what it wishes, as it wishes.[28] That position is obviously wrong. On the other side, originalists of a libertarian bent insist that the Commerce Clause must be restored to its constitutional contours, by which they mean something like the "Old" Constitution and its categorical distinctions between commerce and manufacture, state-internal and national matters, state police-powers and national enumerated powers, direct and indirect effects. Their bête noire is *Wickard v. Filburn*, with its expansion of the commerce power over in-state activities that "in the aggregate" somehow "affect" interstate commerce.[29] That position is also wrong, but more subtly so than the New Deal position. The reasons have to do with the Constitution's structure and political economy, and with its text.

Structure and Political Economy. The affirmative powers of Congress are two-sided; they can be used for pro- or anticompetitive purposes. Congress may secure creditors' rights, or abrogate them; build post roads that connect the eastern seaboard, or bridges to nowhere; break down barriers to interstate commerce, or create them; coordinate commerce on competitive terms, or make it "regular" by suppressing competition. This ambivalence exists regardless of the breadth of enumerated powers. Construe the powers "strictly," "broadly," or fairly: on any view, they will lend themselves to pro- or anticompetitive purposes.

Aware of this difficulty, the Founders created institutional checks and balances to limit the legislature's output and, moreover, bias it in a competitive direction. But while supermajoritarian impediments (bicameralism, presentment and veto) have performed tolerably well on the output dimension, the Founders' hope that those obstacles, coupled with electoral filtration, would also improve the ratio of public-regarding legislation to factional dross has been sorely disappointed. Hence, our grim fate—a Congress that microregulates local affairs or "harmonizes" interstate commerce while routinely failing to protect it on competitive terms.

Against this backdrop, a strategy of controlling Congress by means of judicially enforced enumerated powers limitations attempts, in a functional sense, to substitute a textual "parchment barrier" for political, institutional dynamics that have failed. One has to doubt whether *external* enforcement mechanisms can replace *self*-enforcing norms for any length of time, and one can have a long discussion over the Founders' intents and expectations in this regard. However, we can safely put the freighted question aside. Even *if* the Supreme Court were institutionally capable of curtailing the powers of Congress, the net effect would be anything but procompetitive.

The notion that a Commerce Clause within its supposedly natural, original meaning—something like the categorical distinctions of the pre–New Deal era—will be procompetitive rests on two related calculations.

First, federal legislation will almost invariably be anticompetitive. Reducing the scope of the commerce power thus promises to reduce the overall mischief. Second, the states will have to compete in all the domains that are beyond the reach of Congress. No federal power over agriculture or manufacture means no federally sponsored agriculture, industry, or labor cartels. However, the constitutional history reviewed in earlier chapters illustrates the shortsightedness of a calculus that ignores the negative, dormant side of the Commerce Clause. In an integrated economy, the states' "internal" or "police-power" regulations lend themselves readily to protectionist and exploitative state purposes. To block abuses, the negative commerce power must reach into the interior of each state. But the judiciary's authority can reach no further than the authority of Congress under the affirmative Commerce Clause. Reintroduce categorical Commerce Clause distinctions on the affirmative side: they will simultaneously shield state protectionism and exploitation from judicial scrutiny.[30]

The Commerce Clause problem has never been to limit the powers of Congress; it has always been to identify the competitive balance. Precisely that calculus led the Supreme Court to treat "commerce" as a seamless web well before the New Deal. The Old Court was very well aware of the price to be paid—a very broad affirmative Commerce Clause. Very probably, however, that is the procompetitive rule.

Constitutional Text. Contemporary attempts to reestablish categorical Commerce Clause limitations derive their surface plausibility chiefly by way of contrast with *Wickard*, which took "commerce among the several states" to encompass purely in-state conduct that, in the "aggregate," "affects" interstate commerce. In *Lopez*, the Supreme Court relied on *Wickard* but sought to cabin its reach. The alleged effects on interstate commerce, the Court said, must not be so contrived as to open effectively any activity to congressional regulation; and Congress may not "aggregate" *non*-economic activities to conjure up a "substantial effect" on interstate commerce. In that fashion, *Lopez* purported to immunize against federal legislation private conduct that is *neither* interstate *nor* commerce. But the well-intentioned analysis misses the constitutional mark. Apart from the difficulty of telling "economic" from "noneconomic" activities (illustrated by the fact, delicately unmentioned by the *Lopez* Court, that Mr. Lopez had brought his gun to school for the purpose of *selling* it), the construction does violence to the constitutional language; there is no "substantially affecting" clause in the Constitution. In this respect, *Lopez* is insufficiently bold. In another respect, however, *Lopez* is excessively bold. It ignores the Necessary and Proper Clause.[31]

The Necessary and Proper analysis was there in the beginning. It was *that* analysis, not the (actually rather restrictive) definition of "commerce," that gave *Gibbons v. Ogden* the "breadth" celebrated by the New Dealers. Justice Story and the Taney Court likewise relied on the Necessary and Proper Clause in construing the authority of Congress.[32] The clause disappeared from Commerce Clause cases at the turn of the twentieth century because it would have thwarted the Supreme Court's efforts to limit congressional power. (There is no point to categorical distinctions if Congress can necessary-and-proper its way around them.) In the helter-skelter years of 1936 and 1937, the New Dealers lacked the imagination to revert to the clause. So it came to pass that *Jones & Laughlin Steel*, a pristine Necessary and Proper case, was instead argued and decided with the conventional Commerce Clause categories as a "stream of commerce" case. Once the New Dealers had won, they no longer needed the Necessary and Proper Clause, and so we inherited the abstruse Commerce Clause of *Wickard*.[33]

Lopez seemingly managed to reimpose Commerce Clause limits not because it departed from but precisely because it adhered to the *Wickard* framework. However, *Gonzales v. Raich* (2003) illustrates the instability of the analysis. In sustaining the federal criminalization of the mere possession of marijuana, including its state-approved cultivation and controlled in-state distribution for purely private, noncommercial purposes, the majority followed the analysis (though perhaps not the spirit) of *Lopez* and its enumerated powers twin, *United States v. Morrison* (2000). In both cases, the majority had of needs conceded that Congress can "immunize" doubtful provisions by enacting them as part of a larger legislative scheme that undoubtedly regulates interstate commerce. Sure enough, *Raich* sustained the prohibition against private marijuana cultivation and possession as an integral part of the federal Controlled Substances Act, which governs all classified illegal drugs.[34]

So long as Commerce Clause analysis remains mired in the conceptual muck of *Wickard* and *Lopez*, the enumerated powers game is pretty much up. That demoralizing conclusion, however, is by no means inevitable. Somewhat paradoxically, the solution to the puzzle lies in the long-ignored Necessary and Proper Clause.

Enumerated Powers, After All. The place to begin is Justice Scalia's concurring opinion in *Raich*. Agreeing with the majority's ruling but pointedly disagreeing with its analysis, Justice Scalia observed that purely local, noncommercial activities, aggregated or not, cannot possibly *be* interstate commerce. The question is whether the federal regulation of those activities is *necessary and proper* to the regulation of that commerce. That cogent analysis tracks the structure of the Constitution and, as just seen, its nineteenth-century understanding. Its drawback, one might think, is to extend the reach of Congress even beyond the bounds of *Lopez*. So long as Congress can conjure up some connection between a regulated activity and interstate commerce, no human activity appears beyond its reach. However, that conclusion is much too fast. By reintroducing the Necessary and Proper Clause, the Scalia analysis clears the decks of *Wickard*'s inanities and reverts to an intelligible Commerce Clause that extends only to matters that are (a) commerce, meaning the voluntary exchange of goods and services; and (b) "among the several states" (including, for reason mentioned, the first and last leg of any interstate transaction). The central inquiry, then, is whether the federal regulation of some activity, regardless of its "economic" or purely in-state nature, is nonetheless "necessary and proper" to the regulation of commerce among the several states. Each part of that inquiry has, or should have, independent meaning. In John Marshall's words, the congressional *end* must be legitimate and within the scope of the Constitution. Thus, the law or regulation in question must be necessary and proper not for the general betterment of the GDP or the ecosphere but the regulation of commercial transactions across state lines. Moreover, the language commands a means-ends test: the law or regulation must be both *necessary* and *proper*.

Run the modern landmark cases through this analysis: with a few arguable exceptions, they prove to be rightly decided or at least well within the constitutional ballpark. *Jones & Laughlin* is surely right, so long as one grants its premise that unionization helps to prevent industrial strife. *Wickard*, despite its preposterous analysis, was rightly decided: grant Congress the power to limit the interstate supply of wheat and other commodities, and the power to suppress local evasion follows directly, albeit depressingly. On the limiting side, neither the Gun Free School Zones Act in *Lopez* nor the civil remedies provision at issue in *Morrison* was plausibly related, let alone necessary, to anything having to do with interstate commerce. Thus, even on very deferential judicial premises, the decisions were right. *Raich* turns out to be a hard case: is the prohibition against the mere possession of marijuana—neither commerce nor interstate—nonetheless "necessary" to a legitimate Commerce Clause objective and a set of interstate transactions? Plainly, Congress may suppress the shipment of marijuana and other drugs into states that do not want them. But the effect of local marijuana cultivation and consumption, under state-imposed restrictions, may be sufficiently remote to warrant the inference that the federal prohibition was simply targeted at suppressing policy competition among states (which differ greatly with respect to their "medical marijuana" policies). Justice Scalia deferred to the judgment of Congress; Justice Thomas believed not a word of it and therefore dissented. Reasonable minds will differ about the outcome and the appropriate level of judicial scrutiny, but at least they will differ over the right question.[35]

The same combination of analytical clarity and uncertainty in application attends to the question of whether federal statutory provisions, although concededly "necessary" to a legitimate end, are also "proper." Like "necessary," "proper" goes to means rather than ends. Unlike the "necessary" analysis, the "proper" analysis implicates—in fact, is shorthand for—the broader constitutional structure; and not all means that Congress might find necessary satisfy the "proper" constraint.[36] This line of thinking has gained great salience in litigation over a provision contained in the 2010 Patient Protection and Affordable Care Act (PPACA) that compels individuals (beginning in 2014) to purchase health insurance, or else pay a financial penalty. Plainly, the statute as a whole regulates interstate commerce; and by constitutional canons the individual health insurance mandate is "necessary" to make the overall scheme work.[37] Still, is the mandate *proper*, in the sense of consistency with the constitutional structure? Against its propriety runs the observation that the Constitution generally contemplates and authorizes laws in the form of prohibitions, as distinct from affirmative commands. Federal laws generally presuppose some affirmative private act as a predicate for compelling further private actions; and the constitutional provisions that suggest a federal authority to "commandeer" private parties are few, institutionally cabined, and calculated to ensure the operation of the government's own institutions (such as the armed forces and the jury system)—not, as under the PPACA, to protect the profitability of private corporations. The *form* in which the government exercises its authority counts a great deal in the "proper" analysis.[38]

The analysis just sketched is not beyond cavil. Suitably fleshed out, however, it has a high degree of structural plausibility. Moreover, it satisfies the irreducible demand of any Commerce Clause and "Proper" analysis: to articulate *some* principled line that sustains the enumerated powers logic and identifies *some* set of transactions that are beyond the reach of Congress. Depending on its stringency, the analysis may prove too demanding for the avatars of unlimited government, too latitudinarian for libertarian fundamentalists, or both. But then, it is the sort of line that we are *supposed* to argue about.

Enumerated Powers: "Directness,"
Exclusivity, and Transparency

The extent or breadth of enumerated federal powers is one part of competitive federalism's equation. The other part is the "depth" of those powers—that is to say, the question of what Congress may or may not do to states, assuming it acts pursuant to its enumerated powers. Here, the crucial task is to clear the field of the accumulated rubble of "balance" calculations. The central principle is the "national operation" of federal powers, unequivocally stated in the Supremacy Clause: in cases of conflict, any valid federal law trumps any state law. That principle, though, has both limits and an inherent logic: again, the *forms* of federal action prove decisive in the competitive federalism analysis (regardless, to repeat, of any "balance" effect). The nineteenth-century Court understood the crucial distinctions perfectly well. The New Deal Constitution erased them, and the Supreme Court has remained sadly wedded to its balance nostrums. One of the Court's decisions, however, rearticulates the constitutional understanding. Rightly understood and read for all it is worth, *Printz v. United States* (1997) provides the basis for a broader constitutional reconstruction.

Printz: *The Holding. Printz* involved a challenge to certain provisions of the Brady Handgun Violence Prevention Act, which commanded state and local law-enforcement officers to conduct background checks on prospective gun purchasers. In *New York v. United States* (1992), the Court had held that Congress may not "commandeer" state legislatures; the question in *Printz* was whether that injunction also applies to federal statutes that purport to commandeer state and local enforcement officers. A closely divided Supreme Court answered in the affirmative and struck down the Brady Act.

In tone, style, and substance, *Printz* differs markedly from the general run of the modern Court's federalism decisions. Foremost, it is an ostentatiously *structural* opinion and decision. Justice Scalia advertises the point:

> [Petitioners] contend that congressional action compelling state officers to execute federal laws is unconstitutional. *Because there is no constitutional text speaking to this precise question*, the answer . . .must be sought in historical understanding and practice, *in the structure of the Constitution*, and in the jurisprudence of this Court.[39]

Justice Scalia eventually concludes that a federal statute purporting to commandeer state officers cannot be "proper" (even if Congress deems it "necessary"). However, the textual hook is simply shorthand for the structural arguments that dominate the opinion and which distinguish *Printz* both from a narrowly clause-bound originalism and from a federalism of balance and state enclaves. Consistent with Justice Scalia's formalist disposition, the prohibition against commandeering is a federalism *rule*, not a judicially engineered standard, and a categorical rule at that.[40] And in explicating that rule, the opinion hearkens back to pre–New Deal modes of argument.

Although the term "commandeering" is a modern coinage, the anticommandeering rule has a highly respectable pedigree in the Marshall Court's jurisprudence. In *New York*, the Court had declined to rely on those precedents and instead introduced the anticommandeering rule as a state-protective Tenth Amendment derivation. Somewhat curiously, *Printz* still fails to cite the old precedents, but it revives them in substance.[41] The opinion gives very short shrift to balance-and-enclave considerations and hangs its holding, not on the Tenth Amendment, but on "proper" as shorthand for structure. Justice Scalia reaffirms, as a matter of constitutional principle, that the Constitution establishes a system of "dual sovereignty," wherein the states and the national government occupy separate "spheres."[42] That principle implies limited, enumerated powers (not implicated in *Printz* because no one doubted that those powers extend to gun registration requirements) and "directness": under the Constitution, the national government governs citizens, not states. That precept entails that Congress lacked the constitutional authority to enact the background check requirements.

The Forms of Federal Action. In practical terms, *Printz* was a bit of a joke. At the time, most states already required the background checks mandated by the Brady Act (which, moreover, were scheduled to expire with the then-imminent establishment of a federal computer system). More broadly, true commandeering statutes are quite rare—among other reasons, because Congress has ready alternatives. It may preempt the states, and it may induce their cooperation by means of spending legislation. By its terms, the anticommandeering prohibition does not apply to either of these forms of federal legislation.[43]

For reasons of this sort, scholars—and justices—have criticized *Printz* as both overwrought and ineffectual.[44] Such criticisms, however, assume the premise that *Printz* disavows—to wit, that the point of judicial federalism interventions is to protect a "balance" and the "states as states." If instead one reads *Printz* as an attempt to reestablish the formal baselines of a competitive constitutional architecture, its force and import become perfectly intelligible. Rightly understood, *Printz* distinguishes three forms of federal action and federal-state relations: commandeering, prohibition/preemption, and bargaining/spending. The key to these distinctions and their constitutional logic is the derivation of the anticommandeering or "directness" principle.

Everyone, including the dissenters in *Printz*, agrees that the national government's power to act directly upon individuals spells the difference between the Articles of Confederation and the Constitution. The question is whether that *power* implies a corresponding *prohibition* against legislating indirectly and upon states. That common formulation, though, is a bit misleading. Many of the Constitution's clauses (for example, the prohibitions or Article I, § 10) operate on states, and many enumerated powers authorize Congress to do likewise. The crucial distinction, it transpires, is not between acting (or not) on states but rather between a federal *prohibition* and an affirmative federal *command*.[45] The distinction has firm roots in the constitutional text and structure. As just noted, the Constitution imposes many direct limitations on the states, but only six provisions affirmatively commandeer them. Three of these run, not between the national government and the states, but horizontally among the states.[46] Two of the vertical commandeering clauses (the Militia Clauses and Article I, § 4, authorizing Congress to "make or alter" state regulations with respect to the time, place, and manner of holding elections for the House and the Senate) are institutionally cabined. The only arguable exception to the general pattern, the Supremacy Clause, specifies the legal *effect* of federal law, as opposed to creating a new power to run states around the lot; and to the extent that it "commandeers" at all, it extends only to "the Judges in every State," not to legislatures or executives. In short, the Constitution recognizes the difference between prohibitions and commands, and its commands are so few and conspicuous as to warrant the inference that commandeering is prohibited unless explicitly provided for.

The distinction between commands and prohibitions having been drawn, the question remains whether Congress and the states may bargain around the constitutional entitlements—put differently, whether Congress may pay the states or states may exact payment for the performance of affirmative duties that cannot be commandeered. The obvious answer is "yes," but it is important to see why that is so. The point of departure is that intergovernmental bargains are just that—*bargains*. As the Supreme Court has put it in one of the most consequential sentences in modern federalism jurisprudence, conditional funding programs are "in the nature of a contract."[47] They are not literally contracts; if they were, the parties should be able to sue each other for breach and damages.

But they have many elements of a contract, and the "in the nature" circumlocution captures what spending statutes are not: they are *not* preemption or Supremacy Clause statutes. Their force, such as it is, stems from the states' acceptance of the contractual obligations: no acceptance, no consequences. This, we saw earlier, is the crucial reasoning behind a Hamiltonian "Spending Clause." Federal spending *need* not be cabined by enumerated powers because fiscal transfers per se cannot make states do anything at all.

The Logic of Printz. *Why* are these distinction—commandeering, prohibition/preemption, bargaining/spending—so central to the constitutional architecture? A tempting answer is that affirmative commands are more odious to "states as states" and more upsetting to the federal "balance" than mere prohibitions or spending programs. But this is not really so. State and local officials may well prefer commandeering to outright prohibitions, and the anticommandeering rule may actually weaken the states' entitlements vis-à-vis the national government and induce the national government to create oppressive federal bureaucracies for which state agencies might otherwise be available.[48] The answer has to do, not with balance, but with dualism's corollaries, exclusivity and transparency; and it has to do with citizens, not state officials. As Justice Scalia puts it:

> By forcing state governments to absorb the financial burden of implementing a federal regulatory program, Members of Congress can take credit for "solving" problems without having to ask their constituents to pay for the solutions with higher federal taxes. And even when the States are not forced to absorb the costs of implementing a federal program, they are still put in the position of taking the blame for its burdensomeness and for its defects.[49]

Many critics have argued that this accountability principle is mismatched to the anticommandeering rule. The principle, they say, is overinclusive, in that it bars federal commandeering even in circumstances where other important objectives (for example, national emergencies) should trump accountability concerns. Conversely, accountability concerns would appear to apply with equal force to federal preemption statutes and to "cooperative" federalism programs, especially federal funding statutes. Thus, accountability is a lousy rationale for the anticommandeering rule—unless we are to conclude that noncommandeering cooperative arrangements are likewise suspect.[50] The critics' line of argument has some surface plausibility. Upon inspection, however, it illustrates yet again the error of mobilizing free-floating federalism values against the constitutional structure.

The Supreme Court has articulated the "accountability" principle in a number of cases.[51] In some formulations it has a state-protective ring, but that cannot be its actual point. If it were, state consent should make commandeering constitutional—but it doesn't.[52] More important, officials at *all* levels—state and local as well as federal—would rather have less accountability. Thus, the principle looks to the only actors who want more of it—citizens. The point of *Printz* and its anticommandeering rule is not to assist your local sheriff but to reduce citizens' monitoring costs and to give them effective means of holding public officials to account. To those ends, any given act of sovereign, coercive authority must be traceable to, and emanate from, a single sovereign, as opposed to an intergovernmental conspiracy. In other words, the baseline of *Printz*, and the point of Justice Scalia's invocation of "dual" federalism, is exclusivity: one problem, one sovereign. Commandeering compromises exclusivity, directness, and transparency—and therefore accountability .

Against this backdrop, the objection that preemption statutes—that is to say, prohibitions against the states—entail accountability problems comparable to those that attend "commandeering" is difficult to understand. Of course, preemption statutes are often impenetrable for ordinary citizens and occasionally for experts. And of course, officials at all levels will seize on the confusions to shirk and shift blame. The usual cause of those difficulties, however, is that most preemption statutes, as well as the Supreme Court's jurisprudence, *fail* to follow the exclusivity principle. Where the principle is unambiguously enshrined in federal law, federalism accountability problems are highly attenuated. For example, everyone knows that airline services are the Federal Aviation Authority's problem and responsibility because federal law unambiguously protects the agency's exclusive authority.[53]

The criticism that *Printz*'s accountability rationale cuts far too broadly (analytically speaking) has greater force with respect to spending legislation. When Congress enacts such legislation, the conditions attached to the bargain typically take the form of affirmative commands, and derogations from exclusivity, directness, and transparency are a given. Considering the pervasiveness of the practice, any insistence on an anticommandeering rule begins to look trivial. And yet, it isn't. It is the linchpin for a constitutional, competitive spending power jurisprudence.

A loss of directness, exclusivity, and transparency attends even the most beneficial bargain. Precisely because that is so, the bargains are suspect in a way in which ordinary preemption legislation is not. Because spending legislation is not an exercise of federal supremacy but rather "in the nature of a contract," it must in doubtful cases be construed against the party that wrote it—that is, the Congress.[54] Moreover, courts must be leery of construing bilateral bargains for the benefit of third parties; the folks who pay for the transactions, called "taxpayers" or "citizens," have no place at the table.[55] These bare-bones rules roughly correspond to the contemporary Supreme Court's "vertical" federalism rules—the clear statement rule and an aversion to private rights of action (statutorily implied, or under § 1983). For the most part, the Court has grounded its decisions in these venues on state-protective "balance" calculations. I have earlier criticized that reasoning as untenable. Upon examination, however, it turns out that the doctrines have potent, albeit often unarticulated, constitutional and competitive rationale. *Printz* supplies that rationale.

The Wages of Printz. The holding and the reasoning of *Printz* should apply more broadly than the justices have contemplated to date. First, the case law suggests that the prohibition against commandeering applies only to statutes enacted pursuant to some (not all) of Congress's Article I powers, not to Fourteenth Amendment legislation. This compartmentalization—most probably an improvised move to immunize certain provisions of the Voting Rights Act against a commandeering challenge—is a mistake. Although the rule does not apply to grants of power that explicitly authorize federal commandeering, the Fourteenth Amendment power to enforce the provisions of the Amendment by *appropriate* legislation is not among those grants. Commandeering is no more "appropriate" than it is "proper."[56]

Second, the anticommandeering rule is thought to permit so-called conditional preemption statutes—that is, federal statutes that offer states a "choice" between wholesale federal preemption or state administration of federal mandates. (Many environmental statutes work in that fashion.) This, too, is mistaken. Conditional *funding* statutes constitute a federal-state bargain (albeit often an unattractive one), not an imposition. If a state declines the offer, no direct consequence ensues for its citizens. The rejection of a conditional *preemption* statute, in contrast, drags direct federal regulation in its wake. Although Congress plainly possesses the power to regulate and preempt, that power does not—on the logic and reasoning of *New York* and *Printz*—entail the "lesser" power to preempt conditionally.[57]

Third, *Printz* raises serious questions as to whether Congress may "commandeer" state *judges* rather than legislators and administrators. That power is commonly inferred, not from any enumerated power, but rather from the Supremacy Clause, which provides that "the Judges in every State" (but evidently not legislatures and executives) shall be bound by federal law. On the authority of *Martin v. Hunter's Lessee*, the language implies that state judges must administer federal law in cases "arising under" that law. State courts must enforce federal law (including penal provisions), at least so long as they have appropriate jurisdiction. Congress may also prescribe the procedures that state (as well as federal) courts must follow in adjudicating federal rights, and it may preempt state law procedures that conflict with or imposes an undue burden on the effective pursuit of such rights in state court.[58] Those precepts, however, do not answer the question of whether Congress may prescribe producers to be followed by *state* courts in *state* law cases (as it has done in a number of federal "tort reform" statutes). Although the question is close, I believe the answer is no.[59]

A judicial engagement of these difficult questions, and their resolution in consonance with constitutional premises, would not necessarily herald a second coming of constitutional federalism. It would, however, signal a judicial recognition of the central place of *Printz* in the contemporary federalism debate—and, moreover, its indelible rightness. *Printz* abandons "balance" and engages the critical "what federalism" questions. Indeed, those questions surfaced, with refreshing directness, in the opinions. There is nothing wrong, Justice Breyer averred in dissent, with commandeering: European federalisms not only tolerate but affirmatively embrace it as a way of protecting states' (or countries') autonomy. That autonomy translates, not into an independent choice of political ends, but rather in the independent administration of federally predetermined ends. Autonomy in this sense is worth having, as a means of reconciling the demands of the administrative state with the interest in "active liberty." Barring an ill-advised return to the dark days of "dual" federalism, it is the only federalism that can be had.[60]

"Our federalism is not Europe's," Justice Scalia snarled, correctly but elliptically, in response to Justice Breyer. He may have dispensed with a more thoroughgoing reply because he takes too much of our constitutionalism for granted, or because his opinion had reconstructed as much of the constitutional architecture as a majority of that Court would bear, or because he favors succinctness even in landmark opinions. Whatever the reason, *Printz* provides essential elements for rehabilitating the Constitution's competitive logic and genius.

CHAPTER SIXTEEN

Federalism among the States

I allude to the fraudulent laws which have been passed in too many of the states. And though the proposed constitution establishes particular guards against the repetition of those instances, which have heretofore made their appearance, yet it is warrantable to apprehend, that the spirit which produced them, will assume new shapes that could not be foreseen, nor specifically provided against. Whatever practices may have a tendency to disturb the harmony of the states, are proper objects of federal superintendence and control.

Alexander Hamilton

Introduction

The New Deal Constitution methodically depleted the once-rich inventory of horizontal federalism norms. To that state-empowering, exploitation-maximizing strategy, we owe the "polyphonic," centrifugal tendencies of Our Federalism—cascading impositions on interstate commerce, the litigation explosion, the proliferation of semiautonomous power centers. Curbing those tendencies would require the Supreme Court to rediscover that there is such a thing as horizontal federalism and, moreover, that its maintenance requires some form of constitutional common law. This chapter sketches the contours of such a reconstruction in three long-familiar areas: "dormant" commerce, preemption, and federal common law.

The mere mention of those subjects suggests the difficulty of the enterprise. In all three domains, horizontal federalism's erosion is a central commitment of the New Deal Constitution and its modern heirs. Of late, that commitment has been reinforced originalists who deny the very legitimacy of the dormant Commerce Clause, implied preemption, and federal common law. One cannot talk the New Deal's ideological heirs out of empowerment federalism. It may also be too late in the day to dissuade originalists from talking themselves into it; but I shall nonetheless make the effort.

A plausible starting point is the wide (if inch-deep) consensus that each clause of the Constitution must be given independent meaning and content. Our Federalism has extended the New Deal Constitution to the point where judges must either read certain clauses out of the Constitution or else enforce the constitutional language over some range, at the price of discontinuity with the overall constitutional construction. Either way, the embarrassment provides opportunities to argue backwards to a constitutional understanding that makes the clause fit the structure. Especially among originalists, the strategy ought to have traction.

It must, however, contend with the wreckage of decades. While the Constitution teems with explicit, procompetitive horizontal federalism provisions, virtually all of them have been declared unenforceable. The burial of the Contract Clause provides an example; the interment of the Full Faith and Credit Clause as to public acts, another. Even the modest Compact Clause, we have seen, has become constitutional roadkill. One straggler, however, has inexplicably survived the mayhem: the Tonnage Clause, prohibiting states from imposing duties of tonnage without the consent of Congress. Perhaps on account of its very obscurity, though, the clause offers a window into the Constitution's competitive architecture.

Commerce among the States

Competitive federalism's textual beachhead, and the logical place to begin its rehabilitation, is Article I, § 10. Its prohibitions *against* the states govern horizontal relations *among* them, and several provisions are explicitly procompetitive. Because the clauses are right there in the text, and because they plainly envision enforcement by the judiciary in the first instance, it is hard—far harder than with respect to the dormant Commerce Clause—to maneuver their faithful judicial enforcement into the vicinity of *Lochner*. On account of their procompetitive force and purpose, § 10 prohibitions practically disappeared in post–New Deal case law. One recent case, however, has salvaged one of those provisions: the Tonnage Clause.

Tonnage Duties. Polar Tankers v. City of Valdez (2009) arose over an Alaska tax on large ships (almost exclusively tankers) for the duration of their stay in the city's port, in proportion to time spent in other states' ports. The question was whether the tax was consistent with the Tonnage Clause (Art. I, § 10, Cl. 3), providing that no state shall "without the Consent of the Congress, lay any Duty of Tonnage." By a 7–2 vote (Justices Stevens and Souter dissenting), the Court got the clause, the case, and the constitutional construction right.

Alaska's tax fell on (foreign) ships, but it was nominally designated as a *personal property* tax. How do we determine whether it falls under the prohibition against a "Duty of Tonnage"? Justice Breyer's opinion for the Court interpreted "the language of the Clause *in light of its purpose*."[1] The Tonnage Clause and its textual neighbors—in particular, the immediately preceding prohibition against state levies on imports or exports, without the consent of the Congress—are calculated to block states from exercising the taxing power "injuriously to the interests of each other." To that end, the constitutional language must be read beyond its literal terms, as forbidding a state to "do that indirectly which she is forbidden . . . to do directly."[2] An analysis of the tax showed it to be not a service fee (for pilotage, for example), but rather an exaction for the privilege of entering a port, which the Tonnage Clause forbids.[3] Valdez and Alaska cannot escape the constitutional prohibition by calling the prohibited duty by another name; thus, the tax had to fall. Three key elements of sound constitutional construction appear in this nutshell summary: interpretation in light of the purpose of the clause, a closely related interpretive principle against circumvention, and close judicial scrutiny of the state's proffered rationale.

Although the Tonnage Clause is a prohibition against the states, it is not a nationalist imposition. Rather, its purpose is to guard against exploitation—via the abuse of a bottleneck or monopolistic position— among states. Like all other horizontal federalism provisions, then, the clause protects the gains of national collective organization against local opportunistic expropriation. The competitive constitutional commitment serves to protect citizens, not states "as states." It must be respected and enforced even when, as in *Polar Tankers*, state *governments* take their customary position in defense of mutual exploitation.[4]

The constitutional purpose, in turn, would be defeated under a literal reading of the Tonnage Clause. State legislatures generally know how to do indirectly what they are forbidden to do directly. Thus, literalism would deprive constitutional prohibitions of all force and convert them into "a test of whether the legislature has a stupid staff."[5] The constitutional text must therefore be complemented with an interpretive principle against circumvention.[6]

The principle against circumvention has operated from time immemorial in a wide range of statutory settings, and it appeared in English law as soon as British courts began to treat acts of Parliament as authoritative law (roughly the mid-sixteenth century). Sometimes called the "mischief rule," it admonished judges "always to make such [statutory] construction as shall suppress the mischief, and advance the remedy, and to suppress subtle inventions and evasions for continuance of the mischief . . . and to add force and life to the cure and remedy, according to the true intent of the makers of the act."[7] The same logic governs modern legal doctrines far removed from grand constitutional questions, such as patent law. However, the principle applies with special force to the prohibitions of § 10. They are targeted at state measures with a particularly high propensity of menacing sister-states and, hence, the Union; and they "suppose the disposition which will evade it," as Madison put it.[8] Thus, to give force and effect to the clauses and the structure of the Constitution, courts must apply an anticircumvention principle that blocks not only the literally prohibited conduct but also attempts to accomplish the forbidden ends by surreptitious means.[9]

The same logic dictates that the anticircumvention principle must have a limit—defined, like the principle itself, by the purpose of the underlying provision. The Tonnage Clause must cover a property tax that operates as a tonnage duty in drag but not a bona fide (and nondiscriminatory) property tax or a proportionate fee for the use of harbor facilities. There is no way to make that determination except by examining the structure of the tax and the state's police-power justifications. The scrutiny must have bite, lest the state escape the constitutional strictures. But it must also offer the state an opportunity to proffer a legitimate rationale for the challenged tax or regulation.[10]

Prior to *Polar Tankers*, the Tonnage Clause had last been heard of in 1935.[11] The step into a pre–New Deal constitutional universe helped the justices to think like nineteenth-century jurists. Mindful of the constitutional structure and purpose, and armed with an interpretive maxim against circumvention and a healthy skepticism of the states' opportunistic strategies, they got the constitutional structure right. Thus, the case suggests that competitive federalism's recovery requires no newfangled theorem or constitutional "translation"—only, or rather, a recourse to ancient general maxims of constitutional construction. Unfortunately, however, those maxims are promptly abandoned when the judicial inquiry leaves the safe small harbor of the Tonnage Clause and journeys into more expansive, turbulent constitutional waters.

Dormant Commerce. The concerns over state exploitation so deftly addressed in *Polar Tankers* are of a general nature. What if a state manages to maneuver taxes or equivalent regulations outside the ambit of the Tonnage Clause or the Import-Export Clause? Suppose, for instance, that Alaska taxes oil at the point of production with the same effect as the purported property tax in *Polar Tankers*; or suppose Alaska levies a national sales tax. What then? Historically, the concerns encapsulated in but not covered by § 10 prohibitions have been captured by the notion that the "dormant" Commerce Clause forbids discriminatory and exploitative ("extraterritorial") state impositions on interstate commerce. The structural principle is compelling. But it is not easily hung on the *Commerce Clause*, which is formulated as an affirmative grant of power to Congress, not as a prohibition against states. That awkwardness, we have seen, did not trouble the justices of the nineteenth century or the pre–New Deal era. It is, however, decisive for the modern Court's originalists, Justice Scalia and Justice Thomas. In a dissent in *Tyler Pipe Industries, Inc. v. Washington State Department of Revenues* (1987), joined in relevant part by no other justice, Justice Scalia rejected the dormant Commerce Clause except insofar as it forbids facial, "rank" discrimination, thus doing the work of the Privileges and Immunities Clause under a different name. (Justice Scalia has since explained that he would also enforce the dormant Commerce Clause where a state law at issue is indistinguishable from a type of law previously held unconstitutional by the Supreme Court.) Justice Thomas's opposition to the dormant Commerce Clause, stated most explicitly in his dissent in *Camps Newfound/Owatonna, Inc. v. Town of Harrison* (1997), differs from Justice Scalia's in two respects. First, Justice Thomas would abolish rather than limit the dormant Commerce Clause doctrine. Second, he has identified the Import-Export Clause (understood to cover domestic, state-to-state as well as foreign transactions) as the true source of constitutional limitations that the Court has "illegitimately" enforced under the dormant Commerce Clause.[12]

In either version, the originalist position is erroneous. I suggested in chapter 4 that the "dormant" or "negative" Commerce Clause doctrine is at bottom an anticircumvention rule that protects against state evasions of textually specified prohibitions, especially those listed in Article I, § 10. Justice Scalia's and Justice Thomas's own opinions strongly suggest the contours of the argument—even if both justices, for well-intentioned but mistaken reasons, have declined to follow its logic.

Distractions. The history of the dormant Commerce Clause, Justice Scalia acknowledges at the outset of his *Tyler Pipe* dissent, encompasses well over a century's worth of decisions and five decades worth of earlier dicta. However, Justice Scalia avers, the Court's "applications of the doctrine have, not to put too fine a point on the matter, made no sense." He attributes that uncertainty "in no small part to the lack of any clear theoretical underpinning for judicial 'enforcement' of the Commerce Clause." In five pages, he tackles several presumptive theories of the construct.[13]

Obviously, an *exclusive* commerce power would entail a judicially enforceable *dormant* Commerce Clause. However, Justice Scalia argues, several reasons militate against that theory. First, "the language of the Commerce Clause gives no indication of exclusivity." Nor should one assume that congressional powers are generally exclusive: many of them are "plainly" concurrent. (Justice Scalia references the patent and copyright power, the militia, and bankruptcy.) Second, Article I, § 10 denies the states specific powers corresponding to federal powers, such as coining money or negotiating treaties; it contains no such correlative denial of power with respect to commerce. Third, Congress as well as the states assumed "from the date of ratification that at least some state laws regulating commerce were valid." And exclusivity is "infinitely less attractive today," "now that we know interstate commerce embraces such activities as growing wheat for home consumption" and loan sharking.

Justice Scalia next dismisses the notion, originating in *Cooley v. Board of Wardens* (1851), that the Commerce Clause is exclusive not in toto but over some range. It has, he says, "no conceivable basis in the text of the Commerce Clause, which treats 'Commerce . . . among the several States' as a unitary subject." Purpose-based distinctions between the state regulation of commerce and their "police power," he adds, provide no practical means of marking out state and federal powers. Still less plausible to Justice Scalia's mind is the notion, suggested by some late nineteenth-century cases, that the silence of Congress implies a judicially enforceable prohibition against some forms of state legislation.

Finally, Justice Scalia argues that the lack of serious debate over the Commerce Clause during the Convention and ratification counsels against reading the Commerce Clause as anything beyond an authorization of Congress. The *Federalist* wrote often and emphatically about "the virtues of free trade and the need for uniformity and national control of commercial regulation," Justice Scalia notes, but nothing of substance about the Commerce Clause in particular. "Apprehensions," he surmises, surely "would have been 'entertained' if supporters of the Constitution had hinted that the Commerce Clause, despite its language, gave this Court the power it has since assumed." The dissent concludes:

> In sum, to the extent that we have gone beyond guarding against rank discrimination against citizens of other States—which is regulated not by the Commerce Clause but by the Privileges and Immunities Clause [citation omitted]—the Court for over a century has engaged in an enterprise that it has been unable to justify by textual support or even coherent nontextual theory, that it was almost certainly not intended to undertake, and that it has not undertaken very well.[14]

Never mind "in sum." The idea that the dormant Commerce Clause is unjustified is not a conclusion from the legal materials but a conviction that Justice Scalia brings to those materials, whose ambiguities he then construes in a dismayingly one-sided fashion. For example, it is exceedingly unlikely that the illustrious justices who enforced the doctrine throughout our constitutional history made it all up. *Especially* if the doctrine is so obviously an "adverse intellectual possession," a moment's pause over its broad support and its durability should suggest the question of why all those justices thought they needed it.[15] Similarly, many of Justice Scalia's objections apply with equal force to the affirmative Commerce Clause. Of that *"real* Commerce Clause" (as Justice Scalia calls it), too, it could be said that the Court's applications have waxed, waned, and "made no sense." Here, too, purpose-based and categorical distinction between "interstate commerce" and "police-power" regulations could be said to be "more interesting as a metaphysical exercise than useful as a practical technique."[16] And surely, "apprehensions" would have been entertained at the Founding if the Commerce Clause had been understood to grant *Congress* rather than the Court the power it has since assumed.

We can safely put these and other distractions aside.[17] In the end, the *Tyler Pipe* dissent boils down to two principal contentions: a set of structural arguments against a wholly or partially exclusive Commerce Clause, and the claim that the lack of a textual anchor or coherent theory accounts for the dormant Commerce Clause doctrine's protean contours and perennial drift into "inherently legislative" balancing tests. Both arguments, however, are mistaken. The constitutional structure cuts *for* the dormant Commerce Clause, not against it. For closely related reasons, the vision of a strictly clause-bound prohibition against discriminatory state conduct is a mirage.

Structure. Justice Scalia contends (1) that the commerce power cannot be exclusive because the Constitution contains no "correlative denial of power over commerce" to the states and (2) that "rank" state discrimination is prohibited by the Privileges and Immunities Clause. These positions cannot both be right. The Privileges and Immunities Clause primarily protects commerce and those engaged in it; it is a correlative denial of power to the states. The Import-Export Clause, proffered by Justice Thomas as a constitutionally grounded protection against state discrimination, is another (qualified) denial. The structural argument against an exclusive Commerce Clause, then, cannot be that the power to regulate commerce lacks corresponding prohibitions against the states. It must be that the specific denials of power cut against a Commerce Clause that is exclusive *across the board*. When the Founders wanted to block state impositions on commerce without congressional action, the argument goes, they knew how to do so. When they failed to do so, we can infer that no exclusivity was intended unless a federal power is explicitly designated as such.

The inference is not necessarily correct. Hamilton, for one, argued that some powers—though not explicitly exclusive, and unaccompanied by a correlative prohibition—were nonetheless "necessarily" exclusive.[18] But suppose that Hamilton (and with him Webster, Marshall, and virtually the entire antebellum Court) was simply wrong, either on the general principle of construction or with respect to its application to the Commerce Clause: the correlative prohibition argument is still a potent argument *for*, not against, what we have come to call, perhaps unfortunately, the "dormant Commerce Clause." The Constitution's correlative prohibitions, we have seen, require a principle against circumvention. *The dormant Commerce Clause is that principle.*

The historical development of the doctrine, rehearsed in chapters 4 and 5, illustrates the point. A state tax on importers must be captured by the explicit textual prohibition against taxes on imports, even if the taxes have somewhat different attributes. That is the teaching of *Brown v. Maryland*. The Privileges and Immunities Clause protects citizens against "rank discrimination." It is absurd that citizens should lose that protection when they choose to conduct their business in corporate form; that proposition accounts for the rise of the dormant Commerce Clause in the Gilded Age, when the modern corporate form took hold. A state may not evade the prohibition against import *taxes* by erecting *regulatory* tariff barriers: that is the holding of the unanimous decision in *Baldwin v. Seelig* (1935), written at the zenith of the New Deal. States may not evade the prohibition against facial tax discrimination by substituting a formally nondiscriminatory tax with the same effect: that is the holding of—*Tyler Pipe*, among other cases.[19] Time and again, the dormant Commerce Clause doctrine has been deployed to give force and effect to the Constitution's explicit procompetitive prohibitions.

The difficulty, again, lies in determining the proper range and the limits of the anticircumvention principle. The general precept that there must be some limit has special force in the context of a Constitution of limited, enumerated powers. And in fact, the dormant Commerce Clause doctrine has always had its limits, poorly conceived though they may have been some and perhaps much of the time. Viewed from this angle, the partial exclusivity doctrine of *Cooley* notoriety and the categorical, purpose-based commerce distinctions of the Gilded Age weren't the aimless wanderings of a constitutionally homeless doctrine. They were serious, even if ultimately unworkable, efforts to limit the scope of an inescapable principle of sound constitutional construction. Constitutional fidelity requires both an anticircumvention principle and limits to that principle. One can call that a "balancing test" if one wishes, and attempts to discipline the balancing by means of rules will invariably have a whiff of arbitrariness. But so long as one takes the constitutional text and structure seriously, there is no getting away from the hard work of doctrine.[20]

Clauses and Doctrines. If a move to revert to the ground of the Privileges and Immunities Clause or the Import-Export Clause involved nothing more than constitutional nomenclature, we should be inclined "to leave well enough alone."[21] However, originalists insist that the supposedly atextual quality of the dormant Commerce Clause doctrine is the root cause of its erratic contours and application over lo these many decades. Textual anchors, the theory goes, will prevent such errors. This view, too, is mistaken.

An initial difficulty with the proposed back-to-the-text move is that it would tear gaping holes into the commercial Constitution's fabric.[22] The Privileges and Immunities Clause covers only individuals and excludes corporations. The Import-Export Clause covers some—not all—taxes but not equivalent regulations. Perhaps those difficulties could be avoided by revisiting the question of corporate citizenship and the like. (In for an originalist penny, in for a pound.) But it is hard to see the upside of that complicated operation. Unless "back to the text" means literalism and a "stupid staff" test, it means judicial elaboration of the text in case after case, in the teeth of persistent state evasion. It means an anticircumvention principle with both bite and boundaries. And once that necessary step has been taken, textually reanchored analysis will encounter all the difficulties that have rendered the dormant Commerce Clause so seemingly adrift.

Under the Privileges and Immunities Clause, the Supreme Court will have to deal with discrimination that is not facial but nonetheless "rank."[23] It will have to resolve whether subsidies for state citizens constitute discrimination in a constitutionally relevant sense and tell us what exactly is encompassed by the "privileges and immunities" with respect to which states must not discriminate—an inquiry that carries far more of a substantive due process stench than the dormant Commerce Clause ever has, or ever will. It will have to decide what to do about protectionism that runs against commercial transactions rather than actors— the difficulty that prompted Daniel Webster to argue *Gibbons v. Ogden* under the Commerce Clause rather than the Privileges and Immunities

Clause. It will have to decide what to do about state laws that restrict noncitizens' access to a state's own resources. Difficulties of this sort are standard fare under the dormant Commerce Clause. But they have also arisen under the Privileges and Immunities Clause, and the Supreme Court's answers have left legal scholars no happier than the meandering Commerce Clause doctrine.[24]

Similar difficulties would arise under the Import-Export Clause. Justice Thomas's *Camps Newfound* dissent itself suggests two of them. First, the clause does not prohibit all taxes but only "duties" and "imposts." Relying on historical materials, Justice Thomas argues that only indirect taxes, not direct taxes—such as a land tax, at issue in *Camps Newfound*—can be a "duty or impost." Apart from the wisdom of reverting to the messy direct-indirect distinction in this context, the circumvention problem rears its head yet again. What is one to make of a de facto import duty under a different name, as in *Brown v. Maryland*? If that case was wrongly decided, what remains of the constitutional prohibition? If it was rightly decided, where does the prohibition against import taxes end and a state's right to tax begin—when a blog or e-mail attachment has left its "original package"?[25] *Camps Newfound* provides no conclusive answer.[26] It then executes a remarkable maneuver: after 20-plus pages of painstaking exegesis of the terms "export," "import," "duty," and "impost," Justice Thomas flinches at "any," rejects a plaintext reading of the Import-Export Clause as "unnecessarily" broad and, on the authority of a 1976 opinion by Justice Brennan, reads the clause as prohibiting only *discriminatory* duties.[27] I take the antidiscrimination reading to be right, but it is not a natural reading of the text. It is a gloss on the Import-Export Clause—and not any old gloss, but *a dormant Commerce Clause* gloss.

The short of it is that "text" cannot solve the problems that originalists would chalk up to the dormant Commerce Clause doctrine's supposed lack of a textual basis. Conversely, think of the doctrine as an anticircumvention rule: it turns out to have a firm constitutional foundation. In that as in any other derivation, the doctrine will continue to have its perplexities. A prohibition against facial discrimination may not work very well when states can achieve protectionist ends by ostensibly neutral restrictions (for example, on business size or form of organization). One then has to decide whether the threat is sufficiently serious and the practice sufficiently common to warrant a purpose-based inquiry that protects the antidiscrimination rule against evasion.[28] Similarly, "discrimination" may be a bad way of capturing cases of "balkanization"—that is, state disruptions of industries with pronounced network effects. Spatial metaphors capture the constitutional concern over exploitation only imperfectly, and especially in a modern economy, prohibitions that go directly to exploitation might work better. Those difficulties, however, will arise under any constitutional theory that gives force and effect to horizontal federalism. If we have lived with them throughout our constitutional history, that is because analytical perfection is not the true test of the dormant Commerce Clause. The true test is whether the doctrine (in this or that configuration) works well enough over the general run of cases to protect the constitutional structure and its core purposes.[29]

Preemption

Earlier chapters described the New Deal Constitution's preemption "translation"—the move from latent exclusivity to congressional intent as the touchstone of preemption analysis, and the deployment of a presumption against preemption as a means of preserving federalism's "balance." The New Deal Constitution checked the centrifugal, government-empowering tendency of this construction with a doctrine of implied preemption— implied, that is, from the statute at hand and its purposes and objectives, as understood by the reviewing court. This doctrine, canonically stated in *Hines v. Davidowitz* (1941) and *Rice v. Santa Fe Elevator Corp.* (1947), has remained with us to this day. In its contemporary application, it pushes toward empowerment federalism. The uneasy category of implied preemption—the only element of the New Deal formula that provides a check against centrifugal tendencies—has been eroding for the past decade.

In principle, it is not hard to reconstruct a competitive, constitutionally grounded preemption doctrine. Its basic elements are described below, along with a few brief illustrations.[30] The doctrine runs headlong, not only into a federalism of balance and empowerment, but also into recent originalist and textualist contentions. It is nonetheless the best approximation of the constitutional order.

Elements of a Competitive Preemption Doctrine. Although preemption law is first and foremost a matter of statutory interpretation, it cannot operate without some set of background premises and assumptions. A preemption doctrine consonant with the Constitution's competitive architecture and logic requires three such premises: a background assumption of exclusivity, as opposed to concurrent powers or polyphony; a rule against circumvention; and an explicit recognition of horizontal federalism risks.

The background rule of *exclusivity* governed what we now call preemption law from *Gibbons v. Ogden* well into the pre–New Deal era. The dominance of federal law, to the exclusion of any contravening state law, was deemed incident to the enactment of federal law, regardless of whether Congress had expressed its intent to that effect: the Supremacy Clause does the work of its own force. Pre–New Deal enactments, such as the National Bank Act, the Sherman Act, and (for a lesser example) the Warehouse Act of *Rice* notoriety reflected the same understanding. Congress may of course derogate from the background rule—for example, by enacting "savings clauses" in favor of state law. The derogation may also be implied—for example, by a statutory specification of the role of state authorities in the regulatory scheme. But the background rule remains: one problem, one sovereign.[31]

The exclusivity rule reduces the conflicts, confusion, and coordination problems that invariably afflict any regime of concurrent regulation. Its distinctly competitive dimension lies in eliminating the proregulatory bias that attends any system of concurrent regulation. An exclusive federal scheme may be excessively strict or lax. Concurrent state regulation, however, can correct errors in only one direction—more regulation. Short of empowerment federalism's global premise that more regulation is better regulation, there is no reason to trust a unidirectional mechanism of "error correction"; the better part of wisdom is to argue over and, hopefully, to improve the accuracy of a single system.

The most important application of this principle in the modern context is to read federal health and safety standards, as well as product labeling requirements, as an exclusive and preemptive optimum rather than a mere regulatory floor. *Geier v. Honda Motor Co.* (2000) arrived at that proposition by a circuitous route and in heavy reliance on the defendant-agency's deliberative process and the solicitor general's litigation position. The rapid, near-total erosion of *Geier's* holding and reasoning, summarized in chapter 14, has demonstrated the need for a firmer doctrinal basis. "Exclusivity" provides that basis both on account of its constitutional derivation and because it captures, in this context, the common-sense background expectation that Congress, barring an indication to the contrary, would not want its regulatory regime compromised or biased in either direction.

An interpretive *rule against circumvention* is a necessary means of preserving statutory integrity. It is the statutory equivalent of the constitutional maxim recognized in *Polar Tankers*, and it follows the same logic. Once a preemptive statute has been enacted, the regulated parties— states as well as individuals—will search out byways to achieve their illicit objectives without running afoul of the literal statutory language. The rote reply that Congress can easily clarify matters by clearly stating its intent to preempt will not do. States have every incentive and myriad ways to circumvent federal law, which Congress cannot possibly foresee. What preemption law needs, therefore, is not niggling statutory parsing but a rule against circumvention. The hard question, here as in the constitutional context, is how far to extend the statutory reach to block the evasions, without cutting off legitimate conduct that the statute never meant to forbid.

The rule against circumvention is generally recognized, although not under that name, in cases of express preemption. For example, the Supreme Court has often given a broad interpretation to statutory provisions that expressly preempt state laws "relating to" the federally regulated subject matter.[32] Hard questions and great uncertainty have arisen, however, over the interplay of federal preemptive regimes and state tort law, especially where federal statutes contain a savings clause in favor of state tort law. At times, the Supreme Court has read federal health and safety statutes as incomplete regulatory regimes that establish binding ex ante standards that govern deterrence but leave the compensation function of tort law untouched; at other times, it has treated the requirements of state tort law as the equivalent of clearly preempted state administrative requirements.[33] That latter approach is consonant with a rule against circumvention, and it is generally preferable. Historically as well as functionally, there is little doubt that the dominant forms of contemporary tort litigation—especially over design defects and failure to warn and its variants—are calculated attempts to circumvent the unequivocal preemption of state regulatory authority. It strains credulity that a Congress that has carefully blocked state regulators from compromising a federal regulatory regime would nonetheless want state courts and juries to exercise that authority. It is often a difficult question to what extent statutory savings clauses should be understood to signal a departure from that baseline; but that question goes to the reach of the anticircumvention rule, not its soundness or derivation.

Exclusivity and the rule against circumvention dovetail with an understanding of preemption as a *horizontal federalism* doctrine. At first impression, of course, preemption does not look like a horizontal federalism rule at all; it substitutes, so far as it reaches, a federal monopoly for varying state law. Ordinarily, however, the federal monopoly serves to solve some federalism coordination problems—the balkanization of national markets and state protectionism or exploitation. Thus, express preemption (the affirmative exercise of the commerce power) forms a continuum with the dormant Commerce Clause: one governs when Congress has spoken; the other, when it has remained silent. Implied preemption lies between those poles: it governs when Congress has spoken unclearly or elliptically. Its horizontal federalism implications are profound indeed. Implied preemption is the last remaining venue—other than the dormant Commerce Clause—where concerns over state evasion, defection, and exploitation still have some force. Moreover, the doctrine has come to serve as a substitute for defunct doctrines that once structured interstate relations—contractual defenses, full faith and credit, meaningful limits to extraterritorial jurisdiction, and so on.

No preemption doctrine can fully compensate for the demise of those doctrines, and quite arguably, preemption law has been made to carry more weight than it will bear. Surely, though, it would benefit from a more explicit and systematic recognition of horizontal federalism risks. For example, a preemption dispute over state-imposed automobile fuel efficiency standards is not just a dispute between an ecologically minded state and a laggard central government; it also presents a conflict among that state's preferences and the differing preferences of all other states, including those where cars are produced. A dispute over local utility regulators' authority to block mergers and acquisitions among out-of-state energy producers is not simply a matter between those regulators and the Federal Energy Regulatory Commission; it manifestly implicates the interests of others states. A preemption dispute over a Vermont jury's authority to issue liability verdicts in defiance of FDA labeling requirements also implicates other states' interests; they may well prefer a less liability-driven market for medical devices and drugs but, in the event of a liability verdict, have no choice but to play Vermont's game.[34]

Far more often than not, then, preemption is reciprocal; the prohibition against some states is a protection for others. A federalism of balance and empowerment screens out that dynamic and hands a premium to the most aggressive state. However, it is very hard to see any gains, especially including *federalism* gains, from a failure to preempt state regulators who have no incentive to take the external costs of their activity into account and, very often, have a potent incentive to create them. Recognize the horizontal federalism risks: you are driven back to an exclusivity rule that curbs state defections either way, coupled with a rule against clever circumvention.

Preemption, Balance, and Textualism. The analysis just sketched recaptures, albeit through judicial canons rather than direct constitutional argument, a large piece a competitive Constitution. In that important sense, one can call it originalist. Practicing originalists' preemption understanding, however, has of late gone off in a very different direction. It combines an attachment to federalism's "balance" with a commitment to strict textual interpretation. Textualism counsels an abandonment of a judicial presumption against preemption—certainly in cases of express preemption and very probably in cases of implied preemption. In that latter context, however, text-only analysis also produces what can only be called a near-conclusive presumption against preemption. The clearest statement of this position is Justice Clarence Thomas's concurring opinion in *Wyeth v. Levine* (2009), briefly discussed in chapter 14 but well worth a second look.

The opinion strikes a high constitutional note. It quotes Madison's "double security" passage and the "few and defined" federal powers passage from *Federalist* 45; rehearses federalism's "numerous advantages" and characterizes the Supremacy Clause as an "extraordinary power in a federalist system"; and concludes that "in order to protect the delicate balance of power mandated by the Constitution, the Supremacy Clause must operate only in accordance with its terms."[35] That command entails that Congress must act within the compass of its enumerated powers (although that, Justice Thomas has lamented in another preemption case, may be "water over the dam.")[36] It also entails "that pre-emptive effect be given only to those federal standards and policies that are set forth in, or necessarily follow from, the statutory text that was produced through the constitutionally required bicameral and presentment procedures." Put differently, preemption must either be express, or else "turn on whether state law conflicts with the text of the relevant federal statute or with the federal regulations authorized by that text." It must *not* turn on creative judicial constructions of generalized congressional "purposes" or "tensions" with supposed federal "objectives." The "Court's entire body of 'purposes and objectives' pre-emption jurisprudence," Justice Thomas insists, "is inherently flawed." There follows, by way of elaboration, a review of the trajectory of implied preemption from *Hines v. Davidowitz*, which Justice Thomas views as the origin of "freewheeling" implied preemption and, apparently, as wrongly decided, to its apex in *Geier*.[37]

Much of Justice Thomas's discussion is right and constructive. In preemption as in other statutory contexts, the notion that a federal statute should entail whatever might promote its generalized "purposes" (as divined by a reviewing court) "is the slogan of the enthusiast, not the analytical tool of the arbiter."[38] Moreover, Justice Thomas's push to abandon "obstacle preemption" and to put in its place a single "conflicts" test can be understood as a proposal to merge those supposedly distinct strands of preemption analysis—a step that would indeed simplify preemption analysis and, if done right, lead it back into safer doctrinal waters.[39] That result, however, depends on a sensible understanding of preemption doctrine's constitutional context. Wrenched from that context, Justice Thomas's approach actually threatens to compromise any plausible preemption analysis.

In demolishing the presumption against preemption, Justice Thomas's analysis transcends, with commendable rigor and clarity, a balance nostrum of the New Deal Constitution. And yet, the analysis still owes too much to that legacy. The connection is suggested by Justice Thomas's references to federalism's "advantages" and the "extraordinary" nature of the Supremacy Clause. The origin of those averments, quoted and cited in the *Wyeth* concurrence, is *Gregory v. Ashcroft* (1991)—not a pure preemption case, but a "clear statement" case. Justice Thomas would import that rule or its functional equivalent into the preemption context: if Congress wants to assure the preemptive effect, it must say so. As shown in chapter 15, however, under the impeccable logic of *Printz v. United States*, clear statements are required for spending legislation *but not* for preemptive legislation. The Supremacy Clause is the ordinary mode of operation of our Constitution. Preemptive effects naturally flow from and attend—without any explicit congressional declaration—any federal statute enacted pursuant to the Supremacy Clause.[40]

Recognizing this logic, Justice Thomas's *Wyeth* opinion acknowledges that federal law will still impliedly trump state law in cases of direct conflict. However, the initial presumption that Congress could and should have said what it failed to say invariably shades the implied preemption analysis. A "direct conflict" entailing preemption, Justice Thomas acknowledges, must encompass more than sheer physical inability to comply with both federal and state law; following an influential and powerfully argued law review article, he suggests that it may mean something like "logical-contradiction."[41] Justice Thomas's opinion is strangely diffident, though, on whether that is actually the right test and on what it might mean—yet highly confident that a case that pits federal drug-labeling requirements against state juries' liability verdicts does *not* present a direct conflict. That position suggests an exceptionally narrow conception of conflict. If *any* federal policy "necessarily follows from" a statutory text, it is the Food, Drug, and Cosmetics Act's attempt to strike an optimum balance among risks. Every medicine has side effects and can be misused. What is the point of the federal drug-approval process if not to balance these risks against the benefits of a drug that would save lives? What is the point of labeling standards if not to guard against the twin dangers of under- and overwarning? And what remains of the FDA's mission when juries can hold any pharmaceutical company liable for any reason or, as far as federal law is concerned, for no reason at all?

Those questions, to be sure, go to the *purpose* of the federal statute, not its strict text. However, a textualism that would dismiss them for that reason alone is unsustainable even on its own ground. *Express* preemption provisions ("we hereby preempt any state law 'relating to' stuff we care about") demand a purpose analysis—not with respect to the whether of preemption (the text answers that question) but with respect to their scope. There is no way of conducting that analysis without recourse to what an originalist implied preemption analysis would forbid—an inquiry into the purpose of the statute. To give wide berth to purposes in express preemption cases while declining to revert to them in implied preemption cases is to put far too much weight on legislative magic words.[42]

The purpose inquiry must not be "freewheeling"; it has to remain tethered to the statutory text and structure. However, implied preemption analysis cannot make do without some such inquiry; and in truth, it never has. Justice Thomas's extensive discussion of *Hines v. Davidowitz* strongly suggests that he views implied ("obstacle") preemption as a New Deal invention, of one piece with the expansion of the breadth of congressional powers. But this simply is not so. To see the point, and to recognize how far Justice Thomas's approach differs from the traditional understanding, recall *Gibbons v. Ogden*, the Supreme Court's famous first engagement with preemption and the Commerce Clause: although John Marshall's opinion spoke the language of "conflict," *Gibbons* is plainly a case of the implied "purposes" preemption against which Justice Thomas inveighs. The federal statute at issue (which contained no express preemption clause) conferred on American ships an advantage vis-à-vis foreign ships. It is difficult to perceive any direct conflict, physical or logical, between that policy and New York's preference for one flag carrier over another. Marshall considered the argument that the coastal trading license "gives no right to trade; and that its sole purpose is to confer the American character" on ships and their owners—and *rejected* it.[43] *Wyeth* presents a closely analogous problem, and Justice Thomas responds very differently. The federal approval process, he writes, creates no "unfettered right, for all time, to market [a] drug with the specific label that was federally approved."[44] If that is right, *Gibbons* was wrong, or else should have been decided under the dormant Commerce Clause (if, pace Justice Thomas, it exists). If the statutory text in *Gibbons* created a "conflict" in a preemption-relevant sense, then so, a fortiori, does the FDCA.[45] And if the perfunctory licensing approval in *Gibbons* has preemptive force, then so, and again a fortiori, should the FDA's painstaking, one-drug-at-a-time, one-label-sentence-at-a-time approval process.

What does the work in *Gibbons*, and what drops by the wayside in Justice Thomas's inquiry, is a purpose-based analysis that rests on the three premises identified earlier: one problem (navigation), one sovereign; acute awareness of the "horizontal" risk of state interference with interstate commerce; a rule against circumvention that extends the federal protection into each state's harbor and against exclusion by means of monopoly grant as well as direct exclusion. In any given case, it is hard to say how far the rule against circumvention should reach—what constitutes a "conflict" for purposes of the Supremacy Clause or, as we have come to say, preemption. The difficulty is reflected in judicial synonyms and circumlocutions ("repugnance," "obstacle," "impediment"). All those nineteenth-century formulations rest on a recognition that the operative test must reach beyond incontrovertible conflicts (and yet have a limit); all are driven by a purpose analysis that is informed by constitutionally derived background assumptions. Here as under the dormant Commerce Clause, the doctrinal work is hard and messy—but also necessary.

Federal Common Law

Erie Railroad Co. v. Tompkins, I have argued, is the pivotal case of the New Deal Constitution, both on account of its holding and its emanations. *Swift* rested on principles of party autonomy and contract, and it gave force to the central purpose of diversity jurisdiction—to provide parties in interstate commerce with an unbiased judicial forum and law. It respected state autonomy by allowing states to opt out of the general law by means of legislation, and it left Congress free to supplement or supplant the general common law. Properly applied, the *Swift* regime was uniquely suited to a system of competitive federalism. *Erie* demolished that regime and, in its place, erected a vehemently anticompetitive order. It yoked state autonomy to plaintiffs' opportunistic forum choices; disabled federal courts from countermanding those choices; and in that fashion enshrined the preferences of the most exploitative state as the baseline of Our Federalism.

In many ways, *Erie*'s intellectual foundations have eroded. Its statutory basis—that is, its interpretation of § 34 of the Judiciary Act—has been discredited. Its constitutional holding, mystifying even at the time, has become no more plausible with age; scholars variously describe it as "puzzling," "murky," or "cracked" in its foundations. Its promise of eliminating forum shopping, superficially plausible when made, has become laughable. *Erie*'s slender intellectual basis is Mr. Holmes's crude positivism—which, unlike Mr. Spencer's Social Statics, appears to be enshrined by the Constitution. It is difficult to think of any comparably important case so bereft of serious intellectual or constitutional support; only *Roe v. Wade* (1973) comes close.[46]

And yet, *Erie* stands more unassailable even than *Roe*. Progressives have learned to love *Erie* by limiting it to the federal *general* common law—to all intents, interstate commerce. In that domain, *Erie*'s injunction does what Justice Brandeis wanted it to do: it subjects commercial actors to the whims of opportunistic plaintiffs and faction-ridden states. (For every other concern and constituency, the judiciary has an expansive federal common law on offer.) Conservative jurists, and originalists in particular, embrace *Erie* for very different reasons, but no less ardently. They view the decision as the embodiment of their most fundamental orientations: judicial deference to Congress, opposition to judicial policy making in common-law garb, respect for the democratic process in the states and at the federal level.

An assault on *Erie*'s bastion may be a suicide mission; and in practical terms, it is unclear what can be gained from it. Grant, arguendo, that the *Swift* regime provides *in theory* an elegant and profoundly competitive constitutional solution to a difficult federalism problem. Grant even that contemporary federal courts would tend to identify sensible rules of general common law—not because federal judges and justices are free-marketers, but because their institutional status disposes them, unlike state legislatures or courts, to recognize the reciprocal nature of state law.[47] The fact remains that the *Swift* regime proved unstable even in the nineteenth century and is unlikely to fare any better under modern circumstances. *Swift* assumed that states would recognize, in general and over the long run, the good sense of a competitive federal order and the global gains of reliable rules for interstate commerce. That assumption was mistaken then; it is entirely untenable now. (If anything, state rebellion would take more virulent forms today because the federal common-law rules, unlike those of *Swift*, would have preemptive force.) *Swift* also presupposed a Congress that remains largely quiescent and, moreover, has a residual inhibition against treating private contracts as mere targets of regulation. That supposition was correct in *Swift*'s days; it too is untenable now.

At the same time, we may yet learn to live with *Erie*, under a "new" federal common law that compensates for *Erie*'s defects, political and social. Federal courts have learned to infer substantive rulemaking authority from broad, vague, or purely procedural statutes—in the commercial arena, often to good effect. They have created enclaves of federal common law, from maritime law to federal contractor defenses, and they have jealously safeguarded the Federal Rules of Civil Procedure. Preemption often provides a defense against state depredations; under the Federal Arbitration Act, it allows parties to mimic *Swift*'s contractual regime. And perhaps improvisation in light of experience might yield further progress. For example, Judge Friendly thought that then-still-manageable choice of law problems could be addressed by Congress.[48] A half-century later, we know better. In a world of roving plaintiffs' lawyers and a consistently dilatory Congress, the time may have come for the federal judiciary to overrule *Klaxon* and to regenerate a constitutional choice of law regime while leaving *Erie* itself unscathed.

Perhaps. And yet, in *Erie*'s force field, every procompetitive step is arduous, incremental, contestable, and in permanent danger of reversal. A judiciary that believes in *Erie*'s incontrovertible correctness is unlikely to bring itself to overrule *Klaxon*; much more likely, it will continue to play out its exploitative logic and leave the Full Faith and Credit Clause and due process-based extraterritoriality norms to oblivion. *Erie*'s enclaves are conceptually unstable, and one wonders how long the grandfathered and ad hoc exceptions can last. Worst, *Erie* perennially endangers the remnants of a competitive constitutional architecture. It broods in the background and sometimes the foreground of preemption cases and dormant Commerce Clause cases, as unimpeachable authority and as the lodestar of Our Federalism, and it rears its head in cases and contexts where no state law or court is within viewing distance.[49] *Erie* is as unquestionably right as *Lochner* is wrong; hence, any emanation from its penumbras must also be right. *Erie*'s specific holding may be manageable; but unless its myth is overcome, no confident constitutional federalism jurisprudence is possible.

In that light, the central task may be to do to *Erie* what the New Deal Constitution did to *Lochner*—to discredit it, to the point where it need no longer be overruled. *Erie*'s statutory holding, as noted, has already been discredited and, in any event, cannot bear the weight that its defenders would put on the case. Thus, the crux is *Erie*'s constitutional dimension. Here, *Erie*'s apologists confront two related problems: the want of a credible constitutional argument in *Erie*, and the difficulty of explaining *Erie*'s enclaves (that is, the areas where its injunction against federal common law, by broad agreement, does not operate) without simultaneously undercutting its injunction against federal *general* common law. Recognizing the dual difficulty, originalist scholars have done what liberal scholars have done about *their* problematic lodestar case (*Roe v. Wade*)—float a series of ingenious arguments in the hope that one of them will eventually work. Here as there, I doubt the success of the enterprise.

The most promising defense of *Erie* is some combination of separation of powers and federalism arguments. The most forceful and thoughtful contemporary proponent of this approach, professor Bradford R. Clark, rests his case on the Supremacy Clause, understood in the context of the larger constitutional structure. The Supremacy Clause, he observes, establishes "supremacy" only for three forms of federal law—the Constitution itself; treaties; and laws made "in Pursuance" of the Constitution. "In pursuance," Clark rightly observes, must mean in the way prescribed by the Constitution—that is, subject to bicameral consent, presentment, and presidential veto. It must also mean, within the limits of the enumerated powers. A judicially engineered federal common law that transcends these bounds is constitutionally impermissible. It infringes on federalism because the "pursuant to" requirements are an essential safeguard for states against federal usurpation. It infringes on the separation of powers because lawmaking is committed to the political branches, to the wholesale exclusion of the judiciary.[50]

Although, or rather because, Clark's argument has practically nothing to do with the actual *Erie* opinion, it provides a plausible constitutional rationale for a decision and opinion dreadfully bereft of it. It has the additional attraction of refraining from any debate-stopping harangue about excessive judicial power. Clark's argument, in short, is the *right kind* of originalist argument: it takes the Constitution's text and structure seriously. And yet, in substance, the argument proves both too little and too much. As for "too little," Clark acknowledges, more candidly than most *Erie* defenders, that he isn't saying anything that Justice Story did not already know. (He merely insists that *Swift* got out of hand and eventually prompted judges to substitute their own views of sound public policy on the states, without inquiring why that might have happened.) As for "too much," a Supremacy Clause understanding that is sufficiently rigorous to provide firm ground for *Erie* also casts doubt on practices and institutions wholly outside its ambit—for starters, the administrative state, whose raison d'être is to make law outside the constitutional strictures of bicameral approval and presentment.[51] More obviously and directly, the structural Supremacy Clause argument runs up hard against well-recognized enclaves of federal common law. Well aware of the problem, Clark responds that

> many of the "federal common law" rules that fall within these enclaves do not actually constitute "federal judge-made law" because they consist of background principles derived from the law of nations that are necessary to implement basic aspects of the constitutional scheme.[52]

The most pristine example is the adjudication of disputes among states under federal common law: resorting to either state's domestic law would compromise basic norms of state equality, which are presupposed by, but not explicitly stated in, the Constitution. But if that is right, as surely it is, then what exactly is wrong with *Swift* and the law merchant (the most important branch of "the law of nations," as then understood)—and what is right about *Erie*? The only assumption that would render *Swift* wrong and both *Erie* and its interstate dispute enclave right is that commerce among the states, on terms of equality and mutual nonaggression and nondiscrimination, is *not* a basic aspect of the constitutional scheme. That is indeed the premise of *Erie* and its federalism. To state the premise, however, is to demonstrate its absurdity.

The same point emerges from another recent attempt to provide a coherent account of *Erie*'s enclaves. Where the state legislative process can be expected to operate with tolerable fairness vis-à-vis noncitizens, Jay Tidmarsh and Brian Murray have argued in a thoughtful article, no independent body of federal law is required. This will be the case when out-of-state interests are adequately represented, either directly or virtually. (Matters of contract, tort, or property, the authors write, fit that description: state legislatures cannot act on parochial impulses without inflicting collateral damage on in-state constituencies.) In certain situations, however,

> states have such a strong self-interest in a controversy or have erected such high barriers to political participation by some groups that state law cannot be expected to provide a sufficiently detached, reliable, and neutral rule of decision. . . . In these areas, states must resort to another source of law. Unless Congress or the Constitution has created a rule of decision, that law must by default be federal common law.[53]

The authors' account, like Clark's, is ingeniously argued—and like Clark's, fails to explain *Erie*'s enclaves and *Erie* itself. Again, it collapses into *Erie*'s baseline: never mind, for constitutional purposes, the commerce of the United States.

Start with *Erie*'s enclaves: two of them, endorsed and defended by Tidmarsh and Murray (as well as Clark), are established by the decisions in *Clearfield Trust* (1943) and *United Technologies v. Boyle* (1988)—federal common-law trumps for the federal government's institutions and its contractors, respectively, over state law.[54] Grant the authors' stated premise that states have in certain settings an incentive to treat national assets and institutions as a common pool to be raided. Is that force more likely to operate against the national government and its institutions, or (as in the ordinary *Erie* setting) against sister-states and commercial actors domiciled there? Not even close. State attempts to exploit national institutions run directly against those readily identifiable institutions. The scenario is not unknown; see *M'Culloch*. But it is not very common or likely, and for what it is worth, neither *Clearfield Trust* nor *United Technologies* suggested that the displaced state law had anything to do with parochial motivations. In contrast, horizontal exploitation is the states' daily diet. Its costs are dispersed over forty-nine other states, whose governments are similarly inclined and whose citizens may never notice the imposition. That commonplace abuse, more than the occasionally interference with federal institutions, demands redress.

The authors are careful to specify that likely state bias is a necessary but not a sufficient condition for a resort to federal common law. Additional considerations, especially the need for uniformity and the presence of the United States as a party in interest, should inform (and have historically informed) the calculus. But this justification of *Erie*'s enclaves dissolves in consideration of the federal legislature's incentives and disposition. If Congress can be expected to pay attention to anything at all, it is the protection of institutions that the federal government not only regulates but actually owns and operates, such as the Treasury and the armed forces. Yet here, despite a Congress armed to the teeth with enumerated powers and with ample incentives to make its own institutions work, federal common law reigns—mind you, not merely in the form of a prohibition against the states (a dormant army and navy clause) but in the form of affirmative, judicially supplied rules of decision and affirmative defenses. Conversely, if Congress can be expected to space out on any subject, it is the provision of horizontal ordering rules to protect interstate commerce. And yet here, *Erie* reigns. Go figure.[55]

By way of further refinement, Tidmarsh and Murray concede that, while actual or virtual representation of out-of-state interests provides adequate protection against state law bias, one still wants to guard against the biased *application* of that law. The grant of diversity jurisdiction provides against that bias by providing a neutral forum; but no independent law is required. Again, though, the argument falls short. As an initial matter, "representation" as a check against state law bias does not appear to play a very prominent role in the existing federal common-law enclaves. *United Technologies* arose from, of all places, Virginia—home to the Pentagon, innumerable military installations, and an army's worth of federal military contractors. If that level of "representation" cannot arrest vertical state aggression, it is hard to see what it could accomplish in the horizontal context. But the "representation" calculus is untenable at a more fundamental level.

The distinction between the *making* and the *application* of state law is a weird throwback to *Swift*ean metaphysics, in a post-*Erie* age that has woken up to the recognition that judges make law any given day but Sundays. Moreover, it is alarmingly thin. A state court that invents or extends a theory of design defects, unconscionability, or fraud and misrepresentation, will to all intents have *made* law, which federal courts will then have to follow. (Arresting state courts' propensity in that direction would require a very wide berth for diversity jurisdiction and ready recourse for defendants to remove cases to federal court, neither of which we have.) There may be more than one way to curb the most obviously exploitative exercises of state court jurisdiction—a due process clause with extraterritorial bite, perhaps, or a federal judicial review that blocks state judicial law making by holding state courts to the background principles of "their" state law, as distinct from their latest pronouncements in the case at bar.[56] The former strategy mobilizes constitutional common law; the latter borrows from *Swift*'s insistence—not so metaphysical, when you come to think of the real world—that diversity defendants are entitled to the common law as it actually is, as distinct from a state court's opportunistic manipulation in a particular case. It is hard to square either strategy with *Erie*'s holding, let alone its myth.

In the end, the notion of political "representation" as a safeguard against state law bias is a post hoc rationalization. Like *Erie* itself, it substitutes considerations of political *interests* for the calculations of *parties* to commercial transactions and conflicts.[57] Consequently, it misses *Erie*'s appalling genius. Under *Swift*'s logic, producers and consumers, sellers and buyers can sort themselves into a state regime to suit their tastes. If they fail or decline to do so, they can still be confident that in the event of defection by either party, recourse can be had to federal courts and their law. In *Erie*'s universe, in contrast, consumers and buyers are encouraged to migrate to the most aggressive, pro-plaintiff jurisdiction. Producers and sellers, on the other hand, have no exit. They must guard against ex post expropriation by the worst of the lot—not knowing who that might be, but confident in the expectation that some jurisdiction will volunteer. That regime is not simply at odds with a Constitution that entrusts the commerce of the United States to the care of the central government; it is at odds with any kind of lawful, republican government. A legal order that is worth a dang will aim to maximize citizens' gains from trade at one end and minimize their costs of prevention at the other.[58] It will enable individuals to make their own arrangements, reduce transaction costs by providing a menu of off-the-shelves default rules, provide reliable mechanisms to enforce that regime, and block postcontractual opportunism:

see *Swift*. *Erie* inverts the regime and its premises. It blocks the move into mutually beneficial transactions and, in so doing, encourages ex post opportunism and a systematic migration into jurisdictions most open to it. One could still say, as Murray and Tidmarsh say, that Microsoft surely possesses sufficient economic and political resources to guard against the risk of bias and exploitation in state legislatures.[59] That may be true; but it is true in the same way that in a world without police protection, the most resourceful among us can pay for electric fences and bodyguards.

The question is whether one wants to freight the Founders with a constitutional construction that incorporates so lunatic a calculus. *Erie* answered that question. But there remains a doubt whether its answer was right and whether we can still afford it.

CHAPTER SEVENTEEN

Concluding Essay: Federalism at the Crossroads

Introduction

Our Federalism is "ours" in a tautological sense—but not in any other meaningful sense, especially a constitutional sense. Madison's compound republic envisioned a federalism for citizens, not politicians. It put confidence in competitive politics and a self-enforcing structure, not rights; and it sought to contain factional politics, not to unleash it. Our federalism of rents, rights, and empowerment did have its advocates at the time— the Anti-Federalists. They lost, but enough of their heritage survived the Constitution to allow later generations to seize on it—not by changing the Constitution, which in a formal sense has become more competitive; but by exploiting the running room that a Constitution, however well constructed, will provide. And so we have ended up with entrenched practices and institutions that are more commonly associated with European-style federalism than with its American variant—capacious rights guarantees, high levels of transfer payments, intergovernmentalism, and pervasive political and institutional cartelization.

Throughout, I have emphasized Our Federalism's extraordinary resilience and its self-reinforcing tendencies. Evidence from countries around the world (including the United States, as seen in chapter 12) shows that meaningful reforms of encrusted federalism cartels occur only under acute crisis conditions. America and its federalism now confront that condition:

the country is in a perilous financial condition, and federalism is a very large factor in the equation. Therein lies an opportunity, but also a profound challenge. Although we like to tell ourselves that our constitutional story must have a happy ending, entropy—the decline of nations—is a more plausible political story than Calvary. The most one can say is that crises provide opportunities for political entrepreneurs of a constitutional disposition. The opportunities may go unused. Enough is at stake, however, to explore them.

The End of Our Federalism

In most dimensions, Our Federalism has no obvious upper bound. Consociational rights, by their very nature, demand perennial refinement and expansion, and it is difficult to explain how and why the enterprise makes us worse off. Empowerment federalism erodes the advantages of a reliable legal order—in a global economy, arguably the only comparative and competitive advantage on which the United States can, or could, hope to rely. Losses at this front, however, are not easily traced to individual pieces of regulation or legislation that, at the time of their enactment, respond to potent political demands. The exception to this pattern is the fiscal arena, where Our Federalism runs up against a real-world affordability constraint. For several decades, fiscal federalism has served its purpose of driving up state and local taxes and spending. That potential now seems exhausted. State and local governments are chafing under crushing levels of debt, and there appears to be little room for own-source revenue enhancements sufficient to cover annual budget shortfalls, let alone long-term pension and retirement obligations.[1] In response to the 2008/2009 financial crisis, the national government engineered a series of rescue operations, to the point of compromising the nation's longstanding precommitment against bailing out states. Those interventions, however, have only delayed necessary adjustment.[2] The national government's financial predicament precludes any global bailout of distressed state and local governments and their creditors.

Comparable crises have in other countries prompted steps that reverberated far beyond intergovernmental fiscal relations.[3] This would also be true of any meaningful federalism reform in the United States. Fiscal transfers are part of a web of intergovernmental relations that enmeshes much of the business of modern government, from education to the environment to health care and insurance. The payments are closely tied to the modern entitlement state and the social contract—directly, because the conditions that are attached to federal funding streams often take the form of individual entitlements; indirectly, because the warped incentives generated by federal funding have prompted state and local governments to issue unsustainable amounts of debt and to divert revenues from non-funded entitlement programs, especially public employees' pension and retirement benefit plans. The harsh fact that these obligations cannot and will not be paid (at least not in real dollars) will present questions of grave import. For example, we may need a bankruptcy process for states, a step that was contemplated but, on account of perceived constitutional problems, abandoned during the New Deal.[4] The Federal Reserve may have to buy municipal bonds, or the national government may have to guarantee the states' debts or (as in Argentina) roll insolvent state pension plans into the federal system. Any one of these measures would raise the question of what the states would have to give in return and how the burdens are to be distributed among taxpayers, public employees and retirees, and bondholders. In short, thinking about federalism's future is like thinking about the Union's debt and taxes under the Articles of Confederation: think hard enough, and you recognize the futility of trying to revamp fiscal affairs without rethinking the broader federal structure.

More ephemeral but also more important, federalism's fiscal crisis signals broader institutional failures and accompanying popular discontents. Our Federalism is a product of affluence.[5] We could afford to dissipate revenues and political responsibility in an intergovernmental shell game, and we could afford to subject producers to a barrage of conflicting, ever-escalating regulatory demands because and so long as—well, because and so long as we could afford it. In flush times, the "whiplash of prosperity" provided handy rationale for large-scale fiscal transfers.[6] At times when the country felt prosperous, no one really minded—that is, not enough to prompt a groundswell of demand for reform—that a large chunk of the funds spent on a "war on poverty" disappeared in intergovernmental policy silos; that Medicaid's warped incentives put not only the program itself but state and federal budgets on an unsustainable path; that federalism's intergovernmental machinery first rendered New Orleans defenseless against a sure-to-come hurricane, then botched the response, and finally dissipated upwards of $140 billion in reconstruction funds, to little discernible effect; or that decades of intergovernmental school reform have produced no measurable result.[7] And so long as federal monetary policy and implicit federal guarantees for financial institutions inflated Wall Street profits, there seemed to be little direct harm, and perhaps some good, in letting state attorneys general and trial lawyers capture a portion of the outsized returns by means of investigations and settle-or-else lawsuits. In times of economic and fiscal stress, Our Federalism takes on a more menacing coloration.

A fiscal reckoning, one might think, should cut in favor of a more affordable federalism, in the way in which a private household in distress might shift from a BMW to a Chevy. However, on account of institutional path dependencies and embedded incentives, our political system cannot easily put a better product on offer. Our Federalism augments the surplus capacity of government, keeps competitive discipline at bay, and creates potent fiscal illusions and monitoring problems among voters; hence, it enjoys overwhelming support among government actors at all levels.[8] It offers multiple access points for factions, all of which are occupied and defended. It produces a large class of bureaucrats who write and process checks, administer funds and requirements, report to one another, and blame one another for a lack of results; each performance failure will increase that class. And because Our Federalism is the most viable form of redistribution in America, progressives will always champion it.

This witches' brew of institutional pathologies, illusions, interest groups, and ideology has over time produced inchoate public disaffection, but also rendered it impotent. Voters may come to recognize that many of the things they care about—crime protection, schools, parks, traffic congestion, social mores in the neighborhood—are precisely the things about which the national government can do little by way of consistent improvement. But policy makers are not about to inform their constituents of that fact, and an abstract consensus against federal meddling will eventually yield to another federal grant. Similarly, it may still be possible to explain that a polyphony of state regulators is bound to prompt entrepreneurial capital and talent to exit the auditorium. But that recognition, too, quickly yields to the urge of bringing reckless financial speculators and other malefactors to heel. And for the most part, any federalism debate will revolve around the federal "balance"—that is, the distribution of surplus (or debts) among levels of government. That debate is what we are used to, and it matters greatly to Our Federalism's operators and their constituencies. In short, any federalism debate and renegotiation would encounter an unprepared, deeply conflicted electorate.

It is also the case, however, that in America—unlike other federal systems—periods of crisis and transition have tended to provoke fundamental debates over federalism's purposes and foundations—in other words, over the *kind* of federalism we should aspire to and, as a constitutional matter, are supposed to have. Those debates usually produce a confused jumble of constitutional argument, ideological conflict, and partisan agitation. Under present conditions, in light of federalism's dysfunctions and fiscal travails, an agenda for a more competitive, constitutionally grounded federalism might hold broad appeal not only for conservatives but also for the noncommitted. Even progressives might come to recognize that Our Federalism undermines values of transparency, civic engagement, public deliberation, and democratic control and, moreover, threatens *any* government endeavor that requires a high degree of central coordination, including projects such as a global warming program, a comprehensive energy policy, or immigration reform. Appeals to common sense and good government, however, will invariably be overlaid by more partisan ideological forces and considerations.

For most of the post–New Deal era, federalism and "states' rights" had unequivocally conservative connotations. Over time, however, and especially over the past decade, progressive theorists and activists have become increasingly confident in claiming federalism as their own platform. Theirs is a radicalized version of the New Deal Constitution with copious rights, pervasive intergovernmentalism and entitlements, government empowerment at all levels, and mutual exploitation as organizing principles. This federalism has had enormous traction, not only because it feeds off the self-reinforcing tendencies of the New Deal Constitution, but also because it is suited to a Progressivism that has ceased to believe in Progress with a capital *P* or its corollaries, such as the coherent pursuit of national public objectives, bureaucratic expertise, and regard for production values. Contemporary progressivism's signature achievements— health-care reform, financial services reform—combine grand ambition with a resolute refusal to provide any meaningful regulatory order or sense of public priorities. Enacted statutes, running thousands of pages in length, instruct that "the Commission shall" or "the Secretary may" do any one of literally a hundred things. But the schemes are too unwieldy, and regulatory authority is far too splintered, to permit any coherent system of regulation. While the statutes have prompted much furious debate on account of their government-aggrandizing nature, they do not herald a protosocialist central state. They rather expand Our Federalism, relying on its self-propelling and government-empowering tendencies.

A comparably coherent, politically serviceable federalism formula has yet to emerge at the other end of the political spectrum. Conservative insistence on states' rights was born of opposition to the New Deal's ambitions; and the civil rights struggle, the Great Society, and the national government's regulatory initiatives in the 1970s and under the Obama administration reinforced conservatives' reflexive tendency to identify decentralization with smaller government. Only lately, and belatedly, has it begun to dawn on conservatives that an empowerment federalism for trial lawyers and attorneys general is not quite what they had in mind in championing decentralization; and that a "devolutionary" federalism that institutionalizes moral hazard and large-scale transfers to public-sector unions is neither a responsible nor, for a conservative party or movement, a politically plausible program. In that light, and in consideration of federalism's fiscal crisis condition, conservatism confronts the challenge of finding a federalism formula to match its opponents' and to accommodate the divergent demands that confront, and constitute, its political coalition—producer groups' abiding interest in a federal system that is capable of curbing conflicting and compounding state impositions; state officials' demands for fiscal and regulatory autonomy; and the anti-Washington sentiments of an increasingly rebellious, distrustful electorate.

It is an open question whether political conservatism will recognize and respond to this challenge. A habit of equating decentralization with less government, engrained over generations, is very hard to break, and conservatism may lack the intellectual resources to rethink its federalism commitments in any serious way. One can safely predict, however, that any effort in this direction will revert to *constitutional* arguments and tropes—both because that is the default mode of conservative federalism argument and because it is the only basis on which to accommodate political demands that pull in divergent directions. And for reasons mentioned, that reformulation will have to go beyond "states' rights" and "Tenth Amendment" incantations; it will have to re-argue and reinterpret the constitutional structure at a deeper level.

High-level principles, however, are easily lost or confused in the rough-and-tumble of ordinary politics. Moreover, no political coalition can develop a coherent constitutional program on its own. For better or worse, it needs the Supreme Court—not as a vanguard or oracle, but as a focal point and as an institution whose pronouncements on constitutional matters carry over the din of ordinary politics and convey a measure of legitimacy. It is thus worth asking whether the Supreme Court is capable of rearticulating a constitutionally grounded federalism.

The Supreme Court and Our Federalism

The suggestion that the Supreme Court could or should play a central role in federalism's renegotiation is apt to raise deep suspicions. As thousands of aspiring lawyers have learned (figuratively speaking) at Robert McCloskey's feet, the Court cannot hope to resist the dominant political forces in American politics. When it tries, it endangers its own legitimacy; that is the lesson of 1937.[9] Of late, "democratic constitutionalists" have proffered this argument with a cheerful countenance, in support of the Supreme Court's pursuit of an enlightened consociational consensus on controversial moral issues and in shrill opposition to scholarly and, supposedly, judicial attempts to resurrect a pre–New Deal "Constitution in Exile." To scholars inclined in this direction, competitive federalism will look suspiciously like the pre–New Deal Constitution. The justices should know better than to chase that particular rabbit, and scholars should know better than to urge them on that mission.

One need not embrace democratic constitutionalism's more extravagant claims and formulations to acknowledge that the Supreme Court cannot single-handedly sustain, let alone recreate, a constitutional order in defiance of democratic imperatives. Still, one ought to be suspicious of attempts to mobilize McCloskey's New Deal-ish plea for judicial caution in defense of the modern's Court's rights program.[10] Equal caution is warranted with respect to demagogic invocations of the specter of 1937 and its relevance in the contemporary political and institutional context. 1937 pitted the justices in a direct confrontation with the president and the Congress, under conditions of unusually high political consensus and, by all indications, high levels of public confidence in political institutions. Today's justices confront a divided and polarized Congress and a volatile electorate that is united only by a foreboding sense that our public institutions, with the exception of the armed forces and perhaps the Supreme Court, have ceased to work.[11] Moreover, the crucial fronts in 1937 were the enumerated powers question and *Lochner*-style "economic rights." Renewed engagements at these fronts might indeed pose severe problems of judicial legitimacy and capacity. As I have argued, however, enumerated powers and economic rights are less important—at least in a structural, competitive federalism context—than is commonly believed. And in any event, the justices are perfectly aware of the perils at these fronts. The question is what they are going to do, and are willing and able to do, at federalism's other, potentially more decisive fronts—consociational rights, entitlements, empowerment, exploitation. Upon examination, none of those dimensions conjures up a dramatic confrontation between the Court and the political branches of government. A Court with the appropriate disposition might find considerable running room.

Competitive Federalism's Fronts: Incrementalism. At the rights front, no direct institutional obstacle precludes the Supreme Court from declaring that the American people will henceforth be tested, not by following the Court's edicts, but in the constitutionally envisioned fashion, by governing themselves. Surrendering the rights agenda would be an affront the New Deal Constitution's cartel premises, but surely not to the Congress. Were the Court to make more room for competitive politics, "We the People"—were they to object—could elect representatives who are likely to nominate and appoint rights proliferators, and Congress and the Executive could promise to follow that course of action. But it is difficult to perceive these attenuated responses as a threat to the Court's institutional capacity or legitimacy. Much the same holds true of entitlements and vertical federalism.[12]

What of empowerment and exploitation? On some accounts, Supreme Court intervention at this front, with a view toward reestablishing competitive ground rules, would be as futile as a renewed enumerated powers battle. Scholars have argued that the proliferation of multiple, independent jurisdictions with overlapping, conflicting, redundant claims of authority is an inevitable by-product of modernization and economic complexity. However, at any level of complexity, one still has to ask what the ordering rules ought to be—competitive or cartelizing, exclusive or concurrent. The justices could not avoid that choice even if they wanted to. The "business cases" that have preoccupied the Roberts Court predominantly arise over the disintegrating tendencies of American federalism—consumer class-actions under state law, punitive damages, state efforts to circumvent federal preemption, the extraterritorial projection of state authority, discrimination against interstate commerce. The Supreme Court is splendidly positioned to curb those tendencies. By constitutional design, it finds it easier to beat up on states than on the Congress, and it has much more to work with. To be sure, the Court had yet more to work with before the New Deal Court jettisoned the clauses and doctrines that had theretofore constrained the full and free exercise of factionalism. However, it is impossible to fit that abdication into a *1937!* narrative. Conversely, one cannot easily envision any direct institutional obstacle—excepting an occasional statutory override—that would prevent to Court from reverting to a more integrationist, procompetitive course. The question is not whether the justices, in the exercise of their certiorari discretion, will deign to make the "what federalism" problem their own (they have already done so) or whether they will provoke a knock-down, enumerated-powers-style confrontation with the Congress (they won't). The question is whether they can see their way clear to a coherent judicial federalism.

Commitments, Latent Preferences, and Constitutional Memory. The rough-and-ready analysis just sketched dispels the notion of any 1937-ish impediment to a procompetitive federalism jurisprudence. Arguably, however, it slights or ignores less tangible and direct but more deep-seated impediments. They are suggested by Martin Shapiro's question of whether a "Rights Court" can ever revert to becoming a "Structure Court."[13]

Judicial rights proliferation has a self-reinforcing, politicizing tendency. Consociational rights belong to identifiable groups of individuals, who typically form organized political constituencies. Thus, although the Court's expansive rights agenda looks more compulsive than compelled from an institutional angle, a judicial pull-back at this front would signal—not just to the affected interests, but also to the legal establishment and to the public at large—that the Court has let its former constituencies down. Conversely, a judicial course correction at the structure front will have a distinctly "probusiness" flavor—not because competitive federalism is a procorporate agenda, but because business plaintiffs ("the commercial part of America," in Hamilton's phrase) have a potent incentive, not shared by any other institution or interest, to act as constitutional entrepreneurs in defense of competitive constitutional norms.[14] The "business cases" that have become federalism's fulcrum routinely pit producer interests against states and their clientele—trial lawyers and distributional interests. The Roberts Court's sporadic, halfhearted efforts to curb federalism's centrifugal tendencies have prompted shrill denunciations to the effect that the Court has shifted its allegiance from the plebs to the plutocrats.[15] A more serious, determined judicial engagement in this theater would raise the volume of criticism. In the end, then, the judiciary's maneuvering room depends on the extent to which the country and the Court are still capable of distinguishing between the Constitution and constituency politics—put differently, whether the Court is still capable of recognizing, and willing to enforce and articulate, authentically constitutional commitments that run counter to the politics and democratic demands of the day.

Doubts on that score arise not only from the modern Court's sustained rights enthusiasm but also from its federalism. "Balance" federalism is the federalism of a judiciary that, deep down, lacks confidence in a constitutionally grounded federalism. "See," it says, "we can still enforce structure as well as rights, and a Constitution apart from interest group demands." The enterprise, though, seems to demand an improvised federalism that looks politically neutral—of no harm to anyone (especially not the Court's constituencies); of no particular benefit to anyone except perhaps "states as states"; supposedly of great pragmatic "advantage" but a judicial prerogative, even if those advantages are nonexistent; "constitutionally mandated" but so "delicate" that only the justices can intuit it from case to case. None of this so-called federalism has a constitutional reference point; little of it meaningfully constrains the people's agents.

Perhaps this is the price to be paid for maintaining any judicial role above and beyond the periodic adjustment of the social consensus.[16] But if so, the price is high indeed. Balance federalism's aura of neutrality is deceptive; its tendency is to entrench and radicalize the New Deal Constitution. Worse, balance federalism has nothing intelligent to say about contemporary federalism's actual problems and dysfunctions and in some ways exacerbates them.

Can a rights-plus-harmless-structure Court find its way back to constitutional commitments? Hard to say. If the Court were to try, though, it could draw on a deep constitutional reservoir. The commitment to competition is hardwired in our Constitution's structure; and the protection of that structure and the underlying commitment, *as opposed to some present-day democratic consensus or made-up "advantages,"* is the judiciary's federalism task. In everyday politics, constitutional commitments are routinely trumped by opportunistic preferences. The genius of the New Deal's federalism and its contemporary extensions is to institutionalize that tendency and to enshrine it in a "Living Constitution." In principle, however, the competitive commitment is recoverable. The widespread sense that our institutions have ceased to function, and that we might be better off if everyone surrendered the opportunistic demands that drive our politics and Our Federalism, is not just suggestive of the competitive constitutional baseline; it is that baseline. By pushing back to that baseline, a competitive judicial federalism might have what the Rehnquist Court's federalism lacked—an intelligible constitutional rationale and institutional agenda, informed not by the politics of the day but by systemic pathologies of a sort that the Constitution is supposed to contain.

On some accounts, the Supreme Court is quite good at summating diffuse, latent preferences.[17] And by some measures, it may be capable—more capable, certainly, than the juristocracy of other countries—to revert to constitutional structure. America is the only country where judicial rights proliferation has prompted meaningful resistance; where constitutional "originalism"—beyond the trivial position that the constitutional text must count for something—has had intellectual and political traction; and where the demand to subordinate domestic constitutional traditions, especially including federalism, to the supposed demands of international law still meets with skepticism.[18] To be sure, these are conservative sensibilities, and there is no shortage of suggestions, emanating from our highest councils and most illustrious institutions, that we should shed them. But those promptings have to contend with deeper inhibitions. Even in its Brennanesque heyday, the Supreme Court shied away from overtly consociational innovations. For example, the Court flirted with, but eventually rejected, an expansive welfare rights agenda.[19] It permitted racial and gender preferences and quotas but has continued to view them as suspect and, at most, a temporary necessity.[20] Our First Amendment continues to be exceptional not only because it is much broader than other countries' speech protections but also because the Court has repeatedly rejected distributive theories of free speech (for example, in the context of campaign finance law).[21] Time and again, the Court has fallen back on procompetitive neutrality rules. This experience suggests a residual judicial respect for competitive politics and a corresponding reluctance to remake our constitutional order and culture in a European image. And with a bit of effort, one can detect a corresponding intuition on the structure side. Even in full thrall of New Deal suppositions, for example, the justices never let go of the dormant Commerce Clause. And in the course of a misconceived federalism campaign, the Court stumbled upon a transparency principle with a compelling constitutional pedigree and competitive rationale.

Whether the glimmers of constitutional recognition will suffice for a judicial rehabilitation of a competitive constitutional architecture, one cannot say. But one can confidently state a necessary condition of any such project—the reformulation of an originalism that, in some of its forms, has often stood as an obstacle to a deeper understanding of the constitutional structure.

Originalism at the Crossroads

Any rehabilitation of a competitive constitutional order will have to take some form of "originalist" constitutionalism. That is so not only because pragmatic-progressive jurists are committed to an anticompetitive agenda with deep roots in the Anti-Federalist tradition.[22] The deeper reason is a substantive, two-directional affinity between competitive federalism and originalism, both rightly understood. From one direction, I have insisted that "competition" is not some pragmatic federalism "advantage," like "experimentation"; or a made-up metanorm, like "balance" or "dignity." It is shorthand for a set of interlocking principles that structure a coherent text. Neither the principles nor the umbrella term I have chosen— "competition"—are *in* the text. But the construction makes sense *of* the text, leaves none of it out, and insists that each clause must be given its full and fair meaning. One cannot insist (as I do) on the superiority of that construction over any rival without repairing to some (loosely speaking) originalist standard. From the other direction, originalism embodies two substantive orientations that cut for competitive constitutionalism: a commitment to constitutional stability, and an accompanying aversion to consociational rights jurisprudence.

That natural affinity, however, does not necessarily produce harmony. Dominant forms of contemporary originalism place an inordinate emphasis on the interpretive, hermeneutic dimension of the commitments to constitutional stability and structure. Take one step beyond the text: lo, judges roam in a netherworld of disembodied values and aspirations. From that Manichean perspective, the riff of *The Upside-Down Constitution* is beyond the pale—half of it because it engages theories of constitutional politics, the other half because it insists on common-law argument as a legitimate domain of constitutional adjudication. To the extent that these dispositions prevail, originalism will remain incapable of a constitutionally grounded federalism theory and jurisprudence.

Some originalists may well dig in their heels on these grounds. There are good reasons to think, however, that originalism as a whole will reorient itself. It owes its doctrinaire streak, not to any authentically jurisprudential commitment, but rather to its origin in a particular political context. That context has shifted, in ways that render originalism's standard formula obsolete.[23]

Common-Law Constitutionalism. For practical purposes, one can distinguish two contemporary originalist camps: academic and judicial.[24] *Academic* originalism tends to be rights-based and libertarian. It has the artificial clarity and coherence of a theoretical economic or philosophical blackboard model: its baseline is the Bill of Rights and the enumerated powers doctrine, all fortified by a "presumption of liberty."[25] Academic originalism makes no bones about its aspiration to reverse the New Deal. However, its rigor and elegance also threaten academic originalism with political irrelevance. Moreover, academic originalism's rights orientation renders it ambivalent about the constitutional structure and, in particular, the federal structure: firm insistence on strict enumerated powers limitations alternates with equally ardent denunciations of local "grassroots tyranny."[26]

Judicial originalism is what Justice Antonin Scalia has called "fainthearted" originalism. It is hostile to rights proliferation—though not to rights that have firm roots in the constitutional text or seem to fit the structure—and more accommodating than academic originalism to constitutional traditions and well-settled precedent. It recognizes the overriding importance of constitutional structure; indeed, Justice Scalia has insisted that "structure is everything."[27] In practice, however, there is something halfhearted about fainthearted originalism. Hostility to rights proliferation has not translated into sustained support for a more aggressive judicial role on questions of constitutional structure. Originalists have attempted to maneuver the dormant Commerce Clause, however implausibly, into the vicinity of *Lochner*. They have inveighed against implied preemption as if that doctrine were a nationalist New Deal invention, rather than the desiccated remnant of a constitutional order that originalism professes to cherish. And ample evidence that "the Judicial Power," in the conventional understanding of the Founding era, very likely encompassed something very much like federal common law has failed to persuade originalists that the contemporaneous understanding of Article III, not *Erie* and Holmesian positivism, should anchor judicial practice and understanding.[28]

The source of these inhibitions is not difficult to discern. Originalism originated in the 1980s as a response to a particular political and institutional problem of concern to conservatives—the rights activism of the Brennan Court. So conceived, originalism had to supply an intellectually respectable reformulation of the New Deal's Frankfurterian "judicial restraint" tradition, a position that had failed to arrest the Warren-Brennan Court's ambitions; a formula that would mobilize conservative constituencies without scaring the rest of the country; and a platform on which diverse conservative constituencies could find common ground. Judicial originalism promised to tie judges to the constitutional text and to well-established constitutional traditions—in plaintext, the New Deal and *Brown v. Board*. Conversely, it called for judicial resistance to recent, atextual, still-controversial rights inventions—in plaintext, *Roe* and its progeny. In originalism's early years, this formula served its legitimizing and unifying purposes, and it maintained its polemical edge against a Supreme Court that showed little sign of mending its rights-creating ways.

In reformulating the Frankfurter tradition for a Brennanesque world, however, originalism also inherited the New Deal Constitution's foundational commitment against structure as well as rights. There is nothing fainthearted about originalism's embrace of *Erie*; it is rivaled in intensity only by originalism's animosity to *Lochner*.[29] Those orientations are complementary for originalists (as they were for the New Deal), and they converge on a single point: just as the Constitution must not be read as rights-creating beyond its bare text, it *must* be read to enact Justice Holmes's legal positivism, lest judges lose their constitutional bearings. That doctrinaire approach, however, has as a practical matter failed to do its job and is now in danger of losing its integrative force. Perennial shouts of "*Lochner!*" have failed to prevent *Roe v. Wade* from becoming as firmly entrenched as the New Deal Constitution. Sometime soon, fainthearted originalists will have to explain why it does not command comparable respect and acceptance—or else explain their sustained opposition on other grounds. In that posture, originalism has little to offer to social conservatives.[30] Conversely, judicial originalism has sidled up to structural doctrines that threaten to give free rein to corporate America's nemeses, from trial lawyers to state attorneys general. The only constitutional doctrine that is in any danger of being strangled by *Lochner*'s ghost is the dormant Commerce Clause, and that attack has come from originalists. Obviously, a jurisprudence that cannot contain rights proliferation while emboldening the institutional and regulatory agenda of the political Left is not a sustainable basis for a conservative political force, let alone a branch of conservative elite politics that self-consciously aims to provide a coherent, overarching intellectual agenda.

It would be difficult to escape these self-imposed shackles if rigid clause-boundedness were a nonnegotiable originalist commitment. But this is not so. Originalists have in many contexts *embraced* structural, common-law-like forms of argument. Sovereign immunity, for instance, is explicitly inferred from constitutional "silence" and unstated suppositions without which the constitutional structure cannot be made to work. The clear statement rule, for another example, is a judicial default setting that imputes a hypothetical intent of the Congress even when the actual intent points the other way. And originalists have been quite fond of constitutional common-law constructions, from standing to sue to the "unitary executive," that are much at odds with a clause-bound originalism that leaves no legitimate judicial ground between text and politics.

Originalists' embrace of these doctrines may have to do with the fact that they are not purely structural but also rights restraining. Moreover, as just suggested, originalism has inherited not only the New Deal's "restraint" trope but also its more specific jurisprudential traditions. Originalists have trained their fire on precisely the structural doctrines that the New Deal left standing—the dormant Commerce Clause, implied preemption, and constitutional common-law constructions that survive in *Erie*'s shadow. Still, the fact remains that nothing about originalism as such compels opposition to structural, doctrinal, common-law forms of argument. The contemporary political context may prompt an increased emphasis on those arguments.

Political Theory. The recognition that restraint-oriented, fainthearted originalism may have outlived its usefulness has been dawning for some time. It helps to explain the increased appeal of a more rights-oriented, academic originalism, exemplified by conservative agitation over property rights and the Second Amendment. The agenda is textualist; but again, there is nothing fainthearted or "restrained" about it.[31] A greater emphasis on constitutional structure would be in keeping with this reorientation. However, originalism has had a hard time explaining the constitutional structure to itself. Excepting the perennial preoccupation with the enumerated powers doctrine, it is hard to identify any structural principle that has commanded lasting engagement.

Perhaps the constitutional structure is simply too complicated to be of much service in ideological combat. At the risk of overinterpretation, though, I suspect that the real inhibition lies elsewhere. No compelling account of the constitutional structure can make do without a political theory—more precisely, without a dualist theory of constitutional politics and of ordinary, in-period politics. Originalism, in its conventional forms, has refused to allow itself to have either part of that theory. The source of that inhibition is the same morbid fear that also informs originalism's selective hostility to constitutional doctrine: almost by definition, there will be more than one plausible theory of politics, ordinary and constitutional. Open that door, and the judges will be drawn into an argument over political theory—and all bets are off.

At some level, of course, originalism recognizes the incontrovertible need for a normative basis. Self-consciously and ostentatiously, originalism—at least in its judicial versions—is a *democratic* originalism.[32] However, to forestall a drift into political theory, originalists insist on a minimalist notion of "democracy" as meaning simply majority rule. With respect to ordinary, in-period politics, "democracy" is a residual category: it is the maximand because and insofar as judicially minted rights are the minimand. With respect to constitutional politics, the notion that one might need such a theory is very nearly unintelligible to originalists. (Isn't that Bruce Ackerman's playpen?) Originalists of a natural rights disposition do not care whether the Constitution was written by statesmen or monkeys. It is enough that it embodies Lockean rights (and originalism's sole function is to bring us back to those rights). Originalists of a more positivist disposition do not care about constitutional politics, either. We do not really need to know why, how, or to what end "We the People" ordained the Constitution; it is enough that they did so ordain. (More precisely: it is enough that the present, in-period demos believes the story.) Originalism in this formulation is parasitic on a contractarian tradition that it wishes neither to articulate nor to defend.[33]

This resolute opposition to political theory, like the aversion to common-law argument and doctrine, is rooted in originalism's intended function of serving as a barrier to rights proliferation. Initially, the rights-democracy dichotomy had a certain plausibility and, in its simplicity, a certain charm. It works well enough on the "culture war" issues that have driven originalism for the better part of three decades. For practical political reasons, however, it has lost much of its utility. First, there is no evidence that the demos on whose behalf originalism promises to curb judicial rights imperialism entertains any serious misgivings about that form of government, provided that the justices do not stray too far.[34] More important, a minimalist, majority-rule understanding of democracy misses entirely the problematic politics over the economic, bread-and-butter issues that have moved to the center of American public debate and American federalism. The coin of this realm is interest group wrangling and exploitation, institutional dysfunction, and governmental collusion. The notion that we should throttle back on judicial interventionism for *that* kind of "democracy" holds no public appeal, and it greatly weakens originalism's theoretical appeal. Outside the context of culture war issues and rights, democratic originalism has not much to say either for itself or about the role of constitutionalism and courts in American politics. It is beside the point.

The hope that originalism as a political force will rise to this challenge rests on the fact that it has never been into self-marginalization.[35] A shift in the suggested direction would imply a greater emphasis on structural doctrines that protect against institutional dysfunction and the ravages of factional politics—the accountability principle of *Printz*, for instance; or horizontal federalism rules that guard against government collusion and exploitation; perhaps a preemption doctrine that can stem the centrifugal tendencies of our polyphonic federalism. Such a jurisprudence would target the systemic pathologies of ordinary politics—the pathologies that the Constitution anticipates and which it seeks to check. It differs in that crucial respect both from an ostentatiously pragmatic, pseudoempiricist effort to "make our democracy work" and from a "democratic constitutionalism" that clouds its politics of judicial imperialism and interest group muscle with "deliberation" slogans.[36]

To draw those distinctions and to defend a structural, competitive federalism jurisprudence against demagogic charges of the "Constitution in Exile" variety, one has to have *and articulate* a theory of the Constitution's politics and precommitments. The enterprise would take originalism out of its comfort zone—but also into a constitutional universe that ought to be congenial. Historically, legal conservatism has usually run together with constitutional limitations, not with grim majoritarian rule. In that elementary sense and long-term perspective, "democratic originalism" is a historically conditioned anomaly. In rediscovering the constitutional structure, originalism would revert to a more conventional posture—and moreover, to a rock-solid Madisonian foundation.[37] Along the way, it would dismiss false prophets and appreciate anew the Constitution's true heroes. It would abandon Felix Frankfurter, who never understood the first thing about the Constitution, and rediscover John Marshall, who did. It would overcome its intermittent, bizarre infatuation with Thomas Jefferson and the Roosevelts (who all held the Constitution's structure in contempt) and turn to Abraham Lincoln, who understood and perfected it.[38]

Coda

Apropos comfort zones, the preceding speculations are out of my own. Throughout, I have emphasized not only the broad sweep of federalism's political economy but also, in that context and within those constraints, the contingency of constitutional construction—its dependence on the decisions of real-world actors, acting in real time. What those actors will do in our time, let alone the future, is guesswork, not analysis. My topic, moreover, has been American federalism, not jurisprudential metatheory. Still, I hope to have nudged the constitutional debate in a fruitful direction and perhaps to have raised originalists' confidence in directly addressing questions of constitutional construction. A constitutional federalism jurisprudence requires constitutional common law and constitutional theory. But it is not on that account a freewheeling, "living" constitutionalism. Faithful constitutional construction in light of the Constitution's ascertainable commitments and structural principles does not invite, but rather helps to forestall, a lurch into supposed "federalism advantages" and constitutionally unhinged metaprinciples. The point is not to unleash judicial federalism but to reground and discipline it.

That regrounding and discipline, in turn, require a renewed appreciation of the point of departure, lo these many pages and chapters ago: *what* federalism, not how much, is the central question of American politics and constitutionalism. The question is as old as the Constitution, and older still. "There is something noble and magnificent," Alexander Hamilton wrote on July 4, 1782,

> in the perspective of a great Foederal Republic, closely linked in the pursuit of a common interest; tranquil and prosperous at home, respectable abroad; but there is something proportionably diminutive and contemptible in the prospect of a number of petty states, with the appearance only of union, jarring, jealous and perverse, without any determined direction, fluctuating and

unhappy at home, weak and insignificant by their dissentions, in the eyes of other nations.[39]

The spirit of a diminutive, contemptible, petty, jarring, jealous, fluctuating politics, Hamilton knew, would survive the Founding; it would have to be killed day in, day out.[40] Counteracting it would require sustained constitutional construction, political as well as jurisprudential. Surrender that responsibility to "strict" construction or rigid textualism: paradoxically but predictably, the Constitution will get further and further away from you.

And so it has. Whether we are still capable of rediscovering our more noble and magnificent traditions, and the constitutional conditions of a more prosperous and respectable politics, remains to be seen.

Constitutional Structure: Powers and Prohibitions

	Federal		State
	Powers	Prohibitions/duties	Prohibitions/duties
Commerce			
Regulatory	Commerce Clause (Art. I, § 8, Cl. 3)	Port Preference Clause (Art. I, § 9, Cl. 6) Slave Importation Clause (Art. I, § 9, Cl. 1)*	Privileges & Immunities Clause (Art. IV, § 2, Cl. 1) Contract Clause (Art. I, § 10, Cl. 1) Compact Clause (Art. I, § 10, Cl. 3)
	Bankruptcy Clause (Art. I, § 8, Cl. 4		
	Fix weights & measures (Art. I, § 8, Cl. 5)		
	Establish post office & roads (Art. I, § 8, Cl. 7)		
	Patent & Copyright Clause (Art. I, § 8, Cl. 8)		

	Federal		State
	Powers	Prohibitions/duties	Prohibitions/duties
	Necessary & Proper Clause (Art. I, § 8, Cl. 18)		
Tax/fiscal	Lay & collect taxes, duties, imposts & excises (Art. I, § 8, Cl. 1)	Uniformity (Art. I, § 8, Cl. 1); apportionment for direct taxes (Art. I, § 9, Cl. 4)*; no tax/duty on exports from any state (Art. I, § 9, Cl. 5)	Import-Export Clause (Art. I, § 10, Cl. 2) Tonnage Clause (Art. I, § 10, Cl. 3)
	Borrow money (Art. I, § 8, Cl. 2)		
	Coin money, punish counterfeiting (Art. I, § 8, Cl. 5, 6)		Coin money, emit bills of credit, make anything but gold and silver legal tender (Art. I, § 10, Cl. 1)
Common defense & foreign relations	Declare war; grant letters of marque & reprisal (Art. I, § 8, Cl. 11)		No letters of marque & reprisal (Art. I, § 10, Cl. 1)
	Raise and support armies; provide and maintain navy; regulate armed forces (Art. I, § 8, Cl. 12–14)		Keep troops or ships of war in times of peace, or engage in war unless invaded or in imminent danger, without consent of Congress (Art. I, § 10, Cl. 3)
	Treaty Clause (Art. II, § 2, Cl. 2)		No treaty, alliance with foreign nations (Art. I, § 10, Cl. 1); no compact or agreement without consent of Congress (Art. I, § 10, Cl. 3)
	Define, punish piracy etc. (Art. I, § 8, Cl. 10)		
	Militia Clauses (Art. I, § 8, Cl. 15, 16)	Appointment of officers, training reserved to states (Art. I, § 8, Cl. 16)	

	Federal		State
	Powers	Prohibitions/duties	Prohibitions/duties
Citizenship & interstate relations	Naturalization (Art. I, § 8, Cl. 4)		Privileges & Immunities Clause (Art. IV, § 2, Cl. 1)
		No bill of attainder, *ex post facto* law (Art. I, § 9, Cl. 3)	Same (Art. I, § 10, Cl. 1)
		No title of nobility (Art. I, § 9, Cl. 8)	Same (Art. I, § 10, Cl. 1)
		Habeas corpus guarantee (Art. I, § 9, Cl. 2)	
		Trial of all crimes by jury (Art. III, § 2, Cl. 3)	
	Declare punishment of treason (Art. III, § 3, Cl. 2)	Limitations on crime of treason (Art. III, § 3, Cl. 1, 2)	
	Full Faith & Credit Clause (Art. IV, § 1)		Full Faith & Credit Clause (Art. IV, § 1)
			Extradition Clause (Art. IV, § 2, Cl. 2)
			Fugitive Slave Clause (Art. IV, § 2, Cl. 3)*
	Admission of new states (Art. IV, § 3, Cl. 1)	State legislative consent for division or joinder of existing states (Art. I, § 3, Cl. 1)	
		Guarantee Clause (Art. IV, § 4)	

	Federal		State
	Powers	Prohibitions/duties	Prohibitions/duties
Federal property & institutions	District (of Columbia) Clause (Art. I, § 8, Cl. 17)	Cession by particular states (Art. I, § 8, Cl. 17)	Federal legislation exclusive (Art. I, § 8, Cl. 17)
	Dispose of, regulate territory or other property of U.S. (Art. IV, § 3, Cl. 2)	State legislature's consent to purchase (Art. I, § 8, Cl. 17)	Federal legislation exclusive (Art. I, § 8, Cl. 17)

Notes:

Provisions on federal judiciary and constitutional amendments omitted.

*Changed/superseded by amendment.

Notes

Introduction

1. *M'Culloch v. Maryland*, 17 U.S. 316, 415 (1819).
2. For "constitutional development" see, e.g., Ken I. Kersch, *Constructing Civil Liberties: Discontinuities in the Development of American Constitutional Law* (Cambridge: Cambridge University Press, 2004); Donald S. Lutz, "Toward a Theory of Constitutional Amendment," *American Political Science Review* 88 (1994): 355; and Richard H. Fallon Jr., *Implementing the Constitution* (Cambridge, MA: Harvard University Press, 2001). For the "Living Constitution," see esp. Howard Gillman, "The Collapse of Constitutional Originalism and the Rise of the Notion of the 'Living Constitution' in the Course of American State-Building," *Studies in American Political Development* 11 (1997): 191. For the restorative, "originalist" view, see Randy E. Barnett, *Restoring the Lost Constitution: The Presumption of Liberty* (Princeton, NJ: Princeton University Press, 2004). For a splendid exposition of the "unresolved conflicts" perspective—exaggerated to my mind, but refreshingly free from the postmodern nihilism that typically drives theories of constitutional indeterminacy—see Edward A. Purcell, Jr., *Originalism, Federalism, and the American Constitutional Enterprise: A Historical Inquiry* (New Haven, CT: Yale University Press, 2007). For "constitutional revolutions," see, e.g., John J. Janssen, *Dualist Constitutional Theory and the Republican Revolution of 1800*, 12 Const Comm 381 (1995); Barry Cushman, *Rethinking the New Deal Court: The Structure of a Constitutional Revolution* (New York: Oxford University Press, 1998); and Bruce Ackerman, *We the People: Foundations* (Cambridge, MA: Harvard University Press, 1991).

3. For a brief overview of the literature, see Jonathan Rodden, "The Political Economy of Federalism," in *Oxford Handbook of Political Economy*, ed. Barry Weingast and Donald Wittman (Oxford: Oxford University Press, 2006).

4. A particularly informative contribution to this grim literature is Jonathan Rodden's *Hamilton's Paradox: The Promise and Peril of Fiscal Federalism* (Cambridge: Cambridge University Press, 2006).

5. Book-length contributions in this vein include Daniel Treisman, *The Architecture of Government: Rethinking Political Decentralization* (New York: Cambridge University Press, 2007); and Jenna Bednar, *The Robust Federation: Principles of Design* (New York: Cambridge University Press, 2009).

6. The leading modern exponent is William H. Riker, *Federalism: Origin, Operation, Significance* (Boston: Little, Brown, 1964). For sophisticated reformulations of Riker's perspective, see Mikhail Filippov, Peter C. Ordeshook, and Olga Shvetsova, *Designing Federalism: A Theory of Self-Sustainable Federal Institutions* (Cambridge: Cambridge University Press, 2004); and David McKay, "William Riker on Federalism: Sometimes Wrong but More Right than Anyone Else?" *Regional and Federal Studies* 14:2 (2004): 167–186.

7. For the formal specification of this "Leviathan" hypothesis, see Geoffrey Brennan and James M. Buchanan, *The Power to Tax: Analytical Foundations of a Fiscal Constitution* (Indianapolis, IN: Liberty Fund, 2000), 33–35, 162.

8. "Dualism" is Bruce Ackerman's term (*Foundations*, 3–33).

9. For a compelling discussion, see Treisman, *The Architecture of Government*, esp. chap. 1.

10. *Federalist* 51 (Madison) in *The Federalist*, ed. George Carey (Indianapolis, IN: Liberty Fund, 2001), 269.

11. The italicized assumption is crucial. Empirically, virtually all federal systems attempt to accommodate conflicting loyalties and parochial attachments (more or less well), and some theorists have argued that federalism isn't really federalism unless it implicates identity-based differences for which people are willing to kill or be killed. Malcolm M. Feeley and Edward Rubin, *Federalism: Political Identity and Tragic Compromise* (Ann Arbor: University of Michigan Press, 2008), esp. 61–64. As chap. 1 will show, one cannot understand American federalism unless one understands the Founders' insistence that American federalism is not of that kind.

12. The calculus is not entirely straightforward. "Local" and "national" public goods are clearly distinct only in the economists' blackboard models; in the real world, the determinations are endlessly contestable and contested. Moreover, decentralization entails friction and conflicts among local jurisdictions, which in turn imply decision costs that would not accrue under a centralized system. But so long as federalism yields a *net* reduction in decision costs, it is worth having—all else equal.

13. James M. Buchanan and Gordon Tullock, *The Calculus of Consent: Logical Foundations of Constitutional Democracy* (Ann Arbor: University of Michigan Press, 1962), 135–140. The prediction hangs on the assumption that local

jurisdictions are represented at the national level (as they are in practically all federal systems; Bednar, *Robust Federation*, 46–47).

14. After the eponymous author of a pathbreaking 1956 article. Charles Tiebout, "A Pure Theory of Public Expenditure," *Journal of Political Economy* 64:5 (1956): 416–424.

15. For a level-headed discussion, see William W. Bratton and Joseph A. Mc-Cahery, *The New Economics of Jurisdictional Competition: Devolutionary Federalism in a Second-Best World*, 86 Georgetown L J 201 (1997).

16. *Federalist* 1 (Hamilton), 2; Brennan and Buchanan, *Power to Tax*, 33.

17. One can put the point more strongly and the other way around: states will grudgingly accept procompetitive norms and institutions as the price to be paid for locking themselves into a cartel. (European governments' ready acceptance of the European Court of Justice and its vehemently procompetitive jurisprudence may be an example.) However, the point is one of emphasis only; the constitutional choice analytics shake out the same either way.

18. See, for example, Basic Law for the Federal Republic of Germany, Art. 104 (a), 106–107.

19. Albert Breton, "The Existence and Stability of Interjurisdictional Competition," in *Competition Among States and Local Governments: Efficiency and Equity in American Federalism*, ed. Daphne A. Kenyon and John Kincaid (Washington, D.C.: Urban Institute, 1991), 49.

20. Game theorists call this well-established proposition the "folk theorem" because nobody seems to have discovered it first. See Drew Fudenberg and Eric Maskin, "The Folk Theorem in Repeated Games with Discounting or with Incomplete Information," *Econometrica* 54 (1986): 533–454.

21. For a similar interpretation of the New Deal transformation, though with less emphasis on the role of the states, see Jenna Bednar, William N. Eskridge, Jr., and John Ferejohn, "A Political Theory of Federalism," in *Constitutional Culture and Democratic Rule*, ed. John Ferejohn, Jack N. Rakove, and Jonathan Riley (Cambridge: Cambridge University Press, 2001), 223–267.

22. See, e.g., Jonathan Rodden and Susan Rose-Ackerman, *Does Federalism Preserve Markets?* 83 Va L Rev 1521 (1997).

23. Riker, *Federalism*, 140, 155.

24. I have profited greatly from Richard Franklin Bensel's works: *The Political Economy of American Industrialization, 1877–1900* (New York: Cambridge University Press, 2000); and *Sectionalism and American Political Development: 1880–1980* (Madison: University of Wisconsin Press, 1984).

25. Herbert Wechsler, *The Political Safeguards of Federalism: The Role of the States in the Composition and Selection of the National Government*, 54 Colum L Rev 543 (1954).

26. See Hamilton's discussion in *Federalist* 15, 68–75.

27. See Ackerman, *Foundations* and *We the People: Transformations* (Cambridge, MA: Harvard University Press, 1998).

28. See esp. Barry Cushman, *Rethinking the New Deal Court*. I do not know whether Bruce Ackerman would grant the point; his account of the New Deal's federalism covers a single paragraph (Ackerman, *Foundations*, 161).

His account in *Transformations* is not much more extensive (Ackerman, *Transformations*, 372).

29. "The New Deal Constitution" could just as plausibly be called "the Progressive Constitution," inasmuch as virtually all of the New Deal's intellectual foundations had been laid in that earlier era. I have adopted "the New Deal Constitution" because the Progressive era produced few *institutional* innovations with respect to the federal structure. For a good discussion, see Martha Derthick and John J. Dinan, "Progressivism and Federalism," in *Keeping the Compound Republic: Essays on American Federalism*, ed. Martha Derthick (Washington, D.C.: Brookings Institution, 2001), 105–122.

30. *Federalist* 1 (Hamilton), 1.

31. At some level, Ackerman may share the suspicion. The invention of a constitutional moment that never was frees him from having to defend its fruits on the merits. See Suzanna Sherry, *The Ghost of Liberalism Past*, 105 Harv L Rev 918, 923, 928 (1992).

32. The quote is John Marshall's; see *M'Culloch*, 17 U.S. at 407.

33. The unappealing choice has prompted intramural spats. For an originalist critique of faint-hearted originalism see, e.g., Randy E. Barnett, *Scalia's Infidelity: A Critique of "Faint-Hearted" Originalism*, 75 U Cin L Rev 7 (2006).

34. Keith E. Whittington, *Constitutional Construction: Divided Powers and Constitutional Meaning* (Cambridge, MA: Harvard University Press, 1999), 5–9. For other forms of originalism that go beyond the raw text, see Michael W. McConnell, *Contract Rights and Property Rights: A Case Study in the Relationship Between Individual Liberties and Constitutional Structure*, 76 Cal L Rev 267 (1988); Michael W. McConnell, *Textualism and the Dead Hand of the Past*, 66 Geo Wash L Rev 1127 (1998); Michael W. McConnell, *The Right to Die and the Jurisprudence of Tradition*, 1997 Utah L Rev 665; and from a very different perspective, Jack M. Balkin, *Framework Originalism and the Living Constitution*, 103 Nw U L Rev 549 (2009).

35. See, e.g., the German Constitution (Basic Law for the Federal Republic of Germany, Art. 20: "The Federal Republic of Germany is a democratic and social federal state"); the Argentine Constitution (Constitution of the Argentine Nation, § 1: "The Argentine Nation adopts the federal republican representative form of government"); and the South African Constitution (Constitution of the Republic of South Africa, § 40.1: "In the Republic, government is constituted as national, provincial and local spheres of government which are distinctive, interdependent and interrelated").

36. See, e.g., David A. Strauss, *Common Law Constitutional Interpretation*, 63 U Chi L Rev 877 (1996); and Daniel A. Farber and Suzanna Sherry, *Judgment Calls: Principle and Politics in Constitutional Law* (New York: Oxford University Press, 2009). Many other scholars place a heavy emphasis on common law forms of argument as a dominant and legitimate form of constitutional interpretation. For references and a brief discussion see Brannon P. Denning, *The New Doctrinalism in Constitutional Scholarship and* Heller v. District of Columbia, 75 Tenn L Rev 583 (2008).

37. A jurisprudence that tries to make the Constitution "work" is nowadays called "pragmatism." See, most prominently, Stephen Breyer, *Making Our Democracy Work: A Judge's View* (New York: Knopf, 2010). However, unlike modern pragmatism, nineteenth-century constitutional reasoning was oriented toward rules, not situational judgments. Moreover, it was grounded in a sound understanding of the Constitution's structure and purposes.

38. For suggestions to this effect see, e.g., Michael W. McConnell, *Federalism: Evaluating the Founders' Design*, 54 U Chi L Rev 1484, 1491–1492; and Jack N. Rakove, *Original Meanings: Politics and Ideas in the Making of the Constitution* (New York: Knopf, 1996), xv. Hamilton quotes "the equally solid and ingenious" David Hume:

> "To balance a large state or society . . . on general laws is a work of so great difficulty, that no human genius, however comprehensive, is able by the mere dint of reason and reflection, to effect it. The judgments of many must unite in the work: EXPERIENCE must guide their labour: TIME must bring it to perfection: and the FEELING OF inconveniences must correct the mistakes which they *inevitably* fall into, in their first trials and experiments." *Federalist* 85 (Hamilton), 457 (emphases in original).

Part I. Foundations

1. For a list of citations and a trenchant critique see Robert Lipkin, *Federalism as Balance*, 79 Tul L Rev 93 (2004). For an equally trenchant critique of the Court's free-standing federalism from a different perspective, see John F. Manning, *Federalism and the Generality Problem in Constitutional Interpretation*, 122 Harv L Rev 2003 (2009).

2. Even the Tenth Amendment, the most plausible and most frequently invoked source of balance, speaks of *powers*. For a brief discussion, see chap. 3.

3. See, e.g., *Garcia v. San Antonio Metro. Transit Auth.*, 469 U.S. 528, 572 (1985) (Powell, J., dissenting); *Atascadero State Hospital v. Scanlon*, 473 U.S. 234, 242 (1985).

4. See *Gregory v. Ashcroft*, 501 U.S. 452, 460 (1991) ("delicate balance"); *U.S. v. Lopez*, 514 U.S. 549, 583 (1995) ("etiquette of federalism"); *Idaho v. Coeur d'Alene Tribe of Idaho*, 521 U.S. 261, 268 (1997) ("dignity and respect afforded a state"); *Alden v. Maine*, 527 U.S. 706, 714 (1999) ("dignity"). For the Founders' take on state "dignity," see chap. 2.

5. *Gregory*, 501 U.S. at 458.

6. For incompletely theorized agreements, see Cass R. Sunstein, *One Case at a Time: Judicial Minimalism on the Supreme Court* (Cambridge, MA: Harvard University Press, 1999), 249–252; and *Designing Democracy: What Constitutions Do* (New York: Oxford University Press, 2001), 50–66.

7. The originators of this judicial federalism style still recognized the point. "It is one of the happy incidents of the federal system," Justice Louis Brandeis famously wrote in an opinion that has become a federalism lodestar, "that a

single courageous state may, if its citizens choose, serve as a laboratory." *New State Ice Co. v. Liebmann*, 285 U.S. 262, 311 (1932). "Incidents" is precisely right; experimentation is not a constitutional design feature. On the ideological content of "experimentation," see chap. 9.

The constitutional relevance of federalism's supposed advantages is unclear. A few short months after *Gregory*, its author (Justice O'Connor) gave a nod to its litany but continued that the Court's "task would be the same even if one could prove that federalism secured no advantages to anyone." *New York v. United States*, 505 U.S. 144, 157 (1992). The advantages may be makeweight. Then again, they keep appearing in Supreme Court opinions.

8. *Federalist* 31 speaks of "the constitutional equilibrium between the general and the state governments"; *Federalist* 45 warns that "the balance is much more likely to be disturbed by the preponderancy" of state governments than by the federal government. *Federalist* 31 (Hamilton) in *The Federalist*, ed. George Carey (Indianapolis, IN: Liberty Fund, 2001), 154; *Federalist* 45 (Madison), 238. On both Hamilton's and Madison's account, the "balance" has to do with the Constitution's political economy and the people's attachments, not with the Constitution's formal structure and assignments of powers. For a splendid discussion, see Samuel H. Beer, *To Make A Nation: The Rediscovery of American Federalism* (Cambridge, MA: Harvard University Press, 1993), 297–306. To anticipate an argument that runs through the following chapters: "balance" is appropriate to a quasi-feudal federalism, which the Founders denounced as an "imperium in imperio." Our constitutional federalism, in contrast, is the product of a single sovereign people, which has allocated specified powers to different agents.

9. *Federalist* 39 (Madison), 199.

10. Martha Derthick, *Keeping the Compound Republic: Essays on American Federalism* (Washington, D.C.: Brookings Institution, 2001), 1; Jack N. Rakove, *Original Meanings: Politics and Ideas in the Making of the Constitution* (New York: Knopf, 1996), 162.

11. See, for example, *Gregory*, 501 U.S. at 460 (describing the Supremacy Clause as an "extraordinary power in a federal system"). See also Edward L. Rubin and Malcolm Feeley, *Federalism: Some Notes on a National Neurosis*, 41 UCLA L Rev 903, 904 (1994) (observing that the Rehnquist Court tended to view the Supremacy Clause as suspect).

12. *Hale v. Bimco Trading, Inc.*, 306 U.S. 375, 378 (1939).

13. Lawrence Lessig, *Translating Federalism: United States v. Lopez*, 1995 Sup Ct Rev 125 (1995); and Ernest A. Young, *Making Federalism Doctrine: Fidelity, Institutional Competence, and Compensating Adjustments*, 46 Wm & Mary L Rev 1733 (2005).

1. Constitutionalism

1. James M. Buchanan and Gordon Tullock, *The Calculus of Consent: Logical Foundations of Constitutional Democracy* (Ann Arbor: University of Michigan Press, 1962). For a concise discussion of this "constitutional choice"

literature, see Dennis C. Mueller, *Constitutional Democracy* (Oxford: Oxford University Press, 1996), 61–70.

The global resurgence of democracy (especially after the fall of the Soviet Union) has spawned a vast body of empirical minded scholarship on the "constitutional politics" surrounding the adoption of governing charters. For a brief, insightful review, see Nathan J. Brown, "Reason, Interest, Rationality, and Passion in Constitution Drafting," *Perspectives on Politics* 6:4 (2008): 675–689.

2. David Hume, "Of the Original Contract," in *Essays Moral, Political and Literary*, ed. Eugene F. Miller (Indianapolis, IN: Liberty Fund, 1987), 465–487.

3. Friedrich A. Hayek, *Law, Legislation and Liberty*, vol. 3, *The Political Order of a Free People* (Chicago: University of Chicago Press, 1979), 33–35.

4. *Federalist* 1 (Hamilton) in *The Federalist*, ed. George Carey (Indianapolis, IN: Liberty Fund, 2001), 1.

5. Peter C. Ordeshook, "Constitutional Stability," *Constitutional Political Economy* 3:2 (1992), 137–175; and Russell Hardin, "Why a Constitution?" in *The Federalist Papers and the New Institutionalism*, ed. Bernard Grofman and Donald Wittman (New York: Agathon Press, 1989), 100–120.

6. Arend Lijphart, *Patterns of Democracy: Government Forms and Performance in Thirty-Six Countries* (New Haven, CT: Yale University Press, 1999), 4–5, draws substantially the same distinction between "majoritarian" and "consensus" forms of democracy. For a similar distinction with respect to formal constitutions, see Donald Horowitz, "Constitutional Design: Proposals versus Processes," in *The Architecture of Democracy*, ed. Andrew Reynolds (Oxford: Oxford University Press, 2002), 15–36.

7. See James M. Buchanan, "An Economic Theory of Clubs," *Economica* 32:125 (1965): 1–14.

8. Even that option may prove elusive because the groups' preferences may cycle.

9. For the crucial role of an extended time horizon and decision rules as elements of (unanimous) constitutional choice, see Buchanan and Tullock, *Calculus*, 77–80.

10. *Federalist* 51 (Madison), 271 (emphasis added).

11. Arend Lijphart, "Consociational Democracy," *World Politics* 21:2 (1969): 216. Elites play a central role in procuring consensus because they confront lower bargaining costs than unorganized masses of citizens; because in divided societies, they may be more moderate than their constituents (and perhaps have already met one another at Harvard or Oxford); and because they can bargain—unless they are perfectly monitored—with their constituents' assets, which makes compromise possible. All these tenets are problematic. Even "naturally" moderate elites may have strategic incentives to rile up their followers, and empirical evidence on the moderation of elites in divided countries—relative to their followers—is decidedly mixed. See Horowitz, "Constitutional Design," 21.

12. For the distinction, see Horowitz, "Constitutional Design," 20, 24–25.

13. Consociationalism has often been deemed as particularly suitable for societies that are deeply divided along ethnic or religious lines. However, it has also

been held out as a path to a "kinder, gentler" form of democracy for obstinately competitive advanced industrial countries, such as Great Britain and the United States (Lijphart, *Patterns of Democracy*, 275–300).

14. Buchanan and Tullock suggest that pluralist interest groups, as well as individuals, are capable of an authentic and unanimous choice (*Calculus*, 24–25). But that is right only if the groups can be relied on to represents their members' interests, and if those interests are fully homogeneous. Otherwise, agency problems will undermine the legitimacy of the constitutional choice. The deeper affinity between the individualist premises of *Calculus* and Madison's constitutional moment has since been noted. See, e.g., Vincent Ostrom, *The Political Theory of a Compound Republic: Designing the American Experiment*, 2nd ed. (Lincoln: University of Nebraska Press, 1987), 35–37.

15. In addition to a long-term view and an exclusive focus on decision rules, unanimous constitutional choice may be aided by an ex ante expectation that deadweight losses and rent-seeking costs of uninhibited interest group politics may be so large as to compel assent to constitutional constraints (Mueller, *Constitutional Democracy*, 62). The argument is entirely in keeping with Madisonian theory; my sole reason for not making more of it is that it is derivative of the constitutional subjects' long-term horizon.

   An important implication of the analysis is that the constitutional subjects must not try to do *too much* beyond establishing effective but limited stable government. At variance with that prescription, Walter F. Murphy, *Constitutional Democracy: Creating and Maintaining a Just Political Order* (Baltimore, MD: Johns Hopkins University Press, 2007), presents a screenplay of a modern-day convention of sensible, well-intentioned men and women who write a constitution for a postauthoritarian society. Like the Founders, the assembly "reflects and chooses" and learns from history and the experience of countries around the world; unlike the Founders, it is preoccupied with ensuring that in-period politics will produce the "right" results on abortion, social welfare, and much else besides. Its "constitution" is a social compromise that a Princeton graduate seminar or a meeting of European expert-diplomats might produce. It cannot settle anything or command anyone's allegiance.

16. See the splendid discussion by David F. Epstein, *The Political Theory of the Federalist* (Chicago: University of Chicago Press, 2007), 13–34.

17. *Federalist* 1 (Hamilton), 1.

18. Ibid., 2–3.

19. *Federalist* 1 (Hamilton); and *Federalist* 2 (Jay), 3–7.

20. *Federalist* 2 (Jay), 6.

21. The common war experience is essential because it provides ballast for people's identity perceptions. Theorists of the European Union often emphasize Europeans multiple "identities" (as Europeans, Spaniards, Catalans, etc.) and argue that those identities and the attendant "legal pluralism" provide a basis for an "ever-closer Union" and "diversity in unity." See, e.g., Joseph H. H. Weiler, *The Constitution of Europe: "Do the New Clothes Have an Emperor?" and Other Essays* (Cambridge: Cambridge University Press, 1999), 238–239, 327. At first glance, that position may seem to echo Publius's

recognition that identity perceptions can be shaped to some extent. It may also seem to reflect the American notion that we are "citizens" of a state for some purposes and *United States* citizens for others. In truth, however, there is a world of difference. The European identity talk is alarmingly obtuse to the fact that at the end of the day, people with multiple political identities "have only one life to live, and to give." Susan Meld Shell, "Kant's Conception of the Nation State and the Idea of Europe," in *Kant and the Concept of Community*, ed. Charlton Payne and Lucas Thorpe (Rochester, NY: University of Rochester Press, 2011). The Founders were keenly aware of that fundamental political fact, as many of their compatriots had in fact given their lives. *We* the people were those people who had declared their independence and fought a bloody war to make it real.

22. *Federalist* 45 (Madison), 238 (emphasis added). For the centrality of this passage, see Bruce A. Ackerman, *We the People: Foundations* (Cambridge, MA: Harvard University Press, 1991), 179.

23. The intuition is roughly this: "Under our proposal and our opponents' recommended course of action, bad things could happen. If the worst should come to pass, how sorry will you be? Choose the option that minimizes your expected regret, which is ours." William H. Riker, *The Strategy of Rhetoric: Campaigning for the American Constitution* (New Haven, CT: Yale University Press, 1996), chap. 5.

24. *Federalist* 49 (Madison), 262.

25. In his final books, William H. Riker emphasized the Founders' "heresthetic"—that is, the manipulation of choice situations so as to control the outcome. On the point in this paragraph, see Riker, *Strategy of Rhetoric*, 130. See also William H. Riker, *The Art of Political Manipulation* (New Haven, CT: Yale University Press, 1986). On the *Federalist*, constitutional choice, and agenda control, see also Epstein, *Political Theory*, 30–32.

26. *Federalist* 2 (Jay), 6–7.

27. Riker, *Strategy of Rhetoric*, chap. 11. In my judgment, Riker exaggerates the point. The Convention was not a runaway Federalist freight train. The Constitution turned out more states-friendly than many of the options the delegates had considered, and hard-core nationalists (foremost, James Madison) left Philadelphia in a decidedly fretful mood.

28. *Federalist* 40 (Madison), 205. Madison here echoes, without disclosing, James Wilson's reply at the Convention to worries over the scope of its authority: the Convention could *recommend* anything it wanted. Max Farrand, ed., *The Records of the Federal Convention of 1787*, vol. 1, rev. ed. (New Haven, CT: Yale University Press, 1937), 226 (Yates's notes).

29. Part of Madison's answer was that the Articles had already been breached—which, under the law of nations, entitled all other states to revoke their own treaty commitments unilaterally. Bruce A. Ackerman and Neal Katyal, *Our Unconventional Founding*, 62 U Chi L Rev 475, 540–551 (1995) argue that Madison may not have had many followers on this claim.

30. *Federalist* 40 (Madison), 203.

31. Ibid., 205.

32. Riker, *Strategy of Rhetoric*, 19–22.
33. For a detailed, nuanced account of the history, see Pauline Maier, *Ratification: The People Debate the Constitution, 1787–1788* (New York: Simon and Schuster, 2010).
34. *Federalist* 38 (Madison), 187 (all quotes).
35. James Wilson, Speech to the Pennsylvania Convention, November 24, 1787, in *Friends of the Constitution: Writings of the "Other" Federalists, 1787–1788*, ed. Colleen A. Sheehan and Gary L. McDowell (Indianapolis, IN: Liberty Fund, 1998), 71–87.
36. Charles A. Beard, *An Economic Interpretation of the Constitution of the United States* (New York: Macmillan, 1968; originally published in 1913).
37. Beard's historical data were fragmentary (as he readily admitted), and he probably overestimated the salience of economic (rather than military) considerations in the writing and ratification of the Constitution. Contemporary scholars, operating with better data and more sophisticated methods than Beard had available, have rejected his contentions in whole or in part. See, for example, Forrest McDonald, *We the People: The Economic Origins of the Constitution* (Chicago: University of Chicago Press, 1958). See also Robert A. McGuire and Robert L. Ohlsfeldt, "An Economic Model of Voting Behavior Over Specific Issues at the Constitutional Convention of 1787," *Journal of Economic History* 46:1 (1986): 79–111; and Robert A. McGuire, "Constitution Making: A Rational Choice Model of the Federal Convention of 1787," *American Journal of Political Science* 32:2 (1988): 483–522.
38. Hamilton held out that prospect in *Federalist* 34, 164–166.
39. Beard himself saw the point. Having claimed that the constitutional requirement of apportioning direct federal taxes (Art. I, § 9, Cl. 4) was initially intended as a protection for sparsely populated rural regions, Beard describes it as "a curious turn of fortune that this provision prevented the agrarians and populists in 1894 from shifting a part of the burden of taxes to the great cities of the East. Thus the *Zweck im Recht* is sometimes reversed." Perhaps because the concession is fatal to the argument, it appears in a footnote (Beard, *Economic Interpretation*, 169 n. 1).

    The one interest group that could clearly expect to be worse off under the Constitution consisted of state officials. That constituency, the *Federalist* explained, could not be persuaded; it would have to be beaten. The point has substantial federalism implications; they are discussed in chap. 2.
40. James M. Buchanan, *The Limits of Liberty: Between Anarchy and Leviathan* (Chicago: University of Chicago Press, 1975), 35–41, understands constitutions as two-stage contracts. For a similar (less formalized) position, see Richard A. Epstein, *Takings: Private Property and the Power of Eminent Domain* (Cambridge, MA: Harvard University Press, 1985).
41. *Federalist* 1 (Hamilton), 4 (emphasis in original).
42. *Federalist* 51 (Madison), 269.
43. *Federalist* 62 (Madison), 320. Hamilton had even harsher words for the states' "exceptionable" equality of suffrage (*Federalist* 22, 106).
44. *Federalist* 63 (Madison), 329.

45. *Federalist* 10 (Madison), 43, 45.
46. Ibid., 48. For the "probably" interpretation, see Epstein, *Political Theory*, 105.
47. *Federalist* 51 (Madison), 271.
48. The classic exposition is Mancur Olson, *The Logic of Collective Action: Public Goods and the Theory of Groups* (Cambridge, MA: Harvard University Press, 1965). For Madison's theory, see Neil S. Siegel, "Intransitivities Protect Minorities: Interpreting Madison's Theory of the Extended Republic" (unpublished Ph.D. dissertation, University of California, Berkeley, 2001).
49. If one had to identify a single unifying principle of the Constitution, Cass R. Sunstein has rightly observed, the effort to "control the violence of faction" is the most plausible candidate. Sunstein, *Naked Preferences and the Constitution*, 84 Colum L Rev 1689, 1690 (1984).
50. *Federalist* 51 (Madison), 268–269.
51. The locus classicus is Robert A. Dahl, *A Preface to Democratic Theory*, expanded ed. (Chicago: University of Chicago Press, 2006).
52. Ibid., 137.
53. The canonical constitutional statement of this theory is *United States v. Carolene Products Co.*, 304 U.S. 144, 152 n. 4 (1938). Its purest articulation is John Hart Ely's theory of "representation-reinforcing" adjudication in *Democracy and Distrust: A Theory of Judicial Review* (Cambridge, MA: Harvard University Press, 1980).
54. These theories come in different versions, some more plausible than others. See, for example, Jack M. Balkin and Reva B. Siegel, eds., *The Constitution in 2020* (New York: Oxford University Press, 2009), several contributions; Jack M. Balkin, *Original Meaning and Constitutional Redemption*, 24 Const Comment 515 (2007); William N. Eskridge, Jr., *Some Effects of Identity-Based Social Movements on Constitutional Law in the Twentieth Century*, 100 Mich L Rev 2064 (2002); William E. Forbath, *Popular Constitutionalism in the Twentieth Century*, 81 Chi-Kent L Rev 988, 967 (2006); and Reva B. Siegel, *Text in Contest, Gender and the Constitution From a Social Movement Perspective*, 150 U Pa L Rev 297 (2001).
55. The apprehension is clearest in the work of William H. Riker. See especially Riker, *Liberalism Against Populism: A Confrontation Between the Theory of Democracy and the Theory of Social Choice* (San Francisco: W. H. Freeman, 1982). An equally horrified look at the excesses of democratic politics is Buchanan's *Limits of Liberty*, 7–9.
56. *Federalist* 73 (Hamilton), 381.
57. *Federalist* 62 (Madison), 323–324 (all quotes in this paragraph).
58. *Federalist* 62 (Madison), 324.
59. *Federalist* 51 (Madison), 271.
60. *Federalist* 37 (Madison), 181.
61. Ibid.
62. For a recent contribution to this genre, see Sanford Levinson, *Our Undemocratic Constitution: Where the Constitution Goes Wrong* (New York: Oxford University Press, 2006).

63. For an instructive discussion, see Daryl J. Levinson, *Empire-Building Government in Constitutional Law*, 118 Harv L Rev 915 (2005).

2. Federalism

Epigraph: Max Farrand, ed., *The Records of the Federal Convention of 1787*, vol. 1, rev. ed. (New Haven, CT: Yale University Press, 1937), 530–531 (Madison's notes).

1. There are many obvious reasons to celebrate the federalism compromise as a work of genius and to agonize, embarrassedly, over the slavery bargain. But the deepest reason is that the slavery bargain was never a genuinely constitutional choice to begin with. See Bruce A. Ackerman, *We the People: Foundations* (Cambridge, MA: Harvard University Press, 1991), 15.

2. Farrand, *Records 1*, 323 (Madison's notes; emphasis in original).

3. Ibid., 357.

4. *Federalist* 14 (Madison) in *The Federalist*, ed. George Carey (Indianapolis, IN: Liberty Fund, 2001), 65; Jonathan Elliott, ed., *The Debates in the Several State Conventions, of the Adoption of the Federal Constitution*, vol. 3 (Philadelphia: J. B. Lippincott, 1891), 256–261.

5. An extensive discussion of those animosities is Calvin Johnson, *Righteous Anger at the Wicked States: The Meaning of the Founders' Constitution* (Cambridge: Cambridge University Press, 2005).

6. *Federalist* 1 (Hamilton), 1–2.

7. See, e.g., Dennis C. Mueller, *Constitutional Democracy* (New York: Oxford University Press, 1996), 326–328.

8. Their incentives are those of a stationary bandit with a last-period problem, whose rational choice is plunder. Hamilton had a sophisticated understanding of last-period problems. His discussion of re-eligibility restrictions for the president (which he opposed) is a good example. See *Federalist* 72 (Hamilton), 374–378. See also his distinction between the long-term interests of commercial republics and the short-term orientation of their rulers in *Federalist* 6, 23.

9. The formulation of these topics appears in *Federalist* 1 (Hamilton), 4 (italics omitted).

10. Madison rarely resorted to Jeffersonian bombast, both because it was out of character for him and probably because he suspected that he wasn't very good at it. Lance Banning, *The Sacred Fire of Liberty: James Madison and the Founding of the Federal Republic* (Ithaca, NY: Cornell University Press, 1995), 233.

11. *Federalist* 45 (Madison), 238.

12. Ibid.

13. Malcolm M. Feeley and Edward Rubin, *Federalism: Political Identity and Tragic Compromise* (Ann Arbor: University of Michigan Press, 2008), 62.

14. For the difference see Klaus von Beyme, *Föderalismus und regionales Bewusstsein: Ein internationaler Vergleich* (Munich: C. H. Beck, 2007), 21–35.

15. Arend Lijphart, "Consociation and Federalism: Conceptual and Empirical Links," *Canadian Journal of Political Science* 12:3 (1979): 500.
16. Yash Pal Ghai, "Constitutional Asymmetries: Communal Representation, Federalism, and Cultural and Autonomy," in *The Architecture of Democracy*, ed. Andrew Reynolds (Oxford: Oxford University Press, 2002), 158–162. When that is not so, artificial jurisdictional boundaries complicate the task of organizing each constituency underneath a monopolistic umbrella and often pose divisive problems of minority rights within the jurisdictions.
17. See generally Douglas Laycock, *Equal Citizens of Equal and Territorial States: The Constitutional Foundations of Choice of Law*, 92 Colum L Rev 249 (1992). In many of its provisions, the Constitution forbids special preferences or disadvantages for any state. For discussion, see chap. 3.
18. From Tocqueville on, students of American federalism have argued that the colonies' experience with local elections laid the groundwork for America's successful republican project. See Alexis de Tocqueville, *Democracy in America*, ed. Harvey C. Mansfield and Delba Winthrop (Chicago: University of Chicago Press, 2000), 30–41.
19. *Federalist* 9 (Hamilton), 39.
20. *Federalist* 62 (Madison), 320–321.
21. *Federalist* 14 (Madison), 64.
22. *Federalist* 10 (Madison), 47.
23. Even if the Convention had proposed to abolish state governments, Madison writes, it would be easy to show that "the general government would be compelled, by the principle of self preservation, to reinstate [state governments] in their proper jurisdiction." *Federalist* 14 (Madison), 65. It would be "compelled" in the same way in which France is "compelled" to have administrative *départements*, and for the same reasons. See also Madison's and Hamilton's remarks at the Convention.
24. *Federalist* 45 (Madison), 241.
25. Melancton Smith, June 25, 1788, in Herbert Storing, ed., *The Complete Anti-Federalist*, vol. 6 (Chicago: University of Chicago Press, 1981), 166.
26. Madison to Jefferson, Mar. 29, 1789, in *The Papers of James Madison*, ed. Charles F. Hobson, et al. (Charlottesville: University of Virginia Press, 1979) 12:37–40.
27. *Federalist* 51 (Madison), 270.
28. *Gregory v. Ashcroft*, 501 U.S. 452, 458 (1991). The Court (at 459) attempts to support this statement with an out-of-context citation to *Federalist* 28, where Hamilton discusses the states' and the federal government's propensity to resist mutual "usurpations" *by military means*. That is a far cry from a "healthy balance" or the separation of powers.
29. See, e.g., William H. Riker, *Federalism: Origin, Operation, Significance* (Boston: Little, Brown, 1964), 139–145; Daniel Treisman, ed., *The Architecture of Government: Rethinking Political Decentralization* (New York: Cambridge University Press, 2007), 196–197; and Seth F. Kreimer, "Federalism and Freedom," *Annals of the American Academy of Political and Social Science* 574 (2001): 66–80.

30. The precise error is the expectation of state resistance to federal "imposi-tions" *from Congress.* State resistance to federal judicial controls is a different matter. See later chaps. for discussion.

31. The "federalism protects liberty" argument looks no better if one recasts the supposedly protected liberty, from freedom from official oppression into something like self-determination or "active liberty": active liberty to do *what* to *whom?* See, e.g., Stephen Breyer, *Active Liberty: Interpreting Our Democratic Constitution* (New York: Vintage Books, 2005).

32. See, e.g., *Gregory,* 501 U.S. at 452, 458 (1991). Note that this interpretation would considerably advance my case for competitive constitutional federal-ism. The horizontal separation of powers and checks and balances institu-tionalize competition; so does the vertical separation between federal and state powers. Ergo, competitive federalism. But the argument, while conve-nient, is wrong.

33. *Federalist* 51 (Madison), 268. For the parenthetical text, see David F. Epstein, *The Political Theory of the Federalist* (Chicago: University of Chicago Press, 1984), 178.

34. *Federalist* 51 (Madison), 268.

35. See Todd E. Pettys, *Competing for the People's Affection: Federalism's For-gotten Marketplace,* 56 Vand L Rev 329 (2003).

36. John C. Calhoun, Fort Hill Address, July 26, 1831.

37. Epstein, *Political Theory of the Federalist,* 55–56.

38. The best attempt, in my judgment, is Samuel H. Beer, *To Make a Nation: The Rediscovery of American Federalism* (Cambridge, MA: Harvard University Press, 1993), 289–307. Unlike the vast majority of commentators, Beer recog-nizes the faction problem identified in the text. Moreover, he does not settle for "balance" drivel but attempts to identify the mechanisms and pathways through which states are supposed to protect liberty. Beer, like Epstein, recog-nizes that Publius's "strikingly original and emphatically nationalist analysis of how the federal division of authority is to be maintained" derives from the scenario of a *military* confrontation between the national and state gov-ernments. Unlike Epstein, however, Beer argues that Madison (and probably Hamilton) also viewed state governments as a useful check on the national government in ordinary politics, chiefly through the appointment of sena-tors and through the informal means ("just short of interposition" on Beer's account, 305) discussed in *Federalist* 46. Beer is careful, however, not to press the point too hard. Madison, on his account, "recognized that these controls could be used for parochial as well as national interests" but hoped that filtra-tion would prompt the appointment of senators with an enlarged view (ibid.). If that is right, though, Madison must have lost confidence in the federal con-trol mechanism when he lost faith in filtration. Although Beer may be right as a matter of textual exegesis of the *Federalist,* we are as a practical matter back to the faction problem.

39. "All Germans shall have the right to resist any person seeking to abolish this constitutional order, if no other remedy is available" (Basic Law for the Fed-eral Republic of Germany, Art. 20).

40. Ackerman, *Foundations*, 230–243; *Transformations*, chaps. 10–12.
41. The following pages are adapted from Michael S. Greve, *Compacts, Cartels, and Congressional Consent*, 68 Mo L Rev 285, 310–313 (2003).
42. Madison to Jefferson, Mar. 19, 1787, in *The Papers of James Madison*, ed. Robert A. Rutland, et al. (Chicago: University of Chicago, 1975) 9:317–322, 317–318 (emphasis in original).
43. Charles F. Hobson, "The Negative on State Laws: James Madison, the Constitution, and the Crisis of Republican Government," *William and Mary Quarterly*, 3rd ser. 36:2, 215, 219 (1979). For other excellent discussions of Madison's Negative and its fate at the Convention, see Larry D. Kramer, *Madison's Audience*, 112 Harv L Rev 611 (1999); and Alison L. LaCroix, *The Ideological Origins of American Federalism* (Cambridge, MA: Harvard University Press, 2010).
44. Farrand, *Records* 1, 21 (Madison's notes).
45. Madison to George Washington, Apr. 16, 1787, in *Papers of Madison*, 9:382–387, 384.
46. Jack N. Rakove, *Original Meanings: Politics and Ideas in the Making of the Constitution* (New York: Knopf, 1996), 47.
47. The Negative seems so extreme, and so much at variance with the Madison of the *Federalist* (let alone the Madison of the Bank dispute and the Virginia Resolution), that prominent historians have been tempted to downplay its significance or to speculate that Madison did not really mean it. See, e.g., Gordon Wood, "Is There a 'James Madison Problem'?" in *Liberty and American Experience in the Eighteenth Century*, ed. David Womersley (Indianapolis: Liberty Fund, 2006), 425–447, esp. 436–437 (discussing Madison's "bizarre" proposal); Banning, *Sacred Fire of Liberty*, 111–121. It is plain, however, that Madison was deadly serious about the Negative, and he went to extraordinary lengths in its defense.
48. Max Farrand, ed., *The Records of the Federal Convention of 1787*, vol. 2 (New Haven, CT: Yale University Press, 1937), 28 (Madison's notes). See also *Records* 2 at 391: "Mr. Rutledge: If nothing else, this alone would damn and ought to damn the Constitution. Will any State ever agree to be bound hand & foot in this manner" (Madison's notes).
49. Farrand, *Records* 2, 390 (Madison's notes).
50. Hobson, "The Negative on State Laws," 228. As for "clearly understood," the following comment immediately preceding the rejection of the negative proposal on July 17 is instructive: "Mr. Govr. Morris was more & more opposed to the negative. The proposal of it would disgust all the States. A law that ought to be negatived will be set aside in the Judiciary departmt. and if that security should fail; may be repealed by a Nationl. Law." Farrand, *Records* 2, 28 (Madison's notes). Note that the courts, not the Congress, constitute the first line of defense against state defections.
51. *Federalist* 7 (Hamilton), 28–29.
52. James Wilson, speech at the Pennsylvania Convention, December 4, 1787, in *Friends of the Constitution: Writings of the "Other" Federalists, 1787–1788*,

ed. Colleen A. Sheehan and Gary L. McDowell (Indianapolis, IN: Liberty Fund, 1998), 216; *Federalist* 80 (Hamilton), 413.

53. For the latter interpretation, see Kramer, *Madison's Audience*.

54. "Mr. Madison. Whether the States are now [i.e., prior to the adoption of what became the Tonnage Clause, Art. I, § 10, Cl. 3] restrained from laying tonnage duties depends on the extent of the power 'to regulate commerce.' These terms are vague but seem to exclude this power of the States. . . . He was more & more convinced that the regulation of Commerce was *in its nature indivisible and ought to be wholly under one authority*." Farrand, *Records 2*, 625 (Madison's notes; emphasis added). The date of that entry is September 15, 1787—two days before adjournment. Whatever Madison's weaknesses, a lack of tenacity was not among them.

55. Madison to Jefferson, Oct. 24, 1787, in *The Papers of James Madison*, eds. Robert A. Rutland, et al. (Chicago: University of Chicago Press, 1977) 10:205–220, 209.

56. Ibid., 10:212.

57. For example, Hamilton advocated his scheme for the assumptions of the states' debt partly to stem a feared exodus from high-tax to low-tax states. Alexander Hamilton, "Defence of the Funding System," in *The Works of Alexander Hamilton*, ed. Henry Cabot Lodge (New York: G.P. Putnam's Sons, 1904), vols. 8–9. Madison showed a similarly clear grasp of competitive dynamics, e.g.: "The intercourse between different parts [i.e., states] perfectly free, population, industry, arts, and the value of labour, would constantly tend to equalize themselves. . . . Wherever labour would yield most, people would resort, till the competition should destroy the inequality." Farrand, *Records 1*, 585 (Madison's notes).

58. Madison to Jefferson, Oct. 24, 1787, in *Papers of Madison*, 10:205–220, 211.

59. *Federalist* 7 (Hamilton), 29 (emphasis in original).

3. Constitutional Structure

Epigraph: *Nevada v. Hall*, 440 U.S. 410, 433 (1979) (Rehnquist, J., dissenting).

1. Weingast's competitive federalism condition holds that the states must have primary authority over the *economy* within their jurisdiction. Here and in table 3.1, I use a broader formulation because state competition can and does arise in any dimension that might make citizens may prefer one jurisdiction over another, including conflictual issues (such as smoking restrictions or abortion) or the state's politics in general. See Dennis C. Mueller, *Federalist Governments and Trumps*, 83 Va L Rev 1419, 1426–1427 (1997) (federalism may be most useful on "conflict decisions" rather than allocative issues).

2. *New York v. United States*, 505 U.S. 144 (1992); *Printz v. United States*, 521 U.S. 898 (1997). On the close connection between the directness or "anti-commandeering" rule and "dual" federalism, see Roderick M. Hills, Jr., *The Political Economy of Cooperative Federalism: Why State Autonomy Makes Sense and "Dual Sovereignty" Doesn't*, 96 Mich L Rev 813 (1998).

3. Some federalism theorists have argued that the connection between dualism and competition is spurious. Cooperative federal systems may carve out realms of state and local autonomy or even decide to organize jurisdictional competition, much like McDonald's organizes limited competition among its franchisees. See Edward L. Rubin and Malcolm Feeley, *Federalism: Some Notes on a National Neurosis,* 41 UCLA L Rev 903, 915–926 (1994); and Daniel Treisman, *The Architecture of Government: Rethinking Political Decentralization* (New York: Cambridge University Press, 2007), 100. Those, however, are remote possibilities in a system that is *designed* to obliterate competition. A more trenchant objection is that dual federalism does not invariably translate into competition. That well-taken objection, however, has more to do with competitive federalism's stability than with its formal structure. I will attend to the question below.

4. The anticommandeering principle rule also has a closely related, potent transparency or "accountability" rationale. I discuss it later, in the context of governments' authority to bargain around the constitutional entitlements.

5. See Hills, *Political Economy,* 817–818.

6. For example, the European Union's directives and many types of decisions by the European Court of Justice carry with them an affirmative obligation of full implementation by the member-states. The principal attraction of this arrangement is the protection of the member-states' (administrative) autonomy. See Anne van Aaken, "Supremacy and Preemption: A View from Europe," in *Federal Preemption: States' Powers, National Interests,* ed. Richard A. Epstein and Michael S. Greve (Washington, D.C.: AEI, 2007). See also Daniel Halberstam, *Of Power and Responsibility: The Political Morality of Federal Systems,* 90 Va L Rev 731, 800–801 (2004); and Daniel Halberstam, "Comparative Federalism and the Issue of Commandeering," in *The Federal Vision: Legitimacy and Levels of Governance in the United States and the European Union,* ed. Kalypso Nicolaidis and Robert Howse (New York: Oxford University Press, 2001), 213–241, esp. 213–215.

7. *Texas v. White,* 74 U.S. 700, 725 (1868). The case itself, which permitted the State of Texas to reclaim property that had been alienated by the insurgent government during the Civil War, nicely captures both sides of indestructibility. The Court held Texas's attempt to secede to have been wholly ineffective and then rested the right to recovery on the constitutional guarantee of the states' continued existence. See also David L. Shapiro, *Federalism: A Dialogue* (Chicago: Northwestern University Press, 1995), 64.

8. The fitting phrase is Martha Derthick's, in *Keeping the Compound Republic: Essays on American Federalism* (Washington, D.C.: Brookings Institution, 2001), 28.

9. Joseph Story, *Commentaries on the Constitution of the United States* (Boston: Hilliard, Gray, 1833), § 1808. The clause is the only provision in the entire Constitution that commands performance by "the United States."

10. *Federalist* 43 (Madison), 225–227.

11. For a concise (though to my mind overly skeptical) discussion of state size and numerosity in relation to competitive federalism, see Jacob T. Levy,

"Federalism, Liberalism, and the Separation of Loyalties," *American Political Science Review* 101:3 (2007): 461–462. There is, of course, no reason to think that the states will deploy their assets for competitive ends. Later chapters will describe the states' unremitting efforts to form cartels in the teeth of constitutional obstacles. For an intriguing argument to the effect that state numerosity (above a threshold of 34) may exacerbate that tendency, see Steven G. Calabresi and Nicholas Terrell, *The Number of States and the Economics of American Federalism*, 63 Fla L Rev 1 (2011).

12. Competitive federalism may as a practical matter require some outer bounds on state heterogeneity. Up to a point, differences in factor endowments are tolerable, and an attempt to make the system more "efficient" by allowing the central authority to wipe out the locational rents would bring the system to a fall. Beyond certain limits, however, well-endowed jurisdictions may attract *all* valuable factors, leaving rotten borough-jurisdictions unable to compete. For a formal demonstration and some empirical illustrations, see Treisman, *Architecture of Government*, 91–93. Strikingly, something like this intuition seems to have been at work in American federalism. Historically, formal guarantees of state equality have been accompanied by an effort to create state of roughly equal territorial size or population—tolerable proxies for bounding differences when next to nothing is known about a territory's actual factor endowments. Obviously, nothing could be done about the contours of the original states, and geographical factors as well as historical circumstances surrounding the annexation or accession of Texas, California, Alaska, and Hawaii compelled departures from the rule. The general policy, however, has been to create roughly equal states. For discussion see Eric Biber, *The Price of Admission: Causes, Effects, and Patterns of Conditions Imposed on States Entering the Union*, 46 Am J Legal Hist 119 (2004); and Mark Stein, *How the States Got Their Shapes* (New York: Smithsonian, 2008).

13. *Federalist* 45 (Madison) 240. The protections are extremely robust. The Constitution allocates House seats in proportion to the census and protects a "rotten borough" state from losing all representation (Art. I, § 2, Cl. 3, "each State shall have at Least one Representative"). The states' equal representation in the Senate is the most entrenched of all constitutional guarantees. No state can be deprived of its equal representation in that body even by constitutional amendment (Art. V). The amendment process itself, in turn, affords the states a prominent role.

14. Horizontal federalism rules could just as easily be discussed under the immediately following heading "Coordination." I discuss them under the heading "Structure" because competitive federalism theorists identify horizontal federalism's maintenance as one of the central government's essential entitlements. See table 3.1.

15. Strictly speaking, state equality is also compatible with a regime of mutual state aggression. Although that arrangement cannot possibly produce a net gain in "states' rights" or general welfare (and the Constitution manifestly embodies a nonaggression rule), the thought is not idle speculation.

State politicians—"states-as-states"—will strongly prefer a mutual aggression regime, both ex ante and in real time. Our modern Constitution closely approximates their position. For discussion, see chap. 13.

16. See especially the Privileges and Immunities Clause (Art. IV, § 2, Cl.1). The Supreme Court has long—and to my mind correctly—recognized an extratextual "right to travel" that encapsulates the constitutional principle. *Crandall v. Nevada*, 73 U.S. 35 (1868); *Saenz v. Roe*, 526 U.S. 489, 510–511 (1999).

17. The moniker is of recent vintage. See, e.g., Saul Levmore, *Interstate Exploitation and Judicial Intervention*, 69 Va L Rev 563 (1983). However, the Founders understood the principle very well. See Hamilton's perceptive analysis of New York's import tariffs in *Federalist 7*, 29–31.

18. See *Federalist 7* (Hamilton), 31. The notion of exploitative state legislation as acts of aggression is not a Hamiltonian idiosyncrasy. Madison, too, vocally complained of the states' "rival and spiteful measures dictated by mistaken views of interest." Madison to George Washington, Apr. 16, 1787, in *The Papers of James Madison*, ed. Robert A. Rutland, et. al. (Chicago: University of Chicago, 1975) 9:382–387.

19. The only exceptions to this pattern are the Full Faith and Credit Clause (Art. IV, § 1); the Delivery Clause (Art. IV, § 2, Cl. 2); and the long-superseded Fugitive Slave Clause (Art. IV, § 2, Cl. 3).

20. It is a bad mistake to conflate competitive federalism with state friendliness or even a high degree of decentralization. Competitive federalism theorists share a large measure of blame for that common misunderstanding. In Tiebout-inspired economic models, no central government shows up at all. And even theories in the tradition of *The Calculus of Consent* suggest a very high degree of state autonomy and a federal government that plays a residual role. Although competitive federalism *may* take that form, its maintenance may also require a very high degree of central intervention. See Jonathan Rodden, *Hamilton's Paradox: The Promise and Peril of Fiscal Federalism* (Cambridge: Cambridge University Press, 2006) , 24.

21. *Federalist 14* (Madison), 65.

22. "Subsidiarity" holds that government functions should be assigned to the lowest level of government that is capable of providing the service or of internalizing its full costs and benefits. For a similar comparison between Madison's assignment criteria and modern theories of "Fiscal Federalism," see Samuel H. Beer, *To Make A Nation: The Rediscovery of American Federalism* (Cambridge, MA: Harvard University Press, 1993), 293–294.

23. The Supreme Court has characterized the Tenth Amendment as a "truism," per *United States v. Darby*, 312 U.S. 100, 124 (1941); or a "tautology," per *New York*, 505 U.S. at 157 (1992). The canonical source of the Tenth Amendment's understanding as merely declaratory is Chief Justice Marshall's opinion in *M'Culloch v. Maryland*, 17 U.S. 316 (1819). For a rare contrarian view to the effect that the amendment—notwithstanding the deliberate omission of the word "expressly"—was in fact intended to establish a rule of "strict" construction, see Kurt T. Lash, *The Original Meaning of an Omission: The*

Tenth Amendment, Popular Sovereignty and "Expressly" Delegated Power, 83 Notre Dame L Rev 101 (2008).

In modern opinions and cases, the amendment has sometimes been read as a prohibition against congressional exercises of power "in a fashion that impairs the States' integrity or their ability to function effectively in a federal system"; see *Fry v. United States,* 421 U.S. 542, 547 n. 7 (1975); *Nat'l League of Cities v. Usery,* 426 U.S. 833, 843 (1976); *overruled, Garcia v. San Antonio Metro. Transit Auth.,* 469 U.S. 528, 573 (1985). I believe that the Constitution does imply a "political integrity" principle. However, it is largely congruent with the Guarantee Clause and the prohibition against "commandeering," which is best inferred from the general structure rather than the Tenth Amendment. For discussion, see chap. 15.

24. *Federalist* 45 (Madison), 241.
25. *Gibbons v. Ogden,* 22 U.S. 1, 195 (1824).
26. As a historical matter, the federal elements of the Constitution survived because the nationalists had to concede them at the Convention. In that sense, federalism is a compromise, not a strategy. As explained in chap. 2, however, I believe that the post-Convention Madison was right: the "compromise" can be defended on constitutional (ex ante) grounds.
27. For equilibrium and competition, see Beer, *To Make a Nation,* 295–301; and Todd E. Pettys, *Competing for the People's Affection: Federalism's Forgotten Marketplace,* 56 Vand L Rev 329 (2003). For "withering away," see Jean Yarbrough, "Madison and Modern Federalism," in *How Federal is the Constitution?* ed. Robert A. Goldwin and William A. Schambra (Washington, D.C.: AEI, 1987), 84, 87 ("The subtle message of *The Federalist* is that the states will gradually decline").
28. *Federalist* 46 (Madison), 244. See also *Federalist* 17 (Hamilton), 81: "The people of each state would be apt to feel a stronger bias towards their local government, than towards the government of the union; unless the force of that principle should be destroyed by a much better administration of the latter."
29. For the Supremacy Clause as an injunction against the judicial "harmonization" of federal and preexisting state law, see Caleb Nelson, *Preemption,* 86 Va L Rev 225, 232 (2000).
30. Even where federal and state powers are concurrent, they are not shared or joint. The Constitution envisions only two joint federal-state enterprises: the militia and (more arguably) the exercise of the judicial power. The militia clauses deal with anomalous situations wherein the ordinary distinction between public power and primary private conduct breaks down (an anomaly that is also reflected in the Second and Third Amendments; see Robert R. Gasaway and Ashley C. Parrish, "Structural Constitutional Principles and Rights Reconciliation," in *Citizenship in America and Europe: Beyond the Nation-State?* ed. Michael S. Greve and Michael Zoeller (Washington, D.C.: AEI, 2009). The exercise of the judicial power is "joint" but also strictly hierarchical and, moreover, subject to the grim command of the Supremacy Clause.

31. *Federalist* 32 (Hamilton), 155 (capital letters in original); 156, 154.

32. Ibid., 155 (italics in original).

33. For example, Congress may prescribe, and has prescribed, rules governing the state taxation of railroad property: Railroad Revitalization and Regulatory Reform Act of 1976, Pub. L. No. 94–210, Sec. 306, 90 Stat. 31, 54–55 (1976). See also *CSX Transp., Inc. v. Ga. State Bd. of Equalization*, 552 U.S. 9 (2007). As for political economy, Hamilton himself acknowledges that the constitutional tax regime would effectively limit states to poll and property taxes. His real argument is that the states, freed under the Constitution from the necessity of funding wars, would not *need* a lot of revenue (*Federalist* 34, 165).

34. Epstein and Greve, "Conclusion," in *Federal Preemption*, 311–312.

35. Stability, where it exists, appears to be a function of multiple interdependent variables, some of which (such as the party system) have little to do with formal constitutional structures, let alone assignments of powers to one or another level of government. For extensive discussion, see Mikhail Filippov, Peter C. Ordeshook, and Olga Shvetsova, *Designing Federalism: A Theory of Self-Sustainable Federal Institutions* (Cambridge: Cambridge University Press, 2004); and Jenna Bednar, *The Robust Federation: Principles of Design* (New York: Cambridge University Press, 2009).

36. Jonathan Rodden and Susan Rose-Ackerman, *Does Federalism Preserve Markets?* 83 Va L Rev 1521, 1546–1566 (1997).

37. As explained in chap. 2, Publius also envisioned that electoral filtration would bias Congress in a procompetitive direction and, in particular, prevent it from meddling in local affairs. I ignore that intended structural mechanism because it has so obviously failed.

38. John O. McGinnis and Michael B. Rappaport, *Our Supermajoritarian Constitution*, 80 Tex L Rev 703 (2002); Bradford R. Clark, *Separation of Powers as a Safeguard of Federalism*, 79 Tex L Rev 1321 (2001).

39. This may not be so under the most restrictive readings of the Commerce Clause. See, for example, Calvin Johnson, *Homage to Clio: The Historical Continuity from the Articles of Confederation into the Constitution*, 20 Const Comment 463 (2004). However, the objection is of no consequence; the Convention could have written a broader Commerce Clause in lieu of the state prohibitions.

40. For a terrific exposition of this point and its misunderstanding by many modern-day luminaries, see Akhil Reed Amar, *A Neo-Federalist View of Article III: Separating the Two Tiers of Federal Jurisdiction*, 65 BU L Rev 205, 222–228 (1985).

41. I have painted with a broad brush. Some fields with a high potential of state defection and exploitation, such as bankruptcy and patent law, are committed to Congress. Conversely, the prohibitions against the states and their institutional commitment to the federal judiciary may not be exhaustive but rather illustrative of a broader constitutional principle. Chap. 4 discusses these complications; my emphasis here is on the general principle.

42. Gary Libecap, *Open-Access Losses and Delay in the Assignment of Property Rights*, 50 Ariz L Rev 379 (2008).

43. A major caveat: a constitutional court may also become "nationalist" by way of producing constitutional rights that have a monopolizing effect. For discussion, see chaps. 12 and 15.

    With respect to constitutional structure (as opposed to rights), the point is powerfully illustrated by the antebellum Taney Court. Despite a solid majority of Southern justices, it never seriously questioned the Marshall's Court's "nationalist" commitments. See chap. 4.

44. The most commonly discussed tax assignment option at the time, a national tariff coupled with a prohibition against any federal internal tax, was deliberately rejected. Hamilton explains the Federalists' reasoning in *Federalist* 30, 147–148. For discussion, see chap. 7.

45. This unfortunate provision, of course, was materially affected by the Civil War Amendments and repealed entirely with respect to income taxes by the Sixteenth Amendment. For discussion, see chap. 7.

46. In retrospect (and against the backdrop of modern federal constitutions), this structural feature seems nothing short of astounding. Everyone in 1787 knew which states were small and which were large. Everyone was aware of, and had an opinion on, the states' relative advantages and disadvantages; everyone recognized that the Constitution would substantially change the entitlements and the overall economics. Uniformly, however, all but one of the Convention's compromises remained true to constitutional form. In lieu of end-state distributions, we find assignments of powers and prohibitions coupled with nondiscrimination rules. The glaring exception is the tax and representation bargain over slavery.

47. Contemporary theorists often view "overgrazing" as a consequence of unclear or overlapping tax assignments. See Treisman, *Architecture of Government*, 139–146. Hamilton held something close to the opposite view. Although he conceded the "inconvenience" that might arise in consequence of federal-state competition over the same tax base, he argued that mutual forbearance as well as the states' incentive to migrate to taxes that the national government would find difficult to raise (such as land and poll taxes) would keep that inconvenience in bounds. In contrast, exclusive tax assignments would sooner or later produce a mismatch between revenue sources and necessary expenditures. In that event, precisely the exclusive assignment of a tax base would compel its institutional owner to overgraze it (*Federalist* 35, 167–168, 176). Hamilton does not discuss the now-common option of dividing, by constitutional assignment, the proceeds of a single tax among levels of governments. So far as I know, no one at the time floated the idea, but one can speculate what Hamilton might have said in response: a shared tax implies periodic recalibration, lest it produce over time the mismatch attendant to exclusive tax assignments. A formula that one knows ex ante to be unstable has no place in a Constitution.

48. The dominance of those risks explains the distinctly nationalist, Hamiltonian tone of the modern fiscal federalism literature. Rodden, *Hamilton's Paradox*.

49. Article I, § 10, Cl. 1 provides that "no State shall . . . coin Money; emit Bills of Credit; [or] make any Thing but gold and silver Coin a Tender in payments of

Debts." However, even on a highly restrictive reading (see, e.g., *Craig v. Missouri*, 29 U.S. 410 [1830]) the provision does not bar states from borrowing money. Joseph Story, *Commentaries on the Constitution of the United States*, vol. 3 (Boston: Hilliard, Gray , 1833), § 1357.

50. See Treisman, *Architecture of Government*, 126–130.

51. See generally Robert Cooter, "The Cost of Coase," *Journal of Legal Studies* 11 (1982): 1–33.

52. Congress cannot transfer the nation's air traffic-control system to the Commonwealth of Massachusetts. Laurence Tribe, *American Constitutional Law*, vol. 1, 3rd ed. (New York: Foundation, 2000), 1039. Conversely, states cannot consent to being commandeered by the federal government, per *New York*, 505 U.S. at 182 (1992). The difficulties here are considerable; I discuss some of them in chap. 9.

53. See Madison's invective against (state-issued) paper money in *Federalist* 44, 230–231. Of course, our sensibilities and institutional arrangements have changed. Here, however, my emphasis is on the logic of the Founders' Constitution.

54. *Pennhurst State School and Hospital v. Halderman*, 451 U.S. 1, 17 (1981).

55. *New York*, 505 U.S. at 168–169 (1992); *Printz*, 521 U.S. at 920 (1997). For discussion, see chaps. 14 and 15.

56. Hamilton forcefully articulated the point in insisting on "the essential difference between a mere NON-COMPLIANCE and a DIRECT and ACTIVE RESISTANCE. If the interposition of the state legislatures be necessary to give effect to a measure of the Union, they have only NOT TO ACT, or TO ACT EVASIVELY, and the measure is defeated. . . . The State leaders may even make a merit of their surreptitious evasions of it. . . .

   But if the execution of the laws of the national government should not require the intervention of the state legislatures; if they were to pass into immediate operation upon the citizens themselves, the particular governments could not interrupt their progress without an open and violent exertion of an unconstitutional power." Federalist 16 (Hamilton), 78–79 (capitals in original).

57. "Among the vices inherent in every federal system the most visible of all is the complication of the means that it employs." Alexis de Tocqueville, *Democracy in America*, ed. Harvey C. Mansfield and Delba Winthrop (Chicago: University of Chicago Press, 2000), 155.

58. Preference revelation was the original point of Charles Tiebout's famous article, "A Pure Theory of Public Expenditure," *Journal of Political Economy* 64:5 (1956): 416–424. See also Christopher C. DeMuth, "Competition in Government," AEI Bradley Lecture, October 2004.

59. For sophisticated critiques of constitutional coherence theories—including "intratextual" theories—see Adrian Vermeule and Ernest A. Young, *Hercules, Herbert, and Amar: The Trouble With Intratextualism*, 113 Harv L Rev 730 (2000); and John F. Manning, *Federalism and the Generality Problem in Constitutional Interpretation*, 122 Harv L Rev 2003 (2009).

Part II. Competitive Federalism

1. Sir Henry Sumner Maine, *Popular Government: Four Essays* (New York: H. Holt, 1886), 247.
2. Alfred D. Chandler, Jr., "The Beginnings of Big Business in American Industry," *Business History Review* 33:1 (1959); and Chandler, *The Visible Hand: The Managerial Revolution in American Business* (Cambridge, MA: Harvard University Press, 1977).
3. G. Edward White, *The Marshall Court and Cultural Change 1815–1835* (New York: Oxford University Press, 1991), 594.

4. Commerce and Competition

1. Boris I. Bittker, *Bittker on the Regulation of Interstate and Foreign Commerce* (Gaithersburg, MD: Aspen Law and Business, 1999), 6–4 n. 5.
2. *Camps Newfound/Owatonna, Inc. v. Town of Harrison*, 520 U.S. 564, 609 n. 1 (1997) (Thomas, J., dissenting: "There is, quite frankly, nothing 'dormant' about our jurisprudence in this area").
3. *Almy v. California*, 65 U.S. (24 How.) 169 (1860), held that a state tax on bills of lading covering interstate shipments held to violate Import-Export Clause. It was subsequently declared to be "well decided" under the Commerce Clause per *Woodruff v. Parham*, 75 U.S. (8 Wall.) 123, 138 (1868). The first unambiguous dormant Commerce Clause case is *In re State Tax on Railway Gross Receipts*, 82 U.S. 284 (1872).
4. Bittker, *Bittker on Regulation*, 6–5.
5. *Baldwin v. G.A.F. Seelig, Inc.*, 294 U.S. 511, 522 (1935). See also *Boston Stock Exchange v. State Tax Commission*, 429 U.S. 318, 336–337 (1977) (state competition "lies at the heart of a free trade policy").
6. See Ernest J. Brown, *The Open Economy: Justice Frankfurter and the Position of the Judiciary*, 67 Yale L J 219, 220 (1957) (Discussing and citing Thayer's views). Contemporary attacks on the Commerce Clause are discussed in chap. 16.
7. *H. P. Hood & Sons, Inc. v. Du Mond*, 336 U.S. 525, 535 (1949).
8. *In haec verba*: "I do not think the United States would come to an end if we lost our power to declare an Act of Congress void. I do think the Union would be imperiled if we could not make that declaration as to the laws of the several States. For one in my place sees how often a local policy prevails with those who are not trained to national views, and how often action is taken that embodies what the Commerce Clause was meant to end." Oliver Wendell Holmes, *Collected Legal Papers* (New York: Harcourt Brace, 1921), 295–296.
9. Brown, *Open Economy*, 219.
10. For extensive discussion of the evidence and the literature, see Brannon P. Denning, *Confederation-Era Discrimination Against Interstate Commerce and the Legitimacy of the Dormant Commerce Clause Doctrine*, 94 Ky L J 37 (2005); and Denning, *Reconstructing the Dormant Commerce Clause Doctrine*, 50 Wm & Mary L Rev 417 (2008).

11. Albert S. Abel, *Commerce Regulation before* Gibbons v. Ogden: *Trade and Traffic (Part II)*, 14 Brook L Rev 215, 243 (1948).

12. Harry N. Scheiber, *Federalism and the American Economic Order, 1789–1910*, 10 Law & Soc'y Rev 57, 71–72 (1975).

13. See David P. Currie, *The Constitution in the Supreme Court: The First Hundred Years, 1789–1888* (Chicago: University of Chicago Press, 1992).

14. For insightful discussions of this style of argument, see G. Edward White, *The Marshall Court and Cultural Change 1815–1835* (New York: Oxford University Press, 1991), 114, 596–602; Currie, *Constitution in the Supreme Court*, 325–327.

15. Madison to Jefferson, Oct. 24, 1787, in *The Papers of James Madison*, ed. Robert A. Rutland, et al. (Chicago: University of Chicago Press, 1977) 10:205–220, 212.

16. *The Steam-boat Thomas Jefferson*, 23 U.S. 428 (1825). For discussion see White, *Marshall Court*, 469–474.

17. Maurice G. Baxter, *The Steamboat Monopoly:* Gibbons v. Ogden, *1824* (New York: Knopf, 1972), chap. 1.

18. *Wickard v. Filburn*, 317 U.S. 111, 120 (1942). Although demonstrably wrong, the proposition continues to be cited. See, e.g., *United States v. Morrison*, 529 U.S. 598, 641 (2000; Souter, J., dissenting).

19. Webster conceded that state monopolies over land-based transportation were constitutional despite the Commerce Clause. *Gibbons v. Ogden*, 22 U.S. 1, 18 (1824).

20. *Willson v. Black-Bird Creek Marsh Co.*, 27 U.S. 245 (1829). For discussion, see Currie, *Constitution in the Supreme Court*, 175–176.

21. As late as 1874, the Supreme Court mused that railroads, unlike navigation, might not be "commerce." *R.R. Co. v. Maryland*, 88 U.S. 456, 474–475 (1874). Those, though, were last gasps. In 1886, the Supreme Court explicitly embraced railroads as a form of commerce among the states (*Wabash, St. Louis and Pac. Ry. Co. v. Illinois,* 118 U.S. 557, 573 (1886)), and the Interstate Commerce Act (1887) was enacted pursuant to the Commerce Clause.

22. *Gibbons*, 22 U.S. at 194, 203.

23. Ibid., 203.

24. *Kansas City S. Ry. Co. v. Kaw Valley Drainage Dist.*, 233 U.S. 75, 79 (1914).

25. *Brown v. Maryland*, 25 U.S. 419, 446 (1827).

26. *United States v. Coombs*, 37 U.S. 72 (1838); *Foster v. Davenport*, 63 U.S. 244 (1859).

27. Unfortunately, later courts and scholars would eschew that analysis and instead rely on a nonexistent "affecting interstate commerce clause." See, e.g., *Wickard*, 317 U.S. 111. One justice has lately rediscovered the Necessary and Proper Clause and, along with it, the right analysis; see *Gonzales v. Raich*, 545 U.S. 1, 34 (2005) (Scalia, J., concurring). See also *United States v. Comstock*, 130 S. Ct. 1949 (2010). For further discussion, see chap. 15.

28. *Brown*, 25 U.S. at 446.

29. See *Gibbons; Paul v. Virginia*, 75 U.S. 168 (1869); *Atlantic Coast Line R. R. Co. v. Wharton*, 207 U. S. 328, 334 (1907); *Ward v. Maryland*, 79 U.S. 418 (1870).

30. Bittker, *Bittker on Regulation*, 8–6; with reference to *Robbins v. Shelby County*, 120 U.S. 489 (1887).

31. *Mayor of New York v. Miln*, 36 U.S. 102 (1837). For discussion, see Bittker, *Bittker on Regulation*, 4–5 to 4–11.

32. For the centrality of that distinction in pre–New Deal constitutional law, see Howard Gillman, *The Constitution Besieged: The Rise and Demise of Lochner Era Police Powers Jurisprudence* (Durham, NC: Duke University Press, 1993), 72–74.

33. "This process is ordinarily called 'balancing,' but the scale analogy is not really appropriate, since the interests on both sides are incommensurate. It is more like judging whether a particular line is longer than a particular rock is heavy." *Bendix Autolite Corp. v. Midwesco Enterprises, Inc.*, 486 U.S. 888, 897 (1988; Scalia, J., concurring). For discussion, see chap. 16.

34. *Gibbons*, 22 U.S. at 203. The following paragraphs are adapted from the introduction to *Federal Preemption: States' Powers, National Interests*, ed. Richard Epstein and Michael S. Greve (Washington, D.C.: AEI, 2007), p. 12–14.

35. An earlier illustration is *Willson*, briefly mentioned earlier. Delaware's dam, authorized as part of a design to drain a marshland, undoubtedly obstructed the traffic of sloops carrying on trade (including interstate trade) on that waterway. But then, the swampy little Black Bird Creek, while navigable, was not the Hudson River; and the dam, while arguably authorized for "private emolument" (*Willson*, 27 U.S. at 248), had a plausible public health justification. The en passant mention of "private emolument" points to the purpose of testing the state's police power justifications—to separate public-regarding measures from protectionist interest group rackets.

36. *Smith v. Turner (The Passenger Cases)*, 48 U.S. 283, 284 (1849).

37. Ibid., 403.

38. *Cooley v. Board of Wardens*, 53 U.S. 299, 313 (1851).

39. Ibid., 312–313.

40. *S.C. State Highway Dept. v. Barnwell Bros.*, 303 U.S. 177 (1938) (discussed in chap. 9).

41. Felix Frankfurter, *The Commerce Clause Under Marshall, Taney, and Waite* (Chapel Hill: University of North Carolina Press, 1937), 37–38; White, *Marshall Court*, 582.

42. *Gibbons*, 22 U.S. at 17.

43. Albert S. Abel, *The Commerce Clause in the Constitutional Convention and in Contemporary Comment*, 25 Minn L Rev 432, 493 (1941) (emphasis added).

44. *Federalist* 32 (Hamilton), 155.

45. *Sturges v. Crowninshield*, 17 U.S. 122 (1819). The Court reached this conclusion despite its earlier holding that the power to enact "uniform" rules of naturalization—Hamilton's original example—*was* exclusive. *Chirac v. Chirac's Lessee*, 15 U.S. 259 (1817).

46. Marshall's opinion in *Sturges* left room for Webster's maneuver: it did *not* say that national powers are exclusive only where the Constitution explicitly makes them so (Currie, *Constitution in the Supreme Court*, 145–150).

47. Marshall alluded to the point that "much inconvenience would result" from holding bankruptcy power to be exclusive (*Sturges*, 17 U.S. at 195). Similar considerations probably led the Court to conclude that there is no dormant Patent and Copyright Clause. *Wheaton v. Peters*, 33 U.S. 591 (1834).

48. *M'Culloch v. Maryland*, 17 U.S. 316 (1819) is often cited for the proposition that such state impositions are "unconstitutional." However, an explicit congressional authorization will render them constitutional. *Balt. Nat'l Bank v. State Tax Comm'n*, 297 U.S. 209 (1936).

49. *Brown*, 25 U.S. at 456–457 (Thompson, J., dissenting). Similarly, the majority left untouched state duties on *retailers* who imported goods—an economic distortion that the Maryland statute, which arguably did no more than to put all sellers on a par, would have avoided. Ibid.,449.

50. Marshall himself was diffident about the doctrine (Ibid., 441). The doctrine invited sneers as soon as it had been formulated (ibid., 457) (Thompson, J., dissenting).

51. The economic point of the original package doctrine was not really the packages but the agents who handled and broke them—wholesalers. That came naturally in *Brown* because the state law itself had targeted that chokepoint. However, the doctrine depends for its plausibility on a "three-tiered" mode of product distribution: wholesalers to retailer to consumer. When market participants began to circumvent that model, the Court insisted that the original package doctrine was meant to protect wholesalers, not retailers who ship small packages to circumvent state law. *Austin v. Tennessee*, 179 U.S. 343, 359–360 (1900). It reaffirmed that holding in *Cook v. County of Marshall*, 196 U.S. 261, 273 (1905) with an air of indignation: the Court would not "lend its sanction to those who deliberately plan to debauch the public conscience and set at naught the laws of a state."

52. *Cooley*, 53 U.S. at 319.

53. The principal objection is that *Cooley* rests on a distinction that the Commerce Clause itself does not articulate. As David Currie has paraphrased the holding, "the commerce power [of Congress is] exclusive only when it ought to be" (Currie, *Constitution in the Supreme Court*, 233). See also Kent Newmyer, *History over Law*, 27 Stan L Rev 1373, 1378 (1975): *Cooley* "was less a doctrinal clarification than it was an agreement to stop looking for one."

54. *Cooley*, 53 U.S. at 318.

55. Bittker, *Bittker on Regulation*, 9–5.

56. See *Air Transp. Ass'n of Am. v. Cuomo*, 520 F.3d 218 (2008).

57. *Wilkerson v. Rahrer*, 140 U.S. 545 (1891); *James Clark Distilling Co. v. W. Md. Ry. Co.*, 242 U.S. 311 (1917). *Gibbons* at 207 had already distinguished between the federal adoption of state law and prospective delegation.

58. The delegation problem survived the New Deal in an attenuated form—to wit, the question of how clearly Congress must speak in constitutionalizing state laws that would otherwise violate the dormant Commerce Clause. *Prudential Ins. Co. v. Benjamin*, 328 U.S. 408 (1946). For a recent extensive discussion of the problem, see Norman R. Williams, *Why Congress May Not "Overrule" the Dormant Commerce Clause*, 53 UCLA L Rev 153 (2005).

59. *Duckworth v. Arkansas*, 314 U.S. 390, 401 (1941) (Jackson, J., concurring).
60. Paul Freund, *Umpiring the Federal System*, 54 Colum L Rev 561, 566 (1954).
61. *Houston v. Moore*, 18 U.S. 1, 5 (1820); *Prigg v. Pennsylvania*, 41 U.S. 539, 541–542 (1842).
62. *Gibbons*, 22 U.S. at 17–18.
63. Frankfurter, *Commerce Clause*, 20.
64. *Gibbons*, 22 U.S. at 231–232. Kent continued to maintain this position in his *Commentaries on American Law*, published after *Gibbons* (White, *Marshall Court*, 578).
65. The statutory construction in *Gibbons* is very probably wrong by the standards that the modern Supreme Court brings to bear on questions of this nature—the text of the statute and the intent of the Congress in enacting it. The current version of the statute at issue in *Gibbons*, as amended and modified, was held to preempt a Virginia law prohibiting nonresidents from fishing the state's portion of the Chesapeake Bay: *Douglas v. Seacoast Prods.*, 431 U.S. 265 (1977), largely on the grounds that Congress had long acquiesced to the *Gibbons* interpretation.
66. *Brown*, 25 U.S. at 448.
67. White, *Marshall Court*, 582–583.
68. For example, the sloop owner-plaintiff in *Willson* carried a federal coastal trading license quite similar to those at issue in *Gibbons*—a detail that Marshall, en route to his finding that the obstruction of the little Black Bird Creek wasn't all that serious, neglected to mention (White, *Marshall Court*, 584).
69. For "latent exclusivity," see Steven Gardbaum, "Breadth vs. Depth of Congress's Commerce Power," in *Federal Preemption*, 56–57. The trajectory of preemption jurisprudence is discussed in chap. 9.
70. *Federalist* 6 (Hamilton), 23.
71. Ibid., 25.

5. Corporations

1. Articles of Confederation, Art. IV, Cl. 1. The remainder of the article contains two limiting provisos not relevant to this discussion.
2. "There is a confusion of language here, which is remarkable." *Federalist* 42 (Madison), in *The Federalist*, ed. George Carey (Indianapolis, IN: Liberty Fund, 2001), 220.
3. For a good account of the framing of the Privileges and Immunities Clause, see David S. Bogen, *The Privileges and Immunities Clause of Article IV*, 37 Case W Res L Rev 794 (1987).
4. In *Federalist* 80, Hamilton emphasizes the close connection: "In order to the inviolable maintenance of that equality of privileges and immunities, to which the citizens of the union will be entitled, the national judiciary ought to preside in all cases, in which one state or its citizens are opposed to another state or its citizens. To secure the full effect of so fundamental a provision against all evasion and subterfuge, it is necessary that its construction should

be committed to that tribunal, which, having no local attachments, will be likely to be impartial between the different states and their citizens, and which, owing its official existence to the union, will never be likely to feel any bias inauspicious to the principles on which it is founded." *Federalist* 80 (Hamilton), 413–414.

5. *Hague v. CIO*, 307 U.S. 496, 514 (1939). Corporations do, however, enjoy protection as "persons" under the Due Process Clause and the Equal Protection Clause. See *Trs. of the Univ. of North Carolina v. Foy*, 5 N.C. (1 Mur.) 58 (1805) for what appears to be the earliest case (Fifth Amendment due process); and *Santa Clara County v. S. Pac. R.R. Co.*, 118 U.S. 394, 396 (1886) for the first United States Supreme Court case (Fourteenth Amendment due process). See also *Metro. Life Ins. Co. v. Ward*, 470 U.S. 869 (1985) (equal protection). *W. and S. Life Ins. Co. v. State Bd. of Equalization*, 451 U.S. 648, 656 (1981), cites *Hemphill v. Orloff*, 277 U.S. 537 (1928) for the conclusion that "the Privileges and Immunities Clause is inapplicable to corporations".

6. A classic, highly polemical and entertaining exposition of those views is a three-part series, *A Supreme Court Fiction*, by Dudley O. McGovney: Part I: *Corporations in the Diverse Citizenship Jurisdiction of the Federal Courts*, 56 Harv L Rev 853; Part II: *The Fiction at Work*, 56 Harv L Rev 1090; and Part III: *How Congress Has Been Dissuaded from Withdrawing the Jurisdiction that is Based upon Fiction*, 56 Harv L Rev 1225 (1943) (hereinafter McGovney, *Supreme Court Fiction: I, II, or III*, respectively).

   This position has never gained much traction. The Progressives' and New Dealers' dominant strategy was to attack diversity jurisdiction in toto, not simply its extension to corporations. For discussion, see chap. 10 of this volume. The current diversity provision includes corporations. 28 U.S.C. § 1332(c)(1) (2006).

7. Of course, a corporation, as a legal entity, cannot claim or enjoy *all* the privileges and immunities of natural citizens. But even with respect to natural persons, the Privileges and Immunities Clause does not compel states to treat noncitizens on an equal basis in all respects. Conspicuously, the right to vote—a supposed touchstone of whether or not, and to whom, the clause can apply—is a privilege with respect to which the states may undoubtedly discriminate against noncitizens.

8. *Bank of the U.S. v. Deveaux*, 9 U.S. 61, 86 (1809) (emphasis added).

9. *Strawbridge v. Curtiss*, 7 U.S. 267 (1806).

10. McGovney, *Supreme Court Fiction: I*, 867–870.

11. For Justice Story and his account of Marshall's views, see his letter to Chancellor James Kent, August 31, 1844, in *Life and Letters of Joseph Story, Associate Justice of the Supreme Court of the United States, and Dane Professor of Law at Harvard University*, ed. William Wetmore Story (Boston: Little, Brown, 1851), 2:469. See also McGovney, *Supreme Court Fiction: I*, 877; R. Kent Newmyer, *Justice Joseph Story's Doctrine of "Public and Private Corporations" and the Rise of the American Business Corporation*, 25 DePaul L Rev 825 (1976).

12. Gerard Carl Henderson, *The Position of Foreign Corporations in American Constitutional Law: A Contribution to the History and Theory of Juristic Persons in Anglo-American Law* (Cambridge, MA: Harvard University Press, 1918), 51. Note, though, that these were not quite the same corporations. Pauline Maier, "The Revolutionary Origins of the American Corporation," *William and Mary Quarterly*, 3rd ser. 50:1 (1993): 51–84.

13. This is Madison's take on the clause (*Federalist* 42, 220–221). Of course, the argument cuts both ways: the United States cannot literally "naturalize" foreign corporations, only "domesticate" them.

14. Sans my editorializing on divorce: Charles Warren, *The Supreme Court in United States History*, vol. 1, *1789 to 1821* (Boston: Little, Brown, 1922), 389–390. It appears that the next nine Supreme Court cases on corporations following *Deveaux* were insurance cases (McGovney, *A Supreme Court Fiction: I*, 869).

15. Henderson, *Foreign Corporations*, 56–57.

16. Warren, *Supreme Court in United States History*, 391–392.

17. *Fletcher v. Peck*, 10 U.S. 87 (1810) was first argued in early March 1809, a brief four weeks after the argument in *Deveaux*.

18. *Bank of Augusta v. Earle*, 38 U.S. 519 (1839). More precisely, it was undisputed that state-chartered banks may not establish branches in other states; thus, the question was whether the bank may employ corporate capital in purchase of bills of exchange in the "foreign" state.

19. *Bank of Augusta*, 38 U.S. at 520.

20. We will encounter the strategy again in chap. 7; it parallels Justice Story's construction of the federal common law in *Swift v. Tyson*, 41 U.S. 1 (1842), decided three years after *Bank of Augusta*.

21. *Louisville, Cincinnati, & Charleston R.R. Co. v. Letson*, 43 U.S. 497, 558 (1844).

22. *Marshall v. Baltimore & Ohio R.R. Co.*, 57 U.S. 314 (1853).

23. Henderson, *Foreign Corporations*, 62.

24. Gerard Henderson's masterful, still-canonical 1918 treatise *Foreign Corporations* quotes, at 63, a (presumably typical) 1851 opinion by the Kentucky Supreme Court: "The apparent reciprocity of the power would prove to be a delusion. The competition for extraterritorial advantages would but aggrandize the stronger to the disparagement of the weaker states. Resistance and retaliation would lead to conflict and confusion, and the weaker states must either submit to have their policy controlled, their business monopolized, their domestic institutions reduced to insignificance, or the peace and harmony of the states broken up destroyed (sic)." *Commonwealth v. Milton*, 51 Ky. (12 B. Mon.) 212 (1851).

25. *Paul v. Virginia*, 75 U.S. 168, 179 (1869).

26. Ibid., 181–182.

27. "Special privileges enjoyed by citizens in their own States are not secured in other States by [the Privileges and Immunities Clause]" (*Paul*, 75 U.S. at 180). That much is surely right: neither drafting history (see Bogen, *Privileges and Immunities Clause*, 841–845) nor federalism logic warrants a private right

to drag monopolistic advantages conferred by state law into another state. Henderson, *Foreign Corporations*, 66–67, argues that nothing short of such an entitlement would have helped the insurers in *Paul*. That is right in the sense that insurers at the time still operated under special charters rather than general incorporation laws. On this theory, the reasoning and holding of *Paul* may not apply to corporations chartered under general laws. (Consistent with this interpretation, general incorporation statutes for insurers began to appear in many states in 1871, as one of the industry's *n* attempts to escape *Paul*.) In substance, however, the insurers seem to have demanded no exclusive privilege or immunity, only the right to operate in a foreign state on nondiscriminatory terms. Field rejected that version of the claim, too, and he seems to have regarded limited liability—which attaches under general incorporation laws as well as special charters—as a "special" privilege.

28. *Paul*, 75 U.S. at 182.
29. Ibid., 183.
30. Insurers' repeated attempts to have the Commerce Clause holding of *Paul* overturned remained unavailing (see, e.g., *N.Y. Life Ins. Co. v. Deer Lodge County*, 231 U.S. 495 (1913)) until its repeal in *United States v. Se. Underwriters Assn.*, 322 U.S. 533 (1944). That ruling was promptly overturned by statute (McCarran-Ferguson Act, 15 U.S.C. §§ 1011–1015 (2006)).
31. Henderson, *Foreign Corporations*, 116.
32. *Pensacola Tel. Co. v. W. Union Tel. Co.*, 96 U.S. 1, 21 (1877) (Field, J., dissenting). "There is nothing in the opinion in *Paul v. Virginia* which gives any support to [the majority's holding]," Field added. Ibid.
33. Until the mid-nineteenth century, foreign attachment remained the usual way of proceeding against foreign corporations (which had a funny way of showing up in the jurisdiction when their assets had been seized). That procedure works poorly, however, when a foreign entity has no physical assets in the jurisdiction, only contractual contacts and perhaps agents. Naturally, firms organized their business accordingly.
34. See *Old Wayne Mut. Life Ass'n v. McDonough*, 204 U.S. 8 (1907); *Simon v. S. Ry. Co.*, 236 U.S. 115 (1915).
35. Henderson, *Foreign Corporations*, 91. For an argument that a quasi-contractual, consent-based theory may yield a substantive body of "unconstitutional conditions" law—as opposed to a "take it or leave it" position—see Richard A. Epstein, *Bargaining With the State* (Princeton, NJ: Princeton University Press,1993); and Epstein, *The Unconstitutional Conditions Puzzle*, 4 Cornell J L & and Pub Pol'y 466 (1995).
36. *Ins. Co. v. Morse*, 87 U.S. 445 (1874).
37. *Doyle v. Cont'l Ins. Co.*, 94 U.S. 535, 543 (1876) (Bradley, J., dissenting) (emphasis added). *Lafayette Ins. Co. v. French*, 59 U.S. 404 (1855), contains an earlier statement and has been occasionally cited as stating the doctrine. See, e.g., *Barron v. Burnside*, 121 U.S. 186, 200 (1887).
38. *Conn. Mut. Life Ins. Co. v. Spratley*, 172 U.S. 602 (1899); *Simon*, 236 U.S. 115.
39. *Allgeyer v. Louisiana*, 165 U.S. 578, 587–588 (1897). See, e.g., *McDonough*, 204 U.S. 8 (Full Faith and Credit); *Simon*, 236 U.S. 115 (Due Process),

40. See, e.g., *Pullman Co. v. Adams*, 189 U.S. 420 (1903) (sustaining state law imposing $100 tax, plus 25 cents per mile of railroad track within the state); *Allen v. Pullman's Palace*, 191 U.S. 171 (1903).

41. *W. Union Tel. Co. v. Kansas*, 216 U.S. 1 (1910); *Pullman Co. v. Kansas ex rel. Coleman*, 216 U.S. 56 (1910).

42. *Terral v. Burke Const. Co.*, 257 U.S. 529, 533 (1922); *Frost v. R.R. Comm'n*, 271 U.S. 583, 595–596 (1926).

43. *Frost*, 271 U.S. 583 (1926).

44. John J. Wallis, "Constitutions, Corporations, and Corruption: American States and Constitutional Change, 1842 to 1852," *Journal of Economic History*, 65:1 (2005): 212–215.

45. Henry N. Butler, *Nineteenth-Century Jurisdictional Competition in the Granting of Corporate Privileges*, 14 J Legal Stud 129 (1985). Unless otherwise indicated, the following pages are based on Butler's fine article, with a slightly different emphasis. Butler identifies two factors to explain the pattern and the timing of corporate law reform: the persistent expansion of interstate commerce and *Paul*. I emphasize the role of the Supreme Court and of legal entrepreneurship in the developments.

46. For an illuminating discussion of the history and dynamics; see Charles M. Yablon, *The Historical Race Competition for Corporate Charters and the Rise and Decline of New Jersey: 1880–1910*, 32 J Corp L 323 (2007).

47. Alfred D. Chandler, *The Visible Hand: The Managerial Revolution in American Business* (Cambridge, MA: Harvard University Press, 1977), 316–317.

48. Ibid., 323–324.

49. For the history and the causes of Delaware's rise, see Yablon, *Historical Race*, 355–376.

50. Owen M. Fiss, *Troubled Beginnings of the Modern State, 1888–1910*, vol. 8 of *History of the Supreme Court of the United States* (Cambridge: Cambridge University Press, 2006), 107–111.

51. For a terrific discussion, see Barry Cushman, *Formalism and Realism in Commerce Clause Jurisprudence*, 67 U Chi L Rev 1089 (2000).

52. See, *Balt. & Ohio R.R. v. Baugh*, 149 U.S. 368, 378–379 (1893); *Howard v. Ill. Cent. R.R. Co.* (*Employers' Liability Cases*) 207 U.S. 463 (1908); *Mondou v. N.Y., New Haven & Hartford R.R. Co.* (*Second Employers' Liability Cases*) 223 U.S. 1 (1912).

53. *Wabash, St. Louis. & Pac. Ry. Co. v. Illinois*, 118 U.S. 557 (1886; railroads); *Kidd v. Pearson*, 128 U.S. 1 (1888; manufacture); *Paul*, 75 U.S. 168 (insurance).

54. For an early case example see *Kidd v. Pearson*, 128 U.S. 1 (1888). For a later case see *Heisler v. Thomas Colliery Co.*, 260 U.S. 245 (1922). On the complicated interplay between federalism and liberty during the era see Fiss, *Troubled Beginnings*, esp. 257–261.

55. Contrary to stubborn Progressive lore, supposed obtuseness to the complexities of a modern, industrial society has nothing to do with it. The justices of the late nineteenth century *knew* the categorical distinctions to be problematic. They routinely characterized interstate commerce, not as a metaphysical

conception, but as a "practical one, drawn from the course of business." *Swift & Co. v. United States*, 196 U.S. 375, 398 (1905). The question is why the Court nonetheless believed that it needed the subject-matter categories. The answer is that the construction was an early attempt to engineer a coherent response to that emerging world. It was soon modified for the same reason.

56. *Woodruff v. Parham*, 75 U.S. 123, 139 (1868).

57. Henderson, *Foreign Corporations*, 118–119. The alternative, Henderson notes, was to scrutinize state legislatures' motives. *Robbins v. Shelby County Taxing Dist.*, 120 U.S. 489 (1887) suggests that move. The Court's dominant strategy, however, was to protect interstate commerce by means of categorical distinctions.

58. *Exxon Corp. v. Governor of Md.*, 437 U.S. 117 (1978) is the leading modern case.

59. My account is based on Charles W. McCurdy, "American Law and the Marketing Structure of the Large Corporation, 1875–1890," *Journal of Economic History* 38:3 (1978): 637–643.

60. The distinction between discrimination against a physical product and discrimination against those who deal in it may seem odd and artificial, and in some ways it is. However, it is still part of Commerce Clause jurisprudence. See, e.g., *Granholm v. Heald*, 544 U.S. 460, 483–484 (2005). See also ibid. at 521–522 (Thomas, J., dissenting and criticizing the distinction).

61. *Welton v. Missouri*, 91 U.S. 275, 277, 281 (1875).

62. *Webber v. Virginia*, 103 U.S. 344 (1880).

63. Chandler, *Visible Hand*, 299–300.

64. Ibid., 300.

65. *Minnesota v. Barber*, 136 U.S. 313 (1890).

66. *Brimmer v. Rebman*, 138 U.S. 78 (1891).

67. See, for example, *Coe v. Town of Errol*, 116 U.S. 517 (1886) (logs); *Bacon v. Illinois*, 227 U.S. 504 (1913) (wheat); *Minnesota v. Blasius*, 290 U.S. 1 (1933) (cows); *Kelley v. Rhoads*, 188 U.S. 1 (1903) (sheep).

68. The first trust, Standard Oil's, formed in 1882 among forty oil companies, incorporated several of its members under separate state laws so as to escape the discriminatory state taxes on foreign corporations. "As local enterprises, [state-chartered subsidiaries] were not subject to restrictions or excessive taxes levied on 'foreign' corporations, similar to those Pennsylvania was seeking to place on Standard Oil of Ohio." (Chandler, *Visible Hand*, 324).

6. Federal Common Law

1. *Erie R.R. Co. v. Tompkins*, 304 U.S. 64, 78 (1938) (overruling *Swift v. Tyson*, 41 U.S. 1 (1842)). The origin of the famous "brooding omnipresence" language is Justice Holmes's dissent in *S. Pac. Co. v. Jensen*, 244 U.S. 205, 222 (1917).

2. Tony Freyer, *Harmony and Dissonance: The* Swift *and* Erie *Cases in American Federalism* (New York: New York University Press, 1981), 18–19.

3. "Primarily," because the Full Faith and Credit Clause (Art. IV, § 1) provides another means of ordering horizontal choice of law problems. I put that

complication aside for discussion in later chapters. For the antibias purpose of diversity jurisdiction, see *Strawbridge v. Curtiss*, 7 U.S. 267 (1806).

4. See Joseph Henry Beale, *A Selection of Cases on the Conflict of Laws* (Cambridge, MA: Harvard University Press, 1900).

5. For a full account of the history, see Freyer, *Harmony and Dissonance*, 4–17.

6. Section 34 has since been codified as the Rules of Decision Act, 28 U.S.C. § 1652 (2006).

7. *Swift*, 41 U.S. at 18.

8. Ibid. 1–2 (numbering added for purposes of exposition).

9. Quotes in this paragraph ibid., 19–20.

10. Lest this look like a backward projection of modern concerns: negotiable instruments of the kind at issue in *Swift* were widely used to escape the strictures of state usury laws. A majority of state courts, especially in Western states, rejected the English common-law rule and allowed an endorser to impeach a note as usurious. The Supreme Court, in contrast, embraced the British (or "general") common-law rule. *Bank of the U.S. v. Dunn*, 31 U.S. 51, 57 (1832). For discussion, see Morton J. Horwitz, *The Transformation of American Law, 1780–1860* (Oxford: Oxford University Press, 1994), 219–220.

11. *Van Reimsdyk v. Kane*, F.Cas. 1062, 1065 (C.C.D.R.I. 1812) (No. 16,871) emphasis added). For a discussion of the case, see Freyer, *Harmony and Dissonance*, 32.

12. The treatment of state statutes marked a point of division between Story and Marshall, who was more circumspect in the exercise of federal commercial law and, resisting any grand theory on that subject, preferred to rely on creative applications of federal process acts (as he would in *Van Reimsdyk*) or on direct constitutional arguments (Freyer, *Harmony and Dissonance*, 42). Horwitz (*Transformation*, 221–223) shows that Marshall was of two minds about the question.

13. It never bothered anybody in the *Swift* era. "That the 'outcome' of a case might differ between the state and federal courts within the same state, was, in and of itself, irrelevant. The relevant concern was the consequences to the parties—that is, the preservation of their [ex ante] expectations." Randall Bridwell and Ralph U. Whitten, *The Constitution and the Common Law: The Decline of the Doctrines of Separation of Powers and Federalism* (Lexington, KY: D.C. Heath, 1977), 31.

14. The distinction between common law as a source of authority and as a means of exercising an authority already delegated was widely accepted at the time. For discussion and references, see Bridwell and Whitten, *Constitution and Common Law*, 31–32.

15. *Swift v. Phila. & Reading R.R. Co.*, 64 Fed. 59 (C.C.N.D. Ill. 1894).

16. It is often impossible for modern readers to tell whether a given case was ultimately decided "under" *Swift* or "under" the Commerce Clause or the Contract Clause. One example, briefly discussed below, is *Rowan v. Runnels*, 46 U.S. 134 (1847). David P. Currie reads the case as a Commerce Clause case: *The Constitution in the Supreme Court: The First Hundred Years, 1789–1888* (Chicago: University of Chicago Press, 1992), 223 n. 171. Others read

it as a general common law case: Bridwell and Whitten, *Constitution and Common Law*, 75–76; Freyer, *Harmony and Dissonance*, 48–49.

17. *Trs. of Dartmouth Coll. v. Woodward*, 17 U.S. 518 (1819).

18. G. Edward White, *The Marshall Court and Cultural Change, 1815–1835* (New York: Oxford University Press, 1991), 174–180.

19. Currie, *Constitution in the Supreme Court*, 141–145.

20. For the demise of the Contract Clause, see *Home Bldg. & Loan Ass'n v. Blaisdell*, 209 U.S. 398 (1934). For the Constitution of Zimbabwe as a judicial reference point, see *Knight v. Florida*, 528 U.S. 990, 463 (1999) (Stevens, J., dissenting from denial of certiorari).

21. *Erie* relied on Charles Warren, *New Light on the History of the Federal Judiciary Act of 1789*, 37 Harv L Rev 49 (1923). For "discredited," see esp. Wilfred J. Ritz, *Rewriting the History of the Judiciary Act of 1789: Exposing Myths, Challenging Premises, and Using New Evidence*, ed. Wythe Holt and L. H. LaRue (Norman: University of Oklahoma Press, 1990). See also Patrick J. Borchers, *The Origins of Diversity Jurisdiction, the Rise of Legal Positivism, and a Brave New World for Erie and Klaxon*, 72 Tex L Rev 79, 105–106 (1993). For further discussion see chap. 10.

22. This may not have been entirely uniform. Charles A. Heckman, *Uniform Commercial Law in the Nineteenth Century Federal Courts: The Decline and Abuse of the* Swift *Doctrine*, 27 Emory L J 45, 48 (1978), reports and quotes an 1841 opinion by Justice McLean (riding circuit) to the effect that state courts "should" follow federal courts on commercial law questions. But that may be merely hortatory and in any event was shortly before *Swift*, albeit reported only thereafter.

23. Currie, *Constitution in the Supreme Court*, 262.

24. Freyer, *Harmony and Dissonance*, 75. Even *Swift*'s modern defenders have been critical of its expansion over the second half of the nineteenth century. See, e.g., Bridwell and Whitten, *Constitution and Common Law*, 115–122.

25. Bridwell and Whitten attribute Swift's extension and constitutionalization to the death of Joseph Story and the rise of formalist jurisprudence (*Constitution and Common Law*, 123). To my mind, the explanation in the following pages is more persuasive.

26. *Carpenter v. Providence Washington Ins. Co.*, 41 U.S. 495 (1842).

27. Bridwell and Whitten, *Constitution and Common Law*, 86, 91. Paul B. Stephan, *What Story Got Wrong—Federalism, Localist Opportunism and International Law*, 73 Mo L Rev 1041 (2008) argues that state competition and other forces, such as private norm entrepreneurs, often constrain local opportunism. Eventually, he notes, states adopted uniform laws—the Uniform Negotiable Instruments Law, and the Uniform Commercial Code, § 3–303(a)(3)—embracing the *Swift* position. Even on Stephan's sanguine account, however, the conditions for such a consensus (in particular, a powerful national banking industry with a stake in uniformity) did not exist at the time of *Swift* or several decades thereafter. Moreover, I doubt that the consensus could have been formed without the preexisting baseline provided by *Swift*.

28. Morton Horwitz's characterization of *Swift* as "an attempt to impose a pro-commercial national legal order on unwilling state courts" is wrong in the sense that *Swift* did not authorize federal courts to *impose* anything at all. Horwitz is right, however, in noting that *Swift* operated principally on state *courts*, and he is equally right in noting their vehement resistance (Horwitz, *Transformation*, 250).

29. Heckman, *Uniform Commercial Law*, 50 n. 29 (citing cases from 1843 to 1903).

30. *Rowan v. Runnels*, 46 U.S. 134; *Groves v. Slaughter*, 40 U.S. 449 (1841). For discussion, see Bridwell and Whitten, *Constitution and Common Law*, 74–76.

31. *Rowan*, 46 U.S. at 139.

32. Freyer, *Harmony and Dissonance*, 48–49.

33. *Watson v. Tarpley*, 59 U.S. 517, 521 (1855).

34. That is Freyer's interpretation of *Watson* (*Harmony and Dissonance*, 53–54). Freyer cites G. Edward White, *The American Judicial Tradition: Profiles of Leading American Judges* (New York: Oxford University Press, 1976), 64–83, in support.

35. "The bonds were, to the knowledge of everyone, exclusively creatures of local law" (Bridwell and Whitten, *Constitution and Common Law*, 119; summarizing and following a line of argument by Charles Fairman). However, early nineteenth-century law drew no clear distinction between municipal bonds and other negotiable instruments (Heckman, *Uniform Commercial Law*, 52). Of course, the bonds could trade at discounts to account for the political risks, and they usually did. But nobody knew how to price the political risks—essentially, random events on the frontier—with any kind of accuracy.

36. *Gelpcke v. City of Dubuque*, 68 U.S. 175, 206–207 (majority) and at 214 (Miller, J., dissenting) (1863).

37. Freyer, *Harmony and Dissonance*, 60–61 (with further extensive references and citations).

38. *Balt. & Ohio R.R. Co. v. Baugh*, 149 U.S. 368, 372, 373 (1893).

39. Ibid., 378.

40. Ibid., 394 (Field, J., dissenting). The break is not quite as decisive as it appears. Where law is unsettled, Field hedged, federal courts retain a right to independent judgment. But where state law is settled, no "law out of the state" has application (*Baugh*, 149 U.S. at 402–403). For discussion, see Freyer, *Harmony and Dissonance*, 69–72.

41. Ibid., (Field, J., dissenting), quoted in *Erie*, 304 U.S. at 78.

42. Freyer, *Harmony and Dissonance*, 173 n. 41. The decision is *Chi., Milwaukee and St. Paul Ry. Co. v. Ross*, 112 U.S. 377 (1884).

43. For a parallel argument with respect to maritime law, see Barry Cushman, Lochner, *Liquor and Longshoremen: A Puzzle in Progressive Era Federalism*, 32 J Mar L & Com 1 (2001).

44. *Howard v. Ill. Cent. R.R. Co.* (*Employers' Liability Cases*), 207 U.S. 463 (1908); *Mondou v. N.Y., New Haven & Hartford R.R. Co.* (*Second Employers' Liability Cases*), 223 U.S. 1 (1912).

45. White, *Marshall Court*, 37–64.
46. *Mondou*, 223 U.S. at 57.
47. I take this to be the standard view. For a far more sophisticated and nuanced interpretation, see Owen M. Fiss, *Troubled Beginnings of the Modern State, 1888–1910*, vol. 8 of *History of the Supreme Court of the United States* (Cambridge: Cambridge University Press, 2006).

7. The Fiscal Constitution

Epigraph: Geoffrey Brennan and James M. Buchanan, *The Power to Tax: Analytical Foundations of a Fiscal Constitution* (Indianapolis, IN: Liberty Fund, 2000), 212. James Buchanan, veto message of February 24, 1859, quoted in John C. Eastman, *Restoring the "General" to the General Welfare Clause*, 4 Chap L Rev 63, 65, 86–87 (2001).

1. See Todd J. Zywicki, *Senators and Special Interests: A Public Choice Analysis of the Seventeenth Amendment*, 73 Or L Rev 1007 (1994). On "Spending Clause" limitations, see Eastman, *General Welfare* Clause, and Lynn A. Baker, *The Spending Power and the Federalist Revival*, 4 Chap L Rev 195 (2001).
2. Every dollar transferred from the federal government is a dollar that the state government need not raise at home. If anything, then, the federal representation of states as states should *raise* the state demand for federal funds, relative to a system of directly elected senators.
3. The only additional tax assignment, the prohibition against federal slave-import taxes in excess of $10, expired of its own force in 1808.

   Here and throughout, I put aside the question of intergovernmental tax immunity. *M'Culloch v. Maryland*, 17 U.S. 316 (1819), famously held that states may not tax the Bank of the United States. *Collector v. Day*, 78 U.S. 113 (1870), was the first of many Supreme Court decisions to limit the national government's authority to tax state entities. It was overruled in *Graves v. New York ex rel O'Keefe*, 306 U.S. 466 (1939). For all its fascination, the question is beyond the scope of this study.
4. The trouble with the arrangement (from the states' vantage) was that property taxes were unpopular, easy to evade, and expensive to administer. The budget constraint was quite hard and the revenue stream modest. Hamilton, writing as Publius, did not bother to deny this; rather, he argued that under the Constitution, states would not need a whole lot of revenue for legitimate public purposes. *Federalist* 34 (Hamilton) in *The Federalist*, ed. George Carey (Indianapolis, IN: Liberty Fund, 2001), 166. For what it is worth, the prediction proved correct; by the early nineteenth century many states administered a system of tax-free finance. John J. Wallis, "Constitutions, Corporations, and Corruption: American States and Constitutional Change, 1842 to 1852," *Journal of Economic History*, 65:1 (2005): 211–256.
5. Max Farrand, ed., *The Records of the Federal Convention of 1787*, vol. 1, rev. ed. (New Haven, CT: Yale University Press, 1937), 592 (Madison's notes). For the remainder of this paragraph, see Robin L. Einhorn, *American Taxation, American Slavery* (Chicago: University of Chicago Press, 2006),

165–173; and Bruce Ackerman, *Taxation and the Constitution*, 99 Colum L Rev 1 (1999).

6. Direct, apportioned taxes imposed in 1813, 1815, and 1861 "offered states 15 percent discounts if they treated the taxes as requisitions by 'assuming' their quotas" (Einhorn, *American Taxation*, 158). Few states took the deal in 1813 and 1815; virtually all did in 1861.

7. "Among tax scholars, the most famous passage in the records of the convention is the one where Rufus King 'asked what was the precise meaning of *direct* taxation? No one answd'" (ibid., 168).

8. Ibid., 159, table 1.

9. Ibid., 196–197. For the legal aspects of *Hylton*, see David P. Currie, *The Constitution in the Supreme Court: The First Hundred Years, 1789–1888* (Chicago: University of Chicago Press, 1992), 31–37.

10. *Pollock v. Farmers' Loan & Trust Co.*, 157 U.S. 429 (1895); *reh'g granted* 158 U.S. 601 (1895). For political maneuvering in and around the case, see see Owen M. Fiss, *Troubled Beginnings of the Modern State, 1888–1910*, vol. 8 of *History of the Supreme Court of the United States* (Cambridge: Cambridge University Press, 2006), 75–100.

11. Fiss, *Troubled Beginnings*, 95.

12. The generally accepted understanding is that "uniformity" does *not* mean an identical rate for all goods (of a certain type). See, e.g., *Edye v. Robertson (Head Money Cases)*, 112 U.S. 580 (1884).

13. "The Constitution grants to Congress the power of imposing a duty on imports for revenue, which power is abused by being converted into an instrument of rearing up the industry of one section of the country on the ruins of another" (John C. Calhoun, *South Carolina Exposition and Protest*, 1828).

14. Daniel J. Elazar, *The American Partnership: Intergovernmental Co-operation in the Nineteenth-Century United States* (Chicago: University of Chicago Press, 1962).

15. For data, see Daniel Walker Howe, *What Hath God Wrought: The Transformation of America, 1815–1848* (New York: Oxford University Press, 2007), 358–366.

16. The public did sour on public improvement schemes after the 1837 panic, when countless public schemes went belly-up and governments defaulted on their bond payments. John Lauritz Larson, *Internal Improvement: National Public Works and the Promise of Popular Government in the Early United States* (Chapel Hill: University of North Carolina Press, 2000), 217.

17. Stephen Minicucci, "Internal Improvements and the Union, 1790–1860," *Studies in American Political Development* 18 (2004): 160.

18. "The power to *raise money* is *plenary*, and *indefinite;* and the objects to which it may be *appropriated* are no less comprehensive, than the payment of the public debts and the providing for the common defense and *'general Welfare.'* The terns *'general Welfare'* were doubtless intended to signify more than was expressed or imported in those which Preceded. . ." Alexander Hamilton, "Report on Manufactures," in *The Works of Alexander Hamilton*, ed. Henry Cabot Lodge (New York: G.P. Putnam's Sons, 1904).

19. Jefferson clearly recognized the problem. In 1796, Madison (then a member of Congress) cheerfully suggested to him that post office revenues could profitably be invested in building new post roads (a continuous road from Maine to Georgia). He got an earful in return. The attempt to treat post office revenues as a dedicated fund (and mailing charges as a de facto user fee or benefit tax), Jefferson warned, would soon be compromised. "Other revenues will soon be called into their aid, and it will be a scene of eternal scramble among the members, who can get the most money wasted in their State; and they will always get most who are meanest." Less plausible was Jefferson's attempt to identify a constitutional barrier to the mischief. The constitutional power to "establish post roads," Jefferson suggested, did not mean that Congress could *make* or *pay for* those roads. It could "only select from those already made, those on which there shall be a post." Jefferson to Madison, Mar. 6, 1796, in *The Founders' Constitution*, ed. Philip B. Kurland and Ralph Lerner (Chicago: University of Chicago Press, 1987), 3:28.

20. Howe, *What Hath God Wrought*, 358; Larson, *Internal Improvement*, 184.

21. That difficulty, too, materialized in the internal improvements debate, occasionally to the point of hilarity. For example, Illinois and Indiana, which had a big stake in a road link to the Eastern seaboard, complained that federal funds for the road were dedicated to Ohio. Perplexed legislators inquired how they were supposed to build a road to Indiana *except* through Ohio (Larson, *Internal Improvement*, 162–163).

22. John Joseph Wallis and Barry R. Weingast, "Dysfunctional or Optimal Institutions? State Debt Limitations, the Structure of State and Local Governments, and the Finance of American Infrastructure," in *Fiscal Challenges: An Interdisciplinary Approach to Budget Policy*, ed. Elizabeth Garrett, Elizabeth Graddy and Howell Jackson (Cambridge: Cambridge University Press, 2008), 331–363.

23. Rep. Williamson inveighed against "set[ting] aside that part of the Constitution which requires equal taxes, *and demands similar distributions*" (quoted in Eastman, *General Welfare Clause*, 79; emphasis added).

24. Howe, *What Hath God Wrought*, 499. Similarly, President Jackson "hoped for a plan that would 'reconcile the diversified interests of the States and strengthen the bonds which unite them.' Perhaps a distribution of the surplus federal revenue to the states according to representation would be the 'safe, just, and federal' solution?" (Larson, *Internal Improvements*, 181).

25. Jefferson to Madison, Mar. 6, 1796, in *Founders' Constitution*, 3:28

26. Howe, *What Hath God Wrought*, 88, 254.

27. Larson, *Internal Improvements*, 173, 61.

28. Ibid., 61.

29. Howe, *What Hath God Wrought*, 88–89.

30. An 1824 Survey Bill, for example, authorized the executive to "cause the necessary surveys, plans and estimates" for a general system of improvements in the hope of removing the difficult locational decisions from Congress. Under the leadership of John C. Calhoun (then secretary of war), Army engineers produced list of reasonable projects, but the House of

Representatives had its own ideas. Implementation "quickly exposed fissures within the improvement community that would tend to fracture the system approach and transform any program into a barrel of pork" (Larson, *Internal Improvements*, 162).

31. Howe, *What Hath God Wrought*, 359.

32. The constraint not only limited spending but also blocked what might look like a way out of the Jeffersonians' dilemma: make universalism your friend and construct a *really* big internal improvements system, everywhere and all at once. Considerations of that sort drove the Gallatin plan. However, given the tax-side budget constraint, big, expensive national projects (such as the Cumberland Road, which absorbed an inordinate share of federal funding) could only be built one at a time.

33. Howe, *What Hath God Wrought*, 365, citing Daniel Feller, *The Public Lands in Jacksonian Politics* (Madison: University of Wisconsin Press, 1984), 136. Virginia's insufferable John Randolph articulated a closely related point in 1824, in the course of denouncing the aforementioned Survey Bill as a menace to "every man who has the misfortune . . . to be born a slaveholder." "If Congress possesses the power to do what is proposed in this bill," Randolph harangued, "they may emancipate every slave in the United States" (Larson, *Internal Improvements*, 143).

34. Larson, *Internal Improvements*, 145–146.

35. For a fine discussion of the debt crisis between 1837 and 1843, see Jonathan Rodden, *Hamilton's Paradox: The Promise and Peril of Fiscal Federalism* (Cambridge: Cambridge University Press, 2006), 58–67. The following paragraphs in the text are based on Rodden's account.

36. Rodden, *Hamilton's Paradox*, 62.

37. Ibid., 66.

38. See, e.g., Thomas Reed Powell, *Indirect Encroachment on Federal Authority by the Taxing Power of the States*, 31 Harv L Rev 321 (1918).

39. The following discussion is based on Richard Franklin Bensel, *The Political Economy of American Industrialization, 1877–1900* (New York: Cambridge University Press, 2000).

40. By an (obviously impressionistic) measure of Supreme Court decisions in Commerce Clause cases, it appears that industrial states' tax and regulatory schemes were contested as often and successfully as were southern and western states'. See Bensel, *Political Economy*, 332, esp. cases listed in n. 139.

41. On pensions, see Richard Franklin Bensel, *Sectionalism and American Political Development 1880–1980* (Madison: University of Wisconsin Press, 1984), 502–503; Theda Skocpol, *Protecting Soldiers and Mothers: The Political Origins of Social Policy in the United States* (Cambridge, MA: Harvard University Press, 1992).

42. E.g., Martha Derthick, "How Many Communities? The Evolution of American Federalism," in Martha Derthick, ed., *Dilemmas of Scale in America's Federal Democracy* (Cambridge: Cambridge University Press, 1999), 125; Stephen Skowronek, *Building A New American State: The Expansion of National Administrative Capacities* (Cambridge: Cambridge University Press, 1982);

Skocpol, *Soldiers and Mothers*, 102–152; Kimberley S. Johnson, *Governing the American State: Congress and the New Federalism, 1877–1929* (Princeton, NJ: Princeton University Press, 2007).

43. "State and local governments, particularly when under the control of Republicans, welcomed the government centralization that the new social programs created. State and local leaders appreciated the way in which the programs satisfied demands for public works and welfare that they would otherwise have had to meet." W. Elliot Brownlee, *Federal Taxation in America: A Short History*, 2nd ed. (Cambridge: Cambridge University Press, 2004), 39.

44. See, e.g., Richard A. Epstein, *How Progressives Rewrote the Constitution* (Washington, D.C.: Cato Institute, 2006); John Marini and Ken Masugi, eds., *The Progressive Revolution in Politics and Political Science: Transforming the American Regime* (Lanham, MD: Rowman & Littlefield, 2005).

45. James Bryce, *The American Commonwealth*, vol. 3 (London: Macmillan, 1888), 233.

46. See, respectively, Thomas M. Cooley, *A Treatise on the Constitutional Limitations Which Rest upon the Legislative Power of the States of the American Union* (Boston: Little, Brown, 1868); and Edward S. Corwin, *The Passing of Dual Federalism*, 36 Va L Rev 1 (1950).

47. Howard Gillman, *The Constitution Besieged: The Rise and Demise of* Lochner *Era Police Powers Jurisprudence* (Durham, NC: Duke University Press, 1993), 20–21.

48. Fiss, *Troubled Beginnings* 48–49.

49. See, e.,g., *Pennoyer v. Neff*, 95 U.S. 714 (1878). For "mismatched" see Richard A. Epstein, *Consent, Not Power, as the Basis of Jurisdiction*, 2001 U Chi Legal F 1 (2001).

50. *Hammer v. Dagenhart*, 247 U.S. 251, 273 (1918).

51. See *Champion v. Ames* (*The Lottery Case*), 188 U.S. 321 (1903); *Caminetti v. U.S.*, 242 U.S. 470 (1917).

52. *Hammer*, 247 U.S. at 279–280 (Holmes, J., dissenting).

53. See, e.g., *Nebbia v. New York*, 291 U.S. 502 (1934).

Part III. Transformation

Epigraph: *The Book of the States*, 1937 ed., vol. II, 143–144.

1. For a fine account, see Howard Gillman, "The Collapse of Constitutional Originalism and the Rise of the Notion of the 'Living Constitution' in the Course of American State-Building," *Studies in American Political Development* 11 (1997): 191–247.

2. I have borrowed the snappy slogan from Richard A. Epstein, *How Progressives Rewrote the Constitution* (Washington, D.C.: Cato Institute, 2006).

3. On analytic narratives, see Norman Schofield, "Evolution of the Constitution," *British Journal of Political Science* 32:1 (2002): 1–20.

4. A wonderful book in line with this last suggestion is Morton Keller, *Regulating a New Economy: Public Policy and Economic Change in America, 1900–1933* (Cambridge, MA: Harvard University Press, 1990).

5. In my telling, the constitutional choice story has a great deal in common with developmental and "revisionist" accounts of the New Deal's constitutional history. See esp. Barry Cushman, *Rethinking the New Deal Court: The Structure of a Constitutional Revolution* (Oxford: Oxford University Press, 1998).

6. See Nathan J. Browne, "Reason, Interest, Rationality, and Passion In Constitution Drafting," *Political Perspectives on Politics* 6:4 (2008): 675–689; and Cass R. Sunstein, *Congress, Constitutional Moments, and the Cost-Benefit State*, 48 Stan L Rev 347 (1996), esp. at 254 n. 23 and sources cited therein.

8. Constitutional Inversion

1. See, for example, Samuel H. Beer, "The Modernization of American Federalism," *Publius* 3:2, (1973): 49; Keith E. Whittington, *Dismantling the Modern State? The Changing Structural Foundations of American Federalism*, 25 Hastings Const L Q 483 (1998); William N. Eskridge, Jr., and John Ferejohn, *The Elastic Commerce Clause: A Political Theory of American Federalism*, 47 Vand L Rev 1355, 1356 (1994) (describing centralization as the most widely accepted account). For additional references, see Stephen Gardbaum, *New Deal Constitutionalism and the Unshackling of the States*, 64 U Chi L Rev 483, 483–484 (1997).

2. John Joseph Wallis, "The Birth of the Old Federalism: Financing the New Deal," *Journal of Economic History* 44 (1984): 144.

3. Only one important program, the old-age insurance title of the 1935 Social Security Act (what we now call Social Security), was structured as a wholly national program. For discussion and references, see chap. 11.

4. Gardbaum, *New Deal Constitutionalism.*

5. Invention of the term is generally credited to Edward S. Corwin. See Edward S. Corwin, *The Twilight of the Supreme Court* (New Haven, CT: Yale University Press, 1934); and Corwin, *The Passing of Dual Federalism*, 36 Va L Rev 1 (1950). The United States Supreme Court has used the term "cooperative federalism" both as denoting a form of conditional preemption (e.g., *Hodel v. Va. Surface Mining and Reclamation Ass'n*, 452 U.S. 264, 289 (1981)) and, more broadly, as denoting the state enforcement of federal policies. It has also employed the term "cooperative judicial federalism," meaning federal judicial deference to state court rulings. *Bush v. Gore*, 531 U.S. 98, 137–140 (2000) (Ginsburg, J., dissenting). Here and throughout, I use the term in the broad, general sense given in the text.

6. For a good discussion, see William Graebner, "Federalism in the Progressive Era: A Structural Interpretation of Reform," *Journal of American History* 64:2 (1977): 331–357.

7. The distinction roughly corresponds to game theorists' distinction between "coordination problems" and "collective action problems." Coordination problems arise over players' difficulties in finding a common solution; once it has been identified and agreed upon, no one has an incentive to defect. (Driving on the left or right side of the roads is the standard example.) Collective action problems arise when players do have an incentive to defect. For reasons

explained below, the central federalism problem—from the vantage of the states and of the New Deal Constitution—is state "players'" propensity to defect to competitive positions.

Wholesale indifference to the distinction was a hallmark of Progressive-New Deal agitation from the get-go. Early on, the uniform law movement sought to harmonize state notarization requirements and divorce procedures—and state laws on labor conditions for the tenement industries in New York, New Jersey, and Connecticut, for the explicit purpose of suppressing interstate competition (Graebner, "Federalism in the Progressive Era," 332–334). In the same vein, Felix Frankfurter and James Landis peddled state compacts as a fine instrument for interstate water resource management—and for tax harmonization. Felix Frankfurter and James M. Landis, *The Compact Clause of the Constitution—A Study in Interstate Adjustments*, 34 Yale L J 685, 696–704 (1925).

8. Edward S. Corwin, *The Commerce Power versus States Rights* (Princeton, NJ: Princeton University Press, 1936)

9. *United States v. E. C. Knight Co.*, 156 U.S. 1 (1895).

10. *Swift & Co. v. United States*, 196 U.S. 375 (1905) (antitrust); *Wilkerson v. Rahrer*, 140 U.S. 545 (1891) (upholding the Wilson Act); *James Clark Distilling Co. v. W. Md. Ry. Co.*, 242 U.S. 311 (1917) (upholding the Webb-Kenyon Act).

11. Franklin D. Roosevelt, "A 'Fireside Chat' Discussing the Plan for Reorganization of the Judiciary in Washington, D.C. (Mar. 9, 1937)," in *The Public Papers and Addresses of Franklin D. Roosevelt*, vol. 6, ed. Samuel I. Rosenman (New York: Random House, 1941), 122.

12. For railroads, see the *Houston, East & West Texas Ry. Co. v. United States* (*Shreveport Rate Cases*), 234 U.S. 342 (1914). For bottlenecks, see *Lemke v. Farmers' Grain Co.*, 258 U.S. 50 (1922). For pharmaceuticals, see *Hippolite Egg Co. v. United States*, 220 U.S. 45 (1911) (sustaining Federal Food and Drugs Act). For state enforcement, see *United States v. P. Koenig Coal Co.*, 270 U.S. 512 (1926).

13. In fact, the "cooperative" portions of the Social Security Act drew the conservative justices' united opposition on account of perceived federalism problems. The wholly national old-age insurance system of the same act did not. *Charles C. Steward Mach. Co. v. Davis*, 301 U.S. 548 (1937); *Helvering v. Davis*, 301 U.S. 619 (1937).

14. *Hammer v. Dagenhart*, 247 U.S. 251 (1918); *United States v. Butler*, 297 U.S. 1 (1936); *Panama Refining Co. v. Ryan*, 293 U.S. 388 (1935); *Schechter Poultry Corp. v. United States*, 295 U.S. 495 (1935); *Carter v. Carter Coal Co.*, 298 U.S. 238 (1936).

15. Wholly national responses to increased complexity and novel social demands presented themselves at the time. For example, the recognition that states are poorly equipped to regulate interstate power or telecommunication networks might have suggested that monopolistic, central administration was the appropriate remedy. Regulated industries often pressed the point, but to little avail. See, e.g., Joel Seligman, *The Obsolescence of Wall Street: A*

Contextual Approach to the Evolving Structure of Federal Securities Regulation, 93 Mich L Rev 649, 652 (1995).

16. Still the best account is James T. Patterson, *The New Deal and the States: Federalism in Transition* (Princeton, NJ: Princeton University Press, 1969). For discussion, see chap. 11 of this volume.

17. See Richard A. Epstein, *The Harm Principle - And How It Grew*, 45 U Toronto L J 369 (1995).

18. The leading contributions are Ralph K. Winter, Jr., *State Law, Shareholder Protection, and the Theory of the Corporation*, 6 J Legal Stud 251 (1977); and Roberta Romano, *The Genius of American Corporate Law* (Washington, D.C.: AEI, 1993). But see William L. Cary, *Federalism and Corporate Law: Reflections upon Delaware*, 83 Yale L J 663 (1974) (arguing that state competition results in a race to the bottom).

19. When local jurisdictions undersupply a local public goods such as environmental protection, they typically do so because they are able to export the costs of pollution to other states. But that is an externality problem, not a collective action problem. See Richard L. Revesz, *Rehabilitating Interstate Competition: Rethinking the "Race to the Bottom" Rationale for Federal Environmental Regulation*, 67 NYU L Rev 1210 (1992). Revesz's pathbreaking article produced a flurry of criticism. The references can be found in Revesz's rejoinder, *The Race to the Bottom and Federal Environmental Regulation: A Response to Critics*, 82 Minn L Rev 535 (1997). In my estimation Revesz has long won the argument, even though the debate continues.

20. *Hammer*, 247 U.S. 251; *Bailey v. Drexel Furniture Co. (Child Labor Tax Case)*, 259 U.S. 20 (1922).

21. Carolyn M. Moehling, "State Child Labor Laws and the Decline of Child Labor," *Explorations in Economic History* 36:1 (1999): 72–106.

22. Unless otherwise noted, the constitutional choice analytics in this section are adapted from Geoffrey Brennan and James M. Buchanan, *The Power to Tax: Analytical Foundations of a Fiscal Constitution* (Indianapolis, IN: Liberty Fund, 2000). For "stationary bandits," see Mancur Olson, "Dictatorship, Democracy, and Development," *American Political Science Review* 87:3 (1993): 569.

23. *Federalist* 1 (Hamilton) in *The Federalist*, ed. George Carey (Indianapolis, IN: Liberty Fund, 2001), 2. The difference between autocrats and self-interested politicians in a democracy is not as large as one might think. For a splendid discussion bearing on the subject at hand, see Jonathan Klick, "Limited Autocracy," *Review of Law and Economics* 1:2 (2005): 293–304.

24. The bargain may depend on some external threat. William Riker's famous "military condition" holds that federal systems typically come about in response to external military threats. William H. Riker, *Federalism: Origin, Operation, Significance* (Boston: Little, Brown, 1964), 12–13. For a review and modification of Riker's view, see David McKay, "William Riker on Federalism: Sometimes Wrong but More Right than Anyone Else?" *Regional and Federal Studies* 14:2 (2004): 167–186.

25. For a discussion of the point in the competitive federalism context, see Revesz, *Rehabilitating Interstate Competition*, 1213–1227.

26. Robert Nozick, *Anarchy, State and Utopia* (New York: Basic Books, 1974), 176–178, coined the term "Lockean proviso" as shorthand for Locke's limit on the right to original acquisition: there must be "enough, and as good, left in common for others." John Locke, *Second Treatise on Government*, ed. C. B. Macpherson (Indianapolis, IN: Hackett, 1980), 19. I use it as shorthand for Locke's objection to the Hobbesian bargain: men are not "so foolish, that they take care to avoid what mischiefs may be done them by *pole-cats* or *foxes*, nay, think it safety, to be devoured by *lions*" (*Second Treatise*, 50). States aren't so foolish, either.

27. For the general proposition, see Brennan and Buchanan, *Power to Tax*, 212–213. The congruence between their seemingly extreme modeling assumptions and the design of at least some federal constitutions is uncanny. For example, the state delegates who deliberated over Germany's Basic Law—not Leviathans but rather honorable officials who had survived a gruesome Leviathan—demanded (with the exception of delegates from Bavaria) a federal system that would leave zero tax autonomy to lower-level governments. The residual level of tax competition in Germany's federal constitutional system has been attributed to Allied intervention. See Jonathan A. Rodden, *Hamilton's Paradox: The Promise and Peril of Fiscal Federalism* (Cambridge: Cambridge University Press, 2006), 254, and sources cited there.

28. Also, the demand will rarely be unanimous. In-period, states are keenly aware of their particular advantages, which may include competitive advantages. A single state may enjoy such advantages; Delaware's corporate law regime is an example. Or, the advantages of an open, competitive economy may consistently accrue to a number of states; the sectional division between "producer states" and "market states" in the pre–New Deal decades and beyond is a dramatic illustration. However, even procompetitive states will want protection in *some* dimensions,. Moreover, politicians' short time horizon implies a steep discount rate for the long-term benefits of a competitive system. For these and other reasons, the demand for cartelization will dominate. The complications are discussed later, under "Patterns of Accommodation."

29. For black labor migration, see Robert Higgs, *Competition and Coercion: Blacks in the American Economy, 1865–1914* (New York: Cambridge University Press, 1977), 24–36. For the significance of well-functioning capital markets as a means of disciplining state governments, see Robert P. Inman, "Transfers and Bailouts: Institutions for Enforcing Local Fiscal Discipline," *Constitutional Political Economy* 12:2 (2001): 141–160.

30. The question of whether the Sherman Act was chiefly inspired by considerations of consumer welfare or rather by—often parochial—producer interests has occupied economists and historians to no end. A decidedly protectionist take is Donald J. Boudreaux and Thomas J. DiLorenzo, "The Protectionist Roots of Antitrust," *Review of Austrian Economics* 6 (1993), 81–96. The best-known consumer welfare view is Robert H. Bork, *The Antitrust Paradox: A Policy at War with Itself* (New York: Basic Books, 1978). For the chain store movement, see Richard C. Schragger, *The Anti-Chain Store Movement,*

Localist Ideology, and the Remnants of the Progressive Constitution, 1920–1940, 90 Iowa L Rev 1011 (2005).

31. *Louis K. Liggett Co. v. Lee*, 288 U.S. 517, 580 (1933) (Brandeis, J., dissenting)

32. Schragger, *Anti-Chain Store Movement*, 1081.

33. Robert H. Jackson, *The Struggle for Judicial Supremacy: A Study of a Crisis in American Power Politics* (New York: Knopf, 1941), 160. I have found only one case in which a state challenged a federal intervention (a rate-making decision by the Interstate Commerce Commission) on Commerce Clause grounds, *Florida v. United States*, 282 U.S. 194 (1931). Even that case, moreover, is a constitutionally larded-up administrative challenge.

Jackson's dichotomy between business and states is a bit misleading. Typically, the stubborn defenders of the "old" Commerce Clause, from *Butler* to *Schechter* to *Wickard* to *Parker*, were not large firms or trade associations but marginal producers who fell outside the industry cartels on whose behalf the New Deal reduced complexity and "stabilized" the economy.

34. For a sophisticated discussion, see Mikhail Filippov, Peter C. Ordeshook, and Olga Shvetsova, *Designing Federalism: A Theory of Self-Sustainable Federal Institutions* (Cambridge: Cambridge University Press, 2004), 1–41.

35. See generally Robert Cooter, *The Cost of Coase*, 11 J Legal Stud 1 (1982).

36. For a similar analysis, see Jenna Bednar, William N. Eskridge Jr., and John Ferejohn, "A Political Theory of Federalism," in *Constitutional Culture and Democratic Rule*, ed. John Ferejohn, Jack N. Rakove, and Jonathan Riley (Cambridge: Cambridge University Press, 2001), 238.

37. For a full treatment, see Richard Franklin Bensel, *Sectionalism and American Political Development, 1880–1980* (Madison: University of Wisconsin Press, 1984), chap. 5.

38. See, e.g., Paul Pierson, "Increasing Returns, Path Dependence, and the Study of Politics," *American Political Science Review* 94:2 (2000): 251–267.

39. Jonathan R. Macey, *Federal Deference to Local Regulators and the Economic Theory of Regulation: Toward a Public-Choice Explanation of Federalism*, 76 Va L Rev 265 (1990).

40. For the history, see John James, *Money and Capital Markets in Postbellum America* (Princeton, NJ: Princeton University Press, 1978); and Charles W. Calomiris, *U.S. Bank Deregulation in Historical Perspective* (Cambridge: Cambridge University Press, 2000).

41. The following paragraphs draw on Michael S. Greve, "Laboratories of Democracy: Anatomy of a Metaphor," AEI Federalist Outlook, March 2001, available online at http://www.aei.org/outlook/12743.

42. *New State Ice Co. v. Liebmann*, 285 U.S. 262, 311 (1932). For an earlier formulation, see Justice Holmes's dissent in *Truax v. Corrigan*, 257 U.S. 312, 344 (1921).

43. See, e.g., Ernest A. Young, *The Conservative Case for Federalism*, 74 Geo Wash L Rev 874, 881 (2006) (arguing, wrongly I believe, that Brandeis's federalism has "Burkean" connotations that should be congenial to conservatives). For adaptive efficiency (which does not necessarily translate into allocative efficiency, as economists understand it), see Douglass North, *Institutions,*

Institutional Change and Economic Performance (Cambridge: Cambridge University Press, 1990), 80–81.

44. Even his hagiographers concede that Brandeis would have held a very different view of state economic experimentation and its judicial review had those experiments run against, say, trade unions. See, e.g., Philippa Strum, *Brandeis: Beyond Progressivism* (Lawrence: University Press of Kansas, 1993), 89.

45. Justice Brandeis himself noted the industry's "unremitting efforts, through trade associations, informal agreements, combination of delivery systems, and in particular through the consolidation of plants, to protect markets and prices against competition of any character." *New State Ice*, 285 U.S. at 293.

46. Oklahoma, like many other states, regulated prices and practices in the ice industry before turning it into a public utility. Writing for the *New State Ice* majority, Justice Sutherland explicitly conceded the constitutionality of those regulations. He would have permitted even the licensing scheme, had it rested on any plausible rationale. *New State Ice* thus stands for a very restrained application of due process review—probably more restrained than a man of George Sutherland's judicial disposition would have wanted. Hadley Arkes, *The Return of George Sutherland: Restoring a Jurisprudence of Natural Rights* (Princeton, NJ: Princeton University Press, 1994), 251–252. Only two years later (and three years before the Court's notorious "switch in time") the Court surrendered that review function and embraced Brandeis's position of wholesale abdication. *Nebbia v. New York*, 291 U.S. 502 (1934) (sustaining a New York dairy cartel that imposed the price of "stabilizing" the industry on consumers).

47. Morton Grodzins, *The American System: A New View of Government in the United States*, ed. Daniel J. Elazar (New Brunswick, NJ: Transaction, 1984), 335. Pluralist federalism scholarship, which is the federalism scholarship of the New Deal, has consistently celebrated federalism's openness to interest groups as one of its chief virtues. See, e.g., Corwin, *Dual Federalism*; and Daniel J. Elazar, "Cooperative Federalism," in *Competition Among States and Local Governments: Efficiency and Equity in American Federalism*, ed. Daphne A. Kenyon and John Kincaid (Washington, D.C.: Urban Institute, 1991), 65–86.

48. See, e.g., *W. Coast Hotel Co. v. Parrish*, 300 U.S. 379 (1937) (sustaining a minimum wage law for female workers). There is a reason why the case featured a *West Coast* hotel: its relative insulation from national labor markets gave the state of Washington the "courage" to raise wages—the better to exclude Chinese labor—without much fear of competition.

49. Recall the discussion of this pluralist tenet in chap. 2.

50. For the distinction between "structure courts" and "rights courts," see Martin Shapiro, "The Success of Judicial Review and Democracy," in *On Law, Politics, and Judicialization*, ed. Martin Shapiro and Alec Stone Sweet (New York: Oxford University Press, 2002), 149–183.

51. *United States v. Carolene Products Co.*, 304 U.S. 144 (1938), widely viewed as a kind of Magna Charta for the post-New Deal Supreme Court, said that the

Supreme Court would assume a deferential posture in reviewing the results of the political process, except where that process might encroach upon the specific guarantees of the Bill of Rights or on the interests of "discrete and insular minorities" that are at a systematic disadvantage in the political process. Upon inspection, this shining monument to judicial restraint looses a great deal of its luster. Geoffrey P. Miller, *The True Story of* Carolene Products, 1987 Sup Ct Rev 397 (1987).

52. For variations on this theme and discussions of the literature see Silika Prohl & Friedrich Schneider, "Does Decentralization Reduce Government Size? A Quantitative Study of the Decentralization Hypothesis," *Public Finance Review* 37:6 (2009): 639–664; Jonathan Rodden, "Reviving Leviathan: Fiscal Federalism and the Growth of Government," *International Organization* 57 (2003): 695–729; "Fiscal Federalism, Collusion, and Government Size: Evidence From the States," *Public Finance Review* 27:3 (1999): 262–281; and Craig Volden, "Intergovernmental Political Competition in American Federalism," *American Journal of Political Science* 49:2 (2005): 327–342.

53. Lawrence Lessig, *Fidelity in Translation*, 71 Tex L Rev 1165 (1993); and Ernest A. Young, *Making Federalism Doctrine: Fidelity, Institutional Competence, and Compensating Adjustments*, 46 Wm & Mary L Rev 1753 (2005).

54. For the general proposition, see Adrian Vermeule, *Hume's Second Best Constitutionalism*, 70 U Chi L Rev 421, 435–437 (2003).

9. Commerce, Cartels, and Concurrent Powers

1. See, e.g., Thomas Reed Powell, *State Income Taxes and the Commerce Clause*, 31 Yale L J 799 (1922).

2. *Wickard v. Filburn*, 317 U.S. 111, 120 (1942). The canonical article is Robert L. Stern, *That Commerce Which Concerns More States than One*, 47 Harv L Rev 1335 (1934).

3. See, e.g. Randy E. Barnett, *The Original Meaning of the Commerce Clause*, 68 U Chi L Rev 101 (2001); Calvin Johnson, *Homage to Clio: the Historical Continuity from the Articles of Confederation into the Constitution*, 20 Const Comment 463 (2004). If the position still has adherents on and off the bench, that is chiefly because it makes it easier to deny, and hence to live with, the true scope of the New Deal transformation. Cass R. Sunstein, *Constitutionalism After the New Deal*, 101 Harv L Rev 421, 438 (1987).

4. *Wickard*, 317 U.S. at 119–125.

5. For this paragraph see Jim Chen, *Filburn's Forgotten Footnote—Of Farm Team Federalism and Its Fate*, 82 Minn L Rev 249, 279–302 (1997).

6. See, e.g., Richard A. Epstein, *The Proper Scope of the Commerce Power*, 73 Va L Rev 1387 (1987); and Epstein, *Constitutional Faith and the Commerce Clause*, 71 Notre Dame L Rev 167 (1996).

7. Recall the discussion in chaps. 4 and 5; and see Barry Cushman, *Formalism and Realism in Commerce Clause Jurisprudence*, 67 U Chi L Rev 1089 (2000).

8. Lawrence Lessig, *Translating Federalism: United States v. Lopez*, 1995 Sup Ct Rev 125, 197–201 (1995). Stephen Gardbaum reads post–New Deal cases as

"necessary and proper" cases; see *Rethinking Constitutional Federalism*, 74 Texas L Rev 795 (1996).

9. Frank R. Strong, *Cooperative Federalism*, 23 Iowa L Rev 459, 459 (1938). A footnote to the sentence cites Edward S. Corwin, *National-State Cooperation—Its Present Possibilities*, 46 Yale L J 599 (1937); and F. D. G. Ribble, *National and State Cooperation Under the Commerce Clause*, 37 Colum L Rev 43 (1937).

10. The classic case is *James Clark Distilling Co. v. W. Md. Ry. Co. .*, 242 U.S. 311 (1917) (sustaining the Webb-Kenyon Act). See also *Whitfield v. Ohio*, 297 U.S. 431 (1936); *Ky. Whip & Collar Co. v. Ill. Cent. R.R. Co.*, 299 U.S. 334 (1937).

11. Strong, *Cooperative Federalism*, 476.

12. Ibid., 476–501.

13. In 1937, twenty-eight states favored a proposed Child Labor Amendment to the Constitution; twenty were opposed (Ibid., 486 n. 121).

14. *Schechter Poultry Corp. v. United States*, 295 U.S. 495, 533–534 (1935). As Strong observes, the Court discussed those differences in the course of holding that the NIRA effected an unconstitutional delegation of powers, not its discussion of the Commerce Clause (*Cooperative Federalism*, 487 n. 127). But that does not affect the point in the text.

15. *Ashton v. Cameron County Water Improvement Dis. No. 1*, 298 U.S. 513, 527, 531 (1936).

16. Ibid., 540–541 (Cardozo, J., dissenting). Compare Cardozo's statement to the same effect, in the context of the Spending Clause and now in the majority, in *Charles C. Steward Mach. Co. v. Davis*, 301 U.S. 548, 588–589 (1937).

17. *Ashton* was probably overruled in 1938. *Prudential Ins. Co. v. Benjamin*, 328 U.S. 408, 433 n. 42 (1946) (citing *United States v. Bekins*, 304 U.S. 27 (1938)).

The general nondelegation principle has remained technically intact. However, its range over is very narrow. Primarily, the question remained salient with respect to "cooperative" federal legislation authorizing states to enact *discriminatory* laws that would, in the absence of such authorization, violate the dormant Commerce Clause. (A prime example is the McCarran-Ferguson Act of 1945, which explicitly authorizes states to enact insurance regulations that discriminate against out-of-state firms). Unsurprisingly, the Court answered that Congress may grant such authority, so long as it clearly states its intent. *Prudential Ins. Co.*, 328 U.S. 408; *U.S. Dept. of the Treasury v. Fabe*, 508 U.S. 491 (1993). A second application of the nondelegation rule is that states may not consent to federal "commandeering." *New York v. United States*, 505 U.S. 144 (1992), discussed in chap.15.

18. See, e.g., *Roper v. Simmons*, 543 U.S. 551, 564–565 (2005), and Ibid., 610–611 (Scalia, J., dissenting, arguing that Justice Kennedy cannot count).

19. Strong, *Cooperative Federalism*, 515.

20. Bruce A. Ackerman, *We the People: Foundations* (Cambridge, MA: Harvard University Press, 1991), 6; Strong, *Cooperative Federalism*, 459.

21. Parts of this section are adapted from Richard A. Epstein and Michael S. Greve, "Preemption Doctrine and its Limits," in *Federal Preemption: States'*

Powers, National Interests, ed. Richard A. Epstein and Michael S. Greve (Washington, D.C.: AEI, 2007), 309–342, esp. 309–318.

22. *N.Y. Cent. R.R. Co. v. Winfield*, 244 U.S. 147, 169 (1917).

23. For a concise exposition of this construct and the trajectory of the Supreme Court's preemption doctrine before and during the New Deal, see Stephen Gardbaum, "The Breadth vs. the Depth of Congress's Commerce Power: The Curious History of Preemption During the *Lochner* Era," in Epstein and Greve, *Federal Preemption*, 48–78.

24. *Rice v. Santa Fe Elevator Corp.*, 331 U.S. 218, 230 (1947) (citations omitted).

25. *Rice*, 331 U.S. at 224, citing statutory language (emphasis added).

26. The Sherman Act applies to conspiracies "in restraint of trade or commerce *among the several states, or with foreign nations*" (Sherman Act, 15 U.S.C. § 1). As the verbatim use of the constitutional language illustrates, the statute was enacted against the backdrop of the "old" understanding. It would operate on interstate conspiracies that were then thought beyond the states' authority while leaving state law to operate on internal commerce. Pre–New Deal courts characterized the statute as "supplemental" in this "dualist" sense. Under the New Deal reinterpretation, in contrast, the Sherman Act— in the teeth of its language—applies to purely local events and effects, and "supplemental" means that states may circumvent, pile on to, or piggyback on federal antitrust authority and enforcement against national and global corporations. See *Summit Health, Ltd. v. Pinhas*, 500 U.S. 322 (1991) (extending the reach of the Sherman Act to purely local transactions with exclusively local price effects); *California v. ARC Am. Corp.*, 490 U.S. 93 (1989) (permitting, under state antitrust law, "indirect purchaser" actions that are barred under federal law).

27. *Rice*, 331 U.S. at 243, 247.

28. *Hines v. Davidowitz*, 312 U.S. 52, 75 (1941) (Stone, J., dissenting).

29. Importantly, these are background rules. Latent exclusivity meant that Congress could protect state surplus by legislation. (This is why the first explicit preemption provisions in federal statutes are "savings clauses" in favor of state law.) Conversely, Congress can and occasionally does signal its intent to make a regulatory regime exclusive. But the background rules matter greatly both in how the legislative process plays out and in how the judiciary will interpret a given statute.

30. *Bethlehem Steel Co. v. N.Y. State Labor Relations Bd.*, 330 U.S. 767, 780 (1947) (Frankfurter, J., concurring).

31. Technically, this is not preemption. True preemption, sometimes called "ceiling preemption" (e.g., William W. Buzbee, *Asymmetrical Regulation: Risk, Preemption, and the Floor/Ceiling Distinction*, 82 NYU L Rev 1547 (2007)), deprives state law above the ceiling of any force and effect. In contrast, "floor preemption" has no legal displacement effect. For example, a $9 federal minimum wage leaves state minima above *and below* that floor in force: if a state has a minimum wage of $8, an employer who pays $7 can still be prosecuted for violating both federal and state law. As a practical matter, however, "floor preemption" wipes out the lower-minimum states' policy choice.

32. *Rice*, 331 U.S. at 230 (citations omitted).

33. Ibid., 230–231.

34. Nary an article on the subject fails to note the consensus that preemption law is a "muddle." See, e.g., Caleb Nelson, *Preemption*, 86 Va L Rev 225, 233 (2000) (noting the point and providing references).

35. See generally Thomas K. McCraw, *Prophets of Regulation* (Cambridge, MA: Harvard University Press, 1984).

36. Some federal agencies, especially the National Labor Relations Board, came to enjoy exceedingly robust preemption doctrines; nothing good could come from letting employers escape from its requirements into competing states. See *Lodge 76, Int'l Ass'n of Machinists v. Wis. Employment Relations Comm'n*, 427 U.S. 132 (1976); *San Diego Bldg. Trades Council v. Garmon*, 353 U.S. 26 (1957).

37. Empirical evidence confirms the point. Congress often overrules Supreme Court statutory interpretations. See William N. Eskridge, Jr., *Overriding Supreme Court Statutory Interpretation Decisions*, 101 Yale L J 331 (1991). It almost *never* overrules Supreme Court interpretations of preemption provisions. Note, *State Collective Action*, 119 Harv L Rev 1855 (2006). The most likely explanation is that preemption provisions aren't statutory details. They *are* the statutes, and Congress cannot revise them without reopening the entire legislative package.

38. *S.C. State Highway Dept. v. Barnwell Bros.*, 303 U.S. 177, 185–186 (1938) (citation omitted).

39. *W. Live Stock v. Bureau of Revenue*, 303 U.S. 250, 254 (1938).

40. The data in this paragraph were collected and cases were coded by Harriet McConnell, under the author's supervision. Available upon request.

41. *Di Santo v. Pennsylvania*, 273 U.S. 34, 43–44 (1927) (Stone, J., dissenting and explaining his project). For an insightful analysis, see Noel T. Dowling, *Interstate Commerce and State Power–Revised Version*, 47 Colum L Rev 547 (1947).

42. For a contemporary case, see, e.g., *United Haulers Ass'n, Inc. v. Oneida-Herkimer Solid Waste Mgmt. Auth.*, 550 U.S. 330, 347, 353–354 (2007). For a post–New Deal case see, e.g., *Duckworth v. Arkansas*, 314 U.S. 390, 397 (1941) (Jackson, J., concurring, rejecting the comparison).

43. Ernest J. Brown, *The Open Economy: Justice Frankfurter and the Position of the Judiciary*, 67 Yale L J 219 (1957).

44. *Morgan v. Virginia*, 328 U.S. 373, 380 (1946) (quoting Justice Holmes's opinion in *Kansas City S. Ry. Co. v. Kaw Valley Drainage Dist.*, 233 U.S. 75, 79 (1914)) invalidated a Virginia state law requiring racial segregation of interstate passengers as a violation of the dormant Commerce Clause.

45. Harlan F. Stone, *Fifty Years' Work of the United States Supreme Court*, 14 ABA J 428, 430 (1928). In *Barnwell*, he determined—probably correctly—that South Carolina had offered a bona fide police-power justification for requiring shorter trucks on its roads. In *S. Pac. Co. v. Arizona ex rel Sullivan*, 325 U.S. 761 (1945), in contrast but consistently, Stone held that Arizona could *not* require shorter trains within its state when grade conditions for

track were constant across the nation and the state's proffered safety rationales seemed unsupported by reliable empirical evidence.

46. *Hale v. Bimco Trading, Inc.*, 306 U.S. 375 (1939). For "amusing irony," and
for an insightful discussion, see Brown, *Open Economy*, 219.

47. Justice Jackson's oft-cited opinion in *H. P. Hood & Sons, Inc. v. Du Mond*,
336 U.S. 525, 535 (1949), dates to this period. See also *Freeman v. Hewit*,
329 U.S. 249 (1946); *Spector Motor Service, Inc. v. O'Connor*, 340 U.S. 602
(1951) (overruled in *Complete Auto Transit, Inc. v. Brady*, 430 U.S. 274, 288–
89 (1977)). See also *Toomer v. Witsell*, 334 U.S. 385 (1948), a Privileges and
Immunities cousin to *Hood*.

48. Justice Robert Jackson repeatedly cautioned against an exaggerated confidence in the ability of Congress to protect interstate commerce. See, e.g.,
Duckworth, 314 U.S. 390; *United States v. Se. Underwriters Ass'n*, 322 U.S.
533, 590–591 (1944) (Jackson, J., dissenting).

49. For a longer discussion, see Michael S. Greve, *The Dormant Commerce
Clause as an Ex Ante Rule*, 3 J L Econ & Pol'y 241 (2007).

50. The dormant Commerce Clause is poorly policed because it fails to capture
many facially neutral but nonetheless discriminatory state laws. See, e.g.,
Exxon Corp. v. Governor of Md., 437 U.S. 117 (1978).

51. For a sophisticated treatment consistent with this analysis, see Maxwell L.
Stearns, *A Beautiful Mend: A Game Theoretical Analysis of the Dormant
Commerce Clause Doctrine*, 45 Wm & Mary L Rev 1 (2003).

52. That demand may be quite high; see Geoffrey Brennan and James M.
Buchanan, *The Power to Tax: Analytical Foundations of a Fiscal Constitution* (Indianapolis, IN: Liberty Fund, 2000), 198–200.

53. Not coincidentally, a lot of exploitation cases involve such entities. See Christopher R. Drahozal, *Preserving the American Common Market: State and
Local Governments in the United States Supreme Court*, 7 Sup Ct Econ Rev
233 (1999).

54. *Parker v. Brown*, 317 U.S. 341 (1943).

55. Ibid., 362.

56. *H. P. Hood*, 336 U.S. at 565, 553.

57. For such pleas see, e.g., Frank H. Easterbrook, *Antitrust and the Economics
of Federalism*, 26 J L & Econ 23 (1983); Saul Levmore, *Interstate Exploitation and Judicial Intervention*, 69 Va L Rev 563 (1983); and John T. Dela-
court and Todd J. Zywicki, *The FTC and State Action: Evolving Views on
the Proper Role of Government*, 72 Antitrust L J 1075 (2005).

58. For recent extension of these doctrines, see *United Haulers Ass'n*, 550 U.S.
330; *Dept. of Revenue of Ky. v. Davis*, 553 U.S. 328 (2008) (upholding Kentucky's income tax law that taxes interest income paid on out-of-state municipal bonds while exempting interest paid on bonds issued by the state and
localities). For discussion, see Norman R. Williams and Brannon P. Denning,
The "New Protectionism" and the American Common Market, 85 Notre
Dame L Rev 247 (2009).

59. *Healy v. Beer Inst.*, 491 U.S. 324 (1989).

60. *Nat'l Bellas Hess, Inc. v. Dept. of Revenue*, 386 U.S. 753 (1967); *Quill Corp. v. North Dakota*, 504 U.S. 298 (1992).
61. Easterbrook, "Antitrust and the Economics of Federalism." For empirical evidence along these lines see Michael S. Greve, *Cartel Federalism? Antitrust Enforcement by State Attorneys General*, 72 U Chi L Rev 99 (2005).
62. Drahozal, *American Common Market*.
63. Ibid., 260.
64. To be sure, that may also be true of the discrimination inquiry. A seemingly straightforward "facial discrimination" test poses a risk of confusing the form of a tax with its incidence, with often aberrant results. See Stephen F. Williams, *Severance Taxes and Federalism: The Role of the Supreme Court in Preserving a National Common Market for Energy Supplies*, 53 U Colo L Rev 281 (1982).
65. See chap. 4.
66. *Duckworth*, 314 U.S. at 400–401 (Jackson, J., concurring).

10. *Erie*'s Federalism

Epigraph: *D'Oench, Duhme & Co. v. FDIC*, 315 U.S. 447, 470 (1942) (Jackson, J., concurring).
1. *Erie Railroad Co. v. Tompkins*, 304 U.S. 64, 78 (1938).
2. *Erie* also applies outside the diversity context. Conversely, there are diversity cases in which its rule does *not* apply. However, the diversity issue is central, and it is often described as "the *Erie* problem."
3. "In Praise of *Erie*—And of the New Federal Common Law," in Henry J. Friendly, *Benchmarks* (Chicago: University of Chicago Press, 1967), 155–195, 156 (footnote omitted).
4. John Hart Ely, *The Irrepressible Myth of Erie*, 87 Harv L Rev 693, 695 (1974).
5. Tony Freyer, *Harmony and Dissonance: The Swift and Erie Cases in American Federalism* (New York: New York University Press, 1981), 105–107.
6. The famous "brooding omnipresence" phrase appears in *S. Pac. Co. v. Jensen*, 244 U.S. 205, 222 (1917) (Holmes, J., dissenting). See also Holmes's dissents in *Kuhn v. Fairmont Coal Co.*, 215 U.S. 349, 370–372 (1910); and *Black & White Taxicab & Transfer Co. v. Brown & Yellow Taxicab & Transfer Co.*, 276 U.S. 518, 532–536 (1928).
7. *Black & White* , 276 U.S. 518. Among the bills in Congress was one drafted by Justice Brandeis, one of the dissenters in *Black & White*. He sent the draft to Felix Frankfurter at Harvard, with instructions on where to forward it. Chief Justice Taft, for his part, lobbied to block those efforts. Freyer, *Harmony and Dissonance*, 105.
8. Charles Warren, *New Light on the History of the Federal Judiciary Act of 1789*, 37 Harv L Rev 49 (1923).
9. *Erie*, 304 U.S. at 74–75.
10. Ibid., 77–78.
11. *Buck v. Bell*, 274 U.S. 200, 208 (1927) (describing equal protection as "the usual last resort of constitutional argument"; opinion by Holmes, J.; Brandeis

supporting). Moreover, the clause was not held applicable to federal institutions until sixteen years after *Erie;* and even after that, the "discrimination" ostensibly at issue in *Erie* is not the sort of discrimination for which the clause provides a remedy. In John Hart Ely's words, *Erie*'s "equal protection" is best understood as a metaphor (Ely, *Irrepressible Myth of Erie,* 713).

12. *Erie,* 304 U.S. at 78 (emphasis added).

13. Ibid., 80.

14. See especially William W. Crosskey, *Politics and the Constitution in the History of the United States* (Chicago: University of Chicago Press, 1953), 1:626–628, 866–871; and Wilfred J. Ritz, *Rewriting the History of the Judiciary Act of 1789: Exposing Myths, Challenging Premises, and Using New Evidence,* ed. Wythe Holt and L. H. LaRue (Norman: University of Oklahoma Press, 1990).

15. Freyer, *Harmony and Dissonance,* 112 (Frankfurter); Edward A. Purcell, Jr., *Brandeis and the Progressive Constitution: Erie, the Judicial Power, and the Politics of the Federal Courts in Twentieth-Century America* (New Haven, CT: Yale University Press, 2000), 364–365 n. 93.

16. Friendly, "In Praise of *Erie,*" 162–163. For contemporary puzzlement over *Erie*'s constitutional holding see, e.g., Walter Wheeler Cook, *The Federal Courts and the Conflict of Laws,* 36 U Ill L Rev 493 (1942). See also Arthur John Keeffe et al., *Weary Erie,* 34 Cornell L Q 494, 497–498 (1949).

17. *Erie,* 304 U.S. at 72 (emphasis added).

18. See, e.g., Louise Weinberg, *Federal Common Law,* 83 Nw U L Rev 805 (1989); and Weinberg, *The Curious Notion That the Rules of Decision Act Blocks Supreme Federal Common Law,* 83 Nw U L Rev 860, 867–868 (1989).

19. Ely, *Irrepressible Myth of Erie,* 701–702. Ely's example is Justice Harlan's famous opinion in *Hanna v. Plumer,* 380 U.S. 460 (1965). *Erie* may seem to suggest an enclave reading in averring that *Swift* interfered with "powers reserved to the States," a language often used when the Supreme Court mobilizes the Tenth Amendment or other federalism constraints independently of enumerated powers limitations.

20. See, e.g., *Cannon v. Univ. of Chi,* 441 U.S. 677 (1979).

21. The earliest version of this argument is Paul J. Mishkin, *Some Further Last Words on* Erie—*The Thread,* 87 Harv L Rev 1682 (1974). Its staunchest and most sophisticated contemporary proponent is Professor Bradford Clark. See, e.g., Bradford R. Clark, *Federal Common Law: A Structural Reinterpretation,* 144 U Penn L Rev 1245 (1996); and Bradford R. Clark, *Erie's Constitutional Source,* 95 Cal L Rev. 1289 (2007). Prominent variations on the theme include Thomas W. Merrill, *The Common Law Powers of Federal Courts,* 52 U Chi L Rev 1 (1985); and Martin H. Redish, *The Federal Courts in the Political Order: Judicial Jurisdiction and American Political Theory* (Durham, NC: Carolina Academic Press, 1991), 29–46.

22. Henry P. Monaghan, *The Supreme Court 1974 Term—Foreword: Constitutional Common Law,* 89 Harv L Rev 1 (1975).

23. See *Baker v. Carr,* 369 U.S. 186 (1962). It is no longer true even of the *Miranda* rules; see *Dickerson v. United States,* 530 U.S. 428 (2000). Thomas W. Merrill, *The Disposing Power of the Legislature,* 110 Colum L Rev 452 (2010),

notes a general erosion of reversible constitutional common-law doctrines in the Supreme Court's decisions—and a corresponding expansion of common-law-like constitutional doctrines that are *not* reversible.

24. Purcell, *Brandeis and the Progressive Constitution*, 132–133. My account relies very heavily on Purcell's splendid book.

25. See Susan Bandes, *Erie and the History of the One True Federalism*, 110 Yale L J 829 (2001).

26. The misleadingly named Federal Employers Liability Act (which governs certain private employers, not federal employers) that tied corporate defendants to the law of the state where claims were brought was a particularly fertile field for interstate forum shopping. Purcell, *Brandeis and the Progressive Constitution*, 150–151.

27. In a much-cited 1928 article, Felix Frankfurter argued for a drastic reduction of the Supreme Court's diversity docket. Felix Frankfurter, *Distribution of Judicial Power Between United States and State Courts*, 13 Cornell L Q 499 (1928). The article abounds with empirical data, collected at considerable cost, to buttress the defects and absurdities of diversity jurisdiction. *Black & White* makes its predictable appearance—*without* supporting data, as a sample of one. The same is true of all the literature and of congressional hearings and testimony of the period; the case appears without fail, and invariably without a cite or reference to a second case like it, let alone evidence of rampant abuse.

    To the extent that diversity abuse was a real problem, far more limited and surgical interventions would have sufficed. One option is the recognition that in the antitrust context, the *effects* of the contract, rather than the situs of incorporation or the formation of a contract, should drive the analysis; see *F. Hoffman-La Roche Ltd. v. Empagran S.A.*, 542 U.S. 155 (2004); *Hartford Fire Ins. Co. v. California*, 509 U.S. 764 (1993). Another option is would have been to scrutinize the bona fides of incorporation. John B. Corr, *Thoughts on the Vitality of* Erie, 41 Am U L Rev 1087, 1107–1108 (1992).

28. Purcell, *Brandeis and the Progressive Constitution*, 162.

29. Obviously, a party needs no protection—at least, none that sounds in constitutional federalism—against being sued in its home state. The risk of a suit in a hostile forum under hostile law is checked by removal to federal courts and its law. If the suit is commenced in that forum, neither party can be said to be disappointed in its expectations.

30. For empirical studies, see Hessel E. Yntema and George H. Jaffin, *Preliminary Analysis of Concurrent Jurisdiction*, 79 U Pa L Rev 869 (1931); and Yntema, *The Jurisdiction of the Federal Courts in Controversies between Citizens of Different States—II*, 19 ABA J 149 (1933).

    Erie was the exceptionally rare instance where an individual plaintiff preferred federal rules and the corporate defendant, state law. That may have been one reason why Brandeis chose *Erie*, rather than a case with a more conventional party alignment, to overrule *Swift*: it would be hard for corporate America to throw a fit over a case in which a corporation prevailed, in the teeth of a century-old precedent.

31. The fact that the federal courts and federal law are not open to in-state defendants is not an unfair anomaly but a logical and compelling corollary of *Swift*. In-state parties bargain in the shadow of the local law and should therefore be held to it. And although the local courts and their law may be biased in such cases, they will not be biased for any *federalism*-related reason.

    In an attempt to undermine this logic, *Erie* quotes Charles Warren to the effect that *Swift* had created difficulties for *businessmen* in predicting what rule the Supreme Court would apply to any given transaction (*Erie*, 304 U.S. at 72–73, 86). Note the climb-down, however: the suggestion now is not systemic unfairness but legal uncertainty. And even that suggestion is a concoction of Progressive myth and snake oil. For the most part, businessmen knew what law would apply (Purcell, *Brandeis and the Progressive Constitution*, 253–254).

32. This contention was a standard refrain in the Progressive and New Deal campaign against diversity jurisdiction. E.g. Henry J. Friendly, *The Historic Basis of Diversity Jurisdiction*, 41 Harv L Rev 483 (1928).

33. State statutes *enlarging* general commercial law were consistently enforced in federal court; see Charles A. Heckman, *Uniform Commercial Law in the Nineteenth Century Federal Courts: The Decline and Abuse of the Swift Doctrine*, 27 Emory L J 45, 49 (1978).

34. See *Erie*, 304 U.S. at 80.

35. E.g. *Bradford Elec. Light Co. v. Clapper*, 286 U.S. 145 (1932).

36. *Klaxon Co. v. Stentor Elec. Mfg. Co.*, 313 U.S. 487 (1941).

37. Although coined in the context of personal jurisdiction and due process, see *International Shoe Co. v. Washington*, 326 U.S. 310, 316 (1945), the standard has been held to apply to choice of law questions and the Full Faith and Credit Clause. See, e.g., *Allstate Ins. Co. v. Hague*, 449 U.S. 302 (1981).

38. *Int'l Shoe*, 326 U.S. 310. Technically, personal jurisdiction remains limited by "traditional notions of fair play and substantial justice" embodied in the Due Process Clause. However, due process is "that process which American society—self-interested American society, which expresses its judgments in the laws of self-interested states—has traditionally considered 'due.'" *Burnham v. Superior Court*, 495 U.S. 604, 627 n. 5 (1990). All states have extended their jurisdiction to the limits of this content-less due process. For further discussion, see chap.13.

39. *Die Deutsche Bank Filiale Nurnberg v. Humphrey*, 272 U.S. 517, 519–520 (1926). See also Holmes's opinions in *Hicks v. Guinness*, 269 U.S. 71 (1925); and *W. Union Tel. Co. v. Brown*, 234 U.S. 542 (1914). For an instructive discussion, see Walter Wheeler Cook, *The Federal Courts and the Conflict of Laws*, 36 U Ill L Rev 493 (1942).

40. See Purcell, *Brandeis and the Progressive Constitution*, 151–153. The leading case example is *Bradford Electric Light*, 286 U.S. 145.

41. William A. Baxter, *Choice of Law and the Federal System*, 16 Stan L Rev 1, 23 (1963).

42. Patrick J. Borchers, *The Origins of Diversity Jurisdiction, the Rise of Legal Positivism, and a Brave New World for* Erie *and* Klaxon, 72 Tex L Rev 79, 105–106 (1993). For precisely this reason, Brainerd Currie—the father of the

"Conflicts Revolution" that replaced the traditional learning over the course of the 1950s and 1960s—insisted that conflicts questions were an essentially legislative domain, about which jurisprudence had nothing to say. Brainerd Currie, *The Constitution and the Choice of Law: Governmental Interests and the Judicial Function*, 26 U Chi L Rev 9 (1958). For closely related reasons, he insisted that courts should almost always apply the law of the forum; presumably, that was the wish of the sovereign that had created them.

43. The Full Faith and Credit Clause arguably provides a constitutional warrant for that exercise. However, the Court's *n*-factor balancing test under that clause (at a time when such tests had not yet become standard Supreme Court fare) made that contention unattractive and, for critics, easily assailable.

44. Brandeis thought that even the Federal Rules of Procedure were constitutionally problematic; see Purcell, *Brandeis and the Progressive Constitution* (218, 221, 287–288).

　　Klaxon itself runs counter to the substance-procedure distinction. It foreshadows the Supreme Court's so-called "outcome" test under *Erie*, which holds that "substantive" rules are all those that "significantly" affect the result of a litigation. *Guaranty Trust Co. v. York*, 326 U.S. 99, 109 (1945). That view, principally championed by Justice Frankfurter (the author of *York*), plainly puts choice of law questions on the substantive side, and *York* cites *Klaxon* to that effect (*York*, 326 U.S. at 110).

45. *N.Y. Times Co. v. Sullivan*, 376 U.S. 254 (1964); *Sola Elec. Co. v. Jefferson Elec. Co.*, 317 U.S. 173 (1942).

46. *Texas Indus., Inc. v. Radcliff Materials, Inc.*, 451 U.S. 630, 640 (1981).

47. For illuminating discussion, see Merrill, *Common Law Powers of Federal Courts*; and Redish, *Federal Courts in the Political Order*.

48. "In Heaven, there will be no law. . . . In Hell there will be nothing but law, and due process will be meticulously observed." Grant Gilmore, *The Ages of American Law* (New Haven, CT: Yale University Press, 1979), 111.

49. By some lights, that was the true (and correct) holding of *Erie* all along. Laurence Tribe, *American Constitutional Law*, vol. 1, 3rd ed. (New York: Foundation, 2000), 472. It is in any event the general pattern.

50. *Hinterlider v. La Plata River & Cherry Creek Ditch Co.*, 304 U.S. 92 (1938).

51. See, respectively, *Clearfield Trust Co. v. United States*, 318 U.S. 363 (1943) (federal instruments); *Boyle v. United Tech. Corp.*, 487 U.S. 500 (1988) (contractor defenses); *Carnival Cruise Lines, Inc. v. Shute*, 499 U.S. 585 (1991) (maritime law); *Banco Nacional de Cuba v. Sabbatino*, 376 U.S. 398 (1964) (foreign relations).

52. *Clearfield Trust*, 318 U.S. at 367.

53. Ibid.

54. *Bank of Am. Nat'l Trust and Sav. Ass'n v. Parnell*, 352 U.S. 29 (1956).

55. Restatement (Second) of Conflict of Laws § 187, cmnt. e (1971); Uniform Computer Information Transactions Act (UCITA; originally proposed as Article 2B of the Uniform Commercial Code) § 109 (1999), available online at http://www.law.upenn.edu/bll/archives/ulc/ucita/ucita200.htm. The holding in *Carnival Cruise Lines* was widely criticized and temporarily overruled

by statute: Eugene F. Scoles et al., *Conflict of Laws*, 4th ed. (St. Paul, MN: West Group, 2004), 485.

An uncharitable supposition that might render *Carnival Cruise Lines* consistent with broader hands-off approach to forum selection is that the Supreme Court may be reluctant to confiscate an identifiable state's locational rents.

56. Many scholars have concluded that the federal common law for maritime "instance" cases (roughly, cases in contract and tort) has outlived its usefulness and that its demise would render the *Erie* regime and its enclaves more coherent. See, e.g., Ernest A. Young, *It's Just Water: Toward the Normalization of Admiralty*, 35 J Mar L & Com 469 (2004); Jay Tidmarsh and Brian J. Murray, *A Theory of Federal Common Law*, 100 Nw U L Rev 585, 638 (2006); and Bradford R. Clark, *Federal Lawmaking and the Role of Structure in Constitutional Interpretation*, 96 Cal L Rev 699 (2008). However, the discontinuity between *Erie* and its enclaves, although particularly pronounced with respect to maritime law, also exists elsewhere. See the contrast between *Clearview Trust* and *Parnell*, discussed earlier; and compare, *Boyle*, 487 U.S. 500 (federal common-law defense for federal contractors in design defect litigation) with *Wyeth v. Levine*, 129 S. Ct. 1187 (2009) (no implied preemption defense for products labeled in accordance with strict federal requirements). See chap. 16 for additional discussion.

57. The theory is that the act authorizes the federal courts (within limits) to prescribe *procedural* rules of decision, whereas the Rules of Decision Act, as interpreted in *Erie*, forbids them from prescribing *substantive* rules. The question of how to harmonize those perceived commands is the bane of every first-year law student's existence, and the subject of a meandering line of decisions and a torrent of legal commentary. For an overview, see any textbook on civil procedure or federal courts.

58. See *Nat'l Soc'y of Prof'l Eng'rs v. United States*, 435 U.S. 679, 688 (1978). See also Merrill, *Common Law Powers of Federal Courts*, 43–46.

59. See, respectively, *Reed v. Pa. R.R. Co.*, 351 U.S. 502 (1956) (expanding the scope of the Federal Employers' Liability Act [FELA]); *Textile Workers Union of Am. v. Lincoln Mills*, 353 U.S. 448 (1957) (purely jurisdictional statutory provision read to provide a basis for judicial development of substantive labor law); *J. I. Case Co. v. Borak*, 377 U.S. 426 (1964); *Blue Chip Stamps v. Manor Drug Stores*, 421 U.S. 723 (1975) (private rights of action, securities); *United Steelworkers of Am. v. Weber*, 443 U.S. 193 (1979) (civil rights).

60. *Sullivan*, 376 U.S. 254.

61. See especially Justice Black's encomia to "Our Federalism" in *Younger v. Harris*, 401 U.S. 37, 44–45 (1971). In addition to *Younger* abstention (barring a federal court from enjoining a pending state prosecution in the absence of extraordinary circumstances) see, e.g., *Pullman* abstention per *R.R. Comm'n v. Pullman Co.*, 312 U.S. 496 (1941) (staying a federal court proceeding during the pendency of state proceedings that may clarify ambiguous state statutes for that particular case); *Burford* abstention per *Burford v. Sun Oil Co.*, 319 U.S. 315 (1943) (federal court sitting in diversity jurisdiction may abstain where the state courts likely have greater expertise in a particular area of state

law); *Colorado River* abstention per *Colo. River Water Conservation Dist. v. United States*, 424 U.S. 800 (1976) (deferring to state courts where parallel litigation is being carried out).

62. Friendly, "In Praise of *Erie*," 195.

63. Consider Friendly's effusions over Brandeis's opinions: "Fact is piled on fact, proposition on proposition, until the right doctrine emerges in heavenly glory and the wrong view is consigned to the lowest circle of hell. . . .In some of the great ones . . . this relentless eloquence is screwed to such a pitch as to become almost agonizing. One hopes, as in listening to some passages of Wagner or Strauss, there is not much more to bear." Henry J. Friendly, "Mr. Justice Brandeis—The Quest for Reason," in *Benchmarks*, 291–307, 294–295. The second ellipsis identifies as one of Brandeis's "great" opinions the *New State Ice* dissent—which, unlike Wagner's music, is as bad as it sounds.

64. See Friendly, "In Praise of *Erie*," 180, and also "The Gap in Lawmaking—Judges Who Can't and Legislators Who Won't," in *Benchmarks*, 41–64.

11. Fiscal Federalism

1. Students of the Progressives and the New Deal have consistently emphasized the states' central role in the formation and administration of those programs. See, e.g., Christopher Howard, "Workers' Compensation, Federalism, and the Heavy Hand of History," *Studies in American Political Development* 16 (2002): 28–47. Comparative studies routinely identify the states' prominence as the most distinctive feature of the American welfare state. See, e.g., Herbert Obinger, Stephan Leibfried, and Francis G. Castles, eds., *Federalism and the Welfare State: New World and European Experiences* (Cambridge: Cambridge University Press, 2005).

2. Richard Franklin Bensel, *Sectionalism and American Political Development 1880–1980* (Madison: University of Wisconsin Press, 1984), chap. 5. Bensel emphasizes two institutional factors that stabilized the system: a congressional committee system that was able (until the 1960s) to bottle up legislation that might have broken the bipolar New Deal coalition, and an administrative apparatus with discretionary means and budgetary resources to negotiate sectional (and thus political, intraparty) conflicts.

3. Frances Perkins, "The Roots of Social Security" (keynote address, Social Security Administration Headquarters, Baltimore, MD, October 23, 1962), available online at www.ssa.gov/history/perkins5.html.

4. For a splendid discussion of the role of lawyers and legal expertise in the New Deal transformation, see Peter H. Irons, *The New Deal Lawyers* (Princeton, NJ: Princeton University Press, 1993).

5. "A resident of New York would now benefit his heirs little by dying in Florida." Jane Perry Clark, *The Rise of a New Federalism: Federal-State Cooperation in the United States* (New York: Columbia University Press, 1938), 261.

6. *Florida v. Mellon*, 273 U.S. 12, 16–17 (1927). The decision is of one piece with Sutherland's opinion in *Massachusetts v. Mellon* and *Frothingham v. Mellon*, 262 U.S. 447 (1923) (decided together).

7. *Bailey v. Drexel Furniture Co.* (*Child Labor Tax Case*), 259 U.S. 20 (1922).

8. *McCray v. United States*, 195 U.S. 27 (1904). See also *United States v. Doremus*, 249 U.S. 86 (1919).

9. *United States v. Butler*, 297 U.S. 1 (1936).

10. *Charles C. Steward Mach. Co. v. Davis*, 301 U.S. 548, 594 (1937). See also *Sonzinsky v. United States*, 300 U.S. 506 (1937). But see *Dep't of Revenue v. Kurth Ranch*, 511 U.S. 767 (1994) (relying on *Child Labor Tax Case*, holding that a nominal tax instead amounted to an unconstitutional penalty under the Double Jeopardy Clause).

11. *Butler*, 297 U.S. at 66. Although the *Butler* Court divided over other issues, its ruling on the scope of the spending power was unanimous.

12. *Steward Mach.*, 301 U.S. at 580–583. For Hamilton's position in the "internal improvements" debate, see chap. 5.

13. *Butler*, 297 U.S. 1. The argument is not without merit. Suppose, by way of analogy, that a state imposes a nondiscriminatory tax on all milk sales, from out-of-state and in-state producers, within its boundaries. And suppose that state then subsidizes its dairy industry, which it may do without running afoul of the dormant Commerce Clause. The *combination* of those measures may well operate as a constitutionally impermissible import tariff on out-of-state producers. *West Lynn Creamery, Inc. v. Healy*, 512 U.S. 186 (1994).

14. See *Steward Mach.*, 301 U.S. at 586.

15. *Massachusetts v. Mellon*, 262 U.S. at 478–480. Both rulings are virtually unquestioned to this day. With respect to the state's claims, *Massachusetts v. Mellon* was undoubted until 2007, when the U.S. Supreme Court decreed that states—including, as it happens, the Commonwealth of Massachusetts as the lead plaintiff—do possess parens patriae authority for purposes of global warming litigation. *Massachusetts v. EPA*, 549 U.S. 497 (2007). With respect to taxpayers, the only (and recently limited) exception is "taxpayer standing" for the purpose of entertaining constitutional claims under the Establishment Clause. *Flast v. Cohen*, 392 U.S. 83 (1968); *Hein v. Freedom From Religion Found., Inc.*, 551 U.S. 587 (2007); *Arizona Free Enter. Club's Freedom Club PAC v. Bennett*, 564. U.S. ___ (2011).

16. *Massachusetts v. Mellon*, 262 U.S. at 482.

17. For an argument to the contrary, see Richard A. Epstein, *The "Necessary" History of Property and Liberty*, 6 Chap L Rev 1 (2003).

18. Recall the discussion in chap. 9. It is not altogether clear why any state should have challenged the Maternity Act. The most likely explanation is that Massachusetts' powerful medical establishment opposed the act on the grounds that it might lead to the federal regulation of the practice of medicine.

19. *Steward Mach.*, 301 U.S. at 588. Recall that legal scholars at the time viewed federal fiscal transfer programs as extensions of, and less problematic than, comparable *regulatory* statutes. See, e.g., Frank R. Strong, *Cooperative Federalism*, 23 Iowa L Rev 459, 495–496 (1938). Although that may now seem odd, the constitutional logic is impeccable. If *implied* state consent helps otherwise doubtful federal regulatory statutes over the constitutional hurdle,

spending statutes that require each individual state's explicit consent to take effect in that state are constitutional a fortiori.

20. *Ashton v. Cameron County Water Improvement Dist. No. 1,* 298 U.S. 513, 540 (1936).

21. Cooperative federalism's progressive roots are stressed in Martha Derthick, "How Many Communities? The Evolution of American Federalism," in *Dilemmas of Scale in America's Federal Democracy,* ed. Martha Derthick (Cambridge: Cambridge University Press, 1999), 125–153. The interpretation of government grants as in-period cartelization in this chapter follows Geoffrey Brennan and James M. Buchanan, *The Power to Tax: Analytical Foundations of a Fiscal Constitution* (Indianapolis, IN: Liberty Fund, 2000), 212–214.

22. The federal estate tax credit, for example, was enacted in response to overwhelming state demand—and predictably over the vehement protest of states (Florida, Nevada, and Alabama) that had adopted a zero-tax policy in an effort to attract wealthy retirees (Clark, *Rise of a New Federalism,* 261). The enactment produced the hoped-for convergence of state inheritance and estate taxes.

23. The dormant Commerce Clause and the doctrine of unconstitutional conditions provide tolerably effective protection against outright exploitation and abuse. See, e.g., *Frost v. R.R. Comm'n,* 271 U.S. 583 (1926); *Buck v. Kuykendall,* 267 U.S. 307 (1925). However, coordination problems arise even when states do not attempt to discriminate but, for one reason or another, defect from a common rule. See, e.g., *Kassel v. Consol. Freightways Corp.,* 450 U.S. 662 (1981). Maxwell L. Stearns, *A Beautiful Mend: A Game Theoretical Analysis of The Dormant Commerce Clause Doctrine,* 45 Wm & Mary L Rev 1 (2003), has conceptualized these cases as dealing with defections from a Nash equilibrium.

24. Jon C. Teaford, *The Rise of the States: Evolution of American State Government* (Baltimore, MD: Johns Hopkins University Press, 2002), 33–34.

25. Economists have identified those bureaucratic incentives as an important factor in cooperative federalism's development and operation. It appears that the perceived competence of state bureaucracies correlated positively with their ability to obtain federal funds; see Don C. Reading, "New Deal Activity and the States, 1933 to 1939," *Journal of Economic History* 33:4 (1973): 804. There is evidence that the lesson was not lost on the states: Southern and Western states that still lacked central highway administrations at the time promptly established them (Teaford, *Rise of the States,* 34).

26. For a characteristic contemporaneous example, in the context of a discussion of federal grants-in-aid, see Louis W. Koenig, *Federal and State Cooperation Under the Constitution,* 36 Mich L Rev 752, 753 (1938).

27. One could attempt to counteract this problem through an equalization formula that advantages poor states—but only at the risk of giving wealthier states an incentive to *reduce* their expenditures. John Joseph Wallis, "The Birth of the Old Federalism: Financing the New Deal 1932–1940," *Journal of Economic History* 44 (1984): 153 n. 27.

28. None voiced their frustrations more memorably than Lorena Hickok, the would-be "Joan of Arc of the Fascist movement in the United States." Having tried to coordinate federal emergency relief in California, she concluded that "we ought to let Japan have this state. Maybe they could straighten it out." James T. Patterson, "The New Deal and the States," *American Historical Review* 73:1 (1967): 75. Patterson's article and his book by the same title, *The New Deal and the States: Federalism in Transition* (Princeton, NJ: Princeton University Press, 1969), contain vivid and more extensive accounts of cooperative federalism's birth pangs.

29. Reading, "New Deal Activity," 793.

30. Christopher Howard, "Workers' Compensation, Federalism, and the Heavy Hand of History," *Studies In American Political Development* 16 (2002): 28–47.

31. Clark, *Rise of a New Federalism*, 233.

32. For the following pages, see Michael S. Greve, *Against Cooperative Federalism*, 70 Miss L J 557, 594–599 (2000), and sources cited therein; esp. Edward A. Zelinsky, *Unfunded Mandates, Hidden Taxation, and the Tenth Amendment: On Public Choice, Public Interest, and Public Services*, 46 Vand L Rev 1355 (1993).

33. Brandeis to Mary E. McDowell, July 8, 1912, in *Letters of Louis D. Brandeis*, ed. Melvin I. Urofsky and David W. Levy (Albany: State University of New York Press, 1972), 2:640.

34. Fiscal federalism theory cannot quite explain the asymmetry; it is usually attributed to interest group dynamics at the state level. For a thorough discussion and review of the literature, see Shama Gamkhar, *Federal Intergovernmental Grants and the States: Managing Devolution* (Northampton, MA: Edward Elgar, 2002).

35. On Germany, see Greve, *Against Cooperative Federalism*, 563–573, and sources cited ibid. On Canada see Canadian Constitution Act, 1982, R.S.C., § 36(2): "Parliament and the government of Canada are committed to the principle of making equalization payments to ensure that provincial governments have sufficient revenues to provide reasonably comparable levels of public services at reasonably comparable levels of taxation."

36. Even more attenuated forms of tax harmonization have remained limited in scope. For example, federal-state general revenue sharing was instituted as part of the Nixon Administration's "New Federalism"; it was unceremoniously buried a few years later, as part of the Reagan administration's even newer federalism. Characteristically, moreover, even that modest experiment left the states' tax autonomy untouched. See generally Timothy Conlan, *From New Federalism to Devolution: Twenty-Five Years of Intergovernmental Reform* (Washington, D.C.: Brookings Institution, 1998), 65–76.

37. For discussion, see chap.13.

38. See, e.g., Advisory Commission on Intergovernmental Relations, *The Federal Role in the Federal System: The Dynamics of Growth* 49 (1981): "Inattention to the problem of fiscal equalization is a distinctive feature of the American intergovernmental aid system"); ibid., 39 ("few analysts believe that the

federal grant-in-aid system has ever reflected a clear conception of appropriate national objectives or national purposes").

39. To be clear about the claim, cooperative federalism has just about always and everywhere "evolved more as a self-interested political strategy than a conscious attempt to increase efficiency or fairness in intergovernmental relations." Jonathan Rodden and Susan Rose-Ackerman, *Does Federalism Preserve Markets?* 83 Va L Rev 1521, 1559 (1997). And short of massive financial collapse, cooperative federalism has proven resilient even to severe exogenous shocks; see, e.g., Charlie Jeffery, "The Non-Reform of the German Federal System After Unification," *West European Politics* 18:2 (1995): 252–272. The observations in the text go to the resilience of cooperative fiscal federalism even under a constitutional system that really is not built for it.

40. Aaron Wildavsky, "Fruitcake Federalism or Birthday Cake Federalism?" in *Federalism and Political Culture*, ed. David Schleicher and Brendon Swedlow (New Brunswick, NJ: Transaction, 1998), 55–64, 58–59.

41. The Supreme Court has occasionally opined on the "preemptive" force of federal spending statutes; see, e.g., *Pharm. Research and Mfrs. of Am. v. Walsh*, 538 U.S. 644 (2003). But the Court is confused about many things.

Part IV. Our Federalism

1. *Lochner* was not formally overruled until 1963. See Bruce A. Ackerman, *We the People: Foundations* (Cambridge, MA: Harvard University Press, 1991), 66.

2. Herbert Wechsler, *The Political Safeguards of Federalism: The Role of the States in the Composition and Selection of the National Government*, 54 Colum L Rev 543 (1954).

3. Roderick M. Hills, Jr., *The Political Economy of Cooperative Federalism: Why State Autonomy Makes Sense and "Dual Sovereignty" Doesn't*, 96 Mich L Rev 813, 821 (1998).

4. "The adversaries to the plan of the convention . . . have exhausted themselves in a secondary inquiry into the possible consequences of the proposed degree of power to the governments of the particular States." *Federalist* 45 (Madison) in *The Federalist*, ed. George Carey (Indianapolis, IN: Liberty Fund, 2001), 237.

12. Federalism after the New Deal

1. For the distinction between rights courts and structure courts see Martin Shapiro, "The Success of Judicial Review and Democracy," in *On Law, Politics, and Judicialization*, ed. Martin Shapiro and Alec Stone Sweet (Oxford: Oxford University Press, 2002), 149, 182–183.

2. *Federalist* 84 (Hamilton) in *The Federalist*, ed. George Carey (Indianapolis, IN: Liberty Fund, 2001), 447 (emphasis in original). For a more extensive discussion of rights and structure, see chap. 15.

3. Conceptually, the distinction between structure courts and rights courts does not quite map the distinction between competitive and consociational

constitutions. However, the connections are very close. For example, Arend Lijphart associates judicial review with federalism; see *Patterns of Democracy: Government Forms and Performance in Thirty-Six Countries* (New Haven, CT: Yale University Press, 1999), 4–5. The judicial role looks structural—until one realizes that federalism, in the consociational framework, is not competitive but rather another means of cartelization. And there is no doubt that the rights that are the bread and butter of modern-day constitutionalism and judicial review are of a consociational nature. For evidence, supplied by an author who misses the connection, see Ran Hirschl, *Towards Juristocracy: The Origins and Consequences of the New Constitutionalism* (Cambridge, MA: Harvard University Press, 2004).

4. *United States v. Carolene Prods. Co.*, 304 U.S. 144, 152 n. 4 (1938).

5. Richard H. Fallon, Jr., *The Dynamic Constitution: An Introduction to American Constitutional Law* (Cambridge: Cambridge University Press, 2004), 142–143.

6. For a particularly incisive discussion, see George Thomas, *The Madisonian Constitution* (Baltimore, MD: Johns Hopkins University Press, 2008), 113–144.

7. See Robert A. Dahl, *Decision-Making in a Democracy: The Supreme Court as a National Policymaker*, 6 J Pub L 279 (1957); John Hart Ely, *Democracy and Distrust: A Theory of Judicial Review* (Cambridge, MA: Harvard University Press, 1980); Cass R. Sunstein, *One Case at a Time: Judicial Minimalism on the Supreme Court* (Cambridge, MA: Harvard University Press, 1999).

8. See Laurence H. Tribe, *The Puzzling Persistence of Process-Based Constitutional Theories*, 89 Yale L J 1063 (1980); Bruce A. Ackerman, *Beyond Carolene Products*, 98 Harv L Rev 713 (1985).

9. The most conspicuous specific rights exception was the Second Amendment right to bear arms, which had to await a rediscovery by a conservative court. See *District of Columbia v. Heller*, 554 U.S. 570 (2008); *McDonald v. City of Chicago*, 130 S. Ct. 3020 (2010). For cases discovering "fundamental interests," values, and unenumerated rights, see *Everson v. Bd. of Educ.*, 330 U.S. 1 (1947) ("wall of separation"); *Brown v. Bd. of Educ.*, 347 U.S. 483 (1954) (education); *Baker v. Carr*, 369 U.S. 186 (1962) (voting); *Griswold v. Connecticut*, 381 U.S. 479 (1965) (privacy); *Roe v. Wade*, 410 U.S. 113 (1973) (same).

10. Compare *McConnell v. Fed. Election Comm'n*, 540 U.S. 93 (2003) (sustaining campaign finance regulation under standard that is "strict" in name only) with *Ashcroft v. ACLU*, 542 U.S. 656 (2004) (striking down federal Internet pornography law under extremely demanding standard). The Supreme Court has since reverted to a strict scrutiny standard for campaign finance regulation. See *Citizens United v. Fed. Election Comm'n*, 130 S. Ct. 876 (2010); *Arizona Free Enter. Club's Freedom Club PAC v. Bennett*, 564 U.S. ___ (2011).

11. Martin Shapiro, "The Supreme Court from Early Burger to Early Rehnquist," in *The New American Political System*, ed. Anthony King, 2nd ed. (Washington, D.C.: AEI, 1990), 47–86.

12. Occasionally, they may also sound in *rights* surrender. First Amendment protections for employers, for example, could easily disrupt labor cartels under the NLRB's superintendence. For this reason, the Supreme Court broke with its aggressive free speech posture in this area and put employer speech cases into a separate, less speech-protective box called "labor law." See, e.g., *National Labor Relations Board v. Gissel Packing Co.*, 395 U.S. 575 (1969).

13. See in substance (though not in these terms) Lucas A. Powe, Jr., *The Warren Court and American Politics* (Cambridge, MA: Belknap, 2002).

14. See, e.g., *Regents of the Univ. of Cal. v. Bakke*, 438 U.S. 265, 269–272 (1978) (discussion of the Harvard Plan, providing for consideration of race in admission decisions); *Grutter v. Bollinger* 539 U.S. 306, 331 (2003) (relying on former officials' averment that "the military cannot achieve an officer corps that is *both* highly qualified *and* racially diverse unless the service academies and the ROTC used limited race-conscious recruiting and admissions policies.")

15. Thomas J. Holmes, "The Location of Industry: Do States' Policies Matter?" *Regulation Magazine* 23:1 (2000): 47–50.

16. Beginning in the late 1960s, litigation and administrative initiatives under federal civil rights statutes—on education, employment, and voting—spilled over from the Jim Crow South into Northern states. The civil rights state has long found means of forging national political alliances that trump any residual state differences.

17. This is so despite increased economic integration. For an argument why cultural heterogeneity might go along with increased economic homogeneity, see Sam Peltzman, "An Economic Interpretation of the History of Congressional Voting in the Twentieth Century," *American Economic Review* 75:656 (1985).

18. For *Lochner* and constitutional structure, see chap. 15. For civil rights, see Richard A. Epstein, *Forbidden Grounds: The Case Against Employment Discrimination Laws* (Cambridge, MA: Harvard University Press, 1992).

19. One could, I suppose, characterize the dissident states' obstinacy as a federalism problem of sorts—to wit, as a "moralism." See generally Guido Calabresi and A. Douglas Melamed, *Property Rules, Liability Rules, and Inalienability: One View of the Cathedral*, 85 Harv L Rev 1089 (1972). Enlightened opinion *feels bad* about those states' practices and might be willing to pay something to have them cease. The indignation is itself an interstate "externality" and an injury to federalism. However, an antimoralism campaign is a strange pursuit for a Court that has ceased to care about state externalities of a tangible and deliberately inflicted sort. Moreover, moralisms tend to run both ways: right-to-life constituencies probably feel worse about pro-choice states' practices, and would pay more to see them ended, than the other way around.

20. See William J. Brennan, *State Constitutions and the Protection of Individual Rights*, 90 Harv L Rev 489 (1977); William J. Brennan, *The Bill of Rights and the States: The Revival of State Constitutions as Guardians of Individual Rights*, 61 NYU L Rev 535 (1986).

21. Chris Edwards, "Federal Aid to the States: Historical Cause of Government Growth and Bureaucracy," Cato Policy Analysis Paper No. 593 (May 2007), 5, fig. 2, available online at http://www.cato.org/pubs/pas/pa593.pdf.

22. Own-source revenue figures are an imperfect measure, especially in cross-country comparative studies. Lorenz Blume and Stefan Voigt, "Federalism and Decentralization: A Critical Survey of Frequently Used Indicators" (available at SSRN: ssrn.com/abstract=1263995). Still, the measure remains useful, and the difficulties do not affect the point in the text.

23. The best account of the ESEA's enactment and the subsequent history and politics of education is Gareth Davies, *See Government Grow: Education Politics from Johnson to Reagan* (Lawrence: University Press of Kansas, 2007), esp. chaps. 1–2.

24. See Budget of the United States Government, Fiscal Year 2009, tables 8–17, available online at http://www.gpoaccess.gov/usbudget/fy09/bis.html.

25. For a splendid account of this rapid turn of events, see Davies, *See Government Grow*, chap. 3.

26. See generally R. Shep Melnick, *Federalism and the New Rights*, 14 Yale L & Pol'y Rev 325 (1996).

27. R. Shep Melnick, *Between the Lines: Interpreting Welfare Rights* (Washington, D.C.: Brookings Institution, 1994); chap. 6 provides an excellent account of welfare rights litigation. For civil rights cases, see *Griggs v. Duke Power Co.*, 401 U.S. 424 (1971); *United Steelworkers of Am. v. Weber*, 443 U.S. 193 (1979). For sexual harassment see, e.g., *Meritor Sav. Bank v. Vinson*, 477 U.S. 57 (1986); *Davis v. Monroe County Bd. of Educ.*, 526 U.S. 629 (1999).

28. See *Monroe v. Pape*, 365 U.S. 167 (1961). For an extensive discussion of the volume and the legal aspects of § 1983 litigation near its zenith, see Note, *Developments in the Law: Section 1983 and Federalism*, 90 Harv L Rev 1135 (1977). See generally Michael G. Collins, *Section 1983 Litigation*, 3rd ed. (St. Paul, MN: Thomson/West, 2006).

29. *Maine v. Thiboutot*, 448 U.S. 1 (1980).

30. See Melnick, *Between the Lines*, chap. 9, for an instructive analysis. On the courts' ability to shift legislative equilibrium points and on the limits of that ability see generally McNollgast, *Structure and Process, Politics and Policy: Administrative Arrangements and the Political Control of Agencies*, 75 Va L Rev 431 (1989).

31. The legal term of art is an "integrated remedial scheme." For a spirited defense of this "inspired" model, in a case that marks a significant retreat from it, see Justice Stevens' dissent in *Alexander v. Sandoval*, 532 U.S. 275, 306–307 (2001).

32. See, e.g., Civil Rights Restoration Act of 1987, Pub. L. No. 100–259, 102 Stat. 28 (1988); Civil Rights Act of 1991, Pub. L. No. 102–166, 105 Stat. 1071 (1991); Lilly Ledbetter Fair Pay Act of 2009, Pub. L. No. 111–2, 123 Stat. 5 (2009).

33. Melnick, *Between the Lines*, 81, 138–148.

34. See generally Ross Sandler and David Schoenbrod, *Democracy by Decree: What Happens When Courts Run Government* (New Haven, CT: Yale University Press, 2003). For an instructive case study, see James F. Blumstein and Frank A. Sloan, *Health Care Reform Through Medicaid Managed Care:*

Tennessee (TennCare) as a Case Study and a Paradigm, 53 Vand L Rev 125 (2000).

35. Melnick, *Federalism and the New Rights*.

36. Advisory Commission on Intergovernmental Relations, *The Federal Role in the Federal System: The Dynamics of Growth* (Advisory Commission on Intergovernmental Relations, 1981), 94.

37. Ibid., 95.

38. President Reagan's 1982 State of the Union address forcefully articulated cooperative federalism's discontents: "Our citizens feel they've lost control of even the most basic decisions made about the essential services of government, such as schools, welfare, roads, and even garbage collection. And they're right. A maze of interlocking jurisdictions and levels of government confronts average citizens in trying to solve even the simplest of problems. They don't know where to turn for answers, who to hold accountable, who to praise, who to blame, who to vote for or against. The main reason for this is the overpowering growth of Federal grants-in-aid programs during the past few decades" (President Ronald Reagan, State of the Union address, January 26, 1982).

39. For an account of the origins and fate of the "swap" proposal, see Timothy Conlan, *From New Federalism to Devolution: Twenty-Five Years of Intergovernmental Reform* (Washington, D.C.: Brookings Institution, 1998) 170–190, esp. 181–184. Conlan suggests that more general federal financing than the administration was willing to offer might have produced some compromise with state and local governments and perhaps the Congress (ibid., 190). His narrative, however, makes it seem highly unlikely that the proposed segregation of functions could have been part of any such compromise.

40. For example, the American Recovery and Reinvestment Act of 2009 (ARRA) allocated nearly half the $580 billion in recovery funds to state and local governments. See Alan Greenblatt, "State Budget Crisis," *CQ Researcher* 19:31 (2009): 741–764; and Robert P. Inman, "States in Fiscal Distress," *Regional Economic Development* 6:1 (2010), Federal Reserve Bank of St. Louis, 65–80. The level of ARRA funding was just sufficient to close the predicted state budget gaps at the time of passage. For further discussion of federal bailouts see Michael S. Greve, "Bailouts or Bankruptcy: Are States too Big to Fail?," AEI Legal Outlook, March 2011, available online at http://www.aei.org/outlook/101035.

41. U.S. Advisory Commission on Intergovernmental Relations, *Federal Statutory Preemption of State and Local Authority: History, Inventory, and Issues*, Commission Report A-121 (1992), iii.

42. State and local regulators were often mollified through fiscal side payments embedded in regulatory regimes. Telephone regulation, with AT&T's federal monopoly over long-distance calls and an assortment of cross-subsidies to local carriers and regulators, is an example. See Robert W. Crandall, *After the Breakup: U.S. Telecommunications in a More Competitive Era* (Washington, D.C.: Brookings Institution, 1991).

43. In fact, the most common disputes arose over labor-law preemption—with *pro*-regulatory interests (labor) taking the "nationalist" position and business agitating against preemption. See, e.g., *San Diego Bldg. Trades Council v. Garmon*, 353 U.S. 26 (1957); *Lodge 76, Int'l Ass'n of Machinists v. Wis. Employment Relations Comm'n*, 427 U.S. 132 (1976).

44. Richard B. Stewart, *The Reformation of American Administrative Law*, 88 Harv L Rev 1669 (1975).

45. *Tenn. Valley Auth. v. Hill*, 437 U.S. 153, 188 n. 34 (1978).

46. As one admirer of that model has put it: "With cooperative federalism structures usually accompanying floor preemption and room left for diverse and more stringent regulation, numerous levels of regulatory action are venues for innovation. Multiple actors remain regulatory players. Little is irrevocably settled, apart from preclusion of more lax standard setting." William W. Buzbee, *Interaction's Promise: Preemption Policy Shifts, Risk Regulation, and Experimentalism Lessons*, 57 Emory L J 145, 162 (2007) (footnote omitted).

47. Erwin Chemerinsky, *Empowering States When It Matters: A Different Approach to Preemption*, 69 Brook L Rev 1313, (2004). See also Erwin Chemerinsky, *Enhancing Government: Federalism for the 21st Century* (Stanford, CA: Stanford University Press, 2008).

48. See generally Martha Derthick and Paul J. Quirk, *The Politics of Deregulation* (Washington, D.C.: Brookings Institution, 1985).

49. The Court narrowly sustained conditional preemption in *F.E.R.C. v. Mississippi*, 456 U.S. 742 (1982); *Hodel v. Va. Surface Mining and Reclamation Ass'n*, 452 U.S. 264 (1981). Even in those initial cases, some states supported position of the federal government as amici curiae.

    States soon learned that cashless "cooperative" programs typically substitute regulatory rents for the fiscal transfers. Conditional preemption statutes permit—and when fully enforced, well-nigh command—the EPA to lay waste to any industry. State administration provides a potential for much-needed slack. The harsher the EPA's posture, though, the greater the state administrators' capacity to extract regulatory rents.

50. This may be the only point of agreement in the increasingly heated "preemption wars." See, e.g., William W. Buzbee, ed., *Preemption Choice: The Theory, Law, and Reality of Federalism's Core Question* (New York: Cambridge University Press, 2009); Richard A. Epstein and Michael S. Greve, eds., *Federal Preemption: States' Powers, National Interests* (Washington, D.C.: AEI, 2007); Thomas O. McGarity, *The Preemption War: When Federal Bureaucracies Trump Local Juries* (New Haven, CT: Yale University Press, 2008).

51. See, e.g. *Massachusetts v. EPA*, 549 U.S. 497 (2007).

52. See, e.g., *Gade v. Nat'l Solid Wastes Mgmt. Ass'n*, 505 U.S. 88 (1992); *Morales v. Trans World Airlines*, 504 U.S. 374 (1992).

53. For an inventory of statutory savings clauses for state common law, see Alan E. Untereiner, *The Preemption Defense in Tort Actions: Law, Strategy and Practice* (U.S. Chamber Institute for Legal Reform, 2008), charts A–E.

54. For empirical evidence, see Michael S. Greve and Jonathan Klick, *Preemption in the Rehnquist Court: A Preliminary Empirical Assessment*, 14 Sup Ct Econ Rev 43, 52–53 (2006).
55. See, e.g., Deborah R. Hensler, *The New Social Policy Torts: Litigation as a Legislative Strategy—Preliminary Thoughts on a New Research Project*, 51 DePaul L Rev 493 (2001). For an exhaustive, insightful analysis and discussion of the trends summarized in this paragraph, see Paul Nolette, *Advancing National Policy in the Courts: the Use of Multistate Litigation by State Attorneys General* (unpublished Ph.D. dissertation, Boston College 2011).

13. From Experiments to Exploitation

Epigraph: *Franchise Tax Bd. of Cal. v. Hyatt*, 538 U.S. 488, 499 (2003) (unanimous opinion).

1. Walter Hellerstein, *State Taxation of Interstate Business: Perspective on Two Centuries of Constitutional Adjudication*, 41 Tax Law 37, 38 (1987).
2. *Robbins v. Shelby County Taxing Dist.*, 120 U.S. 489 (1887).
3. See, e.g., *U.S. Glue Co. v. Town of Oak Creek*, 247 U.S. 321 (1918); *Shaffer v. Carter*, 252 U.S. 37 (1920).
4. See, e.g., *Chassaniol v. City of Greenwood*, 291 U.S. 584 (1934) (sustaining municipal license tax on cotton buyers whose goods were destined for sale in other states). The Court distinguished cases in which it had invalidated state police-power regulations of identically situated enterprises (e.g., *Lemke v. Farmers' Grain Co.*, 258 U.S. 50 (1922)).
5. *Farmers' Loan & Trust Co. v. Minnesota*, 280 U.S. 204, 210 (1930) (citations omitted). The proposition had a long history, (see *Bonaparte v. Tax Court*, 104 U.S. 592, 594 (1881), and the Court considered it so obvious "that no adjudication should be necessary" to establish it. *Union Refrigerator Transit Co. v. Kentucky*, 199 U.S. 194, 204 (1905) (discussing *Cleveland, Painsville, and Ashtabula R.R. Co. v. Pennsylvania* (*In re State Tax on Foreign-held Bonds*), 82 U.S. 300 (1872)).
6. Justice Robert Jackson put the point directly: "I find little difficulty in concluding that exaction of a tax by a state which has no jurisdiction or lawful authority to impose it is a taking of property without due process of law. The difficulty is that the concept of jurisdiction is not defined by the Constitution." *State Tax Comm'n of Utah v. Aldrich*, 316 U.S. 174, 201 (1942) (Jackson, J., dissenting).
7. *W. Live Stock v. Bureau of Revenue*, 303 U.S. 250 (1938).
8. The Supreme Court has developed a four-part dormant Commerce Clause test for state taxation, including a "fair apportionment" demanding that a state's apportionment formula, if applied by all states, would not result in double taxation standard. *Complete Auto Transit, Inc. v. Brady*, 430 U.S. 274, 279 (1977). For an overview of the Supreme Court's application of the test see Walter Hellerstein, Michael J. McIntyre, and Richard D. Pomp, *Commerce Clause Restraints on State Taxation After* Jefferson Lines, 51 Tax L Rev 47 (1995).
9. *Quill Corp. v. North Dakota*, 504 U.S. 298 (1992).

10. The Tax Injunction Act, 28 U.S.C. § 1341 (2006), originally enacted in 1937, prohibits lower federal courts from restraining "the assessment, levy or collection of any tax under State law where a plain, speedy and efficient remedy may be had in the courts of such State." The post–New Deal Court has read the statue very broadly and, moreover, "as but a *partial* codification of the federal reluctance to interfere with state taxation." *Nat'l Private Truck Council, Inc. v. Oklahoma Tax Comm'n*, 515 U.S. 582, 590 (1995) (emphasis added). Principles of judicial "comity" further limit the scope of federal judicial checks on state taxation even where petitioners raise constitutional questions; see *Levin v. Commerce Energy, Inc.*, 130 S. Ct. 2323 (2010). Tax authorities' nexus determinations are reviewable in the first instance only in state courts, whose expansive rulings the U.S. Supreme Court reviews only once in a blue moon.

11. The Court has permitted each state to adopt a "consistent" apportionment formula even if no other state in fact uses it. See, e.g., *Moorman Mfg. Co. v. Bair*, 437 U.S. 267 (1978). Each state is thus free to adopt the formula that maximizes its own portion of the interstate tax take. Even actual proof of double taxation, however, will not doom an individual state's apportionment scheme. *Container Corp. of Am. v. Franchise Tax Bd.*, 463 U.S. 159, 187 (1983); *Barclays Bank v. Franchise Tax Bd.*, 512 U.S. 298, 318–319 (1994) (double taxation does not violate dormant Commerce Clause unless it is the "inevitable result" of state's tax regime).

12. *Henneford v. Silas Mason Co.*, 300 U.S. 577 (1937). I believe this position to be correct, but the question is close. For a critical view see Richard A. Posner, *Economic Analysis of Law*, 5th ed. (New York: Aspen Law & Business, 1998), 702–703.

13. Congress hardly lacked sympathy for the states' fiscal difficulties and their complaints over judicially imposed constraints; witness the 1937 Tax Injunction Act. That act, though, was supported by all states. The sourcing question, in contrast, compelled Congress to choose between protecting the industrial states' rents under an origin rule, or else transferring the rents to the Southern and Western consumer states under a destination rule. A legislative solution to that dilemma was a political impossibility.

Due to technological changes (in particular, the ability of catalogue and Internet sellers to locate just about anywhere), the modern-day divide runs not between industrialized producer states and laggard consumer states but rather between large and small states. For sparsely populated "traitor" states without a sales tax (Montana, Delaware, Washington, New Hampshire, and the special case of Alaska), the "loss" of sales tax revenue is more than compensated by the benefit of attracting export industries. That is not so for large states with high levels of taxable in-state consumption. This constellation, though, only exacerbates the problems of obtaining unanimous state consent or congressional sanction for a tax cartel; the more concentrated the rents, the less likely the prospects of consent in either forum. Jonathan R. Macey, *Federal Deference to Local Regulators and the Economic Theory of Regulation: Toward a Public-Choice Explanation of Federalism*, 76 Va L Rev 265 (1990).

14. We do not know why the producer states opposed that rule in Congress but nonetheless accepted it in a "cooperative" forum, but we can guess: interstate sales will remain effectively tax free unless states have the means and the authority to collect the use tax from the seller—a proposition that was highly doubtful under then-existing rules of jurisdiction. In other words, producer states accepted the bargain in full expectation of their own ability to cheat.

15. For discussion, see Michael S. Greve, *Sell Globally, Tax Locally: Sales Tax Reform for the New Economy* (Washington, D.C.: AEI, 2003).

16. *Nw. States Portland Cement Co. v. Minnesota*, consolidated on appeal with *Williams v. Stockham Valves & Fittings, Inc.*, 358 U.S. 450 (1959).

17. Jerry Sharpe, *State Taxation of Interstate Businesses and the Multistate Tax Compact: The Search for a Delicate Uniformity*, 11 Colum J L & Soc Probs 231, 244 (1975).

18. Ibid., 274 (footnote omitted).

19. Jerome R. Hellerstein and Walter Hellerstein, *State Taxation*, vol. 1: *Corporate Income and Franchise Taxes*, 3rd ed. (Boston: Warren, Gorham, and Lamont, 1998), 9–85 (MTC definition of business income "in the context of dividends appears overbroad both from a statutory and constitutional standpoint").

20. In the early 1970s, for example, a group of state officials and business leaders proposed federal legislation that would have enabled the MTC to make binding decisions for all fifty states (Sharpe, *State Taxation*, 265–266 n. 172). The proposal was never acted upon.

21. Even firm defenders of judicial controls acknowledge the problems of hacking through the mysteries of corporate tax accounting with blunt constitutional instruments. See, e.g. Jesse H. Choper and Tung Yin, *State Taxation and the Dormant Commerce Clause: The Object-Measure Approach*, 1998 Sup Ct Rev 193 (1998); Daniel Shaviro, *An Economic and Political Look at Federalism in Taxation*, 90 Mich L Rev 895 (1992).

22. With very rare exceptions (e.g., *Okla. Tax Comm'n v. Jefferson Lines, Inc.*, 514 U.S. 175 (1995)), the Court's interventions have remained sporadic and highly deferential. See Daniel N. Shaviro, *Federalism in Taxation: The Case for Greater Uniformity* (Washington, D.C.: AEI, 1993), 4 (lamenting Supreme Court's "wholesale retreat from even its limited past efforts in the area").

23. The foreign governments' long-running, progressively apoplectic complaints and the Executive's efforts to manage the diplomatic crisis are described and shrugged off in Justice Ginsburg's majority opinion in *Barclays Bank*, 512 U.S. at 324–331. For an account of the controversy, the *Barclays Bank* litigation, and the resolution of the conflict, see Edward T. Swaine, *Negotiating Federalism: State Bargaining and the Dormant Treaty Power*, 49 Duke L J 1127, 1159–1161 (2000).

24. See Railroad Revitalization and Regulatory Reform Act of 1976, Pub. L. No. 94-210, § 306, 90 Stat. 31, Sec. 306 (1976) (prohibiting "unreasonable and unjust" discriminatory tax treatment of transportation property); Act of Jan. 10, 1996, Pub. L. No. 104-95, 109 Stat. 979 (1996) (barring states from taxing pension income of nonresidents); Act of July 19, 1977, Pub. L. No. 95-67,

91 Stat. 271 (1977) (prohibiting state or local governments, other than jurisdictions from which member of Congress is elected, from treating legislator
as resident for income tax purposes).

25. Kathryn L. Moore, *State and Local Taxation: When Will Congress Inter-vene?*, 23 J Legis 171, 173 (1997).

26. The MSA cannot be found in any code or statute book. It is, however, avail-able online at http://ag.ca.gov/tobacco/pdf/1msa.pdf. Parts of this section are adapted from Michael S. Greve, *Compacts, Cartels, and Congressional Consent*, 68 Mo L Rev 285 (2003).

27. Martha Derthick, *Up In Smoke: From Legislation to Litigation in Tobacco Politics*, 2nd ed. (Washington, D.C.: CQ, 2005), 120–147, provides a bal-anced discussion of the factors that contributed to the failure of the proposed legislation.

28. David S. Samford, *Cutting Deals in Smoke-Free Rooms: A Case Study in Public Choice Theory*, 87 Ky L J 845, 886–892, 899–900 (1999).

29. For discussion of the settlement dynamics, see Derthick, *Up In Smoke*, 163–173; and William H. Pryor, Jr., *A Comparison of Abuses and Reforms of Class Actions and Multigovernment Lawsuits*, 74 Tulane L Rev 1885, 1911 (2000) (Alabama attorney general citing imposition of share of MSA costs on Alabama as reason for signing MSA despite his grave misgivings).

30. See, e.g., Jeremy I. Bulow and Paul D. Klemperer, *The Tobacco Deal*, Brook-ings Papers on Economic Activity (Microeconomics) 1998, 324; Hanoch Dagan and James J. White, *Governments, Citizens, and Injurious Industries*, 75 NYU L Rev 354, 425 (2000); Christopher Schroeder, *The Multistate Set-tlement Agreement and the Problem of Social Regulation Beyond the Power of State Government*, 31 Seton Hall L Rev 612, 613–614 (2001); Ian Ayres, *Using Tort Settlements to Cartelize*, 34 Val U L Rev 595 (2000).

31. Dagan and White, *Governments, Citizens, and Injurious Industries*, 382; Michael DeBow, *The State Tobacco Litigation and the Separation of Powers in State Governments: Repairing the Damage*, 31 Seton Hall L Rev 563, 569 (2001) (consumers will pay roughly 90 percent of the cost of the MSA; citing interview with W. Kip Viscusi). Price increases well in excess of MSA-related costs immediately followed the announcement of the MSA (ibid.).

32. Derthick, *Up In Smoke*, 186–188.

33. Jonathan Rauch, "Can A Little Lawsuit Shut Down a Big Tobacco Racket?" *National Journal*, August 5, 2005.

34. The leading cases are *S&M Brands, Inc. v. Caldwell*, 614 F.3d. 172 (5th Cir. 2010), *cert denied*, 131 S. Ct. 1601 (2011); and *Star Scientific, Inc. v. Beales*, 278 F.3d 339 (4th Cir. 2002), *cert. denied sub nom. Star Scientific, Inc. v. Kilgore*, 537 U.S. 818 (2002).

35. For a much more extensive treatment, see Greve, *Compacts, Cartels, and Congressional Consent*.

36. The proximity to the Tonnage Clause and the parallel Import-Export Clause, as well as the historical context and the *Federalist*'s pronouncements on economic warfare as a prelude to armed conflict, strongly suggest that the intended scope of the Compact Clause reaches well beyond overtly political

and military alliances. Those unequivocal threats to the union are best understood as being *absolutely* prohibited under Art. I, § 10, Cl. 1.

37. Modern compacts often establish regional or even national regulatory regimes that are administered on an ongoing basis by standing compact boards or commissions. Typically, such compacts are formed at the behest of organized interests, an observation that casts doubt on their quality as a "coordination" device. See, e.g., Weldon V. Barton, *Interstate Compacts in the Political Process* (Chapel Hill: University of North Carolina, 1967), 8–33, 164. Very often, compact commissions operate beyond the effective control of state legislatures and executives, let alone voters. See Marian E. Ridgeway, *Interstate Compacts: A Question of Federalism* (Carbondale: Southern Illinois University Press, 1971), 308–309; and Jill Elaine Hasday, *Interstate Compacts in a Democratic Society: The Problem of Permanency*, 49 Fla L Rev 1 (1997). Among the prime examples has been the very first compact commission, the scandal-plagued New York–New Jersey Port Authority. See Emanuel Celler, *Congress, Compacts, and Interstate Authorities*, 26 Law & Contemp Probs 682 (1961).

38. *Florida v. Georgia*, 58 U.S. 478, 494 (1854).

39. *Holmes v. Jennison*, 39 U.S. 540, 572 (1840).

40. See, e.g., *United States v. Rauscher*, 119 U.S. 407, 414 (1886). *Holmes* itself concerned an extradition arrangement between the governor of Vermont and a Canadian official. It is not entirely clear whether Taney derived his comprehensive understanding from the text of the Compact Clause or from an extratextual "one voice" rationale for foreign relations. For an analysis, see Edward T. Swaine, *Negotiating Federalism*, 1224–1236.

41. *Virginia v. Tennessee*, 148 U.S. 503, 518–519 (1893).

42. To illustrate the "absurd" sweep of a literal interpretation of the Compact Clause, Field suggested what seemed to him a quintessential police-power activity—an agreement among neighboring states to drain a border-spanning "malarious and disease-producing district." Ibid., 518. But the drained swamp may well surround a navigable stream, in which case it would be "of interest" to the federal government and, moreover, might injuriously affect downstream states.

43. Felix Frankfurter and James M. Landis, *The Compact Clause of the Constitution—A Study in Interstate Adjustments*, 34 Yale L J 685, 729 (1925).

44. *New York v. O'Neill*, 359 U.S. 1, 6–11 (1959). Although Justice Frankfurter wrote those stirring words, for a unanimous Court, in the course of rejecting a challenge to a state agreement under the Fourteenth Amendment (but not the Compact Clause), his pronouncement has been quoted approvingly in compact cases. See, e.g., *U.S. Steel v. Multistate Tax Comm'n*, 434 U.S. 452, 470 (1978).

45. *U.S. Steel*, 434 U.S. at 470.

46. Ibid., 482.

47. Ibid., 472.

48. Quotes ibid., 472 (emphasis added). A "potential impact" test cannot distinguish between facial and as-applied validity. A showing that this or that

application of a legal provision would constitute a violation is not a basis for a separate "as-applied" challenge but simply a showing that the provision has the forbidden potential.

49. It has been suggested that the risk of state cartelization is too small to warrant judicial insistence on the Compact Clause negative; state cartels should be left to the ordinary forces of cheating and defection that erode such arrangements over time. *To Form a More Perfect Union? Federalism and Informal Interstate Cooperation*, Note, 102 Harv L Rev 842, 860–861 (1989). One can read *MTC* as an implicit embrace of this position; the Court repeatedly stressed that states were free to join or leave the MTC at any time. I doubt that the position is right: the Compact Clause by its terms commits judgments over the potential costs and benefits of compacts to Congress, not to judicial improvisation. But in any event, the argument does not apply to compacts from which states *cannot* defect.

50. See *Ne. Bancorp, Inc. v. Bd. of Governors*, 472 U.S. 159, 175 (1985) (describing the "classic indicia" of a compact: establishment of a joint body, conditional action by other states and bar to unilateral modification or repeal, and mandatory reciprocity). The MSA contains all these elements.

51. See, e.g., Charles Joseph Harris, *State Tobacco Settlement: A Windfall of Problems*, Note, 17 J L & Pol 167, 168, 192–193 (2001).

52. Of *potential* encroachments on federal supremacy, there is no dearth. For example, in addition to the antitrust problems noted in the following paragraph, the MSA regulates tobacco advertising, thus running up against a federal law (the Federal Cigarette Labeling and Advertising Act) that preempts any state regulation "based on smoking and health." If these features of the MSA do not constitute a "potential encroachment," *no* state agreement that is not already unlawful for some independent reason (such as preemption) will ever be found to require congressional consent.

53. Ayres, *Using Tort Settlements to Cartelize*, 598.

54. It is not at all clear that *Parker* would cover the MSA even in that application. Its doctrine permits neither unsupervised cartels (such as the MSA) nor certain "hybrid" restraints (such as the MSA). Phillip E. Areeda and Herbert Hovenkamp, *Fundamentals of Antitrust Law*, 3rd ed. (New York: Aspen, 2006) ¶ 217b4, 366–367; ¶ 217a, 352, 356.

55. The point will appear particularly compelling to those who tend to the view that the antitrust state action doctrine itself should be confined, against the constitutional background, to state cartels whose costs fall principally on in-state residents. See Frank Easterbrook, *Antitrust and the Economics of Federalism*, 26 J L & Econ 23 (1983). The Compact Clause tracks this analysis. If states collude for exploitative purposes, we need not wait for courts to get antitrust law right (or for that matter the negative Commerce Clause); the likelihood of damage is so high that the Constitution calls for congressional review ex ante. Saul Levmore, *Interstate Exploitation and Judicial Intervention*, 69 Va L Rev 563, 570 n. 17 (1983).

56. In addition to Greve's *Compacts, Cartels, and Congressional Consent*, calls for a Compact Clause revision include Matthew Pincus, *When Should*

Interstate Compacts Require Congressional Consent? 42 Colum J L & Soc Probs 511 (2009); Allan Erbsen, *Horizontal Federalism*, 93 Minn L Rev 493, 536–537 (2008); and Erbsen, *State Collective Action*, 119 Harv L Rev 1855 (2006). See also Kathleen M. Sullivan and Gerald Gunther, *Constitutional Law*, 15th ed. (New York: Foundation, 2004), 178–179 (suggesting that the Supreme Court will revisit the Compact Clause in the near future); and Schroeder, *Multistate Settlement Agreement*, 612 (the MSA raises "constitutionally vexing questions" under the Compact Clause and related "horizontal federalism questions").

57. Robert A. Kagan, *Adversarial Legalism: The American Way of Law* (Cambridge, MA: Harvard University Press, 2001); George Priest, *The Invention of Enterprise Liability: A Critical History of the Intellectual Foundations of Modern Tort Law*, 14 J Legal Stud 461 (1985); William M. Landes and Richard A. Posner, *The Positive Economic Theory of Tort Law*, 15 Ga L Rev 851 (1981); Walter K. Olson, *The Litigation Explosion: What Happened When America Unleashed the Lawsuit* (New York: E. P. Dutton / Truman Talley, 1991).

58. See, e.g., Gary T. Schwartz, *Considering the Proper Federal Role in American Tort Law*, 38 Ariz L Rev 917 (1996). I do not suggest that modern liability law has been driven *entirely* by the demise of horizontal federalisms doctrines. For example, the expansion of medical malpractice liability is difficult to attribute to exploitative interstate dynamics, inasmuch as the costs of such litigation accrue mostly in-state. For another example, the "first movers," with respect to both jurisdictional and choice-of-law questions and to substantive tort doctrines, have typically been large, economically "advanced" states—not, as one might expect, small and underindustrialized states that can hope to benefit disproportionately from producer-to-consumer transfers. See, e.g., *Babcock v. Jackson*, 12 N.Y. 2d 473 (1963) (New York, choice of law); *Greenman v. Yuba Power Products, Inc.*, 59 Cal. 2d 57 (1963) (California, design and manufacture defects). That said, many other prominent features of modern American tort law are difficult to explain on any basis other than exploitative state dynamics. The explosive growth of multistate (!) class actions—a development not remotely envisioned by the authors of the 1966 class-action reforms—is a prominent example. The state-to-state migration of tens of thousands of asbestos claims is another. The rapid dispersion of near-uniform jurisdiction- and liability-expanding doctrines over a heterogeneous universe of states likewise militates in favor of the explanation sketched in the text.

59. *Int'l Shoe Co. v. State of Wash.*, 326 U.S. 310, 316 (1945).

60. Robert H. Jackson, *Full Faith and Credit—The Lawyer's Clause of the Constitution*, 45 Colum L Rev 1, 17 (1945).

61. The Full Faith and Credit Clause still commands respect for a sister-state's judgments although that requirement, too, has been softened. *Baker v. Gen. Motors Corp.*, 522 U.S. 222 (1998).

62. Brainerd Currie, *The Constitution and Choice of Law: Governmental Interests and the Judicial Function*, 26 U Chi L Rev 9 (1958).

63. Although not all state courts use Currie's "interest" analysis, their approaches all have the same homeward-bound tendency. Patrick J. Borchers, *The Choice-of-Law Revolution: An Empirical Study*, 49 Wash & Lee L Rev 357 (1992).

64. *Allstate Ins. Co. v. Hague*, 449 U.S. 302 (1981).

65. *Franchise Tax Bd. of Cal.*, 538 U.S. at 499.

66. E.g., *Phillips Petroleum Co. v. Shutts*, 472 U.S. 797 (1985) (choice of law); *BMW v. Gore*, 517 U.S. 559, 585 (1996) (due process); *State Farm Mut. Auto. Ins. Co. v. Campbell*, 538 U.S. 408, 421 (2003); *Philip Morris USA v. Williams*, 549 U.S. 346, 353 (2007).

67. William F. Baxter, *Choice of Law and the Federal System*, 16 Stan L Rev 1 (1963); John Hart Ely, *Choice of Law and the State's Interest in Protecting its Own*, 23 Wm & Mary L Rev 173 (1981); Douglas Laycock, *Equal Citizens of Equal and Territorial States: The Constitutional Foundations of Choice of Law*, 92 Colum L Rev 249 (1992).

68. *Ferens v. John Deere Co.*, 494 U.S. 516, 534 (1990) (Scalia, J., dissenting). Although contained in a dissent, the phrase accurately states the unquestioned principle of *Klaxon* and *Erie*.

69. "West Virginia is a small rural state with .66 percent of the population of the United States. Although some members of this Court have reservations about the wisdom of many aspects of tort law, as a court we are utterly powerless to make the *overall* tort system for cases arising in interstate commerce more rational: nothing that we do will have any impact whatsoever on the set of economic trade-offs that occur in the *national* economy. And, ironically, trying unilaterally to make the American tort system more rational through being uniquely responsible in West Virginia will only punish our residents severely without, in any regard, improving the system for anyone else." *Blankenship v. Gen. Motors Corp.*, 406 S.E.2d 781, 783 (W.Va. 1991) (footnotes omitted).

70. Tellingly, general purpose long-arm statutes that extend state jurisdiction "to the extent permitted by the due-process clause" were principally a creation of state *courts*, not legislatures. Douglas D. McFarland, *Dictum Run Wild: How Long-Arm Statutes Extended to the Limits of Due Process*, 84 BU L Rev 491 (2004). The likely reason is that state legislatures must worry about the economic consequences of exposing out-of-state parties to general jurisdiction in their home courts. Judges are more likely to worry about improving the business climate for local lawyers. Michael E. Solimine, *The Quiet Revolution in Personal Jurisdiction*, 73 Tul L Rev 1, 21 (1998).

McFarland's article describes the dispersion of long-arm jurisdiction in the wake of *International Shoe*. The origin of the "to the limits" language is the Illinois Supreme Court's decision in *Nelson v. Miller*, 143 N.E. 2d 673, 679 (Ill. 1957). It is arguably dictum: *Nelson* arose over an in-state tort that would confer jurisdiction under the most hidebound lex loci doctrine; and the Illinois statute at issue was precisely not a general purpose long-arm statute but conferred specific jurisdiction only with respect to certain classes of activities. Even so, the dictum was soon echoed, now as a holding, in numerous state court decisions that imbued specific-jurisdiction statutes with general and ends-of-the-earth reach. (In many instances, state legislatures subsequently codified those decisions.) In seven states, the transformation was the work of *federal* courts. See, e.g., *Agrashell, Inc. v. Bernard Sirotta Co.*, 344 F.2d 583, 587 (2nd Cir. 1965).

A federal judiciary that affirmatively encourages state agencies to push right up to a constitutional line surely has to countenance the possibility that some states will cross the line. Here, however, the "to the limits" invitation was accompanied by an unmistakable message that the federal courts had absolutely no intention of monitoring the states' conduct. There may be more effective ways of eviscerating constitutional limitations, but they do not easily come to mind.

71. See Borchers, *Choice-of-Law Revolution*, 371; Erin A. O'Hara and Larry E. Ribstein, *The Law Market* (New York: Oxford University Press, 2009), chap. 3. In most business-to-business settings, contractual choice of forum and choice of law clauses are still enforced (though more regularly by federal than by state courts; O'Hara and Ribstein, *Law Market*, 69–70). In the commercial context, there is little Currie-esque snarling against "conceptualism," little talk to the effect that the "interests" of the jurisdiction should trump the contracting parties' ex ante understanding, and no serious suggestion that the plaintiff must in all events have his way. In business-to-consumer contexts, in contrast, contractual choice of forum or choice of law rules are generally unenforceable, and contracts have long given way to once-disfavored, now-omnipresent doctrines of fraud and misrepresentation. Traditional conflicts teaching, it turns out, was not untenable per se. It merely stood in the way of giving the New Deal's constituencies an institutional leg up.

72. See, e.g., Baxter, *Choice of Law*; Michael McConnell, "A Choice-of-Law Approach to Products – Liability Reform," in *New Directions in Liability Law*, ed. Walter Olson (New York: Academy of Political Science, 1988), 90–101; O'Hara and Ribstein, *Law Market*.

73. An example of forum manipulation is the Class Action Fairness Act of 2005, which crammed more class actions into federal courts but conspicuously left the underlying *Erie-Klaxon* structure intact. See Samuel Issacharoff and Catherine M. Sharkey, *Backdoor Federalization*, 53 UCLA L Rev 1353 (2006); Samuel Issacharoff, *Settled Expectations in a World of Unsettled Law: Choice of Law after the Class Action Fairness Act*, 106 Colum L Rev 1839 (2006). See also University of Pennsylvania Law Review Symposium, *Fairness to Whom? Perspectives on the Class Action Fairness Act of 2005*, 156 U Pa L Rev 1439 (2008).

Explicit tort-specific federal protections have remained few and far between, and virtually all of them have been tailored to individual, particularly exposed or politically favored industries. See, e.g., General Aviation Revitalization Act of 1994, Pub. L. No. 103–298, 108 Stat. 1552 (statute of repose for claims against aircraft manufacturers); Securities Litigation Uniform Standards Act of 1998, Pub. L. No. 105–353, 112 Stat. 3227 (addressing the increase in state securities litigation after enactment of the Private Securities Litigation Reform Act of 1995, Pub. L. No. 104–67, 109 Stat. 737).

74. For the latter strategy see esp. Erwin Chemerinsky, *Enhancing Government: Federalism for the 21st Century* (Stanford, CA: Stanford University Press, 2008).

75. A few courageous souls have lamented the Supreme Court's failure to articulate a coherent doctrine of horizontal federalism. See, e.g., Scott Fruehwald, *The Rehnquist Court and Horizontal Federalism: An Evaluation and A Proposal for Moderate Constitutional Constraints on Horizontal Federalism*, 81 Denver U L Rev 289, 291 (2003) (lamenting the Rehnquist Court's "minimal and selective horizontal federalism jurisprudence"); Lynn A. Baker, *Putting the Safeguards Back into the Political Safeguards of Federalism*, 46 Vill L Rev 951 (2001); Erbsen, *Horizontal Federalism*.

14. The Supreme Court's Federalism

1. For a small selection of overwrought commentary see, e.g., Thomas M. Keck, *The Most Activist Supreme Court in History: The Road to Modern Judicial Conservatism* (Chicago: University Of Chicago Press, 2004); Kathleen M. Sullivan, *Dueling Sovereignties:* United States Term Limits, Inc. v. Thornton, 109 Harv L Rev 78 (1995); Linda Greenhouse, "Focus on Federal Power," *New York Times*, May 24, 1995, A1; Jeffrey Rosen, "Terminated," *New Republic*, June 12, 1995. For an excessively optimistic take, see Michael S. Greve, *Real Federalism: Why It Matters, How It Could Happen* (Washington, D.C.: AEI, 1999).

2. See, e.g., Brady Baybeck and William R. Lowry, "Federalism Outcomes and Ideological Preferences: The U.S. Supreme Court and Preemption Cases," *Publius* 30:3 (2000): 73; and Richard H. Fallon, Jr., *The "Conservative" Paths of the Rehnquist Court's Federalism Decisions*, 69 U Chi L Rev 429 (2002). Catherine M. Sharkey, *Against Freewheeling, Extratextual Obstacle Preemption: Is Justice Clarence Thomas the Lone Principled Federalist?* 5 NYU J L & Liberty 63, 64 (2010), describes the explanation of the Court's preemption jurisprudence which attributes everything to ideology and politics as the one "with the greatest staying power." Further quotes and references ibid.

3. *United States v. Lopez*, 514 U.S. 549, 561 (1995).

4. *United States v. Morrison*, 529 U.S. 598, 605 (2000). See *Lopez*, 514 U.S. at 564 ("If we were to accept the Government's arguments, we are hard pressed to posit any activity by an individual that Congress is without power to regulate").

5. *Gonzales v. Raich*, 545 U.S. 1 (2005). Before and shortly after the *Raich* decision, the Court denied certiorari in a number of cases on the question of whether the Commerce Clause permits Congress to regulate, under the Endangered Species Act, land use and other matters pertaining to purely local species and their habitat. The Court issued a highly inconclusive decision with respect to the federal government's authority to regulate local wetlands in *Rapanos v. United States*, 547 U.S. 715 (2006).

6. For the state action requirement, see *City of Boerne v. Flores*, 521 U.S. 507, 532 (1997) (affirming the civil rights cases); *Morrison*, 529 U.S. at 599. Prior

to *City of Boerne*, that limitation had been open to doubt. See, e.g., *United States v. Guest*, 383 U.S. 745 (1966).

For "congruence and proportionality," see *City of Boerne*, 521 U.S. at 520. The derivation of this test is not entirely clear. On one reading, it rests on the notion that § 5 only authorizes Congress to *enforce* Fourteenth Amendment rights, not to create new ones. "Congruence and proportionality" is a rough-and-ready way of assuring that legislation is actually remedial (or prophylactic within bounds of reason), rather than rights-creating. On an alternative reading, congruence and proportionality are derived from the phrase "*appropriate* legislation" in § 5. Just as Article I legislation must be "necessary and proper," so § 5 legislation must be "appropriate" (but not necessarily "necessary"). For a good discussion, see Evan H. Caminker, *"Appropriate" Means-Ends Constraints on Section 5 Powers*, 53 Stan L Rev 1127 (2001).

7. See, e.g., Nicholas Quinn Rosenkranz, *The Subjects of the Constitution*, 62 Stan L Rev 1209, 1284 (2010); William W. Buzbee and Robert A. Shapiro, *Legislative Record Review*, 54 Stan L Rev 87 (2001) (criticizing legislative record review). Justice Scalia, an initial (reluctant) supporter of the test, subsequently disavowed it. *Tennessee v. Lane*, 541 U.S. 509, 557–558 (2004) (Scalia, J., dissenting).

8. *Nw. Austin Mun. Util. Dist. No. One v. Holder*, 129 S. Ct. 2504 (2009).

9. *Garcia v. San Antonio Metro. Transit Auth.*, 469 U.S. 528, 546 (1985).

10. John C. Yoo, *The Judicial Safeguards of Federalism*, 70 S Cal L Rev 1311, 1322 (1997).

11. *Atascadero State Hosp. v. Scanlon*, 473 U.S. 234, 242 (1985). Consistent with a super-strong interpretation, the clear statement rule trumps any other statutory canon, including the canon that statutes in favor of Indians must be liberally construed (see *Blatchford v. Native Vill. of Noatak*, 501 U.S. 775 (1991)) and, evidently, *Chevron* deference to administrative agencies (see *Gregory v. Ashcroft*, 501 U.S. 452 (1991)). For the status of the rule, see Nicholas Quinn Rosenkranz, *Federal Rules of Statutory Interpretation*, 115 Harv L Rev 2085 (2002); and William N. Eskridge, Jr. and Philip P. Frickey, *Quasi-Constitutional Law: Clear Statement Rules as Constitutional Lawmaking*, 45 Vand L Rev 593 (1992).

12. *Dellmuth v. Muth*, 491 U.S. 223, 228 (1989); *Gregory*, 501 U.S. 452.

13. E.g., *Will v. Mich. Dept. of State Police*, 491 U.S. 58 (1989); *Blessing v. Freestone*, 520 U.S. 329 (1997); *Alexander v. Sandoval*, 532 U.S. 275 (2001); *Gonzaga Univ. v. Doe*, 536 U.S. 273 (2002).

14. *Seminole Tribe of Fla. v. Florida*, 517 U.S. 44 (1996). *Seminole Tribe* was followed in a long line of controversial cases. Perhaps the farthest extension is *Federal Maritime Comm'n v. S.C. State Ports Auth.*, 535 U.S. 743 (2002).

15. *Fitzpatrick v. Bitzer*, 427 U.S. 445, 455–456 (1976) (abrogation is permissible under Fourteenth Amendment); *Dellmuth*, 491 U.S. 223 (clear statement requirement). Likewise, a clear statement is required when Congress requires a waiver of state sovereign immunity as a condition of state participation in a federal spending program. *Welch v. Tex. Dept. of Highways and Pub. Transp.*, 483 U.S. 468 (1987) (overruling *Parden v. Terminal Ry.*, 377 U.S. 184 (1964)).

16. *New York v. United States*, 505 U.S. 144 (1992); *Printz v. United States*, 521 U.S. 898 (1997).

17. See, e.g., *Nev. Dept. of Human Res. v. Hibbs*, 538 U.S. 721 (2003); *Lane*, 541 U.S. 509; *Davis v. Monroe County Bd. of Educ.*, 526 U.S. 629 (1999).

18. The best discussion along these lines is Keith E. Whittington, *Taking What They Give Us: Explaining the Court's Federalism Offensive*, 51 Duke L J 477 (2001).

19. Congress reenacted the Gun Free School Zones Act of *Lopez* notoriety by inserting a jurisdictional predicate. Note, *The Lesson of Lopez: The Political Dynamics of Federalism's Political Safeguards*, 119 Harv L Rev 609, 626 (2005). Dissenters in enumerated powers cases as well as vertical federalism cases often provided Congress with a road map to circumvent the majority's rulings. See, e.g., *Lopez*, 514 U.S. at 602–603 (Stevens, J., dissenting); *Morrison*, 529 U.S. at 660–661 (Breyer, J., dissenting).

20. See Whittington, *Taking What They Give Us*, 479 (discussing the "problems and puzzles" of the Court's federalism initiative).

21. *South Dakota v. Dole*, 483 U.S. 203, 207 (1987) (citation omitted).

22. See Thomas W. Merrill, *The Making of the Second Rehnquist Court: A Preliminary Analysis*, 47 St Louis L J 569, 572–574 (2003).

23. E.g., *Planned Parenthood of Se. Pa. v. Casey*, 505 U.S. 833 (1992) (abortion; reaffirming the "essential holding" of *Roe v. Wade*, 410 U.S. 113 (1973)); *Romer v. Evans*, 517 U.S. 620 (1996) (homosexual rights); *Lawrence v. Texas*, 539 U.S. 558 (2003) (sodomy); *United States v. Virginia*, 518 U.S. 515 (1996) (gender discrimination); *Roper v. Simmons*, 543 U.S. 551 (2005) (death penalty).

24. Robert F. Nagel, *The Implosion of American Federalism* (New York: Oxford University Press, 2001), esp. chap. 7. The Rehnquist Court has occasionally intervened when *Congress* enacts "moral" legislation (often with no more operational content than a press release, but high on indignation). See *Morrison*, 529 U.S. 598. But this does not signal any judicial skepticism about dragging the country under a postmodern decency umbrella. It merely means that the Court views the enterprise as a judicial monopoly.

25. See *United States v. Bishop*, 66 F.3d 569, 598 (3rd Cir. 1995) (Becker, J., dissenting in part).

26. See Grant S. Nelson and Robert J. Pushaw, Jr., *Rethinking the Commerce Clause: Applying First Principles to Uphold Federal Commercial Regulations but Preserve State Control Over Social Issues*, 85 Iowa L Rev 1 (1999). For a cautious endorsement of a "moral federalism," see Alan Wolfe, *One Nation, After All: What Middle-Class Americans Really Think About God, Country, Family, Racism, Welfare, Immigration, Homosexuality, Work, the Right, the Left and Each Other* (New York: Viking, 1998).

27. *Lopez*, 514 U.S. at 564.

28. *Hibbs*, 538 U.S. 721, sustained the Family Medical Leave Act as a congruent and proportionate means of redressing such stereotypes.

29. Richard A. Epstein, *Constitutional Faith and the Commerce Clause*, 71 Notre Dame L Rev 167, 180 (1996).

30. The State of Alabama urged a procompetitive federalism position as an amicus in support of the respondents in *Raich*, 545 U.S. 1. None of the opinions in the case addressed the point.

31. For a more extended discussion, see Greve, *Real Federalism*, chap. 5.

32. The exception to this generalization is the Court's occasional invocation of an "accountability" theory, which holds that the judiciary must guard against intergovernmental conspiracies against citizens. As chap. 15 will show, this line of thinking has, or could have, real force. However, the Court has invoked the rationale only sporadically.

33. For suggestions to overrule, see especially *Blessing*, 520 U.S. at 349–350 (Scalia, J., concurring). For cert petitions, see especially *Westside Mothers v. Haveman*, 289 F.3d 852 (6th Cir 2002), *cert. denied*, 537 U.S. 1045 (2002). *Gonzaga*, 536 U.S. 273 came close to overruling *Thibotout: The Supreme Court, 2001 Term—Leading Cases*, 116 Harv L Rev 372, 381 (2002). However, the Court punted repeatedly on opportunities to clarify *Gonzaga* and to embrace a broad interpretation. Sasha Samberg-Champion, *How to Read* Gonzaga: *Laying the Seeds of a Coherent Section 1983 Jurisprudence*, 103 Colum L Rev 1838, 1853–1857 (2003).

34. For the ascent of state-protective doctrine in non- or semi-suspect settings see, e.g., *City of Boerne*, 521 U.S. 507 (religious groups); *Coll. Sav. Bank v. Fla. Prepaid Postsecondary Educ. Expense Bd.*, 527 U.S. 666 (1999) (commercial interests); *Seminole Tribe*, 517 U.S. 44 (Indians); *Kimel v. Fla. Bd. of Regents*, 528 U.S. 62 (2000) (age discrimination). Cases dealing with "suspect" classes confirm the pattern. For example, the Court held that sovereign immunity does not shield school officials from personal damage claims in cases of peer-to-peer sexual harassment among students—a notion that rests not on a "clear statement" from Congress but on an inference from a penumbra of a judicial construction. *Davis*, 526 U.S. 629. Similarly, in sustaining damages remedies under the Family Medical Leave Act as an effective means of countering gender "stereotypes," the justices overruled, sub silentio but effectively, enumerated powers principles articulated in *Morrison*. *Hibbs*, 538 U.S. 721. Note, though, that the pattern is not entirely unbroken. See especially *Sandoval*, 532 U.S. 275 (no private right of action under agency regulations pursuant to Title VI of the Civil Rights Act).

35. See, e.g., Erwin Chemerinsky, *Empowering States: The Need to Limit Federal Preemption*, 33 Pepp L Rev 69 (2005); David C. Vladeck, *Preemption and Regulatory Failure*, 33 Pepp L Rev 95 (2005). For denunciations in a more journalistic vein see, e.g., Doug Kendall, "Big Business's Big Term," *Slate Magazine*, March 5, 2008; David C. Vladeck, "Safety Last," *The Nation*, October 16, 2008; Jeffrey Rosen, "Supreme Court, Inc.," *New York Times Magazine*, March 16, 2008.

36. For some empirics, see "Does the Court Mean Business?," AEI Federalist Outlook, September 2007, available online at http://www.aei.org/outlook/26834. See also Robin S. Conrad, *The Roberts Court and the Myth of a Pro-Business Bias*, 49 Santa Clara L Rev 997 (2009); Jonathan Adler, *Business, the*

Environment, and the Roberts Court: A Preliminary Assessment, 49 Santa Clara L Rev 943 (2009); and additional contributions to that volume.

37. See, e.g., *Merrill Lynch, Pierce, Fenner & Smith Inc. v. Dabit,* 547 U.S. 71 (2006); *Bell Atl. Corp. v. Twombly,* 550 U.S. 544 (2007); *Ashcroft v. Iqbal,* 129 S. Ct. 1937 (2009) (pleading standards); *Stoneridge Inv. Partners, LLC v. Scientific-Atlanta,* 552 U.S. 148 (2008) (private rights of action); *Geier v. Am. Honda Motor Co.,* 529 U.S. 861 (2000) (preemption).

38. For a suggestion that Justice Scalia may not have a genuinely pro-state bone in his body, see Merrill, *Making of the Second Rehnquist Court,* 574. For the connection between federalist and originalist orientations in Justice Thomas's jurisprudence, see especially *Wyeth v. Levine,* 129 S. Ct. 1187 (2009) (discussed later); Sharkey, *Justice Thomas.*

39. See the discussion in chap. 10 and sources cited ibid.

40. For maritime law, see *Carnival Cruise Lines, Inc. v. Shute,* 499 U.S. 585 (1991); *Exxon Shipping Co. v. Baker,* 554 U.S. 471 (2008). For antitrust law see especially *Leegin Creative Leather Prods., Inc. v. PSKS, Inc.,* 551 U.S. 877 (2007). But see Thomas W. Merrill, *The Disposing Power of the Legislature,* 110 Colum L Rev 452, 463 (2010) (arguing that the Court has gradually trimmed back on the use of federal common law).

41. Occasionally, the rules hover to defendants' detriment. See, e.g., *Shady Grove Orthopedic Assocs., P.A. v. Allstate Ins. Co.,* 130 S. Ct. 1431 (2010).

42. The foundational cases are *Southland Corp. v. Keating,* 465 U.S. 1 (1984); and *Allied-Bruce Terminix Cos. v. Dobson,* 513 U.S. 265 (1995). The most far-reaching application of the FAA to date is *AT&T Mobility LLC v. Concepcion,* 563 U.S. ___ (2011).

43. See, e.g., *State Farm Mut. Auto Ins. Co. v. Campbell,* 538 U.S. 408 (2003) (three-tier proportionality regime for state punitive damages); *Caperton v. A.T. Massey Coal Co.,* 129 S. Ct. 2252, 2255 (2009) (elected state judges must recuse themselves if a party to a case before them had a "significant and disproportionate influence" in the judge's election); *J. McIntyre Machinery, Ltd. v. Nicastro,* 564 U.S. ___ (2011).

44. With respect to punitive damages, the Court suggested that state juries may not punish defendants for conduct in other jurisdictions (where that conduct may have been legal), although they *may* take that conduct into account in reaching a verdict with respect to the reprehensibility of in-state conduct. *Philip Morris USA v. Williams,* 549 U.S. 346 (2007). When private litigants pressed that tentative suggestion, the Court proceeded to microanalyze and reject state judges' jury instructions on the point. *Philip Morris USA v. Williams,* 553 U.S. 1093 (2008). On the next iteration, recognizing the rapidly diminishing returns on its venture, the Court dropped the question by dismissing certiorari as improvidently granted. *Philip Morris USA v. Williams,* 129 S. Ct. 1436 (2009).

For class actions and extraterritoriality, see *Phillips Petroleum Co. v. Shutts,* 472 U.S. 797 (1985); and *Sun Oil Co. v. Wortman,* 486 U.S. 717 (1988).

The cases just cited share an additional feature: uniformly, the troublesome exertions of state power come not from state legislatures but from state *courts*, often acting beyond or against a legislative mandate. Short of a direct constitutional due process check, one can think of two ways of monitoring state court abuses. One is *Swift*'s formula of federal common law with a state legislative opt-out. That, of course, is blocked by the *Erie* doctrine. The other path is to correct state court decisions on state law grounds. Nothing in federal statutory law, let alone the Constitution, precludes the exercise of such jurisdiction. What stands in the way is the *judge*-made doctrine of *Murdock v. City of Memphis*, 87 U.S. 590 (1874), an early "clear statement" case that was quite probably wrong the day it was decided. See Jonathan F. Mitchell, *Reconsidering* Murdock: *State-Law Reversals as Constitutional Avoidance*, 77 U Chi L Rev 1335 (2010). Having so disarmed the federal judiciary, the Supreme Court has nothing left in its arsenal except the nuclear constitutional bombs. It will deploy the artillery in extremis (see *Bush v. Gore*, 531 U.S. 98 (2000)), but generally not for the quotidian protection of interstate commerce.

45. Similarly, the Nevada lawsuit was initiated and pursued while the tax dispute was still pending in California administrative and judicial agencies. When federal courts are asked to exercise jurisdiction during the pendency of state proceedings, they commonly exercise *Younger* abstention, a cornerstone of "Our Federalism." *Younger v. Harris*, 401 U.S. 37 (1971). In contrast, there is no suggestion that Full Faith and Credit and interstate comity require something like horizontal *Younger* abstention.

46. *Exxon Corp. v. Governor of Md.*, 437 U.S. 117 (1978).

47. With the arguable exception of *Quill Corp. v. North Dakota*, 504 U.S. 298 (1992), no one appears to have won a case under the *Pike* balancing test. Even *Pike* itself was arguably a discrimination case. Brannon P. Denning, *Confederation-Era Discrimination Against Interstate Commerce and the Legitimacy of the Dormant Commerce Clause Doctrine*, 94 Ky L J 37, 93 (2005–2006).

48. *Healy v. Beer Inst.*, 491 U.S. 324 (1989). For a narrow interpretation of the extraterritoriality test, see *Pharm. Research and Mfrs. of Am. v. Walsh*, 538 U.S. 644 (2003).

49. By way of illustration, an entire federal regulatory scheme may lose preemptive force over state tort law if the federal preemption provision contains the word "a" before the term "state law." *Sprietsma v. Mercury Marine*, 537 U.S. 51, 63 (2002). Literalism, pursued to the point of chasing indefinite articles, tends to drive out a substantive analysis of the regulatory scheme.

50. *Tyler Pipe Indus., Inc. v. Wash. State Dept. of Revenue*, 483 U.S. 232, 265 (1987) (Scalia, J., concurring and dissenting in part); *United Haulers Ass'n v. Oneida-Herkimer Solid Waste Mgmt. Auth.*, 550 U.S. 330, 355 (2007) (Thomas, J., concurring).

51. See especially *Wyeth*, 129 S. Ct. 1187; and *Cuomo v. Clearing House Ass'n*, 129 S. Ct. 2710 (2009).

52. *Geier*, 529 U.S. at 870–871.

53. It is confirmed by the unanimous decision and opinion in *Williamson v. Mazda Motor*, 131 S. Ct. 1131 (2011), and by *Chamber of Commerce v. Whiting*, 131 S. Ct. 1968 (2011). Justice Breyer in particular seems to have

changed his mind about *Geier*. His *Wyeth* concurrence suggests that regulatory agencies *might* still be able to lend preemptive force to their regulations by adopting that position through full-blown notice-and-comment rulemaking, as opposed to the less formal process followed by the FDA. *Wyeth*, 129 S. Ct. at 1204 (Breyer, J., concurring). Any hope that this position might create a safe harbor were dashed in the very next preemption case, *Cuomo*, 129 S. Ct. 2710 (discussed later), where the majority, including Justice Breyer, gave zero deference to just the sort of notice and comment preemption suggested by the *Wyeth* concurrence.

54. *Wyeth*, 129 S. Ct. at 1197–1198.
55. Ibid., 1207–1208 (emphasis added).
56. Ibid., 1211.
57. Recall the discussion in chap. 9: Justice Frankfurter's dissent demanded an unequivocal showing of an affirmative conflict between the state regime and the federal warehouse license. State rate regulation of warehouse operators who had availed themselves of a federal charter—presumably, for the purposes of avoiding such regulation—supposedly posed no such conflict. In a similar fashion, Justice Scalia's *Cuomo* opinion insists, at 2717, that a federal charter protects financial institutions only against state "visitorial" oversight (that is, ongoing regulatory supervision) *but not* against a state's suit in state court. That position is charitably described as unrealistic: the power to sue is the power to visit. Such facile judicial acceptance of a state's characterization of its law—as opposed to judicial scrutiny of its nature, purpose, and effect— provides states a ready escape from preemption. See, in addition to *Cuomo*, *Chamber of Commerce v. Whiting*, 131 S. Ct. 1968 (2011).
58. See, for example, *United Haulers Ass'n*, 550 U.S. at 355 (Thomas, J., concurring) (comparing dormant Commerce Clause to *Lochner*); *Camps Newfound/Owatonna, Inc. v. Town of Harrison*, 520 U.S. 564, 615–616 (1997) (Thomas, J., concurring) (*Erie*). See also Sharkey, *Justice Thomas*, 112 n. 260 (dormant Commerce Clause and implied obstacle preemption are linked in Justice Thomas's mind to the federal common law prohibited by *Erie*).
59. *Lopez*, 514 U.S. at 580 (Kennedy, J., concurring).

Part V. The State of Our Federalism

1. For the hapless toad, see *Rancho Viejo, LLC v. Norton*, 334 F.3d 1158, 1160 (C.A.D.C. 2003) (Roberts, J., dissenting from denial of rehearing en banc). See also *GDF Realty Invs., Ltd. v. Norton, 326 F.3d 622 (5th Cir. 2003), cert. denied, 125 S. Ct. 2898 (2004)*. And see Brian F. Mannix, "The Endangered Species Act and the Descent of Man," *American Enterprise*, Nov/Dec 1992, 58. For domestic violence, see *United States v. Morrison*, 529 U.S. 598 (2000). For the remainder, see Robert F. Nagel, *The Implosion of American Federalism* (New York: Oxford University Press, 2001), 16.
2. For California's policies, see Christopher Swope, "Made In Sacramento," *Governing* 16:10 (2003): 34–38. On regulating ancient, wholly foreign transactions, see *Am. Ins. Ass'n v. Garamendi*, 539 U.S. 396 (2003) (foreign affairs

preemption of California's Holocaust Victims Relief Act). For state climate treaties, see Barry G. Rabe, *Statehouse and Greenhouse: The Emerging Politics of American Climate Change Policy* (Washington, D.C.: Brookings Institution, 2004), 133–134.

3. For Argentina, see Juan Pablo Nicolini et al., "Decentralization, Fiscal Discipline in Subnational Governments and the Bailout Problem: The Case of Argentina," *Inter-American Development Bank Research Network Working Paper #R-467*, August 2002, available online at http://www.iadb.org/research/pub_desc.cfm?pub_id=R-467. For Germany, see Jonathan A. Rodden, *Hamilton's Paradox: The Promise and Peril of Fiscal Federalism* (Cambridge: Cambridge University Press, 2006), 240–244.

4. Jonathan Rodden has noted that "the United States, Canada, and Switzerland are in a class by themselves" in terms of subnational tax autonomy and competition; see Rodden, *Hamilton's Paradox*, 31; see also ibid., chap. 10, table 2.1 (28–29). The United States appears to be an outlier even among these outliers. Unlike Switzerland, it cannot easily import an ethos of international competition into its domestic policies; unlike Canada, it lacks a credible exit threat.

5. With striking frequency, the opinions have come from the pen of Justice Scalia. See *Gonzales v. Raich* 545 U.S. 1, 39–40 (2005) (Scalia, J., concurring) (enumerated powers); *Printz v. United States,* 521 U.S. 898, 904–905 (1997) (federal powers); *Blessing v. Freestone,* 520 U.S. 329, 349–350 (1997) (Scalia, J., concurring) (entitlements). The opinions are discussed in the following text.

15. The Court, the Nation, and the States

Epigraph: *Printz v. United States,* 521 U.S. 898, 921 (1997).

1. The Austrian Constitutional Court of the interwar years—at the time, one of the very few constitutional courts in the world—was a pure structure court. It had no bill of rights to enforce. That institutional rigor has its advantages—among them the fact that a nonexistent bill of rights cannot turn into a judicial bill of goods. Hans Kelsen, the Austrian Court's intellectual father, insisted on the rights-less design to reconcile judicial review with democratic principles. See, e.g., Hans Kelsen, "La Garantie Juridictionnel de la Constitution," *Revue de Droit Public* 44 (1928).

2. *Federalist* 84 (Hamilton) in *The Federalist,* ed. George Carey (Indianapolis, IN: Liberty Fund, 2001), 447.

3. See Akhil Reed Amar, *The Bill of Rights as a Constitution,* 100 Yale L J 1131 (1991). Hamilton's notorious opposition to the Bill of Rights seems to run counter to this strategy—but only at first impression. The *Federalist's* *pre*-ratification opposition was driven by two strategic imperatives: to protect, to the extent possible, a closed-vote, up-or-down ratification process, and to block the introduction of amendments that would compromise the constitutional project. (The rights demands that ranked highest on the Anti-Federalists' agenda—limitations on the central government's taxing powers and prohibitions against a standing army—were of precisely that nature.) The *post*-ratification embrace of a Bill of Rights on the part of the Federalists

reflects, not a change of heart, but the changed strategic calculus and the ability to superintend the framing of amendments that would do no harm to the Union, and might even strengthen it. Madison's agenda in Congress was to bang Bill of Rights demands into a structure-conforming shape. In this, he succeeded admirably. Robert A. Goldwin, *From Parchment to Power: How James Madison Used the Bill of Rights to Save the Constitution* (Washington, D.C.: AEI, 1997), esp. chap. 5; Richard Labunski, *James Madison and the Struggle for the Bill of Rights* (New York: Oxford University Press, 2006).

4. Hamilton drew the minimalism connection directly, although not altogether grammatically: "A minute detail of particular rights, is certainly far less applicable to a constitution like that under consideration, which is merely intended to regulate the general political interests of the nation, than to one which has the regulation of every species of personal and private concern." *Federalist* 84 (Hamilton), 445.

5. For example, the Contract Clause runs against the states but not the national government. In contrast, the seemingly similar protection against takings of private property, and indeed the entire Bill of Rights, run by common (initial) understanding only against the national government. For a good discussion, see Michael McConnell, *Contract Rights and Property Rights: A Case Study in the Relationship Between Individual Liberties and Constitutional Structure*, 76 Ca L Rev 267 (1988). The interplay between right and structure may be contained in a single clause. For example, the Privileges and Immunities Clause protects rights, but it is—in the prevailing understanding—more akin to a structural guarantee.

6. For this important point, see especially Robert R. Gasaway and Ashley C. Parrish, "Structural Constitutional Principles and Rights Reconciliation," in *Citizenship in America and Europe: Beyond the Nation-State?*, ed. Michael S. Greve and Michael Zoeller (Washington, D.C.: AEI, 2009), 206–234.

7. Gillian E. Metzger, *Congress, Article IV, and Interstate Relations*, 120 Harv L Rev 1468 (2007) argues that Congress may waive or derogate from the requirements of the Privileges and Immunities Clause (but not those of the Privileges *or* Immunities Clause of the Fourteenth Amendment). I doubt this is right, and I certainly do not agree that "in general . . . the Constitution assigns the primary role of interstate umpire to Congress" (ibid., 1479; footnote omitted). Even on Metzger's reading, though, the Constitution does not entrust horizontal federalism to Congress *alone* but rather provides a series of judicially enforceable default rules on a general principle of nondiscrimination.

8. Recall the discussion in chaps. 2 and 3. The analysis suggests the error of interpreting the central constitutional commitment as something like "democracy" or "deliberation" and the Court, as its forum-cum-agent. The parties envisioned by Privileges and Immunities Clause—"the commercial part of America"—do not want to participate or deliberate; they want to trade without hindrance. The "participation" or "deliberation" entailed by pursuing that demand in a judicial forum is to them a cost they would rather do without. And their rightful demands can have no other effect but to mow down democratically enacted state laws. Perhaps one could argue that the

mechanism vindicates the democratic will of a collective "We the People" over the parochial demands of local majorities. However, what is actually being enforced is the precommitment to a competitive order, regardless of whether the in-period demos wants it.

9. See *Saenz v. Roe*, 526 U.S. 489, 510–511 (1999). For further discussion and references, see Gasaway and Parrish, "Structural Constitutional Principles," 217–218.

10. *Ex parte Young*, 209 U.S. 123 (1908). For the origin and trajectory of the doctrine, see Barry Friedman, "The Story of *Ex parte Young*: Once Controversial, Now Canon," in *Federal Courts Stories*, ed. Vicki C. Jackson and Judith Resnik (New York: Thomson Reuters, Foundation Press, 2010), 247–274. See also John Harrison, Ex parte Young, 60 Stan L Rev 989 (2008).

11. In the modern era, such claims have been held to be enforceable under § 1983: *Golden State Transit Corp. v.City of L.A.*, 493 U.S. 103 (1989) (preemption); *Dennis v. Higgins*, 498 U.S. 439 (1991) (dormant Commerce Clause). On an alternative theory, they derive from or arise "by virtue of" the Supremacy Clause, "thus present[ing] a federal question which the federal courts have jurisdiction under 28 U.S.C. § 1331 to resolve." *Verizon Md., Inc. v. Pub. Serv. Comm'n*, 535 U.S. 635, 642 (2002) (citing *Shaw v. Delta Air Lines, Inc.*, 463 U.S. 85, 96, n. 14 (1983)). In a post-*Erie* world, the precise derivation is not altogether clear, but the practice is well established.

12. For the constitutional calculus of externality and decision-making costs, see James M. Buchanan and Gordon Tullock, *The Calculus of Consent: Logical Foundations of Constitutional Democracy* (Ann Arbor: University of Michigan Press, 1962), chap. 6, esp. 69–71, 78. To simplify their argument: a sensible constitutional insurance policy will combine protection against catastrophic events with high deductibles for higher-probability but low-cost events.

I do not suggest that an abstract preconstitutional calculus will yield a definitive, exhaustive list of externality rights. In real life, historical experience and circumstances will play a large role. For example, the right against self-incrimination has deep common-law roots and is unknown in many civil (and civilized) legal systems. What matters is not the precise content of the rights, or even their number; it is their consistency with the constitutional calculus and its logic.

13. *Barron v. City of Baltimore*, 32 U.S. 243 (1833).

14. Put differently, rights are typically couched not in terms of protected private spheres but in terms of government "going bad." These are not the same things. For example, Hamilton lists the injunction against titles of nobility as a right (*Federalist* 84, 443); we would be hard-pressed to identify the corresponding private (litigable) claim. The more consequential First Amendment protection against an establishment of religion has the same structure. (Modern standing jurisprudence reflects the tension. I have my opinions on that subject, but I shall keep them to myself.)

15. For example, the accused has a right to confront witnesses against him in *all* criminal trials, however inconvenient that might be to the prosecution. See, e.g., *Coy v. Iowa*, 487 U.S. 1012 (1988).

16. *Kelo v. City of New London*, 545 U.S. 469 (2005) held that the "public use" language of the Takings Clause (providing that private property shall not be taken *"for public use,* without just compensation") provides no protection against compensated takings that redound to the benefit of private parties rather than a truly public use. Although the case is hard, I believe that it was correctly decided, though not necessarily for the reasons supplied by the Court: the insisted-upon "public use restriction" would smuggle a social calculus into a clause that, like the remainder of the Constitution, resists that strategy.

17. For emphatic insistence on this point, see Gasaway and Parrish, "Structural Constitutional Principles." The arguable exception is the First Amendment. But even that protection hangs on a determination that the private activity was speech (or assembly or free exercise) and *not* conduct. Compare, for example, *R.A.V. v. City of St. Paul*, 505 U.S. 377 (1992) (invalidating hate speech ordinance) with *Virginia v. Black*, 538 U.S. 343 (2003) (sustaining law against cross burning with intent to intimidate). In any event, the amendment truly is exceptional both comparatively (see, e.g., Frederick Schauer, "The Exceptional First Amendment," in *American Exceptionalism and Human Rights*, ed. Michael Ignatieff [Princeton, NJ: Princeton University Press, 2005], 29–56); and in the context of American rights jurisprudence (see Stephen Gardbaum, *The Myth and the Reality of American Constitutional Exceptionalism*, 107 Mich L Rev 391, 422 (2008)).

18. Unquestionably, their incorporation had substantial effects on the states' police practices and on federalism on-the-ground; in a balance frame of mind, one could say there was less federalism after the fact. Moreover, a serious argument can be made that we would be better off with a constitutional jurisprudence that focuses on government practices rather than personal rights. See William J. Stuntz, *The Political Constitution of Criminal Justice*, 119 Harv L Rev 780 (2006); Eric J. Miller, *The Warren Court's Regulatory Revolution in Criminal Procedure*, 43 Conn L Rev 1 (2010). However, much of this is probably also true of the textual (and incorporated) Fifth Amendment right against self-incrimination. The structural similarity between textual and atextual rights remains.

19. For *Griswold*, see Richard Posner, *Overcoming Law* (Cambridge, MA: Harvard University Press, 1996), 193–194.

20. Judith N. Shklar, *American Citizenship: The Quest for Inclusion* (Cambridge, MA: Harvard University Press, 1991).

21. *Civil Rights Cases*, 109 U.S. 3 (1883); *Slaughter-House Cases*, 83 U.S. 36 (1872). Both limitations are still operative. See, respectively, *City of Boerne v. Flores*, 521 U.S. 507, 508 (1997) (affirming the *Civil Rights Cases*); *McDonald v. City of Chicago*, 130 S. Ct. 48 (2009) (declining to overrule *Slaughter-House*).

22. See *Plessy v. Ferguson*, 163 U.S. 537 (1896); *United States v. Cruikshank*, 92 U.S. 542 (1875). And compare *Plessy* with *Morgan v. Virginia*, 328 U.S. 373 (1946) (dormant Commerce Clause forbids state segregation law as applied to interstate carriers).

23. Clint Bolick, *David's Hammer: The Case for an Activist Judiciary* (Washington, D.C.: Cato Institute, 2007). In *McDonald*, 130 S. Ct. 3020, amici from across the political spectrum supported the petitioners' (unsuccessful) attempt to revive the Privileges or Immunities Clause.

24. Robert D. Cooter, *The Strategic Constitution* (Princeton, NJ: Princeton University Press, 2000), 132.

25. See *United States v. Morrison*, 529 U.S. 598 (2000). For all our rights enthusiasms, we still recognize the good sense of that proposition. Even supposedly sacrosanct First Amendment rights often depend on local "community standards." See, e.g., *City of Renton v. Playtime Theaters, Inc.*, 475 U.S. 41 (1986).

26. For the significance of this fact, see Gasaway and Parrish, "Structural Constitutional Principles," 213–214.

27. See Michael McConnell, *Federalism: Evaluating the Founders' Design*, 54 U Chi L Rev 1484, 1494 (1987). See also Grant S. Nelson and Robert J. Pushaw, Jr., *Rethinking the Commerce Clause: Applying First Principles to Uphold Federal Commercial Regulations but Preserve State Control Over Social Issues*, 85 Iowa L Rev 1 (1999); and Dennis C. Mueller, *Federalist Governments and Trumps*, 83 Va L Rev 1419 (1997).

28. See *Gibbons v. Ogden*, 22 U.S. 1, 195 (1824) ("the enumeration presupposes something not enumerated"). The New Deal heirs know this. However, in any given case, they can be relied on to find some reason to hold a challenged statute constitutional. The argument that there must be *some* limit to enumerated powers—central to the holding in *Lopez* and *Morrison*—goes unanswered. Jeremiads over "the lessons of 1937" compensate for the unwillingness to articulate any boundary. See, e.g., *Morrison*, 529 U.S. at 646 (Souter, J., dissenting).

29. See, e.g., Randy E. Barnett, *The Original Meaning of the Commerce Clause*, 68 U Chi L Rev 101 (2001); Richard A. Epstein, *The Proper Scope of the Commerce Power*, 73 Va L Rev 1387 (1987).

30. Theoretically, the conclusion is not unavoidable. For example, one could cover some of the lost ground under more expansive interpretations of the Privileges and Immunities Clause and the prohibitions of Article I, § 10. Historically, however, the efficacy of those provisions has always depended on the dormant Commerce Clause backstop. More ambitiously, one could pave the country with economic, substantive due process rights. However, a libertarian juristocracy is not a competitive federalism solution.

31. For the following pages, see Lawrence Lessig, *Translating Federalism: United States v. Lopez*, 1995 Sup Ct Rev 125 (1995).

32. *United States v. Coombs*, 37 U.S. 72 (1838); *Foster v. Davenport*, 63 U.S. 244 (1859)).

33. But see Stephen Gardbaum, *Rethinking Constitutional Federalism*, 74 Tex L Rev 795, 800 (1996) (reading *Jones & Laughlin* and its progeny as Necessary and Proper cases).

34. *Gonzales v. Raich*, 545 U.S. 1, 22 (2005).

35. For several justices' views on the question, see *United States v. Comstock*, 130 S. Ct. 1949 (2010).

36. The principal modern-day precedent for this proposition is *Printz*, 521 U.S. 898, discussed in the immediately following section.

37. The individual mandate is contained in § 1501 of the Patient Protection and Affordable Care Act, Pub. L. 111–148, 124 Stat. 119 (2010), codified at 42 U.S.C. § 18091(a)(1); penalty for noncompliance codified at 26 U.S.C. § 5000A(b). The contention that the mandate is "necessary" is easily stated. In an effort to make health insurance "universal," the statute regulates its terms to make the product unsustainable in an open market. Having done so, the statute practically *must* subsidize and, in the end, compel the purchase. Although there is something highly obnoxious about this bootstrapping of federal powers, it is the logic of *Wickard v. Filburn*, among other cases.

38. We know this because we have read *Printz*, discussed in the immediately following section. Our constitutional traditions reinforce the distinction between restrictions and commands. For all it appears, the federal government has never commandeered private citizens to transact with other private parties, and the scope of affirmative civic duties under the American Constitution is far more limited than elsewhere. For example, there is no duty to vote. And even affirmative duties that are readily inferred from the national government's enumerated powers—prominently, conscription to "raise and support Armies" (Art. I, § 8, Cl. 12) have been construed quite narrowly. See, for example, *Selective Service Cases*, 245 U.S. 366 (1918).

39. *Printz*, 521 U.S. at 905 (italics added).

40. The rule applies even where the perceived benefits of commandeering are very substantial and the cost to state government are negligible. See *Printz*, 521 U.S. at 959 (Stevens, J., dissenting, criticizing the majority on these grounds). Neil Siegel stresses this aspect of *Printz*; see Neil S. Siegel, *Commandeering and its Alternatives: A Federalism Perspective*, 59 Vand L Rev 1629 (2006).

41. The most explicit articulation of the principle is *Prigg v. Pennsylvania*, 41 U.S. 539 (1842). See also *Kentucky v. Dennison*, 65 U.S. 66 (1860). And in *Wayman v. Southard*, 23 U.S. 1, 39–40 (1825), Chief Justice Marshall sidestepped the constitutional question but questioned whether federal law could require state officers to execute federal court judgments. "The laws of the Union may permit such agency," Marshall wrote, "but it is by no means clear that they can compel it." On *Printz*'s curious failure to cite these precedents, see Paul Finkelman, *The Roots of* Printz: *Proslavery Constitutionalism, National Law Enforcement, Federalism, and Local Cooperation*, 69 Brook L Rev 1399, 1400 (2004).

42. The majority opinion also maintains, correctly to my mind, that the congressional commandeering of state and local officers would undermine the federal executive; by dragooning state and local officers into federal law enforcement, Congress could subvert and circumvent the president's constitutional authority to ensure the faithful execution of the law (*Printz*, 521 U.S. at 899). For discussion see Evan H. Caminker, Printz, *State Sovereignty, and the Limits of Federalism*, 1997 Sup Ct Rev 199, 225 n. 82.

43. Moreover, the federal government may commandeer states and localities so long as it regulates them along with private parties and in the same manner

(for example, as with respect to data collection and management). *Reno v. Condon*, 528 U.S. 141 (2000). This follows from the proposition that the Constitution does not create state enclaves.

44. See, e.g. Justice Breyer's dissent in *AT&T Corp. v. Iowa Utls. Bd.*, 525 U.S. 366, 427 (1999) (commandeering is a "gnat" compared to the preemption elephant).

45. In the sense of *prohibiting* conduct, the federal government acts upon the states (rather than individuals) all the time. See *Martin v. Hunter's Lessee*, 14 U.S. 304 (1816). What is constitutionally verboten—outside the textually provided-for exceptions—is the issuance of affirmative *commands*. The difference is hard to deny at a conceptual level, but some have tried. See, e.g., Evan H. Caminker, *State Sovereignty and Subordinacy: May Congress Commandeer State Officers to Implement Federal Law?*, 95 Colum L Rev 1001, 1009 (1995) (federal deregulatory preemption amounts to "requiring state officials to implement a federal policy of nonregulation," citing Susan B. Foote, *Regulatory Vacuums: Federalism, Deregulation, and Judicial Review*, 19 U C Davis L Rev 113, 115–116, 126–162 (1985)). Respectfully, this is mere wordplay. Husbands who respect a legal prohibition against beating their wives do not thereby "implement" a public policy of gender equality. For a good discussion emphasizing the distinction, see William P. Marshall and Jason S. Cowart, *State Immunity, Political Accountability, and* Alden v. Maine, 75 Notre Dame L Rev 1069 (2000).

46. In addition to the Fugitive Slave Clause, states are subject to two affirmative duties: to give "Full Faith and Credit" to sister-states' public acts, records, and proceedings; and to "deliver up" fugitives from justice (Art. IV, § 2, Cl. 2). Note the curious passive voice of the Delivery Clause, mirrored in the Fugitive Slave Clause but strikingly at variance with the candor of the Constitution. Although the two clauses tell us who "shall be delivered up" to whom and upon whose request, they are silent on the crucial question of who exactly shall do the delivering. On account of that difficulty, both clauses proved very awkward. *Prigg*, 41 U.S. 539; *Dennison*, 65 U.S. 66.

47. *Pennhurst State Sch. and Hosp. v. Halderman*, 451 U.S. 1, 17 (1981). The most insistent and persuasive advocate of the position described in this paragraph is David Engdahl. See especially Engdahl, *The Spending Power*, 44 Duke L J 1 (1994).

48. Siegel, *Commandeering and Its Alternatives* (state officials' preferences); *Printz*, 521 U.S. at 976–977 (Breyer, J., dissenting) (federal bureaucracies). Tellingly, thirteen states supported the federal government in *Printz*. None supported the plaintiffs.

49. *Printz*, 521 U.S. at 930.

50. See, for example, Roderick M. Hills, Jr., *The Political Economy of Cooperative Federalism: Why State Autonomy Makes Sense and "Dual Sovereignty" Doesn't*, 96 Mich L Rev 813, 826–828 (1998); Vicki C. Jackson, *Federalism and the Uses and Limits of Law:* Printz *and Principle?* 111 Harv L Rev 2180, 2201–2205 (1998); Caminker, *Sovereignty and Subordinacy*, 1061–1067.

51. In addition to *Printz*, see, e.g., *FERC v. Mississippi*, 456 U.S. 742, 787 (1982) (O'Connor, J., dissenting); *New York v. United States*, 505 U.S. 144, 168–169,

182–183 (1992); *Lopez*, 514 U.S. at 576–577 (Kennedy, J., concurring); *Alden v. Maine*, 527 U.S. 706, 751 (1999).

52. *New York*, 505 U.S. at 181.

53. It is true that few federal statutes assign responsibility in this exclusive, transparent fashion—foremost because officials at all levels shun accountability. But that observation only buttresses the constitutional logic and reasoning. It also provides a potent reason for a preemption jurisprudence in line with *Printz*'s baseline presumptions of exclusivity and transparency. See chap. 16.

54. The single best critique (to my mind) of the contract view is Brian Galle, *Getting Spending: How to Replace Clear Statement Rules with Clear Thinking About Conditional Grants of Federal Funds*, 37 Conn L Rev 155 (2004). Galle explains that the "contract" view is one of several poorly articulated and defended rationales for the clear statement rule. That is precisely right. However, even Galle's shrewd analysis eventually collapses into the contention that the clear statement rule "undermines the partnership between courts and the political branches" and is therefore "inconsistent with our modern Constitution" (213–214). That, too, is right; but to the extent that the "modern Constitution" is the issue, it begs the question.

55. Edward A. Zelinsky, *Unfunded Mandates, Hidden Taxation, and the Tenth Amendment: On Public Choice, Public Interest, and Public Services*, 46 Vand L Rev 1355, 1374–1375 (1993), notes that the accountability argument implies that "cooperative" programs are enacted at the behest of concentrated interests that can trace the benefits to the source, on the backs of taxpayers and voters who cannot.

56. For contrary suggestions see, e.g., *City of Rome v. United States*, 446 U.S. 156, 179 (1980.) ("Principles of federalism that might otherwise be an obstacle to congressional authority are necessarily overridden by the power to enforce the Civil War amendments 'by appropriate legislation'"). For discussion, see Caminker, *State Sovereignty and Subordinacy*, 1042–1059. The Supreme Court sidestepped the question in *Nw. Austin Mun. Util. Dist. No. One v. Holder*, 129 S. Ct. 2504 (2009).

57. The leading cases on conditional preemption are *Hodel v. Va. Surface Mining and Reclamation Ass'n*, 452 U.S. 264 (1981); and *FERC*, 456 U.S. 742. Although *Printz* purports to distinguish these cases, its reasoning renders at least some forms of conditional preemption highly suspect. For extensive discussion in a post-*Printz* case, see *Petersburg Cellular P'ship v. Bd. of Supervisors*, 205 F.3d 688 (2000).

58. *Hunter's Lessee*, 14 U.S. 304; *Testa v. Katt*, 330 U.S. 386 (1947); *Claflin v. Houseman*, 93 U.S. 130 (1876). See also *Felder v. Casey*, 487 U.S. 131 (1988) (§ 1983 preempts state notice-of-claim requirement); *Howlett v. Rose*, 496 U.S. 356 (1990) (sovereign immunity does not protect state actors from § 1983 claim in state court when the defense would not be available in federal court).

59. For statutory examples and discussion, see Wendy E. Parmet, *Stealth Preemption: The Proposed Federalization of State Court Procedures*, 44 Vill L Rev 1 (1999); and Anthony J. Bellia, Jr., *Federal Regulation of State Court*

Procedures, 110 Yale L J 947 (2001). Bellia's compelling article contains an extensive discussion of the literature, including opposing views on this difficult question.

60. *Printz*, 521 U.S. at 976 (Breyer, J., dissenting).

16. Federalism among the States

1. *Polar Tankers, Inc. v. City of Valdez,*, 129 S. Ct. 2277, 2282 (2009) (emphasis added).

2. Ibid., 2282, quoting *Smith v. Turner* (*The Passenger Cases*), 48 U.S. 283, 458 (1849).

3. The *Polar Tankers* majority split over the question of whether docked ships could be subjected to a law that taxes both in-state and out-of-state vessels alongside other property on a nondiscriminatory basis. Justice Breyer, writing for a plurality of four justices, suggested that such a tax might pass constitutional muster. Chief Justice Roberts and Justice Thomas insisted that the Tonnage Clause prohibits any duty, including a nondiscriminatory imposition; Justice Alito would have passed on the question. Although the antidiscrimination reading is probably preferable, the question is close. But one can live with the interpretive difficulty; it arises only after the Tonnage Clause has done most of its work.

4. Sixteen states, as well as the Multistate Tax Commission, supported Alaska's position in *Polar Tankers* as amici.

5. *Lucas v. S.C. Coastal Council*, 505 U.S. 1003, 1025 n. 12 (1992) (Scalia, J., rejecting a "stupid staff" test in the context of the Takings Clause).

6. The following paragraphs are adapted from Richard A. Epstein and Michael S. Greve, "Conclusion: Preemption Doctrine and Its Limits," in *Federal Preemption: States' Powers, National Interests*, ed. Richard A. Epstein and Michael S. Greve (Washington, D.C.: AEI, 2007), 309.

7. *Heydon's Case, (1584)* 76 *Eng. Rep. 637.* In fact, the canon dates back to the even earlier times of Roman law. See Richard A. Epstein, *A Common Lawyer Looks at Constitutional Interpretation*, 72 Boston U L Rev 699 (1992).

8. Madison to Jefferson, Oct. 24, 1787, in *The Papers of James Madison*, ed. Robert A. Rutland, et al. (Chicago: University of Chicago Press, 1977) 10:205–220, 212.

9. Note that the Tonnage Clause itself can be understood as a textually specified anticircumvention rule: it blocks states from evading the prohibition against Import-Export Duties on ships' cargo (Art. I, § 10, Cl. 2) by instead taxing the ships themselves. See *Polar Tankers*, 129 S. Ct. at 2282.

10. The tax at issue in *Polar Tankers* was a pure revenue measure; thus, the Court's scrutiny focused on the structure of the tax, not on any police power purpose. Recall, however, the discussion in chap. 4 of the police-power analysis in the famous and closely analogous *Cooley v. Bd of Wardens*, 53 U.S. 299 (1851).

11. *Clyde Mallory Lines v. Alabama ex rel. State Docks Comm'n*, 296 U.S. 261 (1935).

12. For Justice Scalia's position see *Tyler Pipe Indus., Inc. v. Wash. State Dept. of Revenue*, 483 U.S. 232, 265 (1987); *West Lynn Creamery, Inc. v. Healy*, 512 U.S. 186, 210 (1994) (Scalia, J., concurring). Justice Thomas's call for abolition is strongly suggested by his dissent in *Camps Newfound/Owatonna, Inc. v. Town of Harrison*, 520 U.S. 564, 609 (1997) (Thomas, J., dissenting), and the justice has since made it explicit: *United Haulers Ass'n, Inc. v. Oneida-Herkimer Solid Waste Mgmt. Auth.*, 550 U.S. 330, 349 (2007) (Thomas, J., dissenting); *Dept. of Revenue of Ky v. Davis*, 553 U.S. 328, 361 (2008) (Thomas, J., concurring). Justice Scalia, although agreeing with Justice Thomas on the disposition of both these cases, did not join his opinion in either.

13. *Tyler Pipe*, 483 U.S. at 260–264.

14. Ibid., 265.

15. Justice Scalia quotes Felix Frankfurter's characterization of the dormant Commerce Clause as "an audacious doctrine, which, one may be sure, would hardly have been publicly avowed in support of the adoption of the Constitution." *Tyler Pipe*, 483 U.S. at 264. The reference is curious. First, it is open to the interpretation that the supporters of the Constitution in fact considered the Commerce Clause exclusive, while declining for tactical reasons to state that view. Second, the "audacity" is primarily Frankfurter's. He held, and attributed to John Marshall, a view of the Commerce Clause that most assuredly would have brought the Constitution to fall. Third, the reference raises the question of why *Justice* Frankfurter enforced the "audacious" dormant Commerce Clause. See chap. 9.

16. *Tyler Pipe*, 483 U.S. at 262 (Scalia, J., concurring), discussing Chief Justice Taney's opinion in the *Thurlow v. Massachusetts* (*The License Cases*), 46 U.S. 504 (1847). For the "*real* Commerce Clause," see Justice Scalia's concurrence in *Okla.Tax Comm'n v. Jefferson Lines, Inc.*, 514 U.S. 175, 201 (1995).

17. One more example of the *Tyler Pipe* dissent's tendency to flail at straw men: Justice Scalia lampoons the dormant Commerce Clause for allowing Congress to "reconvey" to states the power to enact laws that would otherwise violate the Commerce Clause. "There is surely no area," he writes, "in which Congress can permit the States to violate the Constitution" (*Tyler Pipe*, 483 U.S. at 263 n. 4). Indeed not, if one chooses to put it that way. But Congress *may* waive its otherwise exclusive authority or permit states to derogate from an otherwise applicable structural background rule. States may not tax the Bank of the United States, per *M'Culloch v. Maryland*, 17 U.S. 316 (1819)— unless Congress permits them to do so, per *Balt. Nat'l Bank v. State Tax Comm'n*, 297 U.S. 209 (1936). Similarly, military contractors enjoy certain federal, nonstatutory immunities against suits under state law per *Boyle v. United Tech. Corp.*, 487 U.S. 500 (1988); that constitutional common-law rule also governs only so long as Congress has not provided otherwise. Nor is there anything conceptually odd about "reconveyance." The Constitution itself employs that strategy with respect to tonnage duties, compacts, and the like; those measures are unconstitutional unless Congress affirmatively permits states to adopt them.

18. *Federalist* 32 (Hamilton), 155. Hamilton's discussion has traditionally served as a reference point for any serious engagement with the exclusivity issue. Justice Scalia's *Tyler Pipe* opinion cites several *Federalist* essays but, conspicuously, not number 32.
19. *Tyler Pipe*, 483 U.S. at 248.
20. The best judicial statement of the conundrum:

> [State taxation] spans a spectrum, ranging from the obviously discriminatory to the manipulative to the ambiguous to the wholly innocent. Courts can avoid arbitrariness in their review only by policing the entire spectrum (which is impossible), by policing none of it, or by adopting rules which subject to scrutiny certain well-defined classes of actions thought likely to come at or near the discriminatory end of the spectrum. We have traditionally followed the last course, confining our disapproval to forms of tax that seem clearly designed to discriminate, and accepting the fact that some amount of discrimination may slip through our net. A credit against intrastate taxes falls readily within the highly suspect category; a reduction of intrastate taxes to take account of increased revenue from a nondiscriminatory axle tax does not.
>
> I acknowledge that the distinction between a credit and a straight reduction is a purely formal one, but it seems to me less absurd than what we will be driven to if we abandon it. . . . A line must be drawn somewhere, and (in the absence of direction from any authoritative text) I would draw it here. *American Trucking Ass'ns, Inc. v. Scheiner*, 483 U.S. 266, 305–306 (1987) (Scalia, J., dissenting) (footnote omitted). Well put, and precisely right.

21. *Camps Newfound*, 520 U.S. at 636 (Thomas, J., dissenting).
22. For discussion, see Brannon P. Denning, *Why the Privileges and Immunities Clause of Article IV Cannot Replace the Dormant Commerce Clause Doctrine*, 88 Minn L Rev 384 (2003).
23. Under current doctrine, the Privileges and Immunities Clause prohibits only facial discrimination (ibid., 400).
24. Justice Thomas's *Camps Newfound* dissent notes, correctly, that the "state resources" problem has received inconsistent treatment under the dormant Commerce Clause, and he alleges that the Court's decisions on the issue have "turned on often subtle policy judgments, not the text of the Constitution" (*Camps Newfound*, 520 U.S. at 620, citing cases). It neglects to mention that the same problem, with the same result, has afflicted the Privileges and Immunities Clause ever since its first authoritative interpretation in *Corfield v. Coryell*, 6 F.Cas. 546 (1823) (C.C.E.D. Pa. 1823) (No. 3230), which held that a state could exclude outsiders from harvesting its oyster beds—inter alia, because the critters were stuck in place. We have since learned that the rule of *Coryell* does not extend to more mobile shrimp, per *Toomer v. Witsell*, 334 U.S. 385 (1948), and the Supreme Court has struggled with the access question in contexts from hunting licenses to college tuition to construction jobs, to no one's great satisfaction. For insightful discussion, see Jonathan

D. Varat, *State "Citizenship" and Interstate Equality*, 48 U Chi L Rev 487 (1981); and John Hart Ely, *Choice of Law and the State's Interest in Protecting its Own*, 23 Wm & Mary L Rev 173 (1981).

25. See *Camps Newfound*, 520 U.S. at 639 (Thomas, J., dissenting) (citing historical materials to the effect "duties" meant especially levies "upon printed books, and written instruments").

26. The text notes that the tax at issue in *Camps Newfound* should escape the Import-Export Clause because it was tied to the value of real property, not the volume of any transborder activity (*Camps Newfound*, 520 U.S. at 640). That, of course, also characterized the tax on importers—not imports—in *Brown v. Maryland*, 25 U.S. 419 (1827). A footnote hints that "a property tax in name only" might receive different treatment (*Camps Newfound*, 520 U.S. at 640 n. 22) (Thomas, J., dissenting).

27. *Camps Newfound*, 520 U.S. at 634 (Thomas, J., dissenting), citing and discussing *Michelin Tire Corp. v. Wages*, 423 U.S. 276 (1976).

28. For modern-day case examples, see *Exxon Corp. v. Governor of Md.*, 437 U.S. 117 (1978); and Brannon P. Denning and Rachel M. Lary, *Retail Store Size-Capping Ordinances and the Dormant Commerce Clause Doctrine*, 37 Urban Lawyer 907 (2005).

29. For defenses of the dormant Commerce Clause reflecting this sentiment, see Mark V. Tushnet, *Scalia and the Dormant Commerce Clause: A Foolish Formalism?*, 12 Cardozo L Rev 1717 (1991); and Daniel A. Farber and Robert E. Hudec, *Free Trade and the Regulatory State: A GATT'S-Eye View of the Dormant Commerce Clause*, 47 Vand L Rev 1401 (1994).

30. For a more detailed exposition, see Epstein and Greve, "Conclusion: Preemption Doctrine and Its Limits," 309. The following pages are partially adapted from this essay.

31. The Supreme Court still recognizes the soundness of the proposition in the horizontal context of coordinating rival federal schemes of regulation. See, e.g., *Verizon Commc'ns Inc. v. Law Offices of Curtis V. Trinko, LLP*, 540 U.S. 398 (2004); *Credit Suisse Sec. (USA) LLC v. Billing*, 551 U.S. 264 (2007).

32. See, e.g., *Morales v. Trans World Airlines*, 504 U.S. 374 (1992); *Rowe v. N.H. Motor Transp. Ass'n*, 552 U.S. 364 (2008); *Egelhoff v. Egelhoff*, 532 U.S. 141 (2001).

33. For a good discussion, see Catherine M. Sharkey, *Products Liability Preemption: An Institutional Approach*, 76 Geo Wash L Rev 449 (2008).

34. See *Engine Mfrs. Ass'n v. S. Coast Air Quality Mgmt. Dist.*, 541 U.S. 246 (2004); *Appalachian Power Co. v. Pub. Servs. Comm'n .*, 812 F.2d 898 (4th Cir. 1987); *Wyeth v. Levine*, 129 S. Ct. 1187 (2009).

35. *Wyeth*, 129 S. Ct. at 1205–1206 (Thomas, J., concurring).

36. *Gonzales v. Oregon*, 546 U.S. 243, 301 (2006) (Thomas, J., dissenting).

37. *Wyeth*, 129 S. Ct. at 1207–1208, 1211.

38. *Babbitt v. Sweet Home Chapter of Cmtys. for a Great Or.*, 515 U.S. 687, 726 (1995) (Scalia, J., dissenting) (footnote omitted).

39. For an explicit proposal to this effect, see Robert R. Gasaway and Ashley C. Parrish, "The Problem of Federal Preemption: Toward a Formal Solution,"

in *Federal Preemption: States' Powers, National Interests*, ed. Richard A. Epstein and Michael S. Greve (Washington, D.C.: AEI, 2007), 219. *PLIVA, Inc. v. Mensing*, 564 U.S. ___ (2011), suggests that this view—a unified conflict/obstacle doctrine of preemption without any presumption against preemption—has gained the support of four and perhaps five justices.

40. Behold the effects of the clear statement rule once it is severed from the constitutional logic and imported from spending statutes into the preemption cases: In the course of its migration, the canon changes its federalism implications. Vertically, clear statement canon has modestly procompetitive effects. In a horizontal context, in contrast, it has vehemently *anti*-competitive effects; the more muscular the judicial canon, the harder it becomes for Congress to arrest centrifugal state tendencies. Vertically, the clear statement rule checks redistributive coalitions; horizontally, it amplifies their power. In federalism's balance vortex, all those differences disappear. For further discussion, see Michael S. Greve, *Federalism's Frontier*, 7 Tex Rev L & Pol 93 (2002).

41. *Wyeth*, 129 S. Ct. at 1209 (Thomas, J., concurring), citing Caleb Nelson, *Preemption*, 86 Va L Rev 225, 260–261 (2000). Justice Thomas's majority opinion in *PLIVA*, 564 U.S. ____, relies yet more extensively on Nelson's article.

42. Catherine M. Sharkey, *Against Freewheeling, Extratextual Obstacle Preemption: Is Justice Clarence Thomas the Lone Principled Federalist?* 5 NYU J L & Liberty 63, 112–113 (2010). As Sharkey notes (95–110), Justice Thomas has construed express preemption provisions very liberally and with a view to the broad purposes of Congress. Rigid textualism produces a sharply discontinuous preemption jurisprudence.

43. *Gibbons v. Ogden*, 22 U.S. 1, 214 (1824)

44. *Wyeth*, 129 S. Ct. at 1210 (Thomas, J., concurring).

45. Nelson argues that "*Gibbons* plainly involved a contradiction between the challenged state law and a federal statute (*as interpreted by the Court*)" (*Preemption*, 272; emphasis added). The parenthesis simply shifts the central problem—what counts as a "conflict"?—into the statutory interpretation part of the analysis.

46. The *Roe v. Wade* comparison is mine. For the remainder of the paragraph, see Suzanna Sherry, *Wrong, Out of Step, and Pernicious:* Erie *as the Worst Decision of All Time*, 39 Pepp L Rev ___ (forthcoming 2012); Craig Green, *Repressing* Erie's *Myth*, 96 Cal L Rev 595, 596 (2008) ("*Erie*'s original foundations are cracked"); Patrick J. Borchers, *The Origins of Diversity Jurisdiction, the Rise of Legal Positivism, and a Brave New World for* Erie *and* Klaxon, 72 Tex L Rev 79, 132 (1993) ("The historical justifications [for the *Erie*-and-*Klaxon* doctrine] never did exist, and the pragmatic justifications no longer exist."); John B. Corr, *Thoughts on the Vitality of* Erie, 41 Am U L Rev 1087 (1992).

47. Modern maritime instance cases provide a striking example of this dynamic. See, e.g., *M/S Bremen v. Zapata Off-Shore Co.*, 407 U.S. 1 (1972); *Carnival Cruise Lines, Inc. v. Shute*, 499 U.S. 585 (1991). There is no reason to think that courts would do worse with respect to commercial arrangements on terra

firma. Similarly, nominally statutory "new" common-law doctrines have often had a decidedly procontractual bent quite at odds with *Erie's* spirit. See, e.g., *Leegin Creative Leather Prods., Inc. v. PSKS, Inc.*, 551 U.S. 877 (2007) (antitrust law, resale price maintenance); *Marquette Nat'l Bank v. First of Omaha Serv. Corp.*, 439 U.S. 299 (1978) (interstate banking).

48. Henry J. Friendly, "In Praise of *Erie*—And of the New Federal Common Law," in Henry J. Friendly, *Benchmarks* (Chicago: University of Chicago Press, 1967), 155–195, 174–175.

49. Catherine M. Sharkey has rightly noted that , to Justice Thomas's mind, opposition to the dormant Commerce Clause and to implied preemption is of one piece with *Erie* (*Justice Thomas*, 112). For a far-afield and particularly emphatic insistence on *Erie*, see *Sosa v. Alvarez-Machain*, 542 U.S. 692, 739 (2004) (Scalia, J., concurring).

50. Bradford R. Clark, *Erie's Constitutional Source*, 95 Cal L Rev 1289 (2007); and Bradford R. Clark, *Federal Lawmaking and the Role of Structure in Constitutional Interpretation*, 96 Cal L Rev 699 (2008). See also Bradford R. Clark, *Federal Common Law: A Structural Reinterpretation*, 144 U Pa L Rev 1245 (1996).

51. Craig Green, Erie *and Problems of Constitutional Structure*, 96 Cal L Rev 661, 682–683 (2008). Clark's reply is that his position "poses no real threat to the administrative state because courts lack competence to enforce the Supremacy Clause's safeguards vigorously in this context" (*Federal Lawmaking*, 716). The administrative state will be pleased to hear this. But "competence," whatever it may mean, wasn't really Professor Green's point—was it?

52. Clark, *Federal Lawmaking*, 711.

53. Jay Tidmarsh and Brian J. Murray, *A Theory of Federal Common Law*, 100 Nw U L Rev 585, 588 (2006).

54. *Clearfield Trust Co. v. United States*, 318 U.S. 363 (1943); *Boyle*, 487 U.S. 500.

  The argument in the text—it is difficult to think of a theory that explains *Erie's* enclaves without undermining *Erie* itself—applies most clearly to the administration of federal common law in maritime instance cases. However, Tidmarsh and Murray (like Clark and numerous other scholars) acknowledge the point and incline to the view that "federal common law in instance cases may be an historical curiosity, a dinosaur that has outlived the reasons for its existence" (*Federal Common Law*, 638). Hence, my emphasis on enclaves that the authors do defend.

55. By any rational standard, the incongruity has reached absurdity. Military contractors enjoy federal common-law defenses so long as their products are built to contractual specifications, on account of doctrines that are explicitly borrowed from preemption law (*Boyle*, 487 U.S. at 512). Pharmaceutical companies must obtain federal approval for their products and label them in accordance with federal specifications. They are very large federal contractors and, to all intents, indistinguishable from public utilities. But there is no federal common-law defense for conforming products; there is no longer even an implied preemption defense. See *Wyeth*, 129 S. Ct. 1187.

The recognition that the national government could readily supply uniform rules for the protection of its own institutions probably played a role in two cases, both arising out of the savings and loan crisis of the 1980s, denying the government's demand for federal common law rules (and both, in my estimation, rightly decided). *O'Melveny & Myers v. FDIC*, 512 U.S. 79 (1994); *Atherton v. FDIC*, 519 U.S. 213 (1997).

56. That principle operates under current law where federal constitutional rights, especially the right against "takings" of private property, depend on state law. *Lucas*, 505 U.S. at 1031–1032.

57. Recall the discussion in chap. 10.

58. For the general argument, see Richard A. Epstein, *Forbidden Grounds: The Case Against Employment Discrimination Laws* (Cambridge, MA: Harvard University Press, 1992).

59. Tidmarsh and Murray, *Federal Common Law*, 650–651.

17. Concluding Essay

1. For pensions, see Robert Novy-Marx and Joshua Rauh, "The Liabilities and Risks of State-Sponsored Pension Plans," *Journal of Economic Perspectives* 23:4 (2009): 191–210; and Robert Novy-Marx and Joshua Rauh, "Public Pension Promises: How Big Are They and What Are They Worth?" *Journal of Finance* (forthcoming). Fiscal data are available online from the Rockefeller Institute of Government: http://www.rockinst.org/government_finance/.

2. For discussion, see Michael S. Greve, "Bailouts or Bankruptcy: Are States too Big to Fail?," AEI Legal Outlook, March 2011, available online at http://www.aei.org/outlook/101035.

3. Argentina has usually opted for inflation as a means of solving its federalism-induced fiscal crisis; Brazil, for a draconian reform that subjected junior governments' budgetary decisions to central superintendence. See Jonathan Rodden, *Hamilton's Paradox: The Promise and Peril of Fiscal Federalism* (Cambridge: Cambridge University Press, 2006), especially chaps. 8–9. The European Union, after a series of member-state bailouts, is contemplating revisions of the European Treaties that would cut in the same direction.

4. For the history, see Omer Kimhi, *Chapter 9 of the Bankruptcy Code: A Solution in Search of a Problem*, 27 Yale J on Regulation 351, 362–365 (2010). For a proposal for state bankruptcy, see David A. Skeel, Jr., "Give States a Way to Go Bankrupt: It's the Best Option for Avoiding a Massive Federal Bailout," *California Journal of Politics and Policy* 3:2 (2011), available online at http://www.bepress.com/cjpp/.

5. For the general theory of institutional pathology as a product of affluence, see Christopher C. DeMuth, "Politics and Government in the Super-Affluent Society," 2000 Francis Boyer Lecture, available online at http://www.aei.org/speech/11289; Sam Peltzman, *Regulation and the Natural Progress of Opulence* (Washington, D.C.: AEI, 2005).

6. Walter Heller, *New Dimensions of Political Economy* (New York: Norton, 1966), 118.

7. No result, that is, that anyone would call a success. In 2010, the U.S. secretary of education publicly thanked the forces of nature for having wiped out the hopelessly dysfunctional New Orleans school district. (Nick Anderson, "Education Secretary Duncan Calls Hurricane Katrina Good for New Orleans schools," *Washington Post*, January 30, 2010, available online at http://www.washingtonpost.com/wp-dyn/content/article/2010/01/29/AR201 0012903259.html.) The district now faces perhaps the brightest prospects of any urban school system, until the bureaucracies that produced the pre-Katrina disgrace reconstitute themselves. See Michael B. Henderson, "In the Wake of the Storm," *Education Next*, March 2010.

8. Jonathan Rodden has argued that institutional actors will often be unable to renegotiate the federalism bargain even when the existing bargain generates large losses for the federal system. Federalism reform appears to require some combination of wide, intense public reform demand; political entrepreneurship; and "electoral externalities" (meaning that a governing party's successful reforms will redound to the benefit of its officeholders and candidates at lower levels of government). Rodden, *Hamilton's Paradox*, chap. 9.

9. Robert G. McCloskey, *The American Supreme Court* (Chicago: University of Chicago Press, 2004), chap. 6.

10. For a particularly disingenuous riff, see Jeffrey Rosen, *The Most Democratic Branch: How the Courts Serve America* (New York: Oxford University Press, 2006). See also Cass R. Sunstein, *One Case at a Time: Judicial Minimalism on the Supreme Court* (Cambridge, MA: Harvard University Press, 1999). For a more judicious account, see Barry Friedman, *The Will of the People: How Public Opinion Has Influenced the Supreme Court and Shaped the Meaning of the Constitution* (New York: Farrar, Straus and Giroux, 2009).

11. While opinion data have fluctuated, polls have consistently shown higher public confidence in the Supreme Court than in the presidency and especially in Congress. See Gallup's annual institutional confidence survey, available online at http://www.gallup.com/poll/148163/Americans-Confident-Military-Least-Congress.aspx.

12. The Court's entitlement-curbing jurisprudence (reviewed in chaps. 12 and 14) furnishes ample empirical evidence. On occasion, the Congress has reversed the Court's limiting decisions. But it is difficult to perceive any loss of prestige on the Court's part or to imagine that any catastrophe would befall the Court if, say, it were to overrule *Maine v. Thibotout*.

13. Martin Shapiro, "The Success of Judicial Review and Democracy," in *On Law, Politics, and Judicialization*, ed. Martin Shapiro and Alec Stone Sweet (Oxford: Oxford University Press, 2002), 176–182.

14. Note, moreover, that if the Supreme Court does nothing than to stem the worst state defections and to reverse errant lower-court rulings, the mere maintenance of the status quo will have a distinctly "probusiness" flavor. (I owe the point to Robert R. Gasaway.) Additionally, the policing function, will be compromised by the judiciary's need to project an aura of neutrality (Shapiro, "Judicial Review," 165).

15. Jeffrey Rosen, "Supreme Court, Inc.," *New York Times Magazine*, March 16, 2008; Erwin Chemerinsky, *Empowering States: The Need to Limit Federal Preemption*, 33 Pepp L Rev 69 (2005); David C. Vladeck, *Preemption and Regulatory Failure*, 33 Pepp L Rev 95 (2005).

16. For an equally cynical view, see Shapiro, "Judicial Review," 176–179 (rights courts will tend to pay a perfunctory tribute at the structure front as a token price for sustained rights invention).

17. Martin Shapiro, "The Supreme Court From Early Burger to Early Rehnquist," in *The New American Political System*, ed. Anthony King, 2nd ed. (Washington, D.C.: AEI, 1990), 47–86.

18. For international law see, e.g., *Medellin v. Texas*, 552 U.S. 491 (2008); and generally Steven G. Calabresi, *"A Shining City on a Hill": American Exceptionalism and the Supreme Court's Practice of Relying on Foreign Law*, 86 BU L Rev 1335 (2006).

19. See Cass R. Sunstein, *The Second Bill of Rights: FDR's Unfinished Revolution and Why We Need It More than Ever* (New York: Basic, 2004), chap. 9.

20. The Court has never embraced a "diversity" or "anti-caste" principle that would legitimize those policies in any context and for all eternity. *Gratz v. Bollinger*, 539 U.S. 244 (2003); *Grutter v. Bollinger*, 539 U.S. 306 (2003).

21. See, e.g., *Citizens United v. Fed. Election Comm'n*, 130 S. Ct. 876 (2010); *Arizona Free Enter. Club's Freedom Club PAC v. Bennett*, 564 U.S. ___ (2011).

22. See Michael McConnell, *Active Liberty: A Progressive Alternative to Textualism and Originalism?*, 119 Harv L Rev 2387, 2394–2395 (2006).

23. Parts of the following discussion are adapted from Michael S. Greve, "Conservatives and the Courts," in *Crisis of Conservatism? The Republican Party, the Conservative Movement and American Politics after Bush*, ed. Joel D. Aberbach and Gillian Peele (New York: Oxford University Press, 2011), chap. 11, by permission of Oxford University Press, Inc. It focuses on originalism's political-institutional forms as distinct from its theoretical formulations. For a similar distinction, see Keith Whittington, *The New Originalism*, 2 Georgetown J L & Pub Pol'y 599 (2004); and from a much more polemical perspective, Robert Post and Reva Siegel, *Originalism as Political Practice: The Right's Living Constitution*, 75 Fordham L Rev 545 (2006).

In emphasizing originalism's political context, I do not mean to suggest that all or even most originalists tailor their jurisprudence to the political demands of the moment. I do suggest, however, that the political context has potent effects on the public, political deployment of originalism—put differently, on the extent to which particular forms of originalism do or do not gain real-world traction. Moreover, the Hegelian in me yelps that an intellectual movement that cannot bring itself to reflect on the contingent conditions of its own origins becomes raw ideology. For a persuasive analysis showing that originalism, although of course politically charged, has never been ideological in that strict sense, see Steven M. Teles, *The Rise of the Conservative Legal Movement: The Battle for Control of the Law* (Princeton, NJ: Princeton University Press, 2008), 275–280.

24. I have borrowed the distinction from Robert R. Gasaway and Ashley C. Parrish, "Structural Constitutional Principles and Rights Reconciliation," in *Citizenship in America and Europe: Beyond the Nation-State?* ed. Michael S. Greve and Michael Zoeller (Washington, D.C.: AEI, 2009), 209–212.

25. Randy E. Barnett, *Restoring the Lost Constitution: The Presumption of Liberty* (Princeton, NJ: Princeton University Press, 2004).

26. In theory, academic originalists bridge this dilemma with an imposing edifice of judicially enforced economic rights; in the real world, where those rights are weak and federalism questions often pose difficult choices between central power and local exploitation, academic originalists often have trouble telling whose side they are on.

27. Antonin Scalia, *Foreword: The Importance of Structure in Constitutional Interpretation*, 83 Notre Dame L Rev 1417, 1418 (2008).

28. See James R. Stoner, Jr., *Common-Law Liberty: Rethinking American Constitutionalism* (Lawrence: University Press of Kansas, 2003), chap. 1; H. Jefferson Powell, *On Not Being "Not An Originalist,"* 7 U St Thomas L J 259 (2010).

29. Originalism has been criticized for its grudging acceptance of constitutional innovations—that is, its inability to recognize that some of them, prominently *Brown*, constitute our finest moments. Jack M. Balkin, *Original Meaning and Constitutional Redemption*, 24 Const Comment 427, 515 (2007). The reverse is probably more true: originalism has failed to recognize, and ardently embraced, some of our worst moments.

30. The disenchantment may be mutual. Social conservatives' support for judicial restraint has been predicated on the idea that a reversal of *Roe v. Wade* would produce victory in the political arena. It is not at all clear that this is true. See Neal Devins, *How* Planned Parenthood v. Casey *(Pretty Much) Settled the Abortion Wars*, 118 Yale L J 1318 (2009).

31. Strikingly, it has focused on constitutional rights that are not only long-forgotten but also, once recognized, would require an imposing body of constitutional common law. For a critique of the Court's recognition of Second Amendment rights on these grounds and from an originalist vantage, see J. Harvie Wilkinson III, *Of Guns, Abortions, and the Unraveling Rule of Law*, 95 Va L Rev 253 (2009).

32. See Cass R. Sunstein, *Justice Scalia's Democratic Formalism*, 107 Yale L J 529 (1997).

33. James A. Gardner, *The Positivist Foundations of Originalism: An Account and Critique*, 71 BU L Rev 1, 8 (1991) ("consent-based positivism"). For the natural rights version, see Randy E. Barnett, *Constitutional Legitimacy*, 103 Colum L Rev 111, 117 (2003) ("Constitutional legitimacy has not been conferred by either the individual or the collective consent of 'We the People'"; what matters is the justice of the constitutional scheme; ibid., 113). For a partial exception, see John O. McGinnis and Michael B. Rappaport, *A Pragmatic Defense of Originalism*, 101 Nw U L Rev 383, 385 (2007) (defending originalism "by reference to the likely consequences flowing from the [supermajoritarian] process" that produced the Constitution, not because process itself legitimizes).

34. For data, see Friedman, *Will of the People*, 374–377. See also Devins, *Abortion Wars*.
35. Teles, *Conservative Legal Movement*, esp. chap. 5.
36. See, respectively, Stephen Breyer, *Making Our Democracy Work: A Judge's View* (New York: Knopf, 2010); and Sunstein, *One Case at a Time*.

    To their credit, progressives understand that "democracy" in the simple sense of majority rule is not an unalloyed good. That insight has prompted a series of adjustments: constitutional democracy needs "representation-reinforcing" mechanisms, a comprehensive "anti-caste principle," a "New Deal for Free Speech," "deliberative" institutions, "active liberty," and "constitutional commitments" in a no-man's-land between rights and politics. Interest group politics is no great shakes; thus, democracy must be "thick" or "liberal" or "constitutional." Constitutional law must take its bearings from "stakeholder democracy" and progressive "social movements." However, progressives do not actually trust the democratic content of any of those theories. They would not otherwise toot their rights horns so loudly or hanker so obviously for the second coming of William Brennan.
37. A very fine book in this vein is George Thomas's *The Madisonian Constitution* (Baltimore, MD: Johns Hopkins University Press, 2008).
38. For a cri de coeur to that effect, see Gasaway and Parrish, "Rights Reconciliation," 223–228.
39. Alexander Hamilton, "The Continentalist No. VI," in *The Works of Alexander Hamilton*, ed. Henry Cabot Lodge (New York: G.P. Putnam's Sons, 1904), 1:286–287.
40. John C. Miller, The Federalist Era, 1789–1801 (New York: Harper and Row, 1960), 52 (quoting Hamilton's response to Virginia's Protest and Remonstrance: "This is the first symptom of a spirit which must either be killed, or will kill the Constitution of the United States").

Acknowledgments

O ver the long gestation of this book, I have incurred enough debts to last a lifetime.

The American Enterprise Institute (AEI) provided me with the institutional and intellectual support to work without staff meetings, fundraising obligations, faculty conferences, or any other chores that distract scholars in even the most hospitable academic environment. AEI also supplied a cadre of exceptionally skilled and dedicated research assistants and interns over lo these many years: Kate Schackai, Philip Wallach, Will Wilson, Harriet McConnell, Luci Hague McLeod, Miriel Thomas, and Elizabeth DeMeo; Nathaniel Yoo, Lauren Blas, Scott Jeffrey, Natascha Born, Danielle Charles, Amber Kirby, Joseph Pullano, and David McDonald.

I thank Michael Aronson of Harvard University Press for his staunch support and advocacy, and Lauren Manoy for her capable editing and, in particular, her respect for my idiosyncratic voice and style.

Portions of the manuscript were presented at workshops at AEI, Boston College, Northwestern University Law School, and the University of Texas Law School. I benefitted greatly from these discussions, and I am especially grateful to the organizers and participants—as well as others—who generously provided helpful comments and suggestions: Jonathan Adler, Jack Balkin, David Bernstein, Henry Butler, Stephen Calabresi, James Ceaser, Martha Derthick, John Dinan, Ted Frank, Barry Friedman, William Galston, Douglas Ginsburg, Rick Hills, Ken Kersch, Jonathan Klick,

Marc Landy, Sandy Levinson, Jacob Levy, Nelson Lund, John McGinnis, R. Shep Melnick, Eugene Meyer, Sidney Milkis, Henry Olsen, Ashley Parrish, Michael Rappaport, Martin Redish, Larry Ribstein, Dan Schweitzer, Suzanna Sherry, Alec Stone Sweet, Steven Teles, Edward Warren, Stephen Williams, and Todd Zywicki.

Teaching engagements at Boston College and Johns Hopkins University allowed me to inflict my unorthodox ideas about constitutional politics and design on seminars of smart, engaged students. Special thanks are due to Boston College's R. Shep Melnick—friend, colleague, federalism expert, and suitably skeptical advisor, who has encouraged my research, writing, and teaching on these matters for the better part of three decades.

Colleen Sheehan and the late Lance Banning did me the favor of engaging in a sustained discussion of James Madison's Convention agenda. The exchange helped me considerably in sharpening my views and presentation. I thank them both and take the opportunity to say a belated but fond farewell to a great scholar and gentleman.

I owe a particular debt of gratitude to Christopher C. DeMuth, ingenious past president and brilliant colleague at AEI; Richard A. Epstein, long-time mentor, teacher, coauthor, and coeditor; and Robert R. Gasaway, counselor and fellow combatant in many a federalism engagement. I have profited not only from their prolific writings but also, and more profoundly, from countless informal conversations—freewheeling, but immeasurably productive because of a shared understanding that is sufficiently deep, and common among us, to skip the first four obvious steps of any constitutional argument. Not that the results now on display will necessarily leave anyone very happy. Chris DeMuth may lament my cynicism about democratic politics; Richard Epstein, my Hamiltonian convictions; Rob Gasaway, wayward remarks about federal common law and federal preemption that may come to bite him, and us. The fifth-step stumbles, however, are mine alone.

Jeremy Rabkin introduced me to American constitutional law and theory three decades ago, almost to the day. Many, perhaps most, of what I like to think of as my insights derive from his thoughts and suggestions. I suspect that I haven't quite managed to think all this stuff through to the very end; may he count this book as a contribution to an ongoing conversation.

By good fortune, I have been privileged to enjoy the generous guidance, inspiration, and support of an older generation: Walter Berns, Irving Kristol, Randy Richardson, Dan Searle, Aaron Wildavsky, and James Q. Wilson. To know or have known any one of them is to realize that we don't seem to make men like them anymore.

That apprehension tracks the fear, palpable throughout this book, that a great constitutional order may disappear in a sea of forgetfulness and an inability to recover or replace what has been lost. The notion that America might lose a convulsive cultural battle and become Europe—by popular choice or elitist connivance—strikes me as implausible. The possibility that it might by force of entropy become another Argentina seems to me very real. I thank Father John DeCelles and above all my beloved wife, who have helped me to keep that melancholy thought in perspective.

Index